The SUNDANCE WRITER

The SUNDANCE WRITER

THIRD EDITION

A Rhetoric, Reader, Handbook

MARK CONNELLY

Milwaukee Area Technical College

THOMSON
∗
WADSWORTH

Australia Brazil Canada Mexico Singapore Spain United Kingdom United States

THOMSON
™
WADSWORTH

The Sundance Writer: A Rhetoric, Reader, Handbook
Third Edition

Mark Connelly

Publisher: Michael Rosenberg
Development Editor: Stephanie Pelkowski
  Carpenter
Technology Project Manager: Tim Smith
Managing Marketing Manager: Mandee Eckersley
Associate Marketing Communications Manager:
  Patrick Rooney
Associate Content Project Manager: Sarah
  Sherman
Senior Art Director: Bruce Bond
Print/Media Buyer: Marcia Locke

Senior Permissions Editor: Isabel Alves
Photo Manager: Sheri Blaney
Text Permissions Editor: Sue Brekka
Photo Researcher: Cheri Throop
Cover Designer: Hespenheide Design
Cover Art: © ThinkStock LLC/RF/Index Stock
  Imagery
Cover Printer: China Translation & Printing Services Ltd
Production Service/Compositor: G & S Book
  Services
Printer: China Translation & Printing Services Ltd

Printed in China
4 5 6 7 09 08 07

Library of Congress Control Number:
2006921470

ISBN-13: 978-1-4130-1538-6
ISBN-10: 1-4130-1538-7

Thomson Higher Education
25 Thomson Place
Boston, MA 02210-1202
USA

For more information about our products,
contact us at:
Thomson Learning Academic Resource
Center
1-800-423-0563
For permission to use material from this
text or product, submit a request online
at **http://www.thomsonrights.com**
Any additional questions about
permissions can be submitted by e-mail
to **thomsonrights@thomson.com**

Credits appear on pages 905–907, which
constitute a continuation of the copyright
page.

For LARRY RILEY

TEACHER • MENTOR • FRIEND

Contents

PART FOUR   WRITING IN COLLEGE

PART FIVE   THE RESEARCH PAPER

PART SIX   GRAMMAR AND HANDBOOK

Expanded Contents

PART THREE   THE READER

18 DESCRIPTION: PRESENTING IMPRESSIONS 262

**20   EXAMPLE: PRESENTING
           ILLUSTRATIONS   363**

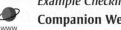

22 COMPARISON AND CONTRAST: INDICATING SIMILARITIES AND DIFFERENCES   445

23   PROCESS: EXPLAINING HOW THINGS WORK AND GIVING DIRECTIONS   487

26   ARGUMENT AND PERSUASION: INFLUENCING READERS   633

PART FOUR   WRITING IN COLLEGE

PART SIX   GRAMMAR AND HANDBOOK

31   GRAMMAR   825

What Is Grammar?   825
Parts of Speech   826
  Nouns   826
  Pronouns   826
  Adjectives   827
  Verbs   827
  Adverbs   829
  Articles   829
  Prepositions   829
  Conjunctions   830
  Interjections   830
Understanding Parts of Speech   830

STRATEGIES for Determining Parts of Speech   831

Phrases and Clauses   832
  Phrases   832
  Clauses   832
Sentences   833
Common Sentence Patterns   833
  Types of Sentences   833
  Other Ways of Looking at Sentences   836
Grammar Review   838
 Companion Website: Grammar   838
www

Preface

Valued for its real-world emphasis and focus on critical thinking, *The Sundance Writer* is the complete textbook for composition courses. Going beyond the standard presentation of readings, grammar, and the writing process, *The Sundance Writer* presents strategies for professional writing, conducting research, analyzing and using images, and interpreting literature. *The Sundance Writer's* balance of theory and strategy, blend of readability and intellectual rigor, critical thinking focus, and practical emphasis on writing for the "real world" make it a flexible teaching and learning tool.

NEW TO THIS EDITION

The third edition was thoroughly reviewed by composition instructors from across the country, who called it "unparalleled to comparable texts" and praised its "impressive" readings and assignments. The new *Sundance Writer* builds on the proven success of previous editions, maintaining its readable style and easy-to-navigate format while offering innovative new features for the ever-evolving needs of today's classroom.

New Design

Now in four colors, *The Sundance Writer* is easier to navigate, and images are reproduced with greater clarity and authenticity.

Hand-edited sentences in the Handbook more clearly demonstrate the difference between an original sentence and a revised one and call attention to easy-to-miss details, such as comma placement.

"Real world writing" now has a "real world" look. Documents appearing in Writing Beyond the Classroom resemble their original context, enhancing discussions of genre and document design.

New and Expanded Visual Chapters

A new Chapter 14, "Writing with Visuals," presents rhetorically based advice on the role of visuals in the writing context, including their use as design features, general illustrations, and specific illustrations. The chapter also guides students in selecting appropriate images, writing captions, and designing documents.

An expanded Chapter 13, "Analyzing Visuals," includes a new section, "The History of an Image," which examines a single photograph in various contexts, demonstrating how an image can become a cultural icon and historical symbol.

New Readings

The third edition features nine new readings, including classic essays, such as Maya Angelou's "Champion of the World" and Rachel Carson's "A Fable for Tomorrow," as well as new pieces, such as Azadeh Moaveni's "Maman and America" and Anna Quindlen's "Uncle Sam and Aunt Samantha."

New E-Readings with Research Assignments

Organized by mode, the reader portion of *The Sundance Writer* includes a thematic anthology of eighty-one electronic readings that you can access through your 1Pass account login. The new edition offers expanded commentary and critical thinking questions. E-readings can be used as controlled resources units for writing research papers, allowing instructors to monitor documentation and plagiarism on nine critical issues:

1. The War on Terrorism
2. The Healthcare Crisis
3. Fatherhood
4. Overcoming TV Addiction
5. Immigration
6. The Job Market
7. Ethics
8. Public Schools
9. The Criminal Justice System

E-Sources

Throughout *The Sundance Writer,* students are referred to reliable online resources that will assist them in every step of the writing process.

KEY FEATURES

The Sundance Writer is divided into six sections: The Rhetoric, Writing in the Information Age, The Reader, Writing in College, The Research Paper, and Grammar and Handbook.

The Rhetoric

The Sundance Writer focuses on critical stages in the writing process, providing students with techniques to improve their writing and overcome common problems. *The Sundance Writer* encourages students to see English as a highly practical course giving them skills they need in future classes and in any field or occupation they pursue—the ability to reason logically, organize ideas, and communicate effectively.

Writing does not occur in a vacuum but in a context that consists of the writer's objective, the reader, the discourse community, and the nature of the document. After introducing strategies for establishing context and enhancing critical thinking, *The Sundance Writer* guides students in developing and supporting a thesis. Students also are given practical directions for revising and editing.

Writing in the Information Age

The Sundance Writer includes chapters on analyzing and using photographs, graphs, tables, and charts in both academic and business writing. In addition, *The Sundance Writer* provides strategies for writing effective e-mail, résumés, letters, and business reports. Strategies are also presented to communicate in a range of special writing contexts:

- collaborative writing
- online writing groups
- writing as the representative of others
- writing to mass audiences
- writing to multiple readers
- giving multimedia and oral presentations

The Reader

Organized by rhetorical mode, this section presents fifty entries, including classic essays by E. B. White, George Orwell, Martin Luther King Jr., and Bruce Catton, as well as recent works by John Taylor Gatto, Barbara Ehrenreich, and Anna Quindlen. Women, African Americans, Asians, and Hispanics are all well represented. The subjects cover a range of issues: public schools, the aftermath of September 11, getting a job, the sinking of the *Titanic*, and the homeless.

The wide variety of topics on science, law, culture, business, and social issues make *The Sundance Writer* suitable for thematic courses. In addition, this textbook has several features that make it a useful teaching tool for college instructors:

A range of readings   Each chapter opens with brief, easy-to-read entries that clearly demonstrate the rhetorical mode, followed by longer, more challenging essays. Instructors have the flexibility to assign readings best suited to their student populations.

Brief entries suitable for in-class reading   Many of the essays are short enough to be read in class and used as writing prompts, thus reducing the need for handouts.

An emphasis on critical thinking   *The Sundance Writer* stresses critical thinking by including essays such as Samuel Scudder's "Take This Fish and Look at It," which dramatizes the importance of detailed observation.

Special Features

Writing beyond the classroom   *The Sundance Writer* places a unique emphasis on the practical value of writing skills. Each chapter ends with a sample of "real-world" writing that illustrates how professionals use the modes in different fields.

Blending the modes   Each chapter highlights an essay that demonstrates how writers use different modes to relate a narrative, make a comparison, or outline a definition.

Opposing viewpoints   Paired essays present different opinions on three critical issues: ethnic identity, the "abuse excuse," and slavery reparations.

Student papers for each mode   Samples of student writing offer models of common assignments.

Collaborative writing   Each reading concludes with directions for group writing.

Responding to images   Classic and contemporary photographs prompt student writing, class discussion, and collaborative analysis.

Writing in College

The Sundance Writer includes chapters on writing essay examinations and writing about literature.

Special Features

- Sample essay examination questions and responses
- An introduction to major literary terms

- A complete short story, two poems, and a dramatic scene
- Sample literary essays

The Research Paper

The Sundance Writer offers students a complete discussion of writing research papers, initially addressing common student misconceptions. Defining *what a research paper is not* is very effective in preventing students from embarking on misguided, time-consuming endeavors. Updated to focus on using Internet sources, *The Sundance Writer* gives guidelines to help students locate, evaluate, and document electronic material.

Special Features

- Strategies for selecting and evaluating sources
- Strategies for overcoming problems with research
- Strategies for evaluating Internet sources
- Strategies for conducting interviews and surveys
- Strategies for locating and documenting visual images
- Separate MLA and APA research papers

Grammar and Handbook

The Sundance Writer presents an overview of grammar, explaining the parts of speech and basic sentence structure in a separate review chapter. The handbook is designed for easy use and focuses on the most common problems in grammar and mechanics.

Special Features

- Strategies for detecting and revising sentence fragments, run-ons, dangling modifiers, faulty parallelism, unnecessary commas, and other errors
- Lists of commonly confused and misspelled words

COMPANION WEBSITE

http://www.thomsonedu.com/english/sundance

The popular Sundance website provides students with an online study guide divided into five sections:

1. The Writing Process
2. Modes of Exposition

3. Research and the Research Paper
4. Special Kinds of Writing
5. Grammar/Sentence Skills

Interactive quizzes offer self-graded support for students in twelve key areas:

1. commonly confused words
2. commonly misspelled words
3. problems with modifiers
4. pronoun agreement
5. parallelism
6. fragments and run-ons
7. punctuation
8. history of English
9. the writing process
10. the comma
11. MLA citations
12. subject-verb agreement

Students receive immediate evaluations and can email results to their instructor.

Sample student papers demonstrate each stage of the writing process from instructor's assignment and prewriting notes through rough and edited drafts to the final essay.

Above all, *The Sundance Writer* has been designed to encourage students to read critically and develop confidence as writers.

ACKNOWLEDGMENTS

This book and previous editions have benefited tremendously from the critiques and recommendations of the following instructors:

Maryann Bencivenga, *Suffolk County Community College*
Robert Beuka, *Louisiana State University*
Edith Borbon, *Devry University*
Alison Caldwell, *University of Tennessee–Martin*
Brenda Craven, *Fort Hays State University*
Carl Curtis, *Liberty University*
Christine Fitzsimons, *Rutgers University–Camden*
Terry Goldmann, *St. Mary's University*

Patrick Goughary, *Camden County College*
Christopher Gould, *University of North Carolina, Wilmington*
Anam Govardhan, *Western Connecticut State University*
Trevor Hodge, *Westfield State College*
Sue Iseman, *Ohio Northern University*
Summer Jackman, *Idaho State University*
Kaye Kolkmann, *Modesta Junior College*
Linda Maifair, *Pennsylvania State University–Mont Alto*
Kathleen McWilliams, *Cuyamaca College*
Michael Mead, *Tomball College*
Scott Redmond, *Cleveland State Community College*
Jenny Sadre-Orafai, *Kennesaw State University*
Madeline Santoro, *Union County College*
Lisa R. Schneider, *Columbus State Community College*
Bernard Selzler, *University of Minnesota, Crookston*
De'Lara Stephens, *Chattanooga State Technical Community College*
Donna Summerlin, *Lee University*
Margaret C. Waguespack, *Amarillo College*

All books are a collaborative effort. My special thanks goes to Michael Rosenberg, publisher; Stephanie Pelkowski Carpenter, development editor; Sarah Sherman, associate production project manager; Karen Judd, development manager; Marcia Locke, manufacturing manager; Mandee Eckersley, managing marketing manager; Bruce Bond, senior art director; Isabel Alves, text permissions manager; and Sheri Blaney, photo manager.

WHY WRITE?

> A writer is someone who writes, that's all.
>
> —Gore Vidal

Few students intend to become writers. You probably think of writers as people who write for a living—reporters, playwrights, and novelists. But all professionals—all educated men and women, in fact—write to achieve their goals. Police officers and nurses document their daily activities in reports and charts, knowing that whatever they write may be introduced in court as evidence months or years in the future. Attorneys spend much of their time writing motions, drafting appeals, and composing letters. Psychiatrists take notes while interviewing patients and then later record a diagnosis and outline a course of treatment. Business lobbyists, labor leaders, environmentalists, and consumer advocates write members of Congress to support or reject proposed legislation. Salespeople send streams of e-mail messages and faxes to announce new products, introduce themselves to new accounts, respond to buyers' questions, and inform management of their progress. Stockbrokers publish investor newsletters and post recommendations on the Internet. A young couple opening a bed and breakfast will find themselves writing to secure financing, contact travel agents, address concerns raised by building inspectors, create sales brochures, and train employees. Men and women entering any profession soon realize that they depend on writing to share ideas, express opinions, and influence people.

WRITERS AT WORK

I don't know any writer who thinks that writing is fun. It's hard work, and the way I do it is just as if I'm doing any other job. I get up in the morning and I have breakfast and read the newspapers and shave and shower and get dressed. But [then] I go down in my cellar, where I have my study, and work. I try to get to my machine by eight or nine o'clock in the morning. Sometimes I'll run out of steam in the afternoon, but sometimes I'll go until midnight. But you have to treat it as a job; you have to be disciplined. You don't sit around waiting for inspiration. If you do, you're never going to get anything done because it's much more fun taking the dog out for a walk along the canal than sitting down there and writing. But the thing that keeps you going, I think, is that you have these peaks in which you really do begin to feel that you're getting the story told and this chapter looks pretty good. Very often it looks good, and you put it aside; you look at it two weeks later and it looks terrible. So you go back and work on it again.

Stanley Karnow, journalist

SOURCE: *Booknotes*

Thinking about your future career, you probably envision yourself in action—a doctor treating patients, an architect walking through a construction site, a choreographer directing a rehearsal. But whether your goal is Wall Street or the Peace Corps, whether you want to help the homeless or develop accounting software, writing will be critical to your success. In the information age, nearly all jobs involve exchanging data. Computers and the Internet link individuals to a global economy. The Internet has created a world community in which nearly everyone can communicate through web pages, e-mail, blogs, and online "chat rooms." Sitting at a keyboard, you write to the world, reaching out to people who share your ideas, values, and interests. Writing is not an academic exercise but a vocational tool useful in every job.

As a college student you will be judged by the papers, essay examinations, research papers, and lab reports you produce. After graduation you will have to write a convincing letter and résumé to secure job interviews. In fact, throughout your career you will encounter challenges and problems that demand a written response.

Learning to write well sharpens your critical thinking skills, improving your ability to communicate. The strategies you learn in a writing course can also enhance your performance in oral arguments, presentations, job interviews, meetings, and telephone calls. By learning to think more clearly, analyze your audience, and organize your ideas, you will be a more effective communicator in any situation.

The Goals of This Book

The Sundance Writer **has been created to**

✔ Increase your awareness of the importance of writing

✔ Help you appreciate the way context shapes writing

✔ Improve your critical thinking skills

✔ Provide practical tips in overcoming common writing problems

✔ Increase your ability to analyze and use visual images

✔ Introduce you to writing research papers, business documents, and literary criticism

Above all, *The Sundance Writer* was created to help you develop the skills needed to succeed in composition, other courses, and your future career. Because no single text can fully address every aspect of writing, *The Sundance Writer* provides links to other sources. Throughout the book the Companion Website logo connects you to online support, while the Comp 21 logo connects you to additional resources available on the CD-ROM *Comp 21: Composition in the 21st Century for the Patterns of Inquiry*.

USING *THE SUNDANCE WRITER*

The Sundance Writer is divided into six parts: the Rhetoric, Writing in the Information Age, the Reader, Writing in College, the Research Paper, and Grammar and Handbook.

The Rhetoric

Rhetoric is the art of communicating effectively. The eleven chapters in Part 1 of *The Sundance Writer* explain stages in the writing process, providing practical strategies to write more effectively. Writing is challenging, and these chapters will help you develop ideas, overcome writer's block, and avoid common problems.

In addition to guiding you in writing a thesis, supporting your ideas, and improving sentence and paragraph structure, *The Sundance Writer* emphasizes the importance of context and critical thinking. **E-Writing** activities help you explore writing resources on the Internet.

Writing in the Information Age

We live in an era in which most jobs involve exchanging information. Increasingly, we communicate in images as well as words. The Internet, camera phones, and desktop publishing allow people to attach photographs, charts, and graphs to e-mail, letters, and reports. Bloggers often include images on their web pages. Digital photography has made it possible for an image to be broadcast around the world almost instantly. The opening chapters in this part explain how to analyze, interpret, and use images to enhance your critical thinking and writing.

Writing outside of college takes place in a special context. To be effective in your future career you need to appreciate the needs of writing in the workplace. *The Sundance Writer* provides strategies for writing e-mail, résumés, cover letters, and reports.

The final chapter of Part 2 provides advice on special writing situations you may encounter in college and your future career:

- writing in groups, in person, and online
- writing as the representative of others
- writing to a mass audience
- writing to multiple readers
- giving oral and multimedia presentations

The Reader

The Sundance Writer includes more than fifty examples of professional and student writing, each illustrating one of nine modes of writing: description, narration, example, definition, comparison/contrast, process, division/classification, cause and effect, and argument and persuasion. These chapters feature works by George Orwell, Malcolm X, Janice Castro, Barbara Ehrenreich, Anna Quindlen, and Martin Luther King Jr. The subjects cover a range of issues: television, reading, job interviews, homelessness, car repairs, and the sinking of the *Titanic*.

Chapters open with a discussion of the mode, pointing out strategies you can use to improve your writing and avoid errors. Sample writings illustrate how writers in different fields or professions use a particular mode to develop their ideas.

Readings are followed by questions focusing on key aspects of good writing:

Understanding Context Analyze the writer's thesis, purpose, and interpretation of events or ideas.

Evaluating Strategy Review the writer's methods, use of support, and appeals to readers.

Appreciating Language Study the writer's choice of words, tone, and style.

Each entry includes writing suggestions, allowing you to use essays as starting points for your own assignments.

Special Features

Blending the Modes   Each chapter highlights an essay demonstrating how writers use different modes to relate a narrative, establish a comparison, or outline a definition.

Writing Beyond the Classroom   All chapters conclude with a brief example of how writers use the modes in "real world" writing such as ads, brochures, and government documents.

Responding to Images   Each chapter includes an image for you to analyze and discuss or write about.

Opposing Viewpoints   Paired essays present differing opinions on three critical issues: ethnic identity, the abuse defense, and slavery reparations.

Student Papers   Each chapter includes a student sample that serves as a model for the kind of paper you may be expected to write in your course.

E-Reading   Each chapter offers a link to articles available online from InfoTrac® College Edition, providing additional readings on nine key issues: the war on terrorism, the healthcare crisis, fatherhood, TV addiction, immigration, the job market, ethics, public schools, and the criminal justice system.

Companion Website: http://sundance.heinle.com provides support for each mode and supplies additional assignments, exercises, checklists, and sample papers. Throughout *The Sundance Writer* the Companion Website will guide you to online support.

comp 21 | Composition in the 21st Century for the Patterns of Inquiry offers interactive "Explicator" tools for analyzing and annotating essays for each mode, along with interactive tutorials on visual rhetoric and each mode.

Writing in College

Writing the Essay Examination

Throughout your college career you may encounter essay examinations. *The Sundance Writer* includes sample questions and strategies for preparing for examinations and writing better responses.

Writing about Literature

Many courses require students to write about works of literature. This chapter offers strategies for reading and analyzing literature and defines common literary terms. Strategies for writing about fiction, poetry, and drama provide advice for reading and responding to each genre.

The Research Paper

The Sundance Writer provides a complete discussion of the research paper, including several strategies to overcome common misconceptions and problems that often frustrate students. Useful guides are provided to aid students in conducting research:

- Two complete research papers in MLA and APA formats
- Strategies for using Internet sources

Grammar and Handbook

The word *grammar* brings to mind complex rules and mysterious terms, such as *gerunds, nonrestrictive elements, faulty parallelism*, and *dangling modifiers*. But grammar is simply a pattern, a way of putting words into sentences that communicate clearly. The grammar chapter provides a simple explanation of sentence structure and the parts of speech.

The handbook focuses on repairing common writing problems and answers questions students frequently ask: When do I capitalize words? Should it be "it's" or "its"? What's a run-on? Where do commas go?

In addition to grammar explanations and writing strategies, *The Sundance Writer* contains glossaries of grammar terms and commonly confused words, lists of writing topics, and frequently misspelled words.

STRATEGIES | for Succeeding in Composition

1. **Review your syllabus and course materials carefully.** Make sure you fully understand policies on dropping the course, obtaining incompletes, late papers, and grading. Record assignment due dates on a calendar.

2. **Read descriptions of *all* the assignments in the syllabus.** By reading about all the assignments at the beginning of the course, you can think ahead and begin noting ideas for future papers. Often you may be able to use material from other courses or job experiences as topics for assignments.

3. **Review all your textbooks carefully.** Become acquainted with indexes, glossaries, and tables of contents so you can quickly locate information and find help.

4. **Read descriptions of assignments carefully.** Make sure you fully understand what your instructors expect before you begin writing. Review these instructions *after* completing your first draft to make sure you are addressing the needs of the assignment.

5. **Experiment with different composing styles and methods.** Writers use a number of strategies to produce effective writing in a timely manner. Experiment with several prewriting strategies to develop ideas. Write at different times of the day or in new locations. You may discover you do your best work at the laundromat rather than the library.

6. **Talk to other students about writing.** Bounce ideas off other students. Ask for comments about your topic, your thesis, your approach. Determine what information they need to accept your point of view. Ask them what evidence might convince them to change their minds or consider a new viewpoint.

7. **Read your papers aloud before handing them in.** The easiest and fastest way to improve your grades is to read your papers aloud. It is easier to *hear* errors than *see* them. If you read your work aloud, you will catch missing and misspelled words, redundant phrases, wordy sentences, illogical statements, sentence fragments, and irrelevant passages.

8. **Keep copies of all your papers.**

9. **Study your returned papers to improve your grades.** If you do poorly on a paper, your first instinct may be to discard it or bury it under some books. But this paper probably holds the key to getting better grades in the future. Read your instructor's comments carefully and list all the mechanical errors you have made. Refer to the handbook section of this book for further assistance. If you have a tendency to write run-ons or overlook needed commas, target these items when you edit future assignments.

10. **Read with a "writer's eye."** Whether reading for class or personal enjoyment, notice how other writers select details, choose words, and organize ideas. When you discover a passage you find interesting, notice how it is constructed.

11. **Write as often as you can.** Like learning to drive a car or play the piano, writing improves with practice. The more you write, the more natural it will feel to express yourself on paper. Although many composition teachers advise students to keep journals, there are many other strategies that can easily squeeze practice writing into your busy schedule:

    - *Take notes in other classes.* Even if you understand the material in lecture courses, take notes. You can easily get in hours of practice writing by listening to a professor's remarks and restating them in your own words.
    - *Write and e-mail friends.*
    - *Chat on the Internet instead of on the phone.* The liveliest chats on the Internet force you to express yourself by writing. Chatting with friends will lead you to appreciate word choice and challenge you to use writing to make a point, to entertain, to advise.
    - *Freewrite whenever you can.* Riding a bus or waiting for the dryer to switch off, scribble your thoughts in a notebook or the blank pages of a textbook.
    - *Keep a daily journal.* Write at least a paragraph a day in a diary. Comment on political events, what you have seen on television, the latest gossip, the way your job is affecting your ability to study.
    - *Blog.* Join the thousands of everyday people who post their thoughts, experiences, opinions, and feelings in cyberspace using words and images. Ask readers to respond to you. Notice how people react to your ideas and your choice of words. Blogging can teach you a great deal about writing by engaging in discourse with real people about issues that matter to you and others.

The
Rhetoric

THE WRITING PROCESS

AN OVERVIEW

WHAT IS WRITING?

Writing is a process as well as a product. Writing requires creativity, concentration, and determination. Even professional writers struggle with the same problems you face in college—setting the right tone, explaining complicated ideas, sharing experiences that are difficult to put into words, deciding which details to add and which to delete, and, often toughest of all, just getting started.

Hollywood has depicted writers as people who work in bursts of inspiration. Tough reporters, usually with cigarettes dangling from their lips, rush to their typewriters and pound out flawless stories that they tear off and hand to copyboys without changing a line. Poets gaze dreamily through a window or at the portrait of a lost love and in a flash of creativity dash out a masterpiece, the soundtrack soaring in the background.

In reality, most writers don't have time to wait until inspiration strikes. Writing, like building a table or creating a computer program, takes effort. Although it helps to think about a topic, it rarely pays to wait, hoping for a sudden insight to automatically guide you. *The best way to begin writing is to write.*

WRITERS AT WORK

In the old days, when I used to write on a type-writer, I would start my drafts on that yellow paper. I just opened my mind and just kept going. I would never know exactly what I was going to say until my fingers were on the keyboard and I'd just type. And a lot of it would be junk, so I'd retype it, and then I'd put in more, and it would get better. These were called "zero minus drafts," and they were on the yellow paper. And then I would cut them up, and cut and paste, and I'd have these cut-and-paste yellow pie sheets. Then finally it would begin to look like it should, and then I'd start typing on white paper, and then I'd have white paper with yellow parts on it. By the time it got to all white paper, that was the first draft. Now I write on a computer, but I just do endless drafts.

Nell Irvin Painter, historian

SOURCE: *Booknotes*

DEVELOPING A COMPOSING STYLE

Writers work in many patterns. Some take extensive notes and develop intricate outlines before writing, while others simply plunge into their subjects and write in all directions, knowing they will discard much of what they produce. Some writers agonize over the first page, unable to move on until the first three or four paragraphs are complete. Others race through half a dozen drafts, slowly revising and reshaping a loose, illogical, misspelled mass of writing into refined prose. The popular novelist Harold Robbins reported he was amazed when he met Jacqueline Suzanne, another best-selling author. Suzanne, he discovered, constructed detailed outlines of her books, listing every episode and character. She wrote passages out of context, then taped them to a timeline she had sketched on the wall. When all of the scenes were completed, she assembled the chapters and wrote a second draft. Robbins, however, began with a few characters in his head and started writing, having no idea who the hero would be or how the novel would end. Driving at night, he pointed out, you don't have to see your final destination, only the next few hundred feet. A writer, he argued, has to think only a page ahead.

Writing is deeply personal. Some writers can work only in the quiet of a library; others are able to plug in their laptops and write in crowded airports and noisy restaurants. Many writers prefer to work at certain times of day, in specific rooms, or in a favorite coffee shop, and use pencils, an antique fountain pen, or a computer. Some writers work in two- or three-hour blocks; others work in fits and starts, continually interrupting themselves to study for a quiz or run an errand.

If you have not been accustomed to writing, it may take you a while to discover when, where, and how you will be most productive. As you get more practice, you may learn that you do your best work under conditions your friends would find impossible. If you find yourself thinking and writing best with a television on, don't feel guilty. Writing does not have to take place in the hushed silence of a book-lined study.

On the other hand, you may have developed some bad habits that hamper your ability to write. If you find writing difficult, consider changing the time, place, and conditions in which you write. Even if you achieve high grades, you may wish to examine the way you compose to see whether you can improve the process.

In the past, composition teachers believed that writing occurred in fixed stages and encouraged students to follow them in strict order. Further research has revealed that writing is a *recursive* process—writers repeat steps, often carrying out two or three simultaneously. Writing on a computer makes it easy to scroll up and down, jotting down ideas for the conclusion, then moving back to change a word or two to polish the introduction. Though they may not follow them in any particular order, most good writers use these six stages:

Prewrite	Explore topics, develop ideas.
Plan	Establish context and outline points.
Write	Get your ideas on paper.
Cool	Put your writing aside.
Revise	Review your draft and rewrite.
Edit	Check your final document.

At first glance, a six-step process may appear complex and time-consuming, but mastering these strategies can improve the speed and quality of your writing:

1. **PREWRITE—Explore topics, develop ideas.** Good writing does more than record what you "feel" about a subject—it explores issues, asks questions, engages readers, and moves beyond the obvious. Writing starts with critical thinking—observing details, testing commonly held assumptions, and distinguishing between fact and opinion. Prewriting takes many forms—making lists, sketching ideas, and noting facts. Prewriting helps you look at the world with new eyes, prompting you to develop fresh ideas and establish a point of view.

2. **PLAN—Establish context and outline ideas.** Once you have established your goal, develop your thesis—your main idea—and supporting ideas in the context formed by the needs of your reader, the standards of the

discourse community (a particular discipline, profession, community, culture, or situation), and the conventions or requirements of the document. If you are responding to an assignment, for example, make sure your plan addresses the instructor's requirements. Develop an outline listing the items you need to achieve your goal and the best way to arrange them. Your opening should attract attention, announce the topic, and prepare readers for the ideas presented in the body of the document. The conclusion should bring the paper to a logical end, using a final observation, quotation, or question to make a lasting impression. An outline does not have to be a formal plan using Roman numerals and capital letters—it can be a list or a diagram that allows you to visualize the essay on a single sheet of paper. Outlining helps to organize ideas, spot missing information, and prevent writing in circles or going off topic.

Long projects should include a budget or timeline. If you are working on a research paper that will take weeks to complete, consult a calendar to break the process into steps. Don't spend six weeks conducting research and expect to write and revise a twenty-page paper over a weekend. Make sure you allot enough time for *each* stage in the writing process.

Later chapters discuss how to recognize and work in specific writing contexts.

3. **WRITE—Get your ideas on paper.** After reviewing your plan, write as much as possible without stopping. As you write, new ideas may occur to you. Record *all* your thoughts. It is easier to delete ideas later rather than try to remember something you forgot to include. Do not pause to check spelling or look up a fact because these interruptions may break your train of thought. Instead, make notes as you go. Underline words you think are misused or misspelled. Leave gaps for missing details. Write quick reminders in parentheses or the margins. Place question marks next to passages that may be inaccurate, unclear, or ungrammatical. *Above all, keep writing!*

4. **COOL—Put your writing aside.** This is the easiest but one of the most important steps in the writing process. It is difficult to evaluate your work immediately after writing because much of what you wish to say is still fresh in your mind. Set your draft aside. Work on other assignments, run an errand, watch television, or read a book to clear your mind. Afterward, you can return to your writing with more objectivity. Just ten minutes of "cooling" can help you gain a new perspective on your work, remember missing details, and eliminate errors you may have overlooked.

5. **REVISE—Review your draft and rewrite.** Before searching your paper for misspelled words or fragments, evaluate it holistically. Review your assignment and your plan. Does what you have created meet the needs of your audience? Does it suit the discourse community? Does it follow the format

expected in this document? If you have developed new ideas, are they relevant? You may find that your first attempt has failed and you must start fresh. Or your first draft may be so well crafted that you can move directly to editing without rewriting. Remember that an essay should have a clear focus—it is not a collection of everything you can think of. Don't be afraid to delete ideas that do not directly support your thesis. You may have developed some interesting points, but they may not belong in this assignment.

6. **EDIT—Check the final document.** When you have completed your last revision, examine it for missing details, grammatical errors, and misspelled words. In addition, review your diction. Eliminate wordy phrases and reduce repetition. Make sure your ideas flow evenly and have clear transitions. Reading a paper aloud can help you spot errors and awkward passages.

Finally, keep in mind that each writing assignment is unique. For example, a narrative requires attention to chronology, a division paper demands clear organization, and persuasion depends on the skillful use of logic. Each discipline represents a distinct discourse community. In literature courses students are expected to provide original interpretations of a play or novel. In the sciences students are required to follow strict standards of gathering data, analyzing results, and presenting conclusions. Undoubtedly, you may find some papers more challenging than others. Because it is often difficult to determine how hard a particular assignment may be, it is advisable to start writing as soon as possible. Just ten minutes of prewriting will quickly reveal how much time and effort you need to devote to this paper.

Creating a Composing Style

✔ **Review your past writing.** Consider how you have written in the past. Which papers received the highest and lowest grades in high school? Why? What can you recall about writing them? What mistakes have you made? What comments have teachers made about your work?

✔ **Experiment with composing.** Write at different times and places, using pen and paper or a computer. See what conditions enhance your writing.

✔ **Study returned papers for clues.** Read your instructors' comments carefully. If your papers lack a clear thesis, devote more attention to prewriting and planning. If instructors fill your papers with red ink, circling misspelled words and underlining fragments, you should spend more time editing.

WRITING ON A COMPUTER

Almost every business and profession today requires computer literacy. If you find yourself overwhelmed by technology, as many professional writers do, consider taking a computer course. Many colleges offer one-credit courses or free seminars. If nothing else, ask a friend or classmate to show you how he or she uses a computer to write.

STRATEGIES | for Writing on a Computer

1. **Appreciate the advantages and limitations of using a computer.** Computers can speed up the writing process, allowing you to add ideas, correct spelling, and delete sentences without having to retype an entire page. But computers will not automatically make you a better writer. They cannot refine a thesis, improve your logic, or enhance critical thinking. Don't confuse the neatness of the finished product with good writing. An attractively designed document must still achieve all the goals of good writing.

2. **Learn the features of your program.** If you are unfamiliar with writing on a computer, make sure you learn how to move blocks of text, change formats, check spelling, and, most important, master the Print and Save functions. Find out whether your program has an Undo option. This can save the day if you accidentally erase or "lose" some of your text. Selecting this option simply undoes your last action, restoring deleted text or eliminating what you just added.

3. **Save your work.** If your program has an automatic Save function, use it. Save your work to a disc, hard drive, portable USB drive, or Internet space (such as Yahoo! Briefcase). For extremely important projects, it is best to save work in more than one place. If you are using a college or library computer and do not have a disc, print your work after a writing session or e-mail it to yourself as an attachment. Don't let a power shortage or a keystroke error cause you to lose your work!

4. **Label your files clearly.** Because some programs limit the number of characters you can use in a file title, choose your names carefully. Develop a clear notation system, such as ENG1 or PSYCH2. If you wish to save a new version of your first English essay, you can make it ENG1A. Maintain a log file that describes each file in detail. This index can save time and prevent you from having to open dozens of similarly named files to find the one you want.

5. **Print drafts of your work as you write.** Computer screens usually allow you to view less than a page of text at a time. Although it is easy to scroll up and down, it can be difficult to revise on the screen. You may find it easier to work with a hard copy of your paper. You may wish to double- or even triple-space before you print, so that you have plenty of room for handwritten notations.

6. **Use spell and grammar checks but recognize their limitations.** Spell checks will go through your document and flag words the computer's dictionary does not recognize, quickly locating many mistakes you might overlook on your own. But spell checks do not locate missing words or recognize errors in usage, such as confusing *there* and *their* or *adopt* and *adapt*. Grammar checks sometimes offer awkward suggestions and flag correct expressions as errors. *Reading your text aloud is still the best method of editing.*

WRITER'S BLOCK

Almost everyone experiences writer's block—the inability to write. With a paper due in a few days, you may find yourself incapable of coming up with a single line, even unable to sit at your desk. You can feel frustrated, nervous, bored, tired, or anxious. The more time passes, the more you think about the upcoming assignment, the more frustrated you can become. There is no magic cure for writer's block, but there are some tactics you can try.

STRATEGIES | for Overcoming Writer's Block

1. **Recognize that writer's block exists.** When you have the time to write, write. Don't assume that if you have two weeks to complete an assignment, you will be able to write well for fourteen days. Get as much writing done as you can, when you can. If you delay work, you may find yourself unable to write as the deadline nears.

2. **Review your assignment.** Sometimes the reason you feel that you have nothing to say is that you have not fully understood the assignment. Read it carefully and turn the instructions into a series of questions to generate ideas.

3. **If you are "stuck" for a topic, review the assignment, select key words, and search the Internet.** See what web pages these words produce. Even wholly unrelated references can sometimes spark your imagination and help identify subjects. Keep in mind that photos and other images you find can also inspire writing.

4. **Write anything.** The more you put off writing, the harder it will be to start. If you have trouble focusing on your assignment, get into the mood and feel of writing by sending an e-mail to a friend. Use instant messaging to get into the rhythm of expressing yourself in writing.

5. **Read what you have already written.** Sometimes looking at an assignment you have completed can give you confidence and remind you how you found a topic, developed ideas, and organized details. If you have managed to complete part of the assignment, read it over several times and try to remember what you were thinking when you were writing these lines.

6. **Talk to a friend and discuss your assignment or goal.** A casual conversation can lead you to see new approaches to your subject. A spirited discussion can spark free associations about your topic. Talking with a friend can often boost your confidence and reduce your anxiety. Post a statement or question in an online chat room or create a weblog (blog) to generate comments.

7. **Force yourself to write for five minutes.** Sit down and write about your topic for five minutes nonstop. Let one idea run into another. Keep writing, even if it is to repeat a nursery rhyme or a radio jingle. Even writing nonsense will help you break the physical resistance you may have to sitting down and working with a pen or keyboard. Try to steer your experimental writing to the assigned task. If your draft is going nowhere, stop after five minutes—but make sure you save it. Take a walk or run some errands, then return to your writing. Sometimes seeing a word or phrase out of context will lead to significant associations.

8. **Lower your standards.** Don't be afraid to write poorly. Write as well as you can, making notes in the margin as you go along to remind yourself of areas that need revision. Remember that writing is recursive and even badly written statements can form the foundation of a good paper.

9. **Don't feel obligated to start at the beginning.** If you find yourself unable to develop a convincing opening line or satisfactory introduction, begin writing the body or conclusion of the paper. Get your ideas flowing.

10. **Switch subjects.** If you are bogged down on your English paper, start work on the history paper due next month. Writing well on a different subject may help you gain confidence to return to an assignment you find difficult.

11. **Record your thoughts on tape or index cards.** If you find writing frustrating, consider talking into a tape recorder or listing ideas on index cards. You may find working with "nonwriting" materials an effective method of getting started.

12. **Try writing in a different location.** If you can't work on the paper at home because of distractions, go to the library or a quiet room. If the library feels stifling, move to a less formal environment. You may find yourself doing your best work drinking coffee in a noisy student union.

13. **If you still have problems with your assignment, talk to your instructor.** Try to identify what is giving you the most trouble. Is it the act of writing itself, finding a topic, organizing your thoughts, or developing a thesis?

WRITING ACTIVITIES

1. Choose a topic from the list on pages 903–904 and use the six-step method described in this chapter to draft a short essay. As you write, note which stages of the process pose the greatest challenges. Alter your composing style in any way that improves your writing.

2. Select an upcoming assignment and write a rough draft. Use this experience to identify areas that require the most attention. Save your notes and draft for future use.

3. Write a letter or e-mail to a friend about a recent experience. Before sending it, set the letter aside, letting it "cool." After two or three days, examine your draft for missing details, awkward or confusing phrases, misspelled words, or repetitious statements. Notice how revision and editing can improve your writing.

e-writing

Exploring Writing Resources Online

The Internet offers an ever-growing variety of resources for student writers: dictionaries, encyclopedias, grammar drills, databases of periodicals, library catalogs, editing exercises, and research guides.

1. Review the Companion Website for *The Sundance Writer* at **www.thomsonedu.com/english/sundance.**

2. Review your library's electronic databases, links, and search engines. Locate online dictionaries and encyclopedias you can use as references while writing assignments.

3. Using a search engine, such as Yahoo!, Google, or Alta Vista, enter key words, such as *prewriting, proofreading, narration, capitalization, thesis statement, comma exercises, editing strategies,* and other terms that appear throughout the book, the index, or your course syllabus. In addition to formal databases, many instructors and writing centers have constructed online tutorials that can help you improve your writing, overcome troubling grammar problems, and aid in specific assignments.

4. Ask your instructors for useful websites. Use your browser's Bookmark function to keep track of these and other sources you find useful.

For Further Reading

Elbow, Peter. *Writing Without Teachers.*

Flesch, Rudolf, and A. H. Lass. *The Classic Guide to Better Writing.*

Strunk, William, and E. B. White. *The Elements of Style.*

Zinsser, William. *On Writing Well: The Classic Guide to Writing Nonfiction.*

E-Sources

Writing in College: A Short Guide to College Writing
http://writing-program.uchicago.edu/resources/collegewriting

Online Writing Lab at Purdue University
http://owl.english.purdue.edu/handouts/general

The Nuts and Bolts of College Writing
http://www.nutsandboltsguide.com

Companion Website

See **http://www.thomsonedu.com/english/sundance** for further information on the writing process.

THE WRITING CONTEXT

> You don't write because you want to say something; you write because you've got something to say.
> —F. Scott Fitzgerald

WHAT IS GOOD WRITING?

No doubt you have read things that break the "rules" of good writing. Advertisements include slang. Novels contain fragments. Scientific journals run multisyllabic terms into paragraph-long sentences. Government reports are filled with indecipherable acronyms.

Writing can be judged only in context. Writing does not occur in a vacuum but in a context shaped by four factors:

1. The writer's purpose and role
2. The knowledge base, attitudes, needs, expectations, and biases of the reader
3. The discipline or profession, community, culture, or event in which the writing takes place
4. The nature of the document or publication

Another way of thinking of context is to think of a "genre"—a kind or type of writing. The genre a writer is working within takes into account all four factors. Genre explains why a story about an airplane crash in the *Chicago Tribune* differs from an FAA report or the airline's condolence letter to the victims' families. Stated simply and printed in narrow columns for easy skimming, a

WRITERS AT WORK

I sit at my computer and write, and then when I have a couple of sentences, I read them over aloud to see how they sound—not what they look like, but how they sound. Could a reader get the meaning of this? Could he follow the words and sound of it? . . . I talk to myself as I write in the hope of getting something of the spoken language into the written page because I think that's the way people read.

David Herbert Donald, Lincoln scholar

SOURCE: *Booknotes*

newspaper account briefly describes current events for general readers. An FAA investigation will produce multivolume reports including extensive test results and testimony of survivors and witnesses. Directed to aviation safety experts, the report is presented in technical language largely incomprehensible to the average reader. In contrast, the airline's letter to victims' families addresses people experiencing confusion, grief, loss, and anger. Carefully drafted by crisis communications experts and reviewed by attorneys, it attempts to inform without admitting liability or appearing falsely sympathetic.

Writing that is successful in one context may not be acceptable in another. The lecture notes you write to prepare for an upcoming examination may be totally useless to other students. If you keep a diary, you may be reluctant to alter the context by allowing your roommate to read it. The essay about sexual harassment that impresses your instructor and classmates in English might be rejected by the editor of the college paper as too "wordy" for the editorial page. A psychology professor may find your essay's comments about male and female sexual behavior simplistic and unsupported by research. An attorney could dismiss your thesis, arguing the policies you urge the university to accept would be unconstitutional.

You unconsciously alter the way you communicate depending on context. Imagine that on your way to class, a van runs a red light and smashes into your car. When you relate the accident to a police officer, you re-create events as accurately as possible. Because you realize that your comments will become part of an official record, you provide details about the position of the vehicles at the time of impact. Taken to the hospital for X-rays, you tell the physician about the accident, focusing on your injuries. Calling your parents, you explain what happened, reassuring them that you are all right. Meeting friends at the student union, however, you might find yourself exaggerating events for dramatic effect. Seeking comfort, you send an e-mail to your best friend, telling her how upset you are by the accident, urging her to call. Later, sitting alone with your diary, you record your private thoughts about the fragility of life.

To be an effective writer, it is important to realize that there is no standard form of "good writing" that is suitable in all circumstances. Understanding the role of context will help you achieve your goals in writing.

Questions

1. Can you recall situations in which you had difficulty expressing yourself because you were unsure how your reader would react? Did you have problems finding the right word or just "getting your ideas on paper"?
2. Have you found that professors have different attitudes about what constitutes "good writing"? How is writing a paper in English literature different than writing one in psychology or economics?
3. Have you noticed that magazines have strikingly different writing styles? What do articles in the *Nation, Car and Driver, Ms., Oprah, Cosmopolitan, Time, People,* and *Rolling Stone* reveal about their readers?

THE WRITER

The Writer's Purpose

Everything you write has a goal. The note you scribble on a Post-it® and stick on your computer screen reminds you of an upcoming test. Research papers demonstrate your skills and knowledge in college courses. The résumé you submit to employers is designed to secure an interview. The announcement stapled on campus bulletin boards alerts students to an upcoming rally or sporting event.

Good writing has a clear goal—to inform, to entertain, or to persuade. Students and professionals in all fields face similar writing tasks. The way they present their ideas, the language they use, and even the physical appearance of the finished document are determined in part by their purpose. Although each writing assignment forms a unique context, most writing tasks can be divided into basic modes or types:

Description   *To create a picture or impression of a person, place, object, or condition.* Description is an element in all writing and usually serves as support of the writer's main goal. Descriptions can be wholly factual and objective, as in an accident report, encyclopedia article, or parts catalog. In other instances, descriptions are highly personal and subjective, offering readers a writer's impression of a person or subject.

Narration   *To relate a series of events, usually in chronological order.* Biographies, histories, and novels use narration. Business and government reports often include sections called *narratives* that provide a historical overview of a problem, organization, or situation. Narration can be fictional or factual, and it can be related in first or third person.

Example   *To present a specific person, place, object, event, or situation as representative or symbolic of a larger subject.* A writer may isolate a particular event and describe it in detail so readers can have a fuller appreciation of a larger or more abstract topic. The fate of a single business may be related in detail to illustrate an economic or technological trend, for example.

Definition   *To explain a term, condition, topic, or issue.* In many instances definitions are precise and standard, such as a state's definition of second-degree murder or a biology book's definition of a virus. Other definitions, such as the definition of a good teacher or parent, may be based on a writer's personal observation, values, experience, and opinion.

Comparison and Contrast   *To examine the similarities and differences between two or more subjects.* Textbooks often employ comparison or contrast to discuss different scientific methods, theories, or subjects. Comparisons may be made to distinguish items or to recommend one theory as superior to others. Consumer magazines, for example, frequently compare competing products.

Process   *To explain how something occurs or to demonstrate how to accomplish a specific task.* Writers can explain how nuclear power plants generate power, how the Internet works, or how the liver functions by breaking the process down into a series of events or stages. Writers also use process to provide directions. Recipes, operator's manuals, and first-aid books provide step-by-step instructions to accomplish specific tasks.

Division   *To name subgroups in a broad class.* Writers seek to make complex topics understandable or workable by dividing them into smaller units. Insurance can be divided into life, health, homeowner's, and auto policies. Biology texts divide the human body into the respiratory, nervous, digestive, and other systems. Writers can develop their own divisions, often creating labels in the process.

Classification   *To place subjects in different classes or levels according to a standard measurement.* Writers use classification to rate subjects. Teachers assign paper grades based on their quality. Homicides are classified as first, second, or third degree according to circumstances and premeditation. As with division, writers often establish subjective classifications, creating a personal system to rate people, products, or ideas.

Cause and Effect   *To trace the reasons for an occurrence or predict the results of an event.* A writer can explain the causes for a decrease in crime, a rise in the stock market, the election of a mayoral candidate, or the extinction of a species. Similarly, he or she could detail the effects a decrease in crime will have on property values, how rising stock values will impact pension funds, how the new mayor will influence the business community, or what effect the loss of a species will have on the environment.

Argument and Persuasion   *To influence opinion and motivate actions.* Writers persuade readers using logical appeals based on evidence and reasoning, ethical appeals based on values or beliefs, and emotional appeals that arouse feelings to support their views. Fund-raising letters motivate readers to donate to charities or political campaigns. Advertisements encourage consumers to try new products. Essayists, columnists, and commentators try to influence readers to accept their views on issues ranging from abortion to casino gambling.

Questions

1. Consider how you have used these modes in the past. How often have you used them to achieve your goals in communicating with people? Can you think of essay questions that directed you to demonstrate your knowledge by writing comparison or cause and effect? Have you used comparison, division, or cause and effect to organize e-mails or business letters?

2. How often do you use modes such as comparison or classification in organizing your ideas and solving problems? Before you buy a product, do you compare it to others? Do you classify the courses you would like to take next semester by their difficulty or desirability? Do you seek solutions to problems by applying cause-and-effect reasoning?

A Note about Modes

Modes refer to a writer's basic goal. Few writing tasks, however, call for use of a single mode. In most instances, writers blend modes to achieve their goals. A biographer's main purpose is to tell a story, to *narrate* the events of a person's life. Within this narrative, the author may use *cause and effect* to explain the forces that molded a person's childhood, draw *comparisons* to illustrate how that person differed from his or her peers, and *persuade* readers to accept the subject as an *example* or role model. Some writing blends modes equally so that E. B. White's essay "Once More to the Lake" is considered *narration* by some readers and *description* by others. The Declaration of Independence uses both *cause and effect* and *persuasion* to motivate readers.

When you write, select the mode or modes that suit your purpose. Don't feel obligated to "fit" your paper into any single pattern. As you will see when you read the essays in *The Sundance Writer,* most writers develop their ideas using a number of modes.

The Writer's Role

The way writers create documents is greatly shaped by their role. An independent blogger may spew out whatever comes into his or her head to amuse, influence, annoy, or infuriate nameless readers in cyberspace. A corporate attorney who is drafting a response to an angry customer demanding a refund is guided by company policy, the standards of the legal profession, and the peers and superiors he or she is representing.

In college your role is like that of a freelance writer. Your essays, reports, and research papers are expected to reflect only your own efforts. In general, your work is judged independently. The grades you receive in psychology have no effect on the way your English papers will be examined. A low grade on your midterm essay does not influence how your final will be evaluated. In addition, college instructors are supposed to be objective. In a composition class, your papers are likely to be graded by *how* you state your views, not *what* they are. Your opinions on controversial views are not likely to be raised in future courses or at job interviews.

The academic environment is unique and very different from what you will encounter after graduation. Beyond the classroom, your role may be more complicated. First, you will be seeking more than an endorsement of your writing ability. Instead of an "A," you will be asking readers to invest money, buy a product, give you a job, accept your idea, or change their opinions on an important issue. In addition, you may have an ongoing relationship with your reader. If you give a client bad news in November, you cannot expect that he or she will read your December letter with much enthusiasm. It is important to consider how one message will affect the way future messages will be evaluated.

In many instances your profession dictates a role that greatly influences the kind of writing you will be expected to produce. Police officers and nurses, for example, are required to provide objective and impersonal records of their observations and actions. Fashion designers, decorators, and advertising copywriters, who are judged by their creativity and originality, are more likely to offer personal insights and write in the first person.

Questions

1. Consider the jobs you have had in the past and organizations you have worked for. What writing style would be considered appropriate for employees in these fields? Was objective reporting more important than personal opinion? Can you consider instances where an employee could jeopardize his or her job by making inappropriate statements to customers or

clients? What image did the organization try to project in its memos, ads, brochures, and other communications to employees and the public?

2. What kind of writing would be effective in your future career? How does writing in engineering or medical malpractice law differ from writing in sales, hotel management, or charities? Does your future profession demand strict adherence to government or corporate regulations or allow for personal expression?

THE READER

Writing is more than an act of self-expression; it is an act of communication. To be effective your message must be understood. The content, form, style, and tone of your writing is shaped by the needs, expectations, and attitudes of your readers. A medical researcher announcing a new treatment for AIDS would write an article for *Immunology* very differently than one for *Newsweek* or *Redbook*. Each magazine represents a different audience, knowledge base, and set of concerns. Doctors and scientists would be interested in the writer's research methods and demand detailed proof of his or her claims. These readers would expect to see extensive data and precise descriptions of experiments and testing methods. Most readers of nonmedical publications would need definitions of scientific terms and explanations of data they would be unable to interpret. Readers of *Newsweek* would be interested in a range of issues such as cost, government policy, and insurance coverage. Subscribers to a women's magazine might wonder if the treatment works equally well for both sexes or if the treatment would be suitable for pregnant women with HIV.

As a writer you have to determine how much knowledge your readers have about your subject. Are you writing to a general audience or specialized readers from the same discipline, profession, or area of interest? Do technical terms require definition? Are there common misunderstandings that should be explained? Do you make historical or biographical references unfamiliar to readers? In addition to your reader's level of knowledge about your subject, you should consider your readers' goals, needs, and expectations. What information do your readers want? Is your audience reading for general interest, curiosity, or entertainment? Or do your readers demand specific details in order to make decisions and plan future actions?

It is also important to take into account how your readers will respond to your ideas. Who are your readers? Are they likely to be friendly, uninterested, or hostile to you, your ideas, or the organization you might represent? What are their interests and concerns? Defense attorneys and police officers have different attitudes toward testimony offered by informers. Environmentalists and real estate developers have conflicting philosophies of land use. Liberals and conservatives have opposing concepts of the proper role of government. When presenting ideas to audiences with undefined or differing attitudes, you will have to work hard to overcome their natural resistance, biases, and suspicions.

Individual Readers

The papers you write in high school and college are usually read by a single instructor evaluating your work within the context of a specific course. Teachers and professors form a special audience because they generally provide clear instructions outlining requirements for each assignment. They are obligated to read your writing and are usually objective in their evaluations.

Beyond the classroom, however, you may have to persuade people to read your work. No one is required to read your résumé or proposal. Your readers will be expected to do more than evaluate how effective your writing is. You will be asking readers to give you a job, buy your product, or accept your opinions. You may ask readers to invest substantial resources on your behalf, conceivably placing their careers in your hands. When you write to individuals, you will have to carefully analyze their needs, concerns, and objections.

The more you learn about the individual you are writing to, the better equipped you will be to shape an effective message. If possible, speak with or e-mail this person to gain greater insight about his or her background, needs, interests, and concerns. Before submitting a long report, you may be able to "test" your ideas by sending a letter or preliminary draft for consideration and discussion before committing yourself to a final document.

Extended Audiences

In college most of your papers are graded and returned. Beyond the classroom, there are often two audiences: immediate readers who receive your documents and a second, extended audience. In most professional situations, letters, reports, and memos are retained for future reference. The angry letter you send to an irate customer may be passed on by the consumer to your supervisor, the Better Business Bureau, or an attorney. At a trial, it may be entered into evidence and read to a jury. The safety inspection report you write in March may be routinely skimmed and filed. But if a serious accident occurs in April, this report will be retrieved and closely examined by insurance investigators, state inspectors, and attorneys for the injured. The handouts you give to high school students may be read by parents and members of the school board. Whenever you write beyond the classroom, realize that many people other than your immediate readers may see your documents. Avoid making remarks that may be misunderstood out of context.

The Perceptual World

To fully appreciate the way readers will respond to your ideas, it is useful to understand what communications experts call the *perceptual world*—the context in which people respond to new information and experiences. As individuals or as members of groups, readers base their responses on a variety of factors that have varying significance. Advertising and marketing executives analyze the perceptual world of consumers to design new products and commercials. Trial attorneys assess the perceptual world of juries to determine their most persuasive argument. Biographers and psychologists often construct the perceptual world of an individual to explain past actions or predict future behavior. Political candidates take polls, conduct interviews, and operate focus groups to establish the perceptual worlds of voters in key districts.

The perceptual world is often depicted as a circle to indicate that its elements are not ranked in any particular order and often operate simultaneously.

Past experiences influence how people react to new information and situations. Readers who have lost money in the stock market will be more skeptical of an investment offer than those who have enjoyed substantial

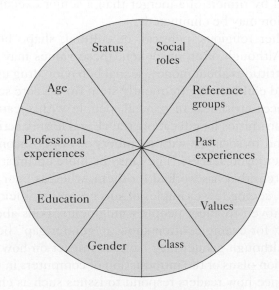

The Perceptual World

profits. People who have a history of conflict with law enforcement may view police officers differently than those who rely on their services to protect their property. The way people behave as parents is often determined by their own childhood.

Education, both formal and informal, shapes the intellectual background against which new ideas are examined and tested. Readers with greater academic training are in a stronger position to measure ideas, evaluate evidence, and analyze the validity of a writer's conclusions. Education in specific disciplines will influence how readers consider the evidence writers present. Scientists and mathematicians, for example, are more likely than the general public to question advertising claims using statistics.

Professional experiences, along with training and career responsibilities, form people's attitudes about a number of issues. An economics professor with tenure may more easily embrace a new tax policy than a struggling business owner worrying about meeting next week's payroll. Occupations expose readers to a range of situations, problems, and people, leading them to develop distinct attitudes and values about the government, success, crime, relationships, money, and technology.

Status influences people's responses, especially to change. A proposed modification in Social Security policies will be of little interest to high school students but of immediate importance to those collecting benefits. An entry-level employee with little invested in a corporation may feel less threatened by rumors of a merger than a senior executive whose hard-won position may be eliminated.

Values, whether religious, political, or cultural, shape how readers react to ideas. Although often unspoken, these values may be deeply held. People's attitudes about money, sexual behavior, drug use, politics, technology, and child rearing frequently stem from a core set of beliefs.

Class influences attitudes. In general, people with greater incomes have more opportunities for education, travel, and leisure activities. Wealthier people tend to socialize with members of upper-income groups, those who have enjoyed success. They may be more optimistic about the economic system that has worked for them, whereas poor people may feel oppressed, seeing few examples of success among their peers.

Gender has proven to affect people's judgments. Polls about a president's popularity, for example, often show a "gender gap" between men and women. Although gender may have no impact on how people evaluate their pension plans or the introduction of computers in the workplace, it can influence how readers respond to issues such as child care, divorce laws, and sexual harassment.

Social roles, such as being a parent, civic leader, or homeowner, influence how people interpret new ideas. A thirty-year-old with two small children has different concerns than someone of the same age with no dependents. Board members of charitable organizations may feel an obligation to represent the interests of those less fortunate than themselves.

Reference groups include people or institutions readers respect and defer to in making judgments. A physician unsure about prescribing a new drug may base his or her decision on recommendations by the American Medical Association. Before leaving college to take a job offer, a student might discuss her decision with friends or advisers.

Age affects how people look at the world and interpret experiences. An eighteen-year-old naturally views life differently than a fifty-year-old. In addition, people's attitudes are influenced by their experiences. People who came of age during the protracted conflict in Vietnam may have different views of using military power than a younger generation whose experience of war was limited to viewing television images of the Gulf War.

Other aspects of the perceptual world can include physical stature, ethnic background, and geography. In determining your readers' perceptual world, it is important to realize that in some instances people will respond to your ideas based on their entire life experiences. In other circumstances, they may react in solely a professional role or because your ideas trigger a specific reaction. In assessing perceptual worlds, avoid basing your assumptions on stereotypes. Not all older people are conservative, and not all minorities support affirmative action. Some Roman Catholics support women's rights to obtain an abortion, and some feminists consider themselves pro-life. Many elements of a reader's perceptual world are unconscious and cannot be easily ascertained. But by learning as much as you can about your readers, you can better determine which strategies will influence them to accept your ideas.

Questions

1. How would you describe your own perceptual world? Which factors most influence the way you respond to new ideas?
2. How would you describe the perceptual world of your parents, coworkers, and friends? Are there sharp individual differences? Are there shared values and experiences that might lead them to respond as a group in some circumstances? How would they respond to a letter urging them to donate money to a homeless shelter, support a handgun ban, or vote for a candidate? Which issues would be difficult to present to them? Why?

3. Have you ever tried to understand someone you hoped to influence? In practicing a presentation, preparing for a job interview, or seeking the right words to discuss a difficult issue with family or friends, do you consider how your audience will react? Is understanding people's perceptual worlds something we engage in every day?
4. Examine the photographs on pages 178, 180, 185, and 186. How do your attitudes, experiences, social roles, and values affect the way you perceive these images? Can you predict how other people might respond to them?

Evaluating Readers

In many situations you will be unable to learn much about your readers. A want ad may offer only a box number to respond to. Foundations and government agencies sometimes have strict policies that limit information given to applicants. In most cases, however, you can learn something about your reader or readers that can guide your writing.

General Readers

1. Envision your readers. Who are you writing to? What kind of person are you addressing? How do you want people to respond to your ideas?
2. Consider your purpose. What are you asking your readers to accept or do? What objections might they have to your thesis? How can you answer their questions or address their concerns? Play the devil's advocate and list all the possible objections people may have to your ideas, evidence, and word choice. How can you overcome these objections?
3. Test your writing. Before printing or mailing an announcement, ad, or brochure, present it to a small group of people who represent your wider audience. Even a group of friends sometimes can detect errors, misleading statements, or inappropriate comments you may have overlooked.

Individual Readers

1. As a college student, ask instructors for further guidelines about upcoming assignments and request comments on an outline or rough draft.
2. For writing beyond the classroom, learn as much as you can about your reader. If you cannot obtain personal information, learn what you can about the organization he or she is associated with. What does your reader's profession suggest about his or her perceptual world?
3. Before submitting a résumé or proposal, call ahead and see whether you can speak to the person who will evaluate your work. Even a brief conversation with a receptionist or assistant can provide insight about your reader.

Extended Readers

1. Determine who else may see your writing. How will the administration respond to an article you write for the student newspaper or a comment about the college you post on the Internet? Will your managers approve of the tone and style of the e-mails you send customers?
2. Review your writing to see if it reflects the kind of image your organization or professional peers feel is appropriate.
3. Realize that your writing may surface months or years later. Think how what you write today will affect your future options. What values do you wish to project in your career? How do you wish to represent yourself? Can anything you write today blemish your future?

THE DISCOURSE COMMUNITY

The communication between writer and reader takes place in a particular environment, discipline, profession, community, culture, situation, or publication. A doctor responding to a reader's question for an advice column in a women's magazine has different concerns and responsibilities than one answering an e-mail from one of his or her patients. A lawyer discussing the first amendment in a law review article may use hypothetical examples and discuss abstract legal principles. The same lawyer drafting a motion for a judge about a specific case will have to limit his or her writing to evidence relevant to a single situation and a single defendant. Effective writers are sensitive to the role the discourse community has on how their ideas will be received and evaluated. Like the perceptual world of the reader, the discourse community may contain several elements operating simultaneously with varying degrees of influence:

Discipline   Each discipline has a unique history that can dictate how writers collect information, evaluate evidence, measure results, and propose ideas. Some disciplines such as literature and mathematics have evolved over thousands of years. In contrast, the Internet and genetic engineering are such recent discoveries that their founders are still actively developing the nature of the discipline. In the humanities, research usually involves an individual's interpretation of specific works. Such fields as physics, biology, and chemistry demand that a thesis result from experiments using standard methods that can be replicated by independent researchers.

Profession   Each profession has its own context of historical experience, technical training, areas of concern, responsibilities, and political outlooks. Advertising executives and designers may be highly individualistic; their success can depend on a willingness to be radical, daring, and inventive. Accountants and engineers must follow government regulations. Law enforcement officers approach a case of suspected child abuse with the goal of determining if there is enough evidence to file charges. Mental health professionals are more interested in the well-being of the child, regardless of whether the situation meets the legal definition of abuse.

Community   People are influenced by those around them. A community may be a geographic region, organization, or collection of people with shared interests. Residents of midtown Manhattan have different interests, concerns, and challenges than Midwestern farmers. The U.S. Navy, IBM, the National Organization for Women, the AFL-CIO, the Catholic Church, and NASA each form a distinct community with a unique history, values, problems, and philosophies. Communities form when people share a common interest. AIDS patients, AOL users, Iraq War veterans, Social Security recipients, Spanish speakers, and adopted children have special concerns leading them to develop common attitudes toward government regulations and public policy.

Culture   National, regional, religious, and ethnic groups have common histories and values that influence how ideas are expressed and evaluated. Traditions and rituals vary between cultures. Although Americans generally respect individuality, other nationalities may value conformity. What may appear to Westerners as frank and honest writing may be viewed by others as brash and disrespectful. Attitudes about immigration, the role of women, or education can be culturally based.

Situation   A discourse community can be altered by a specific event. The way a manager writes to employees will change during a strike. An international crisis will influence the way the president addresses senators opposed to his policies. A crisis may bring writer and reader together as they face a common threat, or it may heighten differences, creating mutual suspicion and hostility.

Questions

1. Examine textbooks from different courses. What do they indicate about the values, standards, and practices in each discipline? Do sociologists write differently than psychologists? What do the books' glossaries reveal about how terms are defined?
2. Consider your future career. What values, attitudes, and skills are important? How will they influence the way you would write to peers? What kind of writing would be considered unprofessional or inappropriate?

3. Think of jobs you have had. Did each workplace form a specific community or culture? Did one office, warehouse, or restaurant have a different atmosphere or spirit than others? Would you word a memo to employees in one business differently than in another?
4. How can a dramatic event shape the way messages are written and evaluated? How would you word a statement announcing the death or injury of a fellow classmate, teammate, or employee?

THE DOCUMENT

The nature of the document influences reader expectations. Memos and e-mail may include informal abbreviations and slang that would be unacceptable in a formal report. Readers expect newspaper articles to be brief and simply stated. Because reporters must write quickly, their readers anticipate that factual errors or inaccurate quotes may appear in print. However, the same readers would have higher expectations of a scholarly journal or a book because the writers have weeks or years to check their sources and verify facts.

Certain documents such as research papers, résumés, wills, legal briefs, military action reports, dissertations, patient histories, and press releases have unique styles and formats. Writers who fail to follow the standard forms may alienate readers by appearing unprofessional.

STRATEGIES | for Writing Specialized Documents

1. **Make sure you understand the form, style, and rigor expected in the document.** Legal documents, grant proposals, and academic dissertations have distinct standards. If no formal directions or guidelines exist, review existing samples, or ask an instructor or manager what is expected.
2. **Determine if the document suits your purpose.** The importance of your message, the amount of information, and the style of writing should match the form. E-mail is suited for routine information and reminders. But announcing salary changes or job reclassifications in an informal document will strike readers as callous and impersonal.
3. **Use more than one document to achieve your goals.** If an accident prompts you to immediately alert employees of new safety regulations, you can state them in a short e-mail. If, however, you find yourself producing

pages of text, consider writing a formal report or set of guidelines. Use e-mail to quickly alert readers of the most important actions they should take and tell them to expect detailed regulations in the near future. Sometimes formal documents restrict your ability to highlight what you consider significant. Attach a cover letter or send a preliminary report that allows greater freedom of expression.

WRITINGS IN CONTEXT

Although the Vietnam War ended thirty years ago, the controversial conflict still resonates in debates about America's foreign policy, values, and history. Notice how the writings of a leading participant and a social commentator are shaped by context—their goal, the reader, the discourse community, and the document.

Lyndon Baines Johnson (1908–1973) served as president from 1963 until 1969. He oversaw the escalation of American involvement in the Vietnam War. As the war dragged on and casualties mounted, his leadership was questioned by a growing number of dissidents. Throughout the war, Johnson made numerous diplomatic overtures to the North Vietnamese, hoping to achieve a peaceful settlement. His inability to resolve the conflict eroded his support with voters and influenced his announcement in March 1968 that he would not seek a second term.

Letter to Ho Chi Minh, April 10, 1967

As you read this diplomatic letter, notice how the American president sought to influence the leader of Communist North Vietnam. Consider Johnson's extended audience— diplomats in both countries, his domestic critics, and the international community.

Dear Mr. President: 1

I am writing to you in the hope that the conflict in Vietnam can be 2 brought to an end. That conflict has already taken a heavy toll—in lives lost, in wounds inflicted, in property destroyed, and in simple human misery. If we fail to find a just and peaceful solution, history will judge us harshly.

Therefore, I believe that we both have a heavy obligation to seek 3 earnestly the path to peace. It is in response to that obligation that I am writing directly to you.

We have tried over the past several years, in a variety of ways and 4 through a number of channels, to convey to you and your colleagues our desire to achieve a peaceful settlement. For whatever reasons, these efforts have not achieved any results.

It may be that our thoughts and yours, our attitudes and yours, have 5 been distorted or misinterpreted as they passed through these various channels. Certainly that is always a danger in indirect communication.

There is one good way to overcome this problem and to move forward in 6 the search for a peaceful settlement. That is for us to arrange for direct talks between trusted representatives in a secure setting and away from the glare of publicity. Such talks should not be used as a propaganda exercise but should be a serious effort to find a workable and mutually acceptable solution.

7   In the past two weeks, I have noted public statements by representatives of your government suggesting that you would be prepared to enter into direct bilateral talks with representatives of the U.S. Government, provided that we ceased "unconditionally" and permanently our bombing operations against your country and all military actions against it. In the last days, serious and responsible parties have assured us indirectly that this is in fact your proposal.

8   Let me frankly state that I see two great difficulties with this proposal. In view of your public position, such action on our part would inevitably produce worldwide speculation that discussions were under way and would impair the privacy and secrecy of those discussions. Secondly, there would inevitably be grave concern on our part whether your government would make use of such action by us to improve its military position.

9   With these problems in mind, I am prepared to move even further towards an ending of hostilities than your Government has proposed in either public statements or through private diplomatic channels. I am prepared to order a cessation of bombing against your country and the stopping of further augmentation of U.S. forces in South Viet-Nam as soon as I am assured that infiltration into South Viet-Nam by land and by sea has stopped. These acts of restraint on both sides would, I believe, make it possible for us to conduct serious and private discussions leading toward an early peace.

10   I make this proposal to you now with a specific sense of urgency arising from the imminent New Year holidays in Viet-Nam. If you are able to accept this proposal I see no reason why it could not take effect at the end of the New Year, or Tet, holidays. The proposal I have made would be greatly strengthened if your military authorities and those of the Government of South Viet-Nam could promptly negotiate an extension of the Tet truce.

11   As to the site of the bilateral discussions I propose, there are several possibilities. We could, for example, have our representatives meet in Moscow where contacts have already occurred. They could meet in some other country such as Burma. You may have other arrangements or sites in mind, and I would try to meet your suggestions.

12   The important thing is to end a conflict that has brought burdens to both our peoples, and above all to the people of South Viet-Nam. If you have any thoughts about the actions I propose, it would be most important that I receive them as soon as possible.

13   Sincerely,
14   Lyndon B. Johnson

MOLLY IVINS

Molly Ivins (1944 –) was a reporter for the **New York Times** before becoming a columnist for the **Dallas Times Herald.** She has written pieces for **Ms., The Nation, The Progressive,** and other magazines. Her often witty and sarcastic commentaries have covered a range of topics, including country music, fashion, politicians, and NFL cheerleaders. Ivins published this article after the dedication of the Vietnam War Memorial in Washington.

A Short Story about the Vietnam War Memorial

As you read this column, consider how newspaper readers might react to this fictional story. The memorial, now a major tourist attraction in Washington, was criticized when it was first unveiled. The long black walls struck many as being grim, depressing, even unpatriotic. How does Ivins try to guide her readers to view the memorial?

She had known, ever since she first read about the Vietnam War Memorial, 1 that she would go there someday. Sometime she would be in Washington and would go and see his name and leave again.

So silly, all that fuss about the memorial. Whatever else Vietnam was, 2 it was not the kind of war that calls for some *Raising the Flag at Iwo Jima* kind of statue. She was not prepared, though, for the impact of the memorial. To walk down into it in the pale winter sunshine was like the war itself, like going into a dark valley and damned if there was ever any light at the end of the tunnel. Just death. When you get closer to the two walls, the number of names start to stun you. It is terrible, there in the peace and the pale sunshine.

The names are listed by date of death. There has never been a time, day 3 or night, drunk or sober, for thirteen years that she could not have told you the date. He was killed on August 13, 1969. It is near the middle of the left wall. She went toward it as though she had known beforehand where it would be. His name is near the bottom. She had to kneel to find it. Stupid clichés. His name leaped out at her. It was like being hit.

4   She stared at it and then reached out and gently ran her fingers over the letters in the cold black marble. The memory of him came back so strong, almost as if he were there on the other side of the stone, she could see his hand reaching out to touch her fingers. It had not hurt for years and suddenly, just for a moment, it hurt again so horribly that it twisted her face and made her gasp and left her with tears running down her face. Then it stopped hurting but she could not stop the tears. Could not stop them running and running down her face.

5   There had been a time, although she had been an otherwise sensible young woman, when she had believed she would never recover from the pain. She did, of course. But she is still determined never to sentimentalize him. He would have hated that. She had thought it was like an amputation, the severing of his life from hers, that you could live on afterward but it would be like having only one leg and one arm. But it was only a wound. It healed. If there is a scar, it is only faintly visible now at odd intervals.

6   He was a biologist, a t.a. at the university getting his Ph.D. They lived together for two years. He left the university to finish his thesis but before he lined up a public school job—teachers were safe in those years—the draft board got him. They had friends who had left the country, they had friends who had gone to prison, they had friends who had gone to Nam. There were no good choices in those years. She thinks now he unconsciously wanted to go even though he often said, said in one of his last letters, that it was a stupid, f——in' war. He felt some form of guilt about a friend of theirs who was killed during the Tet offensive. Hubert Humphrey called Tet a great victory. His compromise was to refuse officer's training school and go as an enlisted man. She had thought then it was a dumb gesture and they had a half-hearted quarrel about it.

7   He had been in Nam less than two months when he was killed, without heroics, during a firefight at night by a single bullet in the brain. No one saw it happen. There are some amazing statistics about money and tonnage from that war. Did you know that there were more tons of bombs dropped on Hanoi during the Christmas bombing of 1972 than in all of World War II? Did you know that the war in Vietnam cost the United States $123.3 billion? She has always wanted to know how much that one bullet cost. Sixty-three cents? $1.20? Someone must know.

8   The other bad part was the brain. Even at this late date, it seems to her that was quite a remarkable mind. Long before she read C. P. Snow, the ferociously honest young man who wanted to be a great biologist taught her a great deal about the difference between the way scientists think and the way humanists think. Only once has she been glad he was not with her. It was at

one of those bizarre hearings about teaching "creation science." He would have gotten furious and been horribly rude. He had no patience with people who did not understand and respect the process of science.

She used to attribute his fierce honesty to the fact that he was a Yankee. 9 She is still prone to tell "white" lies to make people feel better, to smooth things over, to prevent hard feelings. Surely there have been dumber things for lovers to quarrel over than the social utility of hypocrisy. But not many.

She stood up again, still staring at his name, stood for a long time. She 10 said, "There it is," and turned to go. A man to her left was staring at her. She glared at him. The man had done nothing but make the mistake of seeing her weeping. She said, as though daring him to disagree, "It was a stupid, f——in' war," and stalked past him.

She turned again at the top of the slope to make sure where his name is, 11 so whenever she sees a picture of the memorial she can put her finger where his name is. He never said goodbye, literally. Whenever he left he would say, "Take care love." He could say it many different ways. He said it when he left for Vietnam. She stood at the top of the slope and found her hand half-raised in some silly gesture of farewell. She brought it down again. She considered thinking to him, "Hey, take care, love" but it seemed remarkably inappropriate. She walked away and was quite entertaining for the rest of the day, because it was expected of her.

She thinks he would have liked the memorial. He would have hated the 12 editorials. He did not sacrifice his life for his country or for a just or noble cause. There just were no good choices in those years and he got killed.

Questions

1. What context shaped these documents?
2. How does the president's letter to the leader of a belligerent nation differ from Ivins's essay written for a mass audience of Americans?
3. Does the style and tone of the writings reveal something about the nature of the message, the intended audience, and the writer's purpose?
4. What discourse community existed between two world leaders? Who would have been Johnson's extended readers? What value would the letter have to bolster the president's image with his critics at home? How would people react today if they discovered that President Bush had written a similar letter to Saddam Hussein before the Iraq War?
5. What kind of reader would respond favorably to Molly Ivins's article? Can you think of people who would respond negatively?
6. What can you learn about writing by examining these two documents?

STRATEGIES | for Establishing Context

Whenever you write, consider the context.

Your Purpose and Role

1. What is your goal? To provide information, change opinions, or motivate action? Have you clearly determined what you want to express?
2. Are you expressing your own ideas or those of others? If you serve as a representative of a larger group, does your writing reflect the needs, style, attitudes, and philosophies of your peers or superiors? Do you avoid making statements that might jeopardize your position or expose the organization to liability? Will your peers and superiors approve of your ideas and the way you express them?

Your Reader

1. Define your readers. What is their perceptual world?
2. What objections might your readers have to your ideas?
3. Are there potential extended readers? Who else may see this writing? Have you made any statements that could be misunderstood out of context?

The Discourse Community

1. Are you operating in a general or specific discourse community? What is expected in this discipline, community, or profession?
2. Is your writing affected by a specific event or situation that could change in the future? Should you qualify your remarks so they will not be misunderstood if read out of context later?

The Document

1. Does the document have any special requirements? Do you fully understand what is required, what your readers expect?
2. Does the document suit your purpose? For example, are you using e-mail to transmit a message better stated in a personal letter?
3. Should you use more than one document? Would preliminary messages, attachments, or cover letters assist in communicating to your reader?

WRITING ACTIVITIES

Choose one or more of the following situations and develop writing that addresses the needs of the writer, immediate and extended readers, the discourse community, and the document.

1. You serve on a student committee concerned with underage and binge drinking formed after a fraternity party erupted in violence and led to dozens of arrests and a serious drunk driving accident. Write a brief statement to each of the following readers, urging greater responsibility. Consider their perceptual worlds and invent any needed details. Keep the extended audience in mind. How will other students, student organizations, the administration, and local media respond to your messages?

   - The president of the fraternity
   - The liquor distributor who promoted the event
   - Incoming freshmen
   - A local disc jockey who had repeatedly urged listeners to "crash the party and get blasted"

2. Write a short letter asking for funds to support a shelter for homeless and battered women. Consider how each reader's perceptual world will influence responses:

   - The director of women's studies at a university
   - Small business owners in a neighborhood that has become a collecting point for homeless people
   - Local ministers
   - The chamber of commerce
   - A local organization of women entrepreneurs

3. An employer has asked you for references. Write a brief note to the following people, requesting they write a letter on your behalf. Prompt each one to comment on your ability to solve problems. Invent needed details and consider how each person had opportunities to observe your attributes:

   - A high school coach
   - The head of a volunteer organization you assisted in major fund-raising drives
   - A former employer who frequently asked you to manage the business in his or her absence
   - Your parents' attorney, who once congratulated you for helping settle financial problems arising after the death of a relative

e-writing

Exploring Context Online

The Internet offers a quick lesson in the diversity of writing contexts: academic journals, corporate websites, commercial catalogs, political messages, and personal expressions.

1. Using InfoTrac College Edition or one of your library's databases, enter a search word, such as *diabetes, racial profiling, terrorism,* or *income tax,* or any topic in the news. Scan down the list of articles and select a variety to review. How do the style, format, vocabulary, and tone of a medical journal or law review differ from an article in a popular magazine? What does the language reveal about the intended audience? Can you determine the kinds of readers the writers were trying to reach?

2. If you use e-mail, review recent messages you have received. Do e-mails from friends reflect their personality, their way of speaking? Do personal e-mail messages have a different tone than ads you might receive?

3. Analyze the language used in chat rooms on America Online or other Internet services. Have these electronic communities produced their own slang or jargon? Do chat rooms of car enthusiasts differ from those dedicated to child care or investments? Do people with special interests bring their particular terminology and culture into cyberspace?

4. Using a search engine, such as Yahoo!, Alta Vista, or Google, enter the following search terms to locate current sites you might find helpful:

perception   *audience analysis*
persuasion   *perceptual world*
making presentations   *influencing readers*
reader analysis   *communications skills*
writing genres

E-Sources

Writer, Reader, Purpose—The Writing Context
    http://www.powa.org/revise/context.htm
Who Is My Audience and What Will They Expect?
    http://owl.english.purdue.edu/ workshops/hypertext/reportW/ audience.html
Audience
    http://www.unc.edu/depts/wcweb/ handouts/audience.html

Companion Website

See **http://www.thomsonedu.com/ english/sundance** for additional information on context.

CRITICAL THINKING
SEEING WITH A WRITER'S EYE

It is part of the business of the writer ... to examine attitudes, to go beneath the surface, to tap the source.

—*James Baldwin*

WHAT IS CRITICAL THINKING?

Good writing is not a repeat of what you have read or seen on television, and it is more than a rush of thoughts and feelings. Too often we tend to respond to ideas and experiences based solely on our existing perceptual worlds. We allow our emotions to color our judgment and guide our decisions. We buy a product because we like the name or admire the celebrity featured on the box. We confuse opinions with facts, accept statistics without question, and allow stereotypes to influence our evaluations. In short, we let our perceptual world short-circuit our thinking and rush to judgment:

> Ted had a heart attack—he should have stopped smoking ten years ago.
> Rahmin's parents sent him to an Islamic school in Pakistan—I had no idea they supported terrorism.
> This trade agreement with China is bad for the United States; Ford says it will have to lay off 10,000 workers.
> Shelly's law practice must be doing well; she's driving a BMW.

All these statements probably made sense to the people who made them, but close inspection reveals flaws in logic. Smoking is bad for the heart, but it is not the only cause of heart disease. Ted's weight or an inherited condition may be more to blame for his heart attack than smoking. Madrassahs in Pakistan have

45

WRITERS AT WORK

There are difficult moments where you think you're never going to get a handle on it. You end up with a bulging computer with all these little disparate items of information. Some of them you got four years ago and you can't figure out where in the world they fit. They look like they belong to a different jigsaw puzzle, and [as if] you shouldn't be bothering with them at all. Until you get a handle on it, it can be very difficult. I always write a first draft that has everything in it, and it reads about as interesting as a laundry list—"first he did this, and then he did this." I just have a chronological laundry list of everything that happened to him and that he did on a given day. Only after dealing with that, and wrestling with that by just getting it down on the page, which is a chore, do murky shapes begin to appear. Then you just go with those, and you test them and make sure that they work before you finally decide to use them. It's really feeling in the dark for a while, and it can be discouraging. But I always knew he was there somewhere for me, and so I wasn't going to let him go.

Clare Brandt, biographer of Benedict Arnold

SOURCE: *Booknotes*

been known to be operated by radical Islamists, but not all Islamic schools in Pakistan are extremist and not everyone who sends a child to a religious school in Pakistan supports terrorism. A trade agreement might be bad for Ford, but it might be good for the economy overall. It could cost 10,000 jobs in the automotive industry but generate 100,000 jobs in other fields. BMWs are expensive, but that does not prove that Shelly's law practice is doing well. She could be driving a friend's car or a vehicle given to her by her parents or a cash-poor client. Even if Shelly bought the car herself, there is no proof the money was earned through her law practice and not other sources.

Good writing goes beneath the surface to see things others may have overlooked or misunderstood. To determine your purpose, analyze the perceptual world of your readers, develop effective strategies, and achieve your goals, you will have to develop critical thinking skills.

Critical thinking moves beyond casual observation and immediate reactions. Instead of simply responding with what you *feel* about a subject, critical thinking guides you to *think*—to examine issues fully and objectively, test your own assumptions for bias, seek additional information, consider alternative interpretations, ask questions, and delay judgment.

How to See with a Writer's Eye

Good writers are not passive—they don't simply record immediate responses. They *look closely, ask questions, analyze, make connections,* and *think.* Learning to see with a writer's eye benefits not just those who write for a living but all professionals. In any career you choose, success depends on keen observation and in-depth analysis. An information-driven society depends on people who can examine and solve problems instead of simply responding with memorized behaviors learned from strict training. A skilled physician detects minor symptoms in a physical or follows up on a patient's complaint to ask questions that lead to a diagnosis others might miss. A successful stockbroker observes overlooked trends and conducts research to detect new investment opportunities. The school administrator with critical thinking skills can develop new programs despite reduced resources.

Close observation is the first step in critical thinking. Hemingway believed that people could become better writers by sharpening their skills as observers:

> When you walk into a room and you get a certain feeling or emotion, remember back until you see exactly what it was that gave you the emotion. Remember what noises and smells were and what was said. Then write it down, making it clear so the reader will see it too, and have the same feeling you had. And watch people, try to put yourself in somebody else's head. If two men argue, don't just ask who is right and who is wrong. Think about what both their sides are. . . . As a writer, you should not judge, you should understand.

Detailed observation helps not only novelists but scientists. In his essay "Take This Fish and Look at It" (p. 324), Samuel Scudder relates the lesson taught him by Professor Louis Agassiz. Instead of lecturing, Agassiz told his new student to take a fish from a specimen jar, stating, "Look at it . . . by and by I will ask what you have seen." After examining the specimen for ten minutes, Scudder felt he "had seen all that could be seen in that fish" and sought out his professor. Learning that Agassiz had left the building, he returned to the fish and looked at it for over an hour. When Agassiz came back to question Scudder, the professor was unimpressed with his student's observations. "You have not looked very carefully . . . you haven't even seen one of the most conspicuous features of the animal, which is plainly before your eyes as the fish itself; look again, look again!" Still dissatisfied with his student's observations, Agassiz instructed Scudder to try the next day and the next:

> For three long days he placed that fish before my eyes, forbidding me to look at anything else, or to use any artificial aid. "Look, look, look," was his repeated injunction.
>
> This was the best . . . lesson I ever had—a lesson whose influence has extended to the details of every subsequent study; a legacy the Professor had left to me, as he has left it to so many others, of inestimable value, which we could not buy, with which we cannot part.

By examining his subject closely, moving beyond first impressions, Scudder was able to identify the subtle complexities of his specimen.

Asking questions can also stimulate critical thinking. May Sarton believed that even ordinary events could lead to meaningful insights if you get into the habit of asking questions:

> Say you've burned something in a pot, and you are standing at the sink scrubbing it. What comes to your mind as you are doing this? What does it mean to you in a funny way? Are you angry because you burn pots all too often? You can rage against the fact that it seems to be women who are mostly having to scrub pots, or you can ask yourself why are you bothering about this pot anyway. Why not throw it away if you can afford to get another? Is there something wrong with you that you are so compulsive you must try to clean something that is beyond repair?

Questions can help you become a critical consumer of information and a better writer as you test the validity of assumptions. Consider a passage from a freshman essay:

> America must restrict immigration. Millions of people are coming to this country, taking jobs and running businesses while Americans are out of work. A lot of these people don't even speak English. With a recession deepening, this country should promise jobs to people who have lived here and paid taxes, not to new arrivals who are willing to work cheap.

The thesis—that America must restrict immigration—is clearly stated. But where is the proof? The student mentions "millions of immigrants"—but is there a more precise number? Just how many people are we talking about? What evidence is there that immigrants "take jobs" from others? Could they create jobs that others wouldn't take? Does the country "promise" jobs to anyone? What relationship is there between paying taxes and being qualified for a job? Do immigrants really "work cheap"? A thesis makes an assertion; it states a point of view. But without credible support, it remains only an opinion.

If America limited immigration, would the unemployed be hired in the place of immigrants? Do immigrants become valuable consumers? Because few Americans learn foreign languages, do we depend on immigrants to help us communicate and compete in a global marketplace? Do immigrant-run businesses create jobs for American-born citizens?

Critical thinking reveals that the student needs to conduct research and refine his or her arguments. Should the paper make a distinction between legal and illegal immigrants? In addition, the writer should consider what opponents will say. Can he or she call for restrictions on immigration without appearing to be racist? What proof can be offered to support the need for restrictions?

Critical thinking can help generate insight into even minor subjects. Instead of commenting on "more important" women's issues such as sexual harassment or abortion, Emily Prager considers the Barbie doll (see p. 256). In analyzing the significance of a popular toy, she reveals much about the way females are programmed to identify themselves as women. This short piece about a plastic toy is of more interest than a two-page article about sexual assault that only repeats widely held opinions.

STRATEGIES | for Increasing Critical Thinking

There is no quick method of enhancing critical thinking, but you can challenge yourself to develop a writer's eye by asking questions to improve your prewriting, drafting, and editing skills.

1. **Why have you selected this topic?** Students often feel obligated to write about "important" issues such as capital punishment, gun control, or global warming. But unless you have developed a unique thesis, discovered a new angle, or uncovered an overlooked question, you are likely to produce only a summary of previously stated ideas. Look around and write about topics that might have been forgotten or ignored.
2. **Have you looked at your topic closely?** First impressions can be striking but misleading. Examine your subject closely, asking questions, probing beneath the surface. Look for patterns; measure similarities and differences.
3. **Have you rushed to judgment?** Postpone making evaluations or judgments until you have examined your subject objectively. Collect evidence but avoid drawing conclusions until you have analyzed your findings and observations.
4. **Do you separate facts from opinions?** Don't confuse facts, evidence, and data with opinions, claims, and assertions. Opinions are judgments that must be supported with adequate proof; they are not evidence.
5. **Are you aware of your assumptions?** Assumptions are ideas we accept or believe to be true. It is nearly impossible to divorce ourselves from what we have been taught, but you can sharpen your critical thinking skills if you acknowledge your assumptions. Avoid relying too heavily on a single assumption—that IQ tests measure intelligence, that poverty causes crime, that television is a bad influence on children.

COMMON ERRORS IN CRITICAL THINKING

When you attempt to understand problems, evaluate evidence, draw conclusions, and propose solutions, it is easy to make mistakes. These lapses in critical thinking include *logical fallacies*. In establishing your reader's perceptual world, developing your ideas, and interpreting information, avoid these common mistakes.

Ignoring the Role of Coincidence

The degree of coincidence in life is usually underestimated. Random or accidental occurrences are often viewed as being significant, evidence of a cause-and-effect relationship, an ability to predict the future, or proof of some grand conspiracy:

> "My sister had a dream of a plane crashing into the sea. The very next day, Flight 800 crashed off Long Island." (Given that 300 million Americans have as many as five dreams a night, how unlikely would it be that someone would dream of a plane crash shortly before an accident? Did the dream predict the crash?)

> "Tom has flipped that coin ten times and each time it came up heads. I'll bet a hundred dollars next time it comes up tails." (Each toss of a coin provides a fifty-fifty chance of one side facing up. Because each flip of the coin is a separate event, one toss or a thousand previous tosses have no influence on future attempts. The chance that the coin will turn up tails on the eleventh try is still 50 percent.)

> "Don't trust Ted Matthews! Three of his past employers reported thefts while he worked for them." (Although this statement may suggest further investigation, there is no proof that Ted Matthews is guilty of anything. No evidence is presented that links him to the thefts, which may have preceded his employment and continued after he quit.)

Mathematicians use this simple example to show how frequently coincidences occur. Counting February 29, there are 366 possible birthdays. To have a 100 percent guarantee that at least two people in a group share the same birthday, the smallest number of people needed is 367. With 367 people, it is clear that at least two people must have the same birthday since there are only 366 days to go around. If you ask a class, "What's the smallest number of people needed to guarantee that there is a 50 percent probability that two people share the same birthday?" most students would guess 183, or half of 367. The actual number is only 23. With only 23 people there is a 50/50 chance that two people in the group were born on the same day. Coincidence occurs far more often than the general public and many experts realize.

Hasty Generalizations or Jumping to Conclusions

If we believe or suspect something to be true, we may be tempted to make a rash judgment based on limited evidence:

> "My new Toyota needs brakes after 1,000 miles. My cousin's Nissan is six months old and needs a new transmission. The quality of Japanese cars has slipped." (Japan manufactured millions of vehicles last year. This conclusion is based on two cars and fails to consider owner misuse. A fast check of the ratings in *Consumer Reports* might disprove this conclusion.)

> "Tom Watson has a drinking problem. On my way home from work I've seen him stopping at a bar three or four times a week. Last Saturday I saw him coming out of a liquor store." (This hasty generalization ignores other possibilities. First, there is no indication of how much Tom Watson is drinking, if at all. Both bars and liquor stores sell nonalcoholic beverages. Tom Watson may be a friend or partner of the owner. Perhaps he dropped by a liquor store to buy chewing gum. Gossip and rumor often begin with just such "facts.")

> "Hawaii is a rip-off! Everyone I know who has vacationed there had a terrible time." (The evidence seems overwhelming because "everyone" you know who has visited Hawaii regrets the trip. But just how many people does "everyone" amount to— three, five, even fifty? Because Hawaii has been a popular tourist attraction for millions of return visitors, can we automatically assume that it is a "rip-off"?)

> "Child abuse has risen to epidemic proportions! Reports of child abuse have grown 450 percent in the last twenty years. The number of children recommended for foster care has risen from 1 in 5,000 to 1 in 1,500." (The numbers are disturbing—but do they support the conclusion that child abuse has *risen*? Does the increase in cases reflect more instances of child abuse—or better reporting methods? Have the definitions of child abuse changed so that more children are counted as abused?)

> "The governor has pardoned more than 75 convicted murderers. How can anyone vote for someone who lets killers walk free?" (First, not all people convicted of murder are killers. The driver of a getaway car can be convicted of murder even if he or she did not know his or her partner would use a weapon in a robbery. Second, before judging the governor, one would have to examine how many murderers were pardoned by his or her predecessors or governors in other states.)

To avoid jumping to conclusions, ask yourself if you have assembled enough data, then examine alternative interpretations. *Don't rush to judgment.*

Relying on Anecdotal Evidence

One form of jumping to conclusions often appears in misleading advertisements and fraudulent claims:

> "Smoking can't be that bad for your health. Both my grandfathers were heavy smokers, and they lived past eighty and never developed cancer or heart disease." (These grandfathers may be among the lucky smokers—along with George Burns and Winston Churchill. But a few exceptions fail to counter the overwhelming evidence that smoking causes fatal diseases. The fact that some people win at Russian roulette does not diminish its danger.)

> "These seventeen smiling people made over $1,000,000 each last year selling Vitatex. Invest in a franchise now!" (Before investing, you might want to know how many people lost money last year selling Vitatex. And did these lucky seventeen actually earn a million dollars selling the product or selling franchises to other investors?)

> "Crime is a major problem on our campus. At last week's hearing, over two dozen students reported being victims of crime in the last year. The crimes ranged from auto theft to sexual assault." (Personal accounts may be emotionally wrenching, but do they add up to a "major problem"? A student survey or review of police records might reveal the campus has a lower crime rate than some of the safest suburbs in the country.)

Avoid relying on testimonials or a parade of test cases. Individual stories can be impressive but misleading. You might unearth half a dozen homeless Harvard graduates and argue that an Ivy League education is worthless. Likewise, the fact that a number of celebrities dropped out of high school does not prove that dropouts face a successful future. A collection of exceptions does not refute a general truth or trend. The majority of people who gamble lose—no matter how many winners are featured in casino commercials.

Mistaking Time Relationships for Cause and Effect (*post hoc, ergo propter hoc*)

Events occur in time, whether measured in nanoseconds or millions of years. Just because something precedes an event does not mean it was a causal factor. This mistake, often referred to in Latin terms, is easy to make because dramatic events or compelling evidence appear to support a claim:

> "Don't take your car to Quikee Lube! I took my car in for an oil change and the transmission went out three days later." (The evidence seems clear-cut. Your car

ran fine until those mechanics at Quikee Lube touched it. Now it needs major repairs. But changing the oil would have nothing to do with the transmission— which may have been destined to fail in a few days.)

"Mayor Jackson deserves to be reelected; in her first term unemployment dropped 25 percent!" (Unemployment may have dropped—but did the mayor's administration have anything to do with it? Did changes in the national economy or decisions in the private sector create jobs? Did some people out of work simply stop looking for jobs and cease to be counted as being unemployed?)

"Gramma Barnes's elixir really works. I had a splitting migraine, but after one sip of her home remedy my headache was gone in ten minutes." (The elixir may have "cured" a ten-minute headache in ten minutes. An apple, a massage, or watching the evening news might have been just as effective. Gramma Barnes's elixir would have to be the subject of a blind study to determine its efficacy.)

As with hasty generalizations, look for alternative explanations.

Making Faulty Comparisons (False Analogies)

Comparisons are the weakest form of argument. Because no two situations are exactly alike, avoid making judgments based on limited or selected evidence:

"We should adopt Britain's policy of decriminalizing heroin to lower crime. Last year London had fifty homicides while New York had more than eight hundred." (The comparison fails to take into account other differences between Britain and the United States. Could the lower murder rate be caused by another factor, such as Britain's tight gun control laws?)

"If we can fly to the moon, why can't we cure AIDS?" (This reasoning ignores the complex differences between engineering and medicine.)

"We should legalize marijuana because Prohibition failed against alcohol." (The same reasoning could be used to justify legalizing anything—crack, child pornography, machine guns, or prostitution.)

Assuming Trends Will Continue, Making "Slippery Slope" Judgments

We often look to past performance to judge future events. Good students can be counted on to do well on upcoming tests. A winning NFL team can be predicted as a serious Super Bowl contender. But conditions and individuals change, and trends cannot be assumed to continue without alteration:

> "My baseball card collection is worth more than $2,000. Think how much it will be worth when our three-year-old is ready for college!" (Perhaps a baseball card collection is a good investment for college. But what gives those pieces of cardboard their value is demand. The fact that a baseball card collection has soared in value in the past is no guarantee that its value will continue to rise.)

> "If we legalize doctor-assisted suicide of the terminally ill, soon we will be killing the handicapped and elderly." (This position assumes that one action necessarily leads to another. The legalization of abortion did not lead women to have the right to kill children with birth defects. Adopting the death penalty for murder did not lead to executing car thieves or cutting off the hands of shoplifters.)

Trends do not always continue. Economists once predicted that world markets would be threatened by an impending shortage of copper, then used in virtually all telephone and electronic data transfer lines. As copper became more expensive, telephone prices would rise, driving up costs and limiting the development of Third World economies. Their warnings were dire, but they failed to consider that science would develop a replacement for copper—silicon. Studying the amount of wood currently being burned for fuel, nineteenth-century scientists once calculated that America would run out of trees by the 1920s. They could not anticipate that within a few decades coal and oil would be used for energy and that millions of fireplaces would become ornaments.

Creating "Either-Or" Dilemmas

Often complex issues are oversimplified and only two alternatives are given, when in fact there are many others:

> "Employees must accept a 10 percent pay cut or the company will go bankrupt and close. A pay cut is better than losing a job." (The company may have problems and need more money, but cutting wages is only one remedy. Raising prices, increasing sales, selling assets, and limiting purchases could also be solutions.)

> "We must pass the new school bond issue or watch our educational system disintegrate into a morass of mediocrity, drugs, and violence." (The merits of the school bond have not been demonstrated, and no evidence is provided to prove that the schools will disintegrate if it fails.)

False dilemmas are often used to coerce people into accepting something unpleasant by making it appear to be the lesser of two evils.

Relying on False Authorities, Attacking Personalities, and Guilt by Association

Celebrity endorsements often attempt to use a person's image or popularity to lend credibility to an issue or product:

> "Vote for Maria Mendez. Her anticrime proposals were supported by Angelina Jolie, Madonna, and Stephen King." (An actress, a singer, and a novelist may be authorities in their fields but they are not experts in law enforcement. Endorsements by lesser-known lawyers, police officers, and judges might carry more weight.)

Often negative associations are used to discredit something without genuine proof:

> "We shouldn't support any block watch group started by Louis Farrakhan." (Louis Farrakhan may be controversial, but his political views have nothing to do with the merits of the block watch. Using the same logic, one could argue against superhighways and national health care because both were policies of the Third Reich.)

> "How can we consider accepting a budget offered by a man who just pleaded guilty to drunk driving?" (The issue at hand is the budget, not the behavior of the person who developed it.)

Using Circular Reasoning (Begging the Question)

Don't assume that a premise is true or offer a definition as proof:

> "This inefficient plant should be closed to save energy costs." (No proof is offered to demonstrate that the plant is inefficient.)

> "Typewriters are obsolete, so the university should purchase only computers." (The obsolescence of typewriters is assumed, not proven.)

> "We should abolish our entrance tests because they are racially biased." (Are the tests racially biased? Before you can argue about abolishing them, you must prove the tests unfair and invalid.)

Making Emotional and Irrelevant Statements (Red Herrings)

The term *red herring* comes from the ancient practice of farmers dragging fish across their fields to disrupt fox hunts. Chasing the scent of the fox, hunting dogs would be confused by the pungent smell and run in circles, putting an end to the stampede of hunters about to trample a farmer's crop. People some-times attempt to dodge issues by raising emotionally charged but unrelated issues:

> "Perhaps my estimates aren't as accurate as Alderwoman Brown suggests, but are you going to believe me or a racist who wants to shut down the only clinic serving minorities?" (Bringing up issues such as sex, race, and violence is bound to press emotional hot buttons and distract people from the issue being discussed.)

> "Requiring public school students to wear uniforms is repulsive in a democracy. We should encourage individual expression, not conformity. We don't need a na-tion of brown-shirted Hitler Youth goose-stepping on our playgrounds." (Con-juring up images of Nazism offers no proof that school uniforms have a negative influence on students or society.)

Red herring arguments often stem from desperation. Losing one argument, people will raise issues from past arguments, usually ones where they have been proven right, to distract attention.

WRITING ACTIVITIES

1. Select a recent editorial and examine it for lapses in critical thinking. Does the writer make statements that rest on untested assumptions, false analogies, or insufficient data? Write a critique, commenting on the writer's use of logic to support his or her views.

2. Select a topic from the list on pages 903–904 and identify the types of errors in critical thinking you might face in addressing this issue.

3. Examine an evening or two of cable news talk shows. How many guests engage in arguments that are laced with errors in critical think-ing? Can you identify people who attack personalities, use anecdotal evidence, and faulty comparisons? Do interviewers or guests try to persuade viewers by using circular reasoning or creating false "either-or dilemmas"?

Critical Thinking Checklist

Examine your writing for evidence of critical thinking.

✔ Have you carefully examined your subject or relied solely on casual observation?

✔ Is your main idea clearly and logically stated?

✔ Have you collected enough information to make judgments?

✔ Are your sources reliable and unbiased?

✔ Have you considered alternative interpretations?

✔ Have you avoided errors in critical thinking such as imprudent, hasty generalizations?

e-writing

Exploring Critical Thinking Online

The Internet presents a range of sources dedicated to critical thinking, ranging from sites maintained by academic organizations to those created by individual teachers posting information for their students.

1. Using InfoTrac College Edition or one of your library's databases, enter *critical thinking* as a search term and locate articles that may assist you in your writing course and other classes.

2. Locate the online version of a national or local newspaper and review recent editorials. Can you detect any lapses in critical thinking? Do any editorials rely on hasty generalizations, anecdotal evidence, faulty comparisons, circular reasoning, or false authorities?

3. To learn more about critical thinking, enter *critical thinking* as a search term in a general search engine, such as Yahoo!, Alta Vista, or Google, or enter one or more of the following terms:

coincidence   *anecdotal evidence*
post hoc   *circular reasoning*
red herrings   *guilt by association*
hasty generalizations   *fact and opinion*

For Further Reading

Barnet, Sylvan, and Hugo Bedau. *Critical Thinking: Reading and Writing.*

Dauer, Francis Watanabe. *Critical Thinking: An Introduction to Reasoning.*

Hirschberg, Stuart. *Essential Strategies of Argument.*

Packer, Nancy Huddleston, and John Timpane. *Writing Worth Reading: The Critical Process.*

Paulos, John Allen. *Innumeracy: Mathematical Illiteracy and Its Consequences.*

Rosenwasser, David, and Jill Stephens. *Writing Analytically.*

E-Sources

The Critical Thinking Community
http://www.criticalthinking.org/ resources/articles/

Logical Fallacy
http://www.answers.com

Companion Website

See **http://www.thomsonedu.com/ english/sundance** for additional information on critical thinking.

PREWRITING STRATEGIES
GETTING STARTED

5

I think best with a pencil in my hand.

—Anne Morrow Lindbergh

WHAT IS PREWRITING?

Writing is more than a means to create a document; it can be a method to discover topics and explore ideas. *Prewriting* refers to practice or experimental writing— writing that helps you get started and measure what you know, identify new ideas, and indicate areas requiring further research. It is a way of putting critical thinking into action. Prewriting can help sharpen your skills of observation and evaluation. Like an artist making quick sketches before beginning a mural, you can test ideas, explore a range of topics, list ideas, and get a feel for your subject. Prewriting can help you save time by quickly determining which ideas are worth developing and which should be discarded. *Prewriting puts critical thinking in action.*

PREWRITING STRATEGIES

Writers use a number of strategies to discover and develop ideas. Prewriting can be highly focused or totally open. You may wish to target a specific assignment or simply explore some ideas that might generate topics for a number of

I write by longhand. I like to see the words coming out of the pen. And once they distribute themselves, one has the stylistic struggle to try and turn that clumsy sentence on the page into something lucid. That can take a long time. I remember once spending seven hours on one sentence—seven hours. And I looked at it the next morning, it was a pretty banal sentence. That's writing. Writing is a reduction to essentials, elimination, and that takes time.

Edmund Morris, historian

SOURCE: *Booknotes*

papers. Prewriting a business letter can help you identify information needed to support your position. If your composition instructor assigns a comparison paper, prewriting can help you examine a range of possible subjects before you select and develop a specific topic.

People think in different ways. Review these methods and experiment with them. Feel free to combine strategies to create your own method. If you are responding to a specific assignment, read the instructions carefully. Make sure you understand what your instructor expects and how your paper will be evaluated. If you are unsure, talk to your instructor or other students. Sometimes even a casual conversation about an upcoming assignment will reveal different perspectives and insights.

Freewriting

Freewriting records your thoughts, ideas, impressions, and feelings without interruption and without any concern for spelling, grammar, punctuation, or even logic. Don't confuse freewriting with writing a rough draft of an essay—instead, it is a method of discovering ideas. Freewriting is not unlike talking to yourself. It has no direction: it can skip from one topic to another without rational transitions; it may contain contradictory statements. Freewriting produces "running prose," like the tape recording of a rambling telephone conversation. The goal is to sketch out ideas as fast as you can write.

Sit down with a piece of paper or at a computer and start writing. Some experts suggest writing nonstop for at least five minutes. If you can't think of anything to write, draw O's and X's or type gibberish. The main thing is to keep the process going until you can think of something to say. Let one idea remind you of another. Remember, there are no bad ideas.

Having spent the evening searching the Internet for material for a paper, a student switched to a word processing program and rapidly recorded her thoughts on the information superhighway:

> The information superhighway links anyone to the world. A college student, sitting in a dorm or libary, can connect to sources in New York, London, or Tokio. Web pages link you to sources you would nevre find on your own or now about. Within fifteen minutes tonight I printed off twenty pages of infomation that would take hours to find in a conventional libary. The interent is the ultimate consumer guide. I could find on-line catalogs and read product descriptions and prices for things I thought about buying for xmas gifts and presents. I could even check sticker prices on new cars. Xxxxxxxxxxxxxxx xxxxxxxxx.
>
> But switching from web page to web page, bieng hit with all kinds of data from around the owrld wears off after a while. The internet is exciting but like having cable TV, you get used to having 80 channels instead of four or five.
>
> Years ago Clinton promised to have every shcool in America wired to the interent.
>
> But one wonders. If children have trouble reading, what will the internet provide books don't? The information super highway bombards us with statistics and facts. The real question is can people analyze it? Do we have the wisdom to know what to make of all this material. I see students in the lib. Get excited as they see the stacks of information slipping from the printers. But like students forty years ago who were the first to be able to use a Xerox machine and copy an article instead of haivng to take notes— I wonder what will they do with all this informaiton when they get home?
>
> Wisdom vs. Knowledge. X xxxxxxxx x xxxx x Being able to synehisize data. xxxxxxxxxx
>
> CNN tells us about a crisis in Iraq or a stock plunge in Korea in seconds. The TV screen flashes with images and numbers. We hear sound-bites from experts. But do we know enough history of the Middle east to now what this crisis means? Do we know enough about international business and trading to know how the Korean markets effect ours? What does information mean if we don't appreciate what it means?

This freewriting is a loose, repetitive, and misspelled collection of ideas, switching from the Internet to cable television without connection. But within the text there are the germs of ideas that could lead to a good essay about the information superhighway.

Advantages

- Freewriting is a good technique to help you overcome writer's block. By giving yourself the freedom to write anything—even meaningless symbols— you can force yourself to overcome the idea that every time you sit down to write you must come up with significant insights and flawless prose.
- Freewriting is useful when you simply have no idea what to write about. It can help you discover a subject by free association.

Disadvantages

- Because of its unrestricted nature, freewriting can spin off a lot of interesting but inappropriate ideas. You may find yourself writing off track, getting further from the writing needed to meet the needs of your readers. You can focus your freewriting by considering the needs of your readers. Study your instructor's guidelines for the paper before starting to write. Write with your reader in mind.
- Freewriting can be tiring. Feel free to list or cluster ideas to save time. Don't feel obligated to write in complete sentences.

WRITING ACTIVITY

Freewriting

Select one of the following issues and write about it for at least five minutes without stopping. Don't worry about making sense, keeping on topic, or connecting ideas. Remember, this is not a rough draft, but an exploration of ideas. The topic is simply a catalyst, a jumping-off point. Let your free associations flow. If the topic of your hometown leads you to comment on your neighbors' divorce, go with it. Keep writing!

your hometown	campus child care	roommates	reality TV shows
job interviews	blind dates	student loans	death penalty
best friends	success	cable news	first day at work
gay rights	binge drinking	the Internet	outsourcing

Brainstorming

Brainstorming is another method of finding ideas to write about. Brainstorming can take different forms, the most simple being making lists. As in freewriting, there is no attempt to be selective. You write down every idea you can come up with, whether it makes sense or not. The purpose is not to plan a paper but to develop ideas. As with freewriting, there is no need to worry about spelling and grammar at this point.

You can use brainstorming to discover ideas for a personal essay or a research paper. A psychology student searching for a subject for a term paper might begin listing thoughts and topics:

mental illness—schizophrenia
inability to function in society
insanity defense
mental illness/homelessness
mentally ill off medication
public disturbances by mental patients
institutions/group homes
commitment laws decision to protect patients against their will
human rights versus incarceration without trial
committing the homeless to mental health institutions for their own safety

Through brainstorming the student moves from the general topic of mental illness and legal issues to a subject suitable for a research paper—institutionalizing homeless mentally ill patients. With further prewriting, he or she can develop this topic to compare past and present practices, argue for more group homes, study the causes of homelessness, or debate the merits of a local ordinance.

Brainstorming can help you develop writing even when the topic is clearly defined and the context is fixed. Having observed a shoplifter race out of her store with a jacket, the owner of a dress shop plans to write an incident report to the manager of the shopping mall:

time/date of incident
item(s) stolen—get values wholesale/retail
location of video cameras? (Check)
security guard took 6 minutes to respond
guards never at north end of mall
problems at other stores—check video & computer stores
need for security
lease expires in three months/may not renew

From this list, the store owner identifies the information needed to document the problem and comes up with the threat of leaving the mall to dramatize her position and prompt a response.

Advantages

- Like freewriting, brainstorming can help you get started when you have no topic in mind.
- Brainstorming allows you to jot down ideas rapid fire, freeing you from the need to write complete sentences.
- Brainstorming can quickly identify information needed to support your point of view.

Disadvantages

- You may find that brainstorming produces nothing more than a shopping list of unrelated ideas, a stream of topics that are identified but not developed or narrowed. You can, however, combine other techniques such as freewriting to flesh out superficial ideas and clustering to organize and prioritize ideas.
- Because it rests on free associations, brainstorming can lead you far astray from an assigned topic. If you are working on a specific assignment, keep your syllabus or instructor's guidelines in front of you to help focus your train of thought.

WRITING ACTIVITY

Brainstorming

Select a column of topics from below and build on it, adding your own ideas. Jot down your thoughts as quickly as possible. Allow your thoughts to flow freely. Do not worry about changing direction or coming up with an entirely different subject.

men/women	success	campus housing
attitudes about relationships	careers	dorms/off campus
ending relationships	salaries	having your own apt.
how men and women cope with failed relationships	the perfect first job	advantages/disadvantages of living alone

Asking Questions

Asking questions is a method of exploring ideas that can focus your thoughts and identify not only a thesis but needed support. For over a century reporters, writers who work with tight deadlines, have been trained to approach a news story by asking the Five W's—Who? What? Where? When? Why? Asking questions can help you avoid writing in circles and can highlight important issues.

A student in a literature class has been assigned to write about a short story. Selecting the story she found most interesting, she lists questions about Willa Cather's "Paul's Case":

> Why did Paul commit suicide at the end?
> Why didn't Paul have any friends?
> Why did Paul like his job at the opera house?
> Cather tells readers that Paul had sisters, but he never thinks about them—what does that reveal about his character?
> What kind of relationship does Paul have with his father?
> Was Paul's father a good parent?
> Was Paul gay?
> Cather wrote this story about a teenage suicide in 1904—what relevance does it have today?
> Is Paul like today's teens who attempt/commit suicide?

Asking questions can help identify ideas and focus assignments such as narration and description. Thinking about writing a narrative essay about her cousin's wedding, a student uses questions to trigger her memories and to highlight the significance of the event:

> Carol's wedding.
> —What do I remember about the wedding?
> —What does it mean to me now?
> —What was the most moving moment of the day?
> —How did my aunt and uncle act?
> —Why did my sister behave the way she did?
> —How did guests respond to Carol's vows?
> —Why did Carol insist on a church wedding?
> —Did growing up with divorced parents shape Carol's & my own attitudes about marriage, weddings?

Asking questions can help target other forms of prewriting, giving direction to your freewriting and brainstorming. In addition, questions can help spark critical thinking. Exploring the "why's" and "how's" of people, places, and events can help you move beyond simply recording first impressions and superficial observations.

Advantages

- Asking questions can help transform a topic into a thesis by directing you to state an opinion or take a position.
- Questions, if carefully worded, force you to think and test your preconceived notions and attitudes.
- Questions reveal needed information, guiding you to conduct research.

Disadvantages

- Questions in themselves are not necessarily effective in provoking thought. Unless you are careful, you may find yourself simply creating pat questions that lead to simple answers. If your answers simply restate what you already know or believe, write tougher questions or try another prewriting method.
- Asking too many questions, especially misdirected ones, can lead you on a scattered mission, finding unrelated or trivial information. Edit your questions when you complete your list. Don't feel obligated to consider every question you develop.

WRITING ACTIVITY

Asking Questions

Select one of the topics below and develop as many questions as you can. If you find yourself blocked, choose another topic or create one of your own. List as many questions as you can and don't worry about repeating yourself.

campus crime	credit cards	computers	medical insurance
prisons	stalking laws	online dating	fashion
cell phone etiquette	health clubs	divorce	media images of women

Look over your questions and circle those that suggest interesting topics for papers.

Clustering

Clustering is a type of freewriting that helps people who are visually oriented. If you have an artistic or technical background, you may find it easier to explore ideas by blocking them on a sheet of paper or computer screen. Clustering is a form of directed doodling or informal charting. Instead of listing ideas or writing in paragraphs, sketch your ideas on paper, as if arranging index cards on a table. People who use clustering often develop unique visual markers—using rectangles, arrows, and circles to diagram their ideas.

Thinking about his sister's decision to adopt a baby from China, a student clustered a series of observations and questions:

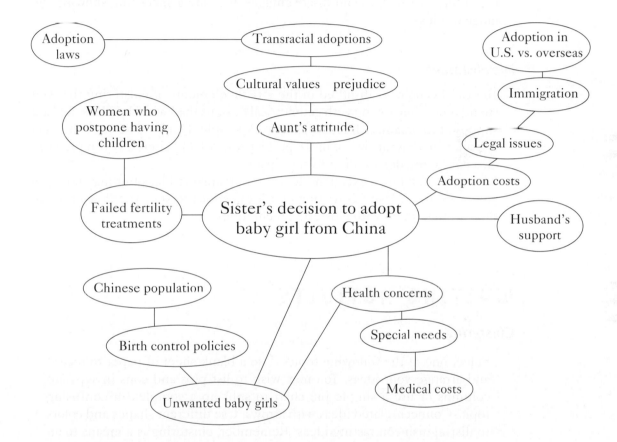

In this case clustering helps chart the positive and negative elements of transracial adoptions.

Advantages

- Clustering is suited to people who think spatially and find it easier to draw rather than write.
- Clustering is a good method to explore topics for comparison and division/classification papers.

■ Clustering can save time. Freewriting, brainstorming, and asking questions list ideas in the order in which they occur to the writer rather than in relationship to each other. These ideas have to be examined and reorganized. Clustering allows you to create several lists or groupings, ranking ideas in importance and immediately showing links between related ideas.

■ Clustering can help place ideas in context. You can group ideas in columns to contrast advantages and disadvantages or create a spectrum, showing the range of ideas.

Disadvantages

■ You can become so absorbed in the artistic elements of clustering that you spend more time toying with geometrical designs than with the ideas they are supposed to organize. Keep your artwork simple. Don't waste your time using rulers to draw arrows or make perfect squares and circles. If you prewrite on a computer, don't bother using clip art.

■ Clustering can be an excellent device for organizing ideas but may not help you get started. Use freewriting or ask questions to start the flow of ideas, then arrange them with clustering techniques.

WRITING ACTIVITY

Clustering

Select one of the following topics. Use a blank sheet of paper to record and arrange your ideas. You may wish to list pros and cons in separate columns or use a simple pie chart to split up a complex or confusing topic. Connect related ideas with arrows. Use different shapes and colors to distinguish contrasting ideas. Remember, clustering is a means to an end. Don't allow your artwork to get in the way of your thinking or take too much time. Neatness does not count.

computer hackers	being laid off	worst/best jobs
role models	airport security	teen pregnancy
violence on TV	singles' bars	fast food
the stock market	poverty	eating disorders
diets	having children	video games

STRATEGIES | for Prewriting

1. Write as often as you can.
2. Get in the habit of asking questions and listing ideas and observations.
3. Make notes of interesting items you see on television and clip newspaper and magazine articles that could serve as writing prompts.
4. Review upcoming assignments and make lists of possible topics.
5. Experiment with different forms of prewriting and feel free to blend them to develop your own style.
6. Save your notes. Ideas that you might discard for one paper might aid you in developing a topic for a future assignment.

e-writing

Exploring Prewriting Strategies Online

The Internet offers a number of valuable prewriting resources. Websites range from those maintained by academic organizations to those created by individual teachers posting information for their students.

1. Using InfoTrac College Edition or one of your library's databases, enter *prewriting strategies* as a search term to locate articles that may assist you in your writing course and other classes.
2. Using a search engine, such as Yahoo!, Alta Vista, or Google, enter such terms as *prewriting, freewriting,* and *brainstorming* to locate current websites.
3. Familiarize yourself with your library's online databases and resources, such as encyclopedias. Often checking a fact or reference can help trigger ideas for an assignment or prevent you from wasting time.

For Further Reading

Lamm, Kathryn. *10,000 Ideas for Term Papers, Projects, Reports, and Speeches.*

E-Sources

The University of Kansas Writing Center
http://www.writing.ku.edu/students/guides/.shtml
Online Writing Lab at Purdue University
http://owl.english.purdue.edu/handouts/general

Companion Website

See **http://www.thomsonedu.com/english/sundance** for additional information on prewriting strategies.

6

DEVELOPING A THESIS

> I write because there is some lie I want to expose, some fact to which I want to draw attention, and my initial concern is to get a hearing.
>
> —George Orwell

WHAT IS A THESIS?

Good writing has a clear purpose. An essay is never just "about" something. Whether the topic is global warming, your first job, Iraq, a high school football coach, or *A Streetcar Named Desire*, your writing should make a point or express an opinion. The *thesis* is a writer's main or controlling idea. A *thesis statement* presents the writer's position in a sentence or two and serves as the document's mission statement. *A thesis is more than a limited or narrowed topic—it expresses a point of view. It is a declaration, summarizing your purpose.*

Topic	Narrowed Topic	Thesis Statement
gun control	handgun ban	*The city's proposed handgun ban will not prevent gang violence.*
computer crime	consumer fraud	*Consumers will resist shopping on the Web until credit card security is assured.*
campus housing	rehabbing dorms	*Given the demand for more on-campus housing, the fifty-year-old men's dorm should be rehabilitated.*
terrorism	cyber-terrorism	*Federal security agencies must take steps to protect the Internet from cyber-terrorism.*

WRITERS AT WORK

I write in my studio. I've got a little studio in Brooklyn, a couple of blocks from my house— no telephone, nothing there. When I go there, the only thing I ever do there is work, so it's wonderful. I'm like a dog with a conditioned reflex. There is no television, no telephone, nothing. My wife wants me to get a portable telephone. I refuse. I don't want to be tempted. There's an old Jewish belief that you build a fence around an impulse. That's not good enough, you build a fence around the fence, so no telephone.

Norman Mailer, novelist

SOURCE: *Booknotes*

WRITING ACTIVITIES

Develop a thesis statement for each of the following topics. Use prewriting techniques such as asking questions and clustering to explore ideas. Remember, your thesis should state a viewpoint, express an opinion, make an appeal, or suggest a solution, not simply make a factual statement or limit the subject.

1. Stem cell research
2. Social Security
3. Car prices
4. The Internet's impact on journalism
5. The aging baby boom generation
6. Welfare reform and day care
7. America's role in the twenty-first century
8. The current job market for college graduates
9. DNA testing and criminal investigations
10. Minimum wage jobs

ELEMENTS OF A THESIS STATEMENT

Effective thesis statements share common characteristics:

■ **They are generally stated in a single sentence.** This statement forms the core of the paper, clearly presenting your point of view. Writing a thesis statement can be a critical part of the prewriting process, helping you move from a list or cluster of ideas to a specific paper. Even if the thesis statement does not appear in the final paper, writing this sentence can focus your ideas and direct your writing.

- **They express an opinion, not a topic.** What distinguishes a thesis statement from a topic is that it does not announce a subject but expresses a viewpoint. The statement "There is a serious shortage of campus parking" describes a problem, but it does not express an opinion. "Shuttle bus service should be expanded to alleviate the campus parking problem" serves as a thesis statement, clearly asserting a point of view.

- **They limit the topic.** Part of the job of a thesis statement is to focus the paper, limiting the scope of the writer's area of concentration. "Television is bad for children" states an opinion, but the subject is so broad that any essay would probably be limited to a list of superficial observations. A thesis such as "Television action heroes teach children that violence is an acceptable method of resolving conflicts" is limited enough to create a far more engaging paper.

- **They indicate the kind of support to follow.** Opinions require proof. "Because of declining enrollment, the cinema course should be canceled" indicates a clear cause-and-effect argument based on factual evidence, leading readers to expect a list of enrollment and budget figures.

- **They often organize supporting material.** The thesis statement "Exercise is essential to control weight, prevent disease, and maintain mental health" suggests that the body of the paper will be divided into three segments.

- **Effective thesis statements are precisely worded.** Because they express the writer's point of view in a single sentence, thesis statements must be accurately stated. General terms, such as *good, bad, serious,* and *important* weaken a thesis. Absolute statements can suggest that the writer is proposing a panacea. "Deadbolt locks should be installed in all dorm rooms to *prevent crime*" implies that a single mechanism is a foolproof method of totally eradicating all crime. "Deadbolt locks should be installed in all dorm rooms to *deter break-ins*" is far more accurate and easier to support.

WRITING ACTIVITIES

Revise the following thesis statements, increasing their precision.

1. The Internet provides students with a lot of educational opportunities.

2. Providing employee health insurance is a challenge for many businesses.

3. Employers should assist employees with small children.

4. Public schools must prepare students for the twenty-first century.

5. Attitudes about fatherhood have changed in the last twenty years.

6. The media stereotypes minorities.

7. Hollywood has given foreigners distorted views of American society.

8. Americans suffer from their lack of understanding of other cultures.

9. Illegal immigration remains a problem for many reasons.

10. Peer pressure can be negative.

LOCATING THE THESIS

To be effective, thesis statements must be strategically placed. The thesis statement does not have to appear in the introduction but can be placed anywhere in the essay:

- **Placing the thesis at the opening** starts the essay with a strong statement, providing it with a clear direction and an outline of the supporting evidence. However, if the thesis is controversial, it may be more effective to open with supporting details and confront readers' objections before formally announcing the thesis. An essay that opens with the statement "We must legalize heroin" might easily be dismissed by people who would think the writer must be naive or insensitive to the pain of addiction, the spread of AIDS, and other social problems stemming from drug abuse. However, if the essay first demonstrates the failure of current policies and argues that addiction should be treated as a medical rather than a legal issue, more readers might be receptive to the writer's call for legalization.
- **Placing the thesis in the middle of the essay** allows a writer to introduce the subject, provide support, raise questions, and guide the reader into accepting a thesis that is then explained or defended. However, placing the thesis somewhere within the essay may weaken its impact because reader attention is strongest at the opening and closing paragraphs. Writers often highlight a thesis statement in the middle of an essay by placing it in a separate paragraph or using italics.
- **Placing the thesis at the end** allows a writer to close the essay with a strong statement. Delaying the thesis allows the writer to address reader objections and bias, providing narratives, examples, and statistics to support the con-

clusion. However, postponing the thesis will disappoint some readers who want a clear answer. Delaying the thesis can suggest to some readers that the writer's position cannot stand on its own and depends on a great deal of qualification.

EXPLICIT, EVOLVING, AND IMPLIED THESES

Many textbooks suggest that every essay should have an easily identifiable thesis statement, a sentence you should be able to locate and underline, but this is not always the case. Most writers present explicit thesis statements, but others use a series of sentences to develop their opinions. In some instances, the writer's thesis is not formally stated but only implied or suggested.

Explicit Thesis Statements

Alan M. Dershowitz opens his essay "The 'Abuse Excuse' Is Detrimental to the Justice System" with a boldly stated, explicit thesis statement:

> The "abuse excuse"—the legal tactic by which criminal defendants claim a history of abuse as an excuse for violent retaliation—is quickly becoming a license to kill and maim.

Explicit theses are best used in writing in the modes of argument and persuasion, comparison, and division and classification.

Advantages

- An explicit thesis statement is clear and concise. The writer's purpose is stated directly so that readers are not confused.
- An explicit thesis can be used to make a strong opening or closing statement.
- A concise, strongly worded statement is easily understood so that even a casual reader will quickly grasp the writer's main idea.

Disadvantages

- Explicit thesis statements can present a narrow interpretation or solution to a complex situation or problem. In many instances an evolving or implied thesis gives the writer greater freedom to discuss ideas and address possible objections.

■ Because they are clear and direct, explicit theses can easily alienate readers with differing opinions. A developing thesis allows the writer to explain or qualify opinions.

Evolving Thesis Statements

In "Grant and Lee," Bruce Catton compares the two Civil War generals meeting at Appomattox Court House to work out terms for the South's surrender. But instead of stating his thesis in a single sentence, he develops his controlling ideas in a series of statements:

> They were two strong men, these oddly different generals, and they represented the strengths of two conflicting currents that, through them, had come into final collision.

After describing the life and social background of each general, Catton expands his thesis:

> So Grant and Lee were in complete contrast, representing two diametrically opposed elements in American life. Grant was the modern man emerging; beyond him, ready to come on the stage, was the great age of steel and machinery, of crowded cities and a restless burgeoning vitality. Lee might have ridden down from the old age of chivalry, lance in hand, silken banner fluttering over his head. Each man was the perfect champion of his cause, drawing both his strengths and his weaknesses from the people he led.

Catton concludes his essay with a final controlling statement:

> Two great Americans, Grant and Lee—very different, yet under everything very much alike.

Evolving thesis statements are best suited for complex or controversial subjects. They allow you to address an issue piece by piece or present a series of arguments.

Advantages

■ An evolving thesis lets a writer present readers with a series of controlling ideas, allowing them to absorb a complex opinion point by point.

■ An evolving thesis can be useful in presenting a controversial opinion by slowly convincing readers to accept less threatening ideas first.

■ An evolving thesis can help a writer tailor ideas to suit different situations or contexts. An evolving thesis can also be organized to address separate reader objections.

Disadvantages

■ Because the statements are distributed throughout an essay, they can appear "scattered" and have less impact than a single direct sentence.

■ Evolving theses can make a writer appear unsure of his or her points, as if he or she is reluctant to state a direct opinion.

Implied Thesis Statements

In describing Holcomb, Kansas, Truman Capote supplies a number of facts and observations without stating a thesis. Although no single sentence can be isolated as presenting the controlling idea, the description is highly organized and is more than a random collection of details:

> The village of Holcomb stands on the high wheat plains of western Kansas, a lonesome area that other Kansans call "out there." Some seventy miles east of the Colorado border, the countryside, with its hard blue skies and desert-clear air, has an atmosphere that is rather more Far Western than Middle West. The local accent is barbed with a prairie twang, a ranch-hand nasalness, and the men, many of them, wear narrow frontier trousers, Stetsons, and high-heeled boots with pointed toes. The land is flat, and the views are awesomely extensive; horses, herds of cattle, a white cluster of grain elevators rising as gracefully as Greek temples are visible long before a traveler reaches them.

Having carefully assembled and arranged his observations, Capote allows the details to speak for themselves and give readers a clear impression of his subject.

Implied thesis statements work best when the writer's evidence is so compelling that it does not require an introduction or explanation. Writers also use an implied thesis to challenge readers by posing an idea or presenting a problem without suggesting an interpretation or solution. Although you may not state a clear thesis statement in writing a description or telling a story, your essay should have a clear purpose, a direction. A thesis statement, though it may not appear on the page, can prevent an essay from becoming a list of random facts or a chain of unrelated events.

Advantages

■ An implied thesis allows the writer's images and observations to represent his or her ideas. Implied thesis statements are common in descriptive and narrative writing.

■ An implied thesis does not dictate an opinion but allows readers to develop their own responses.

■ An implied thesis does not confront readers with bold assertions but allows a writer to slowly unfold controlling ideas.

Disadvantages

■ Writing without an explicitly defined thesis can lead readers to assume ideas unintended by the writer. Capote's description of a small town may provoke both positive and negative responses, depending on the readers' perceptual world.

■ Writing that lacks a clear thesis statement requires careful reading and critical thinking to determine the writer's purpose. A strong thesis sentence at the opening or closing of an essay makes the author's goal very clear.

STRATEGIES | for Developing Thesis Statements

1. **Develop a thesis statement while planning your essay.** If you cannot state your goal in a sentence or two, you may not have a clear focus regarding your purpose. Even if you decide to use an implied thesis, a clearly worded statement on your outline or top of the page can help keep your writing on track.

2. **Write your thesis statement with your reader in mind.** The goal of writing is not only to express your ideas—but to share them with others. Choose your words carefully. Be sensitive to your readers' perceptual world. Avoid writing biased or highly opinionated statements that may alienate readers.

3. **Make sure that your thesis statement expresses an opinion.** Don't confuse making an announcement or a factual statement with establishing a thesis. Review the wording of the statement to see if it includes action verbs. Readers should be directed to take action, change their ideas, or alter their behavior.

4. **Determine the best location for your thesis.** If you believe that most of your readers will be receptive to your views, placing the thesis at the opening may be appropriate. If your position is controversial or depends on establishing a clear context of support, delay your thesis by placing it in the middle or at the conclusion.

5. **Make sure your thesis matches your purpose.** Persuasive arguments demand a strongly worded thesis statement, perhaps one that is restated throughout the essay. If your position is complex, you may wish to develop it by making partial thesis statements throughout the essay. If you are not motivating your readers to take specific action, you may wish to use an implied thesis. State your observations or evidence and permit readers to develop their own conclusions.

6. **Test your thesis.** It is not always easy to find people willing to read a draft of your essay, but you can usually find someone who will listen to a sentence or two. Ask a friend or acquaintance to consider your thesis statement. Is it precise? Does it seem logical? What kind of evidence would be needed to support it? Are there any words or phrases that seem awkward, unclear, or offensive? If your thesis statement seems weak, review your prewriting notes. You may need to further limit your topic or choose a new subject.

7. **Avoid making simple announcements or presenting narrowed topics.** The most common errors writers make in developing thesis statements include simply announcing the subject of a paper or presenting a narrowed topic:

ANNOUNCEMENTS:	My paper is about racial profiling. Snowboarding is a popular sport.
NARROWED TOPICS:	Police departments have been accused of racial profiling. Snowboarders are regarded as outlaws by traditional skiers.
IMPROVED THESIS STATEMENTS:	Police departments must develop methods to combat crime and prevent terrorism without resorting to racial profiling. Snowboarders and traditional skiers must learn to respect each other on the slopes.

WRITING ACTIVITIES

1. Select three to five topics from pages 903–904 and write thesis statements to guide possible rough drafts. Make sure your statements are opinions, not merely narrowed topics.

2. Skim through the entries in the reader section of the book and locate thesis statements. Note where they are located and whether they are explicit, implied, or evolving.

3. Select an issue you have thought about over a period of time and write a series of thesis statements illustrating your evolving viewpoints.

⋯ e-writing ⋯

Exploring Thesis Statements Online

You can use the Internet to learn more about developing thesis statements.

1. Using a search engine, such as Alta Vista, Yahoo!, or Google, enter *thesis statement* as a term and review the range of sources. You may wish to print out helpful websites.

2. Locate one or more newspapers online and scan through a series of recent editorials. Select a few articles on topics you are familiar with and examine the thesis statements. Which sentence summarizes the editorial's main point or assertion? Where is it placed? Are the thesis statements explicit, evolving, or implied? Are they carefully worded?

3. Using InfoTrac College Edition or one of your library's online databases, search for articles on gun control, abortion, capital punishment, or any other controversial topic. Can you identify the writers' thesis statements? Are they effective?

E-Sources

How to Write a Thesis Statement
    http://www.indiana.edu/~wts/ pamphlets/thesis_statement.shtml
Using Thesis Statements
    http://www.utoronto.ca/writing/thesis/ html
Developing a Thesis Statement
    http://www.wisc.edu/writing/ Handbook/Thesis.html

Companion Website

See **http://www.thomsonedu.com/ english/sundance** for additional information on thesis statements.

7

SUPPORTING
A THESIS

WHAT IS SUPPORT?

Whether your thesis is explicitly stated or only implied, it must be supported with evidence. Readers will share your views, appreciate your descriptions, understand your stories, accept your solutions, change their opinions, or alter their behavior only if you provide sufficient proof to convince them. The type of evidence you select depends on context—your goal, your reader, the discourse community, and the nature of the document. Most people associate *evidence* with persuasive or argumentative writing, but all writers—even those composing personal essays or memoirs—provide support for their ideas.

A student proposing a new computer system would have to provide factual support to create a convincing argument:

> *The college must improve its computer system.* This semester four hundred students did not receive mid-term grades because of a computer break down. The college e-mail system, which is critical to the distance learning department, malfunctioned for two weeks, preventing students from electronically submitting research papers. The eight-year old system simply does not have the speed and capacity needed to serve the faculty, students, and administration. Students were told two years ago that online reg-

WRITERS AT WORK

One day I lost my fountain pen, and I could not find another decent fountain pen. Phyllis Wright has this wonderful store where I live . . . called East End Computers. She is a wonderful woman. I walked in there, and I said, "All right, it's time for me to change my life. I can't find a fountain pen in this town." She really not only taught me how to do it [use a computer], she helped me to do it. Every time I had a problem and I couldn't get my document up, I would call Phyllis Wright. She gave me her home number so I could call her day or night for that period of transition that drives writers crazy. Now I'm all plugged in. Now I have a computer everywhere and a laptop that I take everywhere. I still have a fountain pen. Someone bought me one, but the fountain pen era is over.

Blanche Wiesen Cook, biographer

SOURCE: *Booknotes*

istration would save the college money and make it possible to sign up for courses from home. But this service has been postponed for another year because the computers can't support it. If the college is to attract students, maintain its programs, and offer new services, it must upgrade its computers.

The same student writing a personal narrative would use supporting details to paint a picture, set a mood, and express a feeling:

I spent two years in Paris and hated it! Most people raise their eyebrows when I say that, but it is true.

My Paris was not the Paris shown in the movies or the Paris seen by tourists. I lived with my mother in a cramped high rise built for low income workers. My Paris was a noisy, dark two-room apartment with bad heat, banging pipes, and broken elevators. The hallways were filled with trash and spattered with graffiti. Neighbors blasted us night and day with bad rock music. Punks and druggies harassed my Mom every time she left for school. I could not wait for her to finish her degree, so we could move back to New Jersey. I lived in Paris for two years and never saw the Eiffel Tower.

Writers verify their theses using various types of evidence, ranging from personal observations to statistics. Because each type of evidence has limitations (as you will see in the following sections), writers usually present a blend of personal observations and testimony, statistics and examples, or facts and analogies.

Personal Observations

Personal observations are descriptive details and sensory impressions about a person, place, object, or condition. Writers can support a thesis or controlling idea by supplying readers with specific details. The thesis that "Westwood High School must be renovated" can be supported with detailed observations about leaking roofs, faulty wiring, broken elevators, and defective plumbing. A personal description of your hometown might include observations about its neighborhoods and residents so that readers will understand and share your attitudes.

Advantages

- Personal observations can be powerful as long as they are carefully selected and well organized. To be effective, writers must choose words carefully, being aware of their connotations.
- Personal observations can be used to balance objective facts by adding human interest and personal narratives, allowing the writer to inject himself or herself into the writing.

Disadvantages

- Because they are chosen by the writer, personal observations are biased. They often require outside evidence such as facts, statistics, or testimony to be convincing.
- Personal observations may be inappropriate in objective reports. Writers often include material they observed without using first-person references such as "I" or "me."

Personal Experiences

Like personal observations, accounts of your own life can be convincing support. As a college student, you have great authority in discussing higher education. A veteran's comments about the military are likely to have greater credibility than those of a civilian. A single working mother is an authority on day care. A patient's account of battling a serious disease can be as persuasive as an article by a physician or medical researcher.

Advantages

- Personal experiences can be emotionally powerful and commanding because the writer is the sole authority and expert.
- Personal experiences are effective support in descriptive and narrative writing.
- Individual accounts can humanize abstract issues and personalize objective facts and statistics.

Disadvantages

- Personal experience, no matter how compelling, is only one person's story. As with personal observations, personal experience can be supported with the introduction of outside evidence such as expert testimony, facts, and statistics.
- Personal experience, unless presented carefully, can seem self-serving and can weaken a writer's argument. Before including your own experiences, consider whether readers will think you are making a self-serving appeal, asking readers to accept ideas or take actions that primarily benefit only you.

Examples

Examples are specific events, persons, or situations that represent a general trend, type, or condition. A writer supporting the right to die might relate the story of a single terminally ill patient to illustrate the need for euthanasia. The story of a single small business could illustrate an economic trend.

Advantages

- Specific cases or situations can illustrate an issue and humanize a complex or abstract problem. They often make effective introductions.
- Examples can be used to demonstrate facts and statistics that tend to be static lists.
- Examples allow you to introduce narratives that can make a fact-filled paper more interesting and readable.

Disadvantages

- Examples can be misleading or misinterpreted. Examples must be representative. For instance, a single mugging, no matter how violent, does not prove that a crime wave is sweeping a college campus. To be effective, examples should illustrate something larger. Avoid selecting isolated incidents or exceptions to a general condition. Stating that your ninety-year-old great grandfather has not seen a doctor in seventy-five years does not disprove the value of having regular checkups.

- Because they are highlighted, examples can sometimes be distorted into being viewed as major events instead of illustrations. Another danger is that examples can create false generalizations and overlook complex subtleties. Examples can be placed in context with statistics or a disclaimer:

> Mary Smith is one of five thousand teachers who participated in last year's strike. Though some of her views do not reflect the opinions of her colleagues, her experiences on the picket line were typical.

Facts

Facts are objective details that are either directly observed or gathered by the writer. The need to renovate a factory can be demonstrated by presenting evidence from inspection reports, maintenance records, and a manufacturer's repair recommendations.

Advantages

- Facts provide independent support for a writer's thesis, suggesting that others share his or her conclusions.
- Facts are generally verifiable. A reader who may doubt a writer's personal observations or experiences can check factual sources.
- Because of their objectivity, facts can be used to add credibility to personal narratives.

Disadvantages

- Facts, like examples, can be misleading. Don't assume that a few isolated pieces of information can support your thesis. You cannot disprove or dismiss a general trend by simply identifying a few contradictory facts. Citing a list of celebrities who dropped out of high school does not disprove the value of education.
- Facts, in some cases, must be explained to readers. Stating that "the elevator brakes are twenty years old" proves little unless readers understand that the manufacturer suggests replacing them after ten years. Lengthy or technical explanations of facts may distract or bore readers.

Testimony (Quotations)

Testimony, the observations or statements by witnesses, participants, or experts, allows writers to interject other voices into their document, whether in the form of direct quotations or paraphrases.

Advantages

- Testimony, like factual support, helps verify a writer's thesis by showing that others share his or her views and opinions.
- Testimony by witnesses or participants adds a human dimension to facts and statistics. Comments by a victim of child abuse can dramatize the problem, compelling readers to learn more and be willing to study factual data.
- Expert testimony, usually in the form of quotations, enhances a writer's credibility by indicating that highly respected individuals agree with his or her thesis.

Disadvantages

- Comments by people who observed or participated in an event are limited by the range of their experiences. An eyewitness to a car accident sees the crash from one angle. Another person, standing across the street, may report events very differently.
- Witnesses and participants interpret events based on their perceptual worlds and may be less than objective.
- Expert testimony can be misleading. Don't take quotes out of context. Don't assume that you can impress readers by simply sprinkling a paper with quotations by famous people. Statements by experts must be meaningful, relevant, and accurate.

Analogies (Comparisons)

Analogies compare similar situations, people, objects, or events to demonstrate the validity of the thesis. The thesis "AIDS prevention programs will reduce the incidence of infection" can be supported by pointing to the success of similar programs to combat venereal disease or teenage pregnancy. An argument about privatizing Social Security could be supported by comparisons to nations that have privatized their pension systems.

Advantages

- Analogies can introduce new topics by comparing them to ones readers find familiar or understandable.

■ Comparisons can counter alternative theses or solutions by showing their failures or deficiencies in contrast to the writer's ideas.

Disadvantages

■ Analogy is a weak form of argument. Because no two situations are exactly alike, analogy is rarely convincing in itself. Arguing that school uniforms reduced violence in one school does not prove it would work in another with different student populations, teachers, and social challenges.

■ Comparisons depend on readers' perceptual worlds. Suggesting that an urban planner's design should be adopted because it will transform a city's business district into another Fifth Avenue assumes that readers find Fifth Avenue desirable.

✴ Statistics

Statistics are factual data expressed in numbers and can validate a writer's thesis in dramatic terms readers can readily appreciate. However, you must be careful because although statistics represent facts and not an opinion, they can be very deceptive. The statement "Last year the number of students apprehended for possessing cocaine tripled" sounds alarming until you learn the arrests went from one to three students at a university with an enrollment of 30,000. Numbers can be used to provide strikingly different perceptions. Suppose the state of California pays half a million welfare recipients $800 a month. A proposal to increase these benefits by 2 percent can be reported as representing $16 a month to the poor or $96 million a year to taxpayers. Both figures are accurate, and one can easily imagine which numbers politicians will use to support or reject the proposal.

Advantages

■ Statistics can distill a complex issue into a single dramatic statement:
One out of three American children grows up in poverty.
Each cigarette takes seven minutes off a smoker's life.
Twenty-one thousand instances of domestic violence are reported every week.

■ Statistics can be easily remembered and repeated to others. Readers may be unable to remember lengthy paragraphs or sophisticated reasoning but can easily recall a statistic and share it with others.

Disadvantages

■ Because they are often misused, statistics are often distrusted by readers. Whenever you quote statistics, be prepared to explain where you obtained them and why they are reliable.

■ Although statistics can be dramatic, they can quickly bore readers. Long lists of numbers can be difficult for readers to absorb. Statistics can be made easier to understand if presented in graphs, charts, and diagrams.

STRATEGIES for Using Statistics

In gathering and presenting statistics, consider these questions:

1. **Where did the statistics come from?** Who produced the statistics? Is the source reliable? Statistics about the safety of nuclear power plants released by utility companies or antinuclear organizations may be suspect. If the source might be biased, search for information from additional sources.

2. **When were the statistics collected?** Information can become obsolete very quickly. Determine whether the numbers are still relevant. For example, surveys about such issues as capital punishment can be distorted if they are conducted after a violent crime.

3. **How were the statistics collected?** Public opinion polls are commonly used to represent support or opposition to an issue. A statement such as "Ninety percent of the student body think Dean Miller should resign" means nothing unless you know how that figure was determined. How many students were polled—ten or a thousand? How were they chosen—at an anti-Miller rally or by random selection? How was the question worded? Was it objective or did it provoke a desired response? Did the polled students reflect the attitudes of the entire student body?

4. **Are the units being counted properly defined?** All statistics count some item—drunk driving arrests, housing starts, defaulted loans, student dropouts, teenage pregnancies, or AIDS patients. In some cases confusion can occur if the items are not precisely defined. In polling students, for instance, the term *student* must be clearly delineated. Who will be counted? Only full-time students? Undergraduates? Senior citizens auditing an elective art history course? Unless there is a clear definition of *alcoholic* or *juvenile delinquent*, comparing studies will be meaningless.

5. **Do the statistics measure what they claim to measure?** The units being counted may not be accurate indicators. Comparing graduates' SAT scores

assumes that the tests accurately measure achievement. If one nation's air force is 500 percent larger than its neighbor's, does it mean that it is five times as powerful? Counting aircraft alone does not take quality, pilot skill, natural defenses, or a host of other factors into account.

6. **Are enough statistics presented?** A single statistic may be accurate but misleading. The statement that "80 percent of Amalgam workers own stock in the company" makes the firm sound employee owned—until you learn that the average worker has half a dozen shares. Ninety percent of the stock could be held by a single investor.

7. **How are the statistics being interpreted?** Numbers alone do not tell the whole story. If one teacher has a higher retention rate than another, does it mean he or she is a better instructor or an easy grader? If the number of people receiving services from a social welfare agency increases, does it signal a failing economy or greater effort and efficiency on the part of an agency charged with aiding the disadvantaged?

WRITING ACTIVITIES

List the types of evidence needed to support the following thesis statements.

1. The city's proposed handgun ban will not prevent gang violence.

2. Consumers will resist shopping on the Web until credit card security is assured.

3. Given the demand for more on-campus housing, the fifty-year-old dorm for men should be rehabilitated.

4. Women must learn to express intolerance toward sexual harassment without appearing humorless or fanatical.

5. Vote for Sandy Mendoza!

DOCUMENTING SOURCES

No matter how dramatic, evidence is not likely to impress readers unless they know its source. Chapter 30 details methods of using academic documentation styles, such as MLA (Modern Language Association) and APA (American

Psychological Association) formats. Documentation, usually mandatory in research papers, is useful even in short essays. Even informal notations can enhance your credibility:

> According to a recent *Newsweek* poll, 50 percent of today's freshmen plan to own their own business.
>
> Half of today's freshmen plan to open their own businesses someday (*Newsweek,* March 10, 2003).

STRATEGIES | for Using Evidence

Use these questions to evaluate the evidence you have assembled to support your thesis.

1. **Is the evidence suited to your thesis?** Review the writing context to determine what evidence is appropriate. Personal observations and experiences would support the thesis of an autobiographical essay. However, these subjective elements could weaken the thesis of a business report. The thesis "My aunt taught me the meaning of courage" can be supported by personal observations and narratives. But a thesis such as "America must protect itself from the threat of biological terrorism" demands expert testimony, statistics, and factual data to be convincing.

2. **Is the evidence accurate?** It may be possible to find evidence that supports your thesis—but are these quotations, facts, and statistics accurate? Are they current? Figures that were relevant in 2002 may be irrelevant today. Quotations taken out of context can distort the writer's original intent. Statements made by experts in the past may have been retracted in light of later events or research.

3. **Are the sources reliable?** Evidence can be gathered from innumerable sources but not all proof is equally reliable or objective. Many sources of information have political biases or economic interests and only produce data that support their views. If you are writing about gun control, avoid taking all your information from either the National Rifle Association or antigun activists. In gathering information about minimum wage, balance data from labor unions and antipoverty groups with government statistics and testimony from business owners.

In some instances, reliable and objective evidence is difficult to obtain. Highly partisan and controversial issues generate a great deal of information, much of it produced to support a particular viewpoint. You can persuade readers to accept your thesis if you balance sources and openly state that some evidence may be biased and subject to alternative interpretations.

4. **Is sufficient evidence presented?** To convince readers, you must supply enough evidence to support your thesis. A few isolated facts or quotations from experts are not likely to be persuasive. A single extended example might influence readers to accept your thesis about a close friend or relative but would not be likely to alter their views on such issues as immigration, recycling, divorce laws, or public schools. Such topics require facts, statistics, and expert testimony.

Examine your thesis carefully to see whether it can be separated into parts, and determine whether you have adequate proof for each section:

The university should offer more Internet courses to increase enrollment.

- The thesis suggests the current enrollment is unacceptable and must be increased—is there enough factual support to document this view?
- Internet courses are offered as a proposed solution—are sufficient data offered to indicate their success in attracting new students?
- Does the essay document why Internet courses are a better vehicle for increasing enrollment than alternative proposals such as advertising existing courses, expanding night school offerings, or creating new classes?

5. **Is the evidence representative?** To be intellectually honest, writers have to use evidence that is representative. You can easily assemble isolated facts, quotations taken out of context, and exceptional events to support almost any thesis. Books about UFOs, the Bermuda Triangle, and assassination conspiracies are often filled with unsupported personal narratives, quotations from questionable experts, and isolated facts.

If you can support your thesis only with isolated examples and atypical instances, you may wish to question your conclusions.

6. **Is the evidence presented clearly?** Although evidence is essential to support your thesis, long quotations and lists of statistics can be boring and counterproductive. Evidence should be readable. Outside sources should blend well with your own writing.

Read your paper out loud to identify awkward or difficult passages.

7. **Does the evidence support the thesis?** Finally, ask yourself if the evidence you have selected really supports your thesis. In listing personal

observations, collecting statistics, or searching for quotations, it is easy to be led astray from your original goal. Before including a particular piece of evidence, test it against your thesis.

If your evidence does not directly support your thesis, review your prewriting notes and consider revising your thesis statement.

WRITING ACTIVITIES

1. If you developed any thesis statements in the exercises on page 79, list the types of sources that would prove the best support.

2. Select a topic from pages 903–904 and list the kind of evidence readers would expect writers to use as support.

e-writing

Exploring Thesis Support Online

You can use the Internet to learn more about supporting a thesis.

1. Locate resources about specific types of evidence online or in your library's databases by using *statistics* and *personal testimony* as search terms.

2. Search newspapers and journals online and select a few articles and editorials. After identifying the thesis, note how the authors presented supporting evidence.

3. Ask instructors in your various courses for websites to locate useful sources in various disciplines.

E-Sources

Supporting Your Thesis
**http://www.powa.org/thesis/
supporting.html**
Evaluating Web Pages
**http://www.lib.berkeley.edu/TeachingLib/
Guides/Internet/Evaluate.html**
Evaluating Information Found on the Internet
**http://www.library.jhu.edu/
researchhelp/general/evaluating/**

Companion Website

See **http://www.thomsonedu.com/
english/sundance** for information on supporting a thesis.

8

ORGANIZING IDEAS

Planning a work is like planning a journey.

—H. J. Tichy

WHAT IS ORGANIZATION?

Whenever you write, you take readers on a journey, presenting facts, relating stories, sharing ideas, and creating impressions. Readers can follow your train of thought only if you provide them with a clear road map that organizes your thesis and evidence. Even the most compelling ideas will fail to interest readers if placed in a random or chaotic manner. The way you arrange ideas depends on your purpose, the audience, and conventions of the discourse community. Some formal documents dictate a strict format that readers expect you to follow. But in most instances you are free to develop your own method of organization.

As you review the readings in this book, notice how writers organize their essays, providing transitions from one idea to another.

Once you have written a thesis statement and collected supporting material, create a plan for your paper. Prewriting techniques such as brainstorming, writing lists, and clustering can help establish ways to structure your essay. You do not have to develop an elaborate outline with Roman numerals and letters for every paper—a plan can be a simple list of reminders, much like a book's table of contents or a shopping list. A short narrative recalling a recent experience may require only a few notes to guide your first draft. A complex research

I had a tape recorder with me and also had a notebook. I'm scribbling furiously, but . . . what ended up being very beneficial . . . is that I had a little tape recorder with me. For example, the night that we were trapped in the mine field— it's pitch black. You can't see to write a note anywhere. I just turned on the tape recorder, and in doing the research for the book, I just listened to hours and hours of these tapes and could reconstruct entire conversations verbatim.

Molly Moore, Gulf War correspondent

SOURCE: *Booknotes*

paper with numerous sources, however, usually demands a more detailed outline to help you avoid getting lost. Like an artist making a sketch before attempting to paint a large mural, you can use an outline to get an overall view of your essay. Sketching out your ideas can help you identify potential problems, spot missing information, reveal irrelevant material, and highlight passages that would make a good opening or final remark.

INFORMAL AND FORMAL OUTLINES

In most cases, no one sees your outline. It is a means to an end. If prewriting has clearly established the ideas in your mind, you may simply need a few notes to keep your writing on track. The student who worked for an insurance agency for a number of years needs only a few reminders to draft a comparison of two types of policies:

Whole Life and Term Insurance

Whole Life
—explain premiums
—savings & loan options

Term
—no savings
—lower rates

Conclusion—last point

A formal outline, however, can serve to refine your prewriting so that your plan becomes a detailed framework for the first draft. Formal outlines organize details and can keep you from drifting off the topic. In addition, they provide a document an instructor or peer reviewer can work with. Few people may be able to decipher the rough notes you make for yourself, but a standard outline creates a clear picture of your topic, thesis, and evidence for others to review and critique (see the complete essay—based on the following outline—on page 448):

Whole Life and Term Insurance

 I. Introduction: Whole life and term insurance
 II. Whole life insurance
  A. General description
   1. History
   2. Purpose
    a. Protection against premature death
    b. Premium payments include savings
  B. Investment feature
   1. Cash value accrual
   2. Loans against cash value
 III. Term insurance
  A. General description
   1. History
   2. Purpose
    a. Protection against premature death
    b. Premium payments lower than whole life insurance
  B. Investment feature
   1. No cash value accrual
   2. No loans against cash value
  C. Cost advantage
   1. Lower premiums
   2. Affordability of greater coverage
 IV. Conclusion
  A. Insurance needs of consumer
   1. Income
   2. Family situation
   3. Investment goals & savings
   4. Obligations
  B. Investment counselors' advice about coverage

Whether your plan is a simple list or a formal outline, it serves as a road map for the first draft and should focus on three main elements:

Title and introduction
The body
Conclusion

Because new ideas can occur throughout the writing process, your plan does not have to detail each element perfectly. You may not come up with an appropriate title or introduction until final editing. In planning, however, consider the impact you want each part of your paper to make. Consider the qualities of an effective title, introduction, body, and conclusion. Develop as complete a plan as you can, leaving blank spaces for future changes.

WRITING TITLES AND INTRODUCTIONS

Titles

Titles play a vital role in creating effective essays. A strong title attracts attention, prepares readers to accept your thesis, and helps focus the essay. If you find developing a title difficult, simply label the paper until you complete the first draft. As you write you may discover an interesting word or phrase that captures the essence of your essay and would serve as an effective title.

Writers use a variety of types of titles—labels, thesis statements, questions, and creative statements.

Labels

Business reports, professional journals, student research papers, and government publications often have titles that clearly state the subject by means of a label:

Italian Industrial Production—Milan Sector
Bipolar Disorders: Alternative Drug Therapies
Child Abuse Intervention Strategies
Whitman's Democratic Vision

■ Labels should be as precisely worded as possible. Avoid extremely general titles that simply announce a broad topic—*"Death of a Salesman"* or "Urban Crime." Titles should reflect your focus—"Willy Loman: Victim of the American Dream" or "Economic Impact of Urban Crime."

■ Labels are best suited for reports that are addressed to specific audiences, such as a professional association, corporate management, or government agency. Such titles usually fail to generate interest in general readers.

■ Labels are generally objective and are suited to documents that have to reflect the views and values of a large group. Although undramatic, accurate labels are not likely to confuse or alienate readers.

Thesis Statements

Titles can state or summarize the writer's thesis:

> We Must Stop Child Abuse
> Biology Does Not Determine Gender Differences
> Legalizing Drugs Will Not Deter Crime
> Why We Need to Understand Science

■ Thesis statements are frequently used in editorials and political commentaries to openly declare a writer's point of view.

■ Bold assertions attract attention but can also antagonize readers. If you sense that readers may not accept your thesis, it is better to first build your case through introducing background information or supporting details before stating a point of view.

Questions

Writers use questions to arouse interest without revealing their positions:

> Does Recycling Protect the Environment?
> Is There an Epidemic of Child Abuse?
> The Civil Rights Movement: What Good Was It?
> Should This Student Have Been Expelled?

■ Questions stimulate readers' interest, motivating them to consider the writer's answer. Because questions imply different responses, they can spark critical thinking and prompt readers to analyze their existing knowledge, values, and opinions.

■ Questions are useful for addressing controversial issues because readers must evaluate the writer's evidence before learning his or her answer.

■ Questions have to be carefully worded to be effective. Placing a question mark after a label will not make a topic more interesting. Bland titles such as "Is Pollution Bad?" or "Is Murder Wrong?" are not likely to spark genuine interest.

Creative Statements

Writers sometimes use an attention-getting word or creative phrase to attract readers:

> Pink Mafia: Women and Organized Crime
>
> Sharks on the Web: Consumer Fraud on the Internet
>
> The Rascal King: The Life and Times of James Michael Curley (1874–1958)
>
> Climbing the Ebony Tower: Tenure in Black Colleges

- Creative titles, like questions, grab attention and motivate people to read items they might ignore. Magazine writers often use clever, humorous, or provocative titles to stimulate interest.
- Creative titles are usually unsuited to formal documents or reports. Creative wording may appear trivial, inappropriate, or biased and should be avoided in objective writing.
- The language used in a title should match the style and tone established by the publication and discourse community.

Introductions

Introductions should arouse attention, state what your essay is about, and prepare readers for what follows. In addition to stating the topic, the introduction can present background information and provide an overview of the entire essay. A student explaining the different types of Hispanic students on her campus uses the first paragraph to address a misconception and then describes how she will use classification to develop the rest of her essay (see the complete essay on page 548):

> Students, faculty, and administrators tend to refer to "Hispanics" as if all Latino and Latina students belonged to a single homogeneous group. Actually, there are four distinct groups of Hispanic students. Outsiders may only see slight discrepancies in dress and behavior, but there are profound differences which occasionally border on suspicion and hostility. Their differences are best measured by their attitude toward and their degree of acceptance of mainstream American values and culture.

If you don't have a strong introduction in mind, use a thesis statement (see next section) to focus the first draft. In reviewing your initial version, look for quotes, facts, statements, or examples that would make a strong first impression. Avoid making general opening statements that serve as diluted titles: *This paper is about a dangerous trend happening in America today.*

Writers use a number of methods to introduce their essays. You can begin with a thesis statement, a striking fact or statistic, or a quotation, among other possibilities.

Open with a Thesis Statement

> The "abuse excuse"—the legal tactic by which criminal defendants claim a history of abuse as an excuse for violent retaliation—is quickly becoming a license to kill and maim. More and more defense lawyers are employing this tactic and more and more jurors are buying it. It is a dangerous trend, with serious and widespread implications for the safety and liberty of every American.
>
> *Alan Dershowitz, "The 'Abuse Excuse' Is Detrimental to the Justice System"*

- Opening with a thesis creates a strong first impression so even a casual reader quickly understands the message. Declaring your thesis at the outset can inform or persuade an audience that is apathetic and likely to skim or ignore much of the document's text.
- Like a title summarizing the writer's thesis, however, introductions that make a clear assertion may alienate readers, particularly if your topic or position is controversial. You may wish to present evidence or explain reasons before openly announcing your thesis.

Begin with Facts or Statistics

> One out of every five new recruits in the United States military is female. The Marines gave the Combat Action Ribbon for service in the Persian Gulf to 23 women. Two female soldiers were killed in bombing of the USS Cole.
>
> The Selective Service registers for the draft all male citizens between the ages of 18 and 25.
>
> What's wrong with this picture?
>
> *Anna Quindlen, "Uncle Sam and Aunt Samantha: It's Simple Fairness: Women as Well as Men Should be Required to Register for the Draft"*

- In prewriting and planning, you may have come across an interesting fact or example that can quickly demonstrate the importance of your subject.
- The fact or statistic you select should be easy to comprehend and stimulate reader interest.

Use a Quotation

> In 1773, on a tour of Scotland and the Hebrides Islands, Samuel Johnson visited a school for deaf children. Impressed by the students but daunted by their

predicament, he proclaimed deafness "one of the most desperate of human calamities." More than a century later Helen Keller reflected on her own life and declared that deafness was a far greater hardship than blindness. "Blindness cuts people off from things," she observed. "Deafness cuts people off from people."

Edward Dolnick, "Deafness as Culture"

- Quotations allow you to present another voice, giving a second viewpoint. You can introduce expert opinion, providing immediate support for the upcoming thesis.
- Select quotations by authorities readers respect or people they can identify with. Quotations can humanize an issue by presenting a personal experience or opinion.
- Select relevant quotations. Avoid using famous sayings by Shakespeare, Benjamin Franklin, or Martin Luther King Jr. because out of context they can be used to justify almost any point of view.

Open with a Brief Narrative or Example

At first, Robert Maynard thought they were harmless—albeit crude—electronic postings. Most closed with the same poem: "Lord, grant me the serenity to accept the things I cannot change . . . and the wisdom to hide the bodies of the people I had to kill." One claimed that Maynard's employees were liars. Others that his wife, Teresa, was unfaithful. But when the messages, posted on an Internet news group, did not stop, Maynard went to court.

Kevin Whitelaw, "Fear and Dread in Cyberspace"

- A short narrative personalizes complex topics and helps introduce readers to subjects that they might not initially find interesting.
- Narratives should be short and representative. An engaging example may distort readers' understanding and should be balanced with facts and statistics to place it in context.

Pose a Question

Think for a minute. Who were you before this wave of feminism began?

Gloria Steinem, "Words and Change"

- An opening question, like one posed in the title, arouses attention by challenging and engaging readers, prompting them to consider your topic.
- Questions can introduce discussion of controversial topics without immediately revealing your opinion.

ORGANIZING THE BODY OF AN ESSAY

Once you introduce the subject, there are three basic methods of organizing the body of the essay: chronological, spatial, and emphatic. Just as writers often have unique composing styles, they often have different ways of viewing and organizing their material. The way you organize the body of the essay should reflect your thesis and your train of thought. *Remember, place your most important ideas at the opening or ending of your paper. Do not bury the most important information in the middle of the document, which readers are most likely to skip or skim. Within these general methods of organization, you may include portions using different modes. For example, a spatially organized essay may contain chronological sections.*

Chronological: Organizing by Time

The simplest and often the most effective way of structuring an essay is to tell a story, relating events as they occurred. Narrative, process, cause-and-effect, and example essays commonly follow a chronological pattern, presenting evidence on a timeline. Biographies, history books, accident reports, and newspaper articles about current events are often arranged chronologically.

A student discussing the causes of the Civil War might explain the conflict as the result of a historical process, the outcome of a chain of events.

> **THESIS:** The American Civil War resulted from a growing economic, cultural, and ideological division between North and South that could not be resolved through peaceful compromise.

Outline

I. 1776 historical background
   A. Jefferson's deleted anti-slavery statement in Declaration of Independence
   B. Seeds of eventual clash
II. 1820s economic conflict
   A. Growth of Northern commercial and industrial economy
   B. Growth of Southern agrarian economy
III. 1830–40s political feuds stemming from conflicting interests
   A. Northern demand for tariffs to protect infant industries
   B. Southern desire for free trade for growing cotton exports

   IV. 1850s ideological conflict
      A. Growing abolitionist movement in North
         1. John Brown
         2. Underground Railroad
      B. Southern defense of slavery
         1. Resentment of abolitionist actions in South
         2. Resistance to westward expansion and free states
    V. 1860s movement to war
      A. Election of Lincoln
      B. Southern calls for secession
      C. Fort Sumter attack, start of Civil War

■ Readers are accustomed to reading information placed in chronological or-der. Using a narrative form allows writers to demonstrate how a problem de-veloped, relate an experience, or predict a future course of action.

■ Chronological organization does not have to follow a strict time line. Dra-matic events can be highlighted by using flash forwards and flashbacks (see pages 314–315).

■ Arranging evidence in a chronological pattern can mislead readers by sug-gesting cause-and-effect relationships that do not exist.

■ Chronological order may be cumbersome if many unrelated events occur si-multaneously.

Spatial: Organizing by Division · ·

Writers frequently approach complex subjects by breaking them down into parts. Comparison, division, and classification essays are spatially arranged. In-stead of using chronology, another student explaining the causes of the Civil War might address each cause separately.

> **THESIS:** The American Civil War was caused by three major conflicts between the North and the South: economic, cultural, and ideological.

Outline

   I. Economic conflict
      A. Northern commercial and industrial economy
         1. Demand for tariffs to protect infant industries
         2. Need for skilled labor

    B. Southern agrarian economy
      1. Desire for free trade for cotton exports
      2. Dependence on slave labor
  II. Cultural conflict
    A. Northern urban business class
    B. Southern landed aristocracy
  III. Ideological conflict
    A. Growing abolitionist movement in North
      1. John Brown
      2. Underground Railroad
    B. Southern defense of slavery
      1. Resentment of abolitionist actions in South
      2. Resistance to westward expansion and free states

- Spatial organization can simplify complex issues by dividing them into separate elements. By understanding the parts, readers can appreciate the nature of the whole.
- Spatial organization is useful if you are addressing multiple readers. Those with a special interest can quickly locate where a specific issue is discussed. In a chronological paper, this information would be distributed throughout the essay and require extensive searching.
- Divisions in a spatially organized paper must be carefully assigned. Minor ideas can be overemphasized if placed in separate sections and significant concepts overshadowed or overlooked if merged with other topics.

Emphatic: Organizing by Importance

If you believe that some ideas are more notable than others, you can arrange information by importance. Because readers' attention is greatest at the beginning and end of an essay, open or conclude with the most important points. A writer could decide that simply separating the causes of the Civil War fails to demonstrate the importance of what he or she considers the driving reason for the conflict. The student who believes that slavery was the dominant cause of the war could organize a paper in either of two patterns.

> **THESIS:** Although North and South were divided by differing cultural, economic, and ideological conflicts, slavery was the overwhelming issue that directly led to secession and war.

Most Important to Least Important Outline	Least Important to Most Important Outline
I. Slavery, most important cause of Civil War	I. Foreign Trade
A. Jefferson compromise in 1776	A. Northern demand for tariffs
B. Abolitionist movement in North	B. Southern demand for free trade
1. Expansion of abolitionist newspapers	II. Ideological conflict
2. Establishment of Underground Railroad	A. Northern philosophy
3. Protests and riots over Fugitive Slave Act	1. Desire for Western expansion to add free
4. *Uncle Tom's Cabin* & popular culture	states
5. International resentment over slavery	2. Need for stronger federal government
C. Growing Southern dependence on slavery	B. Southern philosophy
1. Growth of militant press	1. Desire for Southern expansion, add slave
2. Rise of King Cotton	states
3. Intellectual defenses of slavery	2. Need to assert states' rights
4. Need for cheap labor	III. Economic conflict
5. Resentment of Northern attacks on slavery	A. Northern economy
II. Economic Conflict	1. Commercial, financial, industrial interests
A. Northern economy	2. Factory owners
1. Commercial, financial, industrial interests	3. Rise of New York as financial center
2. Factory owners	B. Southern economy
3. Rise of New York as financial center	1. Agricultural interests
B. Southern economy	2. Landowners
1. Agricultural interests	3. Resentment of Northern financial power
2. Landowners	IV. Slavery, most important cause of Civil War
3. Resentment of Northern financial power	A. Jefferson compromise in 1776
III. Ideological Conflict	B. Abolitionist movement in North
A. Northern philosophy	1. Expansion of abolitionist newspapers
1. Desire for Western expansion to add	2. Establishment of Underground Railroad
free states	3. Protests and riots over Fugitive Slave Act
2. Need for stronger federal government	4. *Uncle Tom's Cabin* & popular culture
B. Southern philosophy	5. International resentment over slavery
1. Desire for Southern expansion to add	C. Growing Southern dependence on slavery
slave states	1. Growth of militant press
2. Need to assert states' rights	2. Rise of King Cotton
IV. Foreign Trade	3. Intellectual defenses of slavery
A. Northern demand for tariffs	4. Need for cheap labor
B. Southern need for free trade	5. Resentment of Northern attacks on slavery

Advantages: Most Important to Least Important

■ Starting with the most important idea places the most critical information in the first few paragraphs or pages. Readers unable to complete the entire document will absorb the most essential ideas. This can be useful for long, detailed papers or documents that you suspect may not be read in their entirety.

■ You are likely to devote less space and detail to minor ideas, so the reading will become easier to follow and will counter reader fatigue. Because the sections will be shorter and less dense, readers will have the impression of picking up momentum as they read the final sections.

Disadvantages: Most Important to Least Important

■ The principal disadvantage of this method is that the paper loses emphasis and can trail off into insignificant details. An effective conclusion that refers to the main idea can provide the paper with a strong final impression.

■ In some instances, important ideas cannot be fully appreciated without introductory information.

Advantages: Least Important to Most Important

■ Papers concluding with the most important idea build intensity, taking readers to ideas of increasing significance, building a stronger and stronger case for the writer's thesis.

■ Concluding with the most important information is effective in leaving readers with a dominant final impression.

Disadvantages: Least Important to Most Important

■ Readers' attention naturally diminishes over time, so that the ability to concentrate weakens as you present the most important ideas. Because you are likely to devote more space to the significant points, the sentences become more complex and the paragraphs longer, making the essay more challenging to read. Subtitles, paragraph breaks, and transitional statements can alert readers to pay particular attention to your concluding remarks.

■ Readers who are unable to finish the paper will miss the most important ideas. However, you can use the introduction to signal where important ideas are located so that readers unable to read the entire paper will skip ahead to the conclusion.

WRITING CONCLUSIONS

Not all essays require a lengthy conclusion. A short essay does not need a separate paragraph that simply repeats the opening. But all writing should end with an emphatic point, final observation, or memorable comment.

Summarize the Thesis and Main Points

A long, complex essay can benefit from a summary that reminds readers of your thesis and principal considerations:

> Public understanding of science is more central to our national security than half a dozen strategic weapon systems. The sub-mediocre performance of American youngsters in science and math, and the widespread adult ignorance and apathy about science and math, should sound an urgent alarm.
>
> *Carl Sagan, "Why We Should Understand Science"*

- Ending with a summary or restatement of the thesis leaves readers with your main point.
- Summaries in short papers, however, can be redundant and weaken rather than strengthen an essay.

End with a Question

Just as an introductory question can arouse reader interest, so concluding with a question can prompt readers to consider the essay's main points or challenge readers to consider a future course of action:

> So the drumbeat goes on for more police, more prisons, more of the same failed policies. Ever see a dog chase its tail?
>
> *Wilbert Rideau, "Why Prisons Don't Work"*

Some writers pose a last question and provide an answer to reinforce their thesis:

> Can such principles be taught? Maybe not. But most of them can be learned.
>
> *William Zinsser, "The Transaction"*

- Questions can be used to provoke readers to ponder the issues raised in the essay, guiding them to take action or reconsider their views.

■ Questions can lead readers to pause and consider the writer's points. Readers may be tempted to skim through an essay, but a final question provides a test—prompting them to think about what they have just read. A question can lead a reader to review the essay or even read it a second time.

Conclude with a Quotation

A quotation allows writers to introduce a second opinion or conclude with remarks by a noted authority or compelling witness:

> I once had the opportunity to describe father's life to the late, great Jewish American writer Bernard Malamud. His only comment was, "Only in America!"
> *José Antonio Burciaga, "My Ecumenical Father"*

■ Select quotations that are striking, relevant, and that emphasize the main points of the essay.
■ Avoid irrelevant or generic quotations by famous people. Unless it directly addresses your thesis, a quotation by a celebrity or historic figure will not impress readers.

End with a Strong Image

Narrative and descriptive essays can have power if they leave readers with a compelling fact or scene:

> When the others went swimming, my son said he was going in, too. He pulled his dripping trunks from the line where they had hung all through the shower and wrung them out. Languidly, and with no thought of going in, I watched him, his hard little body, skinny and bare, saw him wince slightly as he pulled up around his vitals the small, soggy, icy garment. As he buckled the swollen belt, suddenly my groin felt the chill of death.
> *E. B. White, "Once More to the Lake"*

■ Choose an image that will motivate readers to consider the essay's main points.
■ Concluding images and statements should be suited to the conventions of the discourse community and the nature of the document.

Conclude with a Challenging Statement

Writers of persuasive essays frequently end with an appeal, prediction, warning, or challenge aimed directly at the reader:

Ally yourself with us while you can—or don't be surprised if, one day, you're asking one of *us* for work.

Suneel Rataan, "Why Busters Hate Boomers"

- Direct challenges are effective if you want readers to take action. Make sure that any appeal you use is suited to both your goal and your audience.
- Avoid making statements that are hostile or offensive. Consider possible extended audiences. If you are writing as the agent of others, determine if the remark you make reflects the attitudes, values, and tone of those you represent.

MOVING FROM PREWRITING TO PLANNING

The plan you develop builds upon your prewriting, pulling the relevant ideas into meaningful order. Having read and discussed several essays concerning criminal justice, a student decided to write a short essay debating the merits of a current legal issue. At first she listed topics, then used clustering, freewriting, and questioning to narrow her topic and develop her thesis:

Topics:
    Criminal justice (issues)
    Capital punishment pro/con
    Gun control
    Court TV
    Teenage shootings
    Gangs
    How does the media influence juries?
    Jury nullification—moral or unjust?
    Victims of crime—are they forgotten?
    Who speaks for victims? (victims' rights movement)
    Do prosecutors represent victims or the state?

Victims	TV coverage
Privacy issues	Rape cases
Addresses to judge	Impact statements

Victim impact statements are increasingly a feature of modern trials as people are allowed to state their feelings about the crime and the criminal after he/she has been convicted. Judges can consider the impact of the crime on the victim in sentencing.

Sometimes victims ask for harsh punishment and sometimes they even ask for leniency and give criminals, especially the young, a second chance.

> Who is most impressive?
> What about victims who can't speak well or don't know English?
> What about families of homicide victims?
> Victims without mourners? Less important?

Topic: Victim impact statements

Thesis: Although victim impact statements are designed to empower the victims of crime, they may serve only to further marginalize the most helpless among us.

After reviewing her prewriting notes, she created an outline organizing her essay spatially, presenting positive and then negative effects of victim impact statements. To give her paper a strong conclusion, she decided to end the paper with her thesis.

Outline

I. Introduction
   A. Background of victim impact statements
   B. Definition of victim impact statements
II. Goals of victim impact statements (pro)
   A. Victims granted a voice
   B. Therapeutic benefits for victims
   C. Recommendations for sentencing
III. Negative effects of victim impact statements (con)
   A. Inarticulate victims ignored
   B. Benefits limited to the affluent
IV. Conclusion
   Thesis: Victim impact statements marginalize the poor and helpless

WRITING ACTIVITIES

1. Write a brief plan for the following topics, using each of the three basic methods of organization.
    Topic: Television violence
       Chronological   Spatial   Emphatic
    Topic: Teen smoking
       Chronological   Spatial   Emphatic

Topic: America's role in the twenty-first century
   Chronological   Spatial   Emphatic

2. Review the following prewriting notes and assemble the ideas into an effective outline. (You may use more than one organizational method.)

Topic: Telemarketing fraud

Thesis: State and federal agencies must take greater steps to stem the rapid increase in telemarketing fraud.

> **NOTES:**
> Thousands of victims defrauded of their life savings
> Failure of police and DAs to investigate and prosecute
> History of telemarketing fraud
> Case of Nancy Sims—defrauded of $75,000 in investment scam
> Statements by former telemarketer who admitted preying on the elderly
> Need to change attitudes that fraud is "nonviolent crime"
> Telemarketing scams use long distance to avoid local victims
> Failure of existing state and federal laws
> Telemarketing scams rarely lead to convictions or harsh sentences

Planning Checklist

After you have completed your plan, consider these questions.

✔ **Does your plan fulfill the needs of the writing task?** Review notes, comments, or instructor's guidelines to make sure you have clearly understood the assignment. Are there standard formats that should be followed or are you free to develop your own method of organization? Does your plan address the needs of readers?

✔ **Is your thesis clearly stated?** Does your thesis state a point of view or is it simply a narrowed topic?

✔ **Have you developed enough evidence?** Is the thesis clearly supported by examples, details, facts, quotations, and examples? Is the evidence compelling and clearly stated? Are the sources accurate? Will readers accept your evidence? Should outside sources be documented?

✔ **Have you selected an appropriate method of organization?** Will readers be able to follow your train of thought? Are transitions clearly indicated?

✔ **Does your plan help overcome customary problems?** Review previous assignments or comments instructors have made about your writing in the past. Does your plan provide guidelines for a stronger thesis or more organized support?

✔ **Does your opening arouse attention and introduce readers to your topic? Does your conclusion end the paper with a strong point or memorable image?**

✔ **Does your plan give you a workable guideline for writing your first draft?** Does it include reminders, references, and tips to make your job easier? Do you use a format that you can easily amend? *(Note: Leave space between points so you can make changes as you work.)*

STRATEGIES | for Overcoming Problems in Organization

If you have problems organizing your ideas and developing a plan for your paper, review your prewriting.

1. **Examine your thesis and goal.** The subject and purpose of your writing can suggest an organizational method. Would your ideas be best expressed by telling a story or separating them into parts? Are some ideas more important than others?

2. **Use prewriting strategies to establish a pattern.** Make a list of your main ideas. Use clustering to draw relationships between points. What pattern best pulls these ideas together?

3. **Discuss your paper with your instructor or fellow students.** Like someone who cannot see the forest for the trees, you may be so focused on details that you cannot obtain an overall view of your paper. Another person may be able to examine your notes and suggest a successful pattern.

4. **Start writing.** Although writing without a plan may make you feel like starting a journey without a map, plunging in and starting a draft may help you discover a way of organizing ideas. Although you are writing without a plan, try to stay on target. Review your thesis and focus on your goal. If the introduction gives you trouble, start with the body or conclusion. Developing connections between a few ideas may help you discover a method of organizing your entire essay.

e-writing

Exploring Organization Online

You can use the Internet to learn more about organizing an essay.

1. Using a search engine, such as Google, Yahoo!, or Alta Vista, enter such terms as *organizing an essay, topic outline, sentence outline* or *writing introductions* to locate current sites of interest.

2. Using InfoTrac College Edition or one of your library's databases, look up recent editorials or brief articles and notice how authors organized their ideas. Did writers use a chronological or spatial method? Where did they locate the thesis, the most important evidence? How did they begin and end the article? Could any parts be improved to make the article easier to read or more effective?

E-Sources

Introductions and Conclusions
　　http://www.powa.org/thesis/intros.html
Developing an Outline
　　http://owl.english.purdue.edu/
　　handouts/genereal/gl_outline.html

Companion Website

See **http://www.thomsonedu.com/ english/sundance** for additional information on organizing ideas.

9

DEVELOPING PARAGRAPHS

Just as the sentence contains one idea in all its fullness, so the paragraph should embrace a distinct episode; and as sentences should follow one another in harmonious sequence, so the paragraphs must fit on to one another like the automatic couplings of railway carriages.

—Winston Churchill

WHAT ARE PARAGRAPHS?

Most students can offer an adequate definition of an essay and explain the parts of a sentence. But many are unsure how to describe a paragraph. In writing, they often fail to use paragraphs at all or make periodic indentations every half page or so to break up the essay. But a paragraph is more than a cluster of sentences or a random pause in a block of text. *Paragraphs are groups of related sentences unified by a single idea.* Paragraphs operate much like chapters in a book—they organize related ideas and form cohesive units. Paragraphs have specific functions; they introduce a subject, explain a point, tell a story, compare two ideas, support a thesis, or summarize a writer's main points.

The importance of paragraphs can be demonstrated by removing them from a text. Printed without paragraphs, Walter Lord's foreword to *A Night to*

WRITERS AT WORK

I don't allow anybody around while I'm writing. My wife manages to live with me, and my son and our dog, but I like to be let alone when I'm working. I see these Hollywood movies where the man gets up in the middle of the night and dashes off a few thousand words, and his little wife comes in to make sure he's comfortable and everything. That's all foolishness. It would never be anything like that. In fact, I'm privately convinced that most of the really bad writing the world's ever seen has been done under the influence of what's called inspiration.

Shelby Foote, historian

SOURCE: *Booknotes*

Remember is difficult to comprehend and becomes an unimaginative jumble of facts and numbers:

> In 1898 a struggling author named Morgan Robertson concocted a novel about a fabulous Atlantic liner, far larger than any that had ever been built. Robertson loaded his ship with rich and complacent people and then wrecked it one cold April night on an iceberg. This somehow showed the futility of everything, and in fact, the book was called *Futility* when it appeared that year, published by the firm of M. F. Mansfield. Fourteen years later a British shipping company named the White Star Line built a steamer remarkably like the one in Robertson's novel. The new liner was 66,000 tons displacement; Robertson's was 70,000. The real ship was 882.5 feet long; the fictional one was 800 feet. Both vessels were triple screw and could make 24–25 knots. Both could carry about 3,000 people, and both had enough lifeboats for only a fraction of this number. But, then, this didn't seem to matter because both were labeled "unsinkable." On April 12, 1912, the real ship left Southampton on her maiden voyage to New York. Her cargo included a priceless copy of the *Rubaiyat of Omar Khayyam* and a list of passengers collectively worth two hundred fifty million dollars. On her way over she too struck an iceberg and went down on a cold April night. Robertson called his ship the *Titan;* the White Star Line called its ship the *Titanic.* This is the story of her last night.

Presented as Lord wrote it, the foreword is far more striking:

> In 1898 a struggling author named Morgan Robertson concocted a novel about a fabulous Atlantic liner, far larger than any that had ever been built. Robertson loaded his ship with rich and complacent people and then wrecked it one cold April night on an iceberg. This somehow showed the futility of everything, and in fact, the book was called *Futility* when it appeared that year, published by the firm of M. F. Mansfield.
>
> Fourteen years later a British shipping company named the White Star Line built a steamer remarkably like the one in Robertson's novel. The new liner was 66,000 tons displacement; Robertson's was 70,000. The real ship was 882.5 feet

long; the fictional one was 800 feet. Both vessels were triple screw and could make 24–25 knots. Both could carry about 3,000 people, and both had enough lifeboats for only a fraction of this number. But, then, this didn't seem to matter because both were labeled "unsinkable."

On April 12, 1912, the real ship left Southampton on her maiden voyage to New York. Her cargo included a priceless copy of the *Rubaiyat of Omar Khayyam* and a list of passengers collectively worth two hundred fifty million dollars. On her way over she too struck an iceberg and went down on a cold April night.

Robertson called his ship the *Titan;* the White Star Line called its ship the *Titanic.* This is the story of her last night.

Each paragraph signals a shift, breaking up the text to highlight the parallels between the fictional ocean liner and the real one. The conclusion dramatizes the eerie similarity between the ships' names by placing the final two sentences in a separate paragraph.

Although it is important to provide breaks in your text, random and erratic paragraph breaks interrupt the flow of ideas and create a disorganized list of sentences:

I was born in New Orleans and grew up in a quiet section of Metairie. I had a lot of friends and enjoyed school a lot.

I played football for two seasons. In my sophomore year I won an award at the Louisiana Nationals.

The games are held in Baton Rouge and allow high school athletes from across the state to compete in a number of events.

I came in second out of over fifty high school quarterbacks.

The award guaranteed me a slot on my school's varsity team when I started my junior year. But that summer my Dad was transferred to Milwaukee.

In August we moved to Bayside, a north shore suburb. Our house was larger, and we had a wonderful view of Lake Michigan.

The move was devastating to me personally. I missed my friends. I found out that I would not even be allowed to try out for football until my senior year.

The coach was impressed with my ability, but he told me all positions had been filled.

Improved:

I was born in New Orleans and grew up in a quiet section of Metairie. I had a lot of friends and enjoyed school a lot. I played football for two seasons. In my sophomore year I won an award at the Louisiana Nationals. The games are held in Baton Rouge and allow high school athletes from across the state to compete in a number of events. I came in second out of over fifty high school quarterbacks. The award guaranteed me a slot on my school's varsity team when I started my junior year.

But that summer my Dad was transferred to Milwaukee. In August we moved to Bayside, a north shore suburb. Our house was larger, and we had a wonderful view of Lake Michigan.

The move was devastating to me personally. I missed my friends. I found out that I would not even be allowed to try out for football until my senior year. The coach was impressed with my ability, but he told me all positions had been filled.

WRITING ACTIVITY

Read the following student essay and indicate where you would make paragraph breaks. See page 411 for the student's original essay.

Disneyland Dads

Like half the members of my generation, I am the product of what used to be called a "broken home." My parents divorced when I was eight. I lived with my mother and saw my father on alternate weekends and two weeks during the summer. My father, like many of *his* generation, was a classic Disneyland Dad. The Disneyland Dad is usually found at malls, little league fields, upscale pizza restaurants and ice cream parlors. He is usually accompanied by a child busily eating food forbidden by Mom, trying on clothes, or playing with new toys. The Disneyland Dad dispenses cash like an ATM and provides an endless supply of quarters for arcade games. Whether they are motivated by guilt, frustration, or an inability to parent, Disneyland Dads substitute material items for fatherly advice, guidance, and discipline. While my mother furnished the hands-on, day to day parenting, my father remained distant. My mother monitored my eating habits, my friends, my grades, even the programs I watched on television. But without daily contact with my mother, my father found it difficult to make decisions about my upbringing. He was afraid of contradicting Mom. So he showered me with gifts and trips. He expanded my wardrobe, gave me my first pieces of real jewelry, introduced me to Broadway shows, and took me to Disneyland—but he did not help me with school, teach me about the job market, give me insight into boys, or allow me to be anything more than a spoiled consumer. As I grew older, my relationship with my father became strained. Weekends with him were spent shopping, going to movies, playing tennis, and horseback riding—activities I loved, but activities that limited opportunities for anything but casual conversation. Like most of my friends, I came to view my father as more of an uncle than a parent. He was a beloved family figure, someone who could be counted on for some extra cash, new clothes, or a pizza. And like most of my friends, I was troubled by the gulf that widened between my father and myself. I talked, argued, and made up with my mother as I went through my teens. Both of us changed over the years. But my father remained the same—the generous but distant Disneyland Dad. The Disneyland Dad is a neglected figure. While books and daytime talk shows focus on the plight of single moms, few people offer advice to the fathers. Men in our society are judged by success and conditioned to dispense tokens of their achievement to their children. We kids of divorce *want* all the things the Disneyland Dad can offer, but we really *need* his attention, his guidance, his experience, his mentoring. Someone has to help Disneyland Dads become fathers.

DEVELOPING PARAGRAPHS

Experiment with different ways to develop paragraphs to determine which way best fits your writing context.

Creating Topic Sentences

A topic sentence serves as the thesis statement of a paragraph, presenting the writer's main point or controlling idea. Like a thesis statement, the topic sentence announces the subject and indicates the writer's stance or opinion. The text of the paragraph explains and supports the topic sentence.

Writing about the status of France following the First World War, Anthony Kemp uses strong topic sentences to open each paragraph and organize supporting details:

topic sentence
supporting
details

The French won World War I—or so they thought. In 1918, after four years of bitter conflict, the nation erupted in joyful celebration. The arch-enemy, Germany, had been defeated and the lost provinces of Alsace and Lorraine had been reunited with the homeland. The humiliation of 1870 had been avenged and, on the surface at least, France was the most powerful nation in Europe. Germany was prostrate, its autocratic monarchy tumbled and the country rent by internal dissension.

The reality was different. The northern provinces, as a result of the fighting, had been totally devastated and depopulated. The treasury was empty and saddled with a vast burden of war debt. The French diplomat, Jules Cambon, wrote prophetically at the time, "France victorious must grow accustomed to being a lesser power than France vanquished." *topic sentence*

supporting details

The paradox was that Germany had emerged from the war far stronger. France had a static population of some 40 million, but was confronted by 70 million Germans whose territory had not been ravaged and who had a higher birth-rate. The Austro-Hungarian Empire had been split up into a number of smaller units, none of which could pose a serious threat to Germany. Russia, once the pillar to the Triple Entente, forcing Germany to fight on two fronts, had dissolved into internal chaos. The recreation of an independent Poland after the war produced a barrier between Russia and Germany which meant that the old ally of France no longer directly threatened German territory. *topic sentence*

supporting details

The topic sentence does not always open a paragraph. Like an essay's thesis statement, the topic sentence can appear in the middle or end. Often a writer will present supporting details, a narrative, or a description before stating the topic sentence:

> The airline industry has suffered dramatic losses in the last two years. Lucrative business travel has ebbed, and overseas tourist bookings have dropped by a third. In addition, rising fuel prices and an inability to increase fares has eroded the profit margin on most domestic flights. Reflecting the ongoing concern with terrorism, insurance costs have soared. Four of the largest airlines have announced plans to lay off thousands of employees. *The federal government must take steps to save airlines from bankruptcy.*

Not all paragraphs require an explicit topic sentence, but all paragraphs should have a controlling or central idea, a clear focus or purpose. Although no single topic sentence can be identified in the following paragraphs, the topics are clearly implied. Each paragraph has a clear purpose, a controlling idea:

> It was a bright, clear February afternoon in Gettysburg. A strong sun and layers of down did little to ease the biting cold. Our climb to the crest of Little Round-top wound past somber monuments, barren trees and polished cannon. From the top, we peered down on the wheat field where men had fallen so close together that one could not see the ground. Rifle balls had whined as thick as bee swarms through the trees, and cannon shots had torn limbs from the young men fighting there. A frozen wind whipped tears from our eyes. My friend Amy huddled close, using me as a wind breaker. Despite the cold, it was hard to leave this place.
>
> *James Dillard, "A Doctor's Dilemma," page 339*

Down by the depot, the postmistress, a gaunt woman who wears a rawhide jacket and denims and cowboy boots, presides over a falling-apart post office. The depot itself, with its peeling sulphur-colored paint, is equally melancholy; the Chief, the Super Chief, the El Capitan go by every day, but these celebrated expresses never pause there. No passenger trains do—only an occasional freight. Up on the highway, there are two filling stations, one of which doubles as a meagerly supplied grocery store, while the other does extra duty as a café— Hartman's Café, where Mrs. Hartman, the proprietress, dispenses sandwiches, coffee, soft drinks, and 3.2 beer. (Holcomb, like all the rest of Kansas, is "dry.")

Truman Capote, "Out There," page 286

Using Modes

Just as writers organize essays using modes such as narration and definition, they can use the same patterns of development to unify paragraphs. In writing a comparison, you can use definition, cause and effect, or classification to organize individual paragraphs. You can also number points to make your train of thought easier to follow.

Cornel West uses several modes to analyze views of African American society:

topic sentence
division

definition

contrast
definition

> *Recent discussions about the plight of African Americans—especially those at the bottom of the social ladder—tend to divide into two camps.* On the one hand, there are those who highlight the *structural* constraints on the life chances of black people. Their viewpoint involves a subtle historical and sociological analysis of slavery, Jim Crowism, job and residential discrimination, skewed unemployment rates, inadequate health care, and poor education. On the other hand, there are those who stress the *behavioral* impediments on black upward mobility. They focus on the waning of the Protestant ethic—hard work, deferred gratification, frugality, and responsibility—in much of black America.

topic sentence
transition
examples

contrast

> *Those in the first camp—the liberal structuralists—call for full employment, health, education, and childcare programs, and broad affirmative action practices.* In short, a new, more sober version of the best of the New Deal and the Great Society: more government money, better bureaucrats, and an active citizenry. Those in the second camp—the conservative behaviorists—promote self-help programs, black business expansion, and non-preferential job practices. They support vigorous "free market" strategies that depend on fundamental changes in how black people act and live. To put it bluntly, their projects rest largely upon a cultural revival of the Protestant ethic in black America.

topic sentence
transition
use of
numbered
points

> *Unfortunately, these two camps have nearly suffocated the crucial debate that should be taking place about the prospects for black America. This debate must go far beyond the liberal and conservative positions in three fundamental ways.* First, we must acknowledge that structures and behavior are inseparable, that institutions and values go hand in hand. How people act and live are shaped—though in no way dictated or determined—by the larger circumstances in which they find

themselves. These circumstances can be changed, their limits attenuated, by positive actions to elevate living conditions.

Second, we should reject the idea that structures are primarily economic and political creatures—an idea that sees culture as an ephemeral set of behavioral attitudes or politics; it is rooted in institutions such as families, schools, churches, synagogues, mosques, and supporting and communication industries (television, radio, video, music). Similarly, the economy and politics are not only influenced by values but also promote particular cultural ideals of the good life and good society.

Third, and most important, we must delve into the depths where neither liberals nor conservatives dare to tread, namely, into the murky waters of despair and dread that now flood the streets of black America. To talk about the depressing statistics of unemployment, infant mortality, incarceration, teenage pregnancy, and violent crime is one thing. But to face up to the monumental eclipse of hope, the unprecedented collapse of meaning, the incredible disregard for human (especially black) life and property in much of black America is something else.

The liberal/conservative discussion conceals the most basic issue now facing black America: the nihilistic threat to its very existence. This threat is not simply a matter of relative economic deprivation and political powerlessness—though economic well-being and political clout are requisites for meaningful black progress. It is primarily a question of speaking to the profound sense of psychological depression, personal worthlessness, and social despair so widespread in black America.

topic sentence

supporting detail

topic sentence

supporting detail

thesis statement
example

Emphasizing Transitions

Just as writers use exclamation points to dramatize a sentence, a paragraph break can serve to highlight a transition or isolate an important idea that might be buried or overshadowed if placed in a larger paragraph. In some instances writers will use a one- or two-sentence paragraph to dramatize a shift or emphasize an idea:

> He could remember a time in his early childhood when a large number of things were still known by his family name. There was a Zhivago factory, a Zhivago bank, Zhivago buildings, a Zhivago necktie pin, even a Zhivago cake which was a kind of *baba au rhum*, and at one time if you said "Zhivago" to your sleigh driver in Moscow, it was as if you had said: "Take me to Timbuctoo!" and he carried you off to a fairy-tale kingdom. You would find yourself transported to a vast, quiet park. Crows settled on the heavy branches of firs, scattering the hoarfrost; their cawing echoed and re-echoed like crackling wood. Pure-bred dogs came running across the road out of the clearing from the recently constructed house. Farther on, lights appeared in the gathering dusk.
>
> And then suddenly all that was gone. They were poor.
>
> *Boris Pasternak*

Organizing Dialogue

Dialogue can be difficult to follow unless paragraph breaks show the transition between speakers. Paragraph breaks make dialogue easier to follow and allow you to avoid repeating "he said" or "I said." In "The Fender-Bender," Ramón "Tianguis" Pérez reproduces a conversation that occurred after a minor traffic accident:

> I get out of the car. The white man comes over and stands right in front of me. He's almost two feet taller.
>
> "If you're going to drive, why don't you carry your license?" he asks in an accusatory tone.
>
> "I didn't bring it," I say, for lack of any other defense.
>
> I look at the damage to his car. It's minor, only a scratch on the paint and a pimple-sized dent.
>
> "I'm sorry," I say. "Tell me how much it will cost to fix, and I'll pay for it; that's no problem." I'm talking to him in English, and he seems to understand.
>
> "This car isn't mine," he says. "It belongs to the company I work for. I'm sorry, but I've got to report this to the police, so that I don't have to pay for the damage."
>
> "That's no problem," I tell him again. "I can pay for it."

Paragraph Style

A writer's style or the style of a particular document is shaped by the length of the paragraphs as well as the level of vocabulary. Newspaper articles, which are meant to be skimmed, use simple words, short sentences, and brief paragraphs. Often a paragraph in a newspaper article will contain only two or three sentences. E-mail and memos also use short paragraphs to communicate quickly. Longer and more detailed writing tends to have paragraphs containing 50 to 250 words. In some specialized books, paragraphs will fill an entire page. No matter what their length, however, paragraphs should be well organized and serve a clear purpose.

STRATEGIES | for Developing Paragraphs

1. **Use topic sentences to organize supporting details.** A strong topic sentence can give meaning to details, preventing a paragraph from becoming simply a list of facts and numbers.

   topic sentence   *The French won World War I*—or so they thought. In 1918, after four years of bitter conflict, the nation erupted in joyful supporting details celebration. The arch-enemy, Germany, had been defeated and the lost provinces of Alsace and Lorraine had been reunited with the homeland. The humiliation of 1870 had been avenged and, on the surface at least, France was the most powerful nation in Europe. Germany was prostrate, its autocratic monarchy tumbled and the country rent by internal dissension.

Anthony Kemp

2. **Use modes to unify paragraphs.** Consider unifying paragraphs by using any of the following modes: description, narration, example, definition, comparison and contrast, process, division and classification, cause and effect, and argument and persuasion.

3. **Use paragraphs to highlight transitions.** A paragraph break can highlight a transition or isolate an important idea that might be less noticeable otherwise. One- or two-sentence paragraphs can also create drama or emphasis.

4. **Use paragraphs to distinguish speakers in dialogue.**

I get out of the car. The white man comes over and stands right in front of me. He's almost two feet taller.

"If you're going to drive, why don't you carry your license?" he asks in an accusatory tone.

"I didn't bring it," I say, for lack of any other defense.

I look at the damage to his car. It's minor, only a scratch on the paint and a pimple-sized dent.

Ramón "Tianguis" Pérez

WRITING ACTIVITIES

1. Indicate paragraph breaks in the following section to distinguish speakers. See page 382 for the original version.

Both cops got out. The older one checked out the rental plates. The younger one wanted to see my driver's license. "Where's your hotel?" he asked. Right over there, I said, the Maria Cristina Hotel on Rio Lerma Street. "I don't know any hotel by that name," he said. "Prove it. Show me something from the hotel." I fumbled through my wallet, finally producing a card-key from the hotel. The dance between the cops and me had begun. "I see," the young policeman said. "What are you doing in Mexico?" I'm a journalist, I said. I'd been reporting in Queretaro state. "You know," he said, "for making that illegal turn, we're going to have to take away your driver's license and the plates from the car." I said, What? Why can't you just give me a ticket? He then walked away and asked the other, older, policeman, "How do you want to take care of this?" The veteran officer then took over. "The violation brings a fine of 471 pesos," he told me. "But we still have to take your plates and license. You can pick them up at police head-quarters when you pay the fine. Or, I can deliver them to you tomorrow at your hotel, but only after you pay."

2. Select one or more of the subjects listed and write a paragraph about it. Your paragraph may or may not have a topic sentence—but it should have a controlling idea. It should have a clear purpose and focus and not simply contain a number of vaguely related ideas. After drafting your paragraph, review it for missing details or irrelevant material. Underline your topic sentence or list your controlling thought.
   ■ Describe your first car.
   ■ Compare high school and college instructors.
   ■ Explain one or more reasons why you are attending college.
   ■ State one or more reasons why you admire a certain actor, singer, athlete, or politician.

3. Develop paragraphs using the topic sentences provided. Use each topic sentence as a controlling idea to guide your selection of supporting details and examples.

   Living off-campus provides students with many opportunities.
   However, off-campus housing poses many challenges to young adults.
   Distractions and unexpected responsibilities can interfere with studying.
   Students who plan to live off-campus should think carefully before signing a lease.

4. Write a paragraph supporting the following topic sentences:
   College students must develop self-discipline to succeed.
   The central problem in male–female relationships is a failure to communicate.
   Three steps must be taken to curb teenagers from smoking.
   Proper nutrition is essential for maintaining good health.

5. Develop a conversation between two people and use paragraphs to indicate shifts between the speakers.

6. Write a paragraph organized chronologically about a personal experience.

7. Write a paragraph using comparison to discuss two of your best friends, two local bands, two popular restaurants, or two athletic teams.

8. Write a paragraph that uses division to enumerate at least three points on one of the following topics:

best friends	computers	effects of divorce on children
fast food	health care	the Internet
first dates	talk shows	airlines

e-writing

Exploring Paragraphs Online

You can use the Internet to learn more about developing paragraphs.

1. Using a search engine, such as Google, Yahoo!, or Alta Vista, enter terms such as *paragraph structure* and *topic sentence* to locate current sites of interest.

2. Using InfoTrac College Edition, one of your library's databases, or Comp 21's Media Library, look up recent editorials or brief articles and notice how authors developed paragraphs. Did they use paragraph breaks to signal important transitions, group related ideas, and make the text easier to follow?

   Were individual paragraphs organized by specific modes such as comparison, process, or cause and effect? How many had topic sentences you could underline?

E-Sources

Paragraphs
    http://www.unc.edu/depts/wcweb/ handouts/paragraphs.html

Companion Website

See **http://www.thomsonedu.com/ english/sundance** for additional information on developing paragraphs.

10

WRITING THE FIRST DRAFT

WHAT IS A FIRST DRAFT?

A first draft attempts to capture your ideas on paper and produce a rough version of the final essay. A first draft is not likely to be perfect and will no doubt include awkward sentences, redundant passages, irrelevant ideas, and misspelled words—but it gives you something to build on and refine.

There is no single method of transforming your outline into a completed draft, but there are techniques that can improve your first efforts.

WRITERS AT WORK

The key to turning out good stuff is rewriting. The key to grinding it out is consistency. It sounds silly, but if you write four pages a day, you've written 1,200 pages in a year—or 1,400, whatever it is. You accumulate the stuff. So what I normally do is give myself quotas. They'll vary depending on the depth and complexity of the subject, but somewhere between three and five pages—that's my day's writing. I've got to do it every day. I can't go out and work on my farm until I've done my day's writing, and working on my farm is so pleasurable. So that's my incentive. I hold myself hostage, so to speak, and it gets done.

Forrest McDonald, historian

Source: *Booknotes*

124

STRATEGIES | for Writing the First Draft

1. **Review your plan.** Examine your outline, prewriting notes, and any instructions to make sure your plan addresses the needs of the writing assignment. If you have developed a formal outline, you can follow it as a road map to keep your writing focused.

2. **Focus on your goal.** As you write, keep your purpose in mind. What is your objective—to entertain, inform, or persuade? Do you plan to tell a story, make a comparison, motivate readers to change their behavior, or explain a process?

3. **Write to your reader.** Writing is an act of communication, an exchange between writer and reader. Your job is not simply to fill a computer screen with words but to address people. Think of your essay as a letter. Determine who you are writing to. Consider the readers' perceptual world. What information do readers need to accept your thesis? Anticipate how readers will respond to your ideas. Will they be interested, bored, supportive, or hostile? How can your paper arouse their interest, build on their current knowledge, or address their objections?

4. **Visualize the completed document.** Consider the writing context and what the final product should look like. Are you writing a 500-word personal essay, a ten-page research paper, or a three-paragraph letter? Thinking about the finished document can help you determine whether your plan is suited to the task. Considering how the text should look can guide your decisions about word choice, sentence structure, and paragraph length. Determine whether your document should include photographs, charts, or diagrams.

5. **Support your thesis.** Determine what appeal will best suit your audience—logical, ethical, or emotional? What evidence will convince your readers to accept your ideas?

6. **Amend your plan if needed.** In some cases you will be able to follow a detailed outline point by point, turning words into sentences and adding supporting detail to transform a single line into a half-page. In other instances, you will discover new ideas while writing. One idea may spark others, taking you far from your original plan. Be willing to make changes, but keep your goal, reader, and the nature of the document in mind to keep your writing on course. New ideas that occur to you while writing the first draft may lead you to return to prewriting, to expand or limit the topic, alter your approach, or develop a new thesis.

7. **Start writing.** The most important thing in writing a first draft is getting your ideas on paper. Start writing and produce as much copy as you can.

Don't pause to check your spelling or look up a statistic. Focus on your main points.

- Start with the easiest parts. Don't feel obligated to write the introduction first. You may find it easier to begin with the body or conclusion.
- Give yourself room for changes. You can easily insert text on a computer, but if you are writing on paper, you may wish to skip lines or leave wide margins for last-minute additions.
- Don't edit as you write. Pausing to look up facts or check spelling can interrupt your train of thought, but you can make notes as you write to identify items for future revisions. Underline words you think might be misspelled or misused. Make notes in parentheses to signal missing details.
- Break the paper into manageable parts. Instead of attempting to write a complete draft, you may find it more effective to focus on one section, especially if your paper is long and complex.
- If you get stuck, return to passages you have written and revise them. Keep writing.

8. **Read your work aloud.** Hearing your words can help you evaluate your writing and test the logic of your ideas.

9. **Lower your standards.** Keep writing even if your ideas seem clumsy or repetitive. Don't expect to write flawless copy—this is a rough draft.

10. **Anticipate problems.** Recall comments instructors have made about your writing in the past. Focus on overcoming weaknesses or bad habits.
    - You may not be able to address problem areas during the first draft, but you can make notes in the margin as you write to guide future revisions.

11. **Save everything you write.** Ideas that may seem unrelated to your topic could prove to be valuable in future drafts or other assignments.
    - Make sure you save your work on a disk if working on a computer. If you print a hard copy, you may wish to double- or triple-space the text for easier editing.

AVOIDING PLAGIARISM

Frustrated with an upcoming assignment, you may be tempted to download a paper from the Internet or copy another student's essay. Presenting another writer's work as your own is plagiarism. Plagiarism is a crime. If it is detected, you may face serious consequences. Most colleges and universities have strict policies about plagiarism. Students caught cheating may automatically fail the course or be expelled. Outside academia, plagiarism involves *piracy* and *copyright infringement*—two very serious offenses that expose violators to prosecution and litigation. Individuals and corporations have filed multimillion-dollar lawsuits against people who plagiarize.

If you are having difficulty with writing, talk to your instructor or seek tutorial help before you risk terminating your college career by cheating. Plagiarism involves not only stealing someone's entire essay but also lifting and using sentences and paragraphs. Whenever you use outside material, indicate its source. If you copy the speech or writing of another directly, it should be placed in quotation marks:

ORIGINAL STATEMENT: The airbag is not the most important automotive safety device. It is a sober driver. (Bill Harris, address before the National Safety Council)

STUDENT PAPER: Speaking before the National Safety Council, Bill Harris remarked, "The airbag is not the most important automotive safety device. It is a sober driver."

When you paraphrase or put the idea in your own words, you should indicate the original source:

> Bill Harris has remarked that the most important automobile safety device is not the airbag but a sober driver.

Even an informal acknowledgment can protect you from a charge of plagiarism:

> According to one engineer, the most important automobile safety device is not the airbag but a sober driver.

Under no circumstances should you allow your desperation for completing an assignment on time or getting a good grade lead you to copy another's work.

Outside sources should be documented—see pages 769–776 for guidelines on incorporating outside sources into your work.

MAKING WRITING DECISIONS

In writing the first draft, you will make a series of decisions. In expressing your ideas, you will choose words, construct sentences, and develop paragraphs. The more thought you put into these decisions, the better your rough draft will reflect what you want to say and the less rewriting it will require.

Choosing the Right Words

Words have power. The impact of your writing greatly depends on the words you choose to express your ideas. In writing your first draft, select words that represent your stance and will influence readers. Because the goal of the first draft is to record your ideas, don't stop writing to look up words; instead, underline items for further review.

Use Words Precisely

Many words are easily confused. Should a patient's heart rate be monitored *continually* (meaning at regular intervals, such as once an hour) or *continuously* (meaning without interruption)? Is the city council planning to *adapt* or *adopt* a budget? Did the mayor make an *explicit* or *implicit* statement?

Your writing can influence readers only if you use words that accurately reflect your meaning. There are numerous pairs of frequently confused words:

allusion	An indirect reference
illusion	A false or imaginary impression
infer	To interpret
imply	To suggest
conscience	A sense of moral or ethical conduct
conscious	To be awake or aware of something
principle	A basic law or concept
principal	Something or someone important, as in school *principal*
affect	To change or modify
effect	A result

See pp. 898–900 for a longer list of commonly confused or misused words.

Use Concrete Words

Concrete words communicate more information and make clearer impressions than abstract words, which express only generalized concepts.

Abstract	**Concrete**
motor vehicle	pickup truck
modest suburban home	three-bedroom colonial
individual	boy

protective headgear   helmet
residential rental unit   studio apartment
digestive ailment   heartburn
educational facility   high school

Concrete words make a greater impact on readers:

ABSTRACT: Wherever we went, malnourished individuals lined the road in serious need of assistance.
CONCRETE: Wherever we walked, starving children lined the road like skeletons silently holding empty bowls with bony fingers.

As you write, try to think of effective images and specific details that will suit
your purpose and your reader.

Use Verbs that Create Action and Strong Images

Linking verbs (such as *is* and *are*) join ideas but do not suggest action or present compelling images. Like abstract nouns, generalized verbs, such as *move*,
seem, *appear*, make only vague impressions. Use verbs that express action and
create strong images.

Weak Verbs	**Strong Verbs**
The children *were* homesick and *experienced* sadness.	The children *ached* with home-sickness and *cried*.
The landlord *expressed* little interest in his tenants and *did not repair* the building.	The landlord *ignored* his tenants and *refused to repair* the building.
The firefighters *moved* quickly to the accident scene and then *moved* slowly through the debris *to look* for victims.	The firefighters *raced* to the accident scene then *crept* slowly through the debris *searching* for victims.

Use an Appropriate Level of Diction

The style and tone of your writing are shaped by the words you choose. Your
goal, your reader, the discourse community, and the document itself usually indicate the kind of language that is appropriate. Informal language that might be
acceptable in a note to a coworker may be unsuited to a formal report or article
written for publication.

FORMAL: Sales representatives are required to maintain company vehicles at
their own expense. (employee manual)

STANDARD: Salespeople must pay for routine maintenance of their cars. (business letter)

INFORMAL: Remind the reps to change their oil every 3,000 miles. (e-mail memo)

Slang expressions can be creative and attention-getting, but they may be inappropriate and detract from the credibility of formal documents.

Appreciate the Impact of Connotations

All words *denote*, or indicate, a particular meaning. The words *home, residence,* and *domicile* all refer to where someone lives. Each has the same basic meaning or *denotation*, but the word *home* evokes personal associations of family, friends, and favorite belongings. *Domicile*, on the other hand, has a legalistic and official tone devoid of personal associations.

Connotations are implied or suggested meanings. Connotations reflect a writer's values, views, and attitudes toward a subject. A resort cabin can be described as a *rustic cottage* or a *seedy shack*. The person who spends little money and shops for bargains can be praised for being *thrifty* or ridiculed for being *cheap*. The design of a skyscraper can be celebrated as being *clean and streamlined* or criticized for appearing *stark and sterile*.

The following pairs of words have the same *denotation* or basic meaning but their *connotations* create strikingly different impressions:

young	inexperienced
traditional	old-fashioned
brave	ruthless
casual	sloppy
the homeless	bums
residential care facility	nursing home
unintended landing	plane crash
teenage prank	vandalism
uncompromising	stubborn
strong	dictatorial
delicate	effeminate
street art	graffiti

In selecting words, be sure that your connotations are suited to your task, role, and readers. Avoid terms that your readers may find inappropriate or offensive.

WRITING ACTIVITIES

1. Review papers you have written in previous classes and examine your use of words. Read passages out loud. How does your writing sound? Are there abstract terms that could be replaced by concrete words? Are there connotations that detract from your goal? Does the level of diction fit the assignment?

2. Write a description of your hometown, using as many concrete words as possible to provide sensual impressions. Avoid abstract words like "pleasant" or "noisy" and offer specific details.

3. Use connotations to write a positive and negative description of a controversial personality such as a local politician.

4. Translate this negative description into a positive one by substituting key words:

> Frank Kelso is a reckless, money-grubbing gossip who eagerly maligns celebrities. He is impulsive, stubborn, and insulting. He refuses to show restraint and will exploit anyone's personal misfortune to get ahead while claiming to serve his readers' desire for truth.

Writing Effective Sentences

Writing well is more than a matter of avoiding grammatical errors such as fragments and run-ons. Sentences express thoughts. Your sentences should be clear, logical, and economical. There are several techniques that can increase the power of your sentences.

Emphasize Key Words

Words placed at the beginning and end of sentences receive more attention than those placed in the middle.

Cumulative sentences open with the main idea or key word:

Computer literacy is mandatory for today's high school students.
Alcoholism and drug addiction are contributing causes of child neglect.

Periodic sentences conclude with a key word or major idea:

For today's high school student, success demands *computer literacy*.
Child neglect often stems from two causes: *alcoholism and drug addiction*.

Both cumulative and periodic sentences are more effective than those that bury important words in the middle:

> In today's world *computer literacy* is mandatory for high school students to succeed.
> The problem of child neglect often has *alcoholism and drug addiction* as contributing causes.

Use Parallel Structures to Stress Equivalent Ideas

You can demonstrate that ideas have equal value by placing them in pairs and lists:

> *Coffee and tea* are favorite beverages for dieters.
> *Wilson, Roosevelt, and Johnson* juggled domestic reform while waging war.
> His doctor suggested that *diet and exercise* could *lower his blood pressure and reduce his risk of stroke.*
> A new study revealed that the chief causes of air pollution are *automobile exhaust, industrial emissions, and agricultural pesticides.*

Subordinate Secondary Ideas

Secondary ideas that offer background information such as dates and figures should be subordinated or merged into sentences that stress primary ideas. Combining ideas into single sentences allows writers to demonstrate which ideas they consider significant.

PRIMARY IDEA: *Nancy Chen was accepted into Yale Law School.*
SECONDARY IDEA: Nancy Chen did not learn English until she was twelve.
COMBINED VERSIONS: Although she did not learn English until she was twelve, *Nancy Chen was accepted into Yale Law School.*
Nancy Chen, who did not learn English until she was twelve, *was accepted into Yale Law School.*

Secondary ideas can be placed at the beginning, set off by commas in the middle, or attached to the end of a sentence:

PRIMARY IDEA: *Bayport College will close its doors.*
SECONDARY IDEAS: Bayport College has served this community for a hundred years.
Bayport College was forced to declare bankruptcy.
Bayport College will close on June 15.
COMBINED VERSIONS: On June 15, *Bayport College,* forced to declare bankruptcy, *will close its doors,* after serving this community for a hundred years.

After serving this community for a hundred years, *Bayport College,* forced to declare bankruptcy, *will close its doors* on June 15.

Forced to declare bankruptcy, *Bayport College,* which served this community for a hundred years, *will close its doors* on June 15.

Stress the Relationship Between Ideas

You can make your train of thought easier for readers to follow if your sentences stress how one idea affects another. Coordinating conjunctions—words that join ideas—demonstrate relationships:

and   joins ideas of equal importance:

> The president urged Americans to conserve oil, *and* he denounced Congress for failing to pass an energy bill.

or   indicates choice, suggesting that only one of two ideas is operative:

> The university will raise tuition *or* increase class size.

but   indicates a shift or contrast:

> The company lowered prices, *but* sales continued to slump.

yet   also demonstrates a contrast, often meaning *nevertheless:*

> He studied for hours *yet* failed the exam.

so   implies cause and effect:

> Drivers ignored the stop sign, *so* authorities installed a traffic light.

In addition to coordinating conjunctions, there are transitional expressions that establish the relationship between ideas.

To establish time relationships:

before	*after*	*now*	*then*
today	*further*	*once*	*often*

To demonstrate place relationships:

above	*below*	*over*	*under*
around	*inside*	*outside*	*nearby*
next	*beyond*	*to the left*	

To indicate additions:

again	*also*	*moreover*	*too*
in addition			

To express similarities:

alike	*likewise*	*in the same way*

To stress contrasts:

after all	*different*	*on the other hand*
although	*however*	*still*
unlike	*in contrast*	

To illustrate cause and effect:

as a result   *because*   *therefore*

To conclude or summarize:

finally   *in conclusion*   *in short*

When you write the first draft, try to stress the relationships between ideas as clearly as you can. If trying to determine the best way to link ideas slows your writing down, simply underline related items to signal future revisions and move on to the next point.

Understand How Structure Affects Meaning

Just as the connotations of words you choose shape meaning, so does the structure of your sentences. The way you word sentences can create both dramatic effects and make subtle distinctions. Although the basic facts are the same in the following sentences, notice how altering the words that form the subject (in italics) affects their meaning:

Dr. Green and a group of angry patients are protesting the closing of the East Side Clinic.
(This sentence suggests the doctor and patients are of equal significance.)

Dr. Green, flanked by angry patients, is protesting the closing of the East Side Clinic.
(This sentence emphasizes the role of the doctor. The singular verb "is protesting" highlights the actions of a single person. Set off by commas, the "angry patients" are not even considered part of the subject.)

Angry patients, supported by Dr. Green, are protesting the closing of the East Side Clinic.
(In this version the angry patients are emphasized, and the doctor, set off by commas, is deemphasized, reduced to the status of a bystander.)

Despite protests by Dr. Green and angry patients, *the East Side Clinic* is being closed.
(This wording suggests the protests are futile and that the closing of the clinic is inevitable.)

The closing of the East Side Clinic has sparked protests by Dr. Green and angry patients.
(This sentence indicates a cause-and-effect relationship, implying that the
final outcome may be uncertain.)

WRITING ACTIVITIES

1. Combine the following items into a single sentence that emphasizes
    what you consider the most significant idea.
    A. Alcatraz is located on an island in San Francisco Bay.
        Alcatraz is one of the most famous prisons in American history.
        Alcatraz was closed in 1963.
        Alcatraz is now a tourist attraction.
    B. Arthur Conan Doyle created Sherlock Holmes.
        Arthur Conan Doyle modeled his detective after Dr. Bell.
        Dr. Bell was famous for his diagnostic ability.
        Arthur Conan Doyle was an eye specialist.
    C. Dr. James Naismith was born in Canada.
        He was a YMCA athletic director.
        He invented the game of basketball.
        Naismith wanted to develop a new recreation.

2. Combine the following facts into a single sentence and write three
    versions, placing emphasis on different elements.
    A. The student council proposed a freeze on tuition.
        The faculty accepted the student proposal.
        The alumni accepted the student proposal.
    B. The city was devastated by an earthquake.
        The public responded with calm determination.
        The mayor urged citizens to help authorities.
    C. Job interviews are stressful.
        Applicants fear rejection.
        Interviewers fear hiring the wrong employee.

3. Select a topic from the list on pages 903–904 and freewrite for
    ten minutes. Let the draft cool and then analyze your use of sen-
    tences. Do they emphasize primary ideas? Are minor ideas given too
    much significance? Are the relationships between ideas clearly
    expressed?

Writing Paragraphs

Paragraphs are the building blocks of an essay. If writing the entire paper seems like a confusing or overwhelming task, focus on writing one paragraph at a time.

Use Topic Sentences or Controlling Ideas to Maintain Focus

It is easy to become sidetracked when you write a first draft. You can keep your draft focused by using a topic sentence or controlling idea as a goal. Consider what you want to accomplish in that paragraph. Even if your paragraph does not have a topic sentence, it should have a controlling idea, a clear purpose.

Use the Modes to Organize Paragraphs

Generally, your outline or notes will list *what* you want to write but not *how* to express or organize the ideas. As you develop paragraphs, consider using one or more of the modes. In writing a narrative about moving into your first apartment, for instance, you might use *cause and effect* in one paragraph to explain why you decided to get your own apartment and *comparison* in another paragraph to show how your initial expectations about living alone contrasted with the reality. Later paragraphs in this narrative might be organized by using *process* or *classification*.

Note New Ideas Separately

As you write a first draft, new ideas may come to you. If they do not directly relate to the paragraph you are writing, jot them down on a separate piece of paper or scroll down the computer screen and record them apart from your essay. This way they will not clutter up the paragraph you are working on but remain available for future versions.

Note Possible Paragraph Breaks

Some people find it difficult to make paragraph breaks in the first draft. Narrative and descriptive essays, for example, often seem like a seamless stream of events or details. Because the main goal of the first draft is to get your thoughts on paper, don't agonize over making paragraph breaks. As you write, you might insert a paragraph symbol (¶) or even a pair of slashes (//) to indicate possible breaks.

MOVING FROM PLAN TO FIRST DRAFT

A writer's plan serves as a guide for the first draft, a framework or blueprint that is expanded into a rough version of the final essay. The student writing about victim impact statements used her outline as a guideline for her first draft. In writing her draft, she introduced new ideas, departing from the original plan. At this stage, she does not worry about spelling—the purpose of writing the first draft is not to produce flawless prose, but to get your ideas down on paper.

Outline

I. Introduction
   A. Background of victim impact statements
   B. Definition of victim impact statements
II. Goals of victim Impact statements (pro)
   A. Victims granted a voice
   B. Therapeutic benefits for victims
   C. Recommendations for sentencing
III. Negative effects of victim impact statements (con)
   A. Inarticulate victims ignored
   B. Benefits limited to the affluent
IV. Conclusion
   Thesis: Victim impact statements marginalize the poor and helpless

First Draft

Across America today more and more victims of crime are being allowed to address the court in terms of making what is called a victim impact statment. This written or oral presentation to the court allows victims to express their feelings to the judge after someone has been convicted of a crime.

Advocates of victim impact statements point to key advantages. First, these statements give victims' a voice. For years, victims have felt helpless. Prosecutors represent the state, not the crime victim. Victims have been dismayed when prosecutors have arranged pleas bargains without their knowledge. Some victims are still recovering from their injuries when they learn the person who hurt them has plead to a lesser charge and received probation.

Therapists who work with victims also say that being able to address the court helps with the healing process. Victims of violent crime can feel powerless and vulnerable. Instead of suffering in silence, they are given the chance to addres the criminal, to clear their chests, and get on with the rest of their lives.

Impact statements allows judges to consider what sentences are aproppriate. In one case a judge who planned to fine a teenager for shoplifting excepted the store owners suggestions to waive the fine if the defendent completed his GED.

But giving victims a change to speak raises some issues. What about the victim who is not articulate, who doesn't even speak English? In murder cases the victim's relatives are given a chance to speak? Does this mean that a middle class professional victim with a circle of grieving friends and family members will be granted more signifiacne than the homeless murder victim who leaves no one behind?

Victim impact statements may help empower victims who are educated, personally impressive, and socially promient. But they may also allow forgotten victims to remain voiceless.

STRATEGIES | for Overcoming Problems in the First Draft

When you write the first draft, you may encounter several problems. Remember, your goal is to sketch out your main ideas, not to write flawless prose. Write as well as you can in the first draft—but keep in mind that your objective is to just get your ideas on paper.

1. **Getting started.** You may find yourself unable to write. Perhaps the task seems imposing, your outline too complex, your thoughts unclear.
   - See pages 17–19 for overcoming writer's block.
   - Freewrite on your topic to loosen up and get in the mood to write.
   - Break your essay into parts and start with the easiest section.
   - Flesh out your plan. Write a new version, turning words into phrases and expanding into full sentences. Let the draft emerge from the outline.
2. **Running out of time.** Often you will be writing well, discovering new thoughts as you go. If you cannot write fast enough to capture these ideas or if you run out of time, make notes. A rough draft does not have to be stated in complete sentences.
   - Jot down a list of numbered points so you won't forget new ideas.
   - Use a tape recorder as you work to record ideas you don't have time to write.
3. **Writing in circles.** Even with the best map, you can sometimes get lost and find yourself repeating ideas—discovering that on page three you are restating your introduction.

- Stop writing and read your introduction. Does it set up the rest of the essay? Does it try to say too much? An introduction indicates forthcoming ideas but it does not have to summarize every point.
- List your main ideas or use a diagram to create a pattern you can follow.

4. **Running out of ideas.** Sometimes you may find yourself running out of ideas on the first page of a five-page essay.
   - Review your goal and plan. Are there details that could be added to support your points? Do not add "extra" ideas just to increase the length of your paper. Whatever you write should relate to your thesis.
   - If you can't think of anything else, stop writing and put the draft aside. Do other work, read something about your topic, and let the draft cool. Return to it later and try adding more details. You may find it beneficial to start fresh with a new draft rather than working with an unsuccessful attempt.

5. **Your draft becomes too long.** You might find that the writing goes very well. One idea leads to another. Details and examples come easily. Then you discover that at this rate you will need fifteen pages to cover all the points you planned to discuss in a five-page paper.
   - Read your draft aloud. Are you recording interesting ideas, developing needed support, or merely summarizing the obvious or repeating yourself?
   - Concentrate on capturing main points or continue writing, realizing that much of what you write will be deleted.
   - Narrow the scope of your paper. You may have to limit your subject and refine your thesis. Look over what you have written and determine what section would make the best topic for a more sharply defined essay.

e-writing

Exploring Writing the First Draft Online

You can use the Internet to learn more about writing first drafts.

1. Using a search engine, such as Google, Yahoo!, or Alta Vista, enter such terms as

writing process and *writing first drafts* to locate current sites of interest.

2. Write the draft of an e-mail to a friend. Relate an interesting story about some-

thing that happened at school or at work recently. Write a full draft if you can, but do not send it.

E-sources

Preparing to Write and Drafting the Paper
http://writing-program.uchicago.edu/ resources/collegewriting

Avoiding Plagiarism
http://owl.english.purdue.edu/ handouts/research/r_plagiar.html

Companion Website

See **http://www.thomsonedu.com/ english/sundance** for further information on writing the first draft.

REVISING AND REWRITING

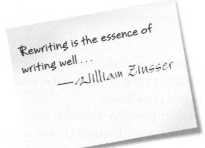

11

Rewriting is the essence of
writing well . . .
—William Zinsser

WHAT IS REVISION?

After completing the first draft, you may be tempted to start rewriting immediately—to reword awkward sentences, to search for that quote that supports
your thesis, to check spelling, or to page through a handbook to determine
whether you need a comma or an apostrophe in the last sentence. If you compose on a computer, you can easily scroll up and down your draft, adding and
deleting sentences, replacing words, inserting punctuation.

But revision is more than correcting mistakes and plugging in missing details. Revision means "to see again." Before you begin to start rewriting, it is
important to examine your draft, to look at it the way your readers will.

DEVELOPING A REVISING STYLE

Just as writers have distinctly personal composing styles, they often use a variety of revision methods. Some writers produce a first draft, then without reading
it, write a second and perhaps a third. Like photographers who shoot a series of
pictures and then select a single exposure, these writers prefer to make a number of attempts, using different styles, wordings, and approaches to their subject.
Later they choose the best version, often blending in elements of the other
drafts. Other writers work in sections, revising and rewriting the introduction

WRITERS AT WORK

I sometimes write in bars in the afternoons. I go out and find a corner of a bar. If the noise is not directed at me—in other words, there's not a phone ringing or a baby crying or something—I quite like it if the jukebox is on and people are shouting the odds about a sports game. I just hunch over a bottle in the corner. I write in longhand anyway, so I can do it anywhere—sometimes in airport terminals. Then when I've got enough [written] down, I start to type it out, editing it as I go. I don't use any of the new technology stuff.

Christopher Hitchens, editor

SOURCE: *Booknotes*

before moving on to the body, perfecting the essay paragraph by paragraph. Still other writers prefer to revise the body of an essay first, then rewrite the introduction and conclusion.

As a composition student you might experiment with different revision methods. You may discover that some papers dictate a specific technique. If the introduction establishes an argument or creates a framework for setting up the evidence, you may find it necessary to concentrate on the opening paragraph in order to make decisions about what should follow. However, you may find it impossible to revise the introduction of a narrative until you determine which events and details will appear in the final essay.

Most writers follow a standard pattern for revising. They begin examining the larger elements, reading through the draft for content and rewriting the paragraphs, before making corrections at the sentence and word levels.

STRATEGIES | for Revising

1. **Let your writing "cool."** Before you can look at your writing objectively, it is important to set it aside. Attempting to revise immediately after writing is difficult because many of your ideas are still fresh in your mind. Let some time pass between writing and revising. Take a walk, watch television, or work on other assignments before attempting to revise.
2. **Print your draft.** Although some students are skilled at revising on a computer, many find it easier to work with hard copy. Printing the draft can allow you to spread out the pages and see the entire text. You may wish to double- or even triple-space the document to provide room for notes and corrections.
3. **Review your goal.** Before looking at your draft, review your plan and instructor's guidelines.

- Review models of the kind of writing you are attempting.
- If your draft is largely off target, it may be easier to review your notes, create a new outline, and write a new draft rather than spend time rewriting a failed attempt.

4. **Examine your draft globally.** Revising is *not* editing. Don't immediately begin to correct spelling and punctuation. Instead, focus on the larger elements of the draft.
   - Review the writing context—does the draft reflect your role, address readers' needs, and suit the discipline or profession?
   - Is the thesis clearly stated?
   - Is the supporting evidence sufficient?
   - Is the paper logically organized?
   - Does the introduction arouse interest and prepare readers for what follows?
   - Does the conclusion leave readers with a strong final impression, question, or challenge?
   - Are sections "off-topic" or redundant?
   - Does this draft meet the needs of the writing assignment?
   - What are the strong and weak points of the essay? What problems should be given priority?

5. **Examine your paper with a "reader's eye."** Consider your readers' perceptual world. What existing knowledge, experiences, values, or attitudes will shape their responses to your paper?
   - Are readers likely to be receptive, indifferent, or hostile to your views? What details will arouse interest or defend your thesis?
   - Do you expect reader objections? Do you anticipate differing opinions?
   - Do readers need any additional background information to appreciate your views? Are there any misunderstandings or misconceptions that should be clarified or dispelled? Do terms or concepts require definitions?
   - Will readers respond favorably to the style and tone of the paper?

6. **Analyze your critical thinking.** In the rush of creating a first draft it can be easy to make lapses in critical thinking. New ideas spring to mind, and you may make connections that lack logical foundation. Review Common Errors in Critical Thinking (pages 50–57).

7. **Consider the nature of the document.** Documents often dictate specific styles and formats. The choppy sentences and short paragraphs expected in a newspaper article are inappropriate for a research paper. The subjective impressions that add color to a personal essay are unsuited to a business report.
   - Does your draft suit the needs of the document?
   - Are the language, style, and "look" of your writing appropriate?

8. **Read your draft aloud.** Hearing how your draft sounds increases your ability to evaluate your draft for clarity, logic, and tone. Awkward sentences, illogical statements, redundant passages, and missing details are far easier to "hear" than read.

9. **Have others read your draft.** Many instructors encourage students to engage in peer review. If you have the opportunity to participate in a writing group, ask fellow classmates to review your work.

   - Let others read your work "cold." If you preface their reading by telling them what you are trying to say, they will have a harder time evaluating your work objectively.
   - If you ask people outside of your composition class to read your paper, however, explain the assignment first. People cannot provide advice if they read your draft in a vacuum. The more they know about your goal and the intended audience, the more valuable their responses will be.
   - Avoid being defensive. Encourage people to react to your work.
   - Encourage feedback by asking targeted questions. If you simply ask, "Do you like it?" or "Is my paper any good?" you are likely to receive polite compliments or vague assurances that your work is "okay." To get helpful advice ask peers specific questions.
   - Ask students what they consider the paper's strong and weak points.
   - Make notes of their remarks and ask how your draft could be improved.

10. **Revise and rewrite.** If you are fortunate, your first attempt will be well written enough to require only minor revisions. In fact, you may be able to make a few improvements and move on to final editing. But most writers, especially those working on complex or challenging assignments, usually discover enough flaws to require extensive revising.

    - Revising is a continuing process. If you write on a computer, it is easy to make subtle changes to your work with each reading.
    - In the light of your first draft, you may wish to review your plan to see whether any changes should be made.
    - If your draft is very unsatisfactory, it may be better to return to your plan and start a fresh draft. Try writing from a different angle, start with a new introduction, use different examples, select different words and images. Often it will take you less time to write a fresh first draft than revise and repair an existing one.
    - If you included images or visual aids in your draft, review their use. Do photographs support your points or simply supply illustrations? Avoid images that will distract or offend readers. Make sure that graphs, charts, and diagrams are accurate and do not oversimplify or distort data.

STRATEGIES | for Peer Review

Writers can greatly benefit from editors, people who can offer a fresh perspective on their work and objective analysis of their writing. Professional writers receive reactions from editors and reviewers who analyze their work for factual errors, lapses in judgments, and mechanical mistakes. Many instructors encourage students to engage in peer review.

1. **Understand the role of editors.** An editor is not a writer. Your job as an editor is not to tell others how you would write the paper but to help a writer craft his or her document. Work with the writer to identify errors and suggest improvements.

2. **Understand the writer's goal and the assignment.** It is difficult to analyze writing in a vacuum. If you are not familiar with the assignment, ask to see any directions the student received from his or her instructor. Read the instructions carefully so that you can provide meaningful advice. Does the paper meet the instructor's requirements?

3. **Review the document globally, then look at specifics.** Before pointing out grammar and spelling errors, focus on the big picture.
   - Does the topic suit the assignment?
   - Does it need to be more clearly focused or limited?
   - Does the paper have a clear thesis?
   - Is the thesis effectively supported with details?
   - Are there irrelevant details that can be deleted?
   - Do paragraphs adequately organize the paper? Could the paragraph structure be more effective?
   - Can you detect sentences that are unclear, illogical, or awkward?
   - Does the paper need proofreading for spelling and grammar errors? As a peer editor, your job is not to correct mechanical errors but indicate to the writer whether the paper needs proofreading.

4. **Be positive.** Make constructive, helpful comments. Don't simply point out errors but indicate how they might be corrected or avoided.

5. **Ask questions.** Instead of stating that a sentence or paragraph does not make sense, ask the writer what he or she was trying to say. Asking questions can prompt a writer to rethink what he or she wrote, remember missing details, or consider new alternatives.

REVISING ELEMENTS OF THE FIRST DRAFT

Although you can correct errors in spelling and punctuation at any point, your main objective in revising is to study the larger elements of your essay, especially the paragraphs.

Look at the Big Picture

Review the Entire Essay

Read the paper aloud. How does it sound? What ideas or facts are missing, poorly stated, or repetitive? Highlight areas that need improvement and delete paragraphs that are off-topic or redundant.

- How does your draft measure up against your goal?
- What prevents this draft from meeting the needs of the writing assignment?
- What are the most serious defects?
- Have you selected an appropriate method of organizing your essay? Would a chronological approach be better than division? Should you open with your strongest point or reserve it for the conclusion?

Examine the Thesis

Most important, focus on the thesis or controlling idea of the essay. Does your paper have a clear thesis, a controlling idea—or is it simply a collection of facts and observations? Does the essay have a point?

- If your paper has a thesis statement, read it aloud. Is it clearly stated? Is it too general? Can it be adequately supported?
- Where have you placed the thesis? Would it be better situated elsewhere in the essay? Remember, the thesis does not have to appear in the opening.
- If the thesis is implied rather than stated, does the essay have a controlling idea? Do details and your choice of words provide readers with a clear impression of your subject?

Review Topic Sentences and Controlling Ideas

Each paragraph should have a clear focus and support the thesis.

- Review the controlling idea for each paragraph.
- Do all the paragraphs support the thesis?

■ Are there paragraphs that are off the topic? You may have developed some interesting ideas, recalled an important fact or quote, or detailed a compelling story—but if they don't directly relate to the thesis, they do not belong in this essay.

Review the Sequence of Paragraphs

While writing, you may have discovered new ideas or diverted from your plan, altering the design of the essay. Study the list of topic sentences and determine whether their order serves your purpose.

■ Should paragraphs be rearranged to maintain chronology or to create greater emphasis?
■ Does the order of paragraphs follow your train of thought? Should some paragraphs be preceded by those offering definitions and background information?

Revise the Introduction

The opening sentences and paragraphs of any document are critical. They set the tone of the paper, announce the topic, arouse reader interest, and establish how the rest of the essay is organized. Because you cannot always predict how you will change the body of the essay, you should always return to the introduction and examine it before writing a new draft.

Introduction Checklist

✔ Does the introduction clearly announce the topic?

✔ Does the opening paragraph arouse interest?

✔ Does the opening paragraph serve to limit the topic, preparing readers for what follows?

✔ If the thesis appears in the opening, is it clearly and precisely stated?

✔ Does the language of the opening paragraph set the proper tone for the paper?

✔ Does the introduction address reader concerns, correct misconceptions, and provide background information so that readers can understand and appreciate the evidence that follows?

Revise Supporting Paragraphs

The paragraphs in the body of the essay should support the thesis, develop ideas, or advance the chronology.

Paragraph Checklist

✔ Does the paragraph have a clear focus?

✔ Is the controlling idea supported with enough evidence?

✔ Is the evidence easy to follow? Does the paragraph follow a logical or-ganization? Would a different mode be more effective in unifying the ideas?

✔ Are there irrelevant ideas that should be deleted?

✔ Are there clear transitions between ideas and between paragraphs?

✔ Do paragraph breaks signal major transitions? Should some para-graphs be combined and others broken up?

Revise the Conclusion

Not all essays require a separate paragraph or group of paragraphs to conclude the writing. A narrative may end with a final event. A comparison may conclude with the last point.

Conclusion Checklist

✔ Does the conclusion end the paper on a strong note? Will it leave readers with a final image, question, quotation, or fact that will chal-lenge them and lead readers to continue thinking about your subject?

✔ Does the conclusion simply repeat the introduction or main ideas? Is it necessary? Should it be shortened or deleted?

✔ If your purpose is to motivate people to take action, does the conclu-sion provide readers with clear directions?

Improving Paragraphs

First drafts often produce weak paragraphs that need stronger topic sentences and clearer support:

First Draft

The automobile changed America. Development increased as distances were reduced. People moved outward from the city to live and work. Highways and bridges were built. Travel increased and greater mobility led to rapid population shifts, causing growth in some areas and declines in others. Cars created new industries and demands for new services.

Revision Notes

too vague, need tighter topic sentence   too general

<u>The automobile changed America.</u> Development increased as distances were reduced.

lack of sentence variety

People moved outward from the city to live and work. Highways and bridges were

explain

built. Travel increased and greater mobility led to rapid population shifts, causing

what areas?   give examples

growth in some areas and declines in others. Cars created new industries and demands

for new services.

Improved

The automobile reshaped the American landscape. As millions of cars jammed crowded streets and bogged down on unpaved roads, drivers demanded better highways. Soon great bridges spanned the Hudson, Delaware, and Mississippi to accommodate the flood of traffic. The cities pushed beyond rail and trolley lines, absorbing farms, meadows, and marshland. The middle class abandoned the polluted congestion of the city for the mushrooming suburbs that offered greater space and privacy. Gas stations, garages, parking structures, drive-in movies appeared across the country. Motels, chain stores, and fast food restaurants catered to the mobile public. Shopping malls, office towers, factories, and schools appeared in the new communities, all of them surrounded by what the cities could not offer—free parking.

Other drafts contain overwritten paragraphs cluttered with redundant statements and irrelevant details. Although they may contain strong controlling statements and impressive evidence, these paragraphs are weakened by unnecessary detail:

First Draft

One of Howard Hughes' early first ventures was the creation of a steam-powered sportscar. Hughes had just recently inherited his father's lucrative tool company, which produced the best oil drill bit of the day. Hughes' father wisely leased rather than sold his "rock eater" to maintain control and increase profits. At nineteen, Hughes could now easily afford to build his dream car. Steam cars, though considered obsolete in 1926, had one advantage over gasoline-powered automobiles. They had as much power at a standing start as they did at full power. But they required ten minutes or more to build up enough steam to run and had to stop for water every fifty miles. Hughes, who would later pour millions into the famed Spruce Goose which made only one test flight after World War II, wanted a state of the art steam car. He hired engineers from Caltech and challenged the engineers to build a steamer that would start in two minutes and be able to drive from Los Angeles to San Francisco on a single tank of water. Hughes went back to making movies and dating starlets as his crack team of Caltech engineers worked in a secret garage. The engineers worked for three years and spent $550,000 to develop a steam car that would start in two minutes and drive from Los Angeles to San Francisco on a single tank of water. Hughes was delighted with his new car and asked the engineers how they had achieved their goals. They explained that a network of radiators ran throughout the body of the car, even the doors. Realizing that even a minor accident could rupture a steam pipe and scald the driver, Hughes ordered his half million dollar dream car, the only one its kind, to be cut to pieces with blow torches.

Revision Notes

One of Howard Hughes' early first ventures was the creation of a steam-powered sportscar. Hughes had just recently inherited his father's lucrative tool company, ~~which~~
needless detail
~~produced the best oil drill bit of the day. Hughes' father wisely leased rather than sold his "rock eater" to maintain control and increase profits.~~ At nineteen, Hughes could now easily afford to build his dream car. Steam cars, though considered obsolete in 1926, had one advantage over gasoline-powered automobiles. They had as much power at a standing start as they did at full power. But they required ten minutes or more to build up enough steam to run and had to stop for water every fifty miles.
delete details
Hughes, ~~who would later pour millions into the famed Spruce Goose which made only one test flight after World War II,~~ wanted a state of the art steam car. He hired engineers from Caltech and challenged the engineers to build a steamer that would start in two minutes and be able to drive from Los Angeles to San Francisco on a single tank of
shorten or delete
water. ~~Hughes went back to making movies and dating starlets as his crack team of Caltech engineers worked in a secret garage.~~ The engineers worked for three years and
shorten
spent $550,000 to develop a steamcar that ~~would start in two minutes and drive from Los Angeles to San Francisco on a single tank of water.~~ Hughes was delighted with his
wordy
new car and asked the engineers how they had achieved their goals. They explained that a network of radiators ran throughout the body of the car, even the doors. Realizing that even a minor accident could rupture a steam pipe and scald the driver, Hughes ordered his half million dollar dream car, the only one its kind, to be cut to pieces with blow torches.

Improved

One of Howard Hughes' first ventures was a steam-powered sportscar. Having recently inherited his father's lucrative tool company at nineteen, Hughes could easily afford to build his dream car. Though considered obsolete in 1926, steam cars had one advantage over gasoline-powered automobiles. They had as much power at a standing start as they did at full power but required ten minutes to build up enough steam to run and had to stop for water every fifty miles. Hughes hired engineers from Caltech and challenged them to build a steamer that would start in two minutes and drive from Los Angeles to San Francisco on a single tank of water. The scientists worked for three years and spent $550,000 to develop a steam car that met Hughes' demanding specifications. Hughes was delighted with his new car until the engineers explained that a network of radiators ran throughout the body, even the doors. Realizing that even a minor accident could rupture a steam pipe and scald the driver, Hughes ordered his half million dollar dream car cut to pieces.

WRITING ACTIVITY

Revise the following paragraphs by restating topic sentences, deleting redundant or irrelevant statements, and adding ideas and observations of your own.

1. The Puritans were and remain controversial. Today we see them as witch-burning bigots, religious zealots, and strict parents. We see them as theology-driven people, almost masochistic in their religious fervor. But the Puritans were also idealistic. Persecuted in England, they came to America to build a community based on a lofty vision of building a society based on piety, unity, and brotherhood. But their vision of brotherhood and harmony was difficult to realize given the fact that they had to face the demands of the New World with its wild terrain and hostile native population. They tended to regard Native

Americans as infidels and savages. Their dealings with them were harsh and violent. Today many people still regard those who are different, who dress differently, worship differently, live differently with contempt and hostility. Their failure to live peaceably with the indigenous people was one of many causes for the failure of the Puritan community.

2. For more than one generation, parents have shown concern about the effects of television on children. Violent television programs expose children to violence, giving them the ideas that complex problems can be easily resolved with the employment of force. Even nonviolent programs grossly simplify complex human issues and suggest that almost any problem can be resolved in thirty or sixty minutes. Commercials brainwash children into seeking quick fixes to problems, seeing products as substitutes for rewards that come from hard work and effort. Television, above all, reduces children to viewers, passive receivers of messages rather than active participants in social interaction and social discussion.

3. In the summer of 1919 a caravan of army trucks left Washington, D.C., to cross America to demonstrate the need for better roads. Twenty-nine-year-old Captain Dwight Eisenhower volunteered, seeking adventure and a chance to explore the West. But the convoy had to toil across trackless wastes, muddy lanes, and rutted paths. The automobile craze had swept America. Henry Ford had produced the inexpensive Model T, which made America a nation of drivers. The First World War had demonstrated the strategic use of trucks for transport. Two decades later, Eisenhower would learn the importance of modern transport when he planned the invasion of Hitler's Europe. But in 1919 few highways had been constructed. Outside of cities and large towns most roads remained unpaved. It took the column of army trucks three months to reach San Francisco. Eisenhower reported they often only progressed three or four miles a day on poor roads. This trip made a lasting impression on Eisenhower. When he became president thirty-three years later, he supported federal funding of the interstate highway system. Eisenhower saw modern highways as critical for transportation in a modern economy. Soon freeways and expressways linked American cities so cars and trucks could cross the nation in days instead of months. This network of modern highways helped expand the economy and fueled the boom in suburban housing and growth of suburban shopping malls. Eisenhower, perhaps, could not see the downside of his vision, that urban sprawl would lead

to traffic jams, chaotic development, the loss of farmland, and damage to the environment. But nevertheless, it reveals how a youthful experience can influence a leader's vision of the future.

REVISING THE FIRST DRAFT

The student writing about victim impact statements reviewed her first draft and read it to several classmates who offered suggestions. As she listened to them, she added notes in the margins and developed a checklist to guide her second draft. At this point, the writer is focusing on the big picture, as well as making some adjustments at the level of word choice. Editing and proofreading will come later.

Revision

wordy/weak   Across America today more and more victims of crime are being allowed to address the court in terms of making what is called a victim impact statment. This written or oral presentation to the court allows victims to express their feelings to the judge after someone has been convicted of a crime.

Advocates of victim impact statements point to key advantages. First, these statements give victim's a voice. For years, victims have felt helpless. Prosecutors represent the state, not the cirme victim. Victim have been dismayed when prosecutors have arranged pleas bargains without their knowledge. Some victims are still recovering from their injuries when they learn the person who hurt them has plead to a lesser charge and received probation.

Therapists who work with victims also say that being able to address the court helps with the healing process. Victims of violent crime can feel powerless and vulnerable. Instead of suffering in silence, they are given the chance to address the criminal,

cliché   to <u>clear their chests</u>, and get on with the rest of their lives.

Impact statements allows judges to consider what sentences are apropptriate. In one case a judge who planned to fine a teenager for shoplifting excepted the store owners suggestions to waive the fine if the defendent completed his GED.

But giving victims a change to speak raises some issues. What about the victim who is not articulate, who doesn't even speak English? In murder cases the victim's relatives are given a chance to speak? Does this mean that a middle class professional victim with a circle of grieving freinds and family members will be granted more significance than the homeless murder victim who leaves no one behind?

Victim impact statements may help empower victims who are educated, personally impressive, and socially promient. But they may also allow forgotten victims to remain voiceless.

Revision Notes

Needs stronger opening—needs attention-getter
Sharper definition
Too short/superficial discussion
Clearer examples/Use real-life trials
Tighter conclusion

Second Draft

The courtroom scene was riveting. One by one, the survivors of a deadly commuter train shooting took the stand and addressed the man who had maimed them. Their voices quivering with emotion, they told the court how the gunman's actions changed their lives forever. Spouses and parents of the dead spoke of loss. There were tears, moments of intense anger, and quiet despair. Victim impact statements have become a common feature of criminal proceedings. Spoken in court or submitted in writing, these statements provide an opportunity for victims to be heard before sentencing.

Advocates of victims impact statements believe these declarations give victims a voice, an opportunity to be heard. Traditionally, victims have appeared in court only as witnesses subject to cross-examination. Prosecutors, victims soon learn, represent the state and not individuals. Still hospitalized after a brutal beating, a New Jersey restaurant owner learned from reading a newspaper that his assailants had plea-bargained to lesser charges and received probation. Joining with other victims, he became an advocate for victims' rights, including impact statements.

Therapists who counsel victims of crime believe that addressing the court and taking an active role in the legal process helps people recover from a sense of helplessness and regain a measure of self-respect.

Impact statements allow judges to consider appropriate sentences. In a Florida case, a judge who intended to fine a teenager for shoplifting agreed with the store owner's suggestion that the fine be waived if the defendant completed his GED.

But giving victims a chance to speak has led to ugly courtroom scenes that seem inappropriate in a democracy. In Milwaukee a sister of a young man murdered by Jeffrey Dahmer wailed and shrieked in contortions of pure rage. The relative of another murder victim shouted that he would execute the killer himself. Bailiffs had to restrain him as he begged the judge, "Just gimme five minutes with him!" Defense attorneys argue these harangues are unnecessary. What need is there to heap abuse upon a person about to lose his or her life or liberty? Can anger and harassment be considered healing?

But even restrained, well-reasoned impact statements raise troubling questions. What about the victim who is too impaired, too frightened, or too wounded to speak? Is his or her absence to be judged as indifference? What about those whose English is limited? What of those without friends or family? Should the drunk driver who kills a young professional missed by friends, family, and colleagues receive a tougher sentence than the drunk driver who kills a homeless man who dies unmourned, unmissed, and uncounted? Do we really want our courts and society to suggest that some lives are more significant than others?

Victim impact statements may help empower victims, especially the educated, the personally impressive, and the socially prominent. But these statements, unintentionally, may also further marginalize the most helpless among us, allowing forgotten victims to remain voiceless.

STRATEGIES for Overcoming Problems in Revising

Revising a draft can be challenging. Writers encounter a range of common problems.

1. **The draft remains unfocused.** If your writing remains too general and seems to lack direction, review your thesis statement.
   - Does your thesis limit the scope of the paper?
   - Does your thesis provide a method of organizing the evidence?
   - Apply prewriting techniques such as lists and clustering to map out the ideas in the draft. Often a list will help you discover a new organizational method and identify ideas that are off-topic.
2. **The draft remains too short.** If, after extensive reading, revising, and rewriting, your essay remains too short, too superficial, return to your plan.
   - Review your thesis and return to prewriting to develop more evidence.
3. **The draft is too long and seems incomplete.** Examine your thesis. Have you attempted to cover too broad a topic given the limit of the assignment?
   - Review your goal and any instructor's guidelines for methods of limiting the paper.
   - An essay that offers an in-depth view of a narrow topic is far more interesting than a longer piece that provides a superficial examination of a broader subject.

····e‑writing ·····

Exploring Revision Online

You can use the Internet to learn more about revising first drafts.

1. Using a search engine, such as Alta Vista, Yahoo, or Google, enter such terms as *writing process* and *revision* to locate current sites of interest.

2. If you wrote an e-mail to a friend, review and revise your draft. What ideas did you forget to add? Are there irrelevant details that could be deleted? Could paragraphs be stronger, better organized? Does your e-mail have the focus, the impact you intended?

3. Review past e-mails you have sent. What changes would you make now? Do you find awkward and wordy sentences? Are there missing details?

For Further Reading

Cook, Claire Kehrwald. *Line by Line: How to Improve Your Writing.*

Venolia, Jan. *Rewrite Right! How to Revise Your Way to Better Writing.*

E-Sources

A Strategy for Analyzing and Revising a First Draft
> **http://writing-program.uchicago.edu/ resources/collegewriting/**

Editing and Proofreading Strategies for Revision
> **http:owl.english.purdue.edu/handouts/ general/**

Companion Website

See **http://www.thomsonedu.com/ english/sundance** for additional information on revising.

12

EDITING AND PROOFREADING

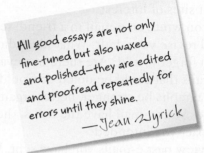

All good essays are not only fine-tuned but also waxed and polished—they are edited and proofread repeatedly for errors until they shine.

—Jean Wyrick

WHAT ARE EDITING AND PROOFREADING?

Editing and proofreading are the final steps in the writing process. In the editing stage, you focus on improving the impact of sentences, correcting errors, eliminating needless phrases, and improving the style and clarity of your writing. Proofreading checks the visual appearance of your document, reviewing the paper for spelling, proper format, pagination, margins, and accuracy of names, dates, and numbers.

Editing and proofreading, though often seen as final steps, can occur throughout the writing process. While writing and revising, you can fix mechanical errors, provided they do not distract you from focusing on the larger elements.

A number of tools can assist you in editing and proofreading:

- a dictionary—to check spelling and definitions
- a thesaurus—to find alternatives for overused or imprecise words
- a handbook—to check grammar, punctuation, mechanics, and documentation styles
- an encyclopedia—to check names, dates, facts, historical and biographical references

WRITERS AT WORK

If I wake up and I've got a deadline looming, it's just awful.

To get through it, you just make coffee. You make a lot of coffee, and you sit down in front of the [computer] screen and you just type out a word. Then you go and talk on the telephone. You go get some more coffee, you come back, and you make yourself type out [a] sentence.

Then, if you're at home, you rearrange your ties or you clean off your dresser. Then you go back and do it again. You make another phone call. And pretty soon your editor's on the phone saying, "Where is my copy? I need your column." So then you sit down, and you just do it.

Andrew Ferguson, editor

SOURCE: *Booknotes*

If you compose on a computer, you may have easy access to online and CD-ROM resources.

STRATEGIES | for Editing

1. **Read your paper aloud.** Listen to your words and sentences. Missing and misspelled words, awkward and redundant phrases, and illogical constructions are easier to hear than see.
2. **Use peer editing.** It is far easier to detect errors in someone else's writing. Switch papers with another student if you can. Read this student's paper aloud if possible, noting mistakes and areas needing revision.
3. **Use spell-check and other computer tools.** Almost all word processing programs include spell-check, which detects items it does not recognize as words.
   - Spell-check systems have limitations. They will not find missing words or always distinguish between homonyms such as "their" and "there." In addition, they will not be able to detect errors in proper names such as "Kowalski" or "Topeka."
4. **Edit backward.** By this time in the writing process, you may have read and reread your paper so many times that it is difficult to look at your sentences objectively. An effective way of spotting errors is to start with the last line and read backward, moving from the conclusion to the introduction.

Working in reverse order isolates sentences so that you can evaluate them out of context.

5. **Focus on identifying and correcting habitual errors.** Students often have habitual errors. You may frequently make spelling errors, forget needed commas, or continually confuse *its* and *it's*.

■ Review previously written papers and instructor comments to identify errors you are likely repeat.

Common Grammar Errors

When editing drafts, look for these common grammar errors.

Fragments

Fragments are incomplete sentences. Sentences require a subject and a verb and must state a complete thought:

Tom works until midnight.	**sentence**
Tom working until midnight	**fragment (incomplete verb)**
Works until midnight.	**fragment (subject missing)**
Because Tom works until midnight.	**fragment (incomplete thought)**

Note that even though the last item has a subject, *Tom*, and a verb, *works*, it does not state a complete thought.

See pages 841–843 for more on fragments.

Run-ons and Comma Splices

Run-ons and comma splices are incorrectly punctuated compound sentences. Simple sentences (independent clauses) can be joined to create compound sentences in two ways:

1. Link with a **semicolon [;]**
2. Link with a **comma [,] + and, or, yet, but,** *or* so

I was born in Chicago, but I grew up in Dallas.	correct
I studied French; Jan took Italian.	correct
We have to take a cab my battery is dead.	run-on
We have to take a cab; my battery is dead.	

Jim is sick, the game is canceled.   comma splice
Jim is sick, so the game is canceled

See pages 843–846 for more about run-ons and comma splices.

Subject and Verb Agreement

Subjects and verbs must match in number. Singular subjects use singular verbs.
Plural subjects use plural verbs:

The boy *walk***s** to school.	Singular
The boy**s** *walk* to school.	Plural
The cost of drugs *is* rising.	Singular (the subject is "cost")
Two weeks *is* not enough time.	Singular (amounts of time and money are singular)
The jury *is* deliberating.	Singular (group subjects are singular)
The teacher or the students *are* invited.	Plural (when two subjects are joined with "or" the subject nearer the verb determines whether it is singular or plural)

See pages 850–854 for more on subject and verb agreement.

Pronoun Agreement

Pronouns must agree or match the nouns they represent:

Everyone should cast *his* or *her* vote.	Singular
The children want *their* parents to call.	Plural

The most misused pronoun is *they*. *They* is a pronoun and should clearly refer to
a noun. Avoid unclear use of pronouns as in, "Crime is rising. Schools are failing. *They* just don't care." Who does *they* refer to?
See pages 854–857 for more on pronoun agreement.

Dangling and Misplaced Modifiers

To prevent confusion, modifiers—words and phrases that add information
about other words—should be placed next to the words they modify.

Rowing across the lake, the moon rose over the water.	(dangling, who was *rowing*? the *moon*?)
Rowing across the lake, *we* saw the moon rise over the water.	(correct)

| She drove the car to the house which was rented. | (misplaced, which was rented?) |
| She drove the car to the rented house. | (correct) |

See pages 866–869 for more about dangling and misplaced modifiers.

Faulty Parallelism

Pairs and lists of words and phrases should match in form:

Jim is tall, handsome, and an athlete.	(not parallel, list mixes adjectives and a noun)
Jim is tall, handsome, and athletic.	(parallel, all adjectives)
We need to paint the bedroom, shovel the walk, and the basement must be cleaned.	(not parallel, the last item does not match with *to paint* and (to) shovel.
We need to paint the bedroom, shovel the walk, and clean the basement.	(parallel, all verb phrases)

See pages 846–849 for more on faulty parallelism.

Awkward Shifts in Person

Avoid illogical shifts in person:

We climbed the tower and you could see for miles.	(illogical shift from *we* to *you*)
We climbed the tower and we could see for miles.	(correct)
If a student works hard, you can get an A.	(illogical shift from *student* to *you*)
If you work hard, you can get an A.	(correct)

Awkward Shifts in Tense

Avoid illogical shifts in tense (time):

| Hamlet hears from a ghost, then he avenged his father. | (awkward shift from present to past) |
| Hamlet heard from a ghost, then he avenged his father. | (correct, both past) |

Hamlet hears from a ghost, then he   (correct, both present)
avenges his father.

Editing Sentences

After revising the larger elements of your draft, examine the sentences in each paragraph. Read each sentence separately to make sure it expresses the thoughts you intended.

Sentence Checklist

✔ Does the sentence support the paragraph's controlling idea? Could it be eliminated?

✔ Are key ideas emphasized through concrete words and active verbs (see pages 128–129)?

✔ Are secondary ideas subordinated (see pages 100–104)?

✔ Are the relationships between ideas clearly expressed with transitional expressions (see pages 133–134)?

✔ Do the tone and style of the sentence suit your reader and nature of the document?

Be Brief

Sentences lose their power when cluttered with unnecessary words and phrases. When writing the rough draft, it is easy to slip in expressions that add nothing to the meaning of the sentence.

ORIGINAL: In today's modern world computer literacy is essential to enter in the job market.
IMPROVED: Computer literacy is essential to get a job.

Phrases that begin with *who is* or *which were* can often be shortened:

ORIGINAL: Viveca Scott, who was an ambitious business leader, doubled profits, which stunned her stockholders.
IMPROVED: Viveca Scott, an ambitious business leader, stunned her stockholders by doubling profits.

Delete Wordy Phrases

Even skilled writers use wordy phrases in trying to express themselves in a first draft. When editing, locate phrases that can be replaced with shorter phrases or single words:

Wordy	Improved
at that period of time	then
at the present time	now
in the near future	soon
winter months	winter
round in shape	round
blue colored	blue
for the purpose of informing	to inform
render an examination of	examine
make an analysis	analyze
in the event of	if

Eliminate Redundancy

Repeating or restating words and ideas can have a dramatic effect, but it is a technique that should be used sparingly and only when you wish to emphasize a specific point.

REDUNDANT: The computer has revolutionized education, revolutionizing delivery systems, course content, and teaching methods.

IMPROVED: The computer has revolutionized educational delivery systems, course content, and teaching methods.

REDUNDANT: He took his medicines, but poor nutrition, bad eating habits, his lack of exercise, and sedentary lifestyle hampered his recovery.

IMPROVED: He took his medicines, but his bad eating habits and sedentary lifestyle hampered his recovery.

Limit Use of Passive Voice

Most sentences state ideas in active voice—the subject performs the action of the verb. In passive voice the order is reversed and the sentence's subject is acted on:

Active	Passive
Mr. Smith towed the car.	The car was towed by Mr. Smith.
The hospital conducted several tests.	Several tests were conducted by the hospital.

The mayor's office announced a new round of budget cuts. / A new round of budget cuts was announced by the mayor's office.

Passive voice is used when the actor is unknown or less important than the object:

My car was stolen.
The door was locked.
His chest was crushed by a rock.

Passive voice, however, can leave out critical information:

After the plane crash, several photographs were taken.

Who took the photographs—investigators, reporters, the airline, survivors, bystanders?

Use passive voice *only* when it emphasizes important elements in a sentence.

Vary Your Use of Sentence Types

You can keep your writing interesting and fresh by altering types of sentences. Repeating a single kind of sentence can give your writing a monotonous predictability. A short sentence isolates an idea and gives it emphasis, but a string of choppy sentences explaining minor details robs your essay of power. Long sentences can subordinate minor details and show the subtle relationships between ideas, but they can become tedious for readers to follow.

UNVARIED: Mary Sanchez was elected to the assembly. She worked hard on the budget committee. Her work won her respect. She was highly regarded by the mayor. People responded to her energy and drive. She became popular with voters. The mayor decided to run for governor. He asked Mary Sanchez to manage his campaign.

VARIED: Mary Sanchez was elected to the assembly. Her hard work on the budget committee won her respect, especially by the mayor. Voters were impressed by her drive and energy. When the mayor decided to run for governor, he asked Mary Sanchez to manage his campaign.

UNVARIED: The mayor believed he could unseat Mike Koepple by attacking what he believed were the governor's two weak points: his failure to reduce property taxes and his reluctance to commit money to urban education. Mary Sanchez conducted in-depth focus groups with voters across the state, devising a series of clever commercials that highlighted Koepple's shortcomings and extolling the mayor's achievements in lowering taxes and aiding schools. Governor Koepple, startled at the mayor's strong showing in the polls, was disappointed by his campaign staff and frustrated by his difficulty in raising funds. Unwilling to spend his own limited resources and fearing a brutal assault in the media, Koepple quietly announced that he would not seek a second term and would accept the president's offer of becoming ambassador to New Zealand.

VARIED: The mayor believed he could unseat Mike Koepple by attacking the governor's two weak points: his failure to reduce property taxes and his reluctance to commit money to urban education. After conducting indepth focus groups with voters across the state, Mary Sanchez devised a series of clever commercials. Mike Koepple's shortcomings were compared to the mayor's achievements in lowering taxes and aiding schools. Governor Koepple, startled by the mayor's strong showing in the polls, was disappointed by his campaign staff. Frustrated by his difficulty in raising funds, he was unwilling to spend his own limited resources. Fearing a brutal assault in the media, Koepple quietly announced that he would not seek a second term. The president had offered him a better job—ambassador to New Zealand.

WRITING ACTIVITIES

Edit the following sentences by eliminating wordy and redundant phrases and emphasizing main ideas.

1. In many ways students must learn to teach themselves to be successful.

2. American automobiles, once threatened by imports from Japan and other countries, are entering and competing in the global car market.

3. Illness and disease can be prevented through proper diet, appropriate exercise, and moderation in the consumption of alcohol.

4. In my personal opinion, the calculus course is too tough for the majority of freshmen students.

5. The exams were distributed by the professor after a brief introduction.

Edit the sentences in the following paragraph to reduce clutter and increase clarity and variety:

Three years ago the writing lab was opened by the English Department. This lab was designed to assist students taking freshman composition courses. The lab was at first staffed by four paraprofessionals with extensive experience in teaching writing and editing. But the budget was cut by the dean of liberal arts. Now only two part-time graduate students serve the students. Neither has teaching or editing experience. The students are no longer getting the assistance they need to improve their writing. The lab is no longer crowded. Often students are found using the computers to send e-mail to friends. Some play solitaire or minesweeper between classes. This should change.

Editing Words

Diction Checklist

✔ Are the words accurate? Have you chosen words that precisely reflect your thinking? (See pages 128–129.)

✔ Is the level of diction appropriate? Do your word choices suit the tone and style of the document? (See pages 129–130.)

✔ Do connotations suit your purpose or do they detract from your message? (See page 130.)

✔ Are technical terms clearly defined?

✔ Do you use concrete rather than abstract words?

Avoid Sexist Language

Sexist language either ignores the existence of one gender or promotes negative attitudes about men or women.

Replace sexist words with neutral terms:

Sexist	Nonsexist
mankind	humanity
postman	letter carrier
policeman	police officer
Frenchmen	the French
Men at Work	Workers Ahead
manmade	synthetic
everyman	everyone
fireman	firefighter
man in the street	average person
chairman	chairperson

Avoid nouns with "female" endings or adjectives. Although the words *actress* and *waitress* are still used, other words designating female professionals are considered largely obsolete:

Sexist	Nonsexist
poetess	poet
authoress	author
lady lawyer	lawyer
woman judge	judge

Avoid using male pronouns when nouns refer to both genders. The single noun *man* takes the single male pronoun *he*. If you are writing about a boys' school, it is appropriate to substitute "he" for the noun "student." But if the school includes both males and females, both should be represented:

Every student should try *his or her* best.
All students should try *their* best.

Plural nouns take the pronouns *they* and *their*, avoiding wordy *he or she* and *his or her* constructions.

Avoid Clichés

Clichés are worn-out phrases. Once creative or imaginative, these phrases, like jokes you have heard more than once, have lost their impact. In addition, clichés allow simplistic statements to substitute for genuine thought.

white as snow	light as a feather	acid test
Mr. Big	in the thick of it	on pins and needles
evil as sin	dead heat	crushing blow
viable option	bottom line	all that jazz
crack of dawn	calm before the storm	dog-tired

WRITING ACTIVITY

Edit the wording of the following sentences to avoid sexism, clichés, awkward phrases, and misused words.

1. Every student should bring his books to class.

2. He jogged at the crack of dawn every morning.

3. The university has listed three mandatory requirements for future revision.

4. We had better get down to brass tacks if we want to get a fresh start.

5. Threatened by drug dealers, the witness required continual security.

6. This dispute must be settled by an uninterested judge.

7. He could manage to explain a difficult problem with childish simplicity.

8. The computer company began to flounder in debt.

9. The president's speech was vague but most implied he favored a tax hike.

10. A voter should use his best judgment.

STRATEGIES | for Proofreading

Proofreading examines writing for errors and concerns itself with the physical appearance—the "look"—of the finished document.

1. **Make a last check for errors in the text.** Read the paper through to make last-minute corrections in grammar, numbers, dates, spellings, usage, punctuation, and capitalization.

2. **Use an appropriate form.** College instructors often dictate specific styles and requirements about paging, margins, spacing, and cover sheets. Business, government, and professional documents may have precise guidelines.

3. **Use standard formats.** Unless you are given specific instructions, follow these standard guidelines.

   ■ Use standard-size 8½ × 11″ white paper. Avoid using onionskin or easily smeared paper.

   ■ Remove any perforated edges.

   ■ Use standard typeface or fonts. Avoid script or fonts smaller than 10 point. Use fonts larger than 14 only for titles and headings.

   ■ Double-space your text, leaving ample margins.

   ■ Use a title page or headline listing your name, instructor's name, course, date, and assignment.

4. **Keep a copy of all your papers.** Papers do get lost. Always make a copy in case your instructor fails to get your assignment.

COMMON MECHANICAL ERRORS

Spelling and Usage Errors

Spell-check programs do not distinguish between words like *there* and *their* or *affect* and *effect*.

Review dictionaries and see pages 894–897 and 901–902.

Punctuation

Use **commas** to separate items in a list, set off introductory and nonrestrictive elements, and join clauses in complex and compound sentences:

We bought pens, pencils, paper, and ink.
After losing the game, we met with the coach to discuss strategy.
My brother, who was born in Manhattan, took us to 21.
Because it was hot, the game was canceled.
We bought the plane tickets, but Hector paid for the hotel.

Use **semicolons** to separate independent clauses in compound sentences:

I flew to San Francisco; Juan took the train.

Use **apostrophes** to indicate contractions and possessives:

Don't let Carlo's truck leave the garage.

See pages 871–888 for more on punctuation.

Capitalization

Capitalize proper nouns such as names of products, organizations, geographical places, and people:

Buick   Yale University   Chicago   Rocky Mountains   Jim Wilson   Jane

Capitalize titles when used before a name:

We called for a doctor just as Dr. Green walked in.

Capitalize *East, North, West, South* when they refer to regions, not directions:

We drove south to the airport and grabbed a flight to the East.

See pages 888–891 for more about capitalization.

WRITING ACTIVITY

Edit and proofread the following essay, correcting errors in wording, spelling, capitalization, and punctuation.

In 1935 two men had a meeting in Akron Ohio that changed their lives and the lives of millions. Both men were Aloholics.

Bill Wilson was a succesful stockbroker but excessive drinking had ruined his prospects. He made repeated pleges to his wife and friends and attempted a variety of "cures." But he was unable to curtale his drinking.

On a business trip to Akron he made a decision that would charge his life. He was alone, far from his family and friends in New York. No one would know if he had a drink. Feeling his willpower to remain sober weaken, Bill Wilson knew what he had to do. He had to talk to another alcoholic. He started phoning churches, and a minister gave him a name of a local alcoholic.

Dr. Smith had been a leading surgeon in Akron. By 1935 alcoholism had nearly destroyed his practice. Friends attempted to help him, but he was unable to stop drinking. The doctor, accustomed to offers of assistence, was surprised when Wilson called, asking him for help.

The two men talked for hours, sharing their common depression, recurring guilt, and ongoing frustration. Afterwards, both realized something special had taken place between them.

Wilson returned to New York and began working with alcoholics in his home. Dr. Smith began working with a group of problem drinkers in Ohio. They did not lecture, they did not offer promises, but they talked to other alcoholics as fellow drunks, as equals.

In 1939 the two groups decided to call themselves Alcholics Anonmous and publish a book about their experiences. Dr. Smith urged the group to keep things simple. There would no officersa and no dues. The group had one goal—sobriety.

STRATEGIES for Overcoming Problems in Editing and Proofreading

1. **Sentences remain awkward.** Even after revising and editing, many sentences may still be awkward or garbled.
   - Think about the ideas you were trying to express and write new sentences without looking at your paper. Try restating your ideas with different words.
   - Use peer review if possible. You can use e-mail or even a phone call to test your sentence with someone else.

2. **Sentences contain redundant phrases and repeated words.**
   - Search a thesaurus for alternative words.
   - Examine your text to see whether subtitles or other devices could substitute for repeating phrases.
   - Read aloud or use peer review to detect needless or awkward repetitions.

3. **You are unable to determine the final format of the document.** Even when your text is perfected, you may find yourself unable to decide whether your paper should be single- or double-spaced, whether diagrams or charts should be included, whether citations should appear at the bottom of the page, within the text, or on a separate page.
   - Review instructions for guidelines or talk with your instructor.
   - Examine any existing examples for guidance.
   - Review official sources such as *The Chicago Manual of Style* or *The MLA Handbook*.

e-writing

Exploring Editing Online

You can use the Internet to learn more about editing.

1. Using a search engine, such as Alta Vista, Yahoo, or Google, enter such terms as *editing drafts* and *editing process* to locate current sites of interest.

2. If you wrote an e-mail to a friend, review and edit your draft. Can you locate any grammar errors such as fragments, run-ons, or dangling modifiers? Have you used standard forms of punctuation and capitalization?

For Further Reading

Fulwiler, Toby, and Alan R. Hayakawa. *The College Writer's Reference.*

Sabin, William A. *The Gregg Reference Manual.*

Stilman, Anne. *Grammatically Correct: The Writer's Essential Guide to Punctuation, Spelling, Style, Usage, and Grammar.*

Sutcliffe, Andrea, ed. *The New York Public Library Writer's Guide to Style and Usage.*

Wilson, Kenneth G. *The Columbia Guide to Standard American English.*

Companion Website

See **http://www.thomsonedu.com/ english/sundance** for further information about editing and proofreading.

E-Sources

Answers.com—online dictionary and encyclopedia
http://www.answers.com

Writing in the Information Age

Image vs. reality

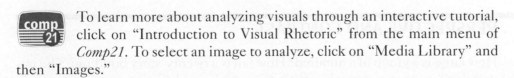

ANALYZING VISUALS
SEEING WITH A "WRITER'S EYE"

13

We increasingly communicate in images. We are bombarded daily with advertisements in newspapers and magazines, on television and billboards. College textbooks, which thirty years ago consisted of only text, now feature graphs and photographs on nearly every page. Websites, once blocks of words, now include streaming video. Satellites allow journalists to broadcast from remote parts of the world. Cable news networks provide images of breaking events twenty-four hours a day. The personal computer and desktop publishing enable students and small-business owners to develop sophisticated multimedia presentations rivaling those created by major corporations. Digital cameras allow people to instantly transmit photos and video worldwide.

Images can be used to grab attention, evoke an emotional response, record events, document conditions, record evidence, illustrate an idea or condition, establish a mood, or develop a context for discussion. Visual images command attention. They can be presented without comment or woven into the text of a written message.

To learn more about analyzing visuals through an interactive tutorial, click on "Introduction to Visual Rhetoric" from the main menu of *Comp21*. To select an image to analyze, click on "Media Library" and then "Images."

PHOTOGRAPHS, FILM, AND VIDEO

Photographs, film, and video are compelling. There is an impression that "the camera does not lie." A written description of a person or a place never seems as objective or as accurate as a photograph. The camera, we believe, hides nothing.

177

The image as icon. Elvis autographs photographs for fans.   © Bettmann/Corbis

It tells the whole truth. It leaves nothing out. People writing reports about a car accident can exaggerate or minimize the damage, but a photograph, we believe, provides us with irrefutable evidence. But visuals can be highly subjective and often misleading. They require careful analysis to determine their meaning and reliability.

The impression a photograph or video makes is shaped by a number of factors: perspective and contrast, context, timing and duplication, manipulation, and captions.

PERSPECTIVE AND CONTRAST

How large is a group of a hundred? How tall is a twenty-story building? The impression we get of events, objects, and people depends on perspective, the angle and distance of the camera and the subject. A hundred protesters photographed in close-up will look like an overwhelming force. Fists raised, faces twisted in emotion, lunging toward the camera, they can appear all-powerful and unstoppable. Photographed from a distance, the crowd can seem small against a landscape of multistory buildings or acres of empty pavement. In contrast to large fixed objects, the protest can appear futile and weak. If ordinary people going about routine business are shown in the foreground, the protesters, in contrast, may appear abnormal, ephemeral, even pathetic. A twenty-story building in a suburban neighborhood of two-story structures will loom over the landscape. Located in midtown Manhattan, dwarfed by skyscrapers, the same structure will seem undersized, less formidable, even homey in contrast. A luxury car photographed in front of a stately country home can appear as a desirable symbol of style, elegance, and taste. Parked next to a migrant farmworker's shack, the same car can appear oppressive, a symbol of tasteless greed, exploitation, and injustice. A mime shown entertaining small children will look wholesome, joyful, and playful. Posed next to a homeless man taking shelter in a cardboard box, a mime will look irrelevant, inane, even offensive.

Charles Lindbergh, 1927   © Bettmann/Corbis

An individual can appear large or small, weak or powerful, depending on perspective. Charles Lindbergh is shown on this page in close-up. His face fills the frame. No other people, structures, or objects detract from his larger-than-life presence. In addition, he is photographed wearing his flight helmet and goggles, emblems of his famous 1927 transatlantic flight. His clear eyes look upward as if gazing to the horizon and the future. This photograph depicts a human being as powerful, in command of his environment. It is the type of image seen in movie posters, postage stamps, official portraits, and celebrity stills. Shown in isolation, any subject can appear dominant because there is nothing else to compare it to.

In contrast to Lindbergh's picture, the photograph of James Dean in Times Square is shot at some distance. Unlike Lindbergh, Dean is shown not in isolation but within an environment. Though he is at the center of the photograph, his stature is diminished by the urban landscape. Tall buildings rise above him. The iron fence on the right restricts his freedom of movement. In addition, the environment is hostile—dark, cold, and

James Dean in Times Square, 1955. © Dennis Stock, 1955/Magnum

Lee Harvey Oswald under arrest, Dallas, 1963   © AP

wet. Dean is hunched forward, his collar turned up against the wind, his hands buried in his pockets against the cold. The picture creates an image of brooding loneliness and alienation, suited to Dean's Hollywood image as a loner and troubled rebel.

The impression created of Lee Harvey Oswald is shaped by perspective. In the press photo taken shortly after his arrest, Oswald looks weak, subdued, cowardly. He is literally cornered, shown off-center at the edge of the frame. Though he is the subject of the photograph, he is markedly smaller in relation to the officers. The angle of the camera distorts the relative sizes of the figures so that the uniformed men in the foreground are oversized, their power and authority emphasized. The officer's badge appears larger than Oswald's head. The room is blank and featureless. Handcuffed and still disheveled from his arrest, Oswald is depicted as a disarmed menace, an assassin rendered harmless.

CONTEXT

Photographs and video images are isolated glimpses of larger events. A camera captures a split second of reality, but it does not reveal what happened before or after the image was taken. The photograph of a baseball player hitting a home run shows a moment of athletic triumph, but it does not reveal the player's batting average or who won the game. Photographs taken during a melee between police and demonstrators can capture a protestor hurling a rock at a police officer or the officer striking back with a nightstick. A single striking image may distort our impressions of a larger event.

Motion picture and video cameras offer us a window onto the world, bringing world events into our homes—but it is a narrow window. During the hostage crisis in Iran in 1979, for example, television cameras continually showed violent demonstrations outside the American embassy, creating the impression that the entire nation was swept by a wave of anti-Americanism. American journalists, however, reported that only a block away they could walk through crowded streets and chat with passersby without incident. Aware of the power of image, protest groups around the world stage demonstrations for cameras to gain maximum media exposure.

Watching an evening of cable network news creates the illusion that you are being informed about world events. In thirty minutes you see a conflict in the Middle East, a White House spokesperson, a senator commenting on the economy, a high-speed car chase in San Diego. But cable news is highly limited to covering visual stories. More complicated stories may not provide gripping visuals or may require too much explanation to make good television. Stories that break in developed countries within easy reach of media crews receive more coverage than events that occur in remote areas. Conflicts in the Middle East and Northern Ireland that claim a few hundred lives a year receive more coverage than a genocidal rebellion that kills hundreds of thousands in Rwanda or ethnic cleansing that destroys hundreds of villages in Sudan.

Juries have acquitted people caught on videotape buying drugs or engaged in violent assaults. Whereas the public often only sees a dramatic segment, juries are often shown a videotape in its entirety. Defense attorneys place the tape in context by providing additional information about the people and events depicted. By raising doubts, they can persuade a jury to rethink what it has seen, questioning the tape's meaning and reliability.

Visual Connotations

Like words, images have connotations. They create emotional responses. Politicians are interviewed with flags and bookshelves in the background to demonstrate patriotism and indicate knowledge. Campaign commercials show candidates with their families, visiting the elderly, shaking hands with firefighters, or visiting veterans to link themselves with positive images. Ads and commercials will use provocative images of sex and violence to arrest people's attention. Book covers and movie posters only vaguely associated with World

Patriotic symbols featured in recruiting ad.
© 2002. Paid for by the United States Army

Osama bin Laden replaces Uncle Sam in political ad.
© TomPaine.com, an online public interest journal, a project of
the nonprofit Florence Fund

War II often feature a large swastika because it is a symbol bound to attract attention.

Certain images become icons, symbols of an event, culture, attitude, or value. Reproduced in books, films, on murals, and T-shirts, they serve to communicate a message with a single image. Marilyn Monroe's upswirled skirt symbolizes sex. The photograph of two African American athletes raising gloved fists at the 1968 Olympic Games became an icon of Black Power. The World Trade Center attack has become an international symbol of terrorism. Often the icon takes on a meaning of its own, so that fiction can become reality. Although John Wayne never served in the military, his picture is often hung in Pentagon offices because his Hollywood image expresses values embraced by the military.

The image for a recruiting ad (above, left) features a close-up of a soldier in a beret, with the Lincoln Memorial in the background, an emblem of democracy. The Pentagon, an actual target in the terrorist attacks of September 11, would no doubt appear too militaristic. Lincoln, though a wartime leader, was also a symbol of unity, humanity, and wisdom.

In contrast, an advertisement opposing administration foreign policy (previous page, right) uses humor and irony. Osama bin Laden replaces Uncle Sam in a historic recruiting poster. The irony of the image grabs attention. The accompanying text is also ironic, urging readers to support what the writers clearly consider the wrong policies.

Both ads appeared in the same issue of *Rolling Stone*.

TIMING AND DUPLICATION

Timing and duplication can enhance an image's impact and distort perceptions. If two celebrities meet briefly at a crowded special event and photographs of them shaking hands are widely reproduced over several months, it can create the impression they are close friends. The two figures become a single image repeatedly imprinted on the public, few recognizing that they are simply seeing the same moment from different angles. Stalin, Roosevelt, and Churchill only met on a few occasions during the Second World War, but the continual reproduction of photographs of them together helped create the image of the Big Three as a solid alliance against Hitler. Cable news reports of a suicide bombing, a shooting spree, or a car chase will recycle scenes over and over, often creating an exaggerated sense of their significance.

MANIPULATING IMAGES

Just as painters in a king's court often depicted royalty in flattering poses without blemishes, photographers and filmmakers can use lighting, perspective, and contrast to alter perceptions of reality. Short actors can be made to seem taller on screen by lowering cameras or placing taller people in the background. Makeup and lighting can magnify or diminish facial features, improving someone's appearance. Even candid images can be carefully selected to show a subject in a positive light. Portraits and photographs of Kaiser Wilhelm and Joseph Stalin camouflaged the fact that both men had one arm noticeably shorter than the other. Wishing to project power and authority, both leaders wished to disguise their physical disability. Although most Americans knew that President Roosevelt had been stricken with polio, few were aware how severely handicapped he actually was. The media did not release films of him in motion. Photographs and newsreels showed him standing or seated. The fact that he often had to be lifted out of cars or carried up steps was not made public. Although suffering from a painful back injury and Addison's disease, President Kennedy

President Wilson and General Pershing. A retoucher has partially erased a figure walking behind the two famous men, altering the perception of a historical event. Frequently, negative or distracting images are removed from pictures to enhance their effect. © TimePix

projected an image of youth and vigor by being shown in athletic contexts, playing touch football, swimming, or boating.

Photographs and film can be edited, revised, cut, and altered after the fact. A group photo can be reduced to focus on a single person. People and objects can be added or removed to alter the record of actual events. Leon Trotsky was once a powerful Soviet leader, often photographed standing next to Lenin. Wishing to obliterate his rival's role in the Russian Revolution, Stalin had thousands of pictures retouched to remove Trotsky from group photographs.

Today with computer technology, images can be easily digitally removed and inserted. Photographs, motion pictures, and videos now have an increasing power to create their own reality, which may exaggerate, minimize, or distort actual events.

GENDER AND CULTURAL ISSUES

Social change reflected by a clash of traditional gender images. Makeup and jewelry are decidedly feminine, in stark contrast to the masculine hard hat. © SuperStock

Images, like language, affect our perceptions. Historically, images have reflected prevailing attitudes and biases. Words like *policeman, mankind, mailman,* and the universal use of *he* as a single pronoun gave English a distinct sexist stance. Historically, photographs focused on male activities, actions, and behaviors, with women generally appearing as family members or sex objects. Photographs taken of minorities often reflected and generated stereotyped views, so that African Americans were often photographed in subservient, patronizing, or comic roles. Advertising has historically presented women as sexual objects or in a secondary role to men. Automobile ads show men standing next to or driving a car, while women are draped across the hood as a kind of ornament. Soap ads depict men taking showers; women are posed lying in tubs. As gender roles change, popular culture and advertising alter our perceptions of men and women.

PERCEPTION AND ANALYSIS

Our analysis of images is shaped by our perceptions, both personal and cultural. A photograph taken in Iran depicts a male professor lecturing female seminary students from behind a screen. To Western eyes, this image can seem a shocking example of oppression and exclusion. To many Iranians, however, the image of women studying Islam represents inclusion and empowerment.

In Iran, a male professor lectures female students from behind a screen   © Lise Sarfati/Magnum

STRATEGIES | for Analyzing Visual Images

1. **Examine the image holistically.** What does it represent? What is your initial reaction? Does it convey a message?

2. **Consider the nature of the image.** Is this a professional portrait or a candid press shot? Was this video taken at a prepared ceremony or a spontaneous event? Were people, images, or objects deliberately posed to make a statement?

3. **Examine perspective.** Is the subject depicted in close-up or at a distance? Does the subject appear in control of the environment, or does the background dominate the frame?

4. **Analyze contrasts and contexts.** Is the background supportive, neutral, or hostile to the subject? Does the image depict conflict or harmony?

5. **Examine poses and body language of human figures.** How are human figures depicted? What emotions do they seem to express?

6. **Look for bias.** Do you sense that the photographers were trying to manipulate the people or events depicted, casting them in either a favorable or negative light?
7. **Consider the larger context.** Does the image offer a fair representation of a larger event, or is it an isolated exception?
8. **Review the image for possible manipulation.** Could camera angles or retouching have altered what appears to be a record of actual events?
9. **Consider the story the image seems to tell.** What is the thesis of this image? What visual details or symbols help tell the story?

CAPTIONS

Images are frequently accompanied by captions that can shape the way people interpret them. Descriptive or narrative captions place an image in a context, often using verbal connotations to shape perceptions.

For example, the news photograph of a riot in India following the assassination of Indira Gandhi in 1984 (page 188) could be accompanied by a range of captions:

New Delhi, India, 1984
Police attack demonstrators
Police quell riot
Protestors clash with police following Gandhi assassination
Violence erupts in India following Gandhi assassination
Police restore order following Gandhi assassination

Each caption would prompt readers of a magazine or newspaper to view the image in a different light. Captions, in many cases, can be as powerful as the image they describe. Captions can turn photojournalism into propaganda or reveal personal and social biases. In the days following Hurricane Katrina one newspaper ran a photograph of a white couple wading through flood waters in New Orleans with a caption describing them as carrying supplies they "found" in a convenience store. Other newspapers ran similar photographs of blacks with captions describing them as carrying supplies they "looted."

© Jacques Langevin/Corbis Sygma

STRATEGIES | for Analyzing Captions

1. **Examine the photograph before reading the caption.** How do you interpret the image? What can you tell from the setting, perspective, contrast, and visual connotations?
2. **Read the caption carefully.** What does it contain—objective information about time, date, and location or a subjective description or commentary?
3. **Review the use of connotations.** Do the words accompanying the image suggest positive or negative interpretations of what is depicted? Is a small residential building described as a "cottage" or a "shack"? Is a bulldozer "destroying" or "clearing" a forest? Is a politician waving off journalists "leaving a press conference" or "ducking reporters"?
4. **Read the accompanying text.** If the photograph appears in a book, article, or e-mail, read the text to determine whether the author reveals any bias.
5. **Reconsider the validity of the image.** If you detect bias in the caption, consider whether the image has been taken out of context and does not fairly represent what it claims to. Search the Internet for other images of the event or situation to discover alternative views of the subject.

The power that images have can be illustrated by examining a single photograph. See "The History of an Image" on pages 194–199.

GRAPHICS

Graphics are a visual representation of numbers and facts. Like photographs, they are compelling because they communicate a fact in an instant. But like photographs, they can alter perceptions by perspective.

For instance, if a company's sales increase 7 percent in a year, it can be accurately demonstrated in a graph:

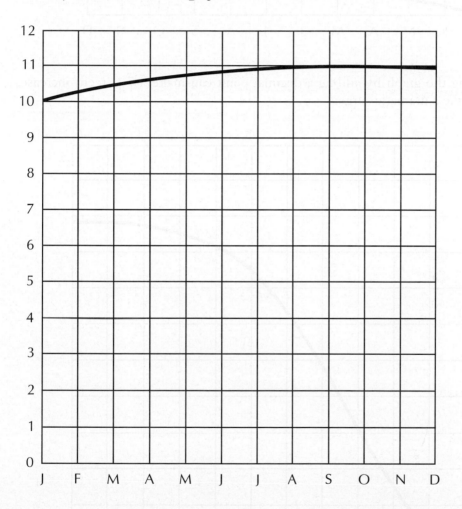

The same 7 percent can look larger by truncating the graph, cutting off the bottom to exaggerate the increase:

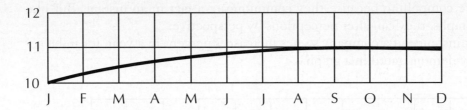

Altering the graph by adding a decimal point can make a 7 percent increase seem like a dramatic surge:

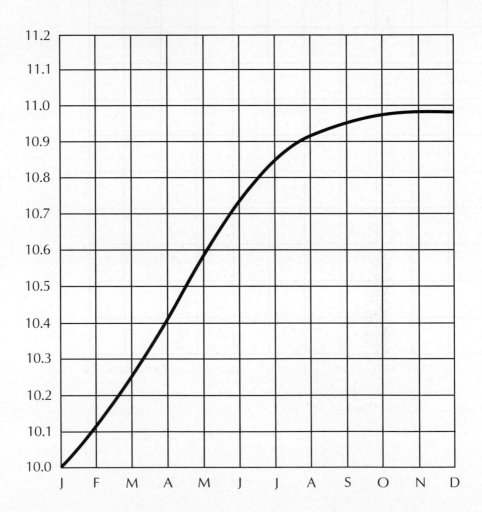

None of these graphs is inaccurate or dishonest, but each alters perceptions for the casual viewer.

An illustration can use a visual illusion to make things seem larger or smaller than they actually are. Suppose a corporation wants to impress investors with the fact that it doubled profits last year from $30 million to $60 million. A simple bar chart demonstrates the difference quite dramatically:

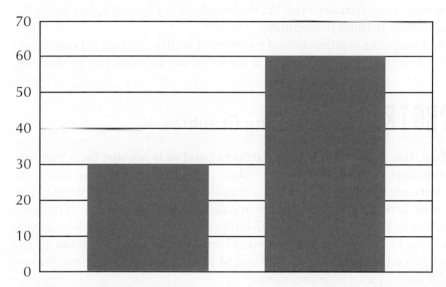

The bar on the right fills twice the space as the bar on the left, accurately showing the relationship between 30 and 60. If the bar, however, is replaced with an image like a money bag, the visual depiction makes a more dramatic impact:

Unlike the one-dimensional bar, the two-dimensional bag of money is enlarged in two directions. The bag representing $60 million is both twice as high and twice as wide as the $30 million bag. If you take the time to look at the numbers on the left side of the chart, you realize the difference is that between 30 and 60. But because the big money bag takes four times, not two times, as much space as the smaller one, it looks four times the size. It would take $240 million to fill this bag. The chart does not lie, the numbers are accurate, but again the visual impression distorts perceptions.

Just as a snapshot captures a brief moment of reality, a visual aid can distort reality by presenting carefully selected data that are accurate but misleading.

STRATEGIES | for Analyzing Graphics

1. **Realize that graphs, charts, and other visual aids are not facts but representations of facts.** Detailed graphics can appear impressive and accurate, but their visuals are based on facts and statistics that require verification.
2. **Examine how facts and numbers are displayed.** Visual aids can magnify or minimize facts. How much is $7 million in sales? Placed on a chart that runs from $1 million to $10 million, $7 million will fill 70 percent of the frame. Placed on a chart that runs from $1 to $100 million, the same amount will fill only 7 percent of the frame.
3. **Determine the source of the visual aid and the numbers or facts it represents.** Visual aids, like statistics, can only be objectively evaluated when you understand their source.
4. **Realize that visual aids, though they communicate at glance, require a dual analysis.** First, you must verify whether the numbers depicted are current, accurate, and meaningful. Second, you must determine if the visual aid distorts the facts, presenting them in such a way to prove a preconceived point of view.

e-writing

Exploring Visual Images Online

The Internet offers a range of sources about analyzing photographs, advertisements, commercials, and film.

1. Using InfoTrac College Edition or one of your library's databases, enter such search terms as *analyzing photographs,*

image analysis, video analysis, manipulating images, and *retouching photographs* to learn more about visual images.

2. Use a search engine, such as Yahoo!, Google, or Alta Vista, enter such terms as *photo analysis, images of women in advertising, political propaganda,* and *graphic design* to locate current sites of interest.

E-Sources

Basic Strategies in Reading Photographs
  **http://nuovo.com/southern-images/
  analyses.html**

Making Sense of Documentary
Photography
  **http://historymatters.gmu.edu/mse/
  Photos/**
Faking Images in Photojournalism
  **http://commfaculty.fullerton.edu/lester/
  writings/faking.html**

THE HISTORY OF AN IMAGE

Iwo Jima, February 23, 1945   © Corbis

If you can get the right moment, the instant, it stays around forever.

Carl Mydans, *Life* photographer

The photograph of the anonymous Marines lifting in poetic unison the flag on Iwo Jima has been read as the final flowering of the collectivist vision of the New Deal, a group of anonymous men unified in a common purpose to restore the nation's glory, the arching flag.

Don Graham, *No Name on the Bullet*

Joe Rosenthal, AP cameraman
© Bettmann/Corbis

First flag raised on Iwo Jima   © Corbis

Capturing the Moment

The most widely reproduced photograph in history is the flag raising on Iwo Jima taken by Joe Rosenthal. On February 19, 1945, thirty thousand U.S. Marines landed on Iwo Jima, a heavily fortified Japanese-held island. The battle lasted thirty-six days and claimed 6,000 American lives. On February 23, 1945, Marines raised a flag atop Mount Suribachi, the highest point on the island. The sight of this flag inspired the men fighting on the beaches. Later that day, it was decided to replace this flag with a larger one.

Joe Rosenthal, an AP photographer, accompanied several Marines and military camera men to the summit. Rosenthal was getting into position when the Marines began to raise the flag. He quickly swung his camera around and snapped a picture. Unsure whether he had taken a usable photo, he asked the Marines to gather around the flagpole for a group picture.

Marines pose for Joe Rosenthal's camera   © Bettmann/Corbis

The Making of an Icon

Rosenthal's film was flown to Guam, where a technician spotted the dramatic picture of the flag raising, cropped off the edges to center the image, and wired it to the United States. Within days the picture appeared on the front pages of hundreds of newspapers. President Roosevelt was impressed by the photograph and ordered millions of copies to boost morale and promote the sale of war bonds. The image appeared on stamps and posters and was recreated in statues.

Confusion and Controversy

The image was so dramatic that it raised doubts. It seemed too perfect to be an action photo of an actual event. A reporter asked Rosenthal, who had no idea the flag raising had become a national sensation, whether he had posed the shot. Thinking the reporter was referring to his group picture (see above), he said yes. A radio program then reported the famous photo was posed, starting a long standing rumor that the image was just a piece of wartime propaganda. For fifty years, Rosenthal repeatedly insisted it was a genuine photograph of a real event.

"Now All Together" War Loan Poster, 1945
© Swim Ink 2, LLC/Corbis

Flag raising statue unveiled in Times Square,
May 1945 © Bettmann/Corbis

Marine Corps War Memorial, dedicated 1954   © William Manning/Corbis

Marines recreate flag raising during Hollywood Christmas Parade, 2004
© Fred Prouser/Reuters/Corbis

Marines re-enact Iwo Jima flag raising, Doss, Texas, 2005 © Bob Daemmrich/Corbis

Historians still debate the validity of the image. Most agree that the photograph, taken by accident, depicts a genuine event, the raising of the second flag on Iwo Jima. It was not the flag that inspired the Marines fighting on the beaches but a replacement that few noticed at the time. There was no question about the bravery and sacrifice of the Marines in the photograph. Of the six flag raisers, three died on Iwo Jima.

The flag raising inspired the USMC memorial and led to many reenactments in subsequent years.

The Other Flag Raising

Throughout the Cold War, textbooks in the United States featured Rosenthal's photograph as a symbol of victory at the end of World War II. Soviet textbooks ran Yevgeny Khaldei's photograph of a Russian solider raising the Red flag over the Reichstag after the fall of Berlin (page 199).

Images snapped in 1/400th of a second can define a war, a nation, and an ideology.

Soviet flag raising over Berlin, May 1945 © Yevgeny Khaldei/Corbis

Soviet photographer Yevgeny Khaldei compares flag raisings, Moscow, 1996 © Peter Turnley/Corbis

14

WRITING WITH VISUALS

Visual images—photographs, diagrams, charts, maps, drawings, and graphs—can enhance written documents. Visually oriented people are more likely to remember what they see than what they read. Pictures can bring a description to life, dramatize a situation, and document an event. Graphs and charts help readers visualize and comprehend data and statistics. Images create immediate impressions that can attract attention, establish a context, and shape reader expectations.

Visuals, however, have to be used carefully. Like the words you choose, any visual image must suit the writing context and not detract from the goal of the document. Visuals that are effective in one document may be inappropriate in another.

 To learn more about writing with visuals through an interactive tutorial, click on "Introduction to Visual Rhetoric" from the main menu of *Comp21*. To select an image to work with, click on "Media Library" and then "Images."

VISUALS AND THE WRITING CONTEXT

Photo software and digital cameras make it very easy to download images or incorporate your own photographs into documents. Effective visuals add depth and rigor to a document. Inappropriate visuals, however, weaken a document by making it appear amateurish and unprofessional. Before including visuals in any document, it is important to consider the writing context or genre.

What is your goal—to inform, persuade, refute an argument, or motivate people to take action? What visuals, if any, will support your purpose?

Who are your readers—what are their needs, attitudes, values, and concerns? Will they respond favorably to your visuals? Images of historical figures, events, or celebrities may provoke different reactions in different people.

Images that some people find amusing may be offensive to others. Will they understand how the images support your text or comprehend the meaning of your graphs or charts?

What is the discipline or situation? Engineers, contractors, and architects will demand far more precise plans or drawings of a proposed building than the general public. Historians and political scientists scrutinize photographs of historical events for signs of bias. Journalists may question the sources of your images. Professors in such subjects as philosophy and literature that stress the written word may find the presence of images in college papers distracting and unprofessional.

What is the nature of the document? An ad for a sports car or a fund-raising e-mail for a charity has to communicate at a glance with a striking and memorable image. A formal research paper or business report may be expected to follow specific guidelines and standards in presenting visuals. Review sample documents to determine what, if any, visuals are considered appropriate.

THE ROLE OF VISUALS

Visuals serve specific purposes. **Design features,** such as photographs, decorative borders, stylistic lettering, logos, and symbols, can identify a subject, idea, or organization, set a tone or mood, and prepare readers to view information in a specific context. A website titled "Famous African Americans," featuring images of W. E. B. Dubois, Martin Luther King, and Thurgood Marshall, instantly creates a different impression and set of expectations than one displaying pictures of Oprah, Beyonce, and Chris Rock. A brochure about homelessness, containing pictures of church volunteers distributing food baskets, immediately states a different purpose and approach than one showing activists marching on city hall. The Sony Corporation uses a colorful image of a young woman using a laptop on its Consumer Electronics website (next page, top) to sell products to the general public. The same company features a world map and gridlike boxes on its Global Headquarters website (next page, bottom) to establish a formal, business-like image.

- Design features are essential in web pages, posters, brochures, ads, newsletters, promotional material, and product packaging.
- Design features in college papers and formal business reports, which are expected to communicate through substance rather than image, are generally limited to text decisions, such as fonts, spacing, and margins. Such visual elements as decorative borders and elaborate logos are avoided.

Sony Consumer Electronics website   © 2006 Sony Corporation of America.

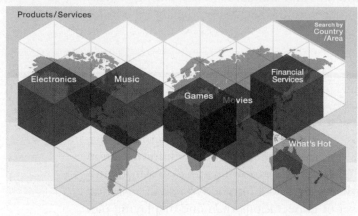

Sony Global Headquarters website   © 2006 Sony Corporation of America.

- Design features should match the tone and style of the document's level of diction and connotation.

General illustrations and attention-getters, such as a striking image, graph, or photograph, can serve to attract attention and illustrate an idea. They often appear without captions in popular magazines, promotional literature, and websites. The student paper "Why They Hate Us" (pages 595–596) uses a photograph of flag burning to identify the topic. The paper itself does not refer to the image explicitly. It serves only to attract attention and reinforce the title. The photograph of Hurricane Katrina victims outside the Superdome (page 203) would provide a gripping image for a fund-raising brochure, magazine cover, or website.

- Illustrations and attention-getters have to be chosen carefully to elicit the response you want. Avoid images that may be controversial, offensive, or confusing.
- If you present illustrations without a caption, make sure that they create the impression you intend. Captions can guide how readers see the image.
- Attention-getters are rarely used in formal academic papers or business reports. Often they are only used as cover art for major documents and are generally conservative in nature. A hundred-page proposal to rehabilitate a college stadium might display a photograph of the existing building or an architect's drawing of the completed restoration on its cover.

Specific illustrations document a specific event or illustrate a particular example. A homeowner filing a flood insurance claim could include a photograph (top right) to document the extent of the damage. A city engineering report might use an aerial photograph of a neighborhood (bottom right) to demonstrate the extent of flood damage.

The photograph on page 497 illustrates a specific step in a process. Graphs, bar charts, and pie charts can highlight important facts and numbers that may be hard to appreciate when expressed in text alone.

■ Specific illustrations are generally consecutively numbered and captioned. Formal reports may only number exhibits or label images with factual details, such as time, place, and location. Informal documents, such as promotional brochures, might use subjective captions to create positive or negative impressions.

■ Specific illustrations are referred to by number or caption to connect them to the text:

New Orleans, September 6, 2005
© Barbara Davidson/Dallas Morning News/Corbis

New Orleans, September 4, 2005   © David J. Phillip/Pool/Reuters/Corbis

Last year sales fell dramatically in all sectors (fig. 6).
Kuwait's oil exports increased greatly last year (see World Oil Exports, 2005).

■ Specific illustrations should clearly represent what is stated in the text. Avoid images that may be controversial, distracting, or subject to varying interpretations. Graphs and charts should be suited to the audience. A report on global warming prepared by scientists at the Environmental Protection Agency may contain complex diagrams that would not be suited for a news magazine or high school textbook.

■ Specific illustrations may require exact details about the time, date, and location of a photograph. For engineers investigating the failure of the levees in New Orleans, photographs of flood waters moving through a neighborhood may be useless unless they can establish a timeline of events. To provide evidence, these photographs would require accurate times and locations. Astronomers' images may have to include the time, date, and type of camera and telescope used to photograph the surface of Mars. A medical journal showing a series of CAT scans documenting a patient's recovery would have to include dates and information about the imaging equipment used to provide accurate data.

It is important to explain the source of images to establish credibility. A report about UFOs that includes images of strange objects flying over a city would gain authority if the pictures come from NASA or the United States Air Force.

■ Documents using specific illustrations often have to follow professional formats of captioning, lettering, or documentation. Many disciplines have style manuals dictating how illustrations should appear in documents. If no manuals exist, follow examples found in professional journals and official reports.

New Orleans Superdome, September 1, 2005   © Michael Ainsworth/Dallas Morning News/Corbis

The kind of visuals you include in a document or presentation depend on your purpose. An ad, website, or newsletter might contain only visual elements to create eye appeal and establish a style or tone for the message. A biology research paper may contain only specific visuals, such as charts and microscopic photographs of cells. A sales brochure for a luxury car, however, might use a striking general illustration on the cover to grab attention, design features to establish and reinforce a mood of style and class, and specific illustrations of leather seats, wood paneling, and a high performance engine to emphasize particular features.

TYPES OF VISUALS

Photographs

Photographs can be compelling support provided they suit the document's context. The picture of the hurricane victims at the Superdome (p. 204) captures the human drama of an actual event. It would make a powerful image for a fund-raising brochure, a Red Cross website, an article in *Time* or *Newsweek*, or a book cover. It would not be suited for a report arguing that the government responded appropriately to the disaster or some kinds of academic papers. Photographs can highlight a specific person, object, or location or provide readers with a "big picture" view. Photographs can capture events as they happen or preserve images carefully posed for the camera.

For all their power, photographs have limitations. They can overemphasize minor events. A dramatic news photo of a demonstration that results in a dozen arrests and a few injuries may be splashed across the front pages of newspapers, while a riot that killed hundreds goes unnoticed because no cameras recorded the events. As Chapter 13 points out, they can be misleading in other ways, as well.

STRATEGIES | for Using Photographs

1. **Select photographs from reliable sources.** Books, news magazines, newspapers, news services, and stock photo websites provide visuals suited for academic and professional writing. Stock photo services often include specific details about photographs, including date, location, and event. *Avoid using visuals that cannot be verified.*

2. **Include photographs that serve specific purposes.** Avoid including images that do not serve to set a tone, illustrate a general idea, attract attention, or document a particular point. You may find interesting and striking images, but if they do clearly relate to your subject, they will confuse or distract readers.
3. **Let the context of the document guide your selection.** Keep your goal, readers, and discipline in mind when you include images.
4. **Avoid cluttering a document with too many images.** Do not let photographs overwhelm or distract from the text. Images should support the writing. You can integrate specific illustrations within the text and supply additional images in an appendix, CD, or supporting website.
5. **Link specific illustrations to text.** To prevent confusion, direct readers to look at specific images by referring to them in the text by figure number, caption, or page number.
6. **Include sources of photographs.** Photographs will have greater impact if sources, dates, and locations are offered in captions or a reference page. Readers may question the validity of images if they are presented without sources.

Tables, Graphs, and Charts

Tables, graphs, and charts express numbers, facts, or statistics in visual form. They can be used to dramatize facts or simply to help people comprehend and remember data. **Tables** present numbers in columns for easy reading and reference. Important tables, such as delivery schedules or price lists, can be placed on a separate page in large type so that they can be detached, scanned, or copied for readers to use as reference tools.

QUARTERLY SALES FIGURES (IN MILLIONS)		
	VHS	DVD
New York	2.5	1.3
Chicago	1.2	1.2
Los Angeles	3.0	2.5

Line graphs show changing numbers over time. They can help readers review and appreciate the rise and fall of sales, prices, cases of flu, homicides, or

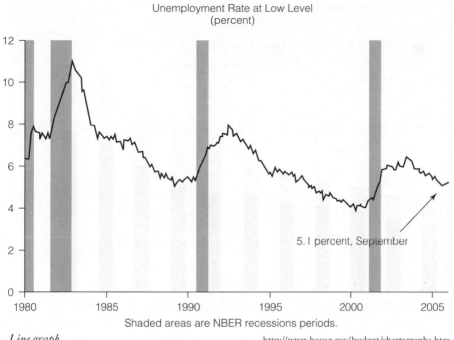

Unemployment Rate at Low Level
(percent)

5.1 percent, September

Shaded areas are NBER recessions periods.

Line graph   http://www.house.gov/budget/chartsgraphs.htm

the earth's temperature over days, weeks, months, or years. Timelines should be clearly presented. Line graphs that include anomalies might need explanations or a footnote to explain a dramatic change that might be misunderstood. A graph showing homicides in Manhattan might have to explain that figures for 2001 include 3,000 victims of the World Trade Center attack.

Bar charts represent data visually by using bars or columns to show differences in values with different heights of bars. Like line graphs, they can show changes over time or comparisons between different topics. A bar chart about high school graduation rates could reflect a ten year period of a single city or last year's statistics for ten different cities. Bars or columns can be coded to show subdivisions.

Pie charts show percentages of a whole by slicing a circle into shaded or colored sections. A pie chart could break immigrants down by their nation of origin, a company's sales by product, or an investor's portfolio by stock type. Because they represent a breakdown of a single subject at one time, more than one chart has to be used to compare different subjects or demonstrate a change over time.

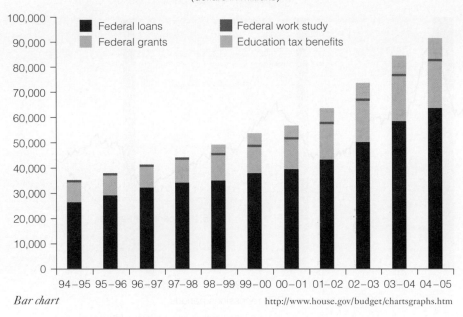

Bar chart

http://www.house.gov/budget/chartsgraphs.htm

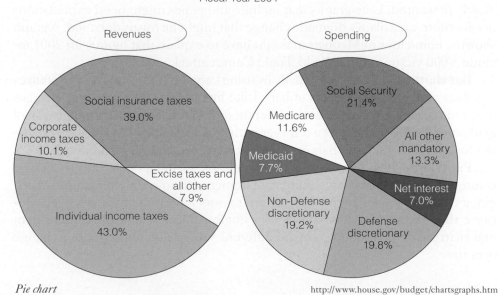

Pie chart

http://www.house.gov/budget/chartsgraphs.htm

STRATEGIES | for Using Tables, Graphs, and Charts

1. **Select tables, graphs, and charts from reliable sources.** Visuals are based on numbers. Statistics can be taken out of context, poorly collected, misinterpreted, or distorted. Use visuals from major news services, government agencies, and nonpartisan organizations.

2. **Use visuals your readers will be able to understand and refer to.** Avoid including overly detailed or complex charts or graphs that require specialized knowledge or training. You may use simplified visuals in the main document for general readers and present more complex visuals in an appendix or supporting website for readers requiring greater detail.

3. **Present tables, charts, and graphs in a readable format.** Avoid shrinking visuals to a size that makes them difficult to see. To prevent large scale charts and graphs from interrupting text, consider placing them in an appendix.

4. **Include sources.** Readers will only accept visuals as accurate if they know where they came from. You can note a graph's source, date, and other important information in a caption or source list.

5. **Link specific illustrations to text.** To prevent confusion, direct readers to look at specific images by referring to them in the text by number, caption, or page number.

6. **Analyze visuals for bias.** Truncated and two-dimensional graphs (see pages 189–191) can be used to distort, inflate, and dramatize numbers. Avoid using or creating graphs and charts that try to maximize or minimize numbers.

CAPTIONS

Captions that accompany visuals can present objective identifications or make subjective statements, guiding reader interpretations.

The photograph of the hurricane victims outside the Superdome (p. 204) could be accompanied by an objective description that simply labels the image:

Superdome, New Orleans, September 1, 2005
Hurricane Katrina victims outside New Orleans Superdome

Subjective captions present readers with an implication of the photograph's meaning:

> *Five days after Hurricane Katrina, victims await rescue*
> *Minority victims crowd outside Superdome*

Captions like these contain descriptive or narrative elements suggesting a delayed or racially biased response to the disaster.

A chart showing a nine percent increase in a company's sales can be labeled with an objective caption:

> *Ford sales, 2006*
> *Ford sales rise 9 percent in 2006*

Subjective captions use connotations to maximize or minimize numbers:

> *Ford sales soar 9 percent in 2006*
> *Ford sales rise less than 10 percent in 2006*

STRATEGIES | for Writing Captions

1. **Use captions for specific illustrations to connect images to the text.**
2. **Make sure captions connect to the text.** Avoid mentioning names, places, or events in the caption that are not explained in the text.
3. **Identify people in photographs from left to right.**
4. **Make sure the tone, style, and wording of captions suit the writing context.** A sales brochure may use colorful language to create favorable impressions of a chart or photograph. Use objective, neutral language in college papers and professional documents.

UNDERSTANDING FAIR USE

Nearly all visual aids you may find in print or online are probably copyrighted and cannot be reproduced or distributed without permission. The concept of fair use allows college students to include a photograph or chart in a research paper as long as the source is identified. However, the same image cannot be used in a website, brochure, ad, packaging, mass e-mail, T-shirt, or poster without permission.

Stock photo and clip art services offer images in the public domain and are therefore available for wider use.

STRATEGIES | for Using Visuals in College Writing

1. **Review the assignment to see whether visuals will enhance your paper.** A research paper in biology, engineering, business, or economics might demand extensive use of visual aids. In other courses, visuals may be nonessential but helpful. In a literature or political science course, visuals may be irrelevant.
2. **Select visuals that support specific points in your paper.** Limit use of attention-getters and general illustrations.
3. **Let your thesis guide your use of visuals.** Visuals should provide illustrations that explain or provide evidence for important points in your paper. Do not include photographs just because they are striking or interesting. Like quotations, visuals should directly support your thesis.
4. **Consider your method of development.** A narrative paper may benefit from a timeline or line graph. Comparisons can be illustrated with tables and bar charts. Diagrams, photographs, and maps can explain a process.
5. **Use objective captions and references to link visuals to your text.** Freestanding images can be distracting or confusing. Consecutively number each image and use parenthetical notes to link them to your text:

    Between 1986 and 2005 the price of oil fluctuated greatly (fig. 12).

6. **Select appropriate sizes.** Simple charts and photographs may be shrunk to the size of an oversized postage stamp and wrapped with text to create a readable text. Detailed photographs, maps, and intricate charts may require a full page to be readable.
7. **Don't allow visuals to overwhelm the text.** If you have a large number of images, especially ones requiring a full page, consider placing some or all of them in an appendix.
8. **Document sources of visuals or information you use to create visuals.** Like quotations, visuals from other sources should be documented. If you create your own graphs or charts, indicate the source for the numbers or statistics they represent. Captions should list sources (see photographs in Chapter 13).
9. **Budget your time carefully.** Locating or creating visuals can be time-consuming. Determine whether your time would be better spent revising and editing your paper.

e-writing

Exploring Images Online

You can use the Internet to learn more about using visuals in writing.

1. Using a search engine, such as Yahoo!, Google, or Alta Vista, enter such terms as *using visuals, locating photographs, designing tables and charts, writing with visuals,* or *using visuals in college writing* to locate current sites of interest.

2. Search websites of news magazines, such as *Time* and *Newsweek*, and cable news channels, such as CNN and FOX, to see how they use visuals in new stories. Can you detect biases in either the images that are selected or their captions?

E-Sources

Stock photo services
   http://www.FotoSearch.com
   http://www.corbis.com
   http://www.indexstock.com
Some Tips for Writing Captions
   **http://www.nyu.edu/classes/
   copyXediting/captions.html**

15

BUSINESS AND PROFESSIONAL WRITING

> You won't work in a vacuum: You'll
> work with and through other people,
> and you'll have to communicate with
> them. Without the ability to inform,
> you will not be successful.
>
> —Thomas Pearsall and
> Donald Cunningham

WHAT IS BUSINESS AND PROFESSIONAL WRITING?

Once you graduate and enter the workforce, you will communicate with others through a variety of documents, ranging from brief e-mail notes to lengthy reports and proposals. Although executives, managers, scientists, and professionals follow the basic rules of English grammar, there are significant differences between academic and business writing.

Business writing occurs in a specific context.   The tone, style, diction, and format of business and professional documents are greatly shaped by the history of the organization, the discipline, the reader, extended audience, and topic. The writing style suited for an ad agency or interior decorator might be considered unprofessional in a law or accounting firm. A branch of the navy facing budget cuts may be more defensive about justifying expenditures than a unit favored by Congress to develop new weapon systems. A corporation that has experienced strikes and layoffs will address employees differently than a firm with good labor relations.

■ When you write, you have to consider the nature of your career, the image and history of the organization, your superiors' concerns, and the needs and expectations of your readers.

Business writing focuses on specific readers.   In college you write for professors in specific disciplines. You do not have to worry about whether they will understand specialized terms or be familiar with background information on the subject. In addition, professors are expected to be objective readers, evaluating your work on the basis of its presentation rather than its point of view.

■ In business writing you may find yourself addressing people with limited knowledge of your particular field or readers hostile to your ideas or the organization you represent. Readers will not be objective. They may have fixed views and resist your recommendations.

Business writing emphasizes results.   College writing demonstrates skills. Your professors are less interested in your opinions and more concerned about the way you develop and support your thesis. In an algebra class, for instance, the numbers are abstract. Getting the right answer is less important than demonstrating the ability to solve problems. In business and industry, ideas and answers mean money.

■ You are seeking not simply to demonstrate your knowledge but to urge readers to accept your recommendations, purchase your products, or accept your proposals. You will be asking people to invest large sums of money or make commitments involving substantial resources.

Business writing is sensitive to legal implications.   Letters, e-mails, reports, and contracts can become legal documents. Writers must be careful to avoid making statements they cannot support. A poorly worded phrase, even a grammar or typographical error, can place writers in legal jeopardy, exposing them and their employers to litigation.

Business writing is carefully designed.   Business documents are carefully designed to follow professional standards and match an organization's image. Writers must consider how the document will look. Law firms, banks, government agencies, and accounting firms will use traditional letterheads, margins, and fonts. Ad agencies, rock radio stations, and hair salons may use colorful designs to attract attention and project a unique image. In addition, business writers use bold headings, white space, and bulleted points to highlight important ideas and help readers follow their train of thought.

Business writing represents the views of others.   In college your papers are individual creations and can express personal views, but in your career you will likely work as a representative of a corporation, organization, partnership, or agency.

- Never write anything that would be unacceptable to your employer.
- Avoid making promises or commitments unless you know that your organization or employer will honor them.
- Never use official stationery for personal letters.

E-MAIL

Today almost every job uses e-mail to communicate. Some people confuse e-mail with "instant messages" or chat room conversations. They write and answer e-mail without thinking, producing a stream of tangled ideas, missing details, grammar errors, and inappropriate comments. E-mail, like any kind of writing, takes thought and planning to be effective.

STRATEGIES | for Writing E-mail

1. **Realize that e-mail is *real mail*.** E-mail can be stored, distributed, and printed. Unlike a note or memo that can be retrieved or corrected, e-mail, once sent, becomes permanent. *Never send e-mail when you are tired or angry. Avoid sending messages you will later regret.*
2. **Follow the prewriting, drafting, revising, and editing strategies you would use in writing a paper document.** Don't let an e-mail message simply record whatever comes into your head. E-mail should have a clear purpose and an easy-to-follow organization. Plan before you write.
3. **Understand what messages *should not* be expressed in e-mail.** E-mail is considered appropriate for short, informative messages. Do not attempt to send a fifteen-page report by e-mail, though it might be sent as an attachment. Do not send personal or sensitive information by e-mail. E-mail is seen as too informal and too public for confidential correspondence.

4. **Respond to e-mail carefully.** Often e-mail messages will list multiple readers. Before sending a reply, determine whether you want everyone or just a few people to see your response.

5. **Make sure you use the correct e-mail address.** E-mail addresses can be complicated and oddly spelled. Often names are shortened or reversed. Donald Peterson might appear as "donald.peterson," "dpeterson," or "petersond." Double-check addresses.

6. **Clearly label your e-mail in the Subject Line.** Spam—unwanted e-mail messages—use misleading headings such as "Following your request" or "next week's conference" to grab attention. To prevent your e-mail from being overlooked or deleted before it is read, use specific identifying details in the subject such as "RE: April 19th health insurance reminder" or "Smithkin Supplies Annual Audit."

7. **Include your reader's full name and the date in your inside address.**

8. **Keep e-mail direct and concise.** People expect e-mail to be brief and easy to read. Avoid complicated sentences and long paragraphs. Use short paragraphs and bulleted or numbered points to increase readability.

9. **End the e-mail with a clear summary, request, or direction.**
   - Summarize important points.
   - If you are asking for information or help, clearly state what you need, when you need it, and how you can be reached.
   - If you want readers to take action, provide clear directions.

10. **Ask readers for an acknowledgement if you want to make sure they received your message.**

11. **Review, edit, and double-check e-mail before sending.** Check your spelling, addresses, names, prices, or figures for accuracy. Read your e-mail aloud to catch missing words, illogical statements, confusing sentences, or awkward phrases.

12. **Print hard copies of important e-mail for future reference.**

Sample E-mail

January 30, 2006
From: John Rio
To: Sales Staff
RE: Expense Account Reports

To all sales staff:

As of March 1, 2006, Pacific Mutual will no longer provide sales representatives with company cars or expense accounts. Instead, sales representatives will be given a flat monthly grant to cover office, travel, and vehicle expenses:

Inside Sales Reps $250 per month

District Sales Reps $500 per month

Regional Sales Reps $750 per month

This policy affects only regular monthly expenses. Pacific Mutual will continue to pay all expenses for those attending regional and national sales conventions.

If you have any questions about the new policy, please contact me at Ext. 7689.

John Rio

RESUMES AND COVER LETTERS

Perhaps the first business documents you will have to produce are a résumé and cover or application letter. Before undertaking this often frustrating task, it is important to understand what a résumé is:

A résumé is a ten-second advertisement. Research has revealed that the average executive spends about ten seconds skimming a résumé before rejecting it or setting it aside for further review. A résumé is not a list of every job you have had or a description of your ultimate goal in life—it is an ad presenting facts and accomplishments relevant to a specific position.

The goal of a résumé is to secure an interview, not a job.   Few, if any applicants, are hired solely on the basis of a one- or two-page document. The goal of a résumé is simply to generate enough interest in the applicant to prompt the employer to schedule an interview. Present only the highlights of your career and education.

Applicants usually benefit from having more than one résumé.   Just as companies design different advertisements to market the same product to different consumers, you may have three or four résumés. An accounting major may have one résumé emphasizing auditing expertise and another stressing tax experience. Because they are read quickly, highly targeted résumés addressing a single job are more effective than general statements.

STRATEGIES | for Writing Résumés

1. **Understand that there are no absolute rules in writing effective résumés—only guidelines.** You may have heard that a résumé must be only one page, that it is useless to list hobbies, or that you should never mention your age. Because there is such a range of jobs and applicants, there are instances in which "breaking" the rules may be the only effective way of getting attention. An actor's résumé is usually accompanied by a photograph. A restaurant manager once secured an interview by designing a résumé in the form of a menu.

2. **Focus your résumé by carefully reading the want ad or job description.** Note the key requirements employers seek and highlight those skills. Pay attention to key words and phrases and determine whether you can repeat them in your résumé.

3. **Include your full name, address, telephone number with area code, or e-mail address.** If you are in the process of moving, you can list two addresses.

4. **Provide a clear, objective statement describing the job you seek.** Avoid using general statements, such as "a position making use of my skills and abilities," or one that lists too many job titles: "Sales Manager/Marketing Manager/Advertising Director." Broad objectives make applicants appear indecisive or desperate. It is better to have specific statements:

   A position in publishing design making use of my experience in graphics
   Assistant Sales Manager

5. **Use a short *summary* or *overview* statement to encapsulate key elements in your background.** A short paragraph describing your background, goals, and skills can personalize a résumé. It can encourage the reader to view your experience in a certain light, showing how seemingly unrelated jobs or education would be relevant to the job you seek:

Textbook Sales
Ten years experience in textbook sales. Increased territory 25 percent in eighteen months. Introduced online marketing. Reduced service budget 18 percent in first six months. Received extensive sales training as agent for New York Life.

Security Consultant
- FBI agent 1985–2000
- Conducted computer fraud investigations for Banker's Life, General Motors Credit Corporation, Miller Brewing, and Westwood Industries.
- Trained New York City detectives in online investigative methods.

You may find it easier to write the summary last, after you have identified your key strengths.

6. **Open your résumé with your strongest and most recent credentials.** If you have professional experience, you may find it more effective to highlight your recent job than to emphasize a new degree. If you are unsure which area to highlight, prepare two résumés, one emphasizing experience and the other stressing education. You can use both résumés, selecting the version that best matches a particular job. Before applying for a number of positions, send out a small number of résumés to identify which version produces the best results.

7. **Arrange education and experience chronologically, beginning with the most recent.**

8. **If you are a recent graduate with little professional experience, list significant courses, awards, grade point averages, and honors.** If you have worked as an intern or completed clinical work, place this under the heading Experience rather than Education:

EXPERIENCE   WESTERN SOFTWARE, San Diego, CA
Intern in marketing program directly assisting two managers introducing new consumer products.
- Wrote two sales brochures for national distribution.
- Edited text of promotional video.
- Attended national sales seminars.

9. **Stress individual accomplishments.** Briefly list dates of employment, title, and general job description; then provide examples of specific skills and experiences. Use action verbs to give your résumé a sense of action:

2005– Sales Manager in Miami's third largest book store, responsible for hiring, training, purchasing, and promotions.
- Lowered employee turnover 25 percent in first year.
- Redesigned promotions to increase point of purchase stationery supplies from $25,000 to $87,500 in first year.
- Organized book signing receptions drawing national media coverage.

10. **List training seminars, volunteer work, hobbies, and military service only if directly related to the position.** A résumé is a fact sheet listing your key skills and experiences. Secondary information can be included in a cover letter or mentioned at a job interview.

Professional Résumé

JOHN BENJAMIN
537 MEADOW LANE
SAN FRANCISCO, CA 94103
(415) 879-8989
jbenjamin@sfnet.com

OBJECTIVE	CONTROLLER	Goal
SUMMARY	More than five years experience as controller of firm with $50 million in sales. Adept at financial reporting, payroll, benefits, insurance. Highly skilled in managing personnel expenditures.	Summary blends experience
EXPERIENCE 2000–Present	FISHERMAN'S MUTUAL INSURANCE COMPANY, San Francisco, CA
Controller responsible for accounts receivable and payable, finance reports, quarterly and annual statements, payroll and benefits, and insurance purchasing. • Created new payroll system, reducing costs 15%. • Developed employee benefits manual. • Negotiated with HMO to maintain level of benefits while achieving 18% savings in era of increasing premiums. • Selected by president to purchase computer and all software for accounting and billing services. • Wrote computer program to centralize personnel files.	Verb phrases highlight specific accomplishments
1993–2000	CITY OF BODEGA BAY, Bodega Bay, CA
<u>Personnel and Safety Director</u> directed by mayor and city council to serve as first safety director of personnel in Bodega Bay. Supervised payroll operations, risk management, and insurance. • Served on team negotiating contracts with Teamsters, firefighter, and police unions. • Oversaw all city insurance programs, including life, health, liability, and casualty. • Established self-insured health program resulting in first-year savings of $100,000.	
1988–1993	BODEGA BAY COMPANY, Bodega Bay, CA
<u>Industrial Engineering and Human Resources Director</u> responsible for risk management, job classification, and training in firm with 2,000 employees. • Created videotape training series, reducing accident rate 22% in six months. • Worked directly with president, controller, and auditing team to centralize records.	Less space devoted to early experience
EDUCATION	SAN FRANCISCO STATE UNIVERSITY
BS in Business Administration, 1988	Education listed last

References Available on Request

Student Résumé Including Previous Experience

MARIA SANCHEZ
1732 St. Charles Avenue
New Orleans, LA 70130
(504) 455-5767
sanchezm@delgado.edu

Goal

OBJECTIVE

Management position in retail printing with opportunities for advancement

Overview blends education and previous experience

OVERVIEW

Five years experience in retail sales management. Fully familiar with state-of-the-art printing equipment and methods. Proven ability to lower overhead and build customer relations.
• Certified to service all Xerox copiers.

Most recent credential

EDUCATION

DELGADO COMMUNITY COLLEGE, New Orleans, LA
Associate Degree, Printing and Publishing, 2006
Completed courses in graphic design, editing, high speed printing, and equipment repair.
• Attended Quadgraphics seminar.
• Assisted in design and publication of college newspaper.

Corporate training

XEROX, New Orleans, LA
Completed service training program, 2004.

EXPERIENCE
2004–

FAST-PRINT, New Orleans, LA
Retail Sales Work twenty hours a week assisting manager in counter sales, customer relations, printing, and inventory.

Current student job

1999–2004

CRESCENT CITY MUSIC, New Orleans, LA
Manager directly responsible for retail record outlet with annual gross sales of $1.8 million.
• Reduced operating costs 15% first year.
• Hired and trained sales staff.
• Prepared all financial statements.
• Developed advertising plan generating 35% increase in sales in first month.

Previous job description emphasizing skills related to desired job

HONORS

Deans List, 2004, 2005, 2006

References and Transcript Available

COVER LETTERS

Cover letters can be as important as the résumés they introduce. Résumés submitted without letters are often dismissed by employers because they assume that applicants who do not take the time to address them personally are not serious. Résumés tend to be rather cold lists of facts; cover letters allow applicants to present themselves in a more personalized way. The letter allows applicants to counter possible employer objections by explaining a job change, a period of unemployment, or a lack of formal education.

STRATEGIES | for Writing Cover Letters

In most instances, cover letters are short sales letters using standard business letter formats.

1. **Avoid beginning a cover letter with a simple announcement:**

   Dear Sir or Madam:
   This letter is to apply for the job of controller advertised in the *San Francisco Chronicle* last week. . . .

2. **Open letters on a strong point emphasizing skills or experiences:**

   Dear Sir or Madam:
   In the last two years I opened fifty-eight new accounts, increasing sales by nearly $800,000.

3. **Use the letter to include information not listed on the résumé.** Volunteer work, high school experiences, or travel that might not be suited to a résumé can appear in the letter—if they are career related.

4. **Refer to the résumé, indicating how it documents your skills and abilities.**

5. **End the letter with a brief summary of notable skills and experiences and a request for an interview.** To be more assertive, state that you will call the employer in two or three days to schedule an appointment.

Letter Responding to Personal Referral

JOHN BENJAMIN
537 MEADOW LANE
SAN FRANCISCO, CA 94103
(415) 879-8989
jbenjamin@sfnet.com

January 1, 2006

Melanie Wong
Pacific Marine Manufacturing
150 Pacific Street
San Francisco, California 94133

Dear Ms. Wong:

Introduction mentions related job not listed in résumé

Ted Fitzgerald mentioned that Pacific Marine is seeking a new controller. In the past six years I have served as controller for a $50 million insurance firm in San Francisco. As you know, Fisherman's Mutual specializes in the insurance needs of commercial boat owners and suppliers. Having begun my career at West Coast Products as a cost estimator, I am fully familiar with the basics of boat building.

Refers to résumé

During the past ten years, I have established a solid record of lowering benefit costs. As my résumé shows, I was able to save the City of Bodega Bay $100,000 in one year by creating a self-insured health program.

Close

Given my experience as a controller, my background in the boat business, and my extensive knowledge of benefits, I believe I would be a valuable asset to Pacific Marine.

I would be interested in discussing my background with you at your convenience. I can be reached at (415) 879-8989.

Sincerely yours,

John Benjamin

Letter Responding to Job Announcement

MARIA SANCHEZ
1732 St. Charles Avenue
New Orleans, LA 70130
(504) 455-5767
sanchezm@delgado.edu

May 24, 2006

Bayou Printing
1500 Magazine Street
New Orleans, LA 70130

RE: Manager position Faxed to Delgado Placement Office
    May 18, 2006   *Identifies position*

Dear Sir or Madam:

This month I will be graduating from Delgado Community College with an associate degree in printing and publishing. As my résumé shows, I have been trained in state-of-the-art publishing and equipment repair. I received additional training in printing at Quadgraphics and Xerox.   *Opens with strong point* / *Refers to résumé*

Before choosing printing and publishing as a career, I managed one of New Orleans's high volume record stores. I hired, trained, and supervised thirty employees. In addition to decreasing turnover, I lowered overhead and increased sales.   *Explains relevance of previous experience*

Given my training in state-of-the-art publishing and my extensive background in retail sales, I think I would be an effective store manager. I would appreciate the opportunity of meeting with you to discuss my abilities at your convenience. I can be reached at (504) 455-5767.   *Close and request for interview*

Sincerely yours,

Maria Sanchez

Putting Your Résumé to Work

Like any advertisement, a résumé is only effective if it reaches the appropriate reader. Don't limit your job search to obvious sources such as the want ads or Internet listings. Talk with instructors in your major courses, contact local recruiters and employment agencies, and investigate professional organizations for networking leads.

BUSINESS AND PROFESSIONAL REPORTS

Business and professional reports differ from academic research papers in purpose and format. Scholarly writing stresses intellectual growth and reflection. A research paper may discuss background details in depth, explore alternative theories, and speculate about the significance of people, historical events, scientific discoveries, or works of art. Documentation is important to distinguish the writer's ideas from outside sources.

In contrast, business writing is result oriented. Although it may stem from scholarly research, the information is presented to guide actions and decisions. The thesis or recommendation is clearly stated. Less attention is paid to formal documentation.

Business reports emphasize results rather than reflection. The thesis or main idea is often stated at the very opening of the report with little or no introduction.

Business reports are terse but thorough. Academic writers may insert interesting asides or references because their goal is to teach. Business writers, however, focus on specific tasks and restrict their commentary to practical details.

Business reports use subtitles. Unlike research papers, which are generally double-spaced and presented with few internal subtitles, business reports contain subtitles for easy reading. Because they may be presented to professionals seeking specific information, business reports serve as reference sources. Readers may not be interested in reading the entire report but only in locating specific facts or numbers.

Business reports may follow industry or corporate formats. In academics, nearly all research papers follow common standards. English students use the Modern Language Association (MLA) style. Psychology and sociology students follow standards set by the American Psychological Association (APA).

But in many jobs, you will be expected to use formats used in a particular industry, corporation, or division.

■ If you are unsure what a report should look like, request samples to use as models.
■ Before turning in a fifty-page proposal only to discover you have used an incorrect format, show a rough draft to your supervisor.
■ Ask experienced employees for advice and samples of their work.

Business reports use informal documentation.   Scientific research reports will include a works cited page, whereas most managers use simple parenthetical notes. Business writers frequently paraphrase the work of others without endnotes. Although readers may not evaluate your use of documentation, it is important to identify those sources that support your point of view.

Business reports are usually written for multiple readers.   Reports are often submitted to boards, committees, employees, regulators, or shareholders. They may have to address the needs and concerns of dozens of experts in different fields. They may be distributed by mail, reviewed by the media, or posted on the Internet.

The extended audience is very important. Consider how your comments will be viewed out of context. Avoid making statements that may appear unprofessional or insensitive to others.

Business reports are often the product of collaborative writing.   In many instances you will have to work with others to produce a report. See Strategies for Collaborative Writing (pages 236–237).

Sample Business Report

RECOMMENDATIONS FOR SELECTION OF CONTRACTORS FOR BID
CONSIDERATION FOR RENOVATION OF HISPANIC CULTURAL CENTER

Prepared by
Kim Gonzalez
Selena Dunn
Abraham Perez

Renovation Committee
Hispanic Cultural Center
El Paso, Texas

April 2006

RECOMMENDATIONS FOR SELECTION OF CONTRACTORS FOR BID CONSIDERATION FOR RENOVATION OF HISPANIC CULTURAL CENTER

I. Recommendation of Three Contractors and Summary

The Renovation Committee recommends that the Hispanic Cultural Center approach three contractors for possible bid consideration. The Renovation Committee unanimously rated these firms in order of preference:

1. Felber & Riley
2. Montano Builders
3. Ortega Design

II. Background

In 2004 the Hispanic Cultural Center, a 503(c) non-profit organization, purchased the former First Methodist Church located at 2727 West Elm Street, El Paso, Texas. The property consists of a 125-year-old church with 25,000 square feet of usable space and an attached two story 12,550 square foot addition constructed in 1910.

The mission of the Hispanic Cultural Center is to operate a facility housing a theater for plays and concerts, a library and cultural center, an art gallery, meeting and banquet rooms, and storage.

The current building provides ample space for storage and meetings and serves as an acceptable venue for artistic performances. However, the lack of a modern kitchen and bar service limit banquet operations, a prime income source for the center. Renovation is necessary to increase attendance at concerts, improve banquet and bar income, create an art gallery, and attract patrons and visitors. In addition, the buildings do not contain the wheelchair ramps and elevators needed to meet ADA (Americans with Disabilities Act) requirements.

III. Charge to the Renovation Committee

Following several board meetings and discussions with city and local business leaders, the directors of the Hispanic Cultural Center created the Renovation Committee to begin selecting architectural firms and contractors to initiate a bidding process for renovation.

Due to the large number of firms suggested by the directors, it was determined that the Renovation Committee should review all suggested firms and present to the board a list of no less than three firms for the board to consider. In soliciting information from contractors it was made clear by the committee that these inquiries were for research purposes only and that any offers or requests for bids, reviews, and proposals would have to be approved by the full board of directors.

IV. <u>Evaluation Methods</u>

The Renovation Committee collected the names of eleven building firms suggested by directors at the January and February board meetings:

Architects 2000	Montano Builders
Arco Builders	Odway & Schmitt
Diaz & Wilson	Pfeiffer & DuChamp
Felber & Riley	Ortega Design
Gulf Coast Construction	Rodriguez Design
Lone Star Builders	

In selecting firms for recommendation, the Renovation Committee was guided by directives approved by the board of directors in a motion at the February meeting:

Recommended firms should be experienced in renovation of structures similar to the existing church, understand the unique needs of a cultural center, and demonstrate experience in working with non-profit organizations.

Members strongly advocated selecting a minority-owned firm.

Given the large number of firms, the committee decided to break the selection process into two phases:

Phase One
1. Contact all named firms by telephone to solicit brochures and lists of recent projects.
2. Review firms based on directions by board of directors' criteria and select six firms for further review.

Phase Two

1. Conduct in-depth interviews with principals of each firm and examine corporate profiles.
2. Select three firms to recommend to the Board of Directors for discussion.

V. Phase One

All firms were contacted for telephone interviews during the second week of March. Two firms—Lone Star Builders and Pfeiffer & DuChamp—are involved in the airport expansion and are not seeking new clients for two years.

The Renovation Committee reviewed brochures and other documents from the remaining nine firms. Further telephone requests for information were made in the last week of March. After examining the nine firms, six were selected:

Architects 2000	Montano Builders
Arco Builders	Ortega Design
Felber & Riley	Rodriguez Design

VI. Phase Two

The Renovation Committee requested further documentation from the six firms and scheduled interviews for the first week of April. In one instance a conference telephone interview was conducted because the principal partners were at a convention in Atlanta.

After conducting the interviews, the Renovation Committee met twice to evaluate the six firms. Architects 2000 and Arco Builders were eliminated because their experience is limited to new residential construction. Rodriguez Design is highly experienced in commercial renovations but has never designed a cultural facility or restored a historic building.

The Renovation Committee identified three finalists, and based on further discussions, the contractors are listed in order of preference:

1. Felber & Riley
   This firm has extensive experience in renovating century old structures, including several churches. They are accustomed to working with non-profit and cultural institutions.

Felber & Riley's renovation projects include St. John's Church, the Montez Art Gallery in Fort Worth, and the Jewish Community Center in Austin. Although not certified as a minority contractor, the firm employs several Hispanics in key positions. Mr. Hector Diaz, who helped transform a turn of the century high school into the Montez Art Gallery, has agreed to work with the Hispanic Cultural Center. The firm's experience in redesigning existing structures to serve as cultural venues distinguishes it from the competition.

The Renovation Committee highly recommends Felber & Riley for consideration.

2. Montano Builders
    This firm is a certified minority contractor with extensive experience in new construction. Recent projects include a number of strip malls and warehouses. Montano Builders has served as a subcontractor on three major renovation projects for the City of El Paso, including the Zoo Administration Building and Symphony Hall. The firm has not worked with non-profit organizations and has no experience in designing cultural facilities.

3. Ortega Design
    This fifty-year-old firm is a certified minority contractor with a national reputation for church renovation. It has rebuilt and restored churches in Austin, Dallas, San Diego, Fort Worth, New Orleans, and Kansas City. The Ortega team includes woodworkers from Germany, stained glass makers from Italy, and masons from Mexico. The firm specializes in restoring old churches to their original specifications rather than converting these structures to serve other purposes. Though highly recommended by community leaders, the firm's expertise lies outside the needs of the Hispanic Cultural Center.

VII. Final Considerations

The Renovation Committee limited its search to the eleven firms suggested by the Board of Directors and strongly suggests further investigations be carried out to locate other qualified firms to insure a favorable bid process.

STRATEGIES for Successful Business and Professional Writing

1. Establish a goal for each document. Make sure your thesis is clearly stated.
2. Address the needs and concerns of both immediate and extended readers.
3. Make sure your writing does not conflict with the policy or image of the organization you represent.
4. Review your document for legal liability. Avoid making commitments or promises you cannot keep.
5. Conform to the standards used in your organization or industry.
6. Use peer review to evaluate documents before submission or publication.
7. Test market documents before mass distribution. After peer review, submit copies to a limited audience and evaluate the response before sending the document to every reader.

FOR FURTHER READING

Baugh, Sue L., Maridell Fryar, and David A. Thomas. *Handbook of Business Writing.*
Beatty, Richard. *The Perfect Cover Letter.*
Bell, Arthur. *Complete Business Writer's Manual: Model Letters, Memos, Reports, and Presentations for Every Occasion.*
Brock, Susan L., and Beverly Manber. *Writing Business Proposals and Reports: Strategies for Success.*
Brown, Leland. *Effective Business Writing.*
Clover, Vernon. *Business Research Methods.*
Frailey, L. E. *Handbook of Business Letters.*
Griffin, Jack. *The Complete Handbook of Model Business Letters.*
Hansen, Katherine. *Dynamic Cover Letters for New Graduates.*
Kupsh, Joyce. *How to Create High Impact Business Reports.*
Ryan, Robert. *Winning Resumes.*
Tepper, Ron. *Power Resumes.*

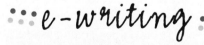 **e-writing**

Exploring Business and Professional Writing Online

You can use the Internet to learn more about business and professional writing.

1. Using a search engine, such as Yahoo!, Google, or AltaVista, enter such terms as *writing email, tips on writing email, resumes, cover letters,* and *writing business reports* to locate current sites of interest.

2. Using InfoTrac College Edition, locate online articles from professional journals to examine how the writing context differs from one discipline to another.

E-Sources

Professional Writing Handouts and Resources
   http://owl.english.purdue.edu/ handouts/pw/

A Beginner's Guide to Effective Email
   http://www.webfoot.com/advice/email .top.html

Writing Résumés and Cover Letters
   http://jobsearchtech.about.com/od/ resumes/

Companion Website

See http://www.thomsonedu.com/ english/sundance for additional information on business and professional writing.

16

SPECIAL WRITING CONTEXTS

WHAT ARE SPECIAL WRITING CONTEXTS?

College courses and your future career may place you in special writing contexts. Instead of working alone to prepare an assignment for an individual instructor, you may have to collaborate with others, participate in an online writing group, write as a representative of others, broadcast a message to a mass audience, address multiple readers, or deliver an oral or multimedia presentation of a report.

COLLABORATIVE WRITING

We think of writers as solitary workers, but many professions require people to work with others to produce a single document. Two business partners may cowrite a sales brochure. A group of engineers or accountants may submit a team report. A committee investigating a problem or proposing a solution usually issues a single document. Even when produced by an individual, writing often incorporates the ideas of a group. Thomas Jefferson wrote the Declaration of Independence, but a committee including John Adams and Benjamin Franklin made forty-seven revisions. More changes occurred when the document was presented to the Continental Congress. By the time John Hancock stepped forward to sign the Declaration of Independence, a quarter of Jefferson's draft had been altered or deleted.

Because collaborative writing is common in many jobs, an increasing number of composition teachers require students to work in groups. Collaborative writing is challenging. Writing is very personal, and few students feel comfortable having their work read and evaluated by others. Because the assignment has to express the ideas of several people, personalities and viewpoints may clash. Even scheduling meeting times can be difficult.

Whether writing alone or in a group, the basic process is the same. The completed document must address the issue, meet the needs of the readers, and respect the conventions of the discourse community, discipline, or situation. To be effective, writing groups must achieve the "Three C's" of group dynamics: *cohesion*, *cooperation*, and *compromise*. Members of a group must be able to meet, communicate, and work together, and must be willing to accept the views and criticism of others. Members must understand that not all of their ideas will be represented in the final product and that their opinions will not always prevail.

STRATEGIES | for Collaborative Writing

1. **Establish cohesion by stressing the common goal, intended readers, and the needs of the discourse community.** Introduce members who may not know each other and focus on the task at hand. Make sure every member has a copy of the assignment.

2. **Keep the group focused on the task by creating a timeline.** People enjoy talking. Discussions can easily degenerate into forums for heated debates or gossip. A timeline can help keep the group on track by outlining expected outcomes and reminding members of the upcoming deadline. The timeline should mark stages in the writing process. Make sure your group allows time for revision and editing.

3. **Use prewriting strategies to develop topics and explore ideas.** Members can take time to individually freewrite, brainstorm, or cluster ideas and then participate in group prewriting.

4. **Designate one member to serve as moderator or recorder.** One member of the group should serve as chair or recorder to document the progress of the group and keep the discussion on target. It can be helpful for the moderator to use the assignment as a reference point for organizing the group's actions.

5. **Avoid topics that are too controversial, require too much research, or cannot be adequately explored in the allotted time.** If members of your group have strikingly different opinions and you find precious time being consumed by arguments and debates, suggest the group select a topic that will prompt cooperation and compromise.

6. **Make meetings productive by setting goals and assigning tasks.** Meetings can become repetitions of previous discussions. Members will have second thoughts and want to express them. Students may also become bored if the group does not seem to make progress.
   - Keep the group on track by opening each meeting with a brief summary of what has been accomplished and a list of what has to be achieved in the current meeting.
   - Summarize points that have been agreed to; then announce tasks for the next meeting.
   - Make sure each member is assigned work and knows what is expected at the next meeting.

7. **Avoid personalizing disagreements.** It is important to discuss opposing viewpoints in neutral terms. Avoid attaching ideas to individuals, which leads to "*us* against *them*" conflicts.

8. **Experiment with different writing methods.** There are a number of ways groups can produce writing:
   - *Individual drafting*
     If the writing is short and not too complex, you might ask each member to prepare a draft and bring copies to the next meeting. Members can then select the best version and suggest alterations, adding items from other drafts.
   - *Parallel drafting*
     For longer documents or those that include specialized information, divide the paper into sections, assigning each one to a different group member.
   - *Team drafting*
     Assign two or more writers to the document or each section. A lead writer begins the first draft, then passes the writing onto subsequent authors when he or she gets stuck or lacks knowledge or data to continue. Drafts are then reviewed by the group.

9. **Take advantage of technology.** Professionals and students alike frequently have difficulty scheduling common times to meet. Use telephone conferences and Internet chat rooms for long-distance meetings. Use e-mail to distribute drafts so that members can read and post comments.

ONLINE WRITING GROUPS

Many college students and professionals use the Internet to expedite the writing process by posting drafts for others to read, criticize, and revise. An increasing number of composition instructors include online writing as a facet of their courses. Online writing groups allow writers to elicit responses from people who cannot meet in person. A marketing executive developing a promotional brochure can easily solicit responses from sales representatives across the country. In addition, online writing groups allow members to respond to a posted draft at their convenience. Students who find it difficult to voice comments in class may feel more comfortable expressing their opinions in writing. Because writing requires more concentration than talking, online writing groups can prompt more thoughtful responses about a draft than a discussion. Members can easily make revisions and suggest alternative versions.

STRATEGIES | for Working in Online Writing Groups

1. **Allow time for members to respond.** Unlike those working collaboratively, members of online writing groups respond individually. Don't post the draft of an essay at midnight and expect to receive feedback the next morning. Budget your time carefully.

2. **Label your documents and restate goals.** If members receive a number of assignments or documents, they can become easily confused. They will be in a better position to respond to your work if you remind them of the assignment or the purpose of your document.
   - You might attach a thesis statement or goal to guide members' responses.

3. **Proofread your document before posting.** Errors in spelling and punctuation, though minor, are distracting. The better-edited your writing is, the more likely it is that readers will be able to respond to the content and analyze your ideas.

4. **Direct responses by asking questions.** Simply posting an essay or letter can generate scattered or otherwise unhelpful commentary that may not enhance the revision process. Provide readers with questions about specific problems or shortcomings you detect in your draft. Encourage them to make suggestions and possible revisions.

5. **Use alternative communications.** Posting and reading e-mail can lead to static exchanges. The work of online writing groups can benefit from personal meetings, chat room conferences, and telephone calls.

6. **Print and save hard copies of posted drafts.** Hard copies allow you to preserve different versions of documents and work while away from your computer.

7. **Observe standards of netiquette.** When you send e-mail or post messages, follow the basic guidelines for electronic messages:

- *Write responsibly*

  E-mail is real mail. Although it can seem informal and casual, e-mail sends messages to readers that cannot be retrieved. Think before you send anyone anything that you might later regret. Consider your professional role and potential extended audiences. A printed letter might be photocopied and passed around to a few people, but an e-mail can easily be reproduced and circulated to thousands.

- *Keep subject lines brief*

  The subject line of your e-mail serves as a title. It should be short and clearly identify the purpose of the message.

- *Keep line length short*

  Many monitors display only forty characters in a line. State messages concisely in short paragraphs using tightly worded sentences. Use attachments to transmit longer, more complex documents.

- *Follow standard capitalization rules*

  Use lowercase and capital letters as you would in a print document. Using all caps is considered SHOUTING and viewed as rude and unprofessional.

- *Proofread your messages*

  Review the spelling and grammar of electronic communication with the same rigor you would apply to a standard letter or research paper.

- *Respect copyrights*

  Do not electronically distribute copyrighted material, including e-mail from others, without permission. Document use of outside sources.

- *Sign your e-mail*

  Include your name, affiliation, and e-mail address at the end of your message.

WRITING AS A REPRESENTATIVE OF OTHERS

Outside of the classroom, you often write as a representative of other people. Your work will not be viewed as a personal creation, an individual opinion, but as the expression of a company, union, board, agency, or institution. When you write as an employee, member, or volunteer of a larger organization, avoid making statements that contradict the mission or philosophy of the organization. Never write anything that might place the organization in jeopardy, expose it to liability, or provoke needless criticism. Keep in mind that whatever you write will be seen as an expression of the corporation, agency, club, or organization. Business letters, memos, reports, newsletters, advertisements, bulletins, and e-mails are assumed to state the views and values of the group, not an individual member or employee. Expressing personal opinions that conflict with corporate practices or administrative policy can jeopardize your position.

STRATEGIES | for Writing as a Representative

1. **Remember that you are writing as a representative of the group, not as an individual.** Keep the values, beliefs, policies, and attitudes of the group in mind as you write. Avoid making statements that conflict with the group's stated goals or common values. Do not make any statements in official correspondence you will not be able to explain or defend to other members of the group.
2. **Clearly distinguish personal opinion from passages expressing ideas of the group.** If you insert personal views in a business letter, clearly label them and indicate to your reader that your views do not reflect those of the group.
3. **Never use official letterhead for personal communications.** Employees have been terminated for using company or government stationery for personal messages. Never write anything on office stationery you would not want your supervisor or manager to read.
4. **Never make profane or even humorous comments that will compromise your professional position.** Even if you are sending a memo to your best friend, be aware that others may read it out of context and draw negative conclusions about your performance or professionalism. Remember that many people who will never see you will see your writing. Whatever you write should reflect the image you wish to project in your career.
5. **Model your writing style on existing documents.** Large organizations provide employees with style manuals containing samples of letters and reports. If official guidelines do not exist, ask your supervisor or fellow employees for examples of what they consider good writing.

BROADCASTING TO MASS AUDIENCES

In many instances you will write something to be distributed to a mass audience—an ad, a website, a sales brochure, or a newsletter. The more people you plan to reach with your document, the more challenging your task becomes. If you make an error or omit a detail in a memo directed to three or four people, you can easily correct yourself by making a few telephone calls. But if you have already mailed five thousand letters or received ten thousand "hits" on a website containing misinformation, any attempt to correct the error will be time-consuming and costly.

In addition, the wider the audience you attempt to reach, the more important it is to measure your readers' perceptual world, particularly their existing knowledge and attitudes. For example, a sales letter directed to urban professionals may alienate rural consumers. A fund-raising brochure that succeeds with Catholics may fail to impress non-Catholics. Consider *all* your readers.

STRATEGIES for Writing to Mass Audiences

1. **Arouse attention.** People customarily receive many letters, mailings, and reports. Don't assume readers will appreciate the importance of your message.
   - Announce the significance of your document at the outset. Tell readers *why* the text is worth reading.
   - If appropriate, use bold headlines, larger font sizes, italics, and underlining to highlight points.
   - Consider including visual aids that can communicate at a glance—diagrams, graphs, cartoons, and photographs. Images should both illustrate your ideas and match the tone and style of the document.
2. **Define your goal clearly.** Whatever document you address to a mass audience must be clearly stated. Most readers will skim rather than read mass-distributed items. Reader attention is limited.
   - Avoid attempting to express too much information in a single document.
   - Make sure your goal is clearly stated at the beginning or end. Do not bury important ideas in the middle of the text.
3. **Keep your document as brief as possible.** Although you must provide support for your ideas, realize that readers respond poorly to long documents.
   - Delete minor details.
   - Use an appendix and attachments for lengthy detail so the primary document can serve as a readable preface or brief overview.

4. **Direct readers to take specific action.** If you wish readers to respond in a certain way, if you desire to motivate them to take action, provide clear directions.

   ■ What is it you want people to do after reading this document?
   ■ Provide instructions, as well as pertinent information—names, dates, and addresses.

5. **Use peer review and focus groups.** Give copies of your document to half a dozen or more people who represent your mass audience and ask for their reactions.

   ■ Direct people to read the document once; then ask questions to test their ability to recall information.
   ■ Ask readers to identify strong and weak points.
   ■ Ask readers to summarize the document's main ideas in their own words. If they can only repeat statements drawn from the text, they may have not fully understood or incorporated the content.

6. **Test market your writing.** Before sending out ten thousand fund-raising letters or e-mails, consider sending out five hundred to a test market and examine the results. If they generate the desired response, continue distribution. If the letter or e-mail fails to achieve your goals, use focus groups and peer review to guide revisions or a change in tactics.

7. **Consider using alternative versions.** There is no reason why you must use only one version of a sales letter, e-mail, or handbill. Different people respond to different ideas, words, and images. Instead of attempting to develop a master document to serve everyone, consider developing multiple versions using varying texts, styles, and images.

   ■ The basic message must be the same if you want people to have a common response. Make sure all facts such as names, dates, prices, and addresses are accurate.
   ■ Track the success rate of each type. If you find that more people respond to a particular version, you might discard others.

WRITING TO MULTIPLE READERS

Often you will send detailed reports to a number of professionals with different interests and responsibilities. In college, most of your papers are directed to a single instructor. In seminars, graduate school, and most organizations you will have a group of readers, many with specific needs and concerns. Although you will, in most cases, be expected to distribute the same report to each member, you can personalize the document to communicate more effectively with a diverse audience.

STRATEGIES | for Writing to Multiple Readers

1. **Include a detailed table of contents and index.** If a number of readers need to look at your document for specific information, make sure they can quickly locate data that interests them. Readers lose patience if they have to page through a report to search for information. Detailed tables of contents and indices can make your document easy to read, making it a resource people can use as a reference.

2. **Attach a cover letter or note.** You can reach different people by attaching letters directing them to specific pages and adding comments unsuited for the basic text:

   Dear Ms. O'Neill:

   Here is the proposal for next year's Chicago Convention.

   Based on your concerns for additional meeting rooms, I have suggested renting an additional ballroom (see diagrams of the Hyatt on page 12).

   In addition, the hotel is only two blocks from our Chicago sales office, which has three conference rooms at our disposal.

   If you have any questions, feel free to call me at extension 7403.

   Sidney Falco

3. **Mark copies for specific readers.** You can aid readers, especially those pressed for time, by highlighting or underlining text, inserting bookmarks, or using Post-it notes.

4. **Alert readers before submitting.** If you have spent a great deal of time and effort in producing an important document, you want to motivate people to read it.

   ■ Send notes, e-mails, or voice mail messages to alert readers when to expect your document. Inform readers of the paper's significance.

   ■ Use attention-getting ideas or facts to arouse interest.

GIVING ORAL AND MULTIMEDIA PRESENTATIONS

Many college courses and your career will require you to make an oral or multimedia presentation. In some instances, this will be simply an introduction or a brief overview of a document. In other instances, it may be a complete alternative to a written report.

Public speaking and writing call on very different skills. An oral presentation occurs in a specific location at a specific time. Environmental factors, such as noise and seating arrangements, affect how messages are received. Listeners, unlike readers, are part of an audience. Their reactions are often shaped by the responses of the people around them. Readers can study a document at their own pace, taking as long as they wish to read and reread. They can skim over familiar information, concentrating on new or difficult material. Listeners, however, receive the message at the same rate and cannot alter the flow of information. Studies reveal that even the most attentive listeners retain much less than readers.

STRATEGIES | for Giving Oral and Multimedia Presentations

1. **Study the environment.** The more you know about the time, place, and conditions of your presentation, the more comfortable and effective you will be.
   - If you are unfamiliar with the location, visit it beforehand if you can. If you cannot survey the site in person, ask what kind of room it is—a seminar room, an auditorium, a lounge? What kind of seating arrangement will be used for the speech? Does it lend itself to a formal or informal presentation? What kind of presentation aids, such as a computer and projector, chalkboard, or microphone, will be available?
   - Find out if you can how many people are expected. Meeting with three or four people around a coffee table calls for a different presentation style than addressing two hundred from a podium.

2. **Learn as much as you can about your audience.** A speech is a public event, an interpersonal exchange. People expect a certain formality or distance in a written document but anticipate that a speaker will connect with them personally. Successful politicians and stand-up comedians acquire the ability to "read" a crowd or measure the "feel" of a room to guide their actions. Learn as much as you can about your listeners and their perceptual world so you can tailor your presentation to address their needs, answer their concerns, and confront their objections.
   - If possible, meet or call people you expect to attend the presentation and ask about their interests or opinions.
   - Go to the meeting early and introduce yourself to people. Ask about their background, ideas, reactions to your subject.

3. **Isolate the key points of your document.** Listeners are unable to grasp the range of details usually presented in written form. Highlight and num-

ber the key points of your paper, emphasizing your thesis, most important evidence, and actions you wish the audience to take.

4. **Prepare a range of presentations.** If you are not sure how long your presentation should be, ask. If you are given thirty minutes, prepare a thirty-minute, a twenty-minute, and a ten-minute version.

   ■ Meetings and seminars often run long. Speakers run over time. If you are pressed for time or recognize that the audience is restless and bored, it is better to deliver a clearly organized short version of your presentation than subject them to the full text.

5. **Do not *read* your speech.** The worst thing a speaker can do is to read a speech. Reading a written document—except for key quotes—has a deadly effect on listeners. Written language, no matter how clear and eloquent on paper, is often difficult to present orally or remember. Spoken English, even in formal circumstances, is usually simpler and delivered in shorter sentences.

   ■ Do not attempt to memorize your speech—*talk* to your audience, using a few notes as reminders.

   ■ Practice your delivery, especially pronunciation of difficult words or phrases.

6. **Maintain eye contact.** The most important skill effective speakers develop is maintaining eye contact with listeners. If looking at people makes you nervous, look above their heads, moving your eyes about the room as you speak.

7. **Use visual aids.** People retain more information if they receive it in more than one medium. Even motivated listeners will recall only about a third of what they hear. A simple outline, a list of talking points, a diagram, or the table of contents of your report can help people follow your presentation.

   ■ If giving a speech makes you nervous, a handout can reduce stress because people will be viewing the document instead of looking in your direction.

   ■ Keep handouts, transparency, and PowerPoint images simple and direct. Avoid distracting artwork. Keep verbal statements short. Emphasize key words that appear in the text of your presentation.

8. **Provide distinct transitions between main points.** In writing, you can use visual indicators such as paragraph or page breaks, titles, or chapters to signal transitions between ideas.

   ■ Listeners have only a flow of words that can easily become confusing. Give your audience clear signals of when your presentation changes course.

   ■ Numbering points makes your speech easier to follow and remember. If you tell people there are five points to consider and they can only recall three, they will realize they have lost something and are more likely to ask questions or refer to your document.

9. **Encourage listeners to write.** One way of getting people to become active listeners is to encourage them to take notes.

10. **If you plan to take questions, mention it at the outset.** Do not give a presentation and then ask, "Are there any questions?" If listeners do not know beforehand that they can ask questions, they may fail to pay attention during your talk. Not knowing they will be able to ask for clarification, they may dismiss ideas they find difficult or confusing.

11. **Motivate listeners to read your document.** Unless your document is a brief letter or memo, no oral presentation is likely to communicate the complete message. Urge your audience to read the paper.

    - Challenge your audience with an interesting fact, question, or statistic, alerting them that more information is contained in the report.
    - Pose questions and concerns shared by the listeners and tell them the answers are in the document.
    - Direct them to look at specific pages of special importance.

12. **Do not waste the audience's time.** Listeners grow impatient with speakers who arrive late or unprepared.

    - Although it is useful to pause between main points to give people an opportunity to absorb ideas, avoid long moments of silence. If you have misplaced or forgotten something, do not take time to search for it. Instead, move to the next point.
    - Anticipate problems and prepare alternative presentations. Don't assume people will bring their reports to the meeting. Consider how you will proceed if a VCR is not available, the bulb burns out on the overhead projector, or the computer won't open your presentation files. Be flexible and ready to adapt to last-minute changes.

e-writing

Exploring Special Writing Contexts Online

You can gather additional insights into special writing contexts by exploring the Internet. Academic and professional organizations, research institutions, and technical journals provide current advice on writing in special situations.

1. Using InfoTrac College Edition or one of your library's databases, search for

current articles about collaborative writing, writing online, giving oral presentations, e-mail, and business writing.

2. Using a general search engine, such as Alta Vista, Yahoo, or Google, enter such terms as *collaborative writing, writing to mass audiences, giving oral presentations, writing online, online writing groups, writing e-mail, using PowerPoint, netiquette,* and *writing to multiple readers* to locate current sites of interest.

3. Review e-mails you have sent and received for "netiquette." Do you detect different standards for online communications? Do you need to change your style of electronic writing?

E-Sources

Collaborative Writing
   http://www.stanford.edu/group/
   collaborate/

Supporting Your Talk with Visuals
   http://www.engineering.utoronto.ca/
   English/page-1-2080-1.html
Presenting Effective Presentations with Visual Aids
   http://www.osha.gov/doc/
   outreachtraining/htmlfiles/traintec.html
Microsoft Office PowerPoint 2003
   http://office.microsoft.com/en-us/
   assistance/CH790018081033.aspx

Companion Website

See http://www.thomsonedu.com/
english/sundance for additional information about special writing contexts.

The Reader

17

BECOMING A CRITICAL READER
READING WITH A "WRITER'S EYE"

If reading is to accomplish anything more than passing time, it must be active.

—Mortimer Adler

WHAT IS CRITICAL READING?

As a student you are accustomed to reading for information. Studying for examinations, you review textbooks, highlighting facts, dates, statistics, quotations, and concepts that you expect to be tested on. Engrossed in a novel, you read for plot, paying little attention to the author's syntax and literary techniques as you follow the story.

As a composition student, however, you need to read critically; you need to read with a "writer's eye." Most diners savor a new gourmet item, but a chef wants to know the recipe. Tourists in Rome marvel at the ancient ruins; an architectural student examines how the columns support the roof. Moviegoers gasp at car chases, but filmmakers study the director's use of camera angles and special effects. The audience in a comedy club laughs as a comic spins out a series of one-liners, while a would-be performer analyzes her timing and delivery.

To increase your skills as a writer, you need to read like a writer, examining *how* something is written. Reading gives you the opportunity to watch other writers at work. When you read, note the way other writers use words, form sentences, and develop paragraphs. Focus on techniques that you can use in your own assignments. How did the author limit the subject? Where did the writer place the thesis statement? What kind of support is used? What kinds of visuals are used? How did the writer organize ideas? What sentence opens the essay? What thought, image, question, or fact did the author choose for the conclusion?

HOW TO READ WITH A WRITER'S EYE

When you pick up a magazine, you rarely read every article. Flipping through the pages, you allow your eyes to guide you. A headline, a photograph, a chart, or a famous name makes you pause and begin reading. If you become bored, you skip to the next article. Reading textbooks, you skim over familiar material to concentrate on new information. If you studied *Death of a Salesman* in high school, you will probably review rather than reread the play for a college literature course.

In a composition course, however, you should read *all* the assigned selections carefully. Reading as a writer, you examine familiar works differently than do readers seeking information. Even if you know a particular essay well, read it closely, observing how it is constructed. As a writer, you read to learn, seeing the essays as models demonstrating strategies that you can use in your own work.

Like writing, critical reading occurs best in stages.

First Reading

1. **Look ahead and skim selections.** Do not wait until the night before a class discussion to read assigned essays. Check your syllabus and skim through upcoming readings to get a general impression. Often, if you think about the authors and their topics, you can approach the essay more critically.
2. **Study the headnote and introduction.** Consider the author, the issue, and the writing context. What readers does the writer seem to be addressing? What can you observe about the discourse community? Measure your existing knowledge about the author and subject.
3. **Suspend judgment.** Try to put your personal views aside as you read. Even if you disagree with the author's choice of topic, tone, or opinion, read the essay objectively. Remember, your goal is to understand *how* the writer states his or her point. Even if you reject an author's thesis, you can still learn useful techniques.
4. **Consider the title.** Titles often provide clues about the author's attitude toward his or her subject. Does the title label the essay, state a thesis, pose a question, or use a creative phrase to attract attention?

5. **Read the entire work.** Just as in writing the first draft, it is important to complete the entire essay in one sitting if possible. Do not pause to look up an unfamiliar word at this stage. Instead, try to get the "big picture."

6. **Focus on understanding the writer's main point.** If possible, summarize the writer's thesis in your own words.

7. **Examine any images or visual aids.** If the author includes photographs, charts, graphs, or illustrations, note whether they serve to arouse attention, provide an illustration, or offer supporting evidence.

8. **Jot down your first impressions.** What do you think of this work? Do you like it? If so, why? If you find it dull, disturbing, or silly, ask why. What is lacking? How did the author fail in your eyes?

Put the essay aside, allowing it to cool. If possible, let two or three days pass before returning to the assignment. If the assignment is due the next day, read the selection early in the day and then turn to other work or run an errand, so that you can come back to it with a fresh outlook.

Second Reading

1. **Review your first impressions.** Determine whether your attitudes are based on biases or personal preferences rather than the writer's ability. Realize that an essay that supports your views is not necessarily well written. If you disagree with the author's thesis, try to put your opinions aside to objectively evaluate how well the writer presented his or her point of view. Don't allow your personal views to cloud your critical thinking. Appreciating an author's writing ability does not require you to accept his or her opinion.

2. **Read with a pen in your hand.** Make notes and underline passages that strike you as interesting, odd, offensive, or disturbing. Reading with a pen will prompt you to write, to be an active reader rather than a passive consumer of words.

 Use the Explicator Tool in *Comp21* to make notes on an electronic text. From the main menu, choose "Build Your Own Occasion for Writing."

3. **Look up unfamiliar words.** Paying attention to words can increase your vocabulary and enhance your appreciation of connotations.

4. **Analyze passages you found difficult or confusing during the first reading.** In many instances a second reading can help you understand complex passages. If you still have difficulty understanding the writer's point, ask why. Would other readers also have problems comprehending the meaning? Could ideas be stated more directly?

5. **Review the questions at the end of the selection.** When available, the questions can help you focus on a closer, more analytical reading of the work. This book's questions are arranged in three groups:

- *Understanding Context:*
  What is the writer's purpose?
  What is the thesis?
  What audience is the writer addressing?
  What is the author trying to share with his or her readers?
- *Evaluating Strategy:*
  How effective is the title?
  How does the writer introduce the essay?
  What evidence supports the thesis?
  How does the writer organize ideas?
  Where does the author use paragraph breaks?
  What role does the writer play? Is the writer's approach subjective or objective?
  How does the writer address possible objections or differing opinions?
  How does the writer conclude the essay?
  Does the author use any special techniques?
- *Appreciating Language:*
  How does the writer use words?
  What does the language reveal about the intended readers?
  What connotations do the words have?
  How do the words establish the writer's tone?

6. **Analyze the use of any visuals.** Do they simply illustrate an idea or provide support? Do the images appear designed to arouse an emotional response or provide objective evidence? Do the images represent what the author claims they do? Are there other interpretations? Does the author explain the context or source of the images? Are graphs and charts accurate or misleading?

7. **Summarize your responses in a point or two for class discussion.** Consider how you will express your opinions of the essay to fellow students. Be prepared to back up your remarks by citing passages in the text.

8. **Most important, focus on what this essay can teach you about writing.** How can this writer's style, way of organizing ideas, or word choice enrich your own writing? Though you may not wish to imitate everything you see, you can learn techniques to broaden your personal composing style.

9. **Think of how writers resolve problems that you have encountered.** If you have trouble making an outline and organizing ideas, study how the essays in this book are arranged. If your instructor returns papers with comments about vague thesis statements and lack of focus, examine how the writers in this book generate controlling ideas.

Before Class Discussion

1. **Before class discussion of an assigned essay, review the reading and your notes.** Identify your main reactions to the piece. What do you consider the essay's strongest or weakest points?
2. **Ask fellow students about their reactions to the writing.** Determine whether their responses to the writer's thesis, tone, approach, and technique match yours. If their reactions differ from yours, review your notes to get a fresh perspective.
3. **Be prepared to ask questions.** Ask your instructor about unfamiliar techniques or passages that you find confusing.

Read the following essay by Emily Prager and study how it has been marked during a critical reading. Notice how the student used the essay to generate ideas for upcoming assignments.

Emily Prager (1952–) graduated from Barnard College with a degree in anthropology. She has written pieces for **National Lampoon** as well as several screenplays. Prager has also appeared in several films. For four years she was a star on **The Edge of Night,** a popular soap opera. She has published three books of fiction: **A Visit from the Footbinder and Other Stories, Clea and Zeus Divorce,** and **Eve's Tattoo.**

Our Barbies, Ourselves

Notice how Prager uses a variety of modes, including comparison, description, narration, and cause and effect, to develop her essay about the Barbie doll. As you read the piece, consider her choice of topics. Is a popular toy a fitting subject to prompt thoughts about gender roles? Is it too trivial? Does Prager give a doll too much significance?

introduction
(obituary as
writing prompt)

1   I read an astounding obituary in *The New York Times* not too long ago. It concerned the death of one Jack Ryan. A former husband of Zsa Zsa Gabor, it said, Mr. Ryan had been an inventor and designer during his lifetime. A man of eclectic creativity, he designed Sparrow and Hawk missiles when he worked for the Raytheon Company, and the notice said, when he consulted for Mattel he designed Barbie.

description
WHY?

female/
feminist
reaction?

2   If Barbie was designed by a man, suddenly a lot of things made sense to me, things I'd wondered about for years. I used to look at Barbie and wonder, What's wrong with this picture? What kind of woman designed this doll? Let's be honest: Barbie looks like someone who got her start at the Playboy Mansion. She could be a regular guest on *The Howard Stern Show.* It is a fact of Barbie's design that her breasts are so out of proportion to the rest of her body that if she were a human woman, she'd fall flat on her face.

3   If it's true that a woman didn't design Barbie, you don't know how much saner that makes me feel. Of course, that doesn't ameliorate the damage.

questions
cause and
effect

There are millions of women who are subliminally sure that a thirty-nine inch bust and a twenty-three inch waist are the epitome of lovability. Could this account for the popularity of breast implant surgery?

4   I don't mean to step on anyone's toes here. I loved my Barbie. Secretly, I still believe that neon pink and turquoise blue are the only colors in which

to decorate a duplex condo. And like so many others of my generation, I've never married, simply because I cannot find a man who looks as good in clam diggers as Ken.

The question that comes to mind is, of course, Did Mr. Ryan design Barbie as a weapon? Because it *is* odd that Barbie appeared about the same time in my consciousness as the feminist movement—a time when women sought equality and small breasts were king. Or is Barbie the dream date of a weapons designer? Or perhaps it's simpler than that: Perhaps Barbie is Zsa Zsa if she were eleven inches tall. No matter what, my discovery of Jack Ryan confirms what I have always felt: There is something indescribably masculine about Barbie—dare I say it, phallic. For all her giant breasts and high-heeled feet, she lacks a certain softness. If you asked a little girl what kind of doll she wanted for Christmas, I just don't think she'd reply, "Please, Santa, I want a hardbody."

On the other hand, you could say that Barbie, in feminist terms, is definitely her own person. With her condos and fashion plazas and pools and beauty salons, she is definitely a liberated woman, a gal on the move. And she has always been sexual, even totemic. Before Barbie, American dolls were flat-footed and breastless, and ineffably dignified. They were created in the image of little girls or babies. Madame Alexander was the queen of doll makers in the '50s, and her dollies looked like Elizabeth Taylor in *National Velvet*. They represented the kind of girls who looked perfect in jodhpurs, whose hair was never out of place, who grew up to be Jackie Kennedy—before she married Onassis. Her dolls' boyfriends were figments of the imagination, figments with large portfolios and three piece suits and presidential aspirations, figments who could keep dolly in the style to which little girls of the '50s were programmed to become accustomed, perhaps what accounts for Barbie's vast popularity in that she was also a '60s woman: into free love and fun colors, anti-class, and possessed a real, molded boyfriend, Ken, with whom she could chant a mantra.

But there were problems with Ken. I always felt weird about him. He had no genitals, and, even at age ten, I found that ominous. I mean, here was Barbie with these humongous breasts, and that was O.K. with the toy company. And then, there was Ken, with that truncated, unidentifiable lump at his groin. I sensed injustice at work. Why, I wondered, was Barbie designed with such obvious sexual equipment and Ken not? Why was he treated as if it were more mysterious than hers? Did the fact that it was treated as such indicate that somehow his equipment, his essential maleness, was considered more powerful than hers, more worthy of the dignity of concealment? And if the issue in the mind of the toy company was obscenity and its possible damage to children, I still object. How do they think I felt, knowing that no matter

5 Barbie as a weapon?

cause and effect

(modern ideal of a hard body!)

6 Barbie as role model?

Barbie = adult doll not a baby or child

comparison

7 Ken sexless? comparison

questions

how many water beds they slept in, or hot tubs they romped in, or swimming pools they lounged by under the stars, Barbie and Ken could never make love? No matter how much sexuality Barbie possessed, she would never turn Ken on. He would be forever withholding, forever detached. There was a loneliness about Barbie's situation that was always disturbing. And twenty-five years later, movies and videos are still filled with topless women and covered men. As if we're all trapped in Barbie's world and can never escape.

Barbie's fate (margin note, left)

conclusion (margin note, left)

final observation (margin note, left)

STUDENT NOTES

First Reading

Barbie as symbol of male domination?
What about GI Joe and boys?
Is Prager really serious about this?
Barbie as paradox—a toy that presents a sexist *Playboy* image of women but a toy that is independent and more "liberated" than traditional baby dolls.
Tone: witty but serious in spots, raises a lot of issues but doesn't really discuss many.

Second Reading

Thesis: The Barbie doll, the creation of a male weapons designer, has shaped the way a generation of women defined themselves. (Get other opinions)
Body: spins off a number of topics and observations, a list of associations, suited for general readers.
Approach: a mix of serious and witty commentary, writer appears to entertain as much as inform or persuade.
Organization: use of modes critical to keeping the essay from becoming a rambling list of contradictory ideas. Good use of description, comparison, cause and effect.
Conclusion—"trapped in Barbie's world" good ending.

Prewriting—Possible Topics

Description—childhood toys—models of cars and planes? games—Monopoly (preparing kids for capitalism?)

Comparison/contrast—boy and girl toys and games, playing house vs. playing ball
   (social roles vs. competition, teamwork)
Cause and effect—we are socialized by our toys and games in childhood, affecting
   how men and women develop (needs support—Psych class notes)
Example—My daughter's old Beanie Baby?

USING THE READER

The reader portion of *The Sundance Writer* is organized in nine modes focusing on writers' goals. The readings in each section illustrate how writers achieve their purpose in different contexts. Each chapter opens with an explanation of the goal or mode. The opening readings in each chapter are brief, clear-cut examples of the mode and can serve as models for many of your composition assignments. Later readings are longer and more complex and demonstrate writing tasks in a range of disciplines and writing situations. Chapters end with samples of applied writings taken from business, industry, and government to illustrate how the mode is used beyond the classroom.

In addition to reading entries assigned by your instructor, perhaps the best way to improve your writing is to flip through the reader and review how different writers state a thesis, support an argument, open an essay, organize ideas, and present a conclusion. Focus on how other writers cope with the problems you encounter in your writing.

Use InfoTrac College Edition to locate additional readings online.

STRATEGIES | for Critical Reading

As you read entries in the reader, ask yourself these questions:

1. **What is the writer's purpose?** Even writers pursuing the same goal—to tell a story or explain a process—have slightly different intentions. What is the purpose of the story—to raise questions, motivate readers to take action, or change people's perceptions?

2. **What is the thesis?** What is the writer's main idea? Is the thesis explicitly stated, developed throughout the essay, or only implied? Can you state the thesis in your own words?

3. **What evidence does the writer provide to support the thesis?** Does the writer use personal observations, narratives, facts, statistics, or examples to support his or her conclusions?

4. **How does the writer organize the essay?** How does he or she introduce readers to the topic, develop ideas, arrange information, and conclude the essay? How does the writer use modes?

5. **Who are the intended readers?** What does the original source of the document tell you about its intended audience? Does the writer direct the essay to a particular group or a general readership? What terms or references are used? Are technical or uncommon terms defined? What knowledge does the writer seem to assume readers already possess?

6. **How successful is the writing—in context?** Does the writer achieve his or her goals while respecting the needs of the reader and the conventions of the discipline or situation? Are there particular considerations that cause the writer to "break" the rules of "good writing"? Why?

7. **What can you learn about writing?** What does this writer teach you about using words, writing sentences, developing paragraphs? Are there any techniques you can use in future assignments?

e-writing

Exploring Reading Online

The Internet offers extensive opportunities to read a variety of articles and documents in a range of professions, disciplines, and organizations.

1. Using InfoTrac College Edition or one of your library's databases, enter a search for the term *critical reading* to access current articles about the reading process.

2. Become familiar with library databases to locate reading material that can assist you not only in composition but in all your college courses.

E-Sources

York University Counseling and Development Centre
Reading Skills for University
http://www.yorku.ca/cdc/lsp/
readingonline/read1.htm

Study Guides and Strategies
  http://www.studygs.net/
Dartmouth Academic Skills Center
Reading Your Textbooks Effectively and
Efficiently
  http://www.dartmouth.edu/~acskills/
  success/reading.html

Companion Website

See **http://www.thomsonedu.com/
english/sundance** for additional information about critical reading.

18

DESCRIPTION
PRESENTING
IMPRESSIONS

WHAT IS DESCRIPTION?

Description captures impressions of persons, places, objects, or ideas. It records what we see, hear, feel, taste, and smell. Description is probably the most basic task that writers encounter. Whether you are writing a short story or a sales proposal, your success depends on your ability to effectively share impressions. Good description not only provides information but brings subjects to life through sensory details. Almost all writing requires a skilled use of description. Before you can narrate events, establish a cause-and-effect relationship, or develop a persuasive argument, you must provide readers with a clear picture of your subject. Dramatists open plays with set descriptions. Homicide detectives begin reports with descriptions of the crime scene. Before proposing expanding an airport, the writers of a government study must first describe congestion in the existing facility.

The way writers select and present details depends on context, particularly their purpose and the needs of their readers.

 To read more about description, along with interactive examples and opportunities to work with interactive texts, click on "The Rhetorical Patterns of Inquiry" from the main menu of *Comp21*.

Objective and Subjective Description

There are two basic types of description. Objective description attempts to create an accurate, factual record, free of personal interpretation or bias. In contrast, subjective description emphasizes a writer's personal reactions, opinions, and values.

Objective Description

Objective description focuses on facts and observable details. Textbooks, newspaper articles, business reports, and professional journals include objective description. Although objective description may avoid highly charged emotional appeals or creative imagery, it is not necessarily lifeless. Objective description is effective when the writer's purpose is to present readers with information required to make an evaluation or decision. In many instances objective description does not attempt to arouse interest or attract attention because it is often written in response to reader demand. *The New Illustrated Columbia Encyclopedia*, for example, includes this description of Chicago:

> The third largest city in the country and the heart of a metropolitan area of almost 7 million people, it is the commercial, financial, industrial, and cultural center for a vast region and a great midcontinental shipping port. It is a port of entry; a major Great Lakes port, located at the junction of the St. Lawrence Seaway with the Mississippi River system; the busiest air center in the country; and an important rail and highway hub.

- Objective description is best suited for providing reference material for a diverse audience seeking reliable, factual information.
- Objective description avoids figurative language that is subject to interpretation. A personal essay or real-estate brochure might describe a home as being a "snug cottage" or "stylish condo." But an insurance underwriter would demand specific facts about age, size, and construction.
- If you are writing as an employee or agent of others, objective description allows you to avoid personalizing a document that must express the views of others.
- Objective description is useful when you are writing to a critical or hostile audience that may demand explanations or justifications of subjective characterizations.
- Objective description is effective when the evidence you are presenting is compelling and dramatic. A description of a plane crash or a famine can be totally factual yet emotionally wrenching to readers. Objective description can be powerful and influential.

Subjective Description

In contrast to objective description, subjective description creates impressions through sensory details and imagery. Short stories, novels, personal essays, advertising copy, memoirs, and editorials use highly personal sensory details and responses to create an individual's sense of the subject. The writer's perceptual world guides the writing. Instead of photographic realism, subjective description paints scenes, creates moods, or generates emotional responses. Providing accurate information is less important than giving readers a "feel" for the subject. In a subjective description of a car, the color, shape, ride, and memories it evokes for the owner are more important than facts about horsepower, resale value, and fuel efficiency.

Attempting to capture his view of Chicago, John Rechy gives the city a personality, comparing it to an expectant mother:

> You get the impression that once Chicago was like a constantly pregnant woman, uneasy in her pregnancy because she has miscarried so often. After its rise as a frontier town, plush bigtime madams, adventurers, and soon the titanic rise of the millionaires, the city's subsequent soaring population—all gave more than a hint that Chicago might easily become America's First City. But that title went unquestionably to New York. Brazenly, its skyscrapers, twice as tall as any in the Midwest city, symbolically invaded the sky. Chicago, in squat self-consciousness, bowed out. It became the Second City.

Rechy uses imagery and unconventional syntax to create a highly personalized view of the city. In the context of his essay, written for a literary magazine, impression is more important than accuracy. Dates and statistics are irrelevant to his purpose. The goal in subjective description is to share a vision, not provide information.

- Subjective description emphasizes the writer's personal impressions rather than accurate reporting. It is best suited for writers who are acting independently, giving readers their personal insights.
- Subjective description relies heavily on the writer's selection and presentation of details. The choice of words and their connotations is critical in achieving the writer's goal.
- Subjective description is widely used when the goal is to entertain and persuade readers rather than to provide information. Humorists, columnists, political commentators, essayists, and advertising copywriters use subjective writing to shape readers' opinion of their subject.

Blended Description

Most description is not purely objective or subjective. Many writers blend subjective elements into objective reporting. Even when trying to be neutral and unbiased, reporters and historians generally cannot avoid being influenced by their personal values and attitudes. Popular nonfiction writers include subjective touches to humanize their writing and enhance the appeal of their work. Best-selling biographers, for instance, frequently employ subjective details to make remote historical figures and events more contemporary and more accessible to readers.

In his description of Chicago's State Street, Russell Miller blends elements of objective realism and subjective impressions to create a striking portrait:

> Summer 1983. State Street, "that great street," is a dirty, desolate, and depressing street for most of its length. It runs straight and potholed from the Chicago city line, up through the black ghettos of the South Side, an aching wasteland of derelict factories pitted with broken windows, instant slum apartment blocks, vandalized playgrounds encased in chain-linked fencing, and vacant lots where weeds sprout gamely from the rubble and the rusting hulks of abandoned automobiles. Those shops that remain open are protected by barricades of steel mesh. One or two men occupy every doorway, staring sullenly onto the street, heedless of the taunting cluster of skyscrapers to the north.

In this description, objective details such as "vandalized playgrounds" are interwoven with expressions granting human emotions to inanimate objects so that wastelands are "aching" and skyscrapers "taunting." Blended descriptions such as this one are useful in strengthening subjective accounts with factual details.

■ Blended descriptions are found in newsmagazines, literary criticism, and most nonfiction books. The degree and intensity of subjective elements depend on the context and may have to conform to stylistic guidelines established by editors.

■ If you are writing as the agent of others or part of a larger organization, examine the use of subjective words carefully. Avoid connotations and characterizations that may offend or displease those you represent. Peer review can help you determine whether you have achieved the right blend of objective and subjective description.

WRITING ACTIVITY

Select sample descriptions from a variety of sources—readings from this chapter, textbooks, magazine articles, brochures, mail-order catalogs, and newspaper advertisements—and review their use of objective and subjective details.

1. Can you detect subjective description in news magazines, such as *Time* or *Newsweek?* Is there a difference between the news stories and personal essays and political commentary pieces?

2. Do you observe different blends of subjective elements in such magazines as *Cosmopolitan, Architectural Digest,* and *Field and Stream?*

3. Circle the subjective details used in ads that describe products.

4. Can you detect subjective description in any of your textbooks?

5. How does the writer's stance affect the blend of objective and subjective elements?

The Language of Description

Diction—the choice of words—is important in all writing, but it has a special role in description. Whether your description is objective, subjective, or a blend, the words you select should be accurate, appropriate, and effective. In choosing words, consider your purpose, readers, and discipline. *Review Chapter 10 to make sure that you have used words accurately and been particularly sensitive to their connotations.*

WRITING ACTIVITIES

1. Read the following pair of descriptions of a village:

> The Yucca tribe lives in dire poverty. Their homes consist of rude shacks clustered around a rotting wooden platform that serves as a stage for primitive rituals. The village has no paved streets, no electricity, no running water. They subsist on fish and roots they dig from the ground with crude sticks. The village women spend their days fashioning coarse garments from tree bark and leaves. Their children wander aimlessly about the village without supervision. Their chief, an illiterate old man, resents the intrusion of outsiders who threaten his hold over his people.

> The Yucca tribe lives simply. Their homes consist of small cottages grouped around an altar that serves as the center of their religious worship. The village has no crime, pollution, or violence. They live on natural fish and vegetables they harvest using the tools of their ancestors. Their children play freely with no fear of traffic or molestation. Their chief, steeped in tradition, resents the intrusion of outsiders who threaten to erode their culture.

■ How do these passages differ? How does word choice affect your impression of the village and its inhabitants?

■ What do word choices reveal about the attitudes and values of the writer?

■ Do you consider these objective, subjective, or blended descriptions?

2. Review a number of advertisements in women's magazines. What words and images are used to sell products to women? Would these connotations appeal to men?

3. Consider words used by advocates on both sides of a controversial issue—abortion, capital punishment, affirmative action, or sexual harassment. Can you draw parallel lists of words and phrases that reflect the views of opposing groups? Why, for instance, do both pro-life and pro-choice groups talk about "rights"?

4. Analyze several popular television commercials. What connotations are used? Do they have any logical connection to the products or services being sold?

STRATEGIES | for Writing Description

Critical Thinking and Prewriting

1. **Use brainstorming and lists to generate possible topics.** Choose subjects you are familiar with—people you know, places you have visited, items you work with.
   - You may find it easier to write about a person you met once than a close friend, or a city you toured on vacation rather than your hometown. Sometimes a subject may have so many memories and complex associations that it is difficult to develop a clear focus for a short paper.
2. **Narrow your list of possible topics and generate details.** Use clustering and freewriting to develop details about your subject.
3. **Use senses other than sight.** Most writers immediately think of description as being visual. But descriptions can be enriched by including impressions of taste, touch, smell, and hearing.
   - You might experiment by building a description based on nonvisual impressions. Describe your job or neighborhood, for instance, by sound rather than sight.

Planning

1. **Determine your purpose.** What is your goal—to entertain a general audience or provide information to colleagues, employees, your boss, or customers? What are the most important details needed to support your thesis?
   - Even if no formal thesis statement appears in the text, your description should have a controlling idea or focus. Good description is not a random collection of facts or observations.

2. **Define your role.** If you are expressing personal opinion or observations, you are free to add subjective elements to your writing. You may wish to include yourself in the description, referring to your actions and writing in the first person. If you are writing as a representative of a larger body, an objective stance is usually more appropriate.

3. **Consider your reader.** Which type of description best suits your audience—subjective impressions or objective facts? What needs and expectations do your readers have? What details, facts, statistics, or observations will help them appreciate your topic and share your impression?

4. **Review the nature of the discourse community.** Determine whether you should use technical or specialized terminology. If you are writing within a profession, academic discipline, government agency, or corporation, use standard methods of presenting information, such as choosing an appropriate genre.

5. **Select key details.** Having determined the context, choose points that will reflect your purpose and impress your readers, and follow any guidelines dictated by the assignment or discourse community. Descriptions should have focus.

   ▪ Eliminate facts that might be interesting in themselves but do not serve your purpose.

6. **Organize details.** Good descriptions are more than collections of facts or lists of characteristics. To be effective, your writing should be logically organized. You may arrange details spatially by describing a house room by room or a city neighborhood by neighborhood. You can present ideas in the order of their importance. If your essay includes both objective and subjective description, these can be blended or placed in separate paragraphs.

   ▪ Use such modes as comparison and contrast, narration, or process to organize details.

Writing the First Draft

1. **Allow details to create a dominant impression.** The description of a room can focus on a single theme:

   > Although I live three hundred miles from the ocean, my apartment has a seagoing motif. Beneath a sweeping seascape, a large antique aquarium dominates the living room, its colorful tropical fish flashing among rocks and shells I brought back from Florida. Miniature schooners, windjammers, and ketches line the window sill. The ornate glass cabinet intended for china houses my collection of Hawaiian seashells.

2. **Describe people and objects in action.** Descriptions of people and objects can become stilted lists of facts. You can bring your subject to life by

introducing short narratives or showing people in action. In writing description, follow the creative writer's advice to "show" not "tell."

Original

Mr. Bryant was the best boss I ever worked for. He supervised the payroll office. He was smart, generous, and patient. He knew the payroll office like the back of his hand. He had a fantastic eye for detail and a great memory. He appeared to have memorized the most complicated IRS regulations and could master any new accounting software in less than an hour. He was a great teacher and trainer. He was always available if anyone in the office had problems with a complex situation. He had excellent communications skills. I never saw him lose his temper no matter how mad employees got when the company made mistakes on their paychecks. He would simply and calmly explain policies and do his best to rectify any errors. He always gave his staff and the employees more than anyone expected. People came away from payroll usually wishing the rest of the company could be run the same way.

Improved

The payroll office came alive the moment Al Bryant stormed in, usually bearing a carton of donuts and a bag of carrot sticks for his employees. Unlike the other supervisors, he rarely used his private office but spent his day roving past our cubicles, answering our questions, showing us shortcuts, and tackling problems we couldn't figure out. Highly patient, he never lost his temper when an employee banged at the door, waving an incorrect check. Instead, he offered the employee a donut and grabbed the nearest computer. He punched in data like a speed typist while juggling a telephone receiver, checking pay schedules, consulting IRS guidelines, and asking the employee about his or her family. He worked with the precision of a surgeon and the speed of a race car driver, bobbing and weaving behind the computer as he sliced through a week of paperwork. Glancing at the clock, he would start to hum, going into overdrive, making it his personal mission to cut a new paycheck before the employee's break was over.

3. **Use dialogue to add action to descriptions involving people.** Allowing people to speak for themselves is more interesting and effective than simply describing their comments.

4. **Avoid unnecessary detail or static descriptions.** Descriptions have focus. A description of your apartment does not have to list every piece of furniture, explain how each room is decorated, or provide dimensions. Descriptions of people do not have to include facts about age, height, and weight. In general, avoid writing descriptions that are static and lifeless or that place unnecessary emphasis on organizational arrangements:

On the left-hand wall is a bookcase. *To the right of the bookcase* is a stereo. *Around the corner of the stereo stands* an antique aquarium with tropical fish. *Above the aquarium* is a large seascape painting. Model ships line the window sill. *A cabinet* to the right of the window *is filled with seashells.*

5. **Keep the length of your paper in mind as you write the first draft.** If you are writing a 500-word essay describing your hometown and discover that by the second page you have covered only two of a dozen items on your outline, you may wish to review your plan.

   ■ Revise your outline, expanding or limiting your topic. It is better to describe a single New York neighborhood in detail than to attempt to create an impression of the entire city that becomes only a bland list of generalities.

Revising

1. **Review your plan and read your draft, focusing on its overall impact.** At this point, ignore such details as word choice or punctuation and concentrate on your draft's general effect.

   ■ Does it capture the true essence of your topic?

   ■ Is the draft too general, too vague? Should the topic be narrowed?

   ■ Does the paper generate interest by telling a story, highlighting overlooked details, or does it read like a shopping list of facts?

2. **Examine the information you have included.**

   ■ Are there minor details that should be deleted?

   ■ Can the description be improved by adding essential or interesting details that you overlooked in the first draft?

   ■ Do you include impressions from senses other than sight?

3. **Does the paper create a dominant impression?**

   ■ Does your paper have a clear focus—can you state a thesis?

   ■ Can ideas be rearranged to add emphasis, suspense, or interest?

4. **Is the description clearly organized?**

   ■ Does the paper's opening arouse interest?

   ■ Are details logically arranged? Do you use other modes to tell a story, create a pattern, or establish contrasts?

   ■ Does the paper end with a strong image, thought, or question that will leave a lasting impression on readers?

5. **Does your paper maintain a consistent point of view?** Avoid shifting from third to first person.

   ■ Determine whether you should change your role in the description. Would it be better stated from an objective or subjective viewpoint? Should you appear in the essay?

6. **Can action and dialogue be added to enliven the description?** Often a first draft will be a list of facts and observations.

   ■ Can you bring facts to life by describing people or things in action or at work?

   ■ Can speech be included?

7. **Can other modes be blended into the description to make it more interesting or easier to follow?**
   - Could the description be revised by adding narrative elements to tell a story?
   - Would comparison and contrast or cause and effect help present the details?
8. **If possible, use peer review to gain an additional perspective.**
   - Ask a friend or fellow student to read your draft. Ask your readers whether your paper creates a vivid picture of your subject. Ask what elements could be added to make the essay more effective.

Editing and Proofreading
1. **Read the paper aloud.** Listen to your sentences.
   - Are there awkward or repetitive phrases that could be revised or deleted?
   - Are the sentences varied in length and complexity, or do they fall into a redundant, humdrum pattern?
2. **Examine your choice of words.**
   - Is your diction fresh and inventive or bland and general?
   - Do you use concrete words?
   - Can clichés be replaced with original statements?
   - Do you use words accurately?
   - Do your connotations create the impressions you intend?
3. **Use a dictionary and thesaurus to examine word choice.**

STUDENT PAPER

This is the second version of a descriptive paper a student wrote in response to an assignment calling for "a brief description of a person, place, or thing."

My Bug

My father was in first grade when my Bug rolled off an assembly line in West Germany thirty-eight years ago. I have no idea what its original color was, but it has gone from gray to rust to black to cream to rust during my time. My '69 VW is not just a car but a family artifact.

My grandfather bought it in May 1969 as a second car for his wife. She drove it along the Jersey shore selling real estate for six years. The car followed the family West to San Francisco in 1975. My uncle then got the car and drove it to college in New Mexico. After graduating and getting a new car, he gave it to my Dad who was just learning how to drive. By now the car bore the tattoos of college bumper stickers, bent fenders, and rusted chrome. My Dad had the car painted a light cream and invested in a new transmission. During a ski trip his freshman year, the Bug skidded off an icy mountain road in Colorado and rolled over. He had the dents pounded out and the car painted gray. It took my parents on their honeymoon. Two years later the battered Bug carried me home from the hospital. After my parents bought a van, the Bug was relegated to being a backup vehicle. When my Mom got a new car, the Bug was retired to the garage.

Now it is mine. The fenders, though repainted, still bear the shallow depressions from the Colorado rollover. The windshield is pitted from stones that flew off a speeding gravel truck that nearly ran me off the road in Elko, Nevada, last year. The door handles are replacements I found on E-Bay. The car seats are patched with tape. Rust holes in the floor have been covered with cookie sheets. The dashboard sports the compass my mother glued on ten years ago so she would not get lost taking me to soccer games. The glove compartment is jammed with rumpled maps and snapshots from decades of family vacations and road trips.

My Bug is not the most glamorous vehicle in the college parking lot, but it has to be the most loved. It looks like a rolling homeless shelter to many. But to me it is a mobile family album. I love every ding and dent.

Questions for Review and Revision

1. How effective is the title?
2. Why is the car more than a vehicle to the student? What does it represent?
3. What method does the student use to organize the essay? How important are paragraph breaks?
4. What details does the student include about the car?
5. How effective is the ending? Would you like to see a more developed conclusion?
6. Read the paper aloud. What revisions would you make?

Writing Suggestions

1. Write a brief description of a common object that has special meaning to you—a car, an old coat, a favorite book, or a piece of furniture. Present as many sensory details as possible.
2. *Collaborative writing:* Discuss this essay with a group of students. Have each member volunteer opinions on its strengths and weaknesses. Do members suggest revisions or a need for added detail?

SUGGESTED TOPICS FOR WRITING DESCRIPTION

General Assignments

Write a description of any of the following topics. Your description may include other modes. Determine whether your description should rely on objective observations and factual detail or subjective impressions. When you select words to describe your topic, be conscious of their connotations. Above all, keep in mind what you are trying to share with your reader.

- Your first apartment
- The people who gather in a place you frequent—a coffee shop, store, nightclub, library, or student union
- Your best or worst boss or professor
- The most desirable/least desirable place to live in your community
- The most dangerous situation you have faced
- The worst day you have had in recent memory
- The type of man or woman you find attractive
- The most serious environmental problem in your region
- The best/worst party you have attended
- Christmas shopping at the mall
- Starting a new job
- Cramming for final exams
- Completing the chore you hate the most
- Most serious problem you face today
- Student attitudes about a specific subject: terrorism, racism, crime, jobs, television
- Violence in America

 To create your own interactive writing project, use the textual, visual, and video libraries on *Comp21*. From the main menu, choose "Build Your Own Occasion for Writing."

Writing in Context

1. Imagine that your college has asked you to write a description of the campus for a brochure designed to recruit students. Write a three- or four-paragraph description that is easy to read and creates a favorable impression. Consider what would appeal to high school seniors or adults returning to school.
2. Assume you are writing a column for an alternative student newspaper. Develop a short, satiric, or sarcastic description of the campus, the administration, or the student body. Draw witty comparisons to create humor and use inventive word choices.
3. Write an open letter to the graduating class of your high school describing college life. You may wish to compare college to high school to prepare students for the problems and challenges they will encounter.
4. Imagine you are trying to sell your car. Write two short ads, one designed for a campus flyer and the other for a newspaper.

STRATEGIES | for Reading Description

As you read the descriptions in this chapter, keep these questions in mind:

Context
1. What is the author's goal—to inform, enlighten, share personal observations, or provide information demanded by others? What is the writer's role? Is he or she writing from a personal or professional stance?
2. What is the intended audience—general or specific readers? How much knowledge does the author assume his or her readers have? Are technical terms defined? Does the description appear to have a special focus?
3. What is the nature of the discourse community? What does the source of the document—news magazine, corporation, personal essay, or book—reveal about the context?

Strategy
1. What details does the writer select? Does he or she appear to be deliberately emphasizing some items while ignoring or minimizing others?
2. Does the description establish a dominant impression? What method does the writer use to create it?

3. How much of the description is objective and how much is subjective?
4. How does the author organize details? Is there any particular method of grouping observations?
5. Does the writer include sensory impressions other than visual details?

Language
1. What level of language does the writer use? Are technical terms explained?
2. What role do connotations have in shaping the description? How do they support the writer's goal?

JONATHAN SCHELL

Jonathan Schell (1943–) is a journalist and antinuclear activist who has written extensively about atomic weapons and the problems of nuclear proliferation and disarmament. In 1981 he published **The Fate of the Earth,** which called for the abolition of nuclear weapons. His other books include **The Time of Illusion** and **The Gift of Time.** Schell was living six blocks from the World Trade Center when the towers collapsed on September 11, 2001.

Letter from Ground Zero

This essay appeared in the Nation *a month after terrorists struck Manhattan. As you read Schell's narrative, consider how this experience must have affected a journalist who had spent decades warning the public about the threat of weapons of mass destruction.*

introduction/
definition of
"ground zero"

sets place

graphic details
of site

1 Of course there can be no such thing as a literal letter from ground zero—neither from the ground zeros of September 11 nor from the potential nuclear ground zero that is the origin of the expression. There are no letters from the beyond. (By now, "zero" has the double meaning of zero distance from the bombardier's assigned coordinates and the nothingness that's left when his work is done.) As it happens, though, I live six blocks from the ruins of the north tower of the World Trade Center, which is about as close as you can be to ground zero without having been silenced. My specific neighborhood was violated, mutilated. As I write these words, the acrid, dank, rancid stink—it is the smell of death—of the still-smoking site is in my nostrils. Not that these things confer any great distinction—they are merely the local embodiment of the circumstance, felt more or less keenly by everyone in the world in the aftermath of the attack, that in our age of weapons of mass destruction every square foot of our globe can become such a ground zero in a twinkling. We have long known this intellectually, but now we know it viscerally, as a nausea in the pit of the stomach that is unlikely to go away. What to do to change this condition, it seems to me, is the most important of the practical tasks that the crisis requires us to perform.

2 It takes time for the human reality of the losses to sink in. The eye is quick but the heart is slow. I had two experiences this week that helped me along. It occurred to me that I would be a very bad journalist and maybe a

worse neighbor if, living just a few blocks from the catastrophe, I did not manage to get through the various checkpoints to visit the site. A press pass was useless; it got me no closer than my own home. A hole in the stormfence circling the site worked better. I found myself in the midst of a huge peaceable army of helpers in a thousand uniforms—military and civilian. I was somehow unprepared by television for what I saw when I arrived at ground zero. Television had seemed to show mostly a low hillock of rubble from which the famous bucket brigade of rescuers was passing out pieces of debris. This proved to be a keyhole vision of the site. In fact, it was a gigantic, varied, panoramic landscape of destruction, an Alps of concrete, plastic and twisted metal, rising tier upon tier in the smoky distance. Around the perimeter and in the surrounding streets, a cornucopia of food, drinks (thousands of crates of spring water, Gatorade, etc.) and other provisions contributed by well-wishers from around the country was heaped up, as if some main of consumer goods on its way to the Trade Center had burst and disgorged its flood upon the sidewalks. The surrounding buildings, smashed but still standing, looked down eyelessly on their pulverized brethren. The pieces of the facade of the towers that are often shown in photographs— gigantic forks, or bent spatulas—loomed surprisingly high over the scene with dread majesty. Entry into the ruins by the rescue workers was being accomplished by a cage, or gondola, suspended by a crane, as if in some infernal ski resort. When I arrived at the southern rim, the rescuers were all standing silent watching one of these cages being lifted out of the ruins. Shortly, a small pile of something not shaped like a human being but covered by an American flag was brought out in an open buggy. It was the remains, a solemn nurse told me, of one of the firemen who had given his life for the people in the building. And then the slow work began again. Although the site was more terrible even than I had imagined, seeing was somehow reassuring. Unvisited, the site, so near my home, had preyed on my imagination.

A few days later—one week after the catastrophe—I took my dog for a 3 walk in the evening in Riverside Park, on the upper West Side. Soft orange clouds drifted over the Hudson River and the New Jersey shore. In the dim, cavernous green of the park, normal things were occurring—people were out for walks or jogging, children were playing in a playground. To the south, a slender moon hung in the sky. I found myself experiencing an instant of surprise: So it was still there! It had not dropped out of the sky. That was good. After all, our local southern mountain peaks—the twin towers— had fallen. The world seemed to steady around the surviving moon. "Peace" became more than a word. It was the world of difference between the bottom half of Manhattan and the top. It was the persistence of all the wonderful, ordinary things before my eyes.

describes what he saw/ TV vs. reality

describes his reaction

contrasting images of normal life

Understanding Context

1. What motivated Schell to visit the disaster site?
2. How did seeing the site in person differ from viewing it on television? What sights had the greatest impact on Schell?
3. What does Schell mean by the statement that the "eye is quick but the heart is slow"?
4. *Critical thinking:* Schell states that though the site was more horrible than he imagined, seeing it was somehow comforting. How did visiting the World Trade Center make the disaster less troubling for him?

Evaluating Strategy

1. What senses besides sight does Schell use in creating his description?
2. What visual details does Schell include to impress readers with the scope of the disaster?
3. What role does the moon play in the final paragraph?

Appreciating Language

1. Schell humanizes the damaged buildings so that they "looked down eyelessly on their pulverized brethren." What impact does this have?
2. What words does Schell use to dramatize the size of the rubble that seems on television to be only a "low hillock"?
3. Schell is a political journalist. How does the tone, style, and diction of this narrative differ from the type of objective reporting you might expect in a newspaper article?

Writing Suggestions

1. Write a description of a disaster scene you have visited—an auto accident, a fire, flood, or blizzard. Use images to help readers visualize the extent of the damage. Remember that your description can include narrative elements, such as action and dialogue.
2. *Collaborative writing:* Working with a group of students, review Schell's article and write a one- or two-paragraph objective description based on his eyewitness testimony.

© Kim Komenich/San Francisco Chronicle/Corbis

e-reading

InfoTrac College Edition
www.infotrac-college.com

THE WAR ON TERRORISM

How can you defeat an enemy who thinks he's on a mission from God? A hundred days and one war later, we know the answer: B-52's, for starters.
Charles Krauthammer

The instinct to retaliate with bombing is an anachronism. Fewer than twenty men had brought us to our national knees. . . . The government's answer was that we were good and love freedom and these people are bad and hate it. That vapid answer came from a national culture that has lost its talent for healthy guilt.

Daniel C. Maguire

Shortly after the attacks of September 11, 2001, President Bush announced a war against terrorism. Speaking to reporters two weeks later,

Paul Wolfowitz, Deputy Secretary of Defense, outlined the direction of the war:

> It's not going to be solved by some limited military action. It's going to take, as the President has said and Secretary Rumsfeld has said, a broad and sustained campaign against the terrorist networks and the states that support those terrorist networks.

Within weeks the United States began military operations that would topple the Taliban regime in Afghanistan, a move that cost few American casualties and was widely supported by the public at home and its Allies abroad.

The passage of the Patriot Act and the invasion of Iraq, however, led critics to question if these actions would defeat terrorists or simply erode civil liberties at home, hurt America's image abroad, create more anger in the Muslim world, encouraging more terrorism. Among those who supported President Bush were columnist Thomas Friedman, who argued that the United States had to project its power in the Middle East:

> The "right reason" for this war was the need to partner with Iraqis . . . to build a progressive Arab regime. Because the real weapons of mass destruction that threaten us were never Saddam's missiles. The real weapons that threaten us are growing number of angry, humiliated young Arabs and Muslims, who are produced by failed or failing Arab states—young people who hate America more than they love life.

Arab and Muslim commentators viewed the invasion differently, seeing it as a dangerous misstep in attempting to curb terrorism. Husain Haqqani, a Pakistani journalist, suggested an alternative strategy to counter extremism in the Muslim world:

> The United States must avoid any impulse to act as an imperial power, dictating its superior ways to "less civilized" peoples. It should be prepared to accept Islamic pride and Arab nationalism as factors in the region's politics, instead of backing narrowly based elites to do its bidding. Patient engagement, rather than the flaunting of military and financial power, should characterize this new phase of U.S. intervention in the heart of the Islamic world.

For some Americans, the concept of a never-ending "war on terrorism" raised concerns. Susan Sontag believed the term "war" itself was inappropriate to describe the actions America must take:

There are no endless wars. But there are declarations of the extension of power by a state that believes it cannot be challenged. America has every right to hunt down the perpetrators of these crimes and their accomplices. But this determination is not necessarily a war. Limited, focused military engagements abroad do not translate into "wartime" at home. There are better ways to check America's enemies, less destructive of constitutional rights and international agreements that serve the public interest of all, than continuing to invoke the dangerous, lobotomizing notion of endless war.

In 2005 members of the Bush Administration began call for a fight against "extremism" rather than a "war on terrorism."

Before reading these articles, consider these questions:

Was the proper response to the attack on September 11 a "war"? What action should the President take to confront international terrorism?

Did toppling regimes in Afghanistan and Iraq make America more or less secure? Did the demonstration of military power shatter the ambitions of extremists or only fuel the humiliation and resentment that breed terrorism?

Why did terrorists target the United States? Do most Americans understand why their nation is viewed with so much hatred throughout Africa and Asia?

When will a war on terror end, if ever? Can we expect the United States to be a nation under threat for next ten, twenty, or fifty years?

Do you think America will suffer another major attack in the future? How likely do think it is that terrorists will cause mass casualties? Is a major attack with biological, chemical, or nuclear weapons probable?

E-Readings Online

Search for each article by author or title after entering InfoTrac College Edition through your 1Pass account login.

Daniel C. Maguire. *When I Boarded the Midwest Express to Washington, D.C., on September 11.*
Following the attacks of September 11, a Christian scholar argues that "to retaliate with bombing is an anachronism." The question we should ask is "Why do the deprived of the world hate us so?"

Charles Krauthammer. *Only in Their Dreams.*
Krauthammer argues that asking "why do they hate us?" misses the point because there is "no assuaging those who see your very existence as a denial of the faith and an affront to God."

Caryle Murphy. *The War on Terrorism: Why It Will Be a Long One.*
Arab Muslims, a Middle East correspondent notes, do not hate us, only our foreign policy. To win the war on terrorism America "must help moderate Muslims find their voices."

Husain Haqqani. *The American Mongols.*
America's victory over Saddam only inspires Islamic fundamentalists who have long believed "that military defeat at the hands of unbelievers results when Muslims embrace pluralism and worldly knowledge." Tolerance and openness to the West, Islamists tell followers, only leads to humiliation.

A. Tariq Karim. *Terrorism: Addressing Its Root Causes.*
Terrorists are bred in unjust and undemocratic societies in which fanatics preaching hatred and bigotry offer the only alternative to oppression.

Howard Zinn. *Operation Enduring War.*
The war against terrorism is a war without end that turns attention away from the most deadly enemies who "are not in caves and compounds abroad but in the corporate boardrooms and governmental offices where decisions are made that consign millions to death and misery . . ."

Susan Sontag. *How Grief Turned into Humbug.*
Sontag argues that while America has real enemies that threaten all that she values, the needed response is limited military operations—not a "war" that limits constitutional rights at home and violates international agreements abroad.

Fareed Zakaria. *How We Can Prevail.*
Leading Muslim scholars and clerics are denouncing terrorism and the United States must work with them to isolate extremists, who are determined to kill anyone, Muslim or non-Muslim, who oppose their ambitions.

Critical Reading and Thinking

1. How do the various authors define "terrorism"?
2. Why was America attacked, according to these authors?
3. What do the authors see as the cause of terrorism?
4. What do these authors see as the proper response to terrorism?

5. Why do some authors believe that the United States must improve its relations with the Muslim world to defeat terrorism?

Writing Suggestions

1. Write an essay about how the war on terrorism has affected your life. Have you witnessed more security at airports? Do you have family or friends serving in the military? What attitudes have you observed among family, friends, coworkers, and other students? Is terrorism something they talk about?
2. *Collaborative writing:* Working with other students, develop an essay outlining what your group believes the best strategies for opposing terrorism. If students disagree, consider drafting opposing essays.
3. *Other modes*
   - Write a *cause-and-effect* essay that explains the causes of terrorism and or the effects it has on society.
   - Develop a *classification* essay that explains what you consider the most to least likely future terrorist attacks or the least to most successful ways of improving national security.
   - Write an essay that uses an *example* of what you consider the best or worst decision the administration has made on the war on terrorism.
   - Write a *process* essay that explains what steps the United States should take to defeat terrorism.

Research Paper

You can develop a research paper about the war on terrorism by conducting further research to explore a range of issues:

- How do different experts, commentators, and governments define "terrorism"?
- How have Europeans responded to America's war on terrorism, especially the invasion of Iraq?
- How has the Muslim world responded to extremism and terrorism?
- What motivates terrorists to attack civilian populations?
- Do historians and political commentators see terrorism as evidence of a "clash of civilizations" between Islam and the West or a conflict between a small group of extremists and the rest of the world, including mainstream Muslims?

For Further Reading

To locate additional sources on terrorism, enter these search terms as InfoTrac subjects:

Terrorism
Subdivisions: analysis
                  beliefs, opinions and attitudes
                  case studies
                  causes of
                  control
                  forecasts and trends
                  investigations
                  prevention

War on Terrorism, 2001–
Subdivisions: analysis
                  beliefs, opinions and attitudes
                  ethical aspects
                  influence
                  international aspects
                  planning
                  political aspects

Additional Sources

Using a search engine, such as Yahoo!, Google, or Alta Vista, enter one or more of the following terms to locate additional sources:

terrorism	Homeland Security
nuclear terrorism	al Qaeda
Osama bin Laden	causes of terrorism
effects of terrorism	war on terrorism
terrorist organizations	suicide bombers

See Evaluating Internet Source Checklist on page 752. See Chapter 30 for using and documenting sources.

Truman Capote (1924–1985) was born in New Orleans and first gained prominence as a writer of short stories. At the age of twenty-four he produced his first novel, **Other Voices, Other Rooms,** which achieved international attention. His other works include **Breakfast at Tiffany's** and **A Tree of Night.** In 1965 he published **In Cold Blood,** which became an immediate best-seller. Based on extensive research and interviews, **In Cold Blood** tells the story of a 1959 mass murder of a Kansas farm family and the fate of the killers. Although nonfiction, Capote's book reads much like a novel. **In Cold Blood** helped shape a new school of journalism that uses the stylistic touches of fiction to relate actual events.

Out There

The opening pages of In Cold Blood *describe the small town of Holcomb, Kansas, where the murders occurred. Capote spent a great deal of time in Holcomb and describes it almost as if it had been his own hometown. Notice how Capote blends objective facts with subjective impressions.*

The village of Holcomb stands on the high wheat plains of western Kansas, a lonesome area that other Kansans call "out there." Some seventy miles east of the Colorado border, the countryside, with its hard blue skies and desert-clear air, has an atmosphere that is rather more Far Western than Middle West. The local accent is barbed with a prairie twang, a ranch-hand nasalness, and the men, many of them, wear narrow frontier trousers, Stetsons, and high-heeled boots with pointed toes. The land is flat, and the views are awesomely extensive; horses, herds of cattle, a white cluster of grain elevators rising as gracefully as Greek temples are visible long before a traveler reaches them.

Holcomb, too, can be seen from great distances. Not that there is much to see—simply an aimless congregation of buildings divided in the center by the main-line tracks of the Santa Fe Railroad, a haphazard hamlet bounded on the south by a brown stretch of the Arkansas (pronounced "Arkan-sas") River, on the north by a highway, Route 50, and on the east and west by prairie lands and wheat fields. After rain, or when snowfalls thaw, the streets, unnamed, unshaded, unpaved, turn from the thickest dust into the direst mud. At one end of the town stands a stark old stucco structure, the roof of which supports an electric sign—Dance—but the dancing has ceased and the advertisement has been dark for several years. Nearby is another building with an irrelevant sign, this one in flaking gold on a dirty window—Holcomb Bank. The bank closed in 1933, and its former counting rooms have been converted into apartments. It is one of the town's two "apartment houses," the second being a ramshackle mansion known, because a good part of the local school's faculty lives there, as the Teacherage. But the majority of Holcomb's homes are one-story frame affairs, with front porches.

3   Down by the depot, the postmistress, a gaunt woman who wears a rawhide jacket and denims and cowboy boots, presides over a falling-apart post office. The depot itself, with its peeling sulphur-colored paint, is equally melancholy; the Chief, the Super Chief, the El Capitan go by every day, but these celebrated expresses never pause there. No passenger trains do—only an occasional freight. Up on the highway, there are two filling stations, one of which doubles as a meagerly supplied grocery store, while the other does extra duty as a café—Hartman's Café, where Mrs. Hartman, the proprietress, dispenses sandwiches, coffee, soft drinks, and 3.2 beer. (Holcomb, like all the rest of Kansas, is "dry.")

4   And that, really, is all. Unless you include, as one must, the Holcomb School, a good-looking establishment, which reveals a circumstance that the appearance of the community otherwise camouflages: that the parents who send their children to this modern and ably staffed "consolidated" school—the grades go from kindergarten through senior high, and a fleet of buses transport the students, of which there are usually around three hundred and sixty, from as far as sixteen miles away—are, in general, a prosperous people. Farm ranchers, most of them, they are outdoor folk of very varied stock—German, Irish, Norwegian, Mexican, Japanese. They raise cattle and sheep, grow wheat, milo, grass seed, and sugar beets. Farming is always a chancy business, but in western Kansas its practitioners consider themselves "born gamblers," for they must contend with an extremely shallow precipitation (the annual average is eighteen inches) and anguishing irrigation problems. However, the last seven years have been years of droughtless beneficence. The farm ranchers in Finney County, of which Holcomb is a part, have done well; money has been made not from farming alone but also from the exploitation of plentiful natural-gas resources, and its acquisition is reflected in the new school, the comfortable interiors of the farmhouses, the steep and swollen grain elevators.

5   Until one morning in mid-November of 1959, few Americans—in fact, few Kansans—had ever heard of Holcomb. Like the waters of the river, like

the motorists on the highway, and like the yellow trains streaking down the Santa Fe tracks, drama, in the shape of exceptional happenings, had never stopped there. The inhabitants of the village, numbering two hundred and seventy, were satisfied that this should be so, quite content to exist inside ordinary life—to work, to hunt, to watch television, to attend school socials, choir practice, meetings of the 4-H Club. But then, in the earliest hours of that morning in November, a Sunday morning, certain foreign sounds impinged on the normal nightly Holcomb noises—on the keening hysteria of coyotes, the dry scrape of scuttling tumbleweed, the racing, receding wail of locomotive whistles. At the time not a soul in sleeping Holcomb heard them—four shotgun blasts that, all told, ended six human lives. But afterward the townspeople, theretofore sufficiently unfearful of each other to seldom trouble to lock their doors, found fantasy re-creating them over and again—those somber explosions that stimulated fires of mistrust in the glare of which many old neighbors viewed each other strangely, and as strangers.

Understanding Context

1. How much of Capote's description can be considered objective, how much subjective?
2. Capote includes a great deal of factual detail—names of highways, the number of students in the high school, and Holcomb's population. Why are these facts important in establishing an impression of the town?
3. What does Capote attempt to capture about this town?

Evaluating Strategy

1. *Critical thinking:* A key element in the opening of any book is to get people's attention and motivate them to continue reading. How does Capote generate interest by describing a nondescript town?
2. What is the impact of the closing lines?

Appreciating Language

1. How does the language of Capote's description differ from that of an encyclopedia or newspaper article?
2. *In Cold Blood* has sold millions of copies. What elements in Capote's style make his story about a crime in a small Kansas town so popular? What phrases strike you as being colorful or interesting?

Writing Suggestions

1. Rewrite a recent article from the local newspaper, adding subjective details to arouse human interest for a national audience. Include observations about your community to give readers a feel for the location.
2. Using Capote's description as a resource, write a purely objective one-paragraph description of Holcomb, Kansas.
3. Attempt to write a one-line thesis statement for "Out There."

Luis Alberto Urrea was born in Tijuana to a Mexican father and American mother. He grew up in San Diego and attended the University of California. After graduation and a brief career as a movie extra, Urrea worked with a volunteer organization that provides food, clothing, and medical supplies to the poor of northern Mexico. In 1982 he taught writing at Harvard. His most recent novel, *In Search of Snow,* was published in 1994, and he published a collection of poems, *Ghost Sickness,* in 1997.

Border Story

In this description of the Mexican-American border from Across the Wire: Life and Hard Times on the Mexican Border *(1993), Urrea uses the device of second person to place his reader in the scene. By making "you" the "illegal," he seeks to dramatize and humanize the plight of the poor seeking a new life in the United States.*

At night, the Border Patrol helicopters swoop and churn in the air all along 1 the line. You can sit in the Mexican hills and watch them herd humans on the dusty slopes across the valley. They look like science fiction crafts, their hard-focused lights raking the ground as they fly.

Borderlands locals are so jaded by the sight of nightly people-hunting 2 that it doesn't even register in their minds. But take a stranger to the border, and she will *see* the spectacle: monstrous Dodge trucks speeding into and out of the landscape; uniformed men patrolling with flashlights, guns, and dogs; spotlights; running figures; lines of people hurried onto buses by armed guards; and the endless clatter of the helicopters with their harsh white beams. A Dutch woman once told me it seemed altogether "un-American."

But the Mexicans keep on coming—and the Guatemalans, the Sal- 3 vadorans, the Panamanians, the Colombians. The seven-mile stretch of Interstate 5 nearest the Mexican border is, at times, so congested with Latin American pedestrians that it resembles a town square.

They stick to the center island. Running down the length of the island is 4 a cement wall. If the "illegals" (currently, "undocumented workers"; formerly, "wetbacks") are walking north and a Border Patrol vehicle happens along, they simply hop over the wall and trot south. The officer will have to drive up to the 805 interchange, or Dairy Mart Road, swing over the overpasses, then drive south. Depending on where this pursuit begins, his detour could entail five to ten miles of driving. When the officer finally reaches the group, they hop over the wall and trot north. Furthermore, because freeway arrests would endanger traffic, the Border Patrol has effectively thrown up its hands in surrender.

5   It seems jolly on the page. But imagine poverty, violence, natural disasters, or political fear driving you away from everything you know. Imagine how bad things get to make you leave behind your family, your friends, your lovers; your home, as humble as it might be; your church, say. Let's take it further—you've said good-bye to the graveyard, the dog, the goat, the mountains where you first hunted, your grade school, your state, your favorite spot on the river where you fished and took time to think.

6   Then you come hundreds—or thousands—of miles across territory utterly unknown to you. (Chances are, you have never traveled farther than a hundred miles in your life.) You have walked, run, hidden in the backs of trucks, spent part of your precious money on bus fare. There is no AAA or Travelers Aid Society available to you. Various features of your journey north might include police corruption; violence in the forms of beatings, rape, murder, torture, road accidents; theft; incarceration. Additionally, you might experience loneliness, fear, exhaustion, sorrow, cold, heat, diarrhea, thirst, hunger. There is no medical attention available to you. There isn't even Kotex.

7   Weeks or months later, you arrive in Tijuana. Along with other immigrants, you gravitate to the bad parts of town because there is nowhere for you to go in the glittery sections where the *gringos* flock. You stay in a rundown little hotel in the red-light district, or behind the bus terminal. Or you find your way to the garbage dumps, where you throw together a small cardboard nest and claim a few feet of dirt for yourself. The garbage-pickers working this dump might allow you to squat, or they might come and rob you or burn you out for breaking some local rule you cannot possibly know beforehand. Sometimes the dump is controlled by a syndicate, and goon squads might come to you within a day. They want money, and if you can't pay, you must leave or suffer the consequences.

8   In town, you face endless victimization if you aren't streetwise. The police come after you, street thugs come after you, petty criminals come after you; strangers try your door at night as you sleep. Many shady men offer to guide you across the border, and each one wants all your money now, and promises to meet you at a prearranged spot. Some of your fellow travelers end their journeys right here—relieved of their savings and left to wait on a dark corner until they realize they are going nowhere.

If you are not Mexican, and can't pass as *tijuanense,* a local, the tough guys find you out. Salvadorans and Guatemalans are routinely beaten up and robbed. Sometimes they are disfigured. Indians—Chinantecas, Mixtecas, Guasaves, Zapotecas, Mayas—are insulted and pushed around; often they are lucky—they are merely ignored. They use this to their advantage. Often they don't dream of crossing into the United States: a Mexican tribal person would never be able to blend in, and they know it. To them, the garbage dumps and street vending and begging in Tijuana are a vast improvement over their former lives. As Doña Paula, a Chinanteca friend of mine who lives at the Tijuana garbage dump, told me, "This is the garbage dump. Take all you need. There's plenty here for *everyone!*"

If you are a woman, the men come after you. You lock yourself in your room, and when you must leave it to use the pestilential public bathroom at the end of your floor, you hurry, and you check every corner. Sometimes the lights are out in the toilet room. Sometimes men listen at the door. They call you "good-looking" and "bitch" and "*mamacita,*" and they make kissing sounds at you when you pass.

You're in the worst part of town, but you can comfort yourself—at least there are no death squads here. There are no torturers here, or bandit land barons riding into your house. This is the last barrier, you think, between you and the United States—*los Yunaites Estaites.*

You still face police corruption, violence, jail. You now also have a wide variety of new options available to you: drugs, prostitution, white slavery, crime. Tijuana is not easy on newcomers. It is a city that has always thrived on taking advantage of a sucker. And the innocent are the ultimate suckers in the Borderlands.

Understanding Context

1. Urrea has called the border a "battlefield." How does his description illustrate this view?
2. What problems do the undocumented aliens face in their attempt to cross the border?
3. How are non-Mexican refugees treated in Tijuana?
4. What is the plight of refugee women on the border?
5. *Critical thinking:* Urrea quotes a Dutch woman who used the term "un-American" to describe the border patrols. What is un-American about fences and helicopter patrols? Does this response to immigration clash with the Statue of Liberty's promise to welcome the tired and poor?

Evaluating Strategy

1. How effective is the use of the second person? Does it really put "you" in the scene? Does it help dramatize the plight of people many readers might choose to ignore?
2. What details does Urrea use to dramatize conditions along the border?

Appreciating Language

1. Throughout the description, Urrea uses lists—"beatings, rape, murder, torture, road accidents. . . ." How effective are they? Can listing words become tedious?
2. Select the words that create the most powerful images of the border. Why do they make strong impressions?

Writing Suggestions

1. Write an essay describing a place that highlights a social problem. Select a location of which you have personal knowledge, and try to convey the conditions residents face through lists of details.
2. *Collaborative writing:* Ask a group of fellow students to respond to Urrea's account. Consider the issues his description of the border raises. Ask members to suggest how conditions could be improved, and then draft a short *persuasion* essay outlining your ideas.

Carl T. Rowan (1925–2000) was born in Tennessee and received degrees from Oberlin College and the University of Minnesota. He worked for years as a columnist for the **Minneapolis Tribune** and the **Chicago Sun-Times,** expressing his views on a variety of issues, especially race relations. Rowan also served as the director of the United States Information Agency and was the ambassador to Finland.

Unforgettable Miss Bessie

This article describing a schoolteacher originally appeared in Reader's Digest, *for which Rowan served as an editor. Rowan's account is personal, and much of his description focuses on the impact this teacher had on him and other disadvantaged students.*

1   She was only about five feet tall and probably never weighed more than 110 pounds, but Miss Bessie was a towering presence in the classroom. She was the only woman tough enough to make me read *Beowulf* and think for a few foolish days that I liked it. From 1938 to 1942, when I attended Bernard High School in McMinnville, Tenn., she taught me English, history, civics— and a lot more than I realized.

2   I shall never forget the day she scolded me into reading *Beowulf.*

3   "But Miss Bessie," I complained, "I ain't much interested in it."

4   Her large brown eyes became daggerish slits. "Boy," she said, "how dare you say 'ain't' to me! I've taught you better than that."

5   "Miss Bessie," I pleaded, "I'm trying to make first-string end on the football team, and if I go around saying 'it isn't' and 'they aren't,' the guys are gonna laugh me off the squad."

6   "Boy," she responded, "you'll play football because you have guts. But do you know what *really* takes guts? Refusing to lower your standards to those of the crowd. It takes guts to say you've got to live and be somebody fifty years after all the football games are over." I started saying "it isn't" and "they aren't," and I still made first-string end—and class valedictorian— without losing my buddies' respect.

7   During her remarkable 44-year career, Mrs. Bessie Taylor Gwynn taught hundreds of economically deprived black youngsters—including my

mother, my brother, my sisters and me. I remember her now with gratitude and affection—especially in this era when Americans are so wrought-up about a "rising tide of mediocrity" in public education and the problems of finding competent, caring teachers. Miss Bessie was an example of an informed, dedicated teacher, a blessing to children and an asset to the nation.

8   Born in 1895, in poverty, she grew up in Athens, Ala., where there was no public school for blacks. She attended Trinity School, a private institution for blacks run by the American Missionary Association, and in 1911 graduated from the Normal School (a "super" high school) at Fisk University in Nashville. Mrs. Gwynn, the essence of pride and privacy, never talked about her years in Athens; only in the months before her death did she reveal that she had never attended Fisk University itself because she could not afford the four-year course.

9   At Normal School she learned a lot about Shakespeare, but most of all about the profound importance of education—especially, for a people trying to move up from slavery. "What you put in your head, boy," she once said, "can never be pulled out by the Ku Klux Klan, the Congress or anybody."

10   Miss Bessie's bearing of dignity told anyone who met her that she was "educated" in the best sense of the word. There was never a discipline problem in her classes. We didn't dare mess with a woman who knew about the Battle of Hastings, the Magna Carta and the Bill of Rights—and who could also play the piano.

11   This frail-looking woman could make sense of Shakespeare, Milton, Voltaire, and bring to life Booker T. Washington and W. E. B. DuBois. Believing that it was important to know who the officials were that spent taxpayers' money and made public policy, she made us memorize the names of everyone on the Supreme Court and in the President's Cabinet. It could be embarrassing to be unprepared when Miss Bessie said, "Get up and tell the class who Frances Perkins is and what you think about her."

12   Miss Bessie knew that my family, like so many others during the Depression, couldn't afford to subscribe to a newspaper. She knew we didn't even own a radio. Still, she prodded me to "look out for your future and find some way to keep up with what's going on in the world." So I became a delivery boy for the Chattanooga *Times*. I rarely made a dollar a week, but I got to read a newspaper every day.

13   Miss Bessie noticed things that had nothing to do with schoolwork, but were vital to a youngster's development. Once a few classmates made fun of my frayed, hand-me-down overcoat, calling me "Strings." As I was leaving school, Miss Bessie patted me on the back of that old overcoat and said, "Carl, never fret about what you *don't* have. Just make the most of what you *do* have—a brain."

Among the things that I did not have was electricity in the little frame 14
house that my father had built for $400 with his World War I bonus. But be-
cause of her inspiration, I spent many hours squinting beside a kerosene
lamp reading Shakespeare and Thoreau, Samuel Pepys and William Cullen
Bryant.

No one in my family had ever graduated from high school, so there was 15
no tradition of commitment to learning for me to lean on. Like millions of
youngsters in today's ghettos and barrios, I needed the push and stimulation
of a teacher who truly cared. Miss Bessie gave plenty of both, as she immersed
me in a wonderful world of similes, metaphors and even onomatopoeia. She
led me to believe that I could write sonnets as well as Shakespeare, or iambic-
pentameter verse to put Alexander Pope to shame.

In those days the McMinnville school system was rigidly "Jim Crow," 16
and poor black children had to struggle to put anything in their heads. Our
high school was only slightly larger than the once-typical little red school-
house, and its library was outrageously inadequate—so small, I like to say,
that if two students were in it and one wanted to turn a page, the other one
had to step outside.

Negroes, as we were called then, were not allowed in the town library, 17
except to mop floors or dust tables. But through one of those secret Old
South arrangements between whites of conscience and blacks of stature,
Miss Bessie kept getting books smuggled out of the white library. That is
how she introduced me to the Brontës, Byron, Coleridge, Keats and Ten-
nyson. "If you don't read, you can't write, and if you can't write, you might
as well stop dreaming," Miss Bessie once told me.

So I read whatever Miss Bessie told me to, and tried to remember the 18
things she insisted that I store away. Forty-five years later, I can still recite
her "truths to live by," such as Henry Wadsworth Longfellow's lines from
"The Ladder of St. Augustine":

> The heights by great men reached and kept
> Were not attained by sudden flight.
> But they, while their companions slept,
> Were toiling upward in the night.

Years later, her inspiration, prodding, anger, cajoling and almost osmotic 19
infusion of learning finally led to that lovely day when Miss Bessie dropped
me a note saying, "I'm so proud to read your column in the Nashville
Tennessean."

Miss Bessie was a spry 80 when I went back to McMinnville and visited 20
her in a senior citizens' apartment building. Pointing out proudly that her
building was racially integrated, she reached for two glasses and a pint of

bourbon. I was momentarily shocked, because it would have been scandalous in the 1930s and '40s for word to get out that a teacher drank, and nobody had ever raised a rumor that Miss Bessie did.

21   I felt a new sense of equality as she lifted her glass to mine. Then she revealed a softness and compassion that I had never known as a student.

22   "I've never forgotten that examination day," she said, "when Buster Martin held up seven fingers, obviously asking you for help with question number seven, 'Name a common carrier.' I can still picture you looking at your exam paper and humming a few bars of 'Chattanooga Choo Choo.' I was so tickled, I couldn't punish either of you."

23   Miss Bessie was telling me, with bourbon-laced grace, that I never fooled her for a moment.

24   When Miss Bessie died in 1980, at age 85, hundreds of her former students mourned. They knew the measure of a great teacher: love and motivation. Her wisdom and influence had rippled out across generations.

25   Some of her students who might normally have been doomed to poverty went on to become doctors, dentists and college professors. Many, guided by Miss Bessie's example, became public-school teachers.

26   "The memory of Miss Bessie and how she conducted her classroom did more for me than anything I learned in college," recalls Gladys Wood of Knoxville, Tenn., a highly respected English teacher who spent 43 years in the state's school system. "So many times, when I faced a difficult classroom problem, I asked myself, *How would Miss Bessie deal with this?* And I'd remember that she would handle it with laughter and love."

27   No child can get all the necessary support at home, and millions of poor children get *no* support at all. This is what makes a wise, educated, warmhearted teacher like Miss Bessie so vital to the minds, hearts and souls of this country's children.

Understanding Context

1. What is Rowan's purpose in describing Miss Bessie? What makes this teacher significant to a middle-aged man?
2. What qualities of Miss Bessie does Rowan admire?
3. Does Rowan offer Miss Bessie as a role model? How does he demonstrate that she is an "asset to the nation"?

Evaluating Strategy

1. Rowan opens his essay with a physical description of Miss Bessie. Why are these details important to his purpose?

2. Why would this article appeal to readers of *Reader's Digest*? What values does it reinforce?

3. *Critical thinking:* Would some people object to Rowan's article as being sentimental? Why or why not? Does this article suggest simple solutions to complex problems? Would a Miss Bessie be able to succeed in a modern urban high school?

Appreciating Language

1. Study the words Rowan uses in describing Miss Bessie. Which words have the most impact?

2. Rowan includes dialogue in his article. What do you notice about Miss Bessie's language? What does this add to the description?

Writing Suggestions

1. Write a brief description of a teacher, employer, or coworker who greatly influenced your development. Provide specific examples of the lessons you learned.

2. *Collaborative writing:* Working with three or four other students, discuss Miss Bessie's statement, "What you put in your head, boy, can never be pulled out by the Ku Klux Klan, the Congress or anybody." Use this quotation as the headline of a poster urging people to read. Keep your message short. Read it aloud to hear how it sounds.

E. B. WHITE

Elwyn Brooks White (1899–1985) was born in Mount Vernon, New York, and attended Cornell University. He was a regular contributor to the **New Yorker** magazine for fifty years. His articles achieved a reputation for their wit and style. White assisted William Strunk in revising his popular book on writing, **The Elements of Style.** He also gained popularity as a writer of children's literature. His books **Stuart Little** and **Charlotte's Web** have become classics.

Once More to the Lake

First published in Harper's *in 1941, "Once More to the Lake" describes White's nostalgic return to a boyhood vacation spot. As you read the essay, notice how White uses comparison and narration in developing his description.*

August 1941

1 One summer, along about 1904, my father rented a camp on a lake in Maine and took us all there for the month of August. We all got ringworm from some kittens and had to rub Pond's Extract on our arms and legs night and morning, and my father rolled over in a canoe with all his clothes on; but outside of that the vacation was a success and from then on none of us ever thought there was any place in the world like that lake in Maine. We returned summer after summer—always on August 1 for one month. I have since become a salt-water man, but sometimes in summer there are days when the restlessness of the tides and the fearful cold of the sea water and the incessant wind that blows across the afternoon and into the evening make me wish for the placidity of a lake in the woods. A few weeks ago this feeling got so strong I bought myself a couple of bass hooks and a spinner and returned to the lake where we used to go, for a week's fishing and to revisit old haunts.

2 I took along my son, who had never had any fresh water up his nose and who had seen lily pads only from train windows. On the journey over to the lake I began to wonder what it would be like. I wondered how time would have marred this unique, this holy spot—the coves and streams, the hills that the sun set behind, the camps and the paths behind the camps. I was sure that the tarred road would have found it out, and I wondered in what other ways it would be desolated. It is strange how much you can remember

about places like that once you allow your mind to return into the grooves that lead back. You remember one thing, and that suddenly reminds you of another thing. I guess I remembered clearest of all the early mornings, when the lake was cool and motionless, remembered how the bedroom smelled of the lumber it was made of and of the wet woods whose scent entered through the screen. The partitions in the camp were thin and did not extend clear to the top of the rooms, and as I was always the first up I would dress softly so as not to wake the others, and sneak out into the sweet outdoors and start out in the canoe, keeping close along the shore in the long shadows of the pines. I remembered being very careful never to rub my paddle against the gunwale for fear of disturbing the stillness of the cathedral.

The lake had never been what you would call a wild lake. There were 3 cottages sprinkled around the shores, and it was in farming country although the shores of the lake were quite heavily wooded. Some of the cottages were owned by nearby farmers, and you would live at the shore and eat your meals at the farmhouse. That's what our family did. But although it wasn't wild, it was a fairly large and undisturbed lake and there were places in it that, to a child at least, seemed infinitely remote and primeval.

I was right about the tar: it led to within half a mile of the shore. But when 4 I got back there, with my boy, and we settled into a camp near a farmhouse and into the kind of summertime I had known, I could tell that it was going to be pretty much the same as it had been before—I knew it, lying in bed the first morning, smelling the bedroom and hearing the boy sneak quietly out and go off along the shore in a boat. I began to sustain the illusion that he was I, and therefore, by simple transposition, that I was my father. This sensation persisted, kept cropping up all the time we were there. It was not an entirely new feeling, but in this setting it grew much stronger. I seemed to be living a dual existence. I would be in the middle of some simple act, I would be picking up a bait box or laying down a table fork, or I would be saying something, and suddenly it would be not I but my father who was saying the words or making the gesture. It gave me a creepy sensation.

We went fishing the first morning. I felt the same damp moss covering 5 the worms in the bait can, and saw the dragonfly alight on the tip of my rod as it hovered a few inches from the surface of the water. It was the arrival of this fly that convinced me beyond any doubt that everything was as it always had been, that the years were a mirage and that there had been no years. The small waves were the same, chucking the rowboat under the chin as we fished at anchor, and the boat was the same boat, the same color green and the ribs broken in the same places, and under the floorboards the same fresh-water leavings and débris—the dead hellgrammite, the wisps of moss, the rusty discarded fish-hook, the dried blood from yesterday's catch. We stared silently at the tips of our rods, at the dragonflies that came and went. I lowered the tip of mine into the water, tentatively, pensively dislodging the fly, which darted two feet away, poised, darted two feet back, and came to rest again a little farther up the rod. There had been no years between the ducking of this dragonfly and the other one—the one that was part of memory. I looked at the boy, who was silently watching his fly, and it was my hands that held his rod, my eyes watching. I felt dizzy and didn't know which rod I was at the end of.

6   We caught two bass, hauling them in briskly as though they were mackerel, pulling them over the side of the boat in a businesslike manner without any landing net, and stunning them with a blow on the back of the head. When we got back for a swim before lunch, the lake was exactly where we had left it, the same number of inches from the dock, and there was only the merest suggestion of a breeze. This seemed an utterly enchanted sea, this lake you could leave to its own devices for a few hours and come back to, and find it had not stirred, this constant and trustworthy body of water. In the shallows, the dark, water-soaked sticks and twigs, smooth and old, were undulating in clusters on the bottom against the clean ribbed sand, and the track of the mussel was plain. A school of minnows swam by, each minnow with its small individual shadow, doubling the attendance, so clear and sharp in the sunlight. Some of the other campers were in swimming, along the shore, one of them with a cake of soap, and the water felt thin and clear and unsubstantial. Over the years there had been this person with the cake of soap, this cultist, and here he was. There had been no years.

7   Up to the farmhouse to dinner through the teeming, dusty field, the road under our sneakers was only a two-track road. The middle track was missing, the one with the marks of the hooves and the splotches of dried, flaky manure. There had always been three tracks to choose from in choosing which track to walk in; now the choice was narrowed down to two. For a moment I missed terribly the middle alternative. But the way led past the tennis court, and something about the way it lay there in the sun reassured me; the tape had loosened along the backline, the alleys were green with plantains and other weeds, and the net (installed in June and removed in September) sagged in the dry noon, and the whole place steamed with midday heat and hunger and emptiness. There was a choice of pie for dessert, and one was blueberry and one was apple, and the waitresses were the same country girls, there having been no passage of time, only the illusion of it as in a dropped curtain—the waitresses were still fifteen; their hair had been washed, that was the only difference—they had been to the movies and seen the pretty girls with the clean hair.

8   Summertime, oh summertime, pattern of life indelible, the fade-proof lake, the woods unshatterable, the pasture with the sweetfern and the juniper

forever and ever, summer without end; this was the background, and the life along the shore was the design, their tiny docks with the flagpole and the American flag floating against the white clouds in the blue sky, the little paths over the roots of the trees leading from camp to camp and the paths leading back to the outhouses and the can of lime for sprinkling, and at the souvenir counters at the store the miniature birch-bark canoes and the postcards that showed things looking a little better than they looked. This was the American family at play, escaping the city heat, wondering whether the newcomers in the camp at the head of the cove were "common" or "nice," wondering whether it was true that the people who drove up for Sunday dinner at the farmhouse were turned away because there wasn't enough chicken.

It seemed to me, as I kept remembering all this, that those times and those summers had been infinitely precious and worth saving. There had been jollity and peace and goodness. The arriving (at the beginning of August) had been so big a business in itself, at the railway station the farm wagon drawn up, the first smell of the pine-laden air, the first glimpse of the smiling farmer, and the great importance of the trunks and your father's enormous authority in such matters, and the feel of the wagon under you for the long ten-mile haul, and at the top of the last long hill catching the first view of the lake after eleven months of not seeing this cherished body of water. The shouts and cries of the other campers when they saw you, and the trunks to be unpacked, to give up their rich burden. (Arriving was less exciting nowadays, when you sneaked up in your car and parked it under a tree near the camp and took out the bags and in five minutes it was all over, no fuss, no loud wonderful fuss about trunks.) 9

Peace and goodness and jollity. The only thing that was wrong now, really, was the sound of the place, an unfamiliar nervous sound of the outboard motors. This was the note that jarred, the one thing that would sometimes break the illusion and set the years moving. In those other summertimes all the motors were inboard; and when they were at a little distance, the noise they made was a sedative, an ingredient of summer sleep. They were one-cylinder and two-cylinder engines, and some were make-and-break and some were jump-spark, but they all made a sleepy sound across the lake. The one-lungers throbbed and fluttered, and the twin-cylinder ones purred and purred, and that was a quiet sound, too. But now the campers all had outboards. In the daytime, in the hot mornings, these motors made a petulant, irritable sound; at night, in the still evening when the afterglow lit the water, they whined about one's ears like mosquitoes. My boy loved our rented outboard, and his great desire was to achieve single-handed mastery over it, and authority, and he soon learned the trick of choking it a little (but not too much), and the adjustment of the needle valve. Watching him I would remember the things you could do with the old one-cylinder engine 10 with the heavy flywheel, how you could have it eating out of your hand if you got really close to it spiritually. Motorboats in those days didn't have clutches, and you would make a landing by shutting off the motor at the proper time and coasting in with a dead rudder. But there was a way of reversing them, if you learned the trick, by cutting the switch and putting it on again exactly on the final dying revolution of the flywheel, so that it would kick back against the compression and begin reversing. Approaching a dock in a strong following breeze, it was difficult to slow up sufficiently by the ordinary coasting method, and if a boy felt he had complete mastery over his motor, he was tempted to keep it running beyond its time and then reverse it a few feet from the dock. It took a cool nerve, because if you threw the switch a twentieth of a second too soon you would catch the flywheel when it still had speed enough to go up past center, and the boat would leap ahead, charging bull-fashion at the dock.

11   We had a good week at camp. The bass were biting well and the sun shone endlessly, day after day. We would be tired at night and lie down in the accumulated heat of the little bedrooms after the long hot day and the breeze would stir almost imperceptibly outside and the smell of the swamp drift in through the rusty screens. Sleep would come easily and in the morning the red squirrel would be on the roof, tapping out his gay routine. I kept remembering everything, lying in bed in the mornings—the small steamboat that had a long rounded stem like the lip of a Ubangi, and how quietly she ran on the moonlight sails, when the older boys played their mandolins and the girls sang and we ate doughnuts dipped in sugar, and how sweet the music was on the water in the shining night, and what it had felt like to think about girls then. After breakfast we would go up to the store and the things were in the same place—the minnows in a bottle, the plugs and spinners disarranged and pawed over by the youngsters from the boys' camp, the Fig Newtons and the Beeman's gum. Outside, the road was tarred and cars stood in front of the store. Inside, all was just as it had always been, except there was more Coca-Cola and not so much Moxie and root beer and birch beer and sarsaparilla. We would walk out with the bottle of pop apiece and sometimes the pop would backfire up our noses and hurt. We explored the streams, quietly, where the turtles slid off the sunny logs and dug their way into the soft bottom; and we lay on the town wharf and fed worms to the tame bass. Everywhere we went I had trouble making out which I was, the one walking at my side, the one walking in my pants.

12   One afternoon while we were there at that lake a thunderstorm came up. It was like the revival of an old melodrama that I had seen long ago with childish awe. The second-act climax of the drama of the electrical disturbance over a lake in America had not changed in any important respect. This

was the big scene, still the big scene. The whole thing was so familiar, the first feeling of oppression and heat and a general air around camp of not wanting to go very far away. In mid-afternoon (it was all the same) a curious darkening of the sky, and a lull in everything that had made life tick; and then the way the boats suddenly swung the other way at their moorings with the coming of a breeze out of the new quarter, and the premonitory rumble. Then the kettle drum, then the snare, then the bass drum and cymbals, then the crackling light against the dark, and the gods grinning and licking their chops in the hills. Afterward the calm, the rain steadily rustling in the calm lake, the return of light and hope and spirits, and the campers running out in joy and relief to go swimming in the rain, their bright cries perpetuating the deathless joke about how they were getting simply drenched, and the children screaming with delight at the new sensation of bathing in the rain, and the joke about getting drenched linking the generations in a strong indestructible chain. And the comedian who waded in carrying an umbrella.

When the others went swimming, my son said he was going in, too. He 13 pulled his dripping trunks from the line where they had hung all through the shower and wrung them out. Languidly, and with no thought of going in, I watched him, his hard little body, skinny and bare, saw him wince slightly as he pulled up around his vitals the small, soggy, icy garment. As he buckled the swollen belt, suddenly my groin felt the chill of death.

Understanding Context

1. What is White's purpose in describing the resort? What lessons or observations does this journey reveal to him?
2. What are the key features of the lake? How much of it had changed in forty years?
3. White comments in the last line that he "felt the chill of death." How does viewing his son give White a sense of his mortality?
4. *Critical thinking:* What role does time play in this description? What is White saying about the passage of time, the passage of life? How does watching a child grow affect a parent?

Evaluating Strategy

1. How does White use his son as a device for recalling his own youth?
2. Descriptions of places can become tedious lists of geographical details. How does White create action and bring the lake to life?

3. Writers usually rely on visual details to develop a description of a place. Locate places where White uses other sensory impressions. How effective are they?
4. *Other modes:* Locate passages where White uses comparison and narration. How do they develop the essay? Could you classify this essay as narration?

Appreciating Language

1. White uses figurative language associated with nonnatural objects to describe the lake. For instance, he describes the lake as having the "stillness of a cathedral" and uses references to musical instruments—"the kettle drum, then the snare, then the brass drum and cymbals"—to capture the sound of a storm. What do these word choices suggest about his audience?
2. White uses brand names throughout his essay. What effect do references to Moxie, Fig Newtons, and Coca-Cola have?

Writing Suggestions

1. Write an essay describing a place you revisited after a considerable lapse of time. Comment on what has and has not changed. Use as many sensory details as you can.
2. *Collaborative writing:* Work with a group of students who share a common memory of a historical event or recent campus incident. Have each member write a brief narrative. Read each paper aloud to see how people recall and interpret events differently.

Target Want Ad

Want ads describe ideal job candidates. This online ad describes openings at a Target facility in Sarasota, Florida.

Team Members & Team Leaders (Area Managers)– Gainesville, FL – Target jobs on EmploymentGuide.com.

http://www.employmentguide.com/browse_employers/33745/jobdetails.html?JobID=1423476&keyword_string=

See what all the **buzz** is about.

See a company like no other. See where risk-taking is applauded.
See a world of opportunity. See the hip new thing. See the new style.
See your future. See yourself in red. See you soon.

See Yourself Here

Team Members
- Deliver fast, fun and friendly service to our guests
- Positions may include: Food Service, Overnight Logistics Backroom and Overnight Logistics Flow (Stocking)

Team Leaders
- Lead a team in different areas of the store to deliver fast, fun and friendly experience for our guests
- Areas may include: Guest Service, Overnight Logistics Backroom, Overnight Logistics Flow (Stocking) and Sales Floor

We're looking for:
- Cheerful and helpful guest service skills
- Friendly and upbeat attitude

See the rewards:
- Target merchandise discount
- Competitive pay
- Flexible scheduling

See Yourself At Target:
Employing more than 270,000 team members in 47 states, we value creativity, diversity and collaboration in all its forms. From stocking our stores' shelves with fantastic products at great prices to a deep commitment to community giving, Target strives for excellence in every way.

To apply:
Click on the **Apply Now Button** to inform us of your interest and visit us at **5350 Fruitville Road, Sarasota, FL 34232** to complete a Target Employment Application on the employment kiosks located near the front of the store.

Target is an equal employment opportunity employer and is a drug-free workplace.

Understanding Context

1. What is the goal of a want ad?
2. How else might a corporation advertise its position?
3. What does this ad suggest about the potential reader? Who is the company seeking to attract?
4. If you were interested in this position, what further information would you want? What questions would you want to ask at a job interview?
5. *Critical thinking:* What are the limits of any want ad? Can a job be fully described in a few paragraphs? Why can't employers address all their interests and concerns? Given the cost to print ads, might the Internet give employers more space to describe jobs?

Evaluating Strategy

1. Why does the ad first describe the job, then list requirements?
2. The ad describes "a world of opportunity." Who might this appeal to and why?
3. Would some potential job seekers be skeptical or suspicious about any job that promises to be "fun"? Might this approach dissuade serious professionals from applying? Why or why not?

Appreciating Language

1. What words does the ad use to describe the ideal candidate?
2. How would you judge the overall tone of the ad? What do words like "hip" and "fun" suggest? Are they powerful words that might grab job seeker's attention?
3. *Critical thinking:* Study the want ads in a local newspaper. Do you detect differences in wording? What ads adopt a conservative tone? Which ads use dramatic phrases and emotional appeals?

Writing Suggestions

1. Write a want ad for a job you once had. Try to model yours after ones you have seen in the newspaper. Keep your ad as short as possible.
2. Write a résumé responding to this ad. Invent any needed biographical details about education and experience. Review Strategies for Writing Résumés in Chapter 15.

3. *Collaborative writing:* Work with a group of students and write a want ad. Imagine you are hiring a part-time employee to act as secretary for your writing group. Determine the skills needed, the major duties, and how the ad should be worded. If members have differences of opinion, craft more than one ad, and ask other students to choose the most effective.

Responding to IMAGES

Seattle Street Youths, 1983   © Mary Ellen Mark

1. Describe your first reactions to this picture. Did you feel anger, disgust, fear, concern? What kind of young people are drawn to guns? Describe the problem these boys represent.

2. This photograph was taken in 1983. What do you assume happened to the boys in the picture? Where might they be today? Describe what you think may have happened to them.

3. *Visual analysis:* What do the hats, clothing, and demeanor suggest about these two boys? What do you see in the face of the boy on the left—defiance, resignation, or anger? What does the position of the weapon imply?

4. *Collaborative writing:* Discuss this picture with a group of students and describe how it might be used in an ad about gun control, juvenile programs, tougher laws, or improved social programs. Write the text to accompany the ad. Pay attention to word choice and connotation.

5. *Other modes*
   - Write a *narrative* to accompany this picture. Invent dialogue for the two boys.
   - Write a *cause-and-effect* essay and outline the causes or effects of youth crime.
   - Develop a *process* paper detailing the steps it would take for a youth program to intervene in these boys' lives.
   - Write a *persuasive* letter to the editor clearly stating your views on gun control. Would handgun bans keep young people from obtaining firearms?

Description Checklist

✔ Have you limited your topic?

✔ Does your support suit your context? Should it be objective, subjective, or a blend?

✔ Is your description focused and clearly organized, or is it only a random list of facts and observations?

✔ Have you avoided including unnecessary details and awkward constructions?

✔ Does sensory detail include more than sight? Can you add impressions of taste, touch, sound, or smell?

✔ Do you avoid overly general terms and focus on specific impressions? Have you created dominant impressions?

✔ Do you *show* rather than *tell*? Can you add action to your description to keep it from being static?

✔ Do you keep a consistent point of view?

✔ Read your paper aloud. How does it sound? Do any sections need expansion? Are there irrelevant details to delete or awkward expressions to revise?

Companion Website

See **http://www.thomsonedu.com/english/sundance** for additional information on writing description.

19

NARRATION
RELATING EVENTS

WHAT IS NARRATION?

Narration relates an event or tells a story. Short stories and novels form narratives, as do fables, legends, biographies, annual reports, and history books. Narratives can be imaginative or factual, fiction or nonfiction. Narrative writing includes most newspaper articles, magazine stories, diaries, and biographies. All narratives seek to answer a simple question—what happened?

Physicians write narratives when they record a patient's history or trace the course of a treatment schedule. Attorneys use narrative writing to relate the details of a crime or justify their client's actions in a civil matter. A store manager filing an accident report will summarize an incident, relating the chain of events preceding the accident.

 To read more about narration, along with interactive examples and opportunities to work with interactive texts, click on "The Rhetorical Patterns of Inquiry" from the main menu of *Comp21*.

The Writer's Purpose and Role

Writers tell stories to inform, entertain, enlighten, or persuade. In some instances the writer's goal is to reconstruct a chain of events as accurately as possible. The purpose of a brief news story or an accident report is to supply readers with an objective statement of facts. In other cases, writers relate a story in order to provide an insight, share an experience, or teach a lesson. The writer will be selective, highlighting key events and describing them in ways to shape readers' perceptions. Some writers prefer to let a story speak for itself, assuming people will understand their point without an actual thesis statement. James

Dillard (page 339), however, provides a clear thesis, stating what he learned after he treated an accident victim. Realizing that a malpractice lawsuit could have ended his medical career, he looks back on the incident, explaining the lesson the accident taught him:

> I took an oath to serve the sick and the injured. I remembered truly believing I would be able to do just that. But I have found out it isn't so simple. I understand now what a foolish thing I did that day. Despite my oath, I know what I would do on that cold roadside near Gettysburg today. I would drive on.

The writer of a narrative can be the central character, an eyewitness, or a researcher who reconstructs a chain of events from remaining evidence or interviews. Narration can be objective or subjective, depending on the writer's goal and context. Objective narration is generally stated in the third person to give the writer's account a sense of neutrality. In objective narration the author is not a participant but a collector and presenter of facts. An article in *Time* or a chapter in a history book usually consists of objective narration. In assembling the final hours of the *Titanic*, Walter Lord presents an objective catalog of facts:

> *April 15, 1912*
> 12:15 a.m. First wireless call for help.
> 12:45 a.m. First rocket fired.
> 12:45 a.m. First boat, No. 7, lowered.
> 01:40 a.m. Last rocket fired.
> 02:05 a.m. Last boat, Collapsible D, lowered.

In contrast, subjective narration highlights the role of the writer, either as an eyewitness to events or as a main participant. James Dillard provides a gripping personal account of trying to resuscitate his victim, focusing not only on the objective appearance of the injured driver but also his own subjective feelings and his role as a participant:

> He was still out cold, limp as a rag doll. His throat was crushed and blood from the jugular vein was running down my arms. He still couldn't breathe. He was deep blue-magenta now, his pulse was rapid and thready. The stench of alcohol turned my stomach, but I positioned his jaw and tried to blow air down into his lungs. It wouldn't go.

Focus

Related closely to the writer's purpose and role is the narrative's focus. A biography of Abraham Lincoln can be a general account of his entire life or a psychological study of his battle with depression during the Civil War. A book about World War II can provide an overview of events or a detailed account of the role of women in the defense industry. An article on recycling may provide a survey of national trends or an in-depth history of carpet recycling in a single city. Focus determines the details the writer includes in the narrative and the kind of evidence he or she relies on. A narrative does not have to include each event and every detail:

> For our tenth anniversary my husband and I planned a trip to Hawaii. The seven-hour flight was exhausting, but as soon as I saw the Easter egg blue of the sky and the bright yellows and reds of the flowers I was energized. We rented a car at the airport and drove to our hotel. On the first day we went to the mountains. The scenery was incredible. The following day it rained, so we took the opportunity to visit a local art museum and dine in a Chinese restaurant. The next day we went to the beach.

Attempting to capture a ten-day vacation in a five-hundred-word essay, the student produces only a catalog, a listing of events. Like a video in fast forward, the narrative sweeps readers through brief scenes that offer only superficial impressions. It is more effective to concentrate on a single event, as if highlighting a single scene from a movie or chapter in a book.

In "The Fender-Bender" (page 329) Ramón "Tianguis" Pérez focuses on a single incident, a minor traffic accident. As an illegal alien without papers, he fears any contact with law enforcement could lead to an investigation of his status and deportation. Pérez does not bother explaining how he immigrated to America, why he left Mexico, or even the date or location of the incident, but immediately plunges his reader into the event:

> One night after work, I drive Rolando's old car to visit some friends, and then head towards home. At a light, I come to a stop too late, leaving the front end of the car poking into the crosswalk. I shift into reverse, but as I am backing up, I strike the van behind me. Its driver immediately gets out to inspect the damage to his vehicle. He's a tall Anglo-Saxon, dressed in a deep blue work uniform. After looking at his car, he walks up to the window of the car I'm driving.
>
> "Your driver's license," he says, a little enraged.
>
> "I didn't bring it," I tell him.
>
> He scratches his head. He is breathing heavily with fury.
>
> "Okay," he says. "You park up ahead while I call a patrolman."
>
> The idea of calling the police doesn't sound good to me, but the accident is my fault. So I drive around the corner and park at the curb. I turn off the motor and hit the steering wheel with one fist. I don't have a driver's license. I've never applied for one. Nor do I have with me the identification card that I bought in San Antonio. Without immigration papers, without a driving permit, and having hit another car, I feel as if I'm just one step from Mexico.

This single, almost incidental, event reveals more about the status of an illegal alien than a three-page summary of the author's life history. By including dialogue Pérez creates an active narrative instead of a summary of events.

WRITING ACTIVITY

Select examples of narrative writing from your textbooks, readings from this chapter, news magazine articles, brochures, short stories, or passages from novels.

1. Can you identify the writer's purpose? Are some narratives written solely to inform, while others also seek to persuade or entertain readers?

2. What role does the author play in these narratives? Are some written in the first person? Is the writer the main participant, a minor character, or a witness of the events?

3. How do the various writers focus their narratives? What details do they leave out? How do they introduce background material?

4. Do the writers include dialogue and action to advance the narratives?

Chronology

Chronology or time is a central organizing element in narrative writing. Writers do not always relate events in a straight timeline. A biography, for instance, does not have to open with birth and childhood. Writers often alter time sequences of their stories to dramatize events or limit their topics. A biographer of Franklin Roosevelt might choose to highlight a key event or turning point in his life. The narrative could open with his polio attack, flash back to his childhood and early political career, then flash forward to his recovery and entry into national and international politics. Other writers find it more dramatic to open a narrative with a final event and explain what led up to it. The first chapter of a biography about Czar Nicholas II could describe his execution and then flash back to the events leading to his downfall and death.

Each method of organizing a narrative has distinct advantages and disadvantages:

■ **Beginning at the beginning** creates an open-ended narrative, providing readers with few hints about later events. Writers who relate complex stories with many possible causes can use a straight chronology to avoid highlighting a single event. Using a direct beginning-to-end approach is the most traditional method of telling a story. One of the difficulties can be determining exactly when the narrative should start. Often the beginning of a story consists of incidental background information that readers may find uninteresting.

- **Beginning at the middle or turning point** can arouse reader interest by opening with a dramatic scene. This method of organizing plunges the reader directly into the narrative and can give the chain of events a clear focus. This is a commonly used pattern in popular biographies. Critics, however, may argue that altering the chronology can be distorting. Not all historians, for instance, might agree that Roosevelt's polio attack was the "turning point" of his life. Some biographers may feel that this approach overemphasizes his physical disability and overshadows the political significance of Roosevelt's career.

- **Beginning at the end** dramatizes the final event. Organizing a narrative in this way can suggest that the conclusion was inevitable. When everything is presented in flashback, readers see events, actions, and thoughts in hindsight. The elements of suspense and randomness are removed, providing a stronger sense of cause and effect. Some readers will object to this method because it implies the final outcome was unavoidable, when, in fact, events just as easily could have led to alternative endings.

WRITING ACTIVITY

Select sample narratives from this chapter or look at one of your favorite books—fiction or nonfiction—and examine how the writers organized the chronology of events.

1. What pattern appears to be the most common?

2. Do any of the authors use flashbacks or flash forwards? If so, what impact do they have? How do they blend these sections into the main narrative without confusing their readers?

3. How do the writers use transitional statements and paragraph breaks to move the narrative and signal changes in time?

4. How do the writers use chronology to establish meaning? Do they use time relationships to indicate cause and effect?

5. How do the writers slow or speed up the narrative to emphasize important events or skim through minor ones?

STRATEGIES | for Writing Narration

Critical Thinking and Prewriting

1. **List topics suitable to your goal.** Consider the nature of the narrative assignment. What subjects would best suit your purpose?
   - Quickly jot down possible topics.
2. **Determine your purpose.** Does your narrative have a goal beyond telling a story? What details or evidence do readers need to accept your point of view?
   - Select experiences in which you learned something or events that represent an issue or problem.
3. **Define your role.** As a narrator you can write in the first person, as either the major participant or the witness to events. You can write in the third person to establish greater objectivity, inserting personal opinion if desired.
4. **Consider your readers.** Define your readers' perceptual world. How much background information will you have to supply for readers to appreciate the significance of events?
5. **Review the discourse community or writing situation.** If you are writing a narrative report as an employee, study samples to determine how you should present your story.
6. **Freewrite for a few minutes on the most likely two or three topics to generate ideas.** Sometimes the only way to identify the topic best suited to your purpose is to begin writing. You may find that one topic sparks a train of thoughts, memories, and associations while others provoke only vague recollections and limited responses.
7. **Determine whether your narrative would benefit from visuals.** If you are writing about an event or personal experience, you may have a photograph or other image that would complement your essay. Avoid using clip art or commercial images that do not directly relate to your narrative or that may confuse or distract readers.

Planning

1. **Develop a clear thesis.** A narrative usually has a goal to do more than simply list a chain of events.
   - What is the purpose of your narrative—to persuade, to entertain, or to teach readers a lesson?
   - Should the thesis be clearly stated or implied?
2. **Identify the beginning and end of your narrative.** You may find it helpful to place background information in a separate foreword or introduction

and limit comments on the ending to an afterword. This can allow the body of the work to focus on a specific chain of events.

3. **Select a chronological pattern.** After reviewing the context of the narrative, determine which pattern would be most effective for your purpose—using a straight chronology, opening with a mid- or turning point, or presenting the final event first.

4. **Select key details that support your thesis.** Focus on those impressions of sight, sound, smell, taste, and touch that will bring your narrative to life.
   - Avoid including specific details about times, dates, and locations unless they serve your purpose.

5. **Draft a timeline, listing main events of the narrative to guide your draft.** Leave space between each item on the timeline for last-minute additions.

Writing the First Draft

1. **Use your plan as a guide, but be open to new ideas.** As you write, new ideas will occur to you. In some cases these may be details supporting your thesis. In other instances you may stray from your original plan.
   - Do not reject ideas, even if they seem irrelevant. If you feel your draft going off track, list ideas or make notations. Do not feel obligated to write whole sentences.

2. **Use dialogue to advance the narrative.** If your narrative contains interactions between people, reconstruct conversations in direct quotations rather than summaries. Allowing people to speak for themselves gives you the opportunity to use word choice to describe a person's level of education, attitude, and lifestyle.

3. **Make use of transitional statements.** To prevent readers from becoming confused, make clear transitional statements to move the narrative. Such statements as "two days later" or "later that afternoon" can help readers follow the passage of time. Clear transitions are important if you alter the chronology with flashbacks and flash forwards.
   - Paragraph breaks can be very important in narratives. They can function like chapters in a book to signal changes, isolate events, and highlight incidents.

4. **Monitor your length as you write.** If your draft begins to run too long, make notes or list points, and try to complete a full version.

Revising

1. **Review your thesis, plan, and goal.** Examine your prewriting notes and outline to determine if changes are needed.

2. **Read the first draft to get an overall view of your narrative.**
   - Does the opening generate interest and plunge readers into the story, or does it simply announce the topic or state the time and location?
   - Does the narrative have a thesis, a clear point?
   - Is the narrative easy to follow? Do transitional statements and paragraph breaks help dramatize shifts between main points?
   - Does the narrative end with a memorable impression, thought, or question?
3. **Examine the draft and isolate the narrative's key events.**
   - Can these elements be heightened or expanded?
   - Should these elements be placed in different order?
4. **Decide whether the narrative should be expanded or narrowed.**
   - If the draft is too short or seems to stall on a minor point or uninteresting detail, consider expanding the scope of the narrative by lengthening the chain of events.
   - If the draft is too long or reads like a summary of events, tighten the focus by eliminating minor events.
5. **Determine whether the narrative can be improved by adding details, including dialogue, or by altering the chronological pattern.**

Editing and Proofreading

1. **Review subsequent drafts for content, style, and tone.** Make sure that your choice of words suits the subject matter, mood, and thesis of the narrative.
   - Review your choice of words to make sure their connotations are appropriate.
2. **Make sure the narrative does not shift tense without reason.** In relating a narrative, you can write in present or past tense. In some cases, you may shift from past to present to express different actions, but you will otherwise want to remain consistent with your choice of tense:
   Acceptable: I *drive* to work every day, but that morning I *took* the bus.
   Awkward: Smith *rushes* into the end zone and the game *was* won.
3. **Avoid shifts in person or stance.** Narratives can be related in first, second, or third person. In most instances, avoid shifts in person, unless there is a clear shift in focus:
   Acceptable: I found working on a farm fascinating, though *you* might find it tedious and boring.
   Awkward: I crossed the bridge where all *you* can see is desert.

STUDENT PAPER

This student prepared the following paper for a freshman composition course in response to the following assignment:

Write a 350–500 word narrative essay based on personal experience or observation. Limit your topic, select details carefully, and use figurative language to create images from the sights, sounds, smells, and moods you experienced.

Spare Change

As I stepped off the San Diego Trolley, I knew that I was going to embark on a great adventure. Tijuana. As I neared the entrance to cross the border there was a priest with a plastic bowl and a picture of some kids. The caption on the picture said, "feed Tijuana's homeless children." Yeah, right, I thought to myself, just another scam, this guy probably isn't even a priest.

Tijuana. Just the name of the city brings back a distinct smell. A smell that you will only know if you have been there. It only takes one time and you can relate to what

Tijuana   Les Stone/Corbis

I am saying. A smell that will permeate my olfactory senses forever. A thousand different scents compounded into one. The smell of fast food, sweat, sewage, and tears. As you cross the border the first thing that hits you is the smell I mentioned earlier. Then you witness the first of many human sufferings you will encounter. The man with no legs begging for money, the woman with her children huddled around her with an old grease stained wax cup hovering in the air waving at you with the eyes of poverty, the children dressed in Salvation Army hand me downs, ripped pants and mismatched shoes surrounding you, begging for money. Their hands searching your pockets for change, a wallet, anything that will get them food for the night.

Once I got past the few blocks of human suffering and handed out all I could, I wandered upon a busy little plaza. This place is reasonably clean and clear of trash, you hear the deafening sounds of the music from the nearby clubs, and see dozens of young drunken Americans stumbling around. A lot of tourists are carrying what seems like 5 bags each and a distressed look, the kind you get when you have been shopping all day long. The children, a score of them holding out these little packs of colored Chiclets, a local gum, sold to you at any price you can haggle them down to. It's pretty pathetic that you should feel the need to haggle over the price of gum with a child, but this is Tijuana. Americans and tourists have come from all over the world to haggle here. That is just the way it is, the way it always will be.

As I continued my journey, I reached a bridge. The bridge was horrible. Along the sides there was trash and rubbish. Towards the midspan of the bridge, I experienced one of the most touching moments of my life, one of those happy ones where you don't know if you should shed a tear from happiness or out of despair. There was this little child playing the accordion and another one playing a guitar. He was singing a Spanish song, well actually it sounded like he was screaming as his compadre was strumming the guitar. He had a little cup in front of him, and I threw a coin into it. He just smiled and kept singing. I turned around and left, but this time as I passed the priest I filled his plastic bowl with the rest of my money.

Questions for Review and Revision

1. This student was assigned a 350–500 word narrative in a composition class. How successfully does this paper meet this goal?
2. How does the student open and close the narrative? Does the opening grab your attention? Does the conclusion make a powerful statement?

3. What devices does the student use to advance the chronology?
4. Most writers focus on visual details. This student includes the senses of sound and smell as well. How effective is this approach?
5. The narrative switches from first person ("I") to second person ("you"); should this be corrected? How does it affect the focus of the narrative?
6. Read the paper aloud. What changes would you make? Can you detect passages that would benefit from revision or rewording?

Writing Suggestions

1. Using this essay as a model, write a short narrative about a trip that exposed you to another culture. Try to recapture the sights, sounds, and smells that characterized the experience.
2. *Collaborative writing:* Ask a group of students to assign a grade to this essay and then explain their evaluations. What strengths and weaknesses does the group identify?

SUGGESTED TOPICS FOR WRITING NARRATION

General Assignments

Write a narrative on any of the following topics. Your narrative may contain passages making use of other modes, such as description or persuasion. Choose your narrative structure carefully and avoid including minor details that add little to the story line. Use flashbacks and flash forwards carefully. Transitional statements, paragraphing, and line breaks can help clarify changes in chronology.

1. Your first job interview
2. Moving into your first apartment
3. The event or series of events that led to you take some action—quitting a job, ending a relationship, or joining an organization
4. A sporting event you played in or observed, perhaps limiting the narrative to a single play
5. A first date, using dialogue as much as possible to set the tone and advance the narrative
6. An event that placed you in danger
7. An experience that led you to change your opinion about a friend or coworker

8. The events of the best or worst day you experienced in a job
9. An accident or medical emergency, focusing on creating a clear, minute-by-minute chronology
10. A telephone call that changed your life, using dialogue as much as possible

    To create your own interactive writing project, use the textual, visual, and video libraries on *Comp21*. For the main menu, choose "Build Your Own Occasion for Writing."

Writing in Context

1. Imagine you are participating in a psychological experiment measuring stressors students face—lack of sleep, deadlines, financial problems, scheduling conflicts, decreased contact with family and friends. Write a diary for a week, detailing instances when you experience stress.
2. Write a letter to a friend relating the events of a typical day in college. Select details your friend may find interesting or humorous.
3. Preserve on paper a favorite story told by your grandparents or other relatives for your children and grandchildren. Include needed background details and identify characters. Consider what you want your descendants to know about their ancestors.
4. You have been accused of committing a crime last Tuesday. Create a detailed log to the best of your recollection of the day's events to establish an alibi.

STRATEGIES | for Reading Narration

When reading the narratives in this chapter, keep these questions in mind:

Context
1. What is the author's narrative purpose—to inform, entertain, enlighten, share a personal experience, or provide information required by the reader? Does the writer have a goal beyond simply telling a story?
2. Does the writer include a thesis statement? If so, where does it appear in the essay?
3. What is the writer's role? Is the writer a participant or a direct witness? Is he or she writing in a personal context, focusing on internal responses, or in a professional context, concentrating on external events?

4. What audience is the narrative directed toward—general or specific? How much knowledge does the author assume readers have?

5. What is the nature of the discourse community or writing situation? Is the narration subjective or objective? Does the original source of the narrative— newsmagazine, book, or professional publication—reveal anything about its context?

Strategy

1. How does the author open and close the narrative?

2. What details does the writer select? Are some items summarized or ignored? If so, why?

3. What kind of support does the writer use—personal observation or factual documentation?

4. Does the author use dialogue or special effects like flashbacks or flash forwards to advance the narrative?

5. What transitional devices does the writer use to prevent confusion? Does the author use paragraph breaks or time references such as "two hours later" or "later that day"?

Language

1. What does the level of vocabulary, tone, and style suggest about the writing context?

2. How is the author's attitude toward the subject or intended readers reflected by his or her choice of words?

Samuel Scudder (1837–1911) attended Williams College. In 1857 he entered Harvard, where he studied under the noted scientist Louis Agassiz. Scudder held various positions and helped found the Cambridge Entomological Club. He published hundreds of papers and developed a comprehensive catalog of three hundred years of scientific publications. While working for the United States Geological Survey, he named more than a thousand species of fossil insects. Much of Scudder's work is still admired for its attention to detail.

Take This Fish and Look at It

Today educators stress critical thinking, which begins with close observation. As you read this essay, consider how effective the professor's teaching method is. Does it rest on the age-old notion that "people learn by doing"?

intro sets time 1 It was more than fifteen years ago that I entered the laboratory of Professor Agassiz, and told him I had enrolled my name in the Scientific School as a student of natural history. He asked me a few questions about my object in coming, my antecedents generally, the mode in which I afterwards proposed to use the knowledge I might acquire, and, finally, whether I wished to study any special branch. To the latter I replied that, while I wished to be well grounded in all departments of zoology, I purposed to devote myself specially to insects.

uses dialogue 2 "When do you wish to begin?" he asked.

3 "Now," I replied.

4 This seemed to please him, and with an energetic "Very well!" he reached from a shelf a huge jar of specimens in yellow alcohol. "Take this fish," he said, "and look at it; we call it a haemulon; by and by I will ask what you have seen."

5 With that he left me, but in a moment returned with explicit instructions as to the care of the object entrusted to me.

6 "No man is fit to be a naturalist," said he, "who does not know how to take care of specimens."

gives direction 7 I was to keep the fish before me in a tin tray, and occasionally moisten the surface with alcohol from the jar, always taking care to replace the stopper tightly. Those were not the days of ground-glass stoppers and elegantly shaped exhibition jars; all the old students will recall the huge neckless glass bottles with their leaky, wax-besmeared corks, half eaten by insects, and begrimed with cellar dust. Entomology was a cleaner science than ichthyology, but the example of the Professor, who had unhesitatingly plunged to the bottom of the jar to produce the fish, was infectious; and though this alcohol had a "very ancient and fishlike smell," I really dared not show any aversion within these sacred precincts, and treated the alcohol as though it were pure water. Still I was conscious of a passing feeling of disappointment, for gazing at a fish did not commend itself to an ardent entomologist. My friends at home, too, were annoyed when they discovered that no amount of eau-de-Cologne would drown the perfume which haunted me like a shadow.

In ten minutes I had seen all that could be seen in that fish, and started 8 in search of the Professor—who had, however, left the Museum; and when I returned, after lingering over some of the odd animals stored in the upper apartment, my specimen was dry all over. I dashed the fluid over the fish as if to resuscitate the beast from a fainting fit, and looked with anxiety for a return of the normal sloppy appearance. This little excitement over, nothing was to be done but to return to a steadfast gaze at my mute companion. Half an hour passed—an hour—another hour; the fish began to look loathsome. I turned it over and around; looked it in the face—ghastly; from behind, beneath, above, sideways, at three-quarters' view—just as ghastly. I was in despair; at an early hour I concluded that lunch was necessary; so, with infinite relief, the fish was carefully replaced in the jar, and for an hour I was free.

first impression

emphasizes boredom

On my return, I learned that Professor Agassiz had been at the Museum, 9 but had gone, and would not return for several hours. My fellow-students were too busy to be disturbed by continued conversation. Slowly I drew forth that hideous fish, and with a feeling of desperation again looked at it. I might not use a magnifying-glass; instruments of all kinds were interdicted. My two hands, my two eyes, and the fish: it seemed a most limited field. I pushed my finger down its throat to feel how sharp the teeth were. I began to count the scales in the different rows, until I was convinced that was nonsense. At last a happy thought struck me—I would draw the fish; and now with surprise I began to discover new features in the creature. Just then the Professor returned.

discovers by drawing

"That is right," said he; "a pencil is one of the best of eyes. I am glad to 10 notice, too, that you keep your specimen wet, and your bottle corked."

With these encouraging words, he added: "Well, what is it like?" 11

He listened attentively to my brief rehearsal of the structure of parts 12 whose names were still unknown to me: the fringed gill-arches and movable operculum; the pores of the head, fleshy lips and lidless eyes; the lateral first impression emphasizes boredom discovers by drawing line, the spinous fins and forked tail; the compressed and arched body. When I finished, he waited as if expecting more, and then, with an air of disappointment:

13   "You have not looked very carefully; why," he continued more earnestly, "you haven't even seen one of the most conspicuous features of the animal, which is plainly before your eyes as the fish itself; look again, look again!" and he left me to my misery.

initial relation 14   I was piqued; I was mortified. Still more of that wretched fish! But now I set myself to my task with a will, and discovered one new thing after another, until I saw how just the Professor's criticism had been. The afternoon passed quickly; and when, towards its close, the Professor inquired:

15   "Do you see it yet?"

16   "No," I replied, "I am certain I do not, but I see how little I saw before."

17   "That is next best," said he, earnestly, "but I won't hear you now; put away your fish and go home; perhaps you will be ready with a better answer in the morning. I will examine you before you look at the fish."

18   This was disconcerting. Not only must I think of my fish all night, studying, without the object before me, what this unknown but most visible feature might be; but also, without reviewing my discoveries, I must give an exact account of them the next day. I had a bad memory; so I walked home by Charles River in a distracted state, with my two perplexities.

19   The cordial greeting from the Professor the next morning was reassuring; here was a man who seemed to be quite as anxious as I that I should see for myself what he saw.

20   "Do you perhaps mean," I asked, "that the fish has symmetrical sides with paired organs?"

21   His thoroughly pleased "Of course! of course!" repaid the wakeful hours of the previous night. After he had discoursed most happily and enthusiastically—as he always did—upon the importance of this point, I ven-

asks for help tured to ask what I should do next.

22   "Oh, look at your fish!" he said, and left me again to my own devices. In a little more than an hour he returned, and heard my new catalogue. "That is good, that is good!" he repeated; "but that is not all; go on"; and so for three long days he placed that fish before my eyes, forbidding me to look

repeated command at anything else, or to use any artificial aid. "Look, look, look," was his repeated injunction.

thesis/value of lesson 23   This was the best entomological lesson I ever had—a lesson whose influence has extended to the details of every subsequent study; a legacy the Professor had left to me, as he has left it to so many others, of inestimable value which we could not buy, with which we cannot part.

A year afterward, some of us were amusing ourselves with chalking out- 24
landish beasts on the Museum blackboard. We drew prancing starfishes;
frogs in mortal combat; hydra-headed worms; stately crawfishes, standing on
their tails, bearing aloft umbrellas; and grotesque fishes with gaping mouths
and staring eyes. The Professor came in shortly after, and was as amused as
any at our experiments. He looked at the fishes.

flash forward to humorous incident

"Haemulons, every one of them," he said; "Mr. —— drew them."   25

True; and to this day, if I attempt a fish, I can draw nothing but 26
haemulons.

The fourth day, a second fish of the same group was placed beside the 27
first, and I was bidden to point out the resemblances and differences between
the two; another and another followed, until the entire family lay before me,
and a whole legion of jars covered the table and surrounding shelves; the odor
had become a pleasant perfume; and even now, the sight of an old, six-inch
worm-eaten cork brings fragrant memories.

The whole group of haemulons was thus brought in review; and, 28
whether engaged upon the dissection of the internal organs, the preparation
and examination of the bony framework, or the description of the various
parts, Agassiz's training in the method of observing facts and their orderly
arrangement was ever accompanied by the urgent exhortation not to be content with them.

"Facts are stupid things," he would say, "until brought into connection 29 *conclusion*
with some general law."

At the end of eight months, it was almost with reluctance that I left 30
these friends and turned to insects; but what I had gained by this outside
experience has been of greater value than years of later investigation in my
favorite groups.

Understanding Context

1. What is Scudder's purpose in this narrative? Why is this essay more than a typical "first day at school" story?
2. What did Professor Agassiz mean when he stated that "a pencil is one of the best of eyes"?
3. *Critical thinking:* How effective was Professor Agassiz's teaching method? By directing a new student to simply "look, look again," did he accomplish more than if he had required Scudder to attend a two-hour lecture on the importance of observation? Does this method assume that students have already acquired basic skills? Would this method work for all students? Why or why not?

4. What has this essay taught you about your future career? How can keen observation and attention to detail help you achieve your goals?

Evaluating Strategy

1. How does Scudder give the narrative focus? What details does he leave out?
2. Scudder does not bother describing Professor Agassiz. Would that add or detract from the narrative?
3. *Other modes:* How does Scudder use *description* of the fish, specimen bottles, and smells to provide readers with a clear impression of the laboratory?

Appreciating Language

1. How much scientific terminology does Scudder use in the narrative? What does this suggest about his intended audience?
2. This essay contains little action. Essentially it is a story about a man interacting with a dead fish. What words add drama and humor to the narrative?

Writing Suggestions

1. Apply Professor Agassiz's technique to a common object you might use every day. Take your clock radio or a can of your favorite soft drink and study it for five minutes. Write a description of what you have observed. List the features you never noticed before.
2. Professor Agassiz gave his student little direction other than a simple command. Write a brief account about a time when a parent, teacher, coach, or boss left you to act on your own. What problems or challenges did you encounter? Did you feel frustrated, afraid, angry, or confident? What did you learn?
3. *Collaborative writing:* Working with three or four other students, select an object unfamiliar to the group. Allow each member to study the object and make notes. Compare your findings, and work to create a single description incorporating the findings of the group.

Ramón "Tianguis" Pérez is an undocumented immigrant and does not release biographical information.

The Fender-Bender

As you read the essay, notice how Pérez uses dialogue to advance the narrative. Pay attention to the role common documents such as a driver's license or a letter play in the drama.

One night after work, I drive Rolando's old car to visit some friends, and 1 then head towards home. At a light, I come to a stop too late, leaving the front end of the car poking into the crosswalk. I shift into reverse, but as I am backing up, I strike the van behind me. Its driver immediately gets out to inspect the damage to his vehicle. He's a tall Anglo-Saxon, dressed in a deep blue work uniform. After looking at his car, he walks up to the window of the car I'm driving.

"Your driver's license," he says, a little enraged. 2

"I didn't bring it," I tell him. 3

He scratches his head. He is breathing heavily with fury. 4

"Okay," he says. "You park up ahead while I call a patrolman." 5

The idea of calling the police doesn't sound good to me, but the acci- 6 dent is my fault. So I drive around the corner and park at the curb. I turn off the motor and hit the steering wheel with one fist. I don't have a driver's license. I've never applied for one. Nor do I have with me the identification card that I bought in San Antonio. Without immigration papers, without a driving permit, and having hit another car, I feel as if I'm just one step away from Mexico.

I get out of the car. The white man comes over and stands right in front 7 of me. He's almost two feet taller.

"If you're going to drive, why don't you carry your license?" he asks in 8 an accusatory tone.

"I didn't bring it," I say, for lack of any other defense. 9

I look at the damage to his car. It's minor, only a scratch on the paint and 10 a pimple-sized dent.

"I'm sorry," I say. "Tell me how much it will cost to fix, and I'll pay 11 for it; that's no problem." I'm talking to him in English, and he seems to understand.

329

12   "This car isn't mine," he says. "It belongs to the company I work for. I'm sorry, but I've got to report this to the police, so that I don't have to pay for the damage."

13   "That's no problem," I tell him again. "I can pay for it."

14   After we've exchanged these words, he seems less irritated. But he says he'd prefer for the police to come, so that they can report that the dent wasn't his fault.

15   While we wait, he walks from one side to the other, looking down the avenue this way and that, hoping that the police will appear.

16   Then he goes over to the van to look at the dent.

17   "It's not much," he says. "If it was my car, there wouldn't be any problems, and you could go on."

18   After a few minutes, the long-awaited police car arrives. Only one officer is inside. He's a Chicano, short and of medium complexion, with short, curly hair. On getting out of the car, he walks straight towards the Anglo.

19   The two exchange a few words.

20   "Is that him?" he asks, pointing at me.

21   The Anglo nods his head.

22   Speaking in English, the policeman orders me to stand in front of the car and to put my hands on the hood. He searches me and finds only the car keys and my billfold with a few dollars in it. He asks for my driver's license.

23   "I don't have it," I answered in Spanish.

24   He wrinkles his face into a frown, and casting a glance at the Anglo, shakes his head in disapproval of me.

25   "That's the way these Mexicans are," he says.

26   He turns back towards me, asking for identification. I tell him I don't have that, either.

27   "You're an illegal, eh?" he says.

28   I won't answer.

29   "An illegal," he says to himself.

30   "Where do you live?" he continues. He's still speaking in English.

31   I tell him my address.

32   "Do you have anything with you to prove that you live at that address?" he asks.

33   I think for a minute, then realize that in the glove compartment is a letter that my parents sent to me several weeks earlier.

34   I show him the envelope and he immediately begins to write something in a little book that he carries in his back pocket. He walks to the back of my car and copies the license plate number. Then he goes over to his car and talks into his radio. After he talks, someone answers. Then he asks me for the name of the car's owner.

He goes over to where the Anglo is standing. I can't quite hear what 35
they're saying. But when the two of them go over to look at the dent in the
van, I hear the cop tell the Anglo that if he wants, he can file charges against
me. The Anglo shakes his head and explains what he had earlier explained
to me, about only needing for the police to certify that he wasn't responsible
for the accident. The Anglo says that he doesn't want to accuse me of anything because the damage is light.

"If you want, I can take him to jail," the cop insists. The Anglo turns him 36
down again.

"If you'd rather, we can report him to Immigration," the cop continues. 37

Just as at the first, I am now almost sure that I'll be making a forced trip 38
to Tijuana. I find myself searching my memory for my uncle's telephone
number, and to my relief, I remember it. I am waiting for the Anglo to say
yes, confirming my expectations of the trip. But instead, he says no, and
though I remain silent, I feel appreciation for him. I ask myself why the Chicano is determined to harm me. I didn't really expect him to favor me, just
because we're of the same ancestry, but on the other hand, once I had admitted my guilt, I expected him to treat me at least fairly. But even against
the white man's wishes, he's trying to make matters worse for me. I've
known several Chicanos with whom, joking around, I've reminded them
that their roots are in Mexico. But very few of them see it that way. Several
have told me how when they were children, their parents would take them
to vacation in different states of Mexico, but their own feeling, they've said,
is, "I am an American citizen!" Finally, the Anglo, with the justifying paper
in his hands, says goodbye to the cop, thanks him for his services, gets into
his van and drives away.

The cop stands in the street in a pensive mood. I imagine that he's try- 39
ing to think of a way to punish me.

"Put the key in the ignition," he orders me.   40

I do as he says.   41

Then he orders me to roll up the windows and lock the doors.   42

"Now, go on, walking," he says.   43

I go off taking slow steps. The cop gets in his patrol car and stays there, 44
waiting. I turn the corner after two blocks and look out for my car, but the
cop is still parked beside it. I begin looking for a coat hanger, and after a
good while, find one by a curb of the street. I keep walking, keeping about
two blocks away from the car. While I walk, I bend the coat hanger into the
form I'll need. As if I'd called for it, a speeding car goes past. When it comes
to the avenue where my car is parked, it makes a turn. It is going so fast that
its wheels screech as it rounds the corner. The cop turns on the blinking
lights of his patrol car and leaving black marks on the pavement beneath it,

shoots out to chase the speeder. I go up to my car and with my palms force a window open a crack. Then I insert the clothes hanger in the crack and raise the lock lever. It's a simple task, one that I'd already performed. This wasn't the first time that I'd been locked out of a car, though always before, it was because I'd forgotten to remove my keys.

Understanding Context

1. What is the author's purpose in telling the story? What do we learn from this experience?
2. Pérez answers the Chicano patrolman in Spanish. Was this a mistake? What does their exchange reveal about cultural conflicts within the Hispanic community?
3. *Critical thinking:* Pérez implies that Chicanos have been offended when he has reminded them of their Mexican heritage; they insist on being seen as American citizens. What does this say about assimilation and identity? Does the Chicano officer's comment about Mexicans reveal contempt for immigrants? Have other ethnic groups—Jews, Italians, the Irish—resented the presence of unassimilated and poorer arrivals from their homelands?

Evaluating Strategy

1. Why is a minor incident like a fender-bender a better device to explain the plight of the undocumented immigrant than a dramatic one?
2. How does Pérez use dialogue to advance the narrative? Is it better to let people speak for themselves?

Appreciating Language

1. What words does Pérez use to trivialize the damage caused by the accident?
2. What word choices and images highlight the importance of documents in the lives of illegal immigrants?

Writing Suggestions

1. Write a short narrative detailing a minor event that taught you something. A brief encounter with a homeless person may have led you to change your opinions of the poor. Perhaps you discovered our dependence on energy

one afternoon when your apartment building lost power and you were unable to use your computer to finish an assignment, watch the evening news, prepare dinner, or even open the garage door to get your car.

2. *Collaborative writing:* Working with a group of students, discuss your views on immigration. Take notes and write a brief statement outlining your group's opinion. If major differences emerge during your discussion, split into subgroups and draft pro and con statements.

Born Marguerite Johnson in Saint Louis, Maya Angelou (1928–) has distinguished herself as a poet, autobiographer, and public performer. *I Know Why the Caged Bird Sings* (1970), the first in a series of memoirs, describes her harrowing youth in Arkansas. She has starred in an off-Broadway play, acted in the television miniseries *Roots,* and directed a feature film. When Bill Clinton was sworn in as president on January 20, 1993, she became only the second poet in American history (after Robert Frost) to read at a presidential inauguration.

Champion of the World

At a time in American history when sports teams were still racially segregated, Joe Louis inspired pride in African Americans when he defeated white men in the boxing ring. Notice how the people gathered together in a small store in a little town in Arkansas in the 1930s feel that the whole future of African Americans in America depends on the outcome of a boxing match.

1 The last inch of space was filled, yet people continued to wedge themselves along the walls of the Store. Uncle Willie had turned the radio up to its last notch so that youngsters on the porch wouldn't miss a word. Women sat on kitchen chairs, dining-room chairs, stools, and upturned wooden boxes. Small children and babies perched on every lap available and men leaned on the shelves or on each other.

2 The apprehensive mood was shot through with shafts of gaiety, as a black sky is streaked with lightning.

3 "I ain't worried 'bout this fight. Joe's gonna whip that cracker like it's open season."

4 "He gone whip him till that white boy call him Momma."

5 At last the talking finished and the string-along songs about razor blades were over and the fight began.

6 "A quick jab to the head." In the Store the crowd grunted. "A left to the head and a right and another left." One of the listeners cackled like a hen and was quieted.

7 "They're in a clinch, Louis is trying to fight his way out."

8 Some bitter comedian on the porch said, "That white man don't mind hugging that niggah now, I betcha."

"The referee is moving in to break them up, but Louis finally pushed 9
the contender away and it's an uppercut to the chin. The contender is hanging on, now he's backing away. Louis catches him with a short left to
the jaw."

A tide of murmuring assent poured out the door and into the yard.   10

"Another left and another left. Louis is saving that mighty right. . . ." 11
The mutter in the Store had grown into a baby roar and it was pierced by the
clang of a bell and the announcer's "That's the bell for round three, ladies
and gentlemen."

As I pushed my way into the Store I wondered if the announcer gave any 12
thought to the fact that he was addressing as "ladies and gentlemen" all the
Negroes around the world who sat sweating and praying, glued to their
"Master's voice."

There were only a few calls for RC Colas, Dr Peppers, and Hires root 13
beer. The real festivities would begin after the fight. Then even the old
Christian ladies who taught their children and tried themselves to practice
turning the other cheek would buy soft drinks, and if the Brown Bomber's
victory was a particularly bloody one they would order peanut patties and
Baby Ruths also.

Bailey and I laid the coins on top of the cash register. Uncle Willie 14
didn't allow us to ring up sales during a fight. It was too noisy and might
shake up the atmosphere. When the gong rang for the next round we
pushed through the near-sacred quiet to the herd of children outside.

"He's got Louis against the ropes and now it's a left to the body and a 15
right to the ribs. Another right to the body, it looks like it was low . . . Yes,
ladies and gentlemen, the referee is signaling but the contender keeps rain-
ing the blows on Louis. It's another to the body, and it looks like Louis is
going down."

My race groaned. It was our people falling. It was another lynching, yet 16
another Black man hanging on a tree. One more woman ambushed and
raped. A Black boy whipped and maimed. It was hounds on the trail of a man
running through slimy swamps. It was a white woman slapping her maid for
being forgetful.

The men in the Store stood away from the walls and at attention. Women 17
greedily clutched the babes on their laps while on the porch the shufflings
and smiles, flirtings and pinching of a few minutes before were gone. This
might be the end of the world. If Joe lost we were back in slavery and beyond
help. It would all be true, the accusations that we were lower types of human
beings. Only a little higher than apes. True that we were stupid and ugly and
lazy and dirty and, unlucky and worst of all, that God Himself hated us and
ordained us to be hewers of wood and drawers of water, forever and ever,
world without end.

18   We didn't breathe. We didn't hope. We waited.

19   "He's off the ropes, ladies and gentlemen. He's moving towards the center of the ring." There was no time to be relieved. The worst might still happen.

20   "And now it looks like Joe is mad. He's caught Carnera with a left hook to the head and a right to the head. It's a left jab to the body and another left to the head. There's a left cross and a right to the head. The contender's right eye is bleeding and he can't seem to keep his block up. Louis is penetrating every block. The referee is moving in, but Louis sends a left to the body and it's an uppercut to the chin and the contender is dropping. He's on the canvas, ladies and gentlemen."

21   Babies slid to the floor as women stood up and men leaned toward the radio.

22   "Here's the referee. He's counting. One, two, three, four, five, six, seven . . . Is the contender trying to get up again?"

23   All the men in the store shouted, "NO."

24   "—eight, nine, ten." There were a few sounds from the audience, but they seemed to be holding themselves in against tremendous pressure.

25   "The fight is all over, ladies and gentlemen. Let's get the microphone over to the referee . . . Here he is. He's got the Brown Bomber's hand, he's holding it up . . . Here he is. . . ."

26   Then the voice, husky and familiar, came to wash over us—"The winnah, and still heavyweight champeen of the world . . . Joe Louis."

27   Champion of the world. A Black boy. Some Black mother's son. He was the strongest man in the world. People drank Coca-Colas like ambrosia and ate candy bars like Christmas. Some of the men went behind the Store and poured white lightning in their soft-drink bottles, and a few of the bigger boys followed them. Those who were not chased away came back blowing their breath in front of themselves like proud smokers.

28   It would take an hour or more before the people would leave the Store and head for home. Those who lived too far had made arrangements to stay in town. It wouldn't do for a Black man and his family to be caught on a lonely country road on a night when Joe Louis had proved that we were the strongest people in the world.

Understanding Context

1. How would you sum up in a single sentence Angelou's thesis statement? What is her purpose in telling this story?

2. What different moods do the people in the store go through as they gather, listen to the fight, and then leave? What are some of the exact words that she uses to let her readers know what the mood in the store is?

3. In paragraph 16, when Joe Louis falls in the boxing ring, Angelou says, "It was our people falling." A few sentences later, in paragraph 17, she says, "This might be the end of the world." Why would a single boxing match have that much importance for African Americans in the 1930s?

4. In the last sentence, Angelou suggests that it would not be safe for an African American family to be traveling on a country road following the fight. Why?

5. *Critical thinking:* Listening to the Joe Louis v. Primo Carnera fight drew Africa Americans together in a sense of community. What events in recent history do you remember that drew members of a group together in a similar way? Did the events you have in mind draw together only members of a single racial or ethnic group? Are there other events that are of such major importance that they draw together people in spite of racial and ethnic differences?

Evaluating Strategy

1. This narrative tells the story of a boxing match, but it also tells how the people in the store reacted to the match. Notice the paragraphs that tell what is going on before the match begins and after it is over. How do those paragraphs help Angelou make her point in the essay?

2. Can you find words in the essay that appeal to all five of the senses: sight, hearing, taste, touch, and smell?

3. Angelou's essay is broken up into many short paragraphs. Why are there so many paragraph breaks? Are your narrative essays likely to have so many paragraphs? How does a narrative writer decide when to start a new paragraph?

Appreciating Language

1. In the second paragraph, Angelou uses a simile, or a comparison using "like" or "as" of two things not usually thought of together. "The apprehensive mood was shot through with shafts of gaiety, as a black sky is streaked with lightning." How was Louis's victory like a streak of lightning for African Americans? Lightning can also be dangerous, of course. How does Angelou suggest the danger in the last paragraph?

2. In paragraph 12, why does Angelou find it ironic that the sports announcer uses the term "ladies and gentlemen"?

Writing Suggestions

1. Choose an event from your past when you felt particularly proud or particularly ashamed. Use first person ("I") to tell the story in an essay modeled on Angelou's. Choose an event that took place in a short period of time, and provide only enough background for your readers to understand the context. Remember that your purpose is to tell what happened and also to make clear how it made you feel.

2. Once you have written a draft of your narrative, go back and see where you might add more details that appeal to the senses of your reader.

3. *Collaborative writing:* Exchange your draft with a student and let him or her point out any places in the story where the facts are not clear. Ask your partner to tell you what he or she thinks your purpose was, and see if that matches what you intended.

James Dillard is a physician who specializes in rehabilitation medicine. In this narrative, first published in the "My Turn" column in *Newsweek,* he relates an incident that nearly ended his medical career.

A Doctor's Dilemma

As you read this narrative, keep in mind how most people expect physicians to respond in an emergency.

It was a bright, clear February afternoon in Gettysburg. A strong sun and layers of down did little to ease the biting cold. Our climb to the crest of Little Roundtop wound past somber monuments, barren trees and polished cannon. From the top, we peered down on the wheat field where men had fallen so close together that one could not see the ground. Rifle balls had whined as thick as bee swarms through the trees, and cannon shots had torn limbs from the young men fighting there. A frozen wind whipped tears from our eyes. My friend Amy huddled close, using me as a wind breaker. Despite the cold, it was hard to leave this place.

Driving east out of Gettysburg on a country blacktop, the gray Bronco 2 ahead of us passed through a rural crossroad just as a small pickup truck tried to take a left turn. The Bronco swerved, but slammed into the pickup on the passenger side. We immediately slowed to a crawl as we passed the scene. The Bronco's driver looked fine, but we couldn't see the driver of the pickup. I pulled over on the shoulder and got out to investigate.

The right side of the truck was smashed in, and the side window was 3 shattered. The driver was partly out of the truck. His head hung forward over the edge of the passenger-side window, the front of his neck crushed on the shattered windowsill. He was unconscious and starting to turn a dusky blue. His chest slowly heaved against a blocked windpipe.

A young man ran out of a house at the crossroad. "Get an ambulance out 4 here," I shouted against the wind. "Tell them a man is dying."

I looked down again at the driver hanging from the windowsill. There 5 were six empty beer bottles on the floor of the truck. I could smell the beer through the window. I knew I had to move him, to open his airway. I had no idea what neck injuries he had sustained. He could easily end up a quadriplegic. But I thought: he'll be dead by the time the ambulance gets here if I don't move him and try to do something to help him.

6   An image flashed before my mind. I could see the courtroom and the driver of the truck sitting in a wheelchair. I could see his attorney pointing at me and thundering at the jury: "This young doctor, with still a year left in his residency training, took it upon himself to play God. He took it upon himself to move this gravely injured man, condemning him forever to this wheelchair . . ." I imagined the millions of dollars in award money. And all the years of hard work lost. I'd be paying him off for the rest of my life. Amy touched my shoulder. "What are you going to do?"

7   The automatic response from long hours in the emergency room kicked in. I pulled off my overcoat and rolled up my sleeves. The trick would be to keep enough traction straight up on his head while I moved his torso, so that his probable broken neck and spinal-cord injury wouldn't be made worse. Amy came around the driver's side, climbed half in and grabbed his belt and shirt collar. Together we lifted him off the windowsill.

8   He was still out cold, limp as a rag doll. His throat was crushed and blood from the jugular vein was running down my arms. He still couldn't breathe. He was deep blue-magenta now, his pulse was rapid and thready. The stench of alcohol turned my stomach, but I positioned his jaw and tried to blow air down into his lungs. It wouldn't go.

9   Amy had brought some supplies from my car. I opened an oversize intravenous needle and groped on the man's neck. My hands were numb, covered with freezing blood and bits of broken glass. Hyoid bone—God, I can't even feel the thyroid cartilage, it's gone . . . OK, the thyroid gland is about there, cricoid rings are here . . . we'll go in right here . . .

10   It was a lucky first shot. Pink air sprayed through the IV needle. I placed a second needle next to the first. The air began whistling through it. Almost immediately, the driver's face turned bright red. After a minute, his pulse slowed down and his eyes moved slightly. I stood up, took a step back and looked down. He was going to make it. He was going to live. A siren wailed in the distance. I turned and saw Amy holding my overcoat. I was shivering and my arms were turning white with cold.

11   The ambulance captain looked around and bellowed, "What the hell . . . who did this?" as his team scurried over to the man lying in the truck.

12   "I did," I replied. He took down my name and address for his reports. I had just destroyed my career. I would never be able to finish my residency with a massive lawsuit pending. My life was over.

13   The truck driver was strapped onto a backboard, his neck in a stiff collar. The ambulance crew had controlled the bleeding and started intravenous

fluid. He was slowly waking up. As they loaded him into the ambulance, I saw him move his feet. Maybe my future wasn't lost.

A police sergeant called me from Pennsylvania three weeks later. Six 14 days after successful throat-reconstruction surgery, the driver had signed out, against medical advice, from the hospital because he couldn't get a drink on the ward. He was being arraigned on drunk-driving charges.

A few days later, I went into the office of one of my senior professors, to tell 15 the story. He peered over his half glasses and his eyes narrowed. "Well, you did the right thing medically of course. But, James, do you know what you put at risk by doing that?" he said sternly. "What was I supposed to do?" I asked.

"Drive on," he replied. "There is an army of lawyers out there who 16 would stand in line to get a case like that. If that driver had turned out to be a quadriplegic, you might never have practiced medicine again. You were a very lucky young man."

The day I graduated from medical school, I took an oath to serve the sick 17 and the injured. I remember truly believing I would be able to do just that. But I have found out it isn't so simple. I understand now what a foolish thing I did that day. Despite my oath, I know what I would do on that cold roadside near Gettysburg today. I would drive on.

Understanding Context

1. What was Dillard's goal in publishing this narrative in a national news magazine?
2. Does this narrative serve to contrast idealism and reality? How does Dillard's oath conflict with his final decision?
3. Does the fact that the victim was drinking have an impact on your reactions to the doctor's actions? Does Dillard seem to show contempt for his patient?
4. *Critical thinking:* Does this essay suggest that there is an undeclared war between doctors and lawyers? Do medical malpractice suits improve or diminish the quality of medicine? Are lawyers to blame for the writer's decision to "drive on"?

Evaluating Strategy

1. *Other modes:* Does this narrative also serve as a persuasive argument? Is the story a better vehicle than a standard argumentative essay that states a thesis and presents factual support?
2. Does this first-person story help place the reader in the doctor's position? Is this a more effective strategy than writing an objective third-person essay about the impact of malpractice suits?

3. Why does Dillard mention that the patient later disobeyed his doctors' orders and left the hospital so he could get a drink?

4. How do you think Dillard wanted his readers to respond to the essay's last line?

Appreciating Language

1. What words does Dillard use to dramatize his attempts to save the driver's life? How do they reflect the tension he was feeling?

2. What language does Dillard use to demonstrate what he was risking by trying to save a life?

3. What kind of people read *Newsweek*? Do you find this essay's language suitable?

Writing Suggestions

1. Relate an emergency situation you experienced or encountered. Using Dillard's essay as a model, write an account capturing what you thought and felt as you acted.

2. Write a letter to the editor of *Newsweek* in response to Dillard's essay. Do you find his position tenable? Are you angry at a doctor who vows not to help accident victims? Or do you blame the legal community for putting a physician in this position?

3. *Collaborative writing:* Discuss Dillard's essay with a number of students and list their reactions to Dillard's final statement. Write a division paper outlining their views.

InfoTrac College Edition
www.infotrac-college.com

THE HEALTH CARE CRISIS

All health systems have pluses and minuses; all ration health care in some way. We ration it, harshly, by income and price. People with money and access command topnotch care. Those without scramble for what

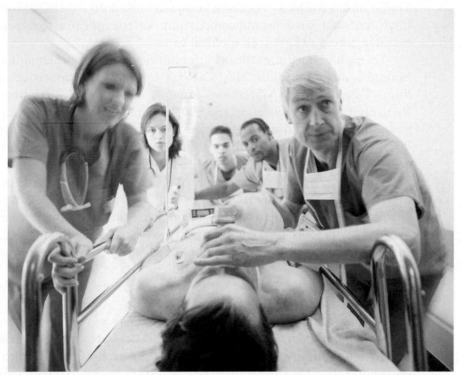

Bernardo Bucci/Corbis

they can get. Big businesses negotiate good group-health insurance. Small businesses are pushed against the wall. The healthy find private policies, the sick get kicked out. That's the American way.

Jane Bryant Quinn

A century ago most physicians in the United States had only a fragmentary knowledge of medicine. Only ten percent had a college degree. Some medical schools did not require applicants to have a high school diploma and granted a license with just six months training. Apprenticed to older doctors, medical students learned by observation. Little connection was made between research and practice. Equipped with dubious medicines and crude surgical techniques, doctors were frequently able to provide their patients with little more than emotional support.

The twentieth century saw a revolution in medical science, education, and technology. Extensive operations that required weeks of hospital care were replaced with minimally invasive procedures performed in out-patient clinics. New generations of drugs improved the quality of life for millions. Doctors became heroic figures, portrayed as selfless role models of skill, wisdom, and compassion. Americans came to expect immediate access to high tech medical care.

Yet each year patients die or suffer injuries from medical malpractice. Surgeons make mistakes. Hospitals fail to follow postoperative procedures. Patients develop infections and drug interactions. According to an Institute of Medicine report, 98,000 hospital patients died from preventable medical errors in 1998. To protect themselves from lawsuits, doctors and hospitals carry malpractice insurance. In recent years many doctors who have never been sued have seen their premiums rise from $30,000 to over $100,000 a year. In response, doctors have refused to treat high risk patients, moved from states with high jury awards, or switched specialties to lower their rates. Leo Boyle argues that "the problem of medical malpractice is that it occurs far too often. . . . killing more people than AIDS, breast cancer, or automobile crashes." Philip K. Howard insists the legal system has failed to address the problem, noting, "Most victims of error get nothing, while others win lottery-like jury awards even when the doctor did nothing wrong."

As medical technology has increased so has its cost. The *Christian Science Monitor* reported in 2005 that U.S. health care costs have reached $1.6 trillion annually, more than $12,000 for each family. Health care costs now represent 15 percent of the nation's economy. Today 45 million Americans lack health insurance, limiting their access to basic medical care. Each year over one million Americans face bankruptcy because of medical expenses. The rising costs of health care are affecting American corporations. In 2005 General Motors reported that health care costs added $1,600 to the price of every vehicle sold. Providing health insurance for employees and retirees has made it harder for American corporations to compete with cheaper imports, further encouraging companies to send jobs overseas where both labor and benefits are cheaper.

Advances in medical technology have also continued to raise ethical questions about providing health care for the poor, using technology to extend the lives of the terminally-ill, the pricing of new drugs, and fetal stem cell research.

Before reading these articles, consider these questions:

Examine the ads for doctors, hospitals, and malpractice attorneys in your local Yellow Pages. How do doctors and lawyers represent themselves to the public?

Is litigation the best way to remedy medical malpractice? Does suing a few doctors on behalf of individual patients lead to reform or simply encourage doctors to practice "defensive medicine" and order unnecessary tests?

Do hospital dramas and drug commercials give the public unrealistic expectations of medical technology?

What kind of health care coverage, if any, do you or members of your family have?

Who should pay for those who can afford health insurance?

Should patients or their families have the right to decide when to withdraw life support from the terminally ill or severely brain damaged?

Should everyone in your family have a living will? If someone becomes incapacitated, who should make decisions about treatment? Do you feel you know how members of your family wish to be cared for in the event they become unable to communicate to their doctors?

E-Readings Online

Search for each article by author or title after entering InfoTrac College Edition through your 1Pass account login.

Katherine Baicker and Amitabh Chandra. *Defensive Medicine and Disappearing Doctors?*
Increases in malpractice insurance premiums and jury awards have led doctors to practice defensive medicine and limit their services.

Leo Boyle. *The Truth About Medical Malpractice.*
The Association of American Trial Lawyers argues the malpractice crisis is not caused by litigation but by preventable medical error. Malpractice, Boyle asserts, kills more Americans each year than AIDS or breast cancer.

David R. Francis. *Why the Healthcare Crisis Won't Go Away.*
The United States now spends $1.6 trillion on health care annually yet the nation lags behinds nearly all other industrialized countries in infant mortality and longevity.

Health & Medicine Week. *Auto Manufacturers Say U.S. Must Solve Healthcare Crisis.*
With corporate health care costs rising 10% a year, the president of the United Auto Workers argues, "Our healthcare crisis is a national problem which demands a national solution" to keep America from losing its industrial base.

Dan Frosch. *Your Money or Your Life: When Getting Sick Means Going Broke.*
The middle class now accounts for nearly 90 percent of medical bankruptcies.

Linda Stern. *Money: Grown Up and Uninsured.*
One third of young adults lack health insurance, leading them to avoid seeing doctors and exposing them to crippling debts in the event of a medical emergency.

Jane Bryant Quinn. *Our 'Kindness Deficit' of Care: We Ration Health Care, Harshly, By Income and Price.*
Those with generous medical benefits or money can afford topnotch care; the poor scramble for what they can get.

Milton Friedman. *How to Cure Health Care.*
A noted economist offers solutions to the rising costs of health care: replacing Medicare and Medicaid with catastrophic insurance coverage for every family and taxing employer-provided medical care.

Liz Halloran. *Of Life and Death.*
Oregon's law that allows physicians to assist terminally ill patients to end their lives heightens the medical and ethical debate about euthanasia.

Jeff Chu. *What If It Happens in Your Family?*
The Terri Schiavo case dramatized the need for families to consider how to make medical decisions for someone who becomes incapacitated.

Critical Reading and Thinking

1. Do you detect a "war" between doctors and lawyers?
2. Is there a better way of identifying and punishing incompetent or irresponsible physicians than costly litigation?
3. Does litigation force medical professionals to raise standards or does it only raise costs?
4. How has the cost of health care affected individuals, corporations, and the national economy?
5. Will upper-income professionals resist change in health care policy because they fear losing some of their benefits in order to create a system that provides care for the uninsured?
6. Should health care coverage be linked to employment?
7. How important are statistics in these articles? Do they provide compelling evidence of a crisis? What role do case histories—stories about specific people—play in these articles? Is one kind of support

more effective? Should writers rely on more than one type of evidence to develop persuasive argument?

Writing Suggestions

1. If you or someone you know has been involved in a medical malpractice case, write a short essay describing what you learned from the experience.
2. Craft a brief letter responding to one or more of the writers agreeing or disagreeing with the views expressed.
3. *Collaborative writing:* Review these articles with a group of students and discuss a single issue, such as medical malpractice, insurance benefits, medical costs, or the right to die. Develop an essay dividing the group's observations into categories or contrasting opposing viewpoints.
4. *Other modes*
   - Write a short *process* paper suggesting a fair method of handling malpractice cases.
   - Write a brief *definition* of "medical malpractice." What distinguishes malpractice from an honest error in judgment?
   - Develop a *cause-and-effect* essay detailing the causes and effects of rising health care costs. What are the causes—incompetent medical professionals, aggressive trial lawyers, patient expectations, or new technology? What are the effects on patients, the medical profession, public health, employers, the federal budget, and the American economy? You may limit your paper by discussing a single cause or effect.
   - Write a *persuasive* essay suggesting or more solutions to one aspect of the crisis in health care.

Research Paper

You can develop a research paper about the health care crisis by conducting further research:

- How much of the health care crisis is related to lifestyle issues such as smoking, obesity, diet, and alcohol and drug use? Can personal choices decrease the incidence of disease and lower family medical expenses?
- Would Americans accept a national health care system that would provide basic coverage for all citizens but limit treatment options?
- Will corporations pressure employees to accept lower healthcare benefits to compete in the global economy?

- How do Americans feel about assisted suicide?
- Can advances in medical technology lower healthcare costs by diagnosing diseases at an earlier stage or identifying conditions that can be prevented with drugs or changes in lifestyle?

For Further Reading

To locate additional sources on health care, enter these search terms as InfoTrac subjects:

Health Insurance
Subdivisions:
    analysis
    comparative analysis
    demographic aspects
    economic aspects
    finance
    forecasts and trends

Medical Malpractice Insurance
Subdivisions:
    analysis
    cases
    economic aspects
    forecasts and trends
    laws, regulations, and rules
    other
    prices and rates
    statistics

Additional Sources

Using a search engine, such as Yahoo!, Google, or Alta Vista, enter one or more of the following terms to locate additional sources:

health care costs	medical malpractice
Medicare	medical malpractice insurance
health care crisis	national health insurance
right to die	euthanasia
living wills	HMOs

See Evaluating Internet Source Checklist on page 752. See Chapter 30 for using and documenting sources.

George Orwell was the pen name of Eric Blair (1903–1950), who was born in India, the son of a British official. Blair attended the prestigious Eton school but joined the Indian Imperial Police instead of attending university. After four years of service in Burma, he left to pursue a writing career. His first book, ***Down and Out in Paris and London,*** explored the plight of the poor and homeless during the depression. His later books included ***Animal Farm*** and ***Nineteen Eighty-Four.***

Shooting an Elephant

As you read the narrative, consider what message about imperialism Orwell was trying to communicate to his British audience. What is his implied thesis? How does he use comparison, description, and persuasion in developing this narrative?

In Moulmein, in Lower Burma, I was hated by large numbers of people— 1 the only time in my life that I have been important enough for this to happen to me. I was sub-divisional police officer of the town, and in an aimless, petty kind of way anti-European feeling was very bitter. No one had the guts to raise a riot, but if a European woman went through the bazaars alone somebody would probably spit betel juice over her dress. As a police officer I was an obvious target and was baited whenever it seemed safe to do so. When a nimble Burman tripped me up on the football field and the referee (another Burman) looked the other way, the crowd yelled with hideous laughter. This happened more than once. In the end the sneering yellow faces of young men that met me everywhere, the insults hooted after me when I was at a safe distance, got badly on my nerves. The young Buddhist priests were the worst of all. There were several thousands of them in the town and none of them seemed to have anything to do except stand on street corners and jeer at Europeans.

All this was perplexing and upsetting. For at that time I had already made 2 up my mind that imperialism was an evil thing and the sooner I chucked up my job and got out of it the better. Theoretically—and secretly, of course— I was all for the Burmese and all against their oppressors, the British. As for the job I was doing, I hated it more bitterly than I can perhaps make clear. In a job like that you see the dirty work of Empire at close quarters. The wretched prisoners huddling in the stinking cages of the lock-ups, the grey, cowed faces of the long-term convicts, the scarred buttocks of the men who had been flogged with bamboos—all these oppressed me with an intolerable sense of guilt. But I could get nothing into perspective. I was young and ill-educated and I had had to think out my problems in the utter silence that is imposed on every Englishman in the East. I did not even know that the British Empire is dying, still less did I know that it is a great deal better than the younger empires that are going to supplant it. All I knew was that I was stuck between my hatred of the empire I served and my rage against the evil-spirited little beasts who tried to make my job impossible. With one part of my mind I thought of the British Raj as an unbreakable tyranny, as something clamped down, *in saecula saeculorum,* upon the will of prostrate peoples; with another part I thought that the greatest joy in the world would be to drive a bayonet into a Buddhist priest's guts. Feelings like these are the normal by-products of imperialism; ask any Anglo-Indian official, if you can catch him off duty.

3   One day something happened which in a roundabout way was enlightening. It was a tiny incident in itself, but it gave me a better glimpse than I had had before of the real nature of imperialism—the real motives for which despotic governments act. Early one morning the sub-inspector at a police station the other end of the town rang me up on the phone and said that an elephant was ravaging the bazaar. Would I please come and do something about it? I did not know what I could do, but I wanted to see what was happening and I got on to a pony and started out. I took my rifle, an old .44 Winchester and much too small to kill an elephant, but I thought the noise might be useful *in terrorem.* Various Burmans stopped me on the way and told me about the elephant's doings. It was not, of course, a wild elephant, but a tame one which had gone "must." It had been chained up as tame elephants always are when their attack of "must" is due, but on the previous night it had broken its chain and escaped. Its mahout, the only person who could manage it when it was in that state, had set out in pursuit, but he had taken the wrong direction and was now twelve hours' journey away, and in the morning the elephant had suddenly reappeared in the town. The Burmese population had no weapons and were quite helpless against it. It had already destroyed somebody's bamboo hut, killed a cow and raided some fruit-stalls and devoured the stock; also it had met the municipal rubbish van, and, when the driver jumped out and took to his heels, had turned the van over and inflicted violence upon it.

4   The Burmese sub-inspector and some Indian constables were waiting for me in the quarter where the elephant had been seen. It was a very poor quarter, a labyrinth of squalid bamboo huts, thatched with palm-leaf, winding all

over a steep hillside. I remember that it was a cloudy stuffy morning at the beginning of the rains. We began questioning the people as to where the elephant had gone, and, as usual, failed to get any definite information. That is invariably the case in the East; a story always sounds clear enough at a distance, but the nearer you get to the scene of events the vaguer it becomes. Some of the people said that the elephant had gone in one direction, some said that he had gone in another, some professed not even to have heard of any elephant. I had almost made up my mind that the whole story was a pack of lies, when we heard yells a little distance away. There was a loud, scandalised cry of "Go away, child! Go away this instant!" and an old woman with a switch in her hand came round the corner of a hut, violently shooing away a crowd of naked children. Some more women followed, clicking their tongues and exclaiming; evidently there was something there that the children ought not to have seen. I rounded the hut and saw a man's dead body sprawling in the mud. He was an Indian, a black Dravidian coolie, almost naked, and he could not have been dead many minutes. The people said that the elephant had come suddenly upon him round the corner of the hut, caught him with its trunk, put its foot on his back and ground him into the earth. This was the rainy season and the ground was soft, and his face had scored a trench a foot deep and a couple of yards long. He was lying on his belly with arms crucified and head sharply twisted to one side. His face was coated with mud, the eyes wide open, the teeth bared and grinning with an expression of unendurable agony. (Never tell me, by the way, that the dead look peaceful. Most of the corpses I have seen looked devilish.) The friction of the great beast's foot had stripped the skin from his back as neatly as one skins a rabbit. As soon as I saw the dead man I sent an orderly to a friend's house nearby to borrow an elephant rifle. I had already sent back the pony, not wanting it to go mad with fright and throw me if it smelled the elephant.

The orderly came back in a few minutes with a rifle and five cartridges, 5 and meanwhile some Burmans had arrived and told us that the elephant was in the paddy fields below, only a few hundred yards away. As I started forward practically the whole population of the quarter flocked out of their houses and followed me. They had seen the rifle and were all shouting excitedly that I was going to shoot the elephant. They had not shown much interest in the elephant when he was merely ravaging their homes, but it was different now that he was going to be shot. It was a bit of fun to them, as it would be to an English crowd; besides, they wanted the meat. It made me vaguely uneasy. I had no intention of shooting the elephant—I had merely sent for the rifle to defend myself if necessary—and it is always unnerving to have a crowd following you. I marched down the hill, looking and feeling a fool, with the rifle over my shoulder and an ever-growing army of people jostling at my heels. At the bottom, when you got away from the huts, there was a metalled road and beyond that a miry waste of paddy fields a thousand yards across, not yet ploughed but soggy from the first rains and dotted with coarse grass. The elephant was standing eighty yards from the road, his left side towards us. He took not the slightest notice of the crowd's approach. He was tearing up bunches of grass, beating them against his knees to clean them and stuffing them into his mouth.

6   I had halted on the road. As soon as I saw the elephant I knew with perfect certainty that I ought not to shoot him. It is a serious matter to shoot a working elephant—it is comparable to destroying a huge and costly piece of machinery—and obviously one ought not to do it if it can possibly be avoided. And at that distance, peacefully eating, the elephant looked no more dangerous than a cow. I thought then and I think now that his attack of "must" was already passing off; in which case he would merely wander harmlessly about until the mahout came back and caught him. Moreover, I did not in the least want to shoot him. I decided that I would watch him for a little while to make sure that he did not turn savage again, and then go home.

7   But at that moment I glanced round at the crowd that had followed me. It was an immense crowd, two thousand at the least and growing every minute. It blocked the road for a long distance on either side. I looked at the sea of yellow faces above the garish clothes—faces all happy and excited over this bit of fun, all certain that the elephant was going to be shot. They were watching me as they would watch a conjuror about to perform a trick. They did not like me, but with the magical rifle in my hands I was momentarily worth watching. And suddenly I realised that I should have to shoot the elephant after all. The people expected it of me and I had got to do it; I could feel their two thousand wills pressing me forward, irresistibly. And it was at this moment, as I stood there with the rifle in my hands, that I first grasped the hollowness, the futility of the white man's dominion in the East. Here was I, the white man with his gun, standing in front of the unarmed native crowd—seemingly the leading actor of the piece; but in reality I was only an absurd puppet pushed to and fro by the will of those yellow faces behind. I perceived in this moment that when the white man turns tyrant it is his own freedom that he destroys. He becomes a sort of hollow, posing dummy, the conventionalised figure of a sahib. For it is the condition of his rule that he shall spend his life in trying to impress the "natives" and so in every crisis he has got to do what the "natives" expect of him. He wears a mask, and his face grows to fit it. I had got to shoot the elephant. I had committed myself to doing it when I sent for the rifle. A sahib has got to act like a sahib; he has got to appear resolute, to know his own mind and do definite things. To come all

that way, rifle in hand, with two thousand people marching at my heels, and then to trail feebly away, having done nothing—no, that was impossible. The crowd would laugh at me. And my whole life, every white man's life in the East, was one long struggle not to be laughed at.

But I did not want to shoot the elephant. I watched him beating his 8 bunch of grass against his knees, with that preoccupied grandmotherly air that elephants have. It seemed to me that it would be murder to shoot him. At that age I was not squeamish about killing animals, but I had never shot an elephant and never wanted to. (Somehow it always seems worse to kill a *large* animal.) Besides, there was the beast's owner to be considered. Alive, the elephant was worth at least a hundred pounds; dead, he would only be worth the value of his tusks—five pounds, possibly. But I had got to act quickly. I turned to some experienced-looking Burmans who had been there when we arrived, and asked them how the elephant had been behaving. They all said the same thing: he took no notice of you if you left him alone, but he might charge if you went too close to him.

It was perfectly clear to me what I ought to do. I ought to walk up to 9 within, say, twenty-five yards of the elephant and test his behaviour. If he charged I could shoot, if he took no notice of me it would be safe to leave him until the mahout came back. But also I knew that I was going to do no such thing. I was a poor shot with a rifle and the ground was soft mud into which one would sink at every step. If the elephant charged and I missed him, I should have about as much chance as a toad under a steam-roller. But even then I was not thinking particularly of my own skin, only the watchful yellow faces behind. For at that moment, with the crowd watching me, I was not afraid in the ordinary sense, as I would have been if I had been alone. A white man mustn't be frightened in front of "natives"; and so, in general, he isn't frightened. The sole thought in my mind was that if anything went wrong those two thousand Burmans would see me pursued, caught, trampled on and reduced to a grinning corpse like that Indian up the hill. And if that happened it was quite probable that some of them would laugh. That would never do. There was only one alternative. I shoved the cartridges into the magazine and lay down on the road to get a better aim.

The crowd grew very still, and a deep, low, happy sigh, as of people who 10 see the theatre curtain go up at last, breathed from innumerable throats. They were going to have their bit of fun after all. The rifle was a beautiful German thing with cross-hair sights. I did not then know that in shooting an elephant one should shoot to cut an imaginary bar running from ear-hole to ear-hole. I ought therefore, as the elephant was sideways on, to have aimed straight at his ear-hole; actually I aimed several inches in front of this, thinking the brain would be further forward.

11   When I pulled the trigger I did not hear the bang or feel the kick—one never does when a shot goes home—but heard the devilish roar of glee that went up from the crowd. In that instant, in too short a time, one would have thought, even for the bullet to get there, a mysterious, terrible change had come over the elephant. He neither stirred nor fell, but every line of his body had altered. He looked suddenly stricken, shrunken, immensely old, as though the frightful impact of the bullet had paralysed him without knocking him down. At last, after what seemed a long time—it might have been five seconds, I dare say—he sagged flabbily to his knees. His mouth slobbered. An enormous senility seemed to have settled upon him. One could have imagined him thousands of years old. I fired again into the same spot. At the second shot he did not collapse but climbed with desperate slowness to his feet and stood weakly upright, with legs sagging and head drooping. I fired a third time. That was the shot that did for him. You could see the agony of it jolt his whole body and knock the last remnant of strength from his legs. But in falling he seemed for a moment to rise, for as his hind legs collapsed beneath him he seemed to tower upwards like a huge rock toppling, his trunk reaching skyward like a tree. He trumpeted, for the first and only time. And then down he came, his belly towards me, with a crash that seemed to shake the ground even where I lay.

12   I got up. The Burmans were already racing past me across the mud. It was obvious that the elephant would never rise again, but he was not dead. He was breathing very rhythmically with long rattling gasps, his great mound of a side painfully rising and falling. His mouth was wide open—I could see far down into caverns of pale pink throat. I waited a long time for him to die, but his breathing did not weaken. Finally I fired my two remaining shots into the spot where I thought his heart must be. The thick blood welled out of him like red velvet, but still he did not die. His body did not even jerk when the shots hit him, the tortured breathing continued without a pause. He was dying, very slowly and in great agony, but in some world remote from me where not even a bullet could damage him further. I felt that I had got to put an end to that dreadful noise. It seemed dreadful to see the great beast lying there, powerless to move and yet powerless to die, and not even to be able to finish him. I went back for my small rifle and poured shot after shot into his heart and down his throat. They seemed to make no impression. The tortured gasps continued as steadily as the ticking of a clock.

13   In the end I could not stand it any longer and went away. I heard later that it took him half an hour to die. Burmans were arriving with dahs and baskets even before I left, and I was told they had stripped his body almost to the bones by the afternoon.

14   Afterwards, of course, there were endless discussions about the shooting of the elephant. The owner was furious, but he was only an Indian and could

do nothing. Besides, legally I had done the right thing, for a mad elephant has to be killed, like a mad dog, if its owner fails to control it. Among the Europeans opinion was divided. The older men said I was right, the younger men said it was a damn shame to shoot an elephant for killing a coolie, because an elephant was worth more than any damn Coringhee coolie. And afterwards I was very glad that the coolie had been killed; it put me legally in the right and it gave me a sufficient pretext for shooting the elephant. I often wondered whether any of the others grasped that I had done it solely to avoid looking a fool.

Understanding Context

1. What is Orwell's goal in relating this incident? What does this event symbolize?
2. What roles does Orwell play in the narrative? How does his behavior as a police officer conflict with his personal views?
3. What are Orwell's attitudes toward the Burmese?
4. Orwell's readers were primarily British. What was he trying to impress upon them?
5. *Critical thinking:* Consider Orwell's statement, "With one part of my mind I thought of the British Raj as an unbreakable tyranny . . . with another part I thought that the greatest joy in the world would be to drive a bayonet into a Buddhist priest's guts." What does this admission reveal?

Evaluating Strategy

1. Orwell opens the essay with the statement, "I was hated by large numbers of people." What impact does that have on readers? Does it do more than simply attract attention?
2. How does Orwell balance his role between narrator and participant?
3. *Other modes:* Can this essay also serve as an example? Is the killing of the elephant representative of a larger issue?

Appreciating Language

1. What metaphors does Orwell use in telling the story?
2. Underline the figurative language Orwell uses on page 354 to describe the labored death of the elephant. What images does he use to create a sense of horror?

3. Orwell calls the Burmese "natives," "coolies," and "Burmans." He describes their huts as "squalid" and the rice paddies as a "miry waste." What does this suggest about his view of Asia?

Writing Suggestions

1. *Critical thinking:* Orwell relates an incident in which he played a role that conflicted with his personal beliefs. Write a brief narrative about an event that placed you in a similar situation. Have your roles as parent, employee, manager, spouse, student, or friend caused you to act against your values? Select a single event and write a short narrative, clearly outlining how the actions you were compelled to take contrasted with what you really felt at the time. Have you ever been compelled to lie on behalf of others?

2. *Collaborative writing:* Work with other students to create a short statement analyzing Orwell's message about political power and the nature of abusive governments. Have each member write a draft and then work to combine ideas into a single statement. If there are major differences in ideas, develop a comparison or division paper to contrast or list these different views.

Walter Lord (1917–2002) was born in Baltimore and studied history at Princeton University. He entered Yale Law School, but his studies were interrupted by World War II. After serving with the Office of Strategic Services, he returned to law school. Lord became the editor-in-chief of a business information service but soon turned to writing history. In the 1950s he tracked down and interviewed sixty-three survivors of the *Titanic* and studied the ship's records to produce *A Night to Remember,* a minute-by-minute account of the doomed luxury liner. Considered unsinkable, the *Titanic* had only twenty lifeboats for its 2,207 passengers. It struck an iceberg on its maiden voyage to New York and sank. Rescuers located 705 survivors, many of them picked up in half-empty boats.

The Reconstructed Logbook of the *Titanic*

To help his readers follow the chronology, Walter Lord reconstructed the logbook of the ship and placed it in the appendix of his book. As you read the document, consider how placing events on a timeline affects how people perceive a narrative.

April 10, 1912		[1]
12 noon	Leaves Southampton dock; narrowly escapes collision with American liner New York.	
7:00 p.m.	Stops at Cherbourg for passengers.	
9:00 p.m.	Leaves Cherbourg for Queenstown.	
April 11, 1912		
12:30 p.m.	Stops at Queenstown for passengers and mail. One crewman deserts.	
2:00 p.m.	Leaves Queenstown for New York, carrying 1,316 passengers and 891 crew.	
April 14, 1912		
9:00 a.m.	Caronia reports ice Latitude 42°N from Longitude 49° to 51°W.	

10	1:42 p.m.	Baltic reports ice Latitude 41°51'N from Longitude 49°52'W.
	1:45 p.m.	Amerika reports ice Latitude 41°27'N, Longitude 50°8'W.
	7:00 p.m.	Temperature 43°.
	7:30 p.m.	Temperature 39°.
	7:30 p.m.	Californian reports ice Latitude 42°3'N, Longitude 49°9'W.
	9:00 p.m.	Temperature 33°.
	9:30 p.m.	Second Officer Lightoller warns carpenter and engine room to watch fresh water supply—may freeze up; warns crow's nest to watch for ice.
	9:40 p.m.	Mesaba reports ice Latitude 42°N to 41°25'N, Longitude 49° to 50°30'W.
	10:00 p.m.	Temperature 32°.
	10:30 p.m.	Temperature of sea down to 31°.
20	11:00 p.m.	Californian warns of ice, but cut off before she gives location.
	11:40 p.m.	Collides with iceberg Latitude 41°46'N, Longitude 50°14'W.
	April 15, 1912	
	12:05 a.m.	Orders given to uncover the boats, muster the crew and passengers.
	12:15 a.m.	First wireless call for help.
	12:45 a.m.	First rocket fired.
	12:45 a.m.	First boat, No. 7, lowered.
	1:40 a.m.	Last rocket fired.
	2:05 a.m.	Last boat, Collapsible D, lowered.
	2:10 a.m.	Last wireless signals sent.
30	2:18 a.m.	Lights fail.
	2:20 a.m.	Ship founders.
	3:30 a.m.	Carpathia's rockets sighted by boats.
	4:10 a.m.	First boat, No. 2, picked up by Carpathia.
	8:30 a.m.	Last boat, No. 12, picked up.
	8:50 a.m.	Carpathia heads for New York with 705 survivors.

Understanding Context

1. What is the purpose of placing events on a timeline?
2. How does a log assist readers to follow events in a complex story involving hundreds of people?
3. Why would this logbook be valuable to a board of inquiry investigating the disaster?

4. *Critical thinking:* According to this record, it took forty minutes to launch the first lifeboat. Although the crew had more than two and one-half hours to evacuate the ship, fifteen hundred people were lost. Do these facts alone raise suspicion of incompetence?

Evaluating Strategy

1. Can a log distort events by emphasizing time relationships instead of causal ones?
2. How can a writer deal with events that do not have a clearly established time reference?

Appreciating Language

1. Why is word choice important in these brief notations?
2. Can you locate words that are not objective?

Writing Suggestions

1. Reconstruct a log of the actions you took yesterday. Consider the problems that arise in attempting to explain events that did not occur in a specific time frame.
2. *Collaborative writing:* Working with a group of students, read the log and discuss your impressions. Should a luxury liner be able to safely evacuate its passengers in two hours? Write a paragraph summarizing your discussion.

Responding to IMAGES

Victims of hurricane Katrina seeking help, New Orleans, 2005
Smiley N. Pool/Dallas Morning News/Corbis

1. Describe your first response to this photograph. What led the people to write a message when their plight would have been obvious? Do you recall your reactions to television coverage of Katrina victims trapped on rooftops, highway overpasses, and the Superdome? Do you believe the criticisms of the government's response were fair or unfair?

2. The victims in New Orleans lived in a world-famous city familiar to many tourists and media personalities. Would victims of a disaster in a remote part of Kansas or Idaho receive as much attention? Does familiarity with a location affect how people perceive images? Millions of people who never visited New York City, for example, had seen the World Trade Center in pictures, movies, and television programs. Did that make its destruction on September 11 more palpable and dramatic? Had terrorists killed the same number of people by flying planes into five story apartment buildings in a smaller city, would the images be as striking? Why or why not?

3. *Visual analysis:* What role do the flags play in this image? What statement do they make? Why would victims use flags to attract attention? Consider the impact of the messages painted on the roofs. Few photographs include text. Do these words create a natural caption?

4. *Collaborative writing:* Work with a group of students and develop a caption for this photograph to be used in a high school history book. Create a caption that is accurate and objective. Pay attention to the use of words and the impact of connotations. If members of your group disagree, develop opposing captions.

5. *Other modes*
   - Write a *description* essay that analyzes the images present in this photograph, such as the flag, the messages, the people's gestures.
   - Write a *cause-and-effect* essay that outlines the impact this image has on the the public. Does an image like this lead many Americans to view the response to Katrina along racial lines?
   - Write a *classification* paper that establishes how you think emergency workers should respond in a disaster. Which victims should be rescued first? Which victims should be rescued last?
   - Write a *persuasive* essay that suggests how local, state, and federal agencies can better coordinate their responses to avoid duplication and indecision.

Narration Checklist

Before submitting your paper, review these points:

✔ Does your narrative have a clear focus?

✔ Can your readers clearly follow the chronology of events?

✔ Do you write in a consistent tense? Does your narrative contain illogical shifts from past to present?

✔ Does the narrative flow evenly, or is it cluttered with unnecessary detail?

✔ Does your narrative maintain a consistent point of view? Do you switch from first to third person without reason?

✔ Does your narrative suit your purpose, reader, and discourse community?

Companion Website

See **http://www.thomsonedu.com/english/sundance** for additional information on writing narration.

EXAMPLE
PRESENTING
ILLUSTRATIONS

20

WHAT IS EXAMPLE?

Examples illustrate an idea, issue, problem, situation, theory, or trait. Examples often serve to establish a definition or support a point of view. An *adjective* can be defined as "a word modifying a noun or pronoun" and illustrated with examples—*red, new, tall, rich*. The achievements of movie directors can be demonstrated with scenes from their films. The case history of a single patient can illustrate the symptoms of a mental disorder. Writers also use examples to support an argument. Attorneys filing claims of sexual harassment may present specific violations to substantiate a client's case. Students demanding greater campus security might list recent thefts in a letter to the dean to substantiate the need for increased protection.

An example differs from a narration or a description in that the details do not characterize a single person, place, or event but supply information about a type. A narrative essay might tell the story of a man or woman winning the Boston Marathon after recovering from a serious accident. An example essay would relate the athlete's story to illustrate how people can overcome challenges. A description essay might provide details about an entrepreneur turning an abandoned church into bookstore. An example essay would use these details as an illustration of recycling abandoned buildings.

To read more about example, along with interactive examples and opportunities to work with interactive texts, click on "The Rhetorical Patterns of Inquiry" from the main menu of *Comp21*.

Purpose: To Inform or Persuade

Examples clarify abstract or complex ideas that are difficult to comprehend or are easily misinterpreted. Because readers have differing perceptual worlds and personal or cultural definitions of general terms, examples offer concrete details:

> Dorm residents may use small electrical devices—*hair dryers, curling irons, clock radios, or electric shavers*—but are prohibited from operating major appliances—*televisions, microwaves, toaster ovens, or refrigerators.*
>
> *—Student Manual*

- Informative examples should be accurate and concrete—ones readers will readily recognize and understand.
- The language used in developing informative examples should be crafted to suit the topic and audience. Writers must choose words carefully and be conscious of how connotations will influence readers.

Writers also use examples to support a thesis:

Thesis
Examples

Fraternities do not promote binge drinking. For example, last month's Greek Week sponsored fifteen separate events that drew 7,500 participants. Alcohol was served only to those of legal drinking age, and IDs were checked by licensed security guards. The campus police reported no drinking-related violations. *On the contrary,* the English Department's Poetry in the Park festival resulted in thirteen citations for illegal drinking and a drunk-driving arrest.

—Letter to the editor

- Persuasive examples should be ones readers will identify and accept. Democrats are not likely to be impressed by a writer who uses only endorsements by Republicans to support a political argument. High school students may lack the sense of history needed to appreciate examples drawn from the Depression or World War II.
- Because examples are often isolated incidents, they should be supported by evidence demonstrating a general trend—statistics, surveys, and expert testimony.

Extended Examples

Writers may use a single extended example—often in the form of a narrative—to explain an idea or support an argument. Extended examples allow writers to tell a story, create human interest, and provide a context for evidence such as quotations and statistics. In "Death of a Dream" (p. 395), Tony Brown uses the failure of a single black business to illustrate the African American community's failure to patronize black entrepreneurs:

> It was a day of celebration when Rick Singletary opened the largest Black-owned supermarket in the country in Columbus, Ohio—a spectacular $4.4 million operation. He had worked for a major grocery chain for fourteen years and started his own store with his life savings, those of his mother, and a government-insured loan from the Reagan administration. He located Singletary Plaza Mart in the Black community because he knew there was a need for a grocery store there, and because he wanted to create jobs for Blacks.
>
> The entrepreneur needed only a $200,000-a-week volume to keep 130 Black people working. And yet, in a tragedy that exemplifies the real reason why Black America has never been able to compete with White America, Singletary's store failed. Although his research has shown that Blacks in Columbus spent $2.5 million per week on groceries, he could not get them to spend even $200,000 of it in the store he had built in their own neighborhood.

Advantages

- Extended examples clarify concepts by telling a story that can arouse interest, build suspense, and dramatize factual detail.
- Extended examples allow writers to explore an issue in depth by creating a microcosm. By understanding a specific item in detail, readers can appreciate the complexity of the larger issue it represents.

Disadvantages

- Readers may dismiss a single example as an anomaly, a random event that has no wider significance. The use of other evidence, such as facts and statistics, can bolster the importance of the example.
- Extended examples may not be representative. Because no two people, objects, or events are exactly alike, no individual example is likely to fully illustrate a subject. An extended example of a child learning to read, an alcoholic seeking sobriety, or a prosecutor preparing a case may be misleading. Readers may assume that a strictly personal trait is shared by the general population. Extended examples require accurate commentary to prevent confusion.

Enumerated Examples

To overcome problems that can occur with a single example, writers often present more than one illustration. By listing a number of examples, they hope that readers will find it easier to identify their subject. In his essay "Odd Enders,"

Larry Orenstein includes a series of short examples of people who die in unusual circumstances:

> Some people become Odd Enders by accident. In 1947, an eccentric U.S. recluse, while carrying food to his equally reclusive brother, tripped a burglar trap in his house and was crushed to death under bundles of old newspapers, three breadboxes, a sewing machine and a suitcase filled with metal. His brother starved to death.
>
> In 1982, a 27-year-old man fired two shotgun blasts at a giant saguaro cactus in the desert near Phoenix. The shots caused a 23-foot section of the cactus to fall and crush him to death. That same year, an elderly Louisiana man with ailing kidneys was waving a gun at quarreling relatives when it went off. The bullet severed a tube from his dialysis machine, and he bled to death.

Advantages

- Using a number of examples demonstrates a range or spectrum of possibilities.
- Readers who might ignore or misinterpret a single example are more likely to gain a balanced view of the subject if more than one illustration is given.

Disadvantages

- Enumerated examples can be too brief to fully explain or represent an issue and offer only superficial illustrations. To counteract this problem, writers often vary the length of examples, listing some while describing others in depth.
- A list of isolated examples can appear to be simply a collection of random events that provides weak support for an argument. The inclusion of facts, testimony, and statistics can provide additional evidence.
- Although a series of brief examples can create a fast-paced essay, they can lack focus. Lists of examples should be carefully organized in a logical pattern.

WRITING ACTIVITY

List examples that would support the following general statements.

1. People will try almost anything to lose weight.
2. Parents must develop methods to spend more time with their children.
3. Consumer decisions affect the environment.
4. The American economy has overcome many challenges.
5. Technology is robbing people of personal privacy.
6. Movies and television present stereotyped images of women.

7. Today's job market demands computer literacy.

8. Automobiles require special attention.

9. Marriage demands compromise.

10. The Internet has influenced journalism.

Hypothetical Examples

Examples can be fictional, usually narratives of possible situations. Writers often use hypothetical examples to explain or dramatize a point:

Thesis	Make sure you report all injuries—even superficial wounds—to your supervisor before leaving the plant. *For example,* if you
Hypothetical example	fall and hurt your knee but fail to inform your supervisor, you may be unable to prove the injury was work related and be unable to receive full benefits if you later discover surgery is required.

Advantages

■ Hypothetical examples are useful when no factual example exists or if actual situations are too complicated to serve as explanations.

■ Hypothetical examples allow writers to speculate about possible events. Typically, factual examples of future events don't exist.

■ Fictional examples are useful when writers wish to avoid bias and subjective judgments. Factual examples may stir controversy or personal interpretations.

Disadvantages

■ Hypothetical examples are not based in fact. They offer only possible events and actions and provide weak evidence for arguments. Hypothetical examples require support from other forms of evidence to support a thesis.

■ Hypothetical examples can seem distant and unrealistic. They can be made effective if they include facts and provide realistic scenarios readers will identify.

Factual Examples

Factual examples use actual events and people to explain an idea or illustrate a point:

Thesis	Make sure you report all injuries—even superficial wounds—to your supervisor before leaving the plant. Last spring a shipping clerk injured her knee on the loading dock. Thinking she had

Factual
example

suffered only a minor bruise, she completed her shift and went home without informing her supervisor. During the night she awoke in great pain and went to the emergency room where doctors discovered a fracture requiring surgery. Because she could not prove the injury occurred at work, she had to pay over $2,500 in insurance co-payments.

Advantages

■ Factual examples command attention because they are based in actual events, involving people readers may know or at least identify with.
■ Factual illustrations can be documented, dramatizing the reality of the issue or problem.

Disadvantages

■ Factual examples may contain specific details that are not generally representative.
■ Because factual examples usually describe past events, some readers may infer that they are irrelevant to current circumstances.

WRITING ACTIVITY

Provide a hypothetical or factual example to support or illustrate the following thesis statements:

1. Peer pressure drives many adolescents to engage in self-destructive behavior.
2. Motion pictures influence fashion trends.
3. Many people purchase pets without considering how they will care for them.
4. Credit cards lead some consumers to spend recklessly.
5. Operating a small business can entail great risk.
6. Public schools are failing to prepare students for college.
7. Attitudes toward child abuse have changed in the last two decades.
8. Many undergraduates find it almost impossible to complete a bachelor's degree in four years.
9. Television gives children unrealistic expectations.
10. A false allegation, even if proved untrue, can ruin a person's reputation.

STRATEGIES | for Writing Example

Critical Thinking and Prewriting

1. **You can begin writing an example essay in two ways:** First, you can think of a specific person, place, situation, event, or object and determine whether it represents something greater. You can turn a description or narrative into an example if it can illustrate a trend or general condition.

   - A power failure prevents you from printing an assignment, illustrating our dependence on energy.
   - A fraudulent charge appears on your credit card statement, providing an example demonstrating the need for consumer awareness.
   - A friend's dedication to her disabled sister illustrates your concept of family values.

   Second, you can select a general concept, idea, or subject and develop a factual or hypothetical example or examples to explain or support your thesis.

   - Describe your concept of a good relationship and support it with examples of people who exhibit these qualities.
   - Outline the qualities of a role model and provide examples of men and women who demonstrate these traits.
   - Determine what you consider to be a major challenge for Americans in the twenty-first century and then provide examples to dramatize the seriousness of this problem.

2. **Consider your readers' perceptual world.** The attitudes, education, values, and experiences of your readers will determine how they will respond to examples you use to inform or persuade your audience. Midwesterners may not understand examples requiring familiarity with New York City politics. Men may not appreciate examples focusing on women. Young people may not recognize famous individuals widely known to their parents.

3. **Engage critical thinking.** Examples, like statistics, can be both persuasive and misleading. Examples, no matter how interesting or compelling, are individual events, persons, or situations and may not be representative of the whole. The fact that a healthy eighty-five-year-old man has smoked heavily since adolescence does not disprove the overwhelming evidence that tobacco causes disease. A casino advertisement featuring a dozen people who have won a million dollars playing slot machines does not change the fact that the majority of gamblers lose. Examples are anecdotal accounts and rarely provide convincing support for an argument unless supplemented with other forms of evidence.

   - Are your examples truly representative, or are they exceptions to a general rule or condition?

■ Can your examples be supported by facts, testimony, surveys, or statistics?

4. **Begin listing examples.** Use brainstorming, listing, and asking questions to generate as many examples as you can. Freewrite to explore longer or extended examples.

Planning

1. **Clearly define the general principle, rule, situation, or fact the example is going to illustrate.** Examples can become simply narratives unless they support a clearly defined subject. Without a clear definition of *la mordida*, Joe Rodriguez's essay (p. 381) is nothing more than an isolated incident.
   ■ Test this thesis or definition through peer editing. Make sure your statement clearly expresses what you are trying to illustrate.
2. **Determine whether your essay would benefit from a single extended example or a series of examples.**
3. **Organize examples using a chronological, spatial, or emphatic pattern.** Create a timeline for longer or extended examples to focus the narrative.
4. **Determine the best placement for the thesis and definitions.** Beginning with an example can arouse interest and present facts before the thesis is stated. This is useful when you are confronting a biased or hostile audience.
5. **Review your thesis before writing.**
   ■ Is it clearly stated?
   ■ Does it express a general idea or principle that can be illustrated or proven by examples?
6. **Review your examples.**
   ■ Do the examples clearly support or illustrate the thesis?
   ■ Are the examples ones readers will understand and appreciate? Do they take the readers' perceptual world into account?
   ■ Are the examples arranged in a logical pattern?

Writing the First Draft

1. **Use the plan as a guide but be open to additional examples.** As you write, you may expand examples, discover new ones, or discard some on your list as irrelevant or unworkable.
   ■ Amend your plan as you write.
   ■ Use notations or phrases to record ideas to capture a full draft in one sitting.
2. **Distinguish between relevant and incidental events.** Because your examples are supposed to illustrate a general situation, it is important that

your text indicate which elements are wholly personal or accidental. Stress items that support the thesis:

> Ted Smith, *like all AIDS patients in the study,* had been HIV positive for at least five years but had not developed outward symptoms beyond slight fatigue. He took the new drug and within six weeks reported increased energy and stamina. *Unlike the other patients,* Smith continued to take AZT. He reported mild to severe headaches lasting ten to fifteen minutes after taking the new drug. This side effect occurred in 20 percent of patients in the study.

3. **Use introductory and transitional statements to link examples and the thesis:**

> Crime is increasing on this campus. Bicycle theft, *for example,* . . .
> Kai Long lost ten pounds in two weeks on this diet, *illustrating* . . .

Revising

1. **Review the plan and thesis.**
   - Is the thesis stated in terms readers can understand?
2. **Review new ideas developed in the first draft.**
   - Do these new examples support the thesis or general point?
3. **Do the examples make a clear point?** You might relate a fascinating narrative or series of illustrations, but if no clear connection is made to the general concept, readers will be left wondering about its significance.
4. **Is other evidence needed to support the main point or make a stronger argument?**
   - Can facts, quotations, or statistics be blended into the essay to offer additional proof?
5. **Can the thesis be refined to more sharply delineate what these examples are supposed to illustrate?**
   - A general principle does not have to be abstract or vague. The more clearly stated the thesis, the more effective its supporting examples will be.
6. **Decide whether your point is better supported by hypothetical or factual examples.**
   - You may wish to mix factual and hypothetical examples to provide actual details and unbiased illustrations.
7. **Measure the number and value of examples.**
   - Are enough examples presented to illustrate all phases of the subject?
   - Do examples provide separate illustrations or are they merely repetitive?
8. **Are examples clearly organized or do they form a random pattern?**
   - You may want to experiment with a different kind of organization (such as chronological, spatial, or emphatic) to be sure you choose the most effective style.

Editing and Proofreading

1. **Examine examples for consistency in voice, tone, style, and tense.** A list of examples can appear chaotic if there are awkward shifts.

   ■ Keep the examples in the same tense and voice. Avoid shifting from first to third person or from past to present unless there are logical transitions.

   ■ Maintain a common tone and style. The examples, though separate items, should form a seamless narrative.

2. **Review diction for unintended connotations.** Because examples are supposed to illustrate and explain an idea, careful word choice is essential to avoid misleading readers.

3. **Examine paragraph breaks and transitions for clarity.** Readers will rely on structure to follow examples and relate them to a general principle.

4. **Make the opening and final examples memorable.** First and last impressions are most likely to influence readers and give them illustrations they can recall and repeat to others.

STUDENT PAPER

This paper was written in response to an assignment in a freshman composition course:

> *Write a 500-word essay that illustrates a current social phenomenon with an example of someone you know or have met. Your paper might illustrate the struggles of single mothers, the perils of dating on the Internet, the dilemma of telling a falsehood. Make sure your paper clearly defines the subject you are illustrating.*

Guerrilla Entrepreneur

Last semester Pauline Feldman gave a talk at the business school promoting her new book *Guerrilla Entrepreneurs*. Her book defined a new breed of small business owner, particularly those in the inner city who often operate in an expanding underground economy. Instead of getting a traditional job, guerrilla entrepreneurs discover an opportunity and launch a business venture.

No one better illustrates this phenomenon than Terrell Williams, my former tennis partner. I say former because Terry stopped coming to the courts in late September.

When I ran into him in the library he explained that in order to pay for tuition and save for a new car, he had started a business.

Terry had discovered, almost by accident, that a company near his father's repair shop purchased wooden fork lift pallets. This firm pays five dollars for pallets in good repair and three dollars for broken ones. Driving to school the next day, Terry noticed abandoned pallets tossed beside dumpsters, stacked in alleys, and leaning against convenience stores. On his way home that afternoon he stopped to ask store managers, landlords, and truck drivers if he could have their discarded pallets. A convenience store owner not only allowed him to take the pallets but agreed to pay him ten dollars a week to get rid of them.

Terry borrowed his father's 1978 Ford van and began picking up pallets on his way home from school. After a week he was earning fifty to a hundred dollars a day. As the semester passed, he developed contacts with local merchants who informed him of major deliveries. Often, he could fill the van with a single trip to a local strip mall. Factory managers began stacking spare pallets in alleys for him.

Terry gave his father fifty dollars a week for use of the van and paid for gas and repairs. The van was put to hard use and soon needed new tires, an exhaust system, and a major tune up. Terry still managed to generate enough profit to pay for school, his books, living expenses, and add to his savings account each week.

Terry represents any number of guerrilla entrepreneurs who seize an opportunity and create a new business. Like the other people chronicled in Pauline Feldman's book, Terry feels a great sense of pride in his accomplishment but also experiences great stress. He knows that the battered van may have to be replaced. He has thought of purchasing a second van and hiring another driver, but insurance costs, liability issues, and the paperwork has led him to decide to stay a one person enterprise. And like many of the guerrilla entrepreneurs Pauline Feldman describes, Terry has no plans to continue his business after he graduates. "It's a means to an end," he says. "After I go to law school, I hope I never see another pallet."

Questions for Review and Revision

1. What is a *guerrilla entrepreneur*?
2. Does the student's example accurately illustrate the definition provided?
3. Do you know people who could also serve as examples of guerrilla entrepreneurs?

4. Is the definition of *guerrilla entrepreneur* clearly stated? Can you restate this concept in your own words?
5. How effectively does the student's example illustrate the subject?
6. Are there some details that could be eliminated from the narrative?
7. The student does not use any visuals in this essay. Do you think it needs one? What kind of image, such as a photo or drawing, might be useful here?
8. The student refers to a book by Pauline Feldman. Does the student rely too much on another source? Is this essay independent? Will it make sense to people unfamiliar with the book?
9. Read this paper aloud. Are there passages you would revise for greater clarity?

Writing Suggestions

1. Using this essay as a model, write an example essay about a person you know who represents a social trend—a downsized executive, a single parent, or a workaholic. Make sure you clearly define the trend you are illustrating.
2. *Collaborative writing:* Working with others, write an essay illustrating how working students balance job and academic responsibilities. Use a number of examples to reveal common problems and solutions.

SUGGESTED TOPICS FOR WRITING EXAMPLE

General Assignments

Write an example paper on any of the following topics. Your example may inform or persuade. You may use both factual and hypothetical examples.

Begin with a point of view. State your opinion on one of the following issues and use examples as illustrations:

1. American materialism
2. Television violence
3. The prevailing attitude on your campus about mandatory drug testing, capital punishment, smoking, abortion, date rape, affirmative action, or any other controversial topic

4. Courage
5. Illegal immigration

Begin with a specific person, place, item, or event and explain its greater significance, demonstrating how it illustrates or symbolizes a general trend or concept:

1. Describe a common behavior you have observed. What does this action represent? You might see road rage as an example of growing selfishness or littering as a sign of disrespect for public property.
2. Write about an incident that taught you a lesson. What does this episode reveal about society, human nature, your family, or friends?
3. Select a location, such as a shopping mall, high school, or summer camp, and explain what it represents about American society.
4. Describe a television program, concert, or movie that represents what you consider to be good or bad in popular culture.
5. Relate a dilemma you have faced in your own life. How does it illustrate a situation faced by others?

 To create your own interactive writing project, use the textual, visual, and video libraries on *Comp21*. For the main menu, choose "Build Your Own Occasion for Writing."

Writing in Context

1. Imagine that you have been asked to explain to foreign students the American attitude toward a specific issue or value—marriage, money, crime, education. Illustrate your response with examples. You may demonstrate a range of opinions by listing differing attitudes and supplying each with at least one example.
2. Write a letter to the editor of a magazine that you read to praise or criticize its coverage. Support your views with examples.
3. Write a response to an essay question that asks for historical examples of movements that changed American society.
4. Write a hypothetical example illustrating the proper course of action in an emergency.

STRATEGIES | for Reading Example

When reading the example essays in this chapter, keep the following questions in mind.

Context

1. What is the author's purpose—to inform or persuade? What does the example illustrate?
2. What is the thesis or general point? Is it clearly defined? Can you restate it in your own words?
3. What can you tell about the intended audience? Are the examples targeted to a specific group of readers? Are the illustrations ones that general readers can recognize and appreciate?

Strategy

1. Does the writer use a single extended example or a series of illustrations?
2. Does the author use other forms of support—facts, testimony, statistics?
3. Are the examples convincing? Do they truly represent a general condition, or are they drawn out of context?
4. How is the essay organized?
5. Where is the thesis or general principle placed in the essay? Would it be more effective if located elsewhere?
6. What transitional devices are used to organize the examples?

Language

1. Do the tone, style, and diction used to relate the example suit the writer's purpose?
2. What role do connotations play in relating examples? How do they shape the reader's perception?

Anna Quindlen (1952–) graduated from Barnard College in 1974 and began working as a reporter in New York. After writing articles for the **New York Post**, she took over the "About New York" column for the **New York Times.** In 1986 she started her own column, "Life in the Thirties." Her collected articles were published in **Living Out Loud** in 1988. She has written numerous op-ed pieces for the **Times** on social and political issues. In 1992 she received the Pulitzer Prize. The following year she published another collection of essays, **Thinking Out Loud: On the Personal, the Political, the Public, and the Private.** Quindlen has also written four novels, **Object Lessons, One True Thing, Black and Blue,** and **Blessings.**

Homeless

In this essay Quindlen illustrates the plight of the homeless by presenting a single example, a woman named Ann whom she discovered living in the Port Authority Terminal. As you read the essay, determine which attributes of this woman's situation are wholly personal and which represent the general homeless population.

Her name was Ann, and we met in the Port Authority Bus Terminal several Januarys ago. I was doing a story on homeless people. She said I was wasting my time talking to her; she was just passing through, although she'd been passing through for more than two weeks. To prove to me that this was true, she rummaged through a tote bag and a manila envelope and finally unfolded a sheet of typing paper and brought out her photographs.

1 introduction of example

They were not pictures of family, or friends, or even a dog or cat, its eyes brown-red in the flashbulb's light. They were pictures of a house. It was like a thousand houses in a hundred towns, not suburb, not city, but somewhere in between, with aluminum siding and a chain-link fence, a narrow driveway running up to a one-car garage and a patch of backyard. The house was yellow. I looked on the back for a date or a name, but neither was there. There was no need for discussion. I knew what she was trying to tell me, for it was something I had often felt. She was not adrift, alone, anonymous, although her bags and her raincoat with the grime shadowing its creases had made me believe she was. She had a house, or at least once upon a time had had one.

2 pictures

home and identity

Inside were curtains, a couch, a stove, potholders. You are where you live. She was somebody.

3   I've never been very good at looking at the big picture, taking the global view, and I've always been a person with an overactive sense of place, the legacy of an Irish grandfather. So it is natural that the thing that seems most wrong with the world to me right now is that there are so many people with no homes. I'm not simply talking about shelter from the elements, or three square meals a day or a mailing address to which the welfare people can send the check—although I know that all these are important for survival. I'm talking about a home, about precisely those kinds of feelings that have wound up in cross-stitch and French knots on samplers over the years.

importance of a home

4   Home is where the heart is. There's no place like it. I love my home with a ferocity totally out of proportion to its appearance or location. I love dumb things about it: the hot-water heater, the plastic rack you drain dishes in, the roof over my head, which occasionally leaks. And yet it is precisely those dumb things that make it what it is—a place of certainty, stability, predictability, privacy, for me and for my family. It is where I live. What more can you say about a place than that? That is everything.

5   Yet it is something that we have been edging away from gradually during my lifetime and the lifetimes of my parents and grandparents. There was a time when where you lived often was where you worked and where you grew the food you ate and even where you were buried. When that era passed, where you lived at least was where your parents had lived and where you would live with your children when you became enfeebled. Then, suddenly where you lived was where you lived for three years, until you could move on to something else and something·else again. And so we have come to something else again, to children who do not understand what it means to go to their rooms because they have never had a room, to men and women whose fantasy is a wall they can paint a color of their own choosing, to old people reduced to sitting on molded plastic chairs, their skin blue-white in the lights of a bus station, who pull pictures of houses out of their bags. Homes have stopped being homes. Now they are real estate.

home vs. real estate

6   People find it curious that those without homes would rather sleep sitting up on benches or huddled in doorways than go to shelters. Certainly some prefer to do so because they are emotionally ill, because they have been locked in before and they are damned if they will be locked in again. Others are afraid of the violence and trouble they may find there. But some seem to want something that is not available in shelters, and they will not compromise, not for a cot, or oatmeal, or a shower with special soap that kills the bugs. "One room," a woman with a baby who was sleeping on her sister's

floor, once told me, "painted blue." That was the crux of it; not size or location, but pride of ownership. Painted blue.

This is a difficult problem, and some wise and compassionate people are working hard at it. But in the main I think we work around it, just as we walk around it when it is lying on the sidewalk or sitting in the bus terminal—the problem, that is. It has been customary to take people's pain and lessen our own participation in it by turning it into an issue, not a collection of human beings. We turn an adjective into a noun: the poor, not poor people; the homeless, not Ann or the man who lives in the box or the woman who sleeps on the subway grate. Sometimes I think we would be better off if we forgot about the broad strokes and concentrated on the details. Here is a woman without a bureau. There is a man with no mirror, no wall to hang it on. They are not the homeless. They are people who have no homes. No drawer that holds the spoons. No window to look out upon the world. My God. That is everything.

Understanding Context

1. What is Quindlen's thesis? Can you state it in your own words?
2. What attitude does Quindlen have about homeless people? What is the worst aspect of their situation?
3. *Critical thinking:* Quindlen states that people use language to lessen their involvement with others by turning "an adjective into a noun: the poor, not poor people." What does she mean? Can you think of other examples?

Evaluating Strategy

1. What role does Ann play in the article? Would an essay about homeless people be as effective without a personal example?
2. Quindlen focuses on the snapshot of Ann's home. What is significant about this detail? What does the picture represent to Ann?
3. What concrete details does Quindlen use to record the condition of homeless people?
4. *Critical thinking:* Quindlen at one point states, "I've never been very good at looking at the big picture, taking the global view." Is it effective for a writer to admit shortcomings or explain his or her approach to the subject? Does this explain why the article does not include statistics or surveys providing a "global view" of the issue?

Appreciating Language

1. What connotation does the word *home* have? What does it bring to mind when you hear or see the word? How does Quindlen use readers' perceptions to highlight what homeless people lack?
2. What words does Quindlen use to describe Ann? What attitude does her word choice reflect?
3. Discuss the different meanings of *home* and *real estate*.

Writing Suggestions

1. Write an essay about a social problem, using a single person to illustrate the issue. Focus on how this one person represents challenges faced by others with the same problem.
2. Select a friend, historical figure, or current celebrity you admire and write an essay using him or her to illustrate a personality trait or quality. A famous athlete might represent determination. A close friend might illustrate selflessness.
3. *Collaborative writing:* Work with a group of students and discuss a social problem, personality trait, political issue, or academic subject. Then select a person, real or hypothetical, to explain it. A local politician arrested on drug charges might illustrate the problem of addiction. A fictional student could portray the problems students face in determining a major.

Joe Rodriguez served as an editorial writer for the **San Jose Mercury News** before becoming one of the newspaper's staff columnists. He has written extensively about life in southern California, commenting on Mexican American identity, bilingual education, gun control, drugs, and city planning. He published several articles about the price of urban renewal, stating, "There's more humanity in one block of real neighborhood than in a square mile of a subdivision."

Mexicans Deserve More Than *La Mordida*

As you read Rodriguez's essay, notice how he uses a minor incident to represent a complex social problem. Consider if this bribery incident illustrates a problem greater than the corruption found in other countries.

"I wouldn't give you a dime for Mexico!" 1

My father used to tell us that every time Mexico broke his heart. He was 2 *muy indio*, with dark reddish brown skin, huge calloused hands and a handsomely hooked nose. On our occasional trips to Tijuana to visit relatives, he'd see Indian women begging on the streets, Indian kids selling Chiclets chewing gum, and white-skinned Mexicans owning and running everything.

"Not a dime for Mexico!" 3

He was more Mexican than I'll ever be, more Mexican than any Harvard 4 educated technocrat, any Spanish-looking *gachupin*, any middle-class Zapatista guerrilla-intellectual, or any bald-headed ex-president crook from Mexico City's ritzy Polanco district. My father wasn't referring to the nation's people, but to a political and social system that still fosters extreme poverty, discrimination and injustice, and to the privileged and the ruthless who benefit by it.

I should have remembered my Dad's dime recently when two Mexico 5 City policemen pulled me over for making an illegal left-hand turn at the Monument of Cuauhtemoc on the famous Paseo de la Reforma boulevard.

I was driving back into the giant city after three days in the countryside. 6

I had escaped a traffic accident only minutes earlier. I was hot, tired, 7 grumpy and jumpy. I was driving a rental car. These conditions made me the perfect *pollo* for these two uniformed coyotes.

8   Both cops got out. The older one checked out the rental plates. The younger one wanted to see my driver's license.

9   "Where's your hotel?" he asked.

10   Right over there, I said, the Maria Cristina Hotel on Rio Lerma Street.

11   "I don't know any hotel by that name," he said. "Prove it. Show me something from the hotel."

12   I fumbled through my wallet, finally producing a card-key from the hotel. The dance between the cops and me had begun.

13   "I see," the young policeman said. "What are you doing in Mexico?"

14   I'm a journalist, I said. I'd been reporting in Queretaro state.

15   "You know," he said, "for making that illegal turn, we're going to have to take away your driver's license and the plates from the car."

16   I said, What? Why can't you just give me a ticket?

17   He then walked away and asked the other, older, policeman, "How do you want to take care of this?"

18   The veteran officer then took over.

19   "The violation brings a fine of 471 pesos," he told me. "But we still have to take your plates and license. You can pick them up at police headquarters when you pay the fine. Or, I can deliver them to you tomorrow at your hotel, but only after you pay."

20   By now, I figured this was all B.S., but I wasn't absolutely sure. Who ever heard of license plate confiscation for minor traffic violations? Still, I didn't know what my rights were as a motorist. Why didn't I prepare myself for something like this?

21   "So, since you say you need the car," the cop said, "*¿Nos podemos arreglar esto de otra manera?* (Can we take care of this another way?)."

22   I would prefer a ticket, I said.

23   The veteran cop stretched his arms upward, relaxed a bit, and then rested his forearms on my door. He leaned in and stuck his face inches from mine, and smiled.

24   "*Lo que tenemos aqui, se llama la corrupción,*" he said. "What we have here is called corruption."

25   So there it was—*la mordida*—the bite, the bribe, a complex government system based not on civil service, but on bribery, political patronage, personal favoritism and individual gain.

26   Everybody in Mexico knows that corruption is rampant among the local, state and federal police forces and the military. A national agency has even taken out full-page newspaper ads asking people not to pay off corrupt cops, saying "*la mordida* spreads as easily as rabies."

27   Just last month, Mexico's national drug czar, a well-respected general, was arrested for protecting a northern drug lord. Corruption at the

top only emboldens the small-fries like these two brown-shirted Mexico City cops.

Mexico's people deserve so much better. It is their personal integrity 28 and family strength that carry the nation, despite the incompetence and dishonesty of the ruling party and corrupt officials big and small. And it's well within the United States' ability to step up the few binational efforts that exist to train Mexican police officers—the honest and sharp ones—in modern methods and ethics.

I wish I had thought about that and my father's dime and refused to play 29 the game as I sat parked on Mexico City's most prominent boulevard, but I didn't.

"What do you say you help us out with 500 pesos?" the veteran cop said. 30

What do you mean, I said. The violation is worth less than that. 31

"400 pesos." 32

I don't have that much, I said, lying through my teeth. 33

"300 pesos." 34

We got stuck on 300 pesos for a while until he came down to 250 pesos, 35 or about $31.25 in American dollars. I thumbed through my wallet for the bills, trying to keep him from seeing that I had much more money.

"Listen," he said. "You're a journalist from the United States. *Tu ganas* 36 *pura lana.* You make lots of money. You can give me 300 pesos easy."

I don't make a lot of money, I said. My newspaper does, not me. I'm not 37 rich. I'm just another Mexican like you trying to get by.

He wasn't moved. 38

Once I had the 250 pesos out of my wallet, he handed me a notebook 39 through the window.

"Put the money in this so people don't see it pass hands." 40

I put the money in the notebook and gave it to him. He asked me once 41 again for more.

"*Andale, hombre,*" he said. "You can give me another 50 pesos. Consider 42 it my tip."

Understanding Context

1. How would you describe *la mordida* in your own words?
2. What attitude toward *la mordida* does the statement "Not a dime for Mexico" reflect?
3. Does this minor request for a bribe—which could occur in any country—illustrate something unique to Mexico?
4. *Critical thinking:* Why is bribery wrong? How does corruption, even in trivial matters, affect people's faith in their government and institutions?

Evaluating Strategy

1. Rodriguez selects a minor incident to reveal the nature of *la mordida*. Would a major bribery scandal involving national elections be a better example?
2. Would a series of shorter examples better represent the extent of *la mordida* in Mexican society?
3. Why is dialogue important in relating this example?
4. What role does the writer play in this example? Why are his reactions important?

Appreciating Language

1. What does the writer's choice of words reveal about his attitude toward *la mordida*?
2. *La mordida* means "the bite" in Spanish. What connotations does "the bite" have?

Writing Suggestions

1. Illustrate a common social problem or incident with a personal experience. You might provide an example of online dating, road rage, recycling, sexual harassment, sports gambling, or binge drinking.
2. *Collaborative writing:* Work with a group of students and develop a list of social problems—discrimination, corruption, alcoholism, and so forth—and then select one and provide one or more examples revealing the nature and extent of the problem.

José Antonio Burciaga (1940–1996) grew up in a synagogue in El Paso, where his father worked as a custodian. Burciaga served in the U.S. Air Force and then attended the University of Texas, where he earned a fine arts degree. Pursuing both art and literature, Burciaga was also active in Chicano affairs. His artwork was first exhibited in 1974. Two years later he published a collection of poetry called ***Restless Serpents,*** followed by a variety of other publications.

My Ecumenical Father

This essay, which first appeared in Drink Cultura, *describes Burciaga's father, a man who maintained his ties to Mexican culture while taking pride in his American citizenship and developing a fierce devotion to the Jewish faith.*

¡Feliz Navidad! Merry Christmas! Happy Hanukkah! As a child, my season's greetings were tricultural—Mexicano, Anglo and Jewish. 1

Our devoutly Catholic parents raised three sons and three daughters in 2 the basement of a Jewish synagogue, Congregation B'nai Zion in El Paso, Texas. José Cruz Burciaga was the custodian and *shabbat goy*. A shabbat goy is Yiddish for a Gentile who, on the Sabbath, performs certain tasks forbidden to Jews under orthodox law.

Every year around Christmas time, my father would take the menorah 3 out and polish it. The eight-branched candleholder symbolizes Hanukkah, the commemoration of the first recorded war of liberation in that part of the world.

In 164 B.C., the Jewish nation rebelled against Antiochus IV Epiphanes, 4 who had attempted to introduce pagan idols into the temples. When the temple was reconquered by the Jews, there was only one day's supply of oil for the Eternal Light in the temple. By a miracle, the oil lasted eight days.

My father was not only in charge of the menorah but for 10 years he also 5 made sure the Eternal Light remained lit.

As children we were made aware of the differences and joys of 6 Hanukkah, Christmas and Navidad. We were taught to respect each celebration, even if they conflicted. For example, the Christmas carols taught in school. We learned the song about the twelve days of Christmas, though I never understood what the hell a partridge was doing in a pear tree in the middle of December.

7   We also learned a German song about a boy named Tom and a bomb— *O Tannenbaum.* We even learned a song in the obscure language of Latin, called "Adeste Fideles," which reminded me of, *Ahh! d'este deo,* a Mexican pasta soup. Though 75% of our class was Mexican-American, we never sang a Christmas song in *Español.* Spanish was forbidden.

8   So our mother—a former teacher—taught us "Silent Night" in Spanish: *Noche de paz, noche de amor:* It was so much more poetic and inspirational.

9   While the rest of El Paso celebrated Christmas, Congregation B'nai Zion celebrated Hanukkah. We picked up Yiddish and learned a Hebrew prayer of thanksgiving. My brothers and I would help my father hang the Hanukkah decorations.

10   At night, after the services, the whole family would rush across the border to Juarez and celebrate the *posadas,* which takes place for nine days before Christmas. They are a communal re-enactment of Joseph and Mary's search for shelter, just before Jesus was born.

11   To the posadas we took candles and candy left over from the Hanukkah celebrations. The next day we'd be back at St. Patrick's School singing, "I'm dreaming of a white Christmas."

12   One day I stopped dreaming of the white Christmases depicted on greeting cards. An old immigrant from Israel taught me Jesus was born in desert country just like that of the West Texas town of El Paso.

13   On Christmas Eve, my father would dress like Santa Claus and deliver gifts to his children, nephews, godchildren and the little kids in orphanages. The next day, minus his disguise, he would take us to Juarez, where we delivered gifts to the poor in the streets.

14   My father never forgot his childhood poverty and forever sought to help the less fortunate. He taught us to measure wealth not in money but in terms of love, spirit, charity and culture.

15   We were taught to respect the Jewish faith and culture. On the Day of Atonement, when the whole congregation fasted, my mother did not cook, lest the food odors distract. The respect was mutual. No one ever complained about the large picture of Jesus in our living room.

16   Through my father, leftover food from B'nai B'rith luncheons, Bar Mitzvahs and Bat Mitzvahs, found its way to Catholic or Baptist churches or orphanages. Floral arrangements in the temple that surrounded a Jewish wedding *huppah* canopy many times found a second home at the altar of St. Patrick's Cathedral or San Juan Convent School. Surplus furniture, including old temple pews, found their way to a missionary Baptist Church in *El Segundo Barrio.*

It was not uncommon to come home from school at lunch time and 17
find an uncle priest, an aunt nun and a Baptist minister visiting our home
at the same time that the Rabbi would knock on our door. It was just as
natural to find the president of B'nai Zion eating beans and tortillas in our
kitchen.

My father literally risked his life for the Jewish faith. Twice he was as- 18
saulted by burglars who broke in at night. Once he was stabbed in the hand.
Another time he stayed up all night guarding the sacred Torahs after anti-
Semites threatened the congregation. He never philosophized about his
ecumenism, he just lived it.

Cruz, as most called him, was a man of great humor, a hot temper and a 19
passion for dance. He lived the Mexican Revolution and rode the rails during the Depression. One of his proudest moments came when he became a
U.S. citizen.

September 23, 1985, sixteen months after my mother passed away, my 20
father followed. Like his life, his death was also ecumenical. The funeral
was held at Our Lady of Peace, where a priest said the mass in English. My
cousins played mandolin and sang in Spanish. The president of B'nai Zion
Congregation said a prayer in Hebrew. Members of the congregation sat
with Catholics and Baptists.

Observing Jewish custom, the cortege passed by the synagogue one last 21
time. Fittingly, father was laid to rest on the Sabbath. At the cemetery, in a
very Mexican tradition, my brothers, sisters and I each kissed a handful of
dirt and threw it on the casket.

I once had the opportunity to describe father's life to the late, great Jew- 22
ish American writer Bernard Malamud. His only comment was, "Only in
America!"

Understanding Context

1. What is a *shabbat goy*?
2. How did the author's family show respect to the congregation?
3. How did the author's family manage to blend respect for several cultures?
4. Burciaga points out that though he learned German and Latin songs in
   school, he was not allowed to sing in Spanish. What does this reveal about
   the educational system?
5. Why is the description of his father's funeral central to Burciaga's story?
6. *Critical thinking:* What values does the ecumenical father represent? Are
   these values rare in our society? What lesson could this essay teach?

Evaluating Strategy

1. Would Bernard Malamud's comment, "Only in America," make a good title for this essay? Why or why not?
2. Burciaga offers an explanation of Hanukkah. What does this suggest about his intended audience?
3. *Other modes:* Can this *description* be seen as an extended *definition* of *ecumenical*?

Appreciating Language

1. How did Burciaga's father define "wealth"?
2. Read through Burciaga's description and highlight his use of non-English words and phrases. How does he define them? What impact do all these unfamiliar words have?

Writing Suggestions

1. Burciaga builds his description largely through details about his father's actions and behavior. Write a few paragraphs describing a person you know well. Try to capture the person's principal attributes by describing actions that reveal their values.
2. *Collaborative writing:* Discuss this essay with a group of other students. What do readers find most striking about this Mexican immigrant? Are his attitudes valuable to society? Is multiculturalism a trend today? Have each member write a few paragraphs explaining the significance of this essay. Read the responses aloud, and work to blend as many as possible in a short *analysis* of this essay.

::e-reading ::::::::::::::::::::::::::::::::::

InfoTrac College Edition
www.infotrac-college.com

FATHERHOOD

Fathers are not expendable, disposable, unnecessary, or replaceable. They are vital to the future of their children.

David Popenoe

Gary Salter/zefa/Corbis

The push for traditional nuclear families remains strong, even if it means bringing abusive dads back where they can do more harm.

Judith Davidoff

In *Fatherless America* David Blankenhorn predicts the United States is rapidly moving toward two societies, separate and unequal, based not on differences of race or income but fatherhood:

> After the year 2000 . . . the United States will be a nation divided into two groups, separate and unequal. The two groups will work in the same economy, speak a common language, and remember the same national history. But they will live fundamentally divergent lives. One group will receive basic benefits—psychological, social, economic, educational, and moral—that are denied to the other group.
>
> The primary fault line dividing the two groups will not be race, religion, class, education, or gender. It will be patrimony. One group will consist of those adults who grew up with the daily presence and provision of fathers. The other group will consist of those who did not. By the early years of the next century, these two groups will be roughly the same size.

David Popenoe echoes many of Blankenhorn's concerns in his article "A World Without Fathers," which argues that fatherlessness is the cause of many social problems, especially delinquency:

> Having a father in the home is no guarantee that a youngster won't commit a crime, but it appears to be an excellent form of prevention. Sixty percent of America's rapists, 72 percent of its adolescent murderers, and 70 percent of its long-term prison inmates come from fatherless homes. Fathers are important to their sons as role models. They are important for maintaining authority and discipline. And they are important in helping their sons develop both self-control and feelings of empathy toward others.

Popenoe challenges the argument that children need not a biological father but caring adults in their lives, citing research that shows that children raised without fathers were more likely to be abused by single mothers and their sexual partners. One study showed that girls were thirty-three times more likely to be sexually abused in households with a stepfather or a mother's live-in boyfriend than a biological father.

Many commentators share the view that the problems of child poverty, youth violence, sexual assault, and domestic violence stem from what David Blankenhorn calls the "flight of males from their children's lives."

Fatherhood became a political issue as faith-based fatherhood programs received federal funding. Designed to motivate men to take responsibility for supporting their children, these programs were criticized by feminists who saw them as reinforcing gender stereotypes and justifying male supremacy. States increasingly sought to crackdown on deadbeat dads who failed to make support payments. Critics argued that blaming fatherlessness on the moral failings of men overlooked the role of poverty and low-wage jobs in preventing fathers from being able to support their children. An Urban Institute report revealed the majority of working fathers of children collecting welfare were earning an average of seven dollars an hour. A third of the fathers would qualify for food stamps after paying child support.

As society wrestles with abortion rights, child support, juvenile delinquency, and the definition of what is considered a family, the role of fatherhood will remain a central concern. Looking to the future, David Popenoe believes that fatherhood, though essential to family unity and social stability, has to be reconciled with changes in society and gender:

> The father's role must also be redefined in a way that neglects neither historical models nor the unique attributes of modern societies, the new roles for women, and the special qualities that men bring to child rearing.

Before reading these articles, consider these questions:

Who is a father? How do you define a father? Is it a man who im-
pregnates a woman, a male who provides financial support, or a
live-in parent?

What social forces have changed the roles of fathers?

Have male attitudes about accepting responsibility for children they
father changed?

How has popular culture depicted fathers?

Has supporting single-parent families made fathers feel less important and less responsible for their children's well-being?

E-Readings Online

Search for each article by author or title after entering InfoTrac College
Edition through your 1Pass account login.

Patricia Fry. *Fathers in America—Yesterday, Today, and Tomorrow.*
Industrialization and divorce have changed the pattern of fatherhood,
but the roles of fathers in their children's lives remains vital.

David Popenoe. *A World Without Fathers.*
To move toward "a more just and humane society," Popenoe argues that
"we must reverse the tide that is pulling fathers apart from their
families."

Jane Eisner. *Where Are the Fathers?*
When children are found dead or neglected, mothers and social workers
are often held accountable. One reporter asks, what responsibility do the
fathers bear for the welfare of their children?

Martin Davis. *Turning the Hearts of Deadbeat Dads.*
Charles Ballard, a former convict, heads a faith-based organization that
seeks to reunite fathers with their abandoned children.

Judith Davidoff. *The Fatherhood Industry.*
Driven by questionable evidence about the importance of fathers, current welfare policies push to maintain two-parent families, "even if it
means bringing abusive dads back to where they can do more harm."

Stephen Baskerville. *Is There Really a Fatherhood Crisis?*
The focus of fatherhood has led both liberals and conservatives to view
restoring fathers to families as a remedy of social ills, creating policies that
criminalize "deadbeat dads" and overlooking the fact that the most common reason men fail to pay child support is low pay and unemployment.

Quassan T. Castro. *My Father, No Show.*
Disillusioned after making contact with his absentee father, a young man determines to become a better parent.

Israel Maldonado. *I'm Not a Deadbeat Dad.*
Although willing to take responsibility for fathering a child, Maldonado publicly protested against being forced to pay 45 percent of his take-home income in child support.

Rickie Windle. *Dad Deeper Than Genetics.*
Windle argues that the true definition of fatherhood has little to do with genetics. Stepfathers, coaches, and mentors can provide the guidance that children need.

Critical Reading and Thinking

1. How do the various authors define fathers?
2. What role do fathers play in childhood development? Can a coach, mentor, or other male figure replace an absentee biological father? Why or why not?
3. Does recognizing the importance of fatherhood suggest that mothers cannot raise children on their own?
4. What roles do "family values" play in the debate over fatherhood?
5. Does focusing on the moral implications of men's failing to take responsibility for their children identify a cause of social problems or a result of poverty?

Writing Suggestions

1. Write an essay presenting your own views on the importance of fatherhood. What role did your father play in your life?
2. *Collaborative writing:* Working with other students, develop a set of questions to measure attitudes about fatherhood: Should a man who gets a woman pregnant be expected to marry her? How much of a man's income should be paid in child support? Do welfare programs encourage fathers to abandon their children? Do young males take fatherhood less seriously than their parents? To get an accurate assessment of attitudes, avoid asking for yes or no answers. Instead, create clear statements and ask respondents whether they strongly disagree, disagree somewhat, have no opinion, agree somewhat, or strongly agree. Discuss the results of your poll and develop an essay presenting the results of your findings.

3. *Other modes*
- *Define* fatherhood. Who, in your view, is a father? What qualities makes a man a father?
- Write a *division* paper that describes different types of fathers.
- *Classify* fathers by their parental involvement, from those who have the greatest involvement in their children's lives to those who play no role at all.
- Write a *cause-and-effect* essay that provides reasons that men fail to provide for the children they father, or outline the effects the lack of a father has on children.
- Write a *comparison* essay describing children who grow up in a home with a father and those who do not. What differences, if any, have you noticed?

Research Paper

You can develop a research paper about fatherhood by conducting further research to explore a range of issues:

- Who considers fatherlessness a crisis? Is this a widely held view, or is it a position advanced by advocates of specific values and policies?
- What are the current statistics about fathers? How many children grow up in homes with fathers today? Have the numbers changed in recent years?
- Have fatherhood programs proven to be effective? Who sponsors them? What do their critics cite as their failures?
- Are attitudes about fatherhood changing in other societies as well? Is this an American issue or has it affected other nations as well?

For Further Reading

To locate additional sources on fatherhood, enter these search terms as Infotrac subjects:

Fatherhood
Subdivisions: analysis
                   influence
                   personal narratives
                   portrayals
                   psychological aspects
                   social aspects
                   surveys

Fathers

Subdivisions:	behavior
	beliefs, opinions and attitudes
	personal narratives
	social policy
	statistics

Additional Sources

Using a search engine, such as Yahoo!, Google, or Alta Vista, enter one or more of the following terms to locate additional sources:

fatherhood	fatherhood programs
child support	father's rights
divorced fathers	fatherlessness
fathers	paternity laws

See Evaluating Internet Source Checklist on page 752. See Chapter 30 for using and documenting sources.

Tony Brown (1933–) is best known as host of **Tony Brown's Journal,** a public television program that first aired in the 1970s. Born in Charleston, West Virginia, Brown attended Wayne State University. Active in civil rights, Brown worked as a social worker and drama critic for the **Detroit Courier.** In 1971 he founded the School of Communications at Howard University in Washington, D.C. In 1995 he published **Black Lies, White Lies: The Truth According to Tony Brown.**

Death of a Dream

As you read Brown's essay, notice how he uses a single illustration to persuade readers to share his views. Highlight places where Brown uses narration, description, and comparison in his essay.

Up! Up! You mighty race. You can accomplish what you will.
—*Marcus Garvey*

It was a day of celebration when Rick Singletary opened the largest Black- 1 owned supermarket in the country in Columbus, Ohio—a spectacular $4.4 million operation. He had worked for a major grocery chain for fourteen years and started his own store with his life savings, those of his mother, and a government-insured loan from the Reagan administration. He located Singletary Plaza Mart in the Black community because he knew there was a need for a grocery store there, and because he wanted to create jobs for Blacks.

The entrepreneur needed only a $200,000-a-week volume to keep 130 2 Black people working. And yet, in a tragedy that exemplifies the real reason why Black America has never been able to compete with White America, Singletary's store failed. Although his research had shown that Blacks in Columbus spent $2.5 million per week on groceries, he could not get them to spend even $200,000 of it in the store he had built for them in their own neighborhood.

I am familiar with the details because I tried to help Singletary, and I 3 tried to help the Blacks in his community realize what was happening. For three days, I joined others in the Buy Freedom campaign of Black economic empowerment in Columbus. But, sadly, we failed to save his store.

4   This is not simply a neighborhood issue, it is a national disgrace. Rick Singletary, a good man who banked on his community, went bankrupt. He lost his life savings and his mother's savings, and 130 Black people lost their jobs. *This story is repeated somewhere in the Black community every day.* This gives credence to my theory that the most successful economic boycott ever conducted in America is the boycott by Blacks of their own businesses.

Making Blacks Competitive

5   The key to making Black America competitive with White America is really quite simple. Black Americans now earn nearly $500 billion annually, according to economist Andrew F. Brommer. This is roughly equivalent to the gross domestic product of Canada or Australia. And yet Blacks spend only 3 percent of their income with a Black business or Black professional. By spending 97 percent of their money outside of their racial community, they exacerbate their own social and economic problems.

6   This is the reason that Blacks do not keep pace economically or socially with the rest of the country. Since 80 percent of Americans are employed in small businesses, it is common sense that if businesses in the Black neighborhoods do not flourish, job opportunities will be greatly reduced.

7   To succeed as a people, Blacks have to invest in and build their community. Other ethnic groups turn their money over multiple times within their communities. If money turns over ten times, it means that for every $100 spent by an individual, nine other individuals or businesses will have access to that same $100. This investment increases the community's economic strength by $1,000 instead of just $100.

8   It works this way. You earn $100 a week and I earn $100 a week. You give me ninety-seven of your dollars. I'm living on $197 and you're living on $3. How can your house be as big as mine? How can your car be as new as mine? How, even, can your IQ be as high as mine? Income affects nearly all aspects of life. A higher paycheck means you can afford to live in a better neighborhood with better schools and more opportunities for intellectual development. Studies have found that the group in America with the highest income is the group with the highest IQ. The group with the second-highest income is the group with the second-highest IQ. The overall IQ of Blacks is low in part because the income retained by Blacks is at the bottom.

Take Back Your Mind

9   Rick Singletary knows this all too well. The problem is not that Blacks don't have money. The problem is what we do with it, or don't do with it. Just as

we waste our votes by not demanding anything in return, we don't spend our money where it pays off.

Over the last twenty-five years, the Black community has had a major thrust in politics and civil rights. We have staged Freedom Marches, but we have never stopped to think about what really buys freedom. It isn't worn-out shoes, and it isn't even civil rights legislation. True freedom springs from economic parity with other Americans.

Money is not everything, but I rate it right up there with oxygen. After almost one hundred years of social engineering, Blacks can sit next to White people in classrooms and restaurants and on airplanes, but can they afford it? *The bottom line is that the only color of freedom is green.* Pride, education, and economic self-sufficiency were the message of Marcus Garvey and Booker T. Washington. But those two great Black men were vilified by the self-serving, self-hating elitists among their own people, and their vital message of self-reliance was blocked. Instead Blacks have spent decades with their arms extended and their hands out, doing the economic death dance to the tune of integration.

Understanding Context

1. What does the failure of Singletary's supermarket represent to Brown? Why does he see it as representing a "national disgrace"?
2. Why do African Americans, in Brown's opinion, "boycott" black businesses?
3. How can blacks achieve economic parity with other Americans in Brown's view?
4. *Critical thinking:* Does Brown's argument reveal the misguided goals of the civil rights movement or does it appear to "blame the victim"? Does an argument for self-reliance necessarily suggest that government action is not needed or that existing programs could be cut?

Evaluating Strategy

1. How effective is the example of Rick Singletary? Does it bring Brown's point to life?
2. Would a hypothetical example be as effective as an actual one?
3. Brown introduces facts and numbers; why are these important?
4. Where does Brown place his thesis? Could it be located elsewhere?
5. *Other modes:* How does Brown use argument in this essay?

Appreciating Language

1. How does Brown describe Singletary? Do Brown's words depict him as a hero or role model?
2. How effective are phrases such as "the color of freedom is green" and "economic death dance"? Do you find them striking or too dramatic?

Writing Suggestions

1. Select a person you consider a role model and describe how his or her actions represent a trend that should be supported or followed by others.
2. *Collaborative writing:* Discuss the actions of Singletary and Brown's analysis with other students. Brainstorm within the group and provide a local example of someone whose efforts failed or succeeded to help his or her community.

COVENANT HOUSE

Covenant House is the nation's largest shelter program for homeless youth. Begun in 1969 by a priest who took in six runaways during a blizzard, the program has grown to serve thousands each year. The agency is supported by almost entirely by donations from individuals.

Covenant House Needs Your Help

As you read this web page soliciting support, notice how examples are used to dramatize the plight of homeless youth and illustrate the program's services.

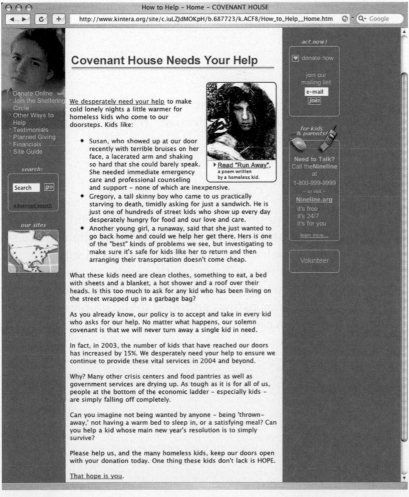

Understanding Context

1. What services does Covenant House provide?
2. Why does Covenant House need financial support?
3. Why do homeless youths face greater challenges today?
4. What is the mission of Covenant House?

Evaluating Strategy

1. What purpose do examples serve? Is it important to provide names of those served? Why or why not?
2. What role do statistics play? Is it important to balance examples with factual detail?
3. How effective is the visual impact of this web page? Do you find it easy to read? Does it communicate at glance? Does the photograph grab attention and demonstrate the severity of the problem of homeless young people?

Appreciating Language

1. Does this level of diction seem appropriate for a mass audience?
2. Do you think using the word "kid" is effective? Why or why not? Might some readers object to this term?

Writing Suggestions

1. Develop the text for a fund raising brochure or web page using examples for support. Determine the best examples that would both dramatize a social problem and demonstrate how the organization works to solve it.
2. *Collaborative writing:* Discuss this web page with a group of students then develop a process essay that explains step by step how you would conduct a national fund raising campaign to draw attention to the problem of homeless youth and encourage donations.

Virgo/zefa/Corbis

1. Describe your immediate reaction to this picture. Do you see it as an example of innocent childhood or a growing social problem?

2. Compare this photograph to the one on page 308. Do you see a connection between them? Would placing these images side by side change people's opinions of two boys playing with toy guns?

3. *Visual analysis:* This picture depicts two white middle-class boys in cowboy hats playing with guns. Would reactions differ if the boys were African American or Latino and wore gang caps? Why or why not?

4. *Collaborative writing:* Discuss this image with a group of students and develop a series of captions that use word choice to create positive and negative connotations.

5. *Other modes*
   - Write a *cause-and-effect* essay that explains the effect that toy guns have on children. Do they lead children to glamorize or trivialize the use of deadly force?
   - *Compare* the effect of children playing cowboy, cops and robbers, or army with other children vs. playing violent video games alone. Is one activity more harmful? Why or why not?
   - Write a *process* paper advising parents how to monitor their children's play activity to identify potential problems, such as a fascination with guns or violence.
   - Write a *persuasive* essay that argues for or against banning the sale of toy guns to children.

Example Checklist

Before submitting your paper, review these points:

✔ Does your example paper have a clearly stated thesis or main point?

✔ Do the examples directly illustrate the thesis? Are there any irrelevant details that may mislead or confuse readers?

✔ If you use a single extended example to persuade, can it be supported with facts, quotations, or statistics?

✔ Are the examples clearly organized? Do they follow a logical pattern?

✔ Should the thesis appear at the opening, middle, or conclusion of the essay?

✔ Read your paper aloud. How does it sound? Do the examples support the thesis? Are there clear transitions between illustrations?

Companion Website

See **http://www.thomsonedu.com/english/sundance** for additional information on writing example essays.

21

DEFINITION
ESTABLISHING MEANING

WHAT IS DEFINITION?

Effective communication requires that writers and readers have a shared language. Words and ideas must be *defined* to eliminate confusion and misinterpretation. Definitions limit or explain the meaning of a word or concept. As a college student you have probably devoted much of your time to mastering new terms and their definitions. Such fields as chemistry, psychology, sociology, economics, law, and anatomy have technical words that must be learned in order to communicate within the discipline.

Clearly stated definitions play a critical role in academic, professional, government, and business writing. To prevent confusion, conflict, and litigation, many union contracts, insurance policies, sales agreements, and leases include definitions so all parties will share a common interpretation of important terms. Government documents, reports, and business proposals frequently include glossaries to familiarize readers with new or abstract terms. Failing to understand a definition can be costly. A tenant who does not understand a landlord's definition of *excessive noise* may face eviction. The car buyer who misinterprets the manufacturer's definition of *normal use* may void his or her warranty.

The word *definition* leads most students to think of a dictionary. But defining involves more than simply looking up the meaning of a word. Definitions are not always precise or universally accepted. Distinctly different definitions exist. To be an effective writer in college and in your future profession, it is important to appreciate the range of definitions:

■ **Standard definitions** are universally accepted and rarely subject to change. Such words as *tibia*, *dolphin*, *uranium*, *felony*, and *turbine* have exact meanings that are understood and shared by scholars, professionals, and the general public. Doctors, nurses, paramedics, biology teachers, and football coaches, for example, all recognize *tibia* as a specific bone in the body. Though different state legislatures might disagree on which specific crime constitutes a *felony*, they all accept its general concept.

- **Regulatory definitions** are officially designated terms that are subject to change. The NFL, IRS, FAA, State of Massachusetts, school boards, labor unions, insurance companies, and the Catholic Church issue definitions to guide policy, control operations, inform the public, and make decisions. The IRS definition of *deductible meal allowance* can change yearly. Congress may pass a bill that changes the Veterans Administration's definition of *service-connected disability*. One health insurance company may pay for a liver transplant while another carrier refuses, defining the procedure as *experimental*. Regulatory definitions may be universally accepted, but they can change or be limited to a specific region, organization, or discipline. The building codes of New York and San Francisco may have varying definitions of what buildings are *structurally sound*. The medical definition of *mental disease* differs greatly from the court-accepted legal definition of *insanity*.

- **Evolving definitions** reflect changes in community attitudes, social values, government policies, and scientific research. In the nineteenth century, striking children was a widely accepted method of discipline called *corporal punishment*. Today, the same behavior would be defined as *child abuse*. The term *date rape* defines incidents that would not have been viewed as criminal assaults in the past. Decades ago medical and psychological texts defined *homosexuality* as a mental disease. In 1973 the American Psychological Association voted to remove homosexuality from its list of psychological disorders. Evolving definitions track social change but rarely shift as abruptly as regulatory definitions.

- **Qualifying definitions** limit meanings of words or concepts that are abstract or subject to interpretation. How does one define *alcoholic*? At what point do doctors label a patient *obese* or *senile*? When does a young person become a *juvenile delinquent*? How does one define *genius*? In some fields organizations provide definitions. The American Medical Association may offer a definition of *alcoholism*. However, physicians and researchers are free to dispute it and apply a different meaning. Some definitions are hotly debated within a discourse community. Researchers, politicians, and social commentators continually argue over whether drug addiction, for example, should be defined as a *disability* that entitles people to receive benefits.

- **Cultural definitions** are shaped by the history, values, and attitudes of a national, ethnic, or religious group. Just as evolving definitions change over time, cultural differences differ from group to group. In some countries it is customary to offer cash or gifts to government officials as a *tribute* in return for their services. In the United States the same action would be considered an illegal *bribe*. People the world over embrace *freedom* but define it differently. For most

Americans *freedom* is defined in personal terms, meaning freedom of movement and expression for individual citizens. In other countries, people may define *freedom* in national terms, as protecting the independence and security of their homeland even if it is maintained by censorship and restricted personal liberties.

■ **Personal definitions** are used by writers to express individual interpretations of words or ideas. A writer can frame an entire essay such as Janice Castro's "Spanglish" (see page 420), in terms of establishing a personal definition. Your concept of a good parent or a desirable career would be a personal definition. Personal definitions are based on the writer's perceptual world and his or her sense of values.

 To read more about definition, along with interactive examples and opportunities to work with interactive texts, click on "The Rhetorical Patterns of Inquiry" from the main menu of *Comp21*.

WRITING ACTIVITY

Determine what type of definition would best suit each of the following topics. In some instances, there may be more than one possible definition.

1. Internal combustion engine

2. Second-degree murder

3. Child abuse

4. Inflation

5. Cyberspace

6. Stalking

7. Existentialism

8. Road rage

9. Pornography

10. Altimeter

The Purpose of Definition

Definitions generally serve to establish meaning, to provide a common or shared understanding. But they can also be persuasive. Writers motivate readers to accept a point of view or particular vision of a problem or issue. Definitions can be used to express an opinion, influence perceptions, or shape the debate over a problem or issue. During criminal trials attorneys employ definition as a way of directing juries' decisions. A prosecutor may define a young defendant's actions as an act of *vandalism*, while the defense attorney may try to influence the jurors by asking them to see his or her client's actions more benignly, defining the incident as a *teenage prank*.

Connotations play a large role in shaping persuasive definitions. To transform public attitudes and change their perceptions, writers frequently urge readers to redefine something—for example, to change their perceptions to see striking a child as *abuse* instead of *spanking* or to accept *graffiti* as *street art*. Because businessowners sensed that *shoplifting* was generally dismissed as a petty offense, many began using the term *retail theft* to emphasize its criminality.

WRITING ACTIVITY

Provide persuasive definitions for the following terms. Your definition can reflect your personal opinions and values.

1. Family values
2. Domestic violence
3. Treason
4. Racism
5. Social justice
6. Capitalism
7. Welfare reform
8. Poverty
9. Gun control
10. Patriotism

Methods of Definition

Writers create definitions using a number of strategies:

1. **Defining through synonyms** is the simplest method of providing meaning for a word or concept. Glossaries and dictionaries customarily define technical terms or foreign words with synonyms. *Costal* refers to *rib*. *Messer* can be translated as *knife*. A *casement* can be explained as a *window*.
   - Because no two words are exact equivalents, be cautious about using a single word in a definition. Be aware of connotations that may distort meanings.

2. **Defining by description** provides details about a subject and gives readers a sense of what it might look, feel, taste, smell, or sound like. Defining *costrel* as "a small flask with a loop or loops that is suspended from a belt" provides readers with a clear picture of the object. Descriptive definitions also can demonstrate how something operates. An *airbag* can be defined as "a rapidly inflated cushion designed to protect automobile passengers in a collision."

   ■ Describing objects in action creates a clear picture. Because some items may have many functions, indicate exceptions or alternative actions to prevent oversimplification.

3. **Defining by example** provides specific illustrations to establish meaning. A *felony* can be defined as "a serious crime such as murder, sexual assault, or burglary." Examples establish meaning through identification. Telling a fourth-grade class that "a verb is a word that expresses action" is not as effective as providing examples children can easily recognize—*run, buy, talk, sell, build, think*.

   ■ Complex or abstract concepts are easier to comprehend if defined by example.

4. **Defining by comparison** uses analogies; this strategy is particularly useful for less familiar terms and concepts. A television reporter covering a space mission might define NASA terminology using comparison. To explain the term *power down*, she remarks that the astronauts are "conserving power by turning off nonessential electrical devices, much like switching off the radio and windshield wipers on a car."

   ■ Because they can oversimplify complex ideas, comparative definitions must be used carefully.

5. **Extended definitions** qualify or limit the meaning of abstract, disputed, or highly complex words or concepts. Such words as *sin, love,* and *racism* cannot be adequately defined through synonyms, brief descriptions, or a few examples. A complete definition might require several paragraphs or pages.

   ■ Extended definitions often use narration.

STRATEGIES for Writing Definition

Critical Thinking and Prewriting

1. **Determine the goal of your definition—to inform or persuade.** Decide whether your purpose is to provide information about a topic, guiding readers to understand a concept or object, or to influence their opinion about a subject or issue.

- If you are responding to a composition assignment, ask your instructor whether a persuasive definition is acceptable.

2. **Write a list of ideas, people, items, concepts, theories, and places.** One way of starting is simply to begin isolating possible topics. At first, list as many ideas as possible. Refer to the list on pages 903–904 for possible ideas.

3. **Review the list and note the best ways of defining selective topics.** Some topics may be challenging to define because they are complex, controversial, or elusive. If you discover a particular subject difficult, explore another idea.

   - Use synonyms for words or concepts that have direct equivalents. Be sure to remind readers of subtle distinctions.
   - Use examples to illustrate your subject.
   - Compare the subject with others that readers may find easier to recognize and comprehend.

Planning

1. **Write a clearly stated one-sentence definition of your subject if possible.** Try to focus your thoughts by stating a working thesis to target your planning.

2. **Define your role.** Your definition can be based on personal observation and opinion or standard principles and methods followed in a specific discipline or profession.

3. **Consider your audience.** What knowledge do your readers have? Your definition should offer recognizable examples in language they will understand. Determine what uses your audience has for the definition. Will readers have to base future decisions based on your definition? Will this definition dictate or guide their actions?

4. **Use a balance of defining methods.** Each method of defining has advantages and disadvantages. It is usually effective to blend descriptions, synonyms, examples, and comparisons.

5. **Determine the best place to locate your thesis—at the beginning, middle, or conclusion.** A controversial issue may alienate or confuse readers. Before stating your thesis, you may wish to present a narrative, a fact, or a statistic.

6. **Organize your essay.** Arrange your material in a logical pattern—spatial, chronological, or emphatic.

   - Address common misconceptions about your topic at the opening.
   - Provide clear transitions between points.
   - Conclude the essay with a memorable statement or shorthand version summarizing the key points of your definition.

Writing the First Draft

1. **Keep extended definitions on target.** Refer to your plan and thesis as you write. Extended examples are designed to illustrate a point. You can easily become enveloped in the narrative and include details that may be interesting but do not advance the purpose of the essay.

    ■ Remember that your goal is to *define* the topic, not tell a story.

2. **Use or refer to existing definitions.** Instead of creating your own definition, you can often adopt or make use of an existing one. If you accept the American Psychological Association's definition of *compulsion*, you can simply restate the definition for readers. When you use existing definitions, acknowledge their sources. If you disagree with an existing official definition, restate it and then demonstrate how your interpretation differs.

3. **Clearly summarize the definition in a sentence or two.** Readers are not likely to recall ideas scattered throughout an essay. If possible, distill your main points into one or two clearly stated sentences that readers can underline for easy reference.

4. **Define abstract or elusive topics by setting boundaries.** John Ciardi suggested that in trying to define an elusive concept like *happiness*, "the best one can do is to try to set some extremes to the idea and then work in toward the middle."

    ■ Openly state what your subject is *not* to set firm boundaries and reduce reader confusion.

    ■ Provide examples in a pro and con fashion, illustrating what does and does not fall within the boundaries of your definition. If you are trying to define *racial profiling*, for instance, you might list those actions that constitute unfair profiling and those that do not.

    ■ Lists of examples or comparisons are effective in providing a personal definition of an abstract concept open to varied interpretations.

Revising

1. **Review your plan; then examine the content of your draft.**

    ■ Does your paper *define* the topic or merely *describe* it? A definition supplies specific limitations to a subject, giving readers an understanding so they can recognize the subject or condition when they encounter it. Your paper must provide more than impressions—it must distinguish what separates this topic from similar ones. A description of a minivan may provide details about its appearance, whereas a definition of a minivan allows readers to distinguish this type of vehicle from vans, station wagons, and pickup trucks.

2. **Review your thesis or summary.**
   - Do you provide a clearly stated definition that readers can remember or highlight for future reference?
3. **Analyze extended definitions for irrelevant or missing details.**
   - Does the narrative simply tell a story or does it *define* the subject by supplying facts, observations, and details needed to inform or persuade readers?
4. **Review informative definitions for clarity.**
   - Are the limits of the definition clearly stated and supported by facts and details?
   - Are readers given measurements, distinguishing features, visual illustrations, or rules to identify the subject when they encounter it on their own?
5. **Review persuasive definitions for critical thinking.**
   - In shaping opinion, do you take your readers' existing knowledge and attitudes into account? Do you address their existing conceptions?
   - Do you show how your definition differs from others?
   - Do you demonstrate why your definition is superior to others?
   - Have you avoided logical fallacies (see page 50)?
6. **Review the introduction and conclusion.**
   - Does the opening introduce the subject and arouse interest? Should the thesis appear in the beginning or follow an initial narrative or fact?
   - Does the conclusion create a strong impression readers will remember?
7. **Review the overall structure of the body.**
   - Is the supporting material clearly organized and joined by transitional statements? Do the separate paragraphs serve to advance the definition?

Editing and Proofreading

1. **Review your choice of words.**
   - Does your paper contain words that require further definition to prevent confusion?
   - Are there any connotations that may alienate or mislead readers?
2. **Read your paper aloud.**
   - Are there awkward, wordy, or repetitive phrases that can be deleted or revised?
3. **Review the thesis statement.**
   - Is your definition clearly stated so readers can grasp a general sense of your thesis without having to read the entire essay?
4. **Use peer editing.**
   - Ask readers whether they can restate your definition in their own words. If they cannot, revise your thesis or add more details and examples.

STUDENT PAPER

This is a working draft of a student paper written in response to the following assignment:

Invent a definition for a social issue or problem you have experienced. You may support your definition through factual research or personal observation. Make sure that your paper clearly defines, and not simply describes, the subject.

Disneyland Dads

Like half the members of my generation, I am the product of what used to be called a "broken home." My parents divorced when I was eight. I lived with my mother and saw my father on alternate weekends and two weeks during the summer.

My father, like many of *his* generation, was a classic Disneyland Dad. The Disneyland Dad is usually found at malls, little league fields, upscale pizza restaurants and ice cream parlors. He is usually accompanied by a child busily eating food forbidden by Mom, trying on clothes, or playing with new toys. The Disneyland Dad dispenses cash like an ATM and provides an endless supply of quarters for arcade games. Whether they are motivated by guilt, frustration, or an inability to parent, Disneyland Dads substitute material items for fatherly advice, guidance, and discipline.

While my mother furnished the hands-on, day to day parenting, my father remained distant. My mother monitored my eating habits, my friends, my grades, even the programs I watched on television. But without daily contact with my mother, my father found it difficult to make decisions about my upbringing. He was afraid of contradicting Mom. So he showered me with gifts and trips. He expanded my wardrobe, gave me my first pieces of real jewelry, introduced me to Broadway shows, and took me to Disneyland—but he did not help me with school, teach me about the job market, give me insight into boys, or allow me to be anything more than a spoiled consumer.

As I grew older, my relationship with my father became strained. Weekends with him were spent shopping, going to movies, playing tennis, and horseback riding—activities I loved, but activities that limited opportunities for anything but casual conversation.

Like most of my friends, I came to view my father as more of an uncle than a parent. He was a beloved family figure, someone who could be counted on for some extra cash, new clothes, or a pizza. And like most of my friends, I was troubled by the gulf that widened between my father and myself. I talked, argued, and made up with my mother as I went through my teens. Both of us changed over the years. But my father remained the same—the generous but distant Disneyland Dad.

The Disneyland Dad is a neglected figure. While books and daytime talk shows focus on the plight of single moms, few people offer advice to the fathers. Men in our society are judged by success and conditioned to dispense tokens of their achievement to their children. We kids of divorce *want* all the things the Disneyland Dad can offer, but we really *need* his attention, his guidance, his experience, his mentoring. Someone has to help Disneyland Dads become fathers.

Questions for Review and Revision

1. What tone does the term *Disneyland Dad* have? Is it suitable for a serious essay? What connotations does it suggest?
2. Does this student really *define* or merely *describe* Disneyland Dads?
3. Does the paper include enough details to outline the qualities of a Disneyland Dad?
4. The student uses italics to highlight certain words. Do you find this an effective technique?
5. *Other modes:* Where does the student use narration and comparison to develop the essay? Does the final paragraph state a persuasive argument?
6. Read the paper aloud. Can you detect awkward or vague passages that would benefit from revision?

Writing Suggestions

1. Invent a term that defines a personality type and illustrate it, using a parent, friend, or coworker as an example.
2. *Collaborative writing:* Discuss this paper with several students and collect ideas for a process paper that offers tips to teenagers on how to communicate with a Disneyland Dad.

SUGGESTED TOPICS FOR WRITING DEFINITION

General Assignments

Write a definition on any of the following topics. Your definition will probably use other modes—narration, description, example, comparison, or persuasion. Choose your terminology carefully and avoid words with misleading connotations. Remember, your main goal is to define, not describe or tell a story. Give your readers ways of recognizing your subject on their own.

- A successful professional in your field, such as a good defense attorney, contractor, nurse, or teacher
- A good relationship
- Pornography (e.g., a definition of the kind of material you might wish to ban from the Internet)
- Addiction
- An educated person
- A healthy lifestyle
- Self-respect
- Racism
- The level of insanity a defendant must exhibit to be held not liable for his or her actions
- Terrorism

 To create your own interactive writing project, use the textual, visual, and video libraries on *Comp21*. For the main menu, choose "Build Your Own Occasion for Writing."

Writing in Context

1. Imagine you have been asked to write a brief brochure about college life to be distributed to disadvantaged high school students. The principal stresses that she fears many of her students lack independent study skills and the discipline needed to succeed in college. Define the characteristics of a good college student, stressing hard work and study habits.
2. You have been asked to participate in a panel on sexual harassment. In preparation, provide two definitions of sexual harassment—one expressing attitudes, feelings, and statements you have encountered from males on campus, the other from females. Try to be objective and state differences fairly.

STRATEGIES for Reading Definition

As you read the definition essays in this chapter, keep these questions in mind:

Context

1. Which type of definition is the author developing—standard, regulatory, evolving, qualifying, cultural, or personal?
2. What is the author's purpose—to inform or persuade?
3. What is the nature of the context, the audience, discipline, or writing situation? Is the writer addressing a general or specific reader?

Strategy

1. What methods of definition does the writer use—synonyms, examples, comparisons, or descriptions?
2. Is the definition limited to a specific incident or context, or can it be applied generally? Is the writer defining a particular person or personality trait that could be shared by millions?
3. Does the writer provide personal examples, or does he or she rely on official sources to establish the definition?

Language

1. What role does word choice and connotation play in establishing the definition?
2. What do the tone and level of language reveal about the writer's purpose and intended audience?

EILEEN SIMPSON

Eileen Simpson is a psychotherapist who struggled for years to overcome dyslexia, a reading disorder that affects more than 20 million Americans. She is the author of several books, including **Poets in Their Youth,** a memoir of her marriage to the poet John Berryman. Other books based on her personal experiences explored problems of children growing up without parents. This section comes from her 1979 book **Reversals: A Personal Account of Victory over Dyslexia.**

Dyslexia

Simpson provides a standard definition of an existing term by examining its Greek and Latin roots and then demonstrates the effects dyslexia has on its victims. Notice that she supplies examples to help readers fully appreciate the implications of a widely misunderstood disorder.

Dyslexia (from the Greek, *dys*, faulty + *lexis*, speech, cognate with the Latin 1 *legere*, to read), developmental or specific dyslexia as it's technically called, the disorder I suffered from, is the inability of otherwise normal children to read. Children whose intelligence is below average, whose vision or hearing is defective, who have not had proper schooling, or who are too emotionally disturbed or brain-damaged to profit from it belong in other diagnostic categories. They, too, may be unable to learn to read, but they cannot properly be called dyslexics.

For more than seventy years the essential nature of the affliction has 2 been hotly disputed by psychologists, neurologists, and educators. It is generally agreed, however, that it is the result of a neurophysiological flaw in the brain's ability to process language. It is probably inherited, although some experts are reluctant to say this because they fear people will equate "inherited" with "untreatable." Treatable it certainly is: not a disease to be cured, but a malfunction that requires retraining.

Reading is the most complex skill a child entering school is asked to de- 3 velop. What makes it complex, in part, is that letters are less constant than objects. A car seen from a distance, close to, from above, or below, or in a mirror still looks like a car even though the optical image changes. The letters of the alphabet are more whimsical. Take the letter *b*. Turned upside

415

down it becomes a *p*. Looked at in a mirror, it becomes a *d*. Capitalized, it becomes something quite different, a *B*. The *M* upside down is a *W*. The *E* flipped over becomes Ǝ. This reversed *E* is familiar to mothers of normal children who have just begun to go to school. The earliest examples of art work they bring home often have I LOVƎ YOU written on them.

4   Dyslexics differ from other children in that they read, spell, and write letters upside down and turned around far more frequently and for a much longer time. In what seems like a capricious manner, they also add letters, syllables, and words, or, just as capriciously, delete them. With palindromic words (was-saw, on-no), it is the order of the letters rather than the orientation they change. The new word makes sense, but not the sense intended. Then there are other words where the changed order—"sorty" for story—does not make sense at all.

5   The inability to recognize that g, *g*, and *G* are the same letter, the inability to maintain the orientation of the letters, to retain the order in which they appear, and to follow a line of text without jumping above or below it—all the results of the flaw—can make of an orderly page of words a dish of alphabet soup.

6   Also essential for reading is the ability to store words in memory and to retrieve them. This very particular kind of memory dyslexics lack. So, too, do they lack the ability to hear what the eye sees, and to see what they hear. If the eye sees "off," the ear must hear "off" and not "of," or "for." If the ear hears "saw," the eye must see that it looks like "saw" on the page and not "was." Lacking these skills, a sentence or paragraph becomes a coded message to which the dyslexic can't find the key.

7   It is only a slight exaggeration to say that those who learned to read without difficulty can best understand the labor reading is for a dyslexic by turning a page of text upside down and trying to decipher it.

8   While the literature is replete with illustrations of the way these children write and spell, there are surprisingly few examples of how they read. One, used for propaganda purposes to alert the public to the vulnerability of dyslexics in a literate society, is a sign warning that behind it are guard dogs trained to kill. The dyslexic reads:

a Wurring
Guard God
Patoly

for

Warning
Guard Dog
Patrol

and, of course, remains ignorant of the danger.

Looking for a more commonplace example, and hoping to recapture the 9 way I must have read in fourth grade, I recently observed dyslexic children at the Educational Therapy Clinic in Princeton, through the courtesy of Elizabeth Travers, the director. The first child I saw, eight-year-old Anna (whose red hair and brown eyes reminded me of myself at that age), had just come to the Clinic and was learning the alphabet. Given the story of "Little Red Riding Hood," which is at the second grade level, she began confidently enough, repeating the title from memory, then came to a dead stop. With much coaxing throughout, she read as follows:

> Grandma you a top. Grandma [looks over at picture of Red Riding Hood]. Red Riding Hood [long pause, presses index finger into the paper. Looks at me for help. I urge: Go ahead] the a [puts head close to the page, nose almost touching] on Grandma

for

> Once upon a time there was a little girl who had a red coat with a red hood. Etc.

"Grandma" was obviously a memory from having heard the story read 10 aloud. Had I needed a reminder of how maddening my silences must have been to Miss Henderson, and how much patience is required to teach these children, Anna, who took almost ten minutes to read these few lines, furnished it. The main difference between Anna and me at that age is that Anna clearly felt no need to invent. She was perplexed, but not anxious, and seemed to have infinite tolerance for her long silences.

Toby, a nine-year-old boy with superior intelligence, had a year of tu- 11 toring behind him and could have managed "Little Red Riding Hood" with ease. His text was taken from the *Reader's Digest's Reading Skill Builder*, Grade IV. He read:

> A kangaroo likes as if he had but truck together warm. His saw neck and head do not . . . [Here Toby sighed with fatigue] seem to feel happy back. They and tried and so every a tiger Moses and shoots from lonesome day and shouts and long shore animals. And each farm play with five friends. . .

He broke off with the complaint, "This is too hard. Do I have to read any 12 more?"

His text was:

> A kangaroo looks as if he had been put together wrong. His small neck and head do not seem to fit with his heavy back legs and thick tail. Soft eyes, a

twinkly little nose and short front legs seem strange on such a large strong animal. And each front paw has five fingers, like a man's hand.

13   An English expert gives the following bizarre example of an adult dyslexic's performance:

> An the bee-what in the tel mother of the biothodoodoo to the majoram or that emidrate eni eni Krastrei, mestriet to Ketra lotombreidi to ra from treido as that.

His text, taken from a college catalogue the examiner happened to have close at hand, was:

> It shall be in the power of the college to examine or not every licentiate, previous to his admission to the fellowship, as they shall think fit.

14   That evening when I read aloud to Auntie for the first time, I probably began as Toby did, my memory of the classroom lesson keeping me close to the text. When memory ran out, and Auntie did not correct my errors, I began to invent. When she still didn't stop me, I may well have begun to improvise in the manner of this patient—anything to keep going and keep up the myth that I was reading—until Auntie brought the "gibberish" to a halt.

Understanding Context

1. What basic definition does Simpson provide? What misinterpretation does she note can occur if a condition is considered "inherited"?
2. How does Simpson summarize controversies in the field of research? What do scientists from different disciplines agree on?
3. What is the implication to dyslexics and their parents that dyslexia is "not a disease to be cured, but a malfunction that requires retraining"?
4. *Critical thinking:* How can this disorder affect a child's development if it is not detected?

Evaluating Strategy

1. Why is it effective to provide an etymology of the word *dyslexia* at the opening? Does this help satisfy reader curiosity about a term many people have heard but do not fully understand?
2. How does Simpson's introduction of personal experience affect the definition? Does this add a human dimension to her definition, or does it detract

from its objectivity? Would the inclusion of personal experience be appropriate in a textbook?

3. Do the examples of dyslexic reading dramatize the effects of this disorder? Would an explanation alone suffice to impress readers with the crippling effects of a reading disorder?

4. *Other modes:* How does Simpson use *description* and *narration* to develop her definition? What role can stories or case studies provide readers seeking to understand a complex subject?

Appreciating Language

1. Simpson is defining a complex disorder. How does her language indicate that she is seeking to address a general audience? Would the vocabulary differ in a definition written for psychology students?

2. Simpson cites an example of a dyslexic reading a warning sign as "propaganda." Does the use of this word weaken her argument that dyslexia is a serious condition? Why or why not?

3. How does Simpson define the term "palindromic"?

Writing Suggestions

1. Write a concisely worded definition of dyslexia in your own words.

2. *Critical writing:* Write an essay expressing your view on how dyslexics should be graded in college. Should students with dyslexia be allowed more time on essay tests, be offered special tutorial services, or be given alternative assignments and examinations? Can students with disabilities be accommodated while maintaining academic standards?

3. *Collaborative writing:* Working with several other students, craft a brief explanation of dyslexia to be incorporated into a brochure for parents of children with learning impairments. Keep your audience in mind, and avoid making negative comments that might upset parents.

JANICE CASTRO,
WITH DAN COOK AND CRISTINA GARCIA

Janice Castro (1949–) is a journalist who became **Time** magazine's first health policy reporter. In 1994 she published **The American Way of Health: How Medicine Is Changing and What It
Means to You.** In addition to writing about medicine, she has published articles on topics ranging from pension plans to home
shopping. The following essay appeared as part of a **Time** cover
story about Hispanics.

Spanglish

*In this essay the writers invent a term to define a blend of English and Spanish spo-
ken by a growing number of Americans. As you read their article, notice how they use
description, example, and comparison to develop their definition.*

1 In Manhattan a first-grader greets her visiting grandparents, happily exclaiming, "Come here, *siéntate!*" Her bemused grandfather, who does not
speak Spanish, nevertheless knows she is asking him to sit down. A Miami
personnel officer understands what a job applicant means when he says,
"Quiero un part time." Nor do drivers miss a beat reading a billboard alongside a Los Angeles street advertising CERVEZA—SIX PACK!

2 This free-form blend of Spanish and English, known as Spanglish, is
common linguistic currency wherever concentrations of Hispanic Americans are found in the U.S. In Los Angeles, where 55% of the city's 3 million
inhabitants speak Spanish, Spanglish is as much a part of daily life as sun-
glasses. Unlike the broken-English efforts of earlier immigrants from Europe,
Asia and other regions, Spanglish has become a widely accepted conversational mode used casually—even playfully—by Spanish-speaking immigrants and native-born Americans alike.

3 Consisting of one part Hispanicized English, one part Americanized
Spanish and more than a little fractured syntax, Spanglish is a bit like a
Robin Williams comedy routine: a crackling line of cross-cultural patter
straight from the melting pot. Often it enters Anglo homes and families
through the children, who pick it up at school or at play with their young
Hispanic contemporaries. In other cases, it comes from watching TV; many
an Anglo child watching *Sesame Street* has learned *uno dos tres* almost as
quickly as one two three.

Spanglish takes a variety of forms, from the Southern California Anglos 4 who bid farewell with the utterly silly "*hasta la* bye-bye" to the Cuban-American drivers in Miami who *parquean* their *carros*. Some Spanglish sentences are mostly Spanish, with a quick detour for an English word or two. A Latino friend may cut short a conversation by glancing at his watch and excusing himself with the explanation that he must "*ir al* supermarket."

Many of the English words transplanted in this way are simply handier 5 than their Spanish counterparts. No matter how distasteful the subject, for example, it is still easier to say "income tax" than *impuesto sobre la renta*. At the same time, many Spanish-speaking immigrants have adopted such terms as VCR, microwave and dishwasher for what they view as largely American phenomena. Still other English words convey a cultural context that is not implicit in the Spanish. A friend who invites you to a *lonche* most likely has in mind the brisk American custom of "doing lunch" rather than the languorous afternoon break traditionally implied by *almuerzo*.

Mainstream Americans exposed to similar hybrids of German, Chinese 6 or Hindi might be mystified. But even Anglos who speak little or no Spanish are somewhat familiar with Spanglish. Living among them, for one thing, are 19 million Hispanics. In addition, more American high school and university students sign up for Spanish than for any other foreign language.

Only in the past ten years, though, has Spanglish begun to turn into a 7 national slang. Its popularity has grown with the explosive increases in U.S. immigration from Latin American countries. English has increasingly collided with Spanish in retail stores, offices and classrooms, in pop music and on street corners. Anglos whose ancestors picked up such Spanish words as *rancho*, *bronco*, *tornado* and *incommunicado*, for instance, now freely use such Spanish words as *gracias*, *bueno*, *amigo* and *por favor*.

Among Latinos, Spanglish conversations often flow more easily from 8 Spanish into several sentences of English and back.

Spanglish is a sort of code for Latinos: the speakers know Spanish, but 9 their hybrid language reflects the American culture in which they live. Many lean to shorter, clipped phrases in place of the longer, more graceful expressions their parents used. Says Leonel de la Cuesta, an assistant professor of modern languages at Florida International University in Miami: "In the U.S., time is money, and that is showing up in Spanglish as an economy of language." Conversational examples: *taipiar* (type) and *winshi-wiper* (windshield wiper) replace *escribir a máquina* and *limpiaparabrisas*.

Major advertisers, eager to tap the estimated $134 billion in spending 10 power wielded by Spanish-speaking Americans, have ventured into Spanglish to promote their products. In some cases, attempts to sprinkle Spanish through commercials have produced embarrassing gaffes. A Braniff airlines ad that sought to tell Spanish-speaking audiences they could settle back *en* (in) luxuriant *cuero* (leather) seats, for example, inadvertently said they could fly without clothes (*encuero*). A fractured translation of the Miller Lite slogan told readers the beer was "Filling, and less delicious." Similar blunders are often made by Anglos trying to impress Spanish-speaking pals. But if Latinos are amused by mangled Spanglish, they also recognize these goofs as a sort of friendly acceptance. As they might put it, *no problema*.

Understanding Context

1. What is Spanglish? Can you define it in a single sentence?
2. How does the concept of Spanglish differ from "broken English"?
3. Who uses Spanglish? What does it indicate about the growing Hispanic influence in the United States?
4. *Critical thinking:* Many Americans advocate "English Only" and oppose bilingual education. What does the emergence of Spanglish reveal about the status of English in America? Is there any danger that immigrants will fail to master English?

Evaluating Strategy

1. How do the authors use examples to create their definition?
2. How do the authors organize details to build a coherent essay?
3. How effective are the opening and closing paragraphs?

Appreciating Language

1. What do the tone and style of the essay suggest about the authors' attitude toward their subject?
2. *Critical thinking:* The writers call Spanglish "slang." What is slang to you? Would you consider it an appropriate label for Spanglish?

Writing Suggestions

1. Invent a word to represent something you have observed and support it with details. You might define "blind datism," "recycling phobia," or "cable TV withdrawal."
2. *Collaborative writing:* Ask three or four students to identify a special kind of language they have encountered. Discuss samples and list examples; then write a short definition of "campus-ese," "first-date euphemisms," "parent-ese," or "online slang."

JOHN CIARDI

John Ciardi (1916–1986) was a poet, literary critic, and translator. After teaching at Harvard, Rutgers, and the University of Kansas, he left academics to pursue a full-time literary career. As poetry editor for the *Saturday Review* for two decades, he attempted to make poetry accessible to a wide audience. Ciardi's most ambitious work was a translation of Dante Alighieri's work, which took him sixteen years. As a poet, critic, and professor, Ciardi was a student of language. For many years he was a guest commentator on National Public Radio, where he offered listeners interesting and amusing anecdotes about the origins and histories of everyday words.

What Is Happiness?

In this essay, which first appeared in Saturday Review, *Ciardi tries to define the elusive concept of happiness. In developing his definition, Ciardi analyzes the role of advertising and the nature of materialism in American life.*

The right to pursue happiness is issued to Americans with their birth 1 certificates, but no one seems quite sure which way it ran. It may be we are issued a hunting license but offered no game. Jonathan Swift seemed to think so when he attacked the idea of happiness as "the possession of being well-deceived," the felicity of being "a fool among knaves." For Swift saw society as Vanity Fair, the land of false goals.

It is, of course, un-American to think in terms of fools and knaves. We 2 do, however, seem to be dedicated to the idea of buying our way to happiness. We shall all have made it to Heaven when we possess enough.

And at the same time the forces of American commercialism are hugely 3 dedicated to making us deliberately unhappy. Advertising is one of our major industries, and advertising exists not to satisfy desires but to create them—and to create them faster than any man's budget can satisfy them. For that matter, our whole economy is based on a dedicated insatiability. We are taught that to possess is to be happy, and then we are made to want. We are even told it is our duty to want. It was only a few years ago, to cite a single example, that car dealers across the country were flying banners that read

"You Auto Buy Now." They were calling upon Americans, as an act approaching patriotism, to buy at once, with money they did not have, automobiles they did not really need, and which they would be required to grow tired of by the time the next year's models were released.

4   Or look at any of the women's magazines. There, as Bernard DeVoto once pointed out, advertising begins as poetry in the front pages and ends as pharmacopoeia and therapy in the back pages. The poetry of the front matter is the dream of perfect beauty. This is the baby skin that must be hers. These, the flawless teeth. This, the perfumed breath she must exhale. This, the sixteen-year-old figure she must display at forty, at fifty, at sixty, and forever.

5   Once past the vaguely uplifting fiction and feature articles, the reader finds the other face of the dream in the back matter. This is the harness into which Mother must strap herself in order to display that perfect figure. These, the chin straps she must sleep in. This is the salve that restores all, this is her laxative, these are the tablets that melt away fat, these are the hormones of perpetual youth, these are the stockings that hide varicose veins.

6   Obviously no half-sane person can be completely persuaded either by such poetry or by such pharmacopoeia and orthopedics. Yet someone is obviously trying to buy the dream as offered and spending billions every year in the attempt. Clearly the happiness-market is not running out of customers, but what is it trying to buy?

7   The idea "happiness," to be sure, will not sit still for easy definition: The best one can do is to try to set some extremes to the idea and then work in toward the middle. To think of happiness as acquisitive and competitive will do to set the materialistic extreme. To think of it as the idea one senses in, say, a holy man of India will do to set the spiritual extreme. That holy man's idea of happiness is in needing nothing from outside himself. In wanting nothing, he lacks nothing. He sits immobile, rapt in contemplation, free even of his own body. Or nearly free of it. If devout admirers bring him food he eats it; if not, he starves indifferently. Why be concerned? What is physical is an illusion to him. Contemplation is his joy and he achieves it through a fantastically demanding discipline, the accomplishment of which is itself a joy within him.

8   Is he a happy man? Perhaps his happiness is only another sort of illusion. But who can take it from him? And who will dare say it is more illusory than happiness on the installment plan?

9   But, perhaps because I am Western, I doubt such catatonic happiness, as I doubt the dreams of the happiness-market. What is certain is that his way of happiness would be torture to almost any Western man. Yet these extremes will still serve to frame the area within which all of us must find some

sort of balance. Thoreau—a creature of both Eastern and Western thought—had his own firm sense of that balance. His aim was to save on the low levels in order to spend on the high.

Possession for its own sake or in competition with the rest of the neigh- 10 borhood would have been Thoreau's idea of the low levels. The active discipline of heightening one's perception of what is enduring in nature would have been his idea of the high. What he saved from the low was time and effort he could spend on the high. Thoreau certainly disapproved of starvation, but he would put into feeding himself only as much effort as would keep him functioning for more important efforts.

Effort is the gist of it. There is no happiness except as we take on life- 11 engaging difficulties. Short of the impossible, as Yeats put it, the satisfactions we get from a lifetime depend on how high we choose our difficulties. Robert Frost was thinking in something like the same terms when he spoke of "The pleasure of taking pains." The mortal flaw in the advertised version of happiness is in the fact that it purports to be effortless.

We demand difficulty even in our games. We demand it because with- 12 out difficulty there can be no game. A game is a way of making something hard for the fun of it. The rules of the game are an arbitrary imposition of difficulty. When the spoilsport ruins the fun, he always does so by refusing to play by the rules. It is easier to win at chess if you are free, at your pleasure, to change the wholly arbitrary rules, but the fun is in winning within the rules. No difficulty, no fun.

The buyers and sellers at the happiness-market seem too often to have 13 lost their sense of the pleasure of difficulty. Heaven knows what they are playing, but it seems a dull game. And the Indian holy man seems dull to us, I suppose, because he seems to be refusing to play anything at all. The Western weakness may be in the illusion that happiness can be bought. Perhaps the Eastern weakness is in the idea that there is such a thing as perfect (and therefore static) happiness.

Happiness is never more than partial. There are no pure states of man- 14 kind. Whatever else happiness may be, it is neither in having nor in being, but in becoming. What the Founding Fathers declared for us as an inherent right, we should do well to remember, was not happiness but the *pursuit* of happiness. What they might have underlined, could they have foreseen the happiness-market, is the cardinal fact that happiness is in the pursuit itself, in the meaningful pursuit of what is life-engaging and life-revealing, which is to say, in the idea of *becoming*. A nation is not measured by what it possesses or wants to possess, but by what it wants to become.

By all means let the happiness-market sell us minor satisfactions 15 and even minor follies so long as we keep them in scale and buy them out of spiritual change. I am no customer for either puritanism or asceticism. But drop any real spiritual capital at those bazaars, and what you come home to will be your own poorhouse.

Understanding Context

1. How does the view "whoever dies with the most toys wins" fit with Ciardi's thoughts on materialism?
2. What seems to be Ciardi's purpose in this essay? How much of this definition is *persuasive*? What does the author mean by the comment that "a nation is not measured by what it possesses or wants to possess, but by what it wants to become"?
3. How does Ciardi *compare* the Eastern mystic's concept of happiness with that of most Americans? Can happiness be achieved by being free of possessions or by owning them all?
4. How does advertising exploit the public hunger for happiness? Does advertising suggest, in Ciardi's view, that happiness can be purchased instead of earned?
5. *Critical thinking:* Although he criticizes what he calls "the happiness-market," Ciardi does not condemn it. However, he advises readers to be cautious consumers. What does he warn readers against? What does he mean by his comment about dropping "any real spiritual capital"?

Evaluating Strategy

1. Ciardi admits that happiness is not easy to define, noting "the best one can do is to try to set some extremes to the idea and then work in toward the middle." Is this an effective method of defining abstract or elusive concepts?
2. Throughout the essay, Ciardi quotes Swift, Bernard DeVoto, and Frost. Is this an effective way of working toward the definition of a difficult subject? Does this add credibility to Ciardi's view?
3. *Blending the modes:* How does Ciardi use *comparison* and *analysis* to develop his definition?

Appreciating Language

1. Ciardi uses simple but abstract words—*happiness, possessions, dream, illusion.* How does he define these terms and give them personal meaning?
2. How does Ciardi paraphrase the language of advertising to reveal its appeals to consumers?

Writing Suggestions

1. Use Ciardi's technique of setting extremes and then working toward the middle to define an elusive or complex subject such as love, friendship, success, wealth or beauty in a short essay.
2. *Critical writing:* Write an essay based on Ciardi's observation that the founding fathers did not promise a right to happiness but a right to the *pursuit* of happiness. Do Americans today seem to believe they have a *right* to happiness? Discuss whether Americans feel cheated if they are not happy and whether this partly explains the epidemic of drug abuse and violence.
3. *Collaborative writing:* Discuss Ciardi's essay with a group of students, and then write a few paragraphs reflecting the group's viewpoint on happiness. You may wish to address a single observation made by Ciardi, such as the partial nature of happiness or the idea that it must derive from a challenge met.

Marie Winn was born in Czechoslovakia (now the Czech Republic) and grew up in New York. After completing her education at Radcliffe College, Winn began a career in publishing, writing and editing a number of children's books. While working with children's literature, she explored the effects television has on childhood development. She has written extensively on children and television, publishing articles in the *New York Times* and *Village Voice.* In 1977 she published an influential study, *The Plug-In Drug: Television, Children and Family,* which was revised in 1985. Her other books include *Children without Childhood* (1983), *Unplugging the Plug-In Drug* (1987), *The Secret Life of Central Park* (1997), and *Red-Tails in Love: A Wildlife Drama in Central Park* (1998). In 2002 Winn published a 25th anniversary edition of *The Plug-In Drug,* subtitled *Television, Computers, and Family Life.*

TV Addiction

In building her case that television has negative effects, Winn first defines the term "addiction," then argues that television, like drugs and alcohol, damages those who allow it to consume their lives.

Cookies or Heroin?

1   The word "addiction" is often used loosely and wryly in conversation. People will refer to themselves as "mystery-book addicts" or "cookie addicts." E. B. White wrote of his annual surge of interest in gardening: "We are hooked and are making an attempt to kick the habit." Yet nobody really believes that reading mysteries or ordering seeds by catalogue is serious enough to be compared with addictions to heroin or alcohol. In these cases the word "addiction" is used jokingly to denote a tendency to overindulge in some pleasurable activity.

2   People often refer to being "hooked on TV." Does this, too, fall into the lighthearted category of cookie eating and other pleasures that people pursue with unusual intensity? Or is there a kind of television viewing that falls into the more serious category of destructive addiction?

Not unlike drugs or alcohol, the television experience allows the partic- 3
ipant to blot out the real world and enter into a pleasurable and passive mental state. To be sure, other experiences, notably reading, also provide a temporary respite from reality. But it's much easier to stop reading and return to
reality than to stop watching television. The entry into another world offered
by reading includes an easily accessible return ticket. The entry via television does not. In this way television viewing, for those vulnerable to addiction, is more like drinking or taking drugs—once you start it's hard to stop.

Just as alcoholics are only vaguely aware of their addiction, feeling that 4
they control their drinking more than they really do ("I can cut it out any
time I want—I just like to have three or four drinks before dinner"), many
people overestimate their control over television watching. Even as they put
off other activities to spend hour after hour watching television, they feel
they could easily resume living in a different, less passive style. But somehow or other while the television set is present in their homes, it just stays
on. With television's easy gratifications available, those other activities seem
to take too much effort.

A heavy viewer (a college English instructor) observes: 5

> I find television almost irresistible. When the set is on, I cannot ignore it. I
> can't turn it off. I feel sapped, will-less, enervated. As I reach out to turn off
> the set, the strength goes out of my arms. So I sit there for hours and hours.

Self-confessed television addicts often feel they "ought" to do other 6
things—but the fact that they don't read and don't plant their garden or sew
or crochet or play games or have conversations means that those activities are
no longer as desirable as television viewing. In a way, the lives of heavy
viewers are as unbalanced by their television "habit" as drug addicts' or alcoholics' lives. They are living in a holding pattern, as it were, passing up the
activities that lead to growth or development or a sense of accomplishment.
This is one reason people talk about their television viewing so ruefully, so
apologetically. They are aware that it is an unproductive experience, that by
any human measure almost any other endeavor is more worthwhile.

It is the adverse effect of television viewing on the lives of so many 7
people that makes it feel like a serious addiction. The television habit distorts the sense of time. It renders other experiences vague and curiously un-
real while taking on a greater reality for itself. It weakens relationships by
reducing and sometimes eliminating normal opportunities for talking, for
communicating.

And yet television does not satisfy, else why would the viewer continue 8
to watch hour after hour, day after day? "The measure of health," wrote the

psychiatrist Lawrence Kubie, "is flexibility . . . and especially the freedom to cease when sated." But heavy television viewers can never be sated with their television experiences. These do not provide the true nourishment that satiation requires, and thus they find that they cannot stop watching.

9   A former heavy watcher, a filmmaker, describes a debilitating television habit:

> I remember when we first got the set I'd watch for hours and hours, whenever I could, and I remember that feeling of tiredness and anxiety that always followed those orgies, a sense of time terribly wasted. It was like eating cotton candy; television promised so much richness, I couldn't wait for it, and then it just evaporated into air. I remember feeling terribly drained after watching for a long time.

10   Similarly a nursery-school teacher remembers her own childhood television experience:

> I remember bingeing on television when I was a child and having that vapid feeling after watching hours of TV. I'd look forward to watching whenever I could, but it just didn't give back a real feeling of pleasure. It was like no orgasm, no catharsis, very frustrating. Television just wasn't giving me the promised satisfaction, and yet I kept on watching. It filled some sort of need, or had to do with an inability to get something started.

11   The testimonies of ex-television addicts often have the evangelistic overtones of stories heard at Alcoholics Anonymous meetings.

12   A handbag repair-shop owner says:

> I'd get on the subway home from work with the newspaper and immediately turn to the TV page to plan out my evening's watching. I'd come home and then we'd watch TV for the rest of the evening. We'd eat our dinner in the living room while watching, and we'd only talk every once in a while, during the ads, if at all. I'd watch anything, good, bad, or indifferent.
>
> All the while we were watching I'd feel terribly angry at myself for wasting all that time watching junk. I could never go to sleep until at least the eleven o'clock news, and then sometimes I'd still stay up for the late-night talk show. I had a feeling that I *had* to watch the news programs, even though most of the time nothing much was happening and I could easily find out what by reading the paper the next morning. Usually my wife would fall asleep on the couch while I was watching. I'd get angry at her for doing that. Actually, I was angry at myself.
>
> I had a collection of three years of back issues of different magazines, but I never got around to reading them. I never got around to sorting or labeling my collection of slides I had made when traveling. I only had time for television. We'd take the telephone off the hook while watching so we wouldn't be interrupted! We like classical music, but we never listened to any, never!

Then one day the set broke. I said to my wife, "Let's not fix it. Let's just see what happens." Well, that was the smartest thing we ever did. We haven't had a TV in the house since then.

Now I look back and I can hardly believe we could have lived like that. I feel that my mind was completely mummified for all those years. I was glued to that machine and couldn't get loose, somehow. It really frightens me to think of it. Yes, I'm frightened of TV now. I don't think I could control it if we had a set in the house again. I think it would take over no matter what I did.

Heavy television viewers often make comparisons between their view- 13 ing habits and substance addictions. Several decades ago, a lawyer reported:

I watch TV the way an alcoholic drinks. If I come home and sit in front of the TV, I'll watch any program at all, even if there's nothing on that especially appeals to me. Then the next thing I know it's eleven o'clock and I'm watching the Johnny Carson show, and I'll realize I've spent the whole evening watching TV. What's more, I can't stand Johnny Carson! But I'll still sit there watching him. I'm addicted to TV, when it's there, and I'm not happy about the addiction. I'll sit there getting madder and madder at myself for watching, but still I'll sit there. I can't turn it off.

Nor is the television addict always blind to the dysfunctional aspects of 14 his addiction. A homemaker says:

Sometimes a friend will come over while I'm watching TV. I'll say, "Wait a second. Just let me finish watching this," and then I'll feel bad about that, letting the machine take precedence over people. And I'll do that for the stupidest programs, just because I *have* to watch, somehow.

In spite of the potentially destructive nature of television addiction, it is 15 rarely taken seriously in American society. Critics mockingly refer to television as a "cultural barbiturate" and joke about "mainlining the tube." A spectacle called *Media Burn* perfectly illustrates the feeling of good fun that often surrounds the issue of television addiction. The event, which took place in San Francisco when television was still a young medium, involved the piling up of forty-four old television sets in the parking lot of the Cow Palace, soaking them with kerosene, and applying a torch. According to the programs distributed before the event, everybody was supposed to experience "a cathartic explosion" and "be free at last from the addiction to television."

The issue of television addiction takes on a more serious air when the 16 addicts are our own children. A mother reports:

My ten-year-old is as hooked on TV as an alcoholic is hooked on drink. He tries to strike desperate bargains: "If you let me watch just ten more minutes, I won't watch at all tomorrow," he says. It's pathetic. It scares me.

17   A number of years ago a mother described her six-year-old son's need to watch:

> We were in Israel last summer where the TV stations sign off for the night at about ten. Well, my son would turn on the set and watch the Arabic stations that were still on, even though he couldn't understand a word, just because he had to watch *something*.

18   Other signs of serious addiction come out in parents' descriptions of their children's viewing behavior:

> We used to have very bad reception before we got on Cable TV. I'd come into the room and see my eight-year-old watching this terrible, blurry picture and I'd say, "Heavens, how can you see? Let me try to fix it," and he'd get frantic and scream, "Don't touch it!" It really worried me, that he wanted to watch so badly that he was even willing to watch a completely blurred image.

19   Another mother tells of her eight-year-old son's behavior when deprived of television:

> There was a time when both TV sets were out for about two weeks, and Jerry reached a point where I felt that if he didn't watch something, he was really going to start climbing the walls. He was fidgety and nervous. He'd crawl all over the furniture. He just didn't know what to do with himself, and it seemed to get worse every day. I said to my husband, "He's having withdrawal symptoms," and I really think that's what it was. Finally I asked one of my friends if he could go and watch the Saturday cartoons at their house.

20   In the early 1980s Robin Smith, a graduate student at the University of Massachusetts in Amherst, conducted a research study on television addiction as part of a doctoral dissertation. Setting out to discover whether television viewing can truly be classified as an addiction according to a particular, narrow definition she had constructed from the work of various social scientists, Smith sent out a questionnaire to 984 adults in Springfield, Massachusetts, in which they were asked to rate their own behavior in regard to television viewing. Using a number of statistical tests to analyze the responses, the author concluded that the results failed to confirm that television addiction exists. "Television addiction does not appear to be a robust phenomenon," Smith wrote in that poetic yet obscure way academics sometimes have of expressing things.

21   Striving to understand why television is so widely considered an addiction, in the conclusion of her research paper Smith noted:

> . . . the popularity of television as "plug-in drug" is enduring. One possible source of this image lies in the nature of viewing experience. The only study to date that examines the nature of the viewing experience in adults found

that television watching, of all life activities measured in the course of one week, was the least challenging, involved the least amount of skill, and was most relaxing.

If television viewing is so bereft of value by most measures of well- 22 being, and yet takes up the greatest part of people's leisure hours, it becomes moot whether it is defined as an addiction or simply a powerful habit. As psychologists Robert Kubey and Mihaly Csikszentmihalyi concluded in their book about the television experience: "A long-held habit becomes so ingrained that it borders on addiction. A person may no longer be watching television because of simple want, but because he or she virtually has to. Other alternatives may seem to become progressively more remote. What might have been a choice years earlier is now a necessity."

Robert Kubey explains further: "While television can provide relaxation 23 and entertainment . . . it still rarely delivers any lasting fulfillment. Only through active engagement with the worlds we inhabit and the people in them can we attain for ourselves the rewards and meaning that lead to psychological well-being."

Understanding Context

1. How does Winn define "addiction"? How does addiction, in her view, differ from overindulgence in something pleasurable?
2. Describe the negative effects Winn sees in habitual television viewing.
3. How does the simple ease and accessibility of watching television versus going out to a movie contribute to making television so addictive?
4. One viewer Winn quotes states, "I had the feeling that I *had* to watch the news programs, that I *had* to know what was happening." Today are more people likely to feel almost obligated to watch television to be informed, to be a good citizen? Can the news be as dangerously addicting as entertainment shows?
5. *Critical thinking:* Do you think that many of Winn's observations about television addiction describe people who feel compelled to spend hours on the Internet? Can cyberspace be just as addictive and just as harmful?

Evaluating Strategy

1. Why is it important for Winn to first define "addiction" before moving to her argument about television?
2. How effective is her use of interviews or case studies of television viewers? Is it important to hear from the "addicts" in their own words?

3. *Other modes:* How much of this definition essay can be considered a *persuasive argument*? What role do *description* and *narration* play in developing the definition?

Appreciating Language

1. Winn quotes one viewer who reports that television leaves him "sapped, will-less, enervated." How important are words like these to argue that television is addictive?
2. Winn repeatedly uses the word "sated." Look this up in a dictionary. Why is it a key word in defining an addiction?
3. *Critical thinking:* Would some people object to applying the word "addiction" to an activity that is not life-threatening? Drugs and alcohol, after all, lead to disease and early death. Does using the term in other contexts weaken its impact?

Writing Suggestions

1. Write a short analysis of your own childhood experiences with television. How many hours did you watch a day? What were your favorite programs? Did television add or detract from your development? Did you forgo studying, playing with other children, reading, or spending time with your family to watch television?
2. *Collaborative writing:* Working with a group of other students, write a paper instructing parents step-by-step how to monitor their children's viewing habits. How can parents prevent their children from becoming television addicts?

···e-reading···

Infotrac College Edition

www.infotrac-college.com

OVERCOMING TV ADDICTION

> The term "TV addiction" is imprecise and laden with value judgments, but it captures the essence of a very real phenomenon. . . . Television can teach and amuse; it can reach aesthetic heights; it can provide much needed distraction and escape. The difficulty arises when people strongly sense that they ought not to watch as much as they do and yet find themselves strangely unable to reduce their viewing.
>
> *Robert Kubey and Mihaly Csikszentmihalyi*

Television has dominated American life for more than half a century, shaping its politics, public opinion, perceptions, and popular culture. Americans turn to television in moments of crisis and triumph, so that people will remember not so much actual events as where they were when they watched them on television. Although television pioneers hoped to create a new medium of information, education, and culture that would enrich public life, television soon became known for soap operas, sitcoms, Westerns, and quiz shows. Speaking before a group of broadcasters in 1961, the FCC chairman Newton Minow told network executives, "I invite you to sit down in front of your television set when your station goes on the air. . . . I can assure you that you will observe a vast wasteland." Forty years later, many critics see a vaster, more violent, more tasteless 500-channel wasteland that is having increasingly negative effects, especially on its habitual users.

Such researchers as Marie Winn, Robert Kubey, and Mihaly Csikszentmihalyi note that television viewing shares many of the addictive properties of drugs and alcohol: using the substance more than intended, making numerous but failed attempts to reduce consumption, giving up other activities, and suffering withdrawal symptoms when stopping.

In recent years, surveys have shown that many teenagers spend more time online than watching television. Although it is argued that the Internet is an interactive medium, Kubey and Csikszentmihalyi point out that it has the same addictive properties as television, so that "for growing numbers of people, the life they lead online may often seem

more important, more immediate and more intense than the life they lead face-to-face."

Before reading these articles, consider these questions:

How did television influence your childhood? How much television did you watch? What were your favorite shows? Did television enlarge your world or preclude you from reading, playing sports, and building relationships?

How much television do you watch now? Do you believe you watch too much television? Do you regret spending time viewing TV shows when you should be studying or working? Does television take up too much time in your life? Do you wish you spent those hours doing something more valuable?

Does television viewing reduce attention span? Does the fast pace of television programs make it hard for people, especially children, to develop the concentration needed to master academic skills?

Do parents have enough control to monitor their children's use of television? When nearly every child has a television set in his or her room, how can parents supervise not only the amount of time children spend watching TV but what they are viewing?

Does television prevent families from communicating? How many evenings do families spend watching television together rather than talking or interacting with each other?

E-Readings Online

Search for each article by author or title after entering InfoTrac College Edition through your 1Pass account login.

Video Age International. *Television Anonymous (Glued to the Tube: The Threat of Television Addiction to Today's Family).*
Cheryl Pawlowski argues that "TV has the potential to destroy the very existence of childhood as a separate and distinct period in human development."

John Taylor Gatto. *Swap Virtual Lives for Real Ones.*
A leading educator became aware of the impact that television had on his students, noting, "I could tell which kids were heavy TV watchers. They showed signs of being radically incomplete as human beings, as if their growth had been artificially retarded."

Dimitri Christakis. *Television Watching and Shortened Attention Spans.*
A pediatrician asserts that early television viewing is responsible for shortened attention spans, noting that "a child who watched two hours of television a day before age three would be 20% more likely to have attention problems at age seven compared to a child who watched none."

Franklin T. Thompson and William P. Austin. *Television Viewing and Academic Achievement Revisited.*
Two education researchers suggest that "TV time be turned into thinking time." Selecting what children watch and discussing it with them can limit television's negative effects.

Kirsetin Karamarkovich Morello. *Think Outside the Box: How to Turn Off the TV and Take Back Your Family Life.*
Today's children spend 1,500 hours a year watching television and 33 hours in meaningful conversation with their parents. Morello offers parents strategies to replace passive viewing with family activities.

Ann Vorisek White. *Breaking Out of the Box. Turn Off TV. Turn On Life.*
Noting that young children who watch television are "transfixed, passive, and nonverbal" as they passively absorb images, White argues it is important to reduce viewing and engage children in conversation that "allows time for reflection, questions, and encouragement."

Critical Reading and Thinking

1. How do authors define "addiction"? Do you feel it is an accurate term or one used simply to arouse attention? Would "obsession" or "compulsion" be more accurate terms?
2. How does television limit children's intellectual and academic development?
3. If television has negative effects on children, how much is caused by the content of programming and how much is caused by the fast pace of the medium itself?
4. Because parents tend to be concerned about drugs, alcohol, and violent behavior, do they see passive viewing as a genuine threat to their children's welfare?
5. Are you convinced by the evidence writers present to support their views of television?
6. Are recommendations to replace television with other activities realistic?

Writing Suggestions

1. Create a TV log, listing your viewing habits or those of your children for a week. How many hours do you watch each day? Did watching television limit time that could have spent studying, working, exercising, playing sports, or meeting friends? Write a brief list of points describing how you would like to change your viewing habits or those of your family.
2. Write a television autobiography. What television programs or events influenced your childhood? How did favorite programs or characters shape your view of the world? Was television beneficial or detrimental to your development? Did it introduce you to other ideas, cultures, and communities? Did it prevent you from forming relationships with others, enjoying activities, or pursuing other interests? Do you look back on your TV viewing with nostalgia or regret?
3. *Collaborative writing:* Working with a group of students, define addiction; then determine whether television watching can be truly considered addictive. Define what addiction is and what addiction is not. Is there a difference between being addicted to television and simply being too lazy to spend time doing anything else?
4. *Other modes*
   - Write a *cause-and-effect* essay about TV addiction. Explore causes—what draws people, especially children, to spend so

much time watching television? Is TV an escape from school pressures, peers, loneliness, family problems? Examine the effects of excessive TV viewing—what impact does it have on children? Does it shorten their attention span, give them distorted views of the world, weaken their ability to concentrate or interact with others? Is there a link between television watching and obesity?

- Write a *classification* paper ranking TV viewers from the most to least selective. Establish clear categories and explain each type with examples.
- Develop a *comparison* paper contrasting what you consider the best and worst television shows for children to view.
- Write a *process* paper that provides practical step-by-step guidelines for parents to reduce excessive TV viewing in children.

Research Paper

You can develop a research paper about television addiction by conducting further research to explore a range of issues:

- How do various disciplines and experts define "addiction."
- What are physiological effects of television on the brain and childhood development?
- Is there a link between excessive television viewing and poor health habits?
- Does excessive television viewing retard children's development or cause attention problems in school?
- Does excessive time online pose the same or different risks? Is the Internet just as addictive, or does its interactive nature engage children in decision making and critical thinking more than passive TV viewing?

For Further Reading

To locate additional sources on television addiction, enter these search terms as InfoTrac subjects:

Television and Children
Subdivisions: analysis
                             health aspects
                             personal narratives
                             psychological aspects
                             research

Television and Family
Subdivisions: analysis
                             health aspects
                             social aspects

Television Viewers
Subdivisions: analysis
                             behavior
                             beliefs, opinions, attitudes
                             health aspects

Additional Sources

Using a search engine, such as Yahoo!, Google, or Alta Vista, enter one or more of the following terms to locate additional sources:

addiction	television and child development
addiction definition	television and attention span
television and children	television and imagination
television addiction	television viewing habits
television and obesity	cyber addiction

See Evaluating Internet Source Checklist on page 752. See Chapter 30 for using and documenting sources.

Don Rosenberg is a psychologist and therapist in Milwaukee. He wrote the following definition of depression for a brochure to be distributed in a mental health clinic.

What Is Depression?

As you read this definition, notice that it is directed to people who may suffer from depression. How does it differ from a definition of depression you might find in a psychology textbook?

Depression is an internal state—a feeling of sadness, loss, "the blues," deep 1 disappointment. *When it is more severe, you may have feelings of irritability, touchiness, guilt, self-reproach, loss of self-esteem, worthlessness, hopelessness, helplessness, and even thoughts of death and suicide.* It may include such other feelings as tearfulness, being sensitive and easily hurt, loss of interests, loss of sexual drive, loss of control in life, feeling drained and depleted, anger at yourself, and loss of the ability to feel pleasure.

It may be accompanied by *physical symptoms* similar to the sense of profound loss, including:

- *loss of appetite*, often with weight loss, but sometimes we find increased eating
- *insomnia or early morning waking*, often 2–4 times per night, nearly every day, but sometimes we see a need to sleep excessively
- moving and speaking slows down, but sometimes we see *agitation*
- *fatigue or loss of energy* nearly every day
- *loss of concentration*, foggy and indecisive
- sometimes includes anxious and headachy feelings and also *frequent crying*

Besides the physical sensations and emotions of depression, depressed 3 people may *withdraw, may brood or ruminate about problems*, have trouble remembering things, wonder if they would be better off dead, and become very concerned about bodily symptoms and pains. They may be grouchy, sulking, restless, and unwilling to interact with family and friends.

Understanding Context

1. What role does definition play in the treatment of any disorder? Do people need to find a name or label for what troubles them? Is that the first step to coping with or resolving a problem?
2. Can you define *depression* in your own words?
3. What are the physical symptoms of depression?

Evaluating Strategy

1. How effective are the techniques used for emphasis—underlining, italics, bulleted points?
2. How is the message directed to its readers? Do you sense that only those experiencing these symptoms are likely to read this document?

Appreciating Language

1. How does Rosenberg describe depression? Do the words create impressions people are likely to recognize?
2. There are few technical or professional terms in this definition. Does this sacrifice accuracy? Why or why not?

Writing Suggestions

1. Take a definition from the glossary section of a textbook and write a general version for an audience of clients, consumers, or students.
2. *Collaborative writing:* Discuss a common problem or issue with fellow students: job insecurity, lack of sleep, stressful family relationships, stalking, or child care. Select a term you often overhear and provide a clear definition for it. Have each member of the group list features of this term. Try to incorporate objective elements. Have the group prepare two versions—one designed for an "official" publication, such as the college catalog or textbook, the other for an informal handout.

Responding to IMAGES

© Tom Stewart/Corbis

1. How do you define patriotism? Do you think people who display the flag are patriotic? Can people disagree with the government and their leaders and still be patriots?

2. Do many people in your neighborhood display a flag? Do they have anything in common? Do you know people who refuse to fly a flag? What reasons do they give for their decision?

3. *Critical thinking:* Do you think some people misuse the flag to camouflage ideas and attitudes than run counter to the Bill of Rights? Why or why not?

4. *Visual analysis:* What does the composition of this photograph suggest to you? Would the image have different meaning if the person flying the flag was a firefighter, a woman in a business suit, an African American, a student with long hair, a biker, or a Muslim woman wearing a scarf? Would the image be different if the structure in the background was a school, a police station, a mobile home, or a yacht? Would your reactions to this photograph differ if the flag were Canadian or Mexican? Why or why not?

5. *Collaborative writing:* Discuss this photograph with a group of students. Ask them to write down their immediate reaction to the image. Share the responses and discuss differences of opinions. What does this image reveal about people's perceptual worlds? Work together to create one or more captions that express the view or views of your group.

Definition Checklist

Before submitting your paper, review these points:

✔ Is your purpose clear—to inform or persuade?

✔ Do you avoid defining a word with the same word, such as "a diffusion pump diffuses"?

✔ Is your level of technical or professional language suited to your audience?

✔ Does your definition provide enough information and examples so that readers can restate your thesis in their own words?

✔ Are there existing definitions you can use for reference or contrast?

✔ Do extended definitions contain illustrations, narratives, or comparisons readers may misinterpret or not recognize?

✔ Do you state the essence of your definition in a short summary statement readers can remember or highlight for future reference?

Companion Website

See **http://www.thomsonedu.com/english/sundance** for additional information on writing definition.

COMPARISON AND CONTRAST
INDICATING
SIMILARITIES AND
DIFFERENCES

22

WHAT IS COMPARISON AND CONTRAST?

Comparison and contrast answers the question, How are things alike or different? What distinguishes a gasoline engine from a diesel engine? Is it cheaper to buy or lease a new car? What separates a misdemeanor from a felony? What is the difference between Sunni and Shia Muslims? How is a viral infection different from a bacterial one? What did Malcolm X and Martin Luther King Jr. have in common? Do men and women define sexual harassment differently? All of these questions can be addressed by examining similarities and differences.

You have probably encountered questions on essay examinations that require comparison-and-contrast responses:

Compare the industrial output of the North and South at the outbreak of the Civil War.

How do the rules of evidence differ in criminal and civil proceedings?

Which arrangement offers businessowners greater protection of personal assets—full or limited partnerships?

Contrast Freud's dream theory with Jung's concept of the unconscious.

At the end of *The Great Gatsby* Nick Carraway decides to return to the West because he is too "squeamish" for the East. What differences did Fitzgerald see between the East and West?

Outline the principal differences between warm- and cold-blooded animals.

Comparison-and-contrast writing is commonly used to organize research papers. You might compare two short stories by Edgar Allan Poe in an English course, explain the differences between methods of depreciation in accounting, or contrast conflicting theories of childhood development in psychology. Comparison-and-contrast writing is also used by engineers to explain the fuel efficiency of different engines, by architects to discuss alternative plans to modernize a building, and by social workers to determine the better program to assist the homeless.

 To read more about comparison and contrast, along with interactive examples and opportunities to work with interactive texts, click on "The Rhetorical Patterns of Inquiry" from the main menu of *Comp21*.

The Purposes of Comparison and Contrast

Writers use comparison and contrast for two basic purposes:

1. **To explain by drawing distinctions between related subjects.** In many instances comparison is used to eliminate confusion. Many people, for instance, mistake an *optician,* who makes and sells eyeglasses, for an *optometrist,* who performs eye examinations and prescribes lenses. Comparison can pair extended definitions to show readers the difference, for example, between air-cooled and water-cooled engines, African and Indian elephants, or cross-country and downhill skiing. When writers draw distinctions, they explain differences between similar subjects but do not choose one over the other.

2. **To persuade readers to make a choice.** In other instances, comparison is used to outline advantages and disadvantages to demonstrate the superiority or desirability of one subject over another. Television commercials compare competing products. Political campaign brochures urge voters to support a candidate over a rival, contrasting their platforms, records, reputations, and achievements. Articles in medical journals argue that one drug is more effective than another. Business proposals recommend one computer program or one security service over competitors. Government studies reject one air-quality standard, arguing that a newer one is preferable.

SELECTING TOPICS FOR COMPARISON-AND-CONTRAST PAPERS

When developing a paper using comparison and contrast, you must be sure your subjects share enough common points for meaningful discussion. You can compare two sports cars, two action adventure films, two diets, or two political theories. But comparing a sports car to a pickup truck or an adventure film to a romantic comedy is not likely to generate more than superficial observations.

In addition, comparisons have to be carefully limited, especially for comparisons of broad or complex subjects. To examine the differences between American and Chinese cultures, Yi-Fu Tuan (p. 461) limits his focus to the different ways Americans and Chinese view space and place. By exploring this limited topic in depth, he reveals more about Chinese culture in a page or two than might be shown in a twenty-page essay attempting to address religion, politics, economics, history, and social customs. To compare two presidents, for instance, you might focus on their relations with the press, their farm policies, or their ability to respond in a crisis.

WRITING ACTIVITY

Use prewriting techniques to develop ideas on the following pairs. If you are unfamiliar with one topic, select another one that stimulates your thoughts. List similarities and note differences. Consider how you might limit the scope of your comparison. Your goal may be to inform or recommend.

1. Buying versus leasing a car

2. Two people you know well: your parents, two bosses, or two close friends

3. American versus Asian attitudes toward family, career, marriage, or government

4. Your generation's attitudes or values versus those of your parents' generation

5. Liberal versus conservative views of government, justice, poverty, or national defense

6. Two opposing views of the Iraq War

7. Two popular bands, filmmakers, fashion designers, or political candidates

8. Best and worst airlines, hotels, landlords, bosses, restaurants, or doctors you have encountered

9. Two regions of the country you have visited or lived in

10. Print versus online journalism

ORGANIZING COMPARISON-AND-CONTRAST PAPERS

Perhaps the most frustrating problem writers face in writing comparison and contrast is organizing ideas. Without careful planning, you may find yourself shifting awkwardly back and forth between subjects. Your reader may have difficulty following your train of thought and may confuse one subject with another. Whether drawing distinctions or making recommendations, writers use two basic methods of organizing comparison-and-contrast writing.

Subject by Subject

The *subject-by-subject* method divides the paper into two sections. Writers state all the information about topic A and then discuss topic B. Usually, the actual comparisons are drawn in the second part of the paper, where B is discussed in relation to A. In a short paper about two types of life insurance, the writer first explains "whole life" insurance and then describes "term" insurance, drawing distinctions between the two types. Because the purpose is to explain, the conclusion does not offer a recommendation:

Whole Life and Term Insurance

Most life insurance companies offer a variety of life insurance products, investments, and financial services. Two of the most common policies provided are whole life and term insurance.

Whole life insurance is the oldest and most traditional form of life insurance. Life insurance became popular in the nineteenth century as a way of protecting the buyer's dependents in the event of premature death. A purchaser would select a policy amount to be paid to his or her beneficiaries after his or her death. Payments called premiums were made on a yearly, quarterly, or monthly basis. As the policyholder paid premiums, the policy gained cash value. Part of the payment earned interest like money in a bank account. Insurance served as an investment tool, allowing people to save for retirement and giving them access to guaranteed loans. For a low interest fee, insurance holders could borrow against the cash value of their policies.

Term insurance, introduced in the twentieth century, serves the same basic purpose as whole life insurance, protecting the buyer's dependents. Unlike whole life, however, no cash value accrues. In a sense, the policyholder is "renting" insurance, purchasing only a death benefit. The advantage of term insurance is its low cost. Because there is no money set aside for investment, the premiums are lower. This allows a person to afford a larger policy. A term policy for $100,000 could be cheaper than a whole life policy for $50,000.

The type of insurance a person needs depends on his or her income, family situation, investment goals, savings, and obligations. Most investment counselors agree, however, that anyone with a spouse or children should have some form of life insurance protection.

Advantages

- The subject-by-subject method is a simple, straightforward method of organizing your essay and thus is useful if you have limited time.
- The subject-by-subject method is suited for short, highly readable papers.
- Abstract topics, such as economic theories, religious beliefs, and scientific principles, are often easier to organize in a subject-by-subject method because few individual features are shared by both subjects.

Disadvantages

- Long papers organized subject by subject are difficult to follow. A twenty-page report, for instance, would read like two ten-page papers fastened together. It would be difficult for readers to recall enough details from the first subject to appreciate how it differs from the second.
- Because subjects are discussed separately, it is difficult to present specific facts side by side. Readers are forced to page back and forth to compare details, such as prices and statistics.

Point by Point

The *point-by-point* method organizes the comparison of A and B on a series of specific subtopics. Following an introduction, A and B are discussed in a number of comparisons. Hotels, for example, have common features: location, appearance, atmosphere, number of rooms, banquet facilities, and rates. In the following paper, the writer organizes information about two hotels in each paragraph. In this instance, the writer makes a recommendation, stating her clear preference for one of the hotels in both the introduction and conclusion:

St. Gregory and Fitzpatrick Hotels
Campus organizations and academic conventions visiting the city hold special events at either the St. Gregory or Fitzpatrick. Both are large convention hotels, but for many reasons the St. Gregory is more desirable.

Opened in 1892, the St. Gregory is the oldest surviving hotel in the city. The Fitzpatrick is the newest, having opened just last spring. The St. Gregory has a commanding view of State Street. The Fitzpatrick is part of the $200 million Riverfront Centre.

The chief attraction of the St. Gregory is its famed domed lobby ornamented with carved mahogany and elaborate brass and marble fittings. Admiral Dewey was presented with the key to the city here following his victory in Manila Bay in 1898. In contrast, the sleek Fitzpatrick is noted for its sweeping thirty-story atrium. The open lobby is banked with massive video screens broadcasting subtitled stock market reports, news, and sports.

The main lounge of the St. Gregory is the Pump Room, a plush, turn-of-the-century Irish bar decorated with gilt-framed paintings of the Emerald Isle. The Fitzpatrick features two bars. Homerun, a sports bar, is popular with local students and young professionals. The Exchange is a smaller, quieter bar that is a favorite of visiting executives. Copiers, fax machines, and computers are available in the nearby Executive Centre.

Both hotels offer a range of room rates. The cheapest rooms at the St. Gregory are $95 a night. Though small, they are comfortable. The Fitzpatrick has only a dozen single traveler rooms for $125. Double rooms at the St. Gregory range from $175 to $259, depending on size and decor. All Fitzpatrick double rooms are identical and cost $195. In addition to convention rates, the St. Gregory offers 20 percent student discounts. The Fitzpatrick offers only corporate discounts.

Both hotels provide excellent convention services. Since most professors and academic delegates have access to university computers and fax machines, they prefer the historic elegance of the St. Gregory. Students especially appreciate discount rates and the availability of public transport to the university.

Advantages

- The point-by-point method is useful in organizing long papers that can be broken into units. Instead of splitting a twenty-page report into two ten-page sections, you can create a series of related comparisons.
- This method allows writers to place specific details side by side so that readers can easily compare prices, dimensions, and figures without having to search through the entire document.
- A point-by-point approach is useful in preparing a document for multiple readers. Because it is organized in sections, a reader can easily isolate the information most relevant to his or her purpose.

Disadvantages

- The point-by-point method can be difficult to use if the subjects are abstract and lack detail. Comparing two philosophies or two films may be easier to organize by discussing each separately.
- The point-by-point method can distort a topic if the specific points of comparison are poorly chosen. Major issues can be overlooked or minimized and minor details overemphasized unless the categories are carefully planned.

Blending the Methods

Writers often blend elements of both methods in a single essay. As you read the comparison-and-contrast entries in this chapter you will notice that few exactly fit either method. But as with all writing, clear organization is essential to avoid confusion, especially when your essay addresses more than one topic.

WRITING ACTIVITY

Select ideas from the previous exercise or develop ones from the following topics and create an outline using the subject-by-subject method, point-by-point method, or a blend of methods.

1. The sense of privacy in a small town versus a large city

2. America before and after a major event—the civil rights movement, World War II, the women's movement, or the Depression

3. The way husbands and wives are depicted on television

4. Media images of New York and California

5. The quality of a football team's offense and defense

6. Reality TV's heroes and villains

7. Male and female attitudes about sex, dating, or relationships

8. Growing up in a single-parent versus two-parent family

9. Two common views of death, abortion, poverty, or a recent campus controversy

10. Imported versus domestic cars, wines, or other products

STRATEGIES for Writing Comparison and Contrast

Critical Thinking and Prewriting

1. **List topics in a tandem fashion.** You can start by developing a series of possible topics by listing pairs of items:

   Personal Digital Assistant (PDA) &   U.S. & Canadian health care
      Paper Day Planner
   English only & bilingual schools   VHS & DVD

   - Leave space beneath each possible topic so that you can list details side by side.

2. **Choose related topics.** The subjects you select must have enough in common to establish meaningful similarities and enough in contrast to distinguish them to establish more than trivial differences.

   - Once you have a list of topics, scan down the pairs to find topics that are suitable for your task.

3. **Select a single topic that has changed.** Instead of comparing two people, two jobs, or two neighborhoods, you might write a before-and-after essay that shows how a subject has changed over time. You might compare today's movie heroes with those featured in classic films or status of a football team before and after the loss of key players. Has your old neighborhood changed? Has a new boss altered the way you work? Has a favorite TV show gotten better or worse?

4. **Avoid superficial comparisons.** Not all subjects are worthy of serious consideration. Although you could develop an essay comparing pet and child care, the information would be of little use because few people seriously debate whether they should adopt a child or purchase a dog.

   - Ask yourself: Who would be interested in reading this? Instead of thinking of your paper as a school assignment, imagine it as an article for a magazine. Is there a market for the information or advice you are presenting?

5. **Determine your purpose.** Is your goal to explain differences between two topics or to recommend one subject over another? Do you wish to inform readers, or do you wish to persuade them to make a choice?

   - Critical thinking is particularly important in persuading readers to accept your opinions. Consider common errors you should avoid (see pages 50–56).

6. **Examine categories for balance.** Because comparisons often measure advantages and disadvantages, it is easy to make lapses in critical thinking by ignoring points of comparison. You can easily demonstrate that nuclear

power is superior to solar energy—as long as you overlook the critical problem of safety and toxic waste.

■ Make sure that you avoid weighting your essay to favor one subject over another by stressing the advantages of one while emphasizing the disadvantages of another.

7. **Consider using visuals.** Can you present contrasting photographs or images to dramatize similarities and differences? Can you create graphs or charts to demonstrate differences in facts, number, or statistics?

8. **Test ideas through peer review.** You may gain new insights on your subject by asking fellow students and friends for their thoughts and reactions.

■ Ask readers whether you have failed to consider important points of comparison. Has the omission led to distortions?

Planning

1. **Consider your audience.** Before you can compare two items, you may have to explain background information. Before comparing two treatments for arthritis, it may be necessary to explain the nature of the illness and define basic medical terms.

2. **Review the scope of the assignment and your thesis.** Because you are discussing more than a single topic, it is important to focus your subject.

■ Could your points be more sharply refined or your recommendations more clearly demonstrated?

3. **Determine which method suits your purpose.** A short, nontechnical paper might be best organized using the subject-by-subject method. Longer works with details that should be placed side by side are better developed using the point-by-point method.

4. **Clearly state your thesis.** Whether your goal is to inform or persuade, your comparison needs a well-stated thesis.

■ Provide a one- or two-sentence thesis statement or summary that readers can highlight for future reference.

5. **Prioritize points.** Determine the most important points of comparison. You may develop many ideas that you may not have space or time to fully develop.

■ Focus your attention on developing the most important points of comparison.

6. **Develop an outline.** Because you are handling two topics, you may find that you need a more detailed outline to write a comparison than to write a narrative or description.

■ If you find it difficult to develop a point-by-point outline, consider developing a subject-by-subject outline for a rough draft.

Writing the First Draft

1. **Focus on the goal of your comparison to guide the draft.** In writing any paper it is easy to get off track and explore unrelated issues. Because you are addressing two subjects, you can easily be distracted.

   ■ Use your thesis to direct your writing. When you discover new ideas, determine whether they will help support the point of your comparison. You may explore interesting ideas but they may not relate to your overall goal.

2. **Get your ideas on paper by writing separate descriptions.** If you find it difficult to get started or follow a detailed outline, it may be easier to describe each subject separately.

   ■ Because you are bound to discover new ideas through writing, consider writing a pair of descriptions to generate points for a second draft.

3. **Most comparisons consist of paired descriptions.** Make your descriptions effective by creating dominant impressions, describing people and objects in action, and including dialogue to give voice to people.

4. **Use parallel structures to organize comparisons.** Readers will find your ideas easier to follow and easier to evaluate if you place ideas in a consistent pattern:

   > Shelly Longwood is a federal prosecutor with no political experience and an outspoken supporter for victims' rights. Her opponent, Sandy Berman, is a judge and former county supervisor who is a strong advocate of community policing.

   Both candidates are described in a matching pattern—current job, political experience, policy.

5. **Be aware of the impact of connotations.** The words you select in describing your topics will influence your readers' interpretations.

   ■ If you are seeking to distinguish differences between related subjects, avoid using words that may suggest unintended preferences. If you don't wish to suggest that one item is superior to the other, use neutral terminology to describe both.

   ■ In making a recommendation, positive and negative connotations and associations will be important tools in pointing out advantages and disadvantages.

6. **Keep the length of your paper in mind as you write.** It is always difficult to measure how many ideas and details you will develop as you write. When you discuss two topics, you may find your essay lengthening.

   ■ If you realize that to cover all the points on your outline, your paper will be far longer than desired, review your outline. You may wish to tighten your thesis, restrict your topic, discard minor points, or possibly abandon your topic for a more workable one.

Revising

1. **Review your plan and read your draft for its overall impact.**
   - Is the thesis clear? Does your paper accurately establish differences or effectively state a recommendation?
   - Is each subject fully developed and fairly described with enough detail?
   - Is the draft focused? Or is it too long, too confused?
   - Does the draft fulfill the needs of the assignment?
2. **Evaluate the way you describe or define each subject.**
   - Do you accurately and precisely define what you are comparing?
   - Have you limited the topics?
   - Are there misconceptions or vague statements that require greater clarity?
3. **Review the organization.**
   - Is the paper logically organized? Should you consider rewriting the paper using a different method?
4. **Examine the information you have included.**
   - Does the essay present enough facts, observations, and details about *both* subjects?
5. **Evaluate transitions between ideas.**
   - Can readers follow your train of thought? Are there clear shifts from one topic to another?
   - Can paragraph breaks and other devices help readers follow your ideas?
6. **Review the emphasis of main points.**
   - Are the main points of the comparison clearly highlighted and easy to remember?
7. **Study the impact of the introduction and conclusion.**
   - Does the introduction set up the comparison and introduce your purpose and thesis?
   - Does the conclusion make a final impression, restate the significant differences, or reinforce your recommendations?
8. **Evaluate the use of any visuals.** If you included visual aids, examine them carefully. Do they clearly illustrate similarities and differences in your subjects? Do the images add value to your writing, or are they unrelated or distracting? Are graphs or charts based on accurate data? Are the visual aids easy to understand?

Editing and Proofreading
1. **Read the paper aloud.** Listen to your sentences.
   - Are there awkward or repetitive phrases?
   - Do any passages require streamlining or greater detail?
2. **Review your choice of words.**
   - Do you accurately define each subject and main points?
   - Do the connotations of your words reflect your meaning?
3. **Use peer editing to identify problems you may have overlooked.**

STUDENT PAPER

This is a draft of a comparison paper a student wrote after reading several articles comparing different cultures. In addition to fulfilling a composition assignment, she considered developing ideas for a talk or display for an upcoming St. Patrick's Day celebration.

Parallel States: Israel and Ireland

Despite obvious historical and cultural differences, Israel and Ireland share striking similarities. Both are small—each has a population of about five million—yet significant nations. Israel is a narrow sliver of desert on the Mediterranean, a Middle Eastern country with negligible oil reserves. Ireland, an island on the fringe of Europe, is a neutral nation which played marginal roles in World War II and the Cold War.

Yet these nations have greater profiles than their larger and more powerful neighbors, largely because they represent homelands to vast Diaspora populations. More Jews live in America than Israel; more Irish live in America than Ireland. American Jews and Irish were significant supporters of the Zionist and Republican movements that helped establish the modern independent states.

Their recent emergence as sovereign states indicates a shared legacy of oppression and occupation. Although both the Jews and the Irish have cultures thousands of years old, Israel and Ireland did not achieve full independence until after the Second World War. Israel was recognized by the United Nations in 1948. Though partitioned in 1922, Ireland was not officially declared a republic until 1949, ending eight hundred years of British influence.

Since their creation, Israel and Ireland have endured decades of violence and terrorism. Both nations have labored to maintain democratic rights while preserving security for their citizenry.

Both nations have dual identities. On one hand, both Israel and Ireland were founded as Western-style Parliamentary democracies. Yet both are religious states. Israel is the Jewish homeland. Ireland is a Catholic nation. The religious authorities—the Catholic bishops and orthodox rabbis—believe citizens should accept their views on marriage, divorce, abortion, censorship, and civil customs. Secular forces, who view the religious orthodoxies as tradition-bound and male dominated, champion diversity and tolerance. Issues such as the role of women and gay rights evoke similar debates in Israel and Ireland as both nations struggle to reconcile their political and religious traditions.

In recent years both nations have engaged in a peace process to resolve long standing conflicts in contested areas. In both Northern Ireland and the West Bank the populations are split by religious, political, and cultural differences.

Presidents of the United States, prompted by the large number of Jews and Irish in America, have played a pivotal role in stimulating stalled peace talks. Negotiations in both regions were difficult to conduct because Israeli and Northern Irish politicians did not wish to recognize leaders of terrorist organizations.

By first inviting Yasser Arafat and Gerry Adams to the White House, Bill Clinton helped transform their public images from terrorists to legitimate leaders so that other democratic leaders could negotiate with them without appearing to endorse violence.

Despite ongoing tensions in both regions, Israel and Ireland enjoy expanding tourism, particularly from millions of American Jews and Irish who enjoy visiting homelands that represent their heritage.

Questions for Review and Revision

1. Is the thesis too general? Does the paper provide genuine insights or merely list obvious observations? Would it be better to fully develop a single issue, such as the role of religion in the two countries?
2. Would a revised introduction and conclusion provide greater focus?
3. What audience does the student seem to address? Who would benefit from reading this essay?
4. *Critical thinking:* To be effective, does a comparison paper have to accomplish more than merely list similarities? Should there be a larger purpose?

5. How effectively does the student organize the comparison? What role does paragraph structure play?
6. Read the paper aloud. Do you detect any passages that could be revised to reduce wordiness and repetition?

Writing Suggestions

1. Write a 500-word essay comparing some aspect of two nations, cities, or neighborhoods. Stress similarities that most readers would be unaware of.
2. *Collaborative writing:* Discuss this student's paper with a group of students. Ask each member to suggest possible changes. Do they identify common areas needing improvement?

SUGGESTED TOPICS FOR WRITING COMPARISON AND CONTRAST

General Assignments

Write a comparison paper on one of the following topics. You may use either subject-by-subject or point-by-point methods of organization. Your paper will likely blend both of these approaches. *Clearly determine your purpose—to inform or persuade.*

- High school and college
- Your best and worst jobs
- Renting versus owning a home
- The two most influential teachers/coaches/supervisors you have known
- Two popular sitcoms/newsmagazines/soap operas/talk shows/reality shows
- Two computer programs
- Your best and worst college courses
- Your parents' values and your own
- Two campus organizations
- Two popular movie stars/singers/bands/films/local personalities
- A subject that has changed over time, such as friend's attitude, a job's appeal, a band's popularity

 To create your own interactive writing project, use the textual, visual, and video libraries on *Comp21*. For the main menu, choose "Build Your Own Occasion for Writing."

Writing in Context

1. Imagine you have been asked by a British newsmagazine to write an article explaining the pro and con attitudes that Americans have about a controversial topic, such as the Iraq War, gun control, capital punishment, abortion, or welfare reform. Your article should be balanced and objective and should provide background information rather than just express your personal opinion.
2. Write the text for a brief pamphlet directed to high school seniors comparing high school and college. You may wish to use a chart format to compare specific points.
3. Write an e-mail to a friend comparing the best and worst aspects of your college, dorm, neighborhood, or job.
4. Examine a magazine article on cars, computers, or entertainment. Write an e-mail to the editor commenting on the magazine's best and worst features.
5. Compare two popular student clubs or restaurants for a review in the campus newspaper. Direct your comments to students who are interested in inexpensive but interesting entertainment.

STRATEGIES | for Reading Comparison and Contrast

In reading the comparison-and-contrast essays in this chapter, keep these questions in mind:

Context
1. What is the writer's goal—to draw distinctions or to recommend a choice?
2. What details does the writer present about each subject?
3. Who is the intended audience? Is the essay directed to a general or a specific reader?
4. Is the comparison valid? Is the writer comparing two subjects in a fair manner? Have any points been overlooked?
5. Does the author have an apparent bias?
6. If the comparison makes a recommendation, does the selection seem valid? What makes the chosen subject superior to others? What evidence is presented?

Strategy
1. What is the basic pattern of the comparison—subject by subject, point by point, or a blend?

2. Does the author use a device to narrow the topic or to advance the comparison?
3. Does the writer use visual aids, such as graphs, charts, or highlighted text?
4. Is the essay easy to follow? Are transitions between subjects clearly established by paragraph breaks and other devices?

Language

1. Does the writer use words with connotations that ascribe positive or negative qualities to one or both of the subjects? How does the author characterize the topics?
2. What does the diction, level of language, and use of technical terms reveal about the intended audience?
3. If the writer is suggesting a choice, how does the language demonstrate his or her preference?

Yi-Fu Tuan (1930–) was born in China and later moved to the United States. Now a geography professor in Madison, Wisconsin, he has studied the cultural differences between America and his native country. He states that he writes "from a single perspective—namely that of experience." In this article published in ***Harper's***, he compares the way people in two cultures view their environments.

Chinese Space, American Space

Cultures as diverse as America's and China's have many points of difference. In attempting to provide insight into their differences in a brief essay, Yi-Fu Tuan focuses on the concept of space and location. Americans, he asserts, are less rooted to place and are future oriented. The Chinese, savoring tradition, are deeply tied to specific locations. Note that Yi-Fu Tuan devotes most of his essay to describing the less-familiar Chinese houses and values.

Americans have a sense of space, not of place. Go to an American home in exurbia, and almost the first thing you do is drift toward the picture window. How curious that the first compliment you pay your host inside his house is to say how lovely it is outside his house! He is pleased that you should admire his vistas. The distant horizon is not merely a line separating earth from sky, it is a symbol of the future. The American is not rooted in his place, however lovely: his eyes are drawn by the expanding space to a point on the horizon, which is his future.

1   thesis

American space

American home

By contrast, consider the traditional Chinese home. Blank walls enclose it. Step behind the spirit wall and you are in a courtyard with perhaps a miniature garden around a corner. Once inside his private compound you are wrapped in an ambiance of calm beauty, an ordered world of buildings, pavement, rock, and decorative vegetation. But you have no distant view: nowhere does space open out before you. Raw nature in such a home is experienced only as weather, and the only open space is the sky above. The Chinese is rooted in his place. When he has to leave, it is not for the promised land on the terrestrial horizon, but for another world altogether along the vertical, religious axis of his imagination.

2   transition

Chinese home

Chinese place

3   The Chinese tie to place is deeply felt. Wanderlust is an alien senti-ment. The Taoist classic *Tao Te Ching* captures the ideal of rootedness in place with these words: "Though there may be another country in the neighborhood so close that they are within sight of each other and the crow-ing of cocks and barking of dogs in one place can be heard in the other, yet there is no traffic between them; and throughout their lives the two peoples have nothing to do with each other." In theory if not in practice, farmers have ranked high in Chinese society. The reason is not only that they are en-gaged in a "root" industry of producing food but that, unlike pecuniary mer-chants, they are tied to the land and do not abandon their country when it is in danger.

4   Nostalgia is a recurrent theme in Chinese poetry. An American reader of translated Chinese poems may well be taken aback—even put off—by the frequency, as well as the sentimentality, of the lament for home. To under-stand the strength of this sentiment, we need to know that the Chinese de-sire for stability and rootedness in place is prompted by the constant threat of war, exile, and the natural disasters of flood and drought. Forcible removal makes the Chinese keenly aware of their loss. By contrast, Americans move, for the most part, voluntarily. Their nostalgia for home town is really long-ing for a childhood to which they cannot return: in the meantime the future beckons and the future is "out there," in open space. When we criticize American rootlessness, we tend to forget that it is a result of ideals we ad-mire, namely, social mobility and optimism about the future. When we ad-mire Chinese rootedness, we forget that the word "place" means both a lo-cation in space and position in society: to be tied to place is also to be bound to one's station in life, with little hope of betterment. Space symbolizes hope; place, achievement and stability.

Final comments on American and Chinese values

Understanding Context

1. How does the author see a difference between "space" and "place"?
2. What do the traditional designs of American and Chinese homes reveal about cultural differences?
3. Why do the Chinese honor farmers?
4. What historical forces have shaped the Chinese desire for "rootedness"? How is American history different?
5. What negative aspects does Yi-Fu Tuan see in the Chinese sense of place?

Evaluating Strategy

1. The writer really devotes only a single paragraph to describing American concepts of space. Why? Is the essay out of balance? Discuss whether a comparison paper should devote half its space to each topic.
2. Is the author objective? Is it possible for a writer to discuss cultures without inserting a measure of bias?

Appreciating Language

1. What words does Yi-Fu Tuan use in describing the two cultures? Do they seem to differ in connotation?
2. Does the word *rootlessness* suggest something negative to most people? How does Yi-Fu Tuan define it?
3. Look up the word *wanderlust*. How does a German term suit an essay comparing American and Chinese cultures?

Writing Suggestions

1. If you have lived in or visited another country or region within the United States, write a brief essay outlining how it differs from your home. Just as Yi-Fu Tuan used the concept of space to focus a short article, you may wish to limit your comparison to discussing eating habits, dress, attitudes toward work, music, or dating practices.
2. *Collaborative writing:* Ask a group of students about their attitudes toward rootlessness and place. Determine how often students have moved in their lives. How many have spent their entire lives in a single house or apartment? Write a few paragraphs outlining the attitudes expressed by the group.

Bruce Catton (1899–1978) grew up listening to stories of Civil War veterans. His own college career was interrupted by service in the First World War. Catton went to work as a reporter for the **Cleveland Plain Dealer** and later served as information director for several government agencies. In 1953 his book **A Stillness at Appomattox** became a best-seller, and Catton received a Pulitzer Prize. He wrote several other books about the Civil War and edited **American Heritage** magazine for two decades.

Grant and Lee

Perhaps no other essay is as widely anthologized as a sample of comparison writing than Catton's "Grant and Lee," which first appeared in a collection, The American Story. *Directed to a general audience, the essay seeks to contrast the two most famous generals of the Civil War.*

1 When Ulysses S. Grant and Robert E. Lee met in the parlor of a modest house at Appomattox Court House, Virginia, on April 9, 1865, to work out the terms for the surrender of Lee's Army of Northern Virginia, a great chapter in American life came to a close, and a great new chapter began.

2 These men were bringing the Civil War to its virtual finish. To be sure, other armies had yet to surrender, and for a few days the fugitive Confederate government would struggle desperately and vainly, trying to find some way to go on living now that its chief support was gone. But in effect it was all over when Grant and Lee signed the papers. And the little room where they wrote out the terms was the scene of one of the poignant, dramatic contrasts in American history.

3 They were two strong men, these oddly different generals, and they represented the strengths of two conflicting currents that, through them, had come into final collision.

4 Back of Robert E. Lee was the notion that the old aristocratic concept might somehow survive and be dominant in American life.

5 Lee was tidewater Virginia, and in his background were family, culture, and tradition . . . the age of chivalry transplanted to a New World which was making its own legends and its own myths. He embodied a way of life that had come down through the age of knighthood and the English country

squire. America was a land that was beginning all over again, dedicated to nothing much more complicated than the rather hazy belief that all men had equal rights and should have an equal chance in the world. In such a land Lee stood for the feeling that it was somehow of advantage to human society to have a pronounced inequality in the social structure. There should be a leisure class, backed by ownership of land; in turn, society itself should be keyed to the land as the chief source of wealth and influence. It would bring forth (according to this ideal) a class of men with a strong sense of obligation to the community; men who lived not to gain advantage for themselves, but to meet the solemn obligations which had been laid on them by the very fact that they were privileged. From them the country would get its leadership; to them it could look for the higher values—of thought, of conduct, of personal deportment—to give it strength and virtue.

Lee embodied the noblest elements of this aristocratic ideal. Through 6 him, the landed nobility justified itself. For four years, the Southern states had fought a desperate war to uphold the ideals for which Lee stood. In the end, it almost seemed as if the Confederacy fought for Lee; as if he himself was the Confederacy . . . the best thing that the way of life for which the Confederacy stood could ever have to offer. He had passed into legend before Appomattox. Thousands of tired, underfed, poorly clothed Confederate soldiers, long since past the simple enthusiasm of the early days of the struggle, somehow considered Lee the symbol of everything for which they had been willing to die. But they could not quite put this feeling into words. If the Lost Cause, sanctified by so much heroism and so many deaths, had a living justification, its justification was General Lee.

Grant, the son of a tanner on the Western frontier, was everything Lee 7 was not. He had come up the hard way and embodied nothing in particular except the eternal toughness and sinewy fiber of the men who grew up beyond the mountains. He was one of a body of men who owed reverence and obeisance to no one, who were self-reliant to a fault, who cared hardly anything for the past but who had a sharp eye for the future.

These frontier men were the precise opposite of the tidewater aristo- 8 crats. Back of them, in the great surge that had taken people over the Alleghenies and into the opening Western country, there was a deep, implicit dissatisfaction with a past that had settled into grooves. They stood for democracy, not from any reasoned conclusion about the proper ordering of human society, but simply because they had grown up in the middle of democracy and knew how it worked. Their society might have privileges, but they would be privileges each man had won for himself. Forms and patterns meant nothing. No man was born to anything, except perhaps to a chance to show how far he could rise. Life was competition.

9   Yet along with this feeling had come a deep sense of belonging to a national community. The Westerner who developed a farm, opened a shop, or set up in business as a trader, could hope to prosper only as his own community prospered—and his community ran from the Atlantic to the Pacific and from Canada down to Mexico. If the land was settled, with towns and highways and accessible markets, he could better himself. He saw his fate in terms of the nation's own destiny. As its horizons expanded, so did his. He had, in other words, an acute dollars-and-cents stake in the continued growth and development of his country.

10   And that, perhaps, is where the contrast between Grant and Lee becomes most striking. The Virginia aristocrat, inevitably, saw himself in relation to his own region. He lived in a static society which could endure almost anything except change. Instinctively, his first loyalty would go to the locality in which that society existed. He would fight to the limit of endurance to defend it, because in defending it he was defending everything that gave his own life its deepest meaning.

11   The Westerner, on the other hand, would fight with an equal tenacity for the broader concept of society. He fought so because everything he lived by was tied to growth, expansion, and a constantly widening horizon. What he lived by would survive or fall with the nation itself. He could not possibly stand by unmoved in the face of an attempt to destroy the Union. He would combat it with everything he had, because he could only see it as an effort to cut the ground out from under his feet.

12   So Grant and Lee were in complete contrast, representing two diametrically opposed elements in American life. Grant was the modern man emerging; beyond him, ready to come on the stage, was the great age of Steel and machinery, of crowded cities and a restless burgeoning vitality. Lee might have ridden down from the old age of chivalry, lance in hand, silken banner fluttering over his head. Each man was the perfect champion of his cause, drawing both his strengths and his weaknesses from the people he led.

13   Yet it was not all contrast, after all. Different as they were—in background, in personality, in underlying aspiration—these two great soldiers had much in common. Under everything else, they were marvelous fighters. Furthermore, their fighting qualities were really very much alike.

14   Each man had, to begin with, the great virtue of utter tenacity and fidelity. Grant fought his way down the Mississippi Valley in spite of acute personal discouragement and profound military handicaps. Lee hung on in the trenches at Petersburg after hope itself had died. In each man there was an indomitable quality. . . . the born fighter's refusal to give up as long as he can still remain on his feet and lift his two fists.

Daring and resourcefulness they had, too; the ability to think faster and 15 move faster than the enemy. These were the qualities which gave Lee the dazzling campaigns of Second Manassas and Chancellorsville and won Vicksburg for Grant.

Lastly, and perhaps greatest of all, there was the ability, at the end, to 16 turn quickly from war to peace once the fighting was over. Out of the way these two men behaved at Appomattox came the possibility of a peace of reconciliation. It was a possibility not wholly realized, in the years to come, but which did, in the end, help the two sections to become one nation again . . . after a war whose bitterness might have seemed to make such a reunion wholly impossible. No part of either man's life became him more than the part he played in their brief meeting in the McLean house at Appomattox. Their behavior there put all succeeding generations of Americans in their debt. Two great Americans, Grant and Lee—very different, yet under everything very much alike. Their encounter at Appomattox was one of the great moments of American history.

Understanding Context

1. What does Catton see as the most striking difference between the generals?
2. How did Grant and Lee differ in background and sense of allegiance?
3. What were the historical forces that shaped the two men?
4. *Critical thinking:* Essentially, Catton is telling the story of a confrontation between victor and vanquished, yet his account does not seem to depict the men as winner and loser. Catton does not dwell on what made Grant victorious or on the causes for Lee's defeat. What does this reveal about his purpose?

Evaluating Strategy

1. How does Catton organize the essay?
2. *Critical thinking:* The Civil War was, in part, a battle over slavery. Catton does not mention this issue. Does his account appear to be ethically neutral, suggesting that neither side was morally superior in its war aims?

Appreciating Language

1. Does Catton appear to be neutral or biased in his description of the two men?
2. What does the tone, level of language, and word choice suggest about Catton's intended audience?

Writing Suggestions

1. Write an essay comparing two people in the same profession. Compare two teachers, coaches, landlords, attorneys, ministers, or coworkers. Try to focus on their personalities and philosophies rather than on their appearance. You may wish to limit your paper to a specific attitude, situation, or behavior.

2. *Collaborative writing:* Work with a group of students to write a short dramatic scene based on Catton's essay. Use set descriptions to establish the locale, and invent dialogue. Discuss with members of the group how Lee and Grant might have sounded. What words might they have chosen? How would their vocabulary indicate their different backgrounds?

Rachel Carson (1907–1964) was a marine biologist known for the literary quality of her writing. She won critical acclaim with her first two books, *The Sea Around Us* (1951) and *The Edge of the Sea* (1955). Then, in 1962, she hit the best-seller list with *Silent Spring,* a frightening exposé of the hazards that insecticides and weed killers were posing to both wildlife and human beings. As much as anything else, this one book can be said to have launched the modern environmental movement.

A Fable for Tomorrow

Rapid industrialization both in manufacturing and agriculture brought unprecedented material advantages to the developed world throughout the first half of the twentieth century. At the same time, insufficient notice was being taken of the damages such industrialization was inflicting on the natural environment. Although Silent Spring *is a well-researched book by a reputable scientist, it is intended for a general audience. The following preface to that book is an imaginative rendering of the eventual consequences of continued indifference to the environment.*

There was once a town in the heart of America where all life seemed to live 1 in harmony with its surroundings. The town lay in the midst of a checkerboard of prosperous farms, with fields of grain and hillsides of orchards where, in spring, white clouds of bloom drifted above the green fields. In autumn, oak and maple and birch set up a blaze of color that flamed and flickered across a backdrop of pines. Then foxes barked in the hills and deer silently crossed the fields, half hidden in the mists of the fall mornings.

Along the roads, laurel, viburnum and alder, great ferns and wildflowers 2 delighted the traveler's eye through much of the year. Even in winter the roadsides were places of beauty, where countless birds came to feed on the berries and on the seed heads of the dried weeds rising above the snow. The countryside was, in fact, famous for the abundance and variety of its bird life, and when the flood of migrants was pouring through in spring and fall people traveled from great distances to observe them. Others came to fish the streams, which flowed clear and cold out of the hills and contained shady pools where trout lay. So it had been from the days many years ago when the first settlers raised their houses, sank their wells, and built their barns.

3   Then a strange blight crept over the area and everything began to change. Some evil spell had settled on the community: mysterious maladies swept the flocks of chickens; the cattle and sheep sickened and died. Everywhere was a shadow of death. The farmers spoke of much illness among their families. In the town the doctors had become more and more puzzled by new kinds of sickness appearing among their patients. There had been several sudden and unexplained deaths, not only among adults but even among children, who would be stricken suddenly while at play and die within a few hours.

4   There was a strange stillness. The birds, for example—where had they gone? Many people spoke of them, puzzled and disturbed. The feeding stations in the backyards were deserted. The few birds seen anywhere were moribund; they trembled violently and could not fly. It was a spring without voices. On the mornings that had once throbbed with the dawn chorus of robins, catbirds, doves, jays, wrens, and scores of other bird voices there was now no sound; only silence lay over the fields and woods and marsh.

5   On the farms the hens brooded, but no chicks hatched. The farmers complained that they were unable to raise any pigs—the litters were small and the young survived only a few days. The apple trees were coming into bloom but no bees droned among the blossoms, so there was no pollination and there would be no fruit.

6   The roadsides, once so attractive, were now lined with browned and withered vegetation as though swept by fire. These, too, were silent, deserted by all living things. Even the streams were now lifeless. Anglers no longer visited them, for all the fish had died.

7   In the gutters under the eaves and between the shingles of the roofs, a white granular powder still showed a few patches; some weeks before it had fallen like snow upon the roofs and the lawns, the fields and streams.

8   No witchcraft, no enemy action had silenced the rebirth of new life in this stricken world. The people had done it themselves.

9   This town does not actually exist, but it might easily have a thousand counterparts in America or elsewhere in the world. I know of no community that has experienced all the misfortunes I describe. Yet every one of these disasters has actually happened somewhere, and many real communities have already suffered a substantial number of them. A grim specter has crept upon us almost unnoticed, and this imagined tragedy may easily become a stark reality we all shall know.

10   What has already silenced the voices of spring in countless towns in America? This book is an attempt to explain.

Understanding Context

1. What sort of a world does Carson describe in the first two paragraphs of the essay?
2. Can you tell exactly what it is that causes the change between the world of the first two paragraphs and the world described next? What do you know about what caused the devastation?
3. What does Carson mean when she says the people had done it themselves?
4. What is Carson's purpose in providing this fictional account of destruction?

Evaluating Strategy

1. Note each reference to silence. How do all of those references relate to the title of the book Carson is introducing, *Silent Spring*?
2. How does Carson use a "before and after" comparison to make her point?

Appreciating Language

1. The first two paragraphs describe the town in almost fairy-tale language. In the remainder of the essay, which specific words help capture the negative atmosphere that Carson is trying to create?
2. Although Carson is a scientist, she chose to use in this introduction language that would be easily understood by the layperson. Why do you think she might have made that choice?

Writing Suggestions

1. You may have seen specific places go through a transformation on a smaller scale of the sort Carson describes. Write two paragraphs in which you first describe a place as you once knew it and then as it exists now.
2. People also go through transformations. Write two paragraphs in which you first describe a person as he or she once was, then describe that person as he or she is now.

AZADEH MOAVENI

Azadeh Moaveni, whose parents left Iran following the fall of
Shah in 1979, was born in Palo Alto, California. She describes the
complex identity she developed as someone growing up in a
community of exiles trying to make lives in a new country in her
book *Lipstick Jihad: A Memoir of Growing Up Iranian in America
and American in Iran.*

Maman and America

In this passage from Lipstick Jihad, *Moaveni uses comparison to dramatize the
differences between her divorced parents, her teenage conflicts with her mother, whom
she calls Maman, and her mother's conflicting opinions of American culture.*

1 When it served her purposes, Maman embraced America and lovingly re-
cited all the qualities that made it superior to our backward-looking Iranian
culture. That Americans were honest, never made promises they didn't intend to keep, were open to therapy, believed a divorced woman was still a
whole person worthy of respect and a place in society—all this earned them
vast respect in Maman's book. It seemed never to occur to her that values do
not exist in a cultural vacuum but are knit into a society's fabric; they earn
their place, derived from other related beliefs. Maman thought values were
like groceries; you'd cruise through the aisles, toss the ones you fancied into
your cart, and leave the unappealing ones on the shelf. When I was a teenager we constantly fought over her pilfering through Iranian and American
values at random, assigning a particular behavior or habit she felt like promoting to the culture she could peg it to most convincingly.

2   Our earliest battle on this territory was over Madonna. Maman called
her *jendeh*, a prostitute, which I considered an offensive way to describe the
singer of "La Isla Bonita." On what grounds, I argued, was she being con-
demned? Was it because she flaunted her sexuality, and if so, did that make
out-of-wedlock sexuality a bad thing? My defense of Madonna seemed to
infuriate Maman; her eyes flashed, and her bearing radiated a grave, ominous disappointment. It was the same disproportionate reaction she'd show
when I would forget which elder in a room full of aging relatives I should
have served tea to first, or when I'd refuse to interrupt an afternoon with a
friend to take vitamins to an elderly Iranian lady who couldn't drive. Certain

472

conversations or requests, unbeknownst to me, would become symbolic tests of my allegiance to that Iranian world, and the wrong response would plunge Maman into dark feelings of failure and regret.

At the prescient age of thirteen, I realized our Madonna arguments sig- 3 naled far more serious confrontations to come. Maman's contempt for Madonna seemed like sheer hypocrisy to me. Was this the same woman who thought it regressive and awful that Iranian culture valued women through their marital status, and rated their respectability according to the success or failure of their marriage? The woman who denounced a culture that considered divorced women criminals? She believed it was only modern to consider women fully equal to men, independent beings with a sacred right to everything men were entitled. Somehow, it became clear through her designation of Madonna as whore, that she also thought it fully consistent to believe premarital sex (for women) was wrong, and that women who practiced it were morally compromised. The men she forgave, offering an explanation worthy of an Iranian villager: "They can't help themselves." Women, it seemed, were physiologically better equipped for deprivation. Often our fights would end with me collapsing in tears, her bitterly condemning my unquestioning acceptance of "this decadent culture's corrupt ways," and my usual finale: "It's all your fault for raising me here; what did you expect?"

In Maman's view, America was responsible for most that had gone wrong 4 in the world. *Een gavhah*, these cows, was her synonym for Americans. She'd established her criticisms early on, and repeated them so often that to this day they are seared on my brain: "Americans have no social skills. . . . They prefer their pets to people. . . . Shopping and sex, sex and shopping; that's all Americans think about. . . . They've figured out how corrupt they are, and rather than fix themselves, they want to force their sick culture on the rest of the world." Since she mostly wheeled out these attitudes to justify why I couldn't be friends with Adam-the-long-haired-guitarist or why I couldn't go to the movies twice in one week, or why I couldn't wear short skirts, I wondered whether they were sincere, or tactical.

Her restrictions were futile, and only turned me into a highly skilled liar 5 with a suspiciously heavy backpack. Every morning she would drop me off at a friend's house, ostensibly so we could walk to school together. Once inside I traded the Maman-approved outfit for something tighter, smeared some cherry gloss on my lips, and headed off to class. Knowing I could secretly evade her restrictions helped me endure the sermons, but sometimes the injustice of her moralizing would provoke me, and I would fling jingoistic clichés designed to infuriate her: "Love it or leave it. . . . These colors don't run. . . . No one's keeping you here." At hearing these words come out of my mouth she'd hurl a piece of fruit at me, dissolve into angry tears, and suddenly the fact that I was torturing my poor, exiled single mother filled me with terrible grief, and I would apologize profusely, begging forgiveness in the formal, filial Farsi I knew she craved to hear. In the style of a traditional Iranian mother, she would pretend, for five days, that I did not exist; thaw on the sixth; and by the seventh have forgotten the episode entirely, privately convinced that my rude friends, who didn't even say *salaam* to her when they came over, were responsible for ruining my manners.

6   When we encountered other second-generation Iranians at Persian parties, I was struck by how much less conflicted they seemed over their dueling cultural identities. I decided my own neurotic messiness in this area was the fault of my divorced parents. The only thing they agreed on was the safety record of the Volvo, and how they should both drive one until I finished junior high. But when it came to anything that mattered, for instance how I should be raised, they didn't even bother to carve out an agreement, so vast was the gulf that separated their beliefs. My father was an atheist (Marx said God was dead) who called the Prophet Mohammad a pedophile for marrying a nine-year-old girl. He thought the defining characteristics of Iranian culture—fatalism, political paranoia, social obligations, an enthusiasm for guilt—were responsible for the failures of modern Iran. He wouldn't even condescend to use the term "Iranian culture," preferring to refer, to this day, to "that stinking culture"; he refused to return to Iran, even for his mother's funeral, and wouldn't help me with my Persian homework, a language, he pronounced direly "you will *never* use." When I announced my decision to move to Iran, his greatest fear, I think, was that something sufficiently awful would happen to me that it would require *his* going back. That he had married Maman, a hyper-ideologue, a reactionary as high-strung as they come, was baffling; little wonder they divorced when I was an infant. Daddy was the benevolent father personified; he couldn't have cared less about curfews, dating, a fifth ear piercing, or whether my hair was purple or not.

Understanding Context

1. How does Moaveni explain her mother's conflicted attitude toward America?
2. Why did Moaveni and her mother fight over Madonna? What did Madonna represent?
3. How does Moaveni describe the differences between her parents? How did her father's attitudes toward Iran differ from her mother's?

4. How did Moaveni's mother view differences between men and women?
5. *Critical thinking:* Do all immigrant parents and their American-born children face a similar clash over cultural values and identity? Could similar mother and daughter arguments occur in Korean, Mexican, or Vietnamese families?

Evaluating Strategy

1. How does Moaveni use an argument over Madonna to highlight her conflict with her mother?
2. Moaveni states that her mother thought of values as being products on a shelf. Is this an effective comparison? Why or why not?
3. How did Moaveni use her parents' attitudes about Farsi, the Iranian language, to dramatize their differences?
4. *Other modes:* How does Moaveni use *description*, *definition*, and *narration* to develop her comparisons?

Appreciating Language

1. What words does Moaveni use to describe her parents?
2. What terms does Maman use to praise and condemn Americans? What connotations do these terms have? Do you think they reflect the positive and negative views many people from other countries have about the United States? Why or why not?

Writing Suggestions

1. Write a comparison essay that describes one or more of your own adolescent conflicts with one or both of your parents. What were the points of contention? What did they symbolize?
2. *Collaborative writing:* Discuss Moaveni's essay with a group of students. Work together to develop a brief essay that outlines the problems immigrant families face living in the United States. Do some people, like Moaveni's father, seek to forget their old country and assimilate, while others, like Moaveni's mother, seek to maintain cultural values and traditions?

© Viviane Moos/CORBIS

 e-reading

InfoTrac College Edition

www.infotrac-college.com

IMMIGRATION

Immigration reform is perhaps the most important challenge facing America. How America resolves this challenge will not only determine what kind of country America will be, but whether or not America will remain a country at all.

Tom Tancredo

I reject the idea that America has used herself up in the effort to help outsiders in, and that now she must sit back exhausted, watching people play the cards fate has dealt them. . . . We have no right to be content, to close the door to others now that we are safely inside.

Mario M. Cuomo

America is a nation of immigrants. Since its founding, the United States has absorbed waves of new arrivals from around the world. Settled primarily by the English, French, and Dutch in the seventeenth century, America attracted large numbers of Germans in the early nineteenth century. During the potato famine of the 1840s and 1850s, 1,700,000 Irish emigrated to the United States. Near the end of the century, millions more arrived from Italy and Eastern Europe. By 1910, 15 percent of American residents were foreign born.

These immigrants filled American cities, adding to their commerce and diversity. European immigrants provided the labor for the country's rapid industrial expansion. Chinese workers laid the railroad tracks that unified the nation and opened the West to economic expansion.

But immigrants also met with resistance. Groups like the Know Nothings opposed the influx of Irish Catholics. As late as the 1920s, help-wanted ads in many newspapers contained the statement "No Irish Need Apply." California passed laws denying rights to the Chinese. Ivy League universities instituted quotas to limit the enrollment of Jewish students. Despite discrimination and hardships, these immigrants and their descendents entered mainstream American society and prospered. Today, some 40 percent of Americans can trace their roots to ancestors who passed through Ellis Island during the peak years of immigration a century ago.

The United States is experiencing the largest increase in immigration in its history. Between 1990 and 2000 the number of foreign-born residents increased 57 percent, reaching 31 million in 2000. Today's immigrants come primarily from Mexico, Asia, and the Middle East. This new wave of immigration is changing the nation's demographics, so that Hispanics, not African Americans, are the largest minority group. Within decades Muslims may outnumber Jews, making Islam America's second-largest religion.

This flow of immigrants, both legal and illegal, has fueled a debate about whether immigration benefits or hurts the United States. Supporters of immigration argue that immigrants set off a declining birthrate, adding new workers and consumers needed to expand the nation's economy. Critics argue that the United States has a limited capacity to absorb immigrants, especially the unskilled. Although immigrants provide employers with cheap labor, they tax the local governments that must provide them and their children with educational and health care services. Because of their numbers and historic ties to the land, Mexicans are changing the cultural fabric of the Southwest. In response, Americans concerned about national identity call for tighter border controls, restricted immigration, and the establishment of English as an official language.

Additionally, the terrorist attacks of September 11, 2001, led to new concerns about immigration, border controls, and national security.

Before reading these articles, consider these questions:

Where did your ancestors come from? Were they immigrants? Did they encounter discrimination when they arrived? Did they struggle to maintain their own language and culture or seek to assimilate into American society?

Should people who entered the country illegally be given legal status? Should amnesty be given to illegal immigrants who have lived and worked in the United States for several years?

Do wealthy countries like the United States have a moral obligation to accept immigrants? The United States has historically accepted immigrants fleeing war and oppression. After Castro assumed power, 250,000 Cubans fled to the United States. Tens of thousands of Vietnamese refugees entered the United States after the fall of South Vietnam. Does a prosperous nation also have an obligation to absorb some of the world's poor?

How should the United States determine the number and type of immigrants allowed to enter the country each year? Should talented immigrants be given priority over the unskilled? Should the number of immigrants be limited during times of recession and high unemployment?

Does admitting immigrants improve the country by adding consumers and workers or weaken it by draining resources and taxing public services?

E-Readings Online

Search for each article by author or title after entering InfoTrac College Edition through your 1Pass account login.

Mario Cuomo. *The American Dream and the Politics of Inclusion: Our Society Must Resist Those Who Would Close Our Doors to Future Immigrants.*
A former governor of New York and the son of immigrants, Cuomo argues that America has historically benefited from immigration.

Robert J. Bresler. *Immigration: The Sleeping Time Bomb.*
Although past waves of immigrants have enriched this country, Bresler argues that unless immigration is limited our population could swell to 500 million in less than fifty years, reducing the quality of life for all citizens.

Christopher Gray. *Alien Nation: Common Sense About America's Immigration Disaster.*

Gray reviews three books analyzing the current immigration policy. America constitutes 5 percent of the world's population but accepts 50 percent of the world's legal immigrants. The influx of a million immigrants a year may profoundly affect America's society, culture, economy, and values.

Robert Samuelson. *The Hard Truth of Immigration: No Society Has a Boundless Capacity to Accept Newcomers, Especially When Many of Them Are Poor and Unskilled Workers.*

Samuelson argues that immigration reform is needed to stem illegal immigration while granting legal status to illegal immigrants already living in the United States. "The stakes are simple," he argues, "will immigration continue to foster national pride and strength or will it cause more and more weakness and anger?"

Peter Duignan. *Do Immigrants Benefit America?*

Duignan believes that most of today's immigrants "will be an integral part of a revised American community" but warns that "past success does not guarantee that history will repeat itself."

Stanley Crouch. *Just Say No for a While to Immigration.*

Noting that past waves of immigration "meant that many skilled black workers were kicked to the curb so some foreigners could get on the gravy train," Crouch calls for restrictions on today's immigrants, especially those from Muslim countries.

August Gribbin. *Flow of Illegals "Inevitable": A Mexican Agency Predicts That the Mexican-born U.S. Population Will at Least Double, up to 18 Million, by the Year 2030.*

The movement of Mexicans back and forth across the United States border follows a two-hundred-year-old pattern that is deeply ingrained in Mexican culture.

Charlie Leduff. *Los Angeles County Weighs Cost of Illegal Immigration.*

Noting the growing costs of providing services for illegal immigrants, a Los Angeles County supervisor has proposed that illegal aliens obtain work permits and that their employers post bonds to pay for their health care.

Steven Camarota. *Our New Immigration Predicament.*

"Rather than changing our society to adapt to existing immigration," Camarota insists, "it would seem to make more sense to change the immigrant stream to fit our society."

Critical Reading and Thinking

1. What do authors see as the major costs and benefits of immigration?
2. What reasons do the authors give for the country's unwillingness to address illegal immigration?
3. What drives immigrants, both legal and illegal, to enter the United States?
4. How will the current wave of immigration change American society?
5. What motivates people to demand restrictions on immigration?

Writing Suggestions

1. Write an essay about your own family history. Were you or your ancestors immigrants? When did they arrive? Did they encounter any discrimination or hardships? Did they assimilate into mainstream American society or seek to maintain ties to their native language, culture, and traditions?
2. *Collaborative writing:* Discuss immigration with other students and develop an essay presenting your group's views on one aspect of immigration—tightening border security, giving amnesty to illegal aliens, developing a guestworker program, or prosecuting employers who hire illegal aliens. If members have differing opinions, consider developing opposing statements.
3. *Other modes*
   - Write an essay that examines the *definitions* used to discuss illegal immigrants, such as "undocumented workers," "illegal immigrants," and "illegal aliens." Note the role that connotation plays in shaping attitudes toward illegal immigrants.
   - *Compare* current immigrants with those who entered Ellis Island a century ago.
   - Use *process* to explain how immigrants can obtain citizenship.
   - Write a *division* essay to outline the major problems that recent immigrants face in finding employment, housing, and health services in the United States.
   - Use *classification* to rank suggestions for immigration reform from the most to the least restrictive or from the most to the least acceptable to the public and politicians.

Research Paper

You can develop a research paper about immigration by conducting further research to explore a range of issues:
- How effectively does law enforcement prosecute companies that hire illegal aliens?

- How has the concern about terrorism affected immigration policies? Do immigrants from Muslim countries face greater scrutiny? Has Homeland Security viewed the borders as potential weakspots?
- What does current research reveal about the status of Mexican Americans? Are immigrants from Mexico entering the middle class at a similar rate to immigrants from other countries?
- How will the new wave of immigrants influence American society, culture, economy, and foreign policy?
- Examine the impact immigration has had on other developed countries, such as Canada, Britain, France, Germany, and Italy. What problems, if any, have immigrants populations posed in these nations?

For Further Reading

To locate additional sources on immigration, enter these search terms as InfoTrac subjects:

> **Immigrants**
> Subdivisions   analysis
> behavior
> cases
> civil rights
> economic aspects
> education
> laws, regulations and rules
> personal narratives
> political activity
> psychological aspects
> social aspects
> statistics

Additional Sources

Using a search engine, such as Yahoo!, Google, or Alta Vista, enter one or more of the following terms to locate additional sources:

> immigration   green cards
> visa lotteries   Ellis Island
> citizenship   bilingual education
> Mexican Americans   English only

See Evaluating Internet Source Checklist on page 752. See Chapter 30 for using and documenting sources.

PEGGY KENNA AND SONDRA LACY

Peggy Kenna and Sondra Lacy are communications specialists based in Arizona who work with foreign-born employees. In addition, they provide cross-cultural training to executives conducting international business. Kenna is a speech and language pathologist who specializes in accent modification. Kenna and Lacy have collaborated on a series of fifty-page booklets that compare American and foreign business organizations, habits, behaviors, and negotiating styles. Widely sold in airports, these booklets give Americans tips on doing business overseas.

Communication Styles: United States and Taiwan

This section from Business Taiwan *contrasts American and Taiwanese styles of communicating. Designing their booklets for quick skimming, Kenna and Lacy use charts to highlight cultural differences.*

UNITED STATES	TAIWAN
• *Frank*	• *Subtle*
Americans tend to be very straightforward and unreserved. The people of Taiwan often find them abrupt and not interested enough in human relationships.	Frankness is not appreciated by the people of Taiwan. They particularly dislike unqualified negative statements.
• *Face saving less important*	• *Face saving important*
To Americans accuracy is important but errors are tolerated. Admitting mistakes is seen as a sign of maturity. They believe you learn from failure and therefore encourage some risk taking.	The Chinese do not like to be put in the position of having to admit a mistake or failure. They also do not like to tell you when they don't understand your point.
Americans believe criticism can be objective and not personal, however, all criticism should be done with tact.	You also should not admit too readily when you don't know something as it can cause you to lose face.

UNITED STATES

- *Direct eye contact*

Direct eye contact is very important to Americans since they need to see the nonverbal cues the speaker is giving. Nonverbal cues are a very important part of the American English language. Americans use intermittent eye contact when they are speaking but fairly steady eye contact when they are listening.

- *Direct and to the point*

Americans prefer people to say what they mean. Because of this they tend to sometimes miss subtle nonverbal cues. Americans are uncomfortable with ambiguousness and don't like to have to "fill in the blanks." They also tend to discuss problems directly.

- *"Yes" means agreement*

Americans look for clues such as nodding of the head, a verbal "yes" or "uh huh" in order to determine if their arguments are succeeding.

TAIWAN

7

- *Avoid direct eye contact*

8

Holding the gaze of another person is considered rude.

9

- *Indirect and ambiguous*

10

People in Taiwan dislike saying "no." They may not tell you when they don't understand. They often hedge their answers if they know you won't like the answer. If they say something like, "We'll think about it," they may mean they aren't interested.

11

They dislike discussing problems directly and will often go around the issue which can be frustrating for Americans.

12

The Chinese language (Mandarin) is so concise that the listener needs to use much imagination to "fill in the gaps."

13

- *"Yes" means "I hear"*

14

People in Taiwan do not judge information given to them so they do not indicate agreement or disagreement; they only nod or say "yes" to indicate they are listening to you.

15

The people of Taiwan believe politeness is more important than frankness so they will not directly tell you "no." The closest they will come to "no" is "maybe."

16

Understanding Context

1. What appear to be the major differences between American and Taiwanese methods of communicating?
2. Why is it important for Americans to be sensitive about making direct eye contact with Taiwanese?
3. How do Americans and Taiwanese accept failure?
4. *Critical thinking:* Why would this booklet be valuable to Americans visiting Taiwan on business? Does such a brief, to-the-point guide risk relying on stereotypes?

Evaluating Strategy

1. How easy is this document to read and review? How accessible would the information be if it were written in standard paragraphs?
2. What does the directness of the document reveal about the intended audience? Would it be suitable for a college classroom?

Appreciating Language

1. What language do the writers use in describing the Taiwanese? Do they attempt to be neutral, or does their word choice favor one nationality over another?
2. Kenna and Lacy suggest that many Taiwanese find Americans to be "abrupt." Is this a good word choice? Does the guide express common prejudices?

Writing Suggestions

1. Using Kenna and Lacy's entry as a source, write a short process paper instructing how an American should present an idea or product in Taiwan. Assume you are writing to sales representatives traveling to Taiwan for the first time. Provide step-by-step suggestions for how they should conduct themselves from the moment they enter a seminar room to make a presentation.
2. *Collaborative writing:* Working with a group of students, discuss the differences between high school teachers and college instructors, then develop a chart contrasting their attitudes toward absenteeism, late homework, tests, and research papers.

Responding to IMAGES

Where the Blame Lies, political cartoon, *1891*   Bettmann/Corbis

1. What is your first reaction to this 1891 cartoon? Does it strike you as racist, silly, or curious?
2. What does the caption suggest? What were immigrants being blamed for?
3. Do you find it ironic that the cartoonist chose to include the Statue of Liberty in the background? Why or why not?
4. *Collaborative writing:* Discuss this cartoon with a group of students. Did any of them have ancestors who emigrated to United States in that era? What do they think motivated people at the time to blame immigration for social problems? Do they see a link between the anti-immigrant sentiments of the 1890s and those expressed today?
5. *Visual analysis:* Study the facial expressions of the immigrants. How would you characterize them? How does the cartoonist position Uncle Sam to give him greater stature?
6. *Other modes*
   ■ Write a *description* to accompany this cartoon in a high school history book or a museum display. Try to objectively explain the attitudes expressed by the cartoonist.
   ■ Write a *cause-and-effect* essay that explains reasons why many Americans, even those descended from immigrants, oppose immigration.
   ■ Develop a *division* essay that details different reasons that people have for calling for immigration reform.
   ■ Write a *persuasive* essay clearly stating your position on immigration.

Comparison and Contrast Checklist

✔ Are your subjects closely related enough to make a valid comparison?

✔ Have you identified the key points of both subjects?

✔ Have you selected the best method of organizing your paper?

✔ Is the comparison easy to follow? Are transitions clear?

✔ Does the comparison meet reader needs and expectations?

✔ Have you defined terms or provided background information needed by readers to fully appreciate the comparison?

✔ Is your thesis clearly stated and located where it will have the greatest impact?

Companion Website

See **http://www.thomsonedu.com/english/sundance** for additional information on writing comparison.

PROCESS
EXPLAINING
HOW THINGS WORK
AND GIVING DIRECTIONS

23

WHAT IS PROCESS?

Process writing shows how things work or how specific tasks are accomplished. The first type of process writing demonstrates how a complex procedure or event occurs. Biology textbooks describe how the heart operates by separating its actions into a series of steps. This chain-of-events explanation also can illustrate how an engine works, how inflation affects the economy, how the IRS audits an account, or how police respond to a 911 call. Process writing is a directed form of narration that explains how an operation takes place.

The second type of process writing gives directions for completing a specific task. Recipes, owners' manuals, textbooks, and home repair articles provide readers with step-by-step directions to bake a cake, rotate tires, create a website, write a research paper, detect a computer virus, or fix a leaking roof. These instructions are challenging to create because writers may be unable to determine how much background information to provide and may easily forget a critical piece of information.

 To read more about process, along with interactive examples and opportunities to work with interactive texts, click on "The Rhetorical Patterns of Inquiry" from the main menu of *Comp21*.

Explaining How Things Work

Just as division writing seeks to explain an abstract or complex subject by separating it into smaller categories, process writing separates the workings of complicated operations into steps or stages. In the essay, "How Our Skins Got Their

Color" (page 512) Marvin Harris explains the role sunlight and Vitamin D played in giving human beings differing complexions:

> Vitamin D can be obtained from a few foods, primarily the oils and livers of marine fish. But inland populations must rely on the sun's rays and their own skins for the supply of this crucial substance. The particular color of a human population's skin, therefore, represents in large degree a trade-off between the hazards of too much versus too little solar radiation: acute sunburn and skin cancer on the one hand, and rickets and osteomalacia on the other. It is this trade-off that largely accounts for the preponderance of brown people in the world and for the general tendency for skin color to be darkest among equatorial populations and lightest among populations dwelling at higher latitudes.

When you write explanations, it is important to consider your readers' existing knowledge. You may need to define technical terms, use illustrative analogies, such as comparing the heart to a pump or a computer virus to an human infection, and relate brief narratives so that readers will understand the process. Some writers will use an extended analogy, comparing a nuclear power plant to a tea kettle or terrorism to a brush fire.

WRITING ACTIVITY

Develop an outline listing ideas for a paper explaining one of the following topics:

1. The admissions procedure at your college

2. The functions of the heart, lungs, or liver

3. The way you perform a task at home, at school, or in your job

4. The formation of a hurricane or tornado

5. The process determining which teams will play in the World Series or Super Bowl

6. The way couples resolve conflicts

7. The process of how a bill becomes a law

8. The procedure of a civil or criminal trial

9. The way children learn to walk, talk, or read

10. The process of getting married, filing for divorce, or adopting a child

STRATEGIES | for Writing Explanations

Critical Thinking and Prewriting

1. **List possible topics.** Choose subjects you are familiar with and that can be fully explained given the scope of the assignment.
2. **Prewrite to explore the most promising topics.** Use freewriting and brainstorming to identify topics best suited to the assignment. Avoid overly complex subjects that require extensive background explanation or are subject to numerous interpretations.
3. **Study your topic carefully.** Note the principal features that need emphasis. Highlight features that are commonly confused or might be difficult for readers to understand.

Planning

1. **Determine how much background information is needed.** Your readers may require, for example, a basic knowledge of how normal cells divide before being able to comprehend the way cancer cells develop. In some instances, you have to address widely believed misconceptions. If you were to explain criminal investigation methods, you might have to point out how actual police operations differ from those depicted on television.
2. **Define clear starting and ending points.** In some cases the process may have an obvious beginning and end. Flowers emerge from buds, grow, turn color, and fall off. But the process of a recession may have no clear-cut beginning and no defined end. If you were to write a paper about the process of getting a divorce, would you stop when final papers are signed or continue to discuss alimony and child visitation rights? When does a divorce end?
3. **Separate the process into logical stages.** Readers will naturally assume all the stages are equally significant unless you indicate their value or importance. Minor points should not be overemphasized by being divided into distinct steps.
4. **Develop an outline listing steps and major points to guide the first draft.** Keep your readers in mind—you are teaching when you write process. Your goal is to transfer your knowledge or experience to your readers so they will share your understanding of a particular operation or event.
5. **Determine whether visual aids such as photographs, diagrams, or charts can illustrate the process.**

Writing the First Draft

1. **Keep your audience in mind as you write.** The key problem in explaining something you are familiar with is assuming that your readers share your knowledge base.

   ▪ Realize that anyone reading your process paper knows less than you.

   ▪ Consider your readers' perceptual world as you explain ideas. What analogies or references will they understand?

2. **Use transitional phrases and paragraph breaks to separate stages.** Statements such as "at the same time" or "two days later" can help readers follow the chronology and direction of events.

3. **Stress the importance of time relationships.** Process writing creates a slow-motion explanation that can be misleading if the chain of events naturally occurs in a short period. You can avoid this confusion by opening with a "real-time" description of the process:

   > The test car collided with the barrier at thirty-five miles an hour. In less than a tenth of a second the bumper crumpled, sending shock waves through the length of the vehicle as the fenders folded back like a crushed beer can. At the same instant sensors triggered the air bag to deploy with a rapid explosion so that it inflated before the test dummy struck the steering wheel.

   The rest of the paper might repeat this process in four or five pages, slowly relating each stage in great detail.

4. **Use images, details, narratives, and examples to enrich the description of each stage.** Give readers a full appreciation of each stage by describing it in details they can grasp. Avoid long strings of nonessential, technical language. Use comparisons and narratives to provide readers with clear pictures of events and situations.

5. **Alert readers to possible variations.** If the process is subject to change or alternative forms, present readers with the most common type. Indicate, either in the introduction or in each stage, that exceptions or variations can occur.

Revising

1. **Review your plan and goals; then read your paper aloud with your reader in mind.**

   ▪ Determine whether your paper provides enough information to explain the process.

   ▪ Examine your paper for terms or concepts that need definition or further explanation.

2. **Review transitions and paragraph breaks for clarity.** Essentially, an explanation paper describes a process in slow motion, breaking a complex chain of events into separate steps.

   - Do not cluster too many important ideas into a single step.
   - Avoid exaggerating the significance of a minor point by isolating it as a single step.

3. **Review the use of visual aids for accuracy.**

4. **Use peer review to test your paper.**

   - Ask others how easy it is for them to understand the process. What improvements could be made?

Editing and Proofreading

1. **Read the paper aloud to test for clarity.** When you explain a process, it is important to use language that readers can understand.

   - Make sure that you define technical or widely misunderstood terms.
   - Examine the level of diction to determine whether it is suited to your readers' existing knowledge.

2. **Use peer editing to locate errors you may have missed.**

GIVING DIRECTIONS

Directions are step-by-step instructions guiding readers through a specific goal or task. Recipes and repair manuals show readers how to prepare a meal or change a tire. Process writing can also include advice on buying a house or negotiating a loan. In "Fender Benders: Do's and Don'ts" (page 507), Armond D. Budish provides tips for drivers involved in a minor collision:

> 1. **Stop! It's the Law.**
>   No matter how serious or minor the accident, stop immediately. If possible, don't move your car—especially if someone has been injured. Leaving cars as they were when the accident occurred helps the police determine what happened. Of course, if your car is blocking traffic or will cause another accident where it is, then move it to the nearest safe location.

Budish, like many other writers, finds it effective to tell people what *not* to do. Negative instructions work best when you are trying to get readers to change their habits or avoid common errors. Budish's last tip warns drivers not to make a frequent mistake:

> **10. Don't Be Too Quick to Accept a Settlement.**
> If the other driver is at fault and there's any chance you've been injured, don't rush to accept a settlement from that person's insurance company. You may not know the extent of your injuries for some time, and once you accept a settlement, it's difficult to get an "upgrade." Before settling, consult with a lawyer who handles personal injury cases.

For giving instructions, you may find it useful to number steps and provide visual aids, such as diagrams, charts, photographs, or maps. Highlighting, bold type, and underlining can dramatize text and make the document easy to read in an emergency.

WRITING ACTIVITY

Select one of the topics below and use prewriting techniques to develop a plan for a short set of directions. Remember to consider each target audience.

1. Provide directions to the campus stadium for out-of-town visitors arriving at the local airport. Give readers visual references, such as landmarks, to identify key intersections.

2. Inform new students how to check out books from the campus library.

3. Tell people how *not* to plan a family vacation.

4. Instruct students how to balance work and school.

5. Direct consumers on using credit wisely; warn them about accumulating debt.

6. Provide safety tips for vacationers renting a sailboat, motorbike, or snowmobile.

7. Warn senior citizens about a common telemarketing scam; provide tips to identify fraudulent offers.

8. Advise new homeowners on the most important actions they can take to protect the environment.

9. Use your own experience to create a list of suggestions to help students study for exams, save money on books, lose weight, read faster, save time, or exercise.

10. Offer tips to parents concerned about their children's use of the Internet. Alert them to potential hazards and suggest remedies.

STRATEGIES for Writing Directions

Critical Thinking and Prewriting

1. **List possible topics under the phrase "How to . . ."**
   - Select subjects you are familiar with and can fully explain in a page or two of directions:
     How to change the oil in your car
     How to write a will without a lawyer
     How to cook in a wok
     How to save money on clothes
     How to choose the right day care center
   - Consider consumer decisions you have recently made. You may already have a great deal of knowledge based on personal experiences in making major purchases or decisions.

2. **Prewrite to explore the most promising topics.**
   - Freewriting and brainstorming can help identify topics best suited to the assignment.
   - Limit the subject to a single task or problem—how to change a tire instead of how to maintain your car.

3. **Consider your audience carefully.** Unlike other types of writing, giving directions requires you to ask people to not only *read* but *act* on your ideas.
   - Determine how much knowledge your readers have.
   - Consider any misconceptions or confusion that must be addressed before proceeding.

Planning

1. **Define the scope of your directions.** Directions must be focused, especially if you are providing step-by-step instructions rather than advice.
   - Clearly define the task or goal—you should be directing readers to accomplish something specific. Directions must be goal centered.

2. **Define clear starting and ending points.** Give readers clear instructions about when to start the process and when to end it. In providing first aid instructions, for example, you must first teach readers to identify situations in which actions must be taken and tell them when to stop.

3. **Make sure directions are self-contained.** A recipe, for example, should list *all* the ingredients, appliances, and instructions required to accomplish the task.
   - Readers should not be directed to another source for information to complete the process.
4. **Break the process into even steps.** Avoid placing too much information or too many actions in a single step.
5. **Consider using numbered steps.** Readers find it easier to follow numbered steps and can mark their places if interrupted.
6. **Consider using visual aids such as charts, graphs, diagrams, maps, or photographs to illustrate the process.** Make sure visuals are clearly labeled and directly connected to specific steps in the written directions.
7. **Prepare a clearly organized outline.**

Writing the First Draft
1. **Using your outline as a guide, write a draft, keeping your goal and your readers in mind.** Write with your readers in mind; consider them strangers to your process who need exact details, such as dates, times, and room numbers.
2. **Provide complete instructions.** Do not tell readers to "remove the flat tire" without explaining the process or to "put the cake in the oven for thirty minutes until it's done" without describing what it is supposed to look like when it is "done."
   - Remember, readers are doing this process for the first time and must rely on your directions; give full details about each step.
3. **Give negative instructions.** Tell people what *not* to do, especially if you know that people are prone to make errors, skip steps, substitute cheaper materials, or ignore potential problems.
4. **Warn readers of possible events that they may misinterpret as mistakes.** If, at some point in the process, the mixture readers are working with suddenly changes color or the machine they are operating makes excess noise, they may assume they have made a mistake and stop. If a person assembling a desk discovers that the legs are wobbly, he or she may think the product is defective. If this is normal—if the legs tighten up when the drawers are installed—let readers know.
5. **Consider using visual aids.** Large print, capital letters, bold or italic type, and underlining can highlight text for easy reading.
   - Remember, readers may have to refer to your document while working, so make it as easy to skim as possible.

6. **Warn readers of any potential hazards to their safety, health, property, or the environment.** When you give directions, you assume a legal liability. Anyone who is injured while following your instructions is in a position to sue for damages.

   - Warn readers about dangerous chemicals, fire hazards, and electrical shocks that could threaten their safety or health.
   - Alert readers to potential property damage that can result from improper use of materials.
   - Inform readers of any legal sanctions they may encounter. Warn car-owners about the proper disposal of used motor oil or old tires.
   - Remind homeowners to check local building codes before starting major projects that may require permits.

Revising

1. **Review your outline and then read your draft for completeness, organization, and readability.**

   - Directions should be stated in short, precise sentences. Delete wordy or unnecessary phrases. Instead of writing "The next thing you should do is . . . ," use numbered steps.
   - Directions should provide clear descriptions of each step. Telling readers to "sand the board" may leave them wondering whether they should simply remove rough edges or work on the surface until it is as smooth as glass.
   - Let readers know when each step ends—each step should have a defined goal.

2. **Review the overall organization and transitions.** Have you broken the process into workable steps? Is too much information placed in a single step?

3. **Examine any visual aids for accuracy.** Make sure any diagrams, maps, or charts are clearly labeled and directly support the text of the document.

4. **Test your writing through peer review.** Writing directions is challenging because it is hard to put yourself in the place of someone lacking what might be second nature to you.

   - Ask people to read your paper; then quiz them on important points.
   - Readers unfamiliar with the process may spot missing critical information that you have overlooked.

Editing and Proofreading

1. **Read the paper aloud to test for clarity.** In explaining a process it is important to use language readers can understand.
   - Make sure you define technical or widely misunderstood terms.
   - Examine the level of diction to determine whether it is suited to your readers' existing knowledge.
2. **Use peer editing to locate errors that you may have missed.**

STUDENT PAPER

This paper was written in response to the following assignment:

Write a 500-word process paper providing directions to accomplish a specific task. You may include graphs, charts, diagrams, or numbered steps.

Securing Your Home

Homeowners frequently think of security only when planning a vacation. Leaving home for a week or two, they install additional locks, set timers to trigger lights, purchase sophisticated monitoring systems, alert neighbors, and hope their homes will not be robbed in their absence. But most homes are not burglarized while their owners are thousands of miles away. And most burglaries do not occur in the dead of night. Most houses are robbed before 9 p.m., often while their owners are near or inside the residence. Your house is more likely to be robbed while you are grilling in the backyard or watching a football game than when you are on a cruise or camping trip.

Although it is impossible to make any home "burglar proof," there are some actions you can take to protect your home and property:

1. **Document your assets.** Make a list of your valuables. Photograph or videotape each room in your home. Keep receipts of major purchases. Store these and other records in a safe deposit box so you can prove any losses. Review your insurance policies to see if special items such as furs, artwork, or coin collections are covered.

2. **Identify valuables.** Engrave computers, television, cameras, stereos, and VCR's with your name or an identifying number. Police often discover stolen property but have no way of contacting the owners.

3. **Always lock your doors.** Nothing attracts a thief more than an open garage or unlatched screen door. Lock up even when you plan to visit a neighbor for "just a minute." That "minute" can easily become half an hour, plenty of time for a burglary to occur. Don't leave doors open if you are going to be upstairs or in the basement.

4. **Install only security systems you will use.** Many homeowners invest in expensive, high-tech systems that are so cumbersome, they leave them off most of the time. A cheap alarm system used twenty-four hours a day provides more protection than a state-of- the-art system used randomly.

5. **Trim shrubbery around entrances and windows.** Don't provide camouflage for burglars. Thieves can easily conceal themselves behind foliage while jimmying doors and windows. Trim hedges and shrubs below window level (see photo).

6. **Network with neighbors.** Let neighbors know if you expect deliveries, house guests, or contractors. Thieves have posed as moving crews, casually looting a house and loading a truck while neighbors look on.

7. **Store valuables in attics and basements.** Thieves are reluctant to venture beyond the ground floor, which usually offers numerous exits in case of detection.

Trim hedges below window level   © Royalty Free/CORBIS

Finally, call the police the moment you discover that a burglary has occurred. If you return home and find evidence of a break-in—*do not go inside!* The thieves, who might be armed, could still be on the premises. Go to a neighbor's and call the police. Never attempt to confront a burglar yourself. No personal possession is worth risking death or a disabling injury.

Questions for Review and Revision

1. The student offers seven directions; would these be easier to recall if emphasized by a subtitle—"Seven tips to keep your home secure"?
2. What misconceptions does the student address?
3. How important is the final warning?
4. The student writes in the second person, directly addressing the readers. Would the paper be less effective if written in the third person?
5. Does the level of language, diction, and tone suit the intended audience?
6. Read the paper aloud. Is this document easy to read, easy to remember? Could revisions increase its clarity?

Writing Suggestions

1. Using this paper as a model, write a set of instructions directed to a general audience about improving the performance of your car, installing a new computer program, planning a trip or a wedding, losing weight, choosing a pet, or preparing for a job interview.
2. *Collaborative writing:* Discuss this paper with other students. Using some of its ideas, work together to write a brief set of instructions on securing a dorm room or apartment.

SUGGESTED TOPICS FOR WRITING PROCESS

General Assignments

Explaining How Things Work

Write a process paper on any of the following topics. Assume you are writing to a general, college-educated audience. You may develop your explanation using narratives, comparisons, and definitions. Explain the process as a clearly stated chain of events. Draw from your own experiences.

- How students register for courses
- The operation of an appliance, such as a microwave, washing machine, or refrigerator
- The process of a disease or disability
- The training of new employees
- How a computer virus works
- The way the body loses fat through diet or exercise
- A method of introducing a new product in the marketplace
- How restaurants prevent food poisoning
- A legal process, such as an arrest, eviction, or bankruptcy
- How real-estate agents sell a house

Giving Directions

Write a process paper giving specific directions to complete a specific task. You may wish to place your instructions in numbered steps rather than standard paragraphs. Remember to highlight potential hazards.

- How to protect your computer against viruses
- How to purchase a new or used car
- How to deter a mugger or attacker
- How to quit smoking
- How to find a job
- How to avoid identity theft
- How to safely operate a piece of industrial or scientific equipment
- How to treat a second-degree burn
- How to teach children to save money, eat properly, read books, or avoid dangerous situations

 To create your own interactive writing project, use the textual, visual, and video libraries on *Comp21*. For the main menu, choose "Build Your Own Occasion for Writing."

Writing in Context

1. Imagine that you have been selected to write a section for a student handbook instructing freshmen how to register for classes. Write a step-by-step paper giving complete instructions. Give exact room numbers, times, and locations. You may wish to refer to a campus map. When you complete a

draft of your paper, review it carefully to see whether you have left out any essential information.

2. Select a process that you have learned on a job and write instructions suitable for training a new employee. Consider how your job may have changed. Give trainees the benefit of your experience and add tips that might not be included in the standard job descriptions. Warn readers, for instance, of common problems that arise.

3. Select a process from one of your textbooks and rewrite it for a sixth-grade class. Simplify the language and use analogies that sixth graders will understand.

STRATEGIES | for Reading Process

As you read the process entries in this chapter, keep these questions in mind:

Context
1. What is the writer's goal—to explain or instruct?
2. Is the goal clearly stated?
3. What are the critical stages or steps in the process?
4. What errors should readers avoid?

Strategy
1. What is the nature of the intended audience? How much existing knowledge does the writer assume that readers have?
2. How are steps or stages separated? Are transitions clearly established?
3. Are the instructions easy to follow?
4. Are any special effects, such as highlighting, numbered steps, and visual aids, skillfully used?

Language
1. Are technical terms clearly defined and illustrated?
2. Does the writer use concrete words to create clear images of what is being explained?

Mortimer Adler (1902–2001) was born in New York City. He taught psychology at Columbia University, then moved to Chicago, where he taught the philosophy of law for more than twenty years. He resigned from the University of Chicago in 1952 to head the Institute for Philosophical Research in San Francisco. His books include **How to Read a Book** and **Philosopher at Large: An Intellectual Autobiography.** Adler became famous as an editor of the **Encyclopedia Britannica** and leader of the Great Books Program of the University of Chicago. This program encouraged adults from all careers to read and discuss classic works. This essay first appeared in the **Saturday Review of Literature** in 1940.

How to Mark a Book

Before reading Adler's essay, consider your own reading habits. Do you read with a pen in your hand? Do you scan a work first or simply begin with the first line? Do you take notes? Do you have problems remembering what you read?

You know you have to read "between the lines" to get the most out of any- 1   introduction
thing. I want to persuade you to do something equally important in the course
of your reading. I want to persuade you to "write between the lines." Unless
you do, you are not likely to do the most efficient kind of reading. I contend,
quite bluntly, that marking up a book is not an act of mutilation but of love.   thesis

    You shouldn't mark up a book which isn't yours. Librarians (or your 2
friends) who lend you books expect you to keep them clean, and you
should. If you decide that I am right about the usefulness of marking books,   disclaimer
you will have to buy them. Most of the world's great books are available today, in reprint editions, at less than a dollar.

    There are two ways in which one can own a book. The first is the prop- 3
erty right you establish by paying for it, just as you pay for clothes and furniture. But this act of purchase is only the prelude to possession. Full own-   defines "full
ership comes only when you have made it a part of yourself, and the best   ownership"
way to make yourself a part of it is by writing in it. An illustration may make
the point clear. You buy a beefsteak and transfer it from the butcher's icebox
to your own. But you do not own the beefsteak in the most important sense

501

until you consume it and get it into your bloodstream. I am arguing that books, too, must be absorbed in your bloodstream to do you any good.

describes "false reverence for paper" 4   Confusion about what it means to *own* a book leads people to a false reverence for paper, binding, and type—a respect for the physical thing—the craft of the printer rather than the genius of the author. They forget that it is possible for a man to acquire the idea, to possess the beauty, which a great book contains, without staking his claim by pasting his bookplate inside the cover. Having a fine library doesn't prove that its owner has a mind enriched by books; it proves nothing more than that he, his father, or his wife, was rich enough to buy them.

classifies three types of book owners 5   There are three kinds of book owners. The first has all the standard sets and best-sellers—unread, untouched. (This deluded individual owns woodpulp and ink, not books.) The second has a great many books—a few of them read through, most of them dipped into, but all of them as clean and shiny as the day they were bought. (This person would probably like to make books his own, but is restrained by a false respect for their physical appearance.) The third has a few books or many—every one of them dogeared and dilapidated, shaken and loosened by continual use, marked and scribbled in from front to back. (This man owns books.)

6   Is it false respect, you may ask, to preserve intact and unblemished a beautifully printed book, an elegantly bound edition? Of course not. I'd no more scribble all over a first edition of *Paradise Lost* than I'd give my baby a set of crayons and an original Rembrandt! I wouldn't mark up a painting or a statue. Its soul, so to speak, is inseparable from its body. And the beauty of a rare edition or of a richly manufactured volume is like that of a painting or a statue.

7   But the soul of a book *can* be separated from its body. A book is more like the score of a piece of music than it is like a painting. No great musician confuses a symphony with the printed sheets of music. Arturo Toscanini reveres Brahms, but Toscanini's score of the C-minor Symphony is so thoroughly marked up that no one but the maestro himself can read it. The reason why a great conductor makes notations on his musical scores—marks them up again and again each time he returns to study them—is the reason why you should mark your books. If your respect for magnificent binding or typography gets in the way, buy yourself a cheap edition and pay your respects to the author.

explains need to write as you read 8   Why is marking up a book indispensable to reading? First, it keeps you awake. (And I don't mean merely conscious; I mean wide awake.) In the second place, reading, if it is active, is thinking, and thinking tends to express itself in words, spoken or written. The marked book is usually the thought-through book. Finally, writing helps you remember the thoughts you had, or the thoughts the author expressed. Let me develop these three points.

If reading is to accomplish anything more than passing time, it must be active. You can't let your eyes glide across the lines of a book and come up with an understanding of what you have read. Now an ordinary piece of light fiction, like say, *Gone with the Wind*, doesn't require the most active kind of reading. The books you read for pleasure can be read in a state of relaxation, and nothing is lost. But a great book, rich in ideas and beauty, a book that raises and tries to answer great fundamental questions, demands the most active reading of which you are capable. You don't absorb the ideas of John Dewey the way you absorb the crooning of Mr. Vallee. You have to reach for them. That you cannot do while you're asleep.
9 defines "active reading"

If, when you've finished reading a book, the pages are filled with your notes, you know that you read actively. The most famous active reader of great books I know is President Hutchins, of the University of Chicago. He also has the hardest schedule of business activities of any man I know. He invariably reads with a pencil, and sometimes, when he picks up a book and pencil in the evening, he finds himself, instead of making intelligent notes, drawing what he calls "caviar factories" on the margins. When that happens, he puts the book down. He knows he's too tired to read, and he's just wasting time.
10

But, you may ask, why is writing necessary? Well, the physical act of writing, with your own hand, brings words and sentences more sharply before your mind and preserves them better in your memory. To set down your reaction to important words and sentences you have read, and the questions they have raised in your mind, is to preserve those reactions and sharpen those questions.
11 why write?

Even if you wrote on a scratch pad, and threw the paper away when you had finished writing, your grasp of the book would be surer. But you don't have to throw the paper away. The margins (top and bottom, as well as side), the end-papers, the very space between the lines, are all available. They aren't sacred. And, best of all, your marks and notes become an integral part of the book and stay there forever. You can pick up the book the following week or year, and there are all your points of agreement, disagreement, doubt, and inquiry. It's like resuming an interrupted conversation with the advantage of being able to pick up where you left off.
12

And that is exactly what reading a book should be: a conversation between you and the author. Presumably he knows more about the subject than you do; naturally, you'll have the proper humility as you approach him. But don't let anybody tell you that a reader is supposed to be solely on the receiving end. Understanding is a two-way operation; learning doesn't
13 reading as conversation

consist in being an empty receptacle. The learner has to question himself and question the teacher. He even has to argue with the teacher, once he understands what the teacher is saying. And marking a book is literally an expression of your differences, or agreements of opinion, with the author.

14   There are all kinds of devices for marking a book intelligently and fruitfully. Here's the way I do it:

uses numbered
steps and italics
for easy reading

1. *Underlining:* of major points, of important or forceful statements.
2. *Vertical lines at the margin:* to emphasize a statement already underlined.
3. *Star, asterisk, or other doo-dad at the margin:* to be used sparingly, to emphasize the ten or twenty most important statements in the book. (You may want to fold the bottom corner of each page on which you use such marks. It won't hurt the sturdy paper on which most modern books are printed, and you will be able to take the book off the shelf at any time and, by opening it at the folded-corner page, refresh your recollection of the book.)
4. *Numbers in the margin:* to indicate the sequence of points the author makes in developing a single argument.
5. *Numbers of other pages in the margin:* to indicate where else in the book the author made points relevant to the point marked; to tie up the ideas in a book, which, though they may be separated by many pages, belong together.
6. *Circling of key words or phrases.*
7. *Writing in the margin, or at the top or bottom of the page, for the sake of:* recording questions (and perhaps answers) which a passage raised in your mind; reducing a complicated discussion to a simple statement; recording the sequence of major points right through the book. I use the end-papers at the back of the book to make a personal index of the author's points in the order of their appearance.

15   The front end-papers are, to me, the most important. Some people reserve them for a fancy bookplate. I reserve them for fancy thinking. After I have finished reading the book and making my personal index on the back end-papers, I turn to the front and try to outline the book, not page by page, or point by point (I've already done that at the back), but as an integrated structure, with a basic unity and an order of parts. This outline is, to me, the measure of my understanding of the work.

16   If you're a die-hard anti-book-marker, you may object that the margins, the space between the lines, and the end-papers don't give you room enough. All right. How about using a scratch pad slightly smaller than the

page-size of the book—so that the edges of the sheets won't protrude? Make your index, outlines, and even your notes on the pad, and then insert these sheets permanently inside the front and back covers of the book.

Or, you may say that this business of marking books is going to slow up 17 your reading. It probably will. That's one of the reasons for doing it. Most of us have been taken in by the notion that speed of reading is a measure of our intelligence. There is no such thing as the right speed for intelligent reading. Some things should be read quickly and effortlessly, and some should be read slowly and even laboriously. The sign of intelligence in reading is the ability to read different things according to their worth. In the case of good books, the point is not to see how many of them you can get through, but rather how many can get through you—how many you can make your own. A few friends are better than a thousand acquaintances. If this be your aim, as it should be, you will not be impatient if it takes more time and effort to read a great book than it does a newspaper.

goal of reading good books

You may have one final objection to marking books. You can't lend them 18 to your friends because nobody else can read them without being distracted by your notes. Furthermore, you won't want to lend them because a marked copy is a kind of intellectual diary, and lending it is almost like giving your mind away.

If your friend wishes to read your *Plutarch's Lives, Shakespeare,* or *The Fed-* 19 *eralist Papers,* tell him gently but firmly to buy a copy. You will lend him your car or your coat—but your books are as much a part of you as your head or your heart.

conclusion

Understanding Context

1. In Adler's view, when do you really *own* a book? What makes a book truly yours? What makes a book like a steak?
2. What does Adler mean by the "soul" of a book? How does respecting it differ from respecting its "body"?
3. Why is it important, in Adler's view, to write as you read?
4. *Critical thinking:* This essay was first published more than sixty years ago. Are Adler's suggestions any different from the study skills you may have learned in high school or college?

Evaluating Strategy

1. What audience is Adler addressing?
2. *Other modes:* Where does Adler use *comparison, description,* and *classification* in developing this essay?

3. Adler provides seven suggestions that are stated in italics and numbered. If this advice were written in a standard paragraph, would it be as effective? Why or why not?

Appreciating Language

1. The *Saturday Review of Literature* had a general but highly literary readership, much like that of today's *New Yorker* or *Vanity Fair*. Does the tone and style of the article seem suited to this audience?
2. Are there any words, phrases, references, or expressions in this sixty-year-old article that need updating?

Writing Suggestions

1. Using Adler's seven suggestions, write a brief one-page guide on active reading directed to high school students.
2. *Collaborative writing:* Adler presents tips for active reading. Work with a group of students and discuss their experiences in studying for examinations. Record your ideas and suggestions, and then write a well-organized list of tips to help new students develop successful study skills.

Armond D. Budish is an attorney and consumer-law reporter. He practices law in Ohio, where he writes columns on consumer issues for the *Cleveland Plain Dealer.* He has also published articles for *Family Circle* magazine. His book *How to Beat the Catastrophic Costs of Nursing Home Care* was published in 1989.

Fender Benders: Do's and Don't's

As you read this article, notice how Budish makes use of numbered steps and bold type to make this Family Circle *article easy to skim.*

The car ahead of you stops suddenly. You hit the brakes, but you just 1 can't stop in time. Your front bumper meets the rear end of the other car. *Ouch!*

There doesn't seem to be any damage, and it must be your lucky day be- 2 cause the driver you hit agrees that it's not worth hassling with insurance claims and risking a premium increase. So after exchanging addresses, you go your separate ways.

Imagine your surprise when you open the mail a few weeks later only to 3 discover a letter from your "victim's" lawyer demanding $10,000 to cover car repairs, pain and suffering. Apparently the agreeable gentleman decided to disagree, then went ahead and filed a police report blaming you for the incident and for his damages.

When automobiles meet by accident, do you know how to respond? 4

Here are 10 practical tips that can help you avoid costly legal and insurance hassles.

1. **Stop! It's the Law.**

    No matter how serious or minor the accident, stop immediately. If 5 possible, don't move your car—especially if someone has been injured. Leaving the cars as they were when the accident occurred helps the police determine what happened. Of course, if your car is blocking traffic or will cause another accident where it is, then move it to the nearest safe location.

    For every rule there are exceptions, though. If, for example, you 6 are rear-ended at night in an unsafe area, it's wisest to keep on going and notify the police later. There have been cases in which people were robbed or assaulted when they got out of their cars.

2. Zip Loose Lips.

7   Watch what you say after an accident. Although this may sound harsh, even an innocent "I'm sorry" could later be construed as an admission of fault. Also be sure not to accuse the other driver of causing the accident. Since you don't know how a stranger will react to your remarks, you run the risk of making a bad situation worse.

8   Remember, you are not the judge or jury; it's not up to you to decide who is or is not at fault. Even if you think you caused the accident, you might be wrong. For example: Assume you were driving 15 miles over the speed limit. What you probably were not aware of is that the other driver's blood-alcohol level exceeded the legal limits, so he was at least equally at fault.

3. Provide Required Information.

9   If you are involved in an accident, you are required in most states to give your name, address and car registration number to: any person injured in the accident; the owner, driver or passenger in any car that was damaged in the accident; a police officer on the scene. If you don't own the car (say it belongs to a friend or your parents), you should provide the name and address of the owner.

10   You must produce this information even if there are no apparent injuries or damages and even if you didn't cause the accident. Most states don't require you to provide the name of your insurance company, although it's usually a good idea to do so. However, *don't* discuss the amount of your coverage—that might inspire the other person to "realize" his injuries are more serious than he originally thought.

11   What should you do if you hit a parked car and the owner is not around? The law requires you to leave a note with your name, and the other identifying information previously mentioned, in a secure place on the car (such as under the windshield wiper).

4. Get Required Information.

12   You should obtain from the others involved in the accident the same information that you provide them with. However, if the other driver refuses to cooperate, at least get the license number and the make and model of the car to help police track down the owner.

5. Call the Police.

13   It's obvious that if it's a serious accident in which someone is injured, the police should be called immediately. That's both the law

and common sense. But what if the accident seems minor? Say you're stopped, another car taps you in the rear. If it's absolutely clear to both drivers that there is no damage or injury, you each can go your merry way. But that's the exception.

Normally, you should call the police to substantiate what 14 occurred. In most cities police officers will come to the scene, even for minor accidents, but if they won't, you and the other driver should go to the station (of the city where the accident occurred) to file a report. Ask to have an officer check out both cars.

If you are not at fault, be wary of accepting the other driver's 15 suggestion that you leave the police out of it and arrange a private settlement. When you submit your $500 car-repair estimate several weeks later, you could discover that the other driver has developed "amnesia" and denies being anywhere near the accident. If the police weren't present on the scene, you may not have a legal leg to stand on.

Even if you *are* at fault, it's a good idea to involve the police. 16 Why? Because a police officer will note the extent of the other driver's damages in his or her report, limiting your liability. Without police presence the other driver can easily inflate the amount of the damages.

6. **Identify Witnesses.**

Get the names and addresses of any witnesses, in case there's a le- 17 gal battle some time in the future. Ask bystanders or other motorists who stop whether they saw the accident; if they answer "yes," get their identifying information. It is also helpful to note the names and badge numbers of all police officers on the scene.

7. **Go to the Hospital.**

If there's a chance that you've been injured, go directly to a hos- 18 pital emergency room or to your doctor. The longer you wait, the more you may jeopardize your health and the more difficult it may be to get reimbursed for your injuries if they turn out to be serious.

8. **File a Report.**

Every driver who is involved in an automobile incident in which in- 19 juries occur must fill out an accident report. Even if the property damage is only in the range of $200 to $1,000, most states require that an accident report be filed. You must do this fairly quickly, usually in 1 to 30 days. Forms may be obtained and filed with the local motor vehicle department or police station in the city where the accident occurred.

9. Consider Filing an Insurance Claim.

20   Talk with your insurance agent as soon as possible after an accident. He or she can help you decide if you should file an insurance claim or pay out of your own pocket.

21   For example, let's say you caused an accident and the damages totaled $800. You carry a $250 deductible, leaving you with a possible $550 insurance claim. If you do submit a claim, your insurance rates are likely to go up, an increase that will probably continue for about three years. You should compare that figure to the $550 claim to determine whether to file a claim or to pay the cost yourself. (Also keep in mind that multiple claims sometimes make it harder to renew your coverage.)

10. Don't Be Too Quick to Accept a Settlement.

22   If the other driver is at fault and there's any chance you've been injured, don't rush to accept a settlement from that person's insurance company. You may not know the extent of your injuries for some time, and once you accept a settlement, it's difficult to get an "upgrade." Before settling, consult with a lawyer who handles personal injury cases.

23   When you *haven't* been injured and you receive a fair offer to cover the damage to your car, you can go ahead and accept it.

Understanding Context

1. What problems can motorists have if they are careless about handling even minor accidents?
2. What are some of the most important things you should do if involved in a fender bender?
3. Why should you go to the hospital even if you have what appears to be a minor injury?
4. *Critical thinking:* Should this article be printed as a pamphlet and distributed to drivers' education classes? Have you known anyone who has gotten into difficulties that could have been avoided if he or she had followed the writer's advice?

Evaluating Strategy

1. How does Budish arouse reader attention in the opening?
2. How effective are the numbered steps? Would the article lose impact if printed in standard paragraphs?

3. How easy is this article to remember? Can you put it down and recall the main points?

Appreciating Language

1. This article was written for *Family Circle*. Does the language appear to be targeted to a female audience?
2. Why does Budish, who is an attorney, avoid legal terminology?
3. Does Budish's language create concrete images that make strong impressions to dramatize his subject?

Writing Suggestions

1. Using this article as a model, provide the general public with a similar list of tips to prevent heart disease, deter muggers, prepare their children for school, or save money for retirement.
2. *Collaborative writing:* Work with a group of students to provide tips for new students on campus. Use peer review to make sure you do not overlook details in guiding students to accomplish a specific goal.

Marvin Harris (1927–2001) was born in Brooklyn and received degrees from Columbia University. After teaching at Columbia for many years, Harris moved to the University of Florida, where he served as a graduate research professor in anthropology. Harris conducted research in Harlem, Africa, South America, and Asia. He published several scholarly works but is best known for books written to general readers such as *Cows, Pigs, Wars, and Witches: The Riddles of Culture* and *Cannibals and Kings: The Origins of Cultures.* Much of Harris's work focused on how people's basic needs for food and shelter influence their culture.

How Our Skins Got Their Color

In this essay from Our Kind: Who We Are, Where We Came From, Where We Are Going *(1988), Harris explains how human beings developed different skin colors. In reading this account, determine how he addresses a topic laden with controversy.*

1 Most human beings are neither very fair nor very dark, but brown. The extremely fair skin of northern Europeans and their descendants, and the very black skins of central Africans and their descendants, are probably special adaptations. Brown-skinned ancestors may have been shared by modern-day blacks and whites as recently as ten thousand years ago.

2 Human skin owes its color to the presence of particles known as melanin. The primary function of melanin is to protect the upper levels of the skin from being damaged by the sun's ultraviolet rays. This radiation poses a critical problem for our kind because we lack the dense coat of hair that acts as a sunscreen for most mammals. Hairlessness exposes us to two kinds of radiation hazards: ordinary sunburn, with its blisters, rashes, and risk of infection; and skin cancers, including malignant melanoma, one of the deadliest diseases known. Melanin is the body's first line of defense

against these afflictions. The more melanin particles, the darker the skin, and the lower the risk of sunburn and all forms of skin cancer. This explains why the highest rates for skin cancer are found in sun-drenched lands such as Australia, where light-skinned people of European descent spend a good part of their lives outdoors wearing scanty attire. Very dark-skinned people such as heavily pigmented Africans of Zaire seldom get skin cancer, but when they do, they get it on depigmented parts of their bodies—palms and lips.

If exposure to solar radiation had nothing but harmful effects, natural se- 3 lection would have favored inky black as the color for all human populations. But the sun's rays do not present an unmitigated threat. As it falls on the skin, sunshine converts a fatty substance in the epidermis into vitamin D. The blood carries vitamin D from the skin to the intestines (technically making it a hormone rather than a vitamin), where it plays a vital role in the absorption of calcium. In turn, calcium is vital for strong bones. Without it, people fall victim to the crippling diseases rickets and osteomalacia. In women, calcium deficiencies can result in a deformed birth canal, which makes childbirth lethal for both mother and fetus.

Vitamin D can be obtained from a few foods, primarily the oils and liv- 4 ers of marine fish. But inland populations must rely on the sun's rays and their own skins for the supply of this crucial substance. The particular color of a human population's skin, therefore, represents in large degree a trade-off between the hazards of too much versus too little solar radiation: acute sunburn and skin cancer on the one hand, and rickets and osteomalacia on the other. It is this trade-off that largely accounts for the preponderance of brown people in the world and for the general tendency for skin color to be darkest among equatorial populations and lightest among populations dwelling at higher latitudes.

At middle latitudes, the skin follows a strategy of changing colors with 5 the seasons. Around the Mediterranean basin, for example, exposure to the summer sun brings high risk of cancer but low risk for rickets; the body produces more melanin and people grow darker (i.e., they get suntans). Winter reduces the risk of sunburn and cancer; the body produces less melanin, and the tan wears off.

The correlation between skin color and latitude is not perfect because 6 other factors—such as the availability of foods containing vitamin D and calcium, regional cloud cover during the winter, amount of clothing worn, and cultural preferences—may work for or against the predicted relationship. Arctic-dwelling Eskimos, for example, are not as light-skinned as expected, but their habitat and economy afford them a diet that is exceptionally rich in both vitamin D and calcium.

7   Northern Europeans, obliged to wear heavy garments for protection against the long, cold, cloudy winters, were always at risk for rickets and osteomalacia from too little vitamin D and calcium. This risk increased sometime after 6000 B.C., when pioneer cattle herders who did not exploit marine resources began to appear in northern Europe. The risk would have been especially great for the brown-skinned Mediterranean peoples who migrated northward along with the crops and farm animals. Samples of Caucasian skin (infant penile foreskin obtained at the time of circumcision) exposed to sunlight on cloudless days in Boston (42°N) from November through February produced no vitamin D. In Edmonton (52°N) this period extended from October to March. But further south (34°N) sunlight was effective in producing vitamin D in the middle of the winter. Almost all of Europe lies north of 42°N. Fair-skinned, nontanning individuals who could utilize the weakest and briefest doses of sunlight to synthesize vitamin D were strongly favored by natural selection. During the frigid winters, only a small circle of a child's face could be left to peek out at the sun through the heavy clothing, thereby favoring the survival of individuals with translucent patches of pink on their cheeks characteristic of many northern Europeans. . . .

8   If light-skinned individuals on the average had only 2 percent more children survive per generation, the changeover in their skin color could have begun five thousand years ago and reached present levels well before the beginning of the Christian era. But natural selection need not have acted alone. Cultural selection may also have played a role. It seems likely that whenever people consciously or unconsciously had to decide which infants to nourish and which to neglect, the advantage would go to those with lighter skin, experience having shown that such individuals tended to grow up to be taller, stronger, and healthier than their darker siblings. White was beautiful because white was healthy.

9   To account for the evolution of black skin in equatorial latitudes, one has merely to reverse the combined effects of natural and cultural selection. With the sun directly overhead most of the year, and clothing a hindrance to work and survival, vitamin D was never in short supply (and calcium was easily obtained from vegetables). Rickets and osteomalacia were rare. Skin cancer was the main problem, and what nature started, culture amplified. Darker infants were favored by parents because experience showed that they grew up to be freer of disfiguring and lethal malignancies. Black was beautiful because black was healthy.

Understanding Context

1. What is Harris's thesis?
2. What is the "natural" color for human skin?
3. What caused people to develop different complexions?
4. What role did sunlight play in human evolution?
5. *Critical thinking:* What impact could this scientific explanation of skin color have on debates about race and discrimination? Can biological aspects of humanity be separated from social, cultural, political, or psychological attitudes?

Evaluating Strategy

1. How does Harris organize his essay?
2. What research does Harris use to support his views?
3. *Blending the modes:* Where does Harris use *narration*, *comparison*, and *definition* in his explanation?

Appreciating Language

1. How does Harris define *melanin*?
2. Does Harris's selection of words describing color contain connotations that suggest a bias? Is his essay wholly objective? How often does he use words such as *white* and *black*?
3. Would the average newspaper reader be able to understand this essay? What does the level of language suggest about the intended audience?

Writing Suggestions

1. Using this essay for background information, draft a brief explanation about skin color for an elementary school brochure on race relations. Use easily understood language, and employ comparisons and short narratives to explain scientific principles. Avoid words that may have negative connotations.
2. *Critical writing:* Write an essay analyzing the effect reading this essay had on you. Did it affect your attitudes toward people of different races? Does the knowledge that all humans probably once shared the same complexion change the way you view yourself?

3. *Collaborative writing:* Discuss Harris's essay with a group of students. What value does a scientific explanation of skin color have in addressing racial problems? Would it be beneficial to share this information with children? Record members' reactions, and create a short statement about the importance of understanding the origins of skin color. If members disagree, consider developing pro and con responses.

Davidyne Mayleas attended the University of Chicago and New York University, where she majored in banking and finance. After college she became a freelance journalist and social critic. She has written articles for popular magazines, such as **Reader's Digest** and **Esquire.** She is most noted for her investment and career advice. She has published several books, including **The Hidden Job Market for the 80s** and **By Appointment Only.**

How to Land the Job You Want

After graduation, you will no doubt enter the job market. As you read this essay, consider how you can make use of Mayleas's instructions.

Louis Albert, 39, lost his job as an electrical engineer when his firm made 1 extensive cutbacks. He spent two months answering classified ads and visiting employment agencies—with zero results. Albert might still be hunting if a friend, a specialist in the employment field, had not shown him how to be his own job counselor. Albert learned how to research unlisted openings, write a forceful résumé, perform smoothly in an interview, even transform a turndown into a job.

Although there seemed to be a shortage of engineering jobs, Albert real- 2 ized that he still persuaded potential employers to see him. This taught him something—that his naturally outgoing personality might be as great an asset as his engineering degree. When the production head of a small electronics company told him that they did not have an immediate opening, Albert told his interviewer, "You people make a fine product. I think you could use additional sales representation—someone like me who understands and talks electrical engineer's language, and who enjoys selling." The interviewer decided to send Albert to a senior vice president. Albert got a job in sales.

You too can be your own counselor if you put the same vigorous effort 3 into *getting* a job as you would into *keeping* one. Follow these three basic rules, developed by placement experts:

1. Find the hidden job market. Classified ads and agency listings reveal 4 only a small percentage of available jobs. Some of the openings that occur through promotions, retirements and reorganization never reach the personnel department. There are three ways to get in touch with this hidden market:

5   *Write a strong résumé with a well-directed cover letter and mail it to the appropriate department manager in the company where you'd like to work.* Don't worry whether there's a current opening. Many managers fill vacancies by reviewing the résumés already in their files. Dennis Mollura, press-relations manager in the public-relations department of American Telephone and Telegraph, says, "In my own case, the company called me months after I sent in my résumé."

6   *Get in touch with people who work in or know the companies that interest you.* Jobs are so often filled through personal referral that Charles R. Lops, executive employment manager of the J. C. Penney Co., says, "Probably our best source for outside people comes from recommendations made by Penney associates themselves."

7   *"Drop in" on the company.* Lillian Reveille, employment manager of Equitable Life Assurance Society of the United States, reports: "A large percentage of the applicants we see are 'walk-ins'—and we do employ many of these people."

8   **2. Locate hidden openings.** This step requires energy and determination to make telephone calls, see people, do research, and to keep moving despite turndowns.

9   *Contact anyone who may know of openings,* including relatives, friends, teachers, bank officers, insurance agents—anyone you know in your own or an adjacent field. When the teachers' union and employment agencies produced no teaching openings, Eric Olson, an unemployed high-school math instructor, reviewed his talent and decided that where an analytical math mind was useful, there he'd find a job. He called his insurance agent, who set up an interview with the actuarial department of one of the companies he represented. They hired Olson.

10   It's a good idea to contact not only professional or trade associations in your field, but also your local chamber of commerce and people involved in community activities. After Laura Bailey lost her job as retirement counselor in a bank's personnel department, she found a position in customer relations in another bank. Her contact: a member of the senior-citizens club that Mrs. Bailey ran on a volunteer basis.

11   *Use local or business-school libraries.* Almost every field has its own directory of companies, which provides names, addresses, products and/or services, and lists officers and other executives. Write to the company president or to the executive to whom you'd report. The vice president of personnel at Warner-Lambert Co. says, "When a résumé of someone we could

use—now or in the near future—shows up 'cold' in my in-basket, that's luck for both of us."

Consult telephone directories. Sometimes the telephone company will send 12 you free the telephone directories of various cities. Also, good-sized public libraries often have many city directories. Fred Lewis, a cabinet maker, checked the telephone directories of nine different cities where he knew furniture was manufactured. At the end of five weeks he had a sizable telephone bill, some travel expenses—and ten interviews which resulted in three job offers.

3. After you find the opening, get the job. The applicants who actually 13 get hired are those who polish these six job-getting skills to perfection:

Compose a better résumé. A résumé is a self-advertisement, designed to get 14 you an interview. Start by putting yourself in an employer's place. Take stock of your job history and personal achievements. Make an inventory of your skills and accomplishments that might be useful from the employer's standpoint. Choose the most important and describe them in words that stress accomplishments. Avoid such phrases as "my duties included . . ." Use action words like planned, sold, trained, managed.

Ask a knowledgeable business friend to review your résumé. Does it 15 stress accomplishment rather than duties? Does it tell an employer what you can do for him? Can it be shortened? (One or two pages should suffice.) Generally, it's not wise to mention salary requirements.

Write a convincing cover letter. While the résumé may be a copy, the cover 16 letter must be personal. Sy Mann, director of research for Aceto Chemical Co., says: "When I see a mimeographed letter that states, 'Dear Sir, I'm sincerely interested in working for your company,' I wonder, 'How many other companies got this valentine?'" Use the name and title of the person who can give you the interview, and be absolutely certain of accuracy here. Using a wrong title or misspelling a prospective employer's name may route your correspondence directly to an automatic turndown.

Prepare specifically for each interview. Research the company thoroughly; 17 know its history and competition. Try to grasp the problems of the job you're applying for. For example, a line in an industry journal that a food company was "developing a new geriatric food" convinced one man that he should emphasize his marketing experience with vitamins rather than with frozen foods.

You'll increase your edge by anticipating questions the interviewer might 18 raise. Why do you want to work for us? What can you offer us that someone else cannot? Why did you leave your last position? What are your salary requirements?

19   An employer holds an interview to get a clearer picture of your work history and accomplishments, and to look for characteristics he considers valuable. These vary with jobs. Does the position require emphasis on attention to detail or on creativity? Perseverance or aggressiveness? Prior to the interview decide what traits are most in demand. And always send a thank-you note immediately after the interview.

20   *Follow-up.* They said you would hear in a week; now it's two. Call them. Don't wait and hope. Hope and act.

21   *Supply additional information.* That's the way Karen Halloway got her job as fashion director with a department store. "After my interview I sensed that the merchandise manager felt I was short on retail experience. So I wrote to him describing the 25 fashion shows I'd staged yearly for the pattern company I'd worked for."

22   *Don't take no for an answer.* Hank Newell called to find out why he had been turned down. The credit manager felt he had insufficient collection experience. Hank thanked him for his time and frankness. The next day, Hank called back saying, "My collection experience is limited, but I don't think I fully emphasized my training in credit checking." They explored this area and found Hank still not qualified. But the credit manager was so impressed with how well Hank took criticism that when Hank asked him if he could suggest other employers, he did, even going so far as to call one. Probing for leads when an interview or follow-up turns negative is a prime technique for getting personal referrals.

23   The challenge of finding a job, approached in an active, organized, realistic way, can be a valuable personal adventure. You can meet new people, develop new ideas about yourself and your career goals, and improve your skills in dealing with individuals. These in turn can contribute to your long-term job security.

Understanding Context

1. What is the "hidden job market"? How can people discover opportunities that are not advertised?
2. What are the best sources of locating openings other than the want ads?
3. How should job seekers prepare résumés and cover letters?
4. *Critical thinking:* Students attend college to prepare for careers, but do colleges effectively train their graduates to enter the job market? Could schools do a better job of giving their students the skills needed to locate and secure employment?

Evaluating Strategy

1. How effective is the opening narrative? Does it dramatize the need for Mayleas's instructions? Does it grab attention?
2. Review Mayleas's use of paragraphing, numbering, and italics. Could the article be made any easier to skim and remember?
3. *Critical thinking:* Process writers often number points and develop short, easy-to-remember instructions so readers can recall advice and apply it later. Is there a risk, however, that a complex concept can be reduced to a superficial slogan?

Appreciating Language

1. Mayleas uses verbs to begin each instruction—"Find the hidden job market" and "Write a convincing cover letter." Why is it important to emphasize verbs in giving directions?
2. Seeking a job can be stressful and depressing. Underline words the writer uses to build reader confidence and create a positive tone.

Writing Suggestions

1. Based on your own experiences, write a short set of instructions for students seeking jobs in a business you have worked in. Make your directions as specific as possible.
2. *Collaborative writing:* Discuss these tips with a group of students. Brainstorm and add suggestions; then write a short list of directions to help new students find part-time jobs on or off campus.

Infotrac College Edition
www.infotrac-college.com

THE JOB MARKET

As much as you may appreciate the love and guidance your parents give you, you must figure out who you are and what you want to do. And your doing so is an absolute requirement if you want to have a fulfilling career.
Pamela M. McBride

College students typically begin looking for jobs during spring break in their senior year, often with little direction or preparation. Many will waste valuable time, miss opportunities, or find themselves "taking jobs" rather than "launching careers." Employment experts note that most jobseekers, especially recent graduates, make common mistakes in searching for jobs, preparing résumés, and interviewing.

Eighty percent of job openings are never advertised. They are not listed in want ads, bulletin boards, or websites. To locate the best of these opportunities, jobseekers have to look for them by networking—locating people who have the job they want or know someone who does.

Students can begin networking long before graduation. Before deciding on a major, they should determine whether their courses and degree will prepare them for the work they want to do and whether they will be prepared to find a job when they graduate. Talking to or e-mailing people who have the job you want can provide valuable advice. Professional organizations, volunteer work, and internships can generate contacts with potential employers.

Developing networking and interviewing skills can help students find jobs and prepare them to make future career shifts. Outsourcing, changing government policies, shifts in the global economy, and constantly advancing technologies will force most of today's graduates to change careers, not jobs, four or five times in their lives.

Before reading these articles, consider these questions:

How did you determine your major? Do you know what you want to do with your life? Do you know what people really do in the careers you want to pursue? Do you know whether jobs in this field are growing or declining and what they pay?

If you were looking for a job today, what method would you use to locate openings?

Do you know what you would include on your résumé? Have you seen copies of successful résumés? Do you know not only what information to include but how to present it?

What questions do you expect to be asked at an interview?

Are you aware of the economic trends that will affect your future career? Are you entering a job market that is expanding or shrinking?

Do you know ways of improving your prospects of getting a job when you graduate? Are there professional organizations you can join? Are there part-time or summer jobs that can give you relevant experience? If you cannot locate a job, are there opportunities for volunteer work that can provide experience or valuable contacts?

E-Readings Online

Search for each article by author or title after entering InfoTrac College Edition through your 1Pass account login.

Pamela M. McBride. *Self-Assessment: Knowing Yourself and What You Want to Do.*
To be successful in their careers, students should devote time to self-assessment to determine what they want to do.

Careers and Colleges. *10 Job-Hunting Mistakes and How Not to Make Them.*
Job seekers must make determined efforts to locate jobs among the 80 percent that are never advertised.

United Press International. *Top 20 Mistakes in Writing Resumes.*
Because résumés are now scanned on computer screens rather than read, "you have only five to ten seconds to say who you are and what you do."

Patient Care Management. *Top Questions Asked at Job Interviews.*
A recent survey of 2,000 recruiters and hiring managers worldwide reveals the most common fifteen job interview questions that applicants face.

The New York Times. *More Jobs, Worse Work.*

More than 80 percent of jobs created in recent years have been in low-end professions, making it harder for applicants to find desirable employment.

Jyoti Thottam. *Where the Good Jobs Are Going.*

Software developers, engineers, and accountants who earned $70,000 or $80,000 a year are increasingly losing jobs to professionals in India who are willing to do the same job for less than $10,000.

Jerry J. Jasinowski. *Manufacturing Is In Crisis.*

In less than three years, two million manufacturing jobs, most paying high wages and providing health insurance, have been lost as factory jobs have moved to cheaper labor markets overseas.

Sean Gregory. *Five Jobs for Our Shores: Afraid of Outsourcing?*
Here Are Some Growing Fields That Won't Be Farmed Out to Overseas Workers.

Oil prospecting, physical training, transportation, health care, and money management offer well-paying jobs that cannot be sent overseas.

Lou Dobbs. *Disorganized Labor.*

Labor unions established the forty-hour workweek, unemployment insurance, medical benefits, and decent wages, but today they have lost influence and political power because only eight percent of private-sector workers are unionized.

InfoWorld. *Off the Record: The Myth of Job Security.*

In one decade the U.S. economy "created 318 million new jobs and destroyed 300 million of them," forcing workers to always "keep one eye on the job market."

The Economist (US). *The Conundrum of the Glass Ceiling.*

Twenty years after the term "glass ceiling" was coined to describe the barriers women face seeking promotion to the highest positions, women still account for only 8 percent of the top managers.

Critical Reading and Thinking

1. How can students prepare themselves for entering the job market?
2. What common mistakes should applicants avoid in looking for jobs and writing résumés?
3. What questions are commonly asked at interviews?

4. What changes are occurring in the American economy, and how do they affect the job market?
5. Why do workers with good jobs have to keep an eye on the job market?

Writing Suggestions

1. Write a self-assessment essay that analyzes your personal strengths and weaknesses, likes and dislikes, skills and abilities and that analyzes the career you intend to pursue. Have you talked with anyone who has the kind of job you want? Do you really know what people do in this profession, or have your impressions been shaped by what you have heard or seen on television?
2. *Collaborative writing:* Working with other students, discuss what you have learned about the job market, interviewing, and writing résumés. Take notes and work together to present your group's advice in a process paper listing suggestions in numbered steps.
3. *Other modes*
   - Write a *cause-and-effect* essay that explains why many companies are outsourcing jobs overseas.
   - Write a *description* of your ideal first job.
   - Develop a *classification* essay that ranks jobs from the most to least desirable.
   - Create a *comparison* essay that shows how technology or economic trends have changed an industry, a specific business, or the nature of a job.
   - Write a personal *definition* of what you consider an ideal career.

Research Paper

You can develop a research paper about the job market by conducting further research to explore a range of issues:

- What economic, political, and technological forces are shaping today's job market?
- How is outsourcing affecting the job market?
- Why have labor unions lost power?
- Do women still face barriers to advancement?
- Do fewer jobs offer health care benefits and pensions? Will more workers be forced to become personally responsible for providing their own health insurance and retirement savings?

For Further Reading

To locate additional sources about the job market, enter these search terms as InfoTrac subjects:

Employment
Subdivisions:
- analysis
- compensation and benefits
- demographic aspects
- economic aspects
- social aspects
- statistics

Employment Forecasting
Subdivisions
- analysis
- forecasts and trends
- reports
- statistics

Résumés (Employment)
Subdivisions:
- analysis
- design and construction
- ethical aspects
- innovations
- planning
- surveys

Employment Interviewing
Subdivisions:
- analysis
- methods
- personal narratives
- research

Labor Unions
Subdivisions:
- aims and objectives
- beliefs, opinions and attitudes
- compensation and benefits
- demographic aspects
- forecasts and trends
- organizing

Outsourcing

Subdivisions:	aims and objectives
	case studies
	causes of
	forecasts and trends

Additional Sources

Using a search engine, such as Yahoo!, Google, or Alta Vista, enter one or more of the following terms to locate additional sources:

employment résumés	job interviews
career trends	outsourcing
labor unions	worker benefits
glass ceiling	employment trends
job forecasts	hidden job market

See Evaluating Internet Sources Checklist on page 752. See Chapter 30 for using and documenting sources.

Malcolm X (1925–1965) was born Malcolm Little in Omaha, Nebraska, where his father worked as a preacher. While in prison for robbery, Malcolm converted to the Black Muslim faith. He changed his last name to X to reject his "slave name" and dramatize African Americans' loss of heritage. He became a rising force in the Nation of Islam and in 1963 was named its first "national minister." After a trip to Mecca, he converted to orthodox Islam and rejected the racial views advocated by Black Muslims. He founded the Muslim Mosque, Inc., in 1964. A year later, he was shot and killed at a Harlem rally.

My First Conk

In this section from his autobiography, Malcolm X explains the process of "conking," or straightening hair, popular with some African Americans in the 1940s and 1950s. As you read this essay, note how Malcolm X explains the process, then uses it as an example in an argument about black identity.

1 Shorty soon decided that my hair was finally long enough to be conked. He had promised to school me in how to beat the barbershops' three- and four-dollar price by making up congolene, and then conking ourselves.

2 I took the little list of ingredients he had printed out for me, and went to a grocery store, where I got a can of Red Devil lye, two eggs, and two medium-sized white potatoes. Then at a drugstore near the poolroom, I asked for a large jar of Vaseline, a large bar of soap, a large-toothed comb and a fine-toothed comb, one of those rubber hoses with a metal spray-head, a rubber apron and a pair of gloves.

3 "Going to lay on that first conk?" the drugstore man asked me. I proudly told him, grinning, "Right!"

4 Shorty paid six dollars a week for a room in his cousin's shabby apartment. His cousin wasn't at home. "It's like the pad's mine, he spends so much time with his woman," Shorty said. "Now, you watch me—"

5 He peeled the potatoes and thin-sliced them into a quart-sized Mason fruit jar, then started stirring them with a wooden spoon as he gradually poured in a little over half the can of lye. "Never use a metal spoon; the lye will turn it black," he told me.

A jelly-like, starchy-looking glop resulted from the lye and potatoes, and ₆ Shorty broke in the two eggs, stirring real fast—his own conk and dark face bent down close. The congolene turned pale-yellowish. "Feel the jar," Shorty said. I cupped my hand against the outside, and snatched it away. "Damn right, it's hot, that's the lye," he said. "So you know it's going to burn when I comb it in—it burns bad. But the longer you can stand it, the straighter the hair."

He made me sit down, and he tied the string of the new rubber ₇ apron tightly around my neck, and combed up my bush of hair. Then, from the big Vaseline jar, he took a handful and massaged it hard all through my hair and into the scalp. He also thickly Vaselined my neck, ears and forehead. "When I get to washing out your head, be sure to tell me anywhere you feel any little stinging," Shorty warned me, washing his hands, then pulling on the rubber gloves, and tying on his own rubber apron. "You always got to remember that any congolene left in burns a sore into your head."

The congolene just felt warm when Shorty started combing it in. But ₈ then my head caught fire.

I gritted my teeth and tried to pull the sides of the kitchen table to- ₉ gether. The comb felt as if it was raking my skin off.

My eyes watered, my nose was running. I couldn't stand it any longer; I ₁₀ bolted to the washbasin. I was cursing Shorty with every name I could think of when he got the spray going and started soap-lathering my head.

He lathered and spray-rinsed, lathered and spray-rinsed, maybe ten or ₁₁ twelve times, each time gradually closing the hot-water faucet, until the rinse was cold, and that helped some.

"You feel any stinging spots?"   ₁₂

"No," I managed to say. My knees were trembling.   ₁₃

"Sit back down, then. I think we got it all out okay."   ₁₄

The flame came back as Shorty, with a thick towel, started drying my ₁₅ head, rubbing hard. *"Easy, man, easy!"* I kept shouting.

"The first time's always worst. You get used to it better before long. You ₁₆ took it real good, homeboy. You got a good conk."

When Shorty let me stand up and see in the mirror, my hair hung down ₁₇ in limp, damp strings. My scalp still flamed, but not as badly; I could bear it. He draped the towel around my shoulders, over my rubber apron, and began again Vaselining my hair.

I could feel him combing, straight back, first the big comb, then the fine- ₁₈ tooth one.

Then, he was using a razor, very delicately, on the back of my neck. ₁₉ Then finally, shaping the sideburns.

20   My first view in the mirror blotted out the hurting. I'd seen some pretty conks, but when it's the first time, on your own head, the transformation, after the lifetime of kinks, is staggering.

21   The mirror reflected Shorty behind me. We both were grinning and on top of my head was this thick, smooth sheen of shining red hair—real red—as straight as any white man's.

22   How ridiculous I was! Stupid enough to stand there simply lost in admiration of my hair now looking "white," reflected in the mirror in Shorty's room. I vowed that I'd never again be without a conk, and I never was for many years.

23   This was my first really big step toward self-degradation: when I endured all of that pain, literally burning my flesh to have it look like a white man's hair. I had joined that multitude of Negro men and women in America who are brainwashed into believing that the black people are "inferior"—and white people "superior"—that they will even violate and mutilate their God-created bodies to try to look "pretty" by white standards.

24   Look around today, in every small town and big city, from two-bit catfish and soda-pop joints into the "integrated" lobby of the Waldorf-Astoria, and you'll see conks on black men. And you'll see black women wearing these green and pink and purple and red and platinum-blonde wigs. They're all more ridiculous than a slapstick comedy. It makes you wonder if the Negro has completely lost his sense of identity, lost touch with himself.

25   You'll see the conk worn by many, many so-called "upper class" Negroes, and, as much as I hate to say it about them, on all too many Negro entertainers. One of the reasons that I've especially admired some of them, like Lionel Hampton and Sidney Poitier, among others, is that they have kept their natural hair and fought to the top. I admire any Negro man who has never had himself conked, or who has had the sense to get rid of it—as I finally did.

26   I don't know which kind of self-defacing conk is the greater shame—the one you'll see on the heads of the black so-called "middle class" and "upper class," who ought to know better, or the one you'll see on the heads of the poorest, most downtrodden, ignorant black men. I mean the legalminimum-wage ghetto-dwelling kind of Negro, as I was when I got my first one. It's generally among these poor fools that you'll see a black kerchief over the man's head, like Aunt Jemima; he's trying to make his conk last longer, between trips to the barbershop. Only for special occasions is this kerchief-protected conk exposed—to show off how "sharp" and "hip" its owner is. The ironic thing is that I have never heard any woman, white or black, express any admiration for a conk. Of course, any white woman with a black man isn't thinking about his hair. But I don't see how on earth a black woman

with any race pride could walk down the street with any black man wearing a conk—the emblem of his shame that he is black.

To my own shame, when I say all of this I'm talking first of all about 27 myself—because you can't show me any Negro who ever conked more faithfully than I did. I'm speaking from personal experience when I say of any black man who conks today, or any white-wigged black woman, that if they gave the brains in their heads just half as much attention as they do their hair, they would be a thousand times better off.

Understanding Context

1. What motivated black people to endure the painful "conking" process?
2. Why does Malcolm X see the conk as an "emblem of shame"?
3. Why is Malcolm X especially disturbed by the sight of conks worn by middle-class and professional African Americans?
4. *Critical thinking:* A century ago, Jewish immigrants were urged, often by American Jews, to shave their beards and discard traditional garments in order to succeed in the New World. Are these changes harmless adaptations to a new culture or do they represent a form of self-loathing? Do you see current examples of men and women altering their identity?

Evaluating Strategy

1. Malcolm X begins the essay with a story, told without any commentary. Do you find it effective to explain the process, then discuss its social significance?
2. How does Malcolm X use dialogue to bring the narrative to life?
3. *Other modes:* Can you consider this essay a blend of process, example, and argument? What parts do these elements play in the essay?
4. *Critical thinking:* Social critics generally comment on social behavior from a distance. How does the story of his own conking give Malcolm X greater insight into black self-degradation? Without introducing his own experiences, what effect would the last four paragraphs have?

Appreciating Language

1. What language does Malcolm X use to dramatize the pain of being conked?
2. At one point, Malcolm X states he was "brainwashed." Why is this a key term? How did popular culture "brainwash" generations of African Americans to admire "whiteness" and despise black identity?
3. Malcolm X uses the word *shame* repeatedly. How do you define *shame*?

Writing Suggestions

1. Write a short essay about a process you have experienced—getting your ears pierced, applying for a loan, trying out for a team, auditioning for a part. First describe the process; then comment on what you learned about yourself and society.

2. *Collaborative writing:* Discuss the last sentence of the essay with a number of students. Do many people—of all races—devote more attention to their hair than their brains? Write a list of examples showing how people seek to alter their appearance to achieve a new identity.

As you read these instructions about leasing a car, determine whether you would find them easy to follow. Are they clearly organized and do they provide enough detail?

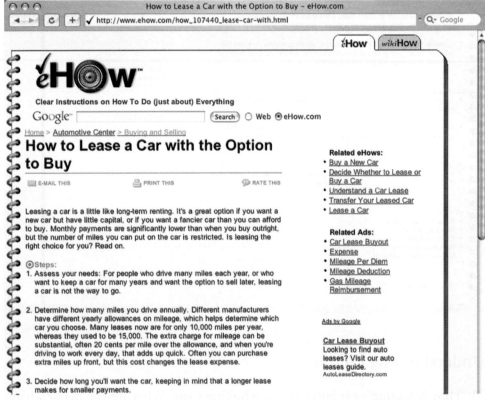

How to Lease a Car with the Option to Buy – eHow.com

http://www.ehow.com/how_107440_lease-car-with.html

eHOW | **wikiHow**

eHOW™

Clear Instructions on How To Do (just about) Everything

Google [_____] (Search) ○ Web ● eHow.com

Home > Automotive Center > Buying and Selling

How to Lease a Car with the Option to Buy

E-MAIL THIS   PRINT THIS   RATE THIS

Leasing a car is a little like long-term renting. It's a great option if you want a new car but have little capital, or if you want a fancier car than you can afford to buy. Monthly payments are significantly lower than when you buy outright, but the number of miles you can put on the car is restricted. Is leasing the right choice for you? Read on.

⊙Steps:

1. **Assess your needs:** For people who drive many miles each year, or who want to keep a car for many years and want the option to sell later, leasing a car is not the way to go.

2. **Determine how many miles you drive annually.** Different manufacturers have different yearly allowances on mileage, which helps determine which car you choose. Many leases now are for only 10,000 miles per year, whereas they used to be 15,000. The extra charge for mileage can be substantial, often 20 cents per mile over the allowance, and when you're driving to work every day, that adds up quick. Often you can purchase extra miles up front, but this cost changes the lease expense.

3. **Decide how long you'll want the car,** keeping in mind that a longer lease makes for smaller payments.

Related eHows:
* Buy a New Car
* Decide Whether to Lease or Buy a Car
* Understand a Car Lease
* Transfer Your Leased Car
* Lease a Car

Related Ads:
* Car Lease Buyout
* Expense
* Mileage Per Diem
* Mileage Deduction
* Gas Mileage Reimbursement

Ads by Google

Car Lease Buyout
Looking to find auto leases? Visit our auto leases guide.
AutoLeaseDirectory.com

© 1999–2006 eHow, Inc.

4. Calculate how large a deposit you can put down up front and how much you can afford to pay monthly. Bankrate.com and other sites offer auto lease payment calculators so you can find out how much you'll have to pay. Factors include manufacturers suggested retail price (MSRP), final negotiated price, down payment, usage tax, length of lease, and new car lending rate.

5. Find a reutable dealership that leases the kind of car you want, in your price range. Take a test drive. Have the dealer explain warranties offered on the car, servicing and fees for overmileage, wear and tear, and early-out for quitting the lease. Always ask if taxes are included in the quoted fee. Make sure you understand everything you can be charged for before you sign the contract.

6. Ask how a buyout at the end of the lease works. You don't have to decide just yet whether or not you will buy out.

7. Negotiate the lowest possible lease price (capitalized cost) to keep payments low. Cars with higher residual values have lower lease costs.

8. Consider getting gap coverage insurance, which is usually included but may not be on your policy. If you don't have it and the car gets stolen, it can cost more than the price of your lease.

✱ Overall Tips:
- For peace of mind, keep your lease's length within the car's warranty period.

- Ask if you can transfer the lease to someone else at some point. This is not legal in some states. See How to Transfer Your Leased Car.

⚠ Overall Warnings:
- If you plan to buy the car at the end of the lease, you often pay more than if you had bought the car in the first place.

↺ What to look for:
- Reputable dealership
- Warranty period
- Extra charges
- High residual value
- Gap coverage insurance

Please Share Your Tips with Us

Understanding Context

1. How is leasing a car different from buying a car? What are the major advantages and disadvantages?
2. Who should *not* lease a car? Why?
3. What questions should consumers ask car dealers before they lease a vehicle?
4. What is a buyout? How does it work?
5. How can consumers reduce their monthly payments?
6. *Critical thinking:* Do you think it is advisable for all consumers to consider their long-term needs and driving habits before buying a vehicle as well? Do many people buy cars based on style or performance alone?

Evaluating Strategy

1. Why are numbered points useful in giving these directions?
2. What role do visuals play in making a web page easy to read and navigate?
3. How do bold fonts emphasize key points? Would two pages of text in standard paragraphs communicate as well? Why or why not?

Appreciating Language

1. What does the level of diction and word choice reveal about the intended audience?
2. Do the authors successfully avoid overly technical language that some readers would find difficult?

Writing Suggestions

1. Write a short set of directions to accomplish a task in an emergency. Give numbered steps to alert dorm residents what to do if they discover a fire, tell parents how to respond if their child is lost, or direct consumers how to protect their identity if their credit cards are stolen.
2. *Collaborative writing:* Work with a group of students and write a short persuasive essay urging car buyers to avoid common mistakes in selecting, financing, or insuring a new or used car.

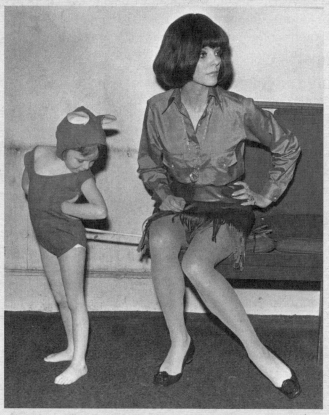

Joan Collins and daughter, 1968   © Hulton Getty

1. What is your first impression of this photograph? Do you find it a charming mother-and-daughter scene, or do you view it as an example of the way girls are socialized into emphasizing their looks?

2. Does this photograph illustrate the process of socialization, the way boys and girls come to see themselves and their gender roles? How are boys and girls told at a very early age about the way they are expected to look, act, and behave?

3. How might a typical father-and-son picture differ from this one (see p. 389)? How might people respond to the image of a father encouraging a son in ballet class or a mother urging a young daughter to play

ice hockey? Do we have expectations about the way parents should raise boys and girls?

4. When you recall your own childhood, who had the greatest impact on your views of yourself, your gender role, your interests, your behavior—your parents, teachers, or other children?

5. *Visual analysis:* Most parent-child images depict an interaction between figures. In this photograph Joan Collins is posed looking away from her child. What does this imply? Does her body language suggest she was posing for the camera?

6. *Collaborative writing:* Ask a group of students about their reactions to this photograph. Do they see it as a universal example of parent and child, or do they focus on Joan Collins as a celebrity? Do children of movie stars and other public personalities face special challenges? Work together to write a brief essay about the way children seek to imitate their parents. Include personal examples to illustrate your group's observations.

7. *Other modes*
   - Write a brief *narrative* essay about the way your father or mother influenced your childhood. Did you see your parent as a role model?
   - Write an essay *comparing* your childhood personality with that of a brother or sister. Why do children by the same parents often act so differently? How much of human behavior seems to be shaped by parents and how much seems genetic?
   - Develop a *cause-and-effect* paper showing how parents influence the way children come to view themselves, their role in society, and their values. What messages do parents give children? How do parents teach children to receive approval?
   - Write a *comparison* essay contrasting the parenting styles of your father and mother.

Process Checklist

Before submitting your paper, review these points:

✔ Is the process clearly defined?

✔ Do you supply background information readers need?

✔ Is the information easy to follow? Is the chain of events or the sequence of steps logically arranged?

✔ Could the text be enhanced by large print, bold or italic type, diagrams, or charts?

✔ Are your instructions complete? Do readers know when one step is over and another begins?

✔ Do your instructions alert readers to normal changes that they might mistake for errors?

✔ Are hazards clearly stated?

✔ Did you use peer review to test your document?

Companion Website

See **http://www.thomsonedu.com/english/sundance** for additional information about writing process.

DIVISION AND CLASSIFICATION
SEPARATING INTO PARTS AND RATING CATEGORIES

24

WHAT ARE DIVISION AND CLASSIFICATION?

Division helps readers understand complex subjects by separating them into parts. Classification, often used to guide decision making, rates subjects by placing them on a scale of differing categories.

 To read more about division and classification, along with interactive examples and opportunities to work with interactive texts, click on "The Rhetorical Patterns of Inquiry" from the main menu of *Comp21*.

DIVISION

If you enter a hospital, you will probably see signs directing you to different departments: cardiology, radiology, psychiatry, and pediatrics. Hospitals are divided into specific services. Universities consist of separate colleges, such as business and liberal arts. American literature can be divided into courses by historical era (nineteenth- and twentieth-century writers), by genre (poetry and drama), or by special interest (women's literature and science fiction). Corporations are separated into departments: design, production, maintenance, marketing, sales, and accounting.

Division makes complicated subjects easier to comprehend and work with. The human body, for example, is overwhelmingly intricate. In order to understand how it functions, medical disciplines divide it into systems: digestive, respiratory, nervous, muscular-skeletal, reproductive, and others. By studying individual systems, medical students come to a fuller understanding of how the whole body functions. Crime is such a vast social problem that writers discuss it in terms of traditional divisions—robbery, car theft, homicide, and fraud—or invent their own categories, dividing crime by causes: power, greed, identity, and revenge. People use the term *depression* to express everything from minor disappointment to suicidal despair. To inform patients about the variety of depressive illnesses, a mental health brochure divides the disorder into specific types:

> *Bereavement*   A two- to nine-week process of grieving with sad and empty feelings after the death of someone important to you. May linger for much longer after the loss of parent, child, or partner, but tends to gradually improve over time. You should observe steady readjustment to your changed world and resumption of social activities and pleasures.
>
> *Adjustment reaction*   A period of up to six months after a major stressful event during which depressed mood or hopeless feelings are more intense than normal and interfere with daily social and school or work activities. Like bereavement, it is often helped by brief crisis therapy or family therapy.
>
> *Major depression*   Depressed mood or loss of interests with a variety of symptoms and feelings of depression, discussed earlier, lasting at least two weeks. Major depression ranges from mild cases with few symptoms to severe cases (known as "clinical depression") marked by a persistent bleak outlook, which may lead to thoughts of escape through suicide. Depression may begin to lift after several weeks or may become chronic, lasting two years or more.

In this case division presents readers with a series of definitions. Division can be used to organize a set of narratives, descriptions, processes, or persuasive arguments.

WRITING ACTIVITY

Select one of the topics and divide it into subtopics. You can use an existing division or invent one of your own.

1. Customers you encountered in a recent job

2. Tests students face in college

3. Student housing on or off campus

4. Blind dates

5. Jobs in a particular career

6. Diets

7. Television programs

8. Current movies

9. Cars

10. Popular night spots

STRATEGIES | for Writing Division

Critical Thinking and Prewriting

1. **Begin by listing possible topics for division.** Not all subjects are suitable for division. Interesting topics can resist easy separation into distinct parts. Begin by listing as many possibilities as you can, using prewriting techniques to discard difficult topics and identify promising ones.

2. **Clearly limit your subject.** If you do not initially limit the overall topic, you will find it difficult to break it down into parts.

   ■ Define your topic, narrowing it to fit the scope of the assignment.

3. **Avoid oversimplifying your subject.** You have no doubt seen magazine articles announcing three kinds of bosses, four types of marriages, or five methods of child rearing. Writers often invent descriptive or humorous labels, warning you to avoid the "toxic controller" or advising you how to negotiate with the "whiny wimp." Although these divisions can be amusing and insightful, they can trivialize or oversimplify a subject. Not all people or situations can neatly fit into three or four types.

   ■ In discussing complex subjects, inform readers of possible exceptions to your categories.

4. **Use methods of division suitable to your subject, task, readers, and assignment to create meaningful distinctions.** There are many methods of making divisions. In a history or political science class you could divide American presidents into liberals, conservatives, and centrists or those sympathetic, hostile, or indifferent toward a particular issue. Few professors or fellow students, however, would be interested in reading a paper dividing presidents by their astrological sign or their pets.

5. **Remember, the goal of division is to make a subject easier to understand and work with.** Your division should have a purpose beyond simply breaking it into parts.

Planning

1. **Write a clear thesis statement or definition at the top of the page to guide planning.**
2. **Select a division method that includes all parts of the whole.** If you divide college students into three types, for example, make sure everyone on campus can be included in one group. Eliminate potential gaps. You cannot simply divide students into Protestants, Catholics, and Jews if some are Muslims or agnostics. Every member of the whole must be addressed, even if only in an introduction acknowledging exceptions to general categories.
3. **Make sure individual parts fit only one category.** If you were to divide businesses by location—North, South, East, and West—how would you address a company with operations on both coasts? If items can fit in more than a single category, your method of division may not suit your subject. It might be better to discuss businesses in terms of products, gross sales, or size rather than location.
4. **Avoid creating categories that include too many differences.** Not all items within a category are going to be identical, but to make sense a division should have a focus. If you were examining people in different age groups, it would be logical to write about people in their twenties, thirties, forties, and fifties. But a category of those in their sixties would include both working and retired people, both those still paying into Social Security and those receiving benefits. It might be more accurate to subdivide this group into those from sixty to sixty-five, and those sixty-six and older.
5. **Determine what other modes you will use.** A division essay is actually a collection of related narratives, definitions, arguments, examples, processes, or descriptions. Study your subject and select the best method of addressing each subtopic.
6. **Develop an outline that clearly divides your topic to guide the first draft.** Without a clear breakdown of your subject, you will find writing very difficult.

Writing the First Draft

1. **Focus your writing by clearly envisioning your purpose.** Divisions should help explain a subject and make it easier to work with.
2. **Follow guidelines for writing other modes—definition, narrative, example, process, and so forth—in developing each category.**
3. **Use parallel structures to develop categories.** Readers will find your categories easier to follow if you provide a common pattern of development.

In discussing three types of cities, you might discuss size, population, major industry, climate, and social life, in that order.

▪ Readers must be able to compare common points of each subject to understand their similarities and differences.

4. **Monitor the length of your draft.** Because of their complexity, division papers can become lengthy. If you realize that your subject is too ambitious, that it would take ten pages to fully address a topic selected for a 500-word essay, you may wish to return to prewriting to narrow your topic or select a different subject.

5. **Be open to new ideas but remain focused.** As you write, new ideas may occur to you. You may add new categories, expand discussion, or restrict your thesis—but avoid going off topic. A division paper has a clear purpose—not every interesting idea or observation you develop belongs in this assignment.

Revising

1. **Examine your thesis and overall draft.**
   ▪ Is the thesis clearly stated? Is your purpose clear?
   ▪ Does your method of division make sense? Does it draw meaningful or only arbitrary distinctions between items?
   ▪ Does the essay help readers understand a complex subject or only confuse the issue?

2. **Review the essay for balance and thoroughness.**
   ▪ Do you describe some categories superficially, whereas others contain extensive examples, narratives, and details?
   ▪ Do some sections need expansion and others trimming?

3. **Analyze the essay for parallel development.**
   ▪ Do you follow a general pattern to discuss each item so that readers can easily compare them, or are the subtopics presented in a jumbled manner that mixes narratives, definitions, and examples without a common thread?

4. **Are the divisions clearly defined?**
   ▪ Can some items be placed in more than one division?

5. **Do the divisions account for every part of the whole?**
   ▪ Are there any items that remain undiscussed or unqualified, leaving readers wondering where to place them? If you discuss three types of students on campus, will every last student clearly fit into one of the categories?

6. **Do you qualify your observations and account for possible exceptions?**
   ▪ Can there be exceptions to your division? You may wish to state in an introduction or conclusion that not every item may fit your pattern of

division or that your division may not be operative at all times or in all conditions.
- Acknowledge any limitations to your thesis.

7. **Use peer review.**
- Ask others to review your essay for clarity and completeness.

Editing and Proofreading

1. **Review word choice for accuracy and connotations.**
- Are your subheadings meaningful and easy to remember?
- Do some words have connotations that may mislead readers?
- Do technical terms require definition or qualification?

2. **Read your paper aloud to identify errors.**

3. **Use peer editing to locate errors you may have missed.**

CLASSIFICATION

Like division, classification breaks a complex subject into parts. But in classification, the categories are rated according to a standard. Burns are classified as first-, second-, and third-degree based on the severity of tissue damage. Teachers grade tests according to the number of correct answers. Geologists classify rocks by their hardness. Insurance companies use classification to determine premiums based on potential loss. Motion pictures are rated G, PG, PG-13, R, or NC-17 based on their depictions of sex and violence. Classification can reflect personal preferences. A food critic may grant a new restaurant one or five stars depending solely on his or her experience.

Perhaps no more serious event occurs in society than when one individual causes the death of another. In addressing this issue, the law identifies a range of situations in which one person is responsible for a fatality and ranks them from the most to least objectionable:

Felonious homicide   The wrongful killing of a human being, of any age or either sex, without justification or excuse in law; of which offense there are two degrees, manslaughter and murder.

Homicide by misadventure   The accidental killing of another, where the slayer is doing a lawful act, unaccompanied by any criminally careless or reckless conduct . . .

Homicide by necessity   A species of justifiable homicide, because it arises from some unavoidable necessity, without any will, intention, or desire, and without any inadvertence or negligence in the party killing, and therefore without any shadow of blame.

Classification assists people to make decisions and direct actions. Classification can set prices, establish salaries, and in some instances save lives. Confronted with a flood of trauma victims, doctors place patients into three triage categories: those who will die with or without immediate medical attention, those who will survive without emergency treatment, and those who will die unless given immediate treatment. The last group is given priority so that doctors will not waste time on the dying or those with minor injuries.

WRITING ACTIVITY

Select one of the following topics and develop at least three classifications. Remember to use a single standard to rate the topic—price, quality, size, performance, severity, and so forth.

1. Home security systems
2. Professional athletes or teams
3. Local restaurants
4. College professors
5. Investments
6. Job security
7. Drug use
8. Friendships
9. Newspapers
10. Courses in your major

STRATEGIES for Writing Classification

Critical Thinking and Prewriting
1. **Understand the difference between division and classification.** Remember that in classification you not only divide a subject into parts but also rate the parts on a scale. Instead of simply describing or defining three

types of professors, your goal is to rate them by their status, their teaching skills, or their interest in students.

2. **List topics that you might be able to classify.** Consider subjects that you customarily rate on a scale. You may have encountered classifications in such courses as biology and accounting or in the workplace where you used a scale to respond to problems or customer requests.

3. **To focus prewriting, start with a scale.** Because classification rates subjects on a standard, you can easily identify workable subjects and discard unusable ones if you work with a scale. You might develop a generic chart to explore topics, using 1–5 stars, an A–F grading system, or a 1–10 scale to rate your topics.

   ■ You may use existing classifications or invent classifications of your own. Based on your experience you might rate customers, professors, or bosses according to your experience and opinion.

Planning

1. **Establish a clearly defined standard of measurement.** If you plan to classify cars by price, determine whether you are going to use wholesale or dealer prices. If you rate cars by resale value, establish the methods used to obtain your figures.

2. **Do not mix standards.** The most common mistake writers make in classification is mixing standards. You can classify cars by price, engine performance, reliability, or safety—but you can't write a paper about cars that discusses one as being safe, another as being expensive, and another as being easy to maintain.

3. **Define each category clearly.** To successfully teach writing, for example, an English professor must provide students with a clear understanding of what distinguishes an A paper from a B paper. Even if you are making up your own categories, each one should be clearly defined so readers can understand what separates each classification.

4. **Arrange categories in order.** Organize the categories so they follow a ladderlike progression, such as judging items from the best to the worst, the cheapest to most expensive, the newest to the oldest.

5. **Provide enough categories or classes to include all parts of the whole.** If you classify cars as being either American or foreignmade, how would you account for Toyotas produced in the United States or Chryslers assembled in Mexico?

6. **Make sure all topics fit only one class.** Every unit should fit only a single category. Make sure you have no leftover items that either can fit in more than one class or cannot be accounted for.

7. **Note any exceptions or variations to the classification.**

Writing the First Draft

1. **As you write, keep your thesis in mind—to rate items on a scale.**
2. **Use concrete language and details to distinguish each class and describe each item.** Avoid vague or general descriptions. Be as accurate as you can in defining standards.
3. **Illustrate each class with examples readers can identify.** Consider your audience carefully to select items they will understand. If you rate films, make references to movies your readers will recognize.
4. **Use parallel structures to develop categories.** Develop common reference points so that readers can distinguish between categories and compare examples.
5. **Monitor the length of your draft.** As with division, a classification paper can easily balloon into a much longer essay. If you realize that to fully classify your subject, your essay will expand beyond the scope of the assignment, consider narrowing your topic or selecting a new subject.
6. **Note new ideas, but remember your goal—to rate items on a common scale.**

Revising

1. **Analyze your thesis.**
   - Is your overall subject clearly defined?
2. **Review your method of classification.**
   - Does your classification make meaningful or only arbitrary distinctions between items? Will your scale help people understand the subject and make decisions?
   - Are your categories clearly defined?
   - Are there any gaps between categories? Do categories overlap?
   - Are the categories arranged in a progressive order, moving from small to large, cheap to costly, worst to best, or strongest to weakest?
3. **Examine the categories for balance and completeness.**
   - Are some categories sharply defined and others vaguely worded?
   - Are some categories illustrated with four examples and others with just one?
4. **Can all items or parts be placed on your scale? Do you account for variations or exceptions?**
5. **Use peer review to identify areas needing improvement.**

Editing and Proofreading

1. **Read your paper aloud.**
   - Is your paper stated in concrete, accurate language?

■ Do any terms require further clarification or definition?
■ Do some words have connotations that may confuse readers?
2. **Consider using visual aids.**
■ Would your classification be easier to understand and recall if the text were supported by a chart, graph, or grid?
3. **Use peer editing to locate errors you may have missed.**

STUDENT PAPER

This paper was written in response to the following assignment:

Write a 500-word paper classifying people, objects, or issues you have observed on campus. Make sure that you choose meaningful divisions and describe each category fully.

Hispanics on Campus

Students, faculty, and administrators tend to refer to "Hispanics" as if all Latino and Latina students belonged to a single homogeneous group. Actually, there are four distinct groups of Hispanic students. Outsiders may only see slight discrepancies in dress and behavior, but there are profound differences which occasionally border on suspicion and hostility. Their differences are best measured by their attitude toward and their degree of acceptance of mainstream American values and culture.

The least assimilated and most alien group of these students are politically active immigrants or children of immigrants. These are the students who sponsored the recent protest against Western Civilization courses. Most of them were born in Mexico or Puerto Rico. English is their second language and a perceived cultural barrier. Because of this, they tend to see European culture as oppressive, an arbitrary hurdle blocking their progress. They are keenly sensitive to negative stereotypes of Hispanics and resent media portrayals of bandits, drug dealers, and gang members.

Equally alien to American culture but less politically active are the foreign students from Latin America. Whether they are from Mexico, Chile, or Argentina, they speak excellent English. Many have lived or studied in Europe. As citizens of their native countries, they have no insecurities about their ethnic identities and seem willing to mix socially with Americans, but only if they share the same class values. Unlike the immigrants, they consider themselves linked to European culture. Many speak French and

German in addition to Spanish and Italian. Often they seem to feel more at home with foreign students from Europe than either Americans or other Hispanic students.

The most assimilated and largest group of Hispanic students are second and third generation Latinos and Latinas. Few speak more than a few Spanish phrases. Many pronounce their names with an Anglo accent, so that they say "Rammer-ez" for Ramirez. They interact with all students and consider themselves Americans. Their parents work for IBM, sell real estate, or own restaurants. These students are not politically active. They use the terms "Chicano," "Latino," and "Spanish" interchangeably. Although many participate in Hispanic cultural activities on campus, they generally avoid political rallies. Only a few consider themselves radical and some, especially the Cuban-Americans, are extremely conservative.

There is a group of Hispanics who are so assimilated into mainstream American culture that I call them invisible. Because of intermarriage, many Hispanics have last names like O'Brien, Edelman, and Kowalski. My father is third generation Irish. While working on an engineering project in Mexico, he met my mother, who ironically had an Irish grandmother. I was born in San Diego but spent almost every summer in Cancun with my aunt. I speak and write Spanish. I subscribe to Mexican magazines. I serve on numerous Hispanic organizations. But because of my blonde hair and my last name, Callaghan, I am frequently viewed as an outsider by Hispanics who don't speak Spanish.

Questions for Review and Revision

1. What is the student's thesis?
2. How does the student define her standard of measurement?
3. What value does this classification have in understanding Hispanic students?
4. Is each class of students clearly defined? Can you think of any students who would not fit in one of the categories?
5. Does the student include enough examples or descriptions to fully explain each category of students?
6. Read the essay aloud. Can you detect weak or awkward passages that need revision?

Writing Suggestions

1. Using this paper as a model, write a similar classification paper about students on your campus. Classify students by academic performance, school

spirit, support of athletic teams, or involvement in campus activities or politics. Remember to use a single standard or method of evaluation.

2. *Collaborative writing:* Discuss this essay with other students. Do students in other ethnic groups fit a pattern similar to the Hispanics at the writer's college? Work together to select a group and write a short paper that classifies them into different types.

SUGGESTED TOPICS FOR WRITING DIVISION AND CLASSIFICATION

General Assignments

Separating into parts

Write a division essay on any of the following topics. Your division may make use of standard categories or ones you invent. Remember to clearly state the way you are dividing your subject. Each subject or example should be supported with definitions, brief narratives, or descriptions.

- Dates you have had
- Basketball, football, or baseball teams
- Career opportunities in your field
- Popular music
- Student housing
- Computer systems you have worked with
- Charitable organizations
- Women's groups
- Local restaurants

Rating categories

Write a classification essay on any of the following topics. Make sure to use a single method rating the subtopics, from best to worst, easiest to hardest, least desirable to most desirable, or least expensive to most expensive.

- Jobs you have had
- Diets
- Talk shows
- Current movies
- Professors, coaches, or bosses you have known

- Football teams
- Cars
- Personal computers
- Hotels

 To create your own interactive writing project, use the textual, visual, and video libraries on *Comp21*. From the main menu, choose "Build Your Own Occasion for Writing."

Writing in Context

1. Assume you have been asked by a national magazine to write about students' political attitudes. You may develop your essay by division or classification. You can discuss politics in general terms of liberal and conservative attitudes or concentrate on a single issue, such as capital punishment or legalizing marijuana.
2. Write a humorous paper about campus fashion by dividing students into types. Invent titles or labels for each group and supply enough details so that readers can readily fit the people they meet into one of your categories.

STRATEGIES | for Reading Division and Classification

As you read the division and classification entries in this chapter, keep these questions in mind:

Context
1. What is the writer trying to explain by dividing or classifying the subject? Does the writer have another goal—to inform, entertain, or persuade?
2. Do the divisions risk oversimplifying the subject?
3. Do the classification essays have a clearly defined scale or standard?
4. Do the standards seem fair or adequate? Do they accurately measure what they claim to evaluate?

Strategy
1. How does the writer introduce or establish the divisions or classes?
2. How does the author illustrate each type with other modes such as example, definition, or narrative?

3. Does the writer use an existing, long-established standard or one he or she invented?
4. Is the goal of the paper to explain items or recommend one over others?

Language
1. What does the level of language reveal about the intended audience?
2. What words does the author use to describe or define categories? Do the connotations of any of these words reveal positive or negative attitudes toward specific items? Do you detect a bias?

Russell Baker (1925 –) was born in Virginia and raised in New Jersey and Maryland. After serving in World War II, he attended Johns Hopkins University. After graduating in 1947, Baker became a reporter for a Baltimore newspaper. In the 1950s he joined the staff of the **New York Times** and covered the White House and the State Department. In 1962 he began writing "Observer," a column that now appears in hundreds of newspapers. In the 1980s he published two autobiographical books, **Growing Up** and **The Good Times.** Many of his columns appeared in the collection **There's a Country in My Cellar** in 1990.

The Plot Against People

In this humorous piece, Baker invents three categories of common objects we encounter. As you read the essay, notice how Baker uses definition, description, *and* example.

Inanimate objects are classified into three major categories—those that don't work, those that break down and those that get lost. 1 thesis

The goal of all inanimate objects is to resist man and ultimately to defeat him, and the three major classifications are based on the method each object uses to achieve its purpose. As a general rule, any object capable of breaking down at the moment when it is needed most will do so. The automobile is typical of the category. 2 examples / categories

With the cunning typical of its breed, the automobile never breaks down while entering a filling station with a large staff of idle mechanics. It waits until it reaches a downtown intersection in the middle of the rush hour, or until it is fully loaded with family and luggage on the Ohio Turnpike. 3 category #1

Thus it creates maximum misery, inconvenience, frustration and irritability among its human cargo, thereby reducing its owner's life span. 4

Washing machines, garbage disposals, lawn mowers, light bulbs, automatic laundry dryers, water pipes, furnaces, electrical fuses, television tubes, hose nozzles, tape recorders, slide projectors—all are in league with the automobile to take their turn at breaking down whenever life threatens to flow smoothly for their human enemies. 5 examples

Many inanimate objects, of course, find it extremely difficult to break down. Pliers, for example, and gloves and keys are almost totally incapable 6 category #2 of breaking down. Therefore, they have had to evolve a different technique for resisting man.

7   They get lost. Science has still not solved the mystery of how they do it, and no man has ever caught one of them in the act of getting lost. The most plausible theory is that they have developed a secret method of locomotion which they are able to conceal the instant a human eye falls upon them.

8   It is not uncommon for a pair of pliers to climb all the way from the cellar to the attic in its single-minded determination to raise its owner's blood pressure. Keys have been known to burrow three feet under mattresses. Women's purses, despite their great weight, frequently travel through six or seven rooms to find a hiding space under a couch.

9   Scientists have been struck by the fact that things that break down virtually never get lost, while things that get lost hardly ever break down.

examples 10   A furnace, for example, will invariably break down at the depth of the first winter cold wave, but it will never get lost. A woman's purse, which after all does have some inherent capacity for breaking down, hardly ever does; it almost invariably chooses to get lost.

11   Some persons believe this constitutes evidence that inanimate objects are not entirely hostile to man, and that a negotiated peace is possible. After all, they point out, a furnace could infuriate a man even more thoroughly by getting lost than by breaking down, just as a glove could upset him far more by breaking down than by getting lost.

12   Not everyone agrees, however, that this indicates a conciliatory attitude among inanimate objects. Many say it merely proves that furnaces, gloves and pliers are incredibly stupid.

category #3 13   The third class of objects—those that don't work—is the most curious of all. These include such objects as barometers, car clocks, cigarette examples   lighters, flashlights and toy train locomotives. It is inaccurate, of course, to say that they never work. They work once, usually for the first few hours after being brought home, and then quit. Thereafter, they never work again.

14   In fact, it is widely assumed that they are built for the purpose of not working. Some people have reached advanced ages without ever seeing some of these objects—barometers, for example—in working order.

15   Science is utterly baffled by the entire category. There are many theories about it. The most interesting holds that the things that don't work have attained the highest state possible for an inanimate object, the state to which things that break down and things that get lost can still only aspire.

conclusion 16   They have truly defeated man by conditioning him never to expect anything of them, and in return they have given man the only peace he receives from inanimate society. He does not expect his barometer to work, his electric locomotive to run, his cigarette lighter to light or his flashlight to illuminate, and when they don't, it does not raise his blood pressure.

Understanding Context

1. What is Baker's purpose?
2. How have objects "defeated" people?
3. Are there objects that you frankly do not expect to work?
4. *Critical thinking:* Humor is often based on acute observation. What is Baker saying about the lives of Americans, who often measure their success or happiness by the number of objects they possess? Do all the things we yearn to have truly enrich or merely complicate our lives?

Evaluating Strategy

1. Why is the essay's introduction important? Is it effective in setting up the body of the essay?
2. How important are the examples Baker uses to define each category? Can readers relate to these?
3. Baker creates three categories. Would the humor of the essay wear thin if he invented four, five, or six categories? Is there a limit to audience attention when reading for entertainment?

Appreciating Language

1. Baker uses the third person to describe people's experiences with objects. Would a first-person approach, emphasizing his personal encounters with things, have the same effect?
2. *Critical thinking:* Throughout this 1968 essay Baker uses male references— "man" and "he." Would a modern editor insist on nonsexist language? Would you suggest making changes? Why or why not?

Writing Suggestions

1. Write a short essay, using Baker's as a model, to humorously classify college courses, professors, local restaurants, garages, or stores. Define each type clearly, and illustrate with examples.
2. *Collaborative writing:* Discuss Baker's essay with a group of students, and work together to create a short, humorous, updated version that includes DVDs, computers, e-mail, or cell phones.

JOHN HOLT

John Holt (1923–1985) wrote several books about children and education, including **How Children Fail** and **How Children Learn.** Having taught in grade and high schools for fourteen years, Holt became a critic of the American educational system. He created and edited **Growing without Schooling,** a magazine dedicated to home schooling.

Three Kinds of Discipline

In this section from his book Freedom and Beyond *(1972), Holt classifies three types of discipline that occur in children's lives. Most people assume discipline comes only from authority figures, such as parents and teachers. Holt reveals that discipline also comes from a child's environment.*

1 A child, in growing up, may meet and learn from three different kinds of disciplines. The first and most important is what we might call the Discipline of Nature or of Reality. When he is trying to do something real, if he does the wrong thing or doesn't do the right one, he doesn't get the result he wants. If he doesn't pile one block right on top of another, or tries to build on a slanting surface, his tower falls down. If he hits the wrong key, he hears the wrong note. If he doesn't hit the nail squarely on the head, it bends, and he has to pull it out and start with another. If he doesn't measure properly what he is trying to build, it won't open, close, fit, stand up, fly, float, whistle, or do whatever he wants it to do. If he closes his eyes when he swings, he doesn't hit the ball. A child meets this kind of discipline every time he tries to *do* something, which is why it is so important in school to give children more chances to do things, instead of just reading or listening to someone talk (or pretending to). This discipline is a good teacher. The learner never has to wait long for his answer; it usually comes quickly, often instantly. Also it is clear, and very often points toward the needed correction; from what happened he can not only see that what he did was wrong, but also why, and what he needs to do instead. Finally, and most important, the giver of the answer, call it Nature, is impersonal, impartial, and indifferent. She does not give opinions, or make judgments; she cannot be wheedled, bullied, or fooled; she does not get angry or disappointed; she does not praise or blame; she does not remember past failures or hold

grudges; with her one always gets a fresh start, this time is the one that counts.

The next discipline we might call the Discipline of Culture, of Society, 2 of What People Really Do. Man is a social, a cultural animal. Children sense around them this culture, this network of agreements, customs, habits, and rules binding the adults together. They want to understand it and be a part of it. They watch very carefully what people around them are doing and want to do the same. They want to do right, unless they become convinced they can't do right. Thus children rarely misbehave seriously in church, but sit as quietly as they can. The example of all those grownups is contagious. Some mysterious ritual is going on, and children, who like rituals, want to be part of it. In the same way, the little children that I see at concerts or operas, though they may fidget a little, or perhaps take a nap now and then, rarely make any disturbance. With all those grownups sitting there, neither moving nor talking, it is the most natural thing in the world to imitate them. Children who live among adults who are habitually courteous to each other, and to them, will soon learn to be courteous. Children who live surrounded by people who speak a certain way will speak that way, however much we may try to tell them that speaking that way is bad or wrong.

The third discipline is the one most people mean when they speak of 3 discipline—the Discipline of Superior Force, of sergeant to private, of "you do what I tell you or I'll make you wish you had." There is bound to be some of this in a child's life. Living as we do surrounded by things that can hurt children, or that children can hurt, we cannot avoid it. We can't afford to let a small child find out from experience the danger of playing in a busy street, or of fooling with the pots on the top of a stove, or of eating up the pills in the medicine cabinet. So, along with other precautions, we say to him, "Don't play in the street, or touch things on the stove, or go into the medicine cabinet, or I'll punish you." Between him and the danger too great for him to imagine we put a lesser danger, but one he can imagine and maybe therefore wants to avoid. He can have no idea of what it would be like to be hit by a car, but he can imagine being shouted at, or spanked, or sent to his room. He avoids these substitutes for the greater danger until he can understand it and avoid it for its own sake. But we ought to use this discipline only when it is necessary to protect the life, health, safety, or well-being of people or other living creatures, or to prevent destruction of things that people care about. We ought not to assume too long, as we usually do, that a child cannot understand the real nature of the danger from which we want to protect him. The sooner he avoids the danger, not to escape our punishment, but as a matter of good sense, the better. He can learn that faster than we think. In Mexico, for example, where people drive their cars with a good deal of spirit, I saw many children no older than five or four walking unattended on the streets. They understood about cars, they knew what to do. A child whose life is full of the threat and fear of punishment is locked into babyhood. There is no way for him to grow up, to learn to take responsibility for his life and acts. Most important of all, we should not assume that having to yield to the threat of our superior force is good for the child's character. It is never good for *anyone's* character. To bow to superior force makes us feel impotent and cowardly for not having had the strength or courage to resist. Worse, it makes us resentful and vengeful. We can hardly wait to make someone pay for our humiliation, yield to us as we were once made to yield. No, if we cannot always avoid using the discipline of Superior Force, we should at least use it as seldom as we can.

4   There are places where all three disciplines overlap. Any very demanding human activity combines in it the disciplines of Superior Force, of Culture, and of Nature. The novice will be told, "Do it this way, never mind asking why, just do it that way, that is the way we always do it." But it probably *is* just the way they always do it, and usually for the very good reason that it is a way that has been found to work. Think, for example, of ballet training. The student in a class is told to do this exercise, or that; to stand so; to do this or that with his head, arms, shoulders, abdomen, hips, legs, feet. He is constantly corrected. There is no argument. But behind these seemingly autocratic demands by the teacher lie many decades of custom and tradition, and behind that, the necessities of dancing itself. You cannot make the moves of classical ballet unless over many years you have acquired, and renewed every day, the needed strength and suppleness in scores of muscles and joints. Nor can you do the difficult motions, making them look easy, unless you have learned hundreds of easier ones first. Dance teachers may not always agree on all the details of teaching these strengths and skills. But no novice could learn them all by himself. You could not go for a night or two to watch the ballet and then, without any other knowledge at all, teach yourself how to do it. In the same way, you would be unlikely to learn any complicated and difficult human activity without drawing heavily on the experience of those who know it better. But the point is that the authority of these experts or teachers stems from, grows out of their greater competence and experience, the fact that what they do *works*, not the fact that they happen to be the teacher and as such have the power to kick a student out of the class. And the further point is that children are always and everywhere attracted to that competence, and ready and eager to submit themselves to a discipline that grows out of it. We hear constantly that children will never do anything unless compelled to by bribes or threats. But in their private lives, or in extracurricular activities in school, in sports, music, drama, art, running

a newspaper, and so on, they often submit themselves willingly and whole-heartedly to very intense disciplines, simply because they want to learn to do a given thing well. Our Little-Napoleon football coaches, of whom we have too many and hear far too much, blind us to the fact that millions of children work hard every year getting better at sports and games without coaches barking and yelling at them.

Understanding Context

1. What lessons in discipline do children learn from experience?
2. How does Holt define discipline? Is learning about the limits of experience in the physical world, such as the effect of gravity, a kind of discipline?
3. What is Holt's opinion of parental authority? When is parental discipline justified in his view?
4. *Critical thinking:* What does Holt's view of discipline reveal about his attitude toward children? How much discipline can children learn on their own? Is strict discipline from parents and teachers effective? Would some consider Holt permissive?

Evaluating Strategy

1. How does Holt organize his classification? What standard of measurement does he use?
2. Holt invents titles to describe each discipline. How effective are they?
3. *Other modes:* Where does Holt use narration and definition to develop his essay?

Appreciating Language

1. What connotations do you associate with the word *discipline*?
2. How does word choice reveal Holt's attitude about each form of discipline?

Writing Suggestions

1. Holt wrote this essay before the recent tide of violence and school shootings. In an era when many public schools search students with metal detectors and require them to wear uniforms, would many teachers and

parents reject his views? Write a short essay expressing your own views on school discipline. Classify schools from the most to least desirable.

2. *Collaborative writing:* Working with a group of students, discuss the issue of raising and disciplining children. Consider your own childhood. If any of the members are parents, ask their honest opinion of Holt's essay. Take notes on the comments and work together to write a definition of good childhood discipline.

STEPHANIE ERICSSON

Stephanie Ericsson (1953–) grew up in California and became a screenwriter and advertising copywriter. She has written books based on her own experiences, including two books about addiction: *Shamefaced: The Road to Recovery* (1985) and *Women of AA: Recovering Together* (1985). She also wrote about the unexpected death of her husband in *Companion Through the Darkness: Inner Dialogues on Grief* (1993). The following year she published *Companion Into the Dawn: Inner Dialogues on Loving,* a collection essays.

The Ways We Lie

Before reading this essay, consider your own views about lying. Do you always tell the truth? Are lies always immoral or deceitful or do they sometimes shield people from unpleasant facts or spare people's feelings? Do you consider failing to inform someone or allowing someone to believe an untruth a lie? Is honesty always the best policy?

The bank called today and I told them my deposit was in the mail, even 1 though I hadn't written a check yet. It'd been a rough day. The baby I'm pregnant with decided to do aerobics on my lungs for two hours, our three-year-old daughter painted the living-room couch with lipstick, the IRS put me on hold for an hour, and I was late to a business meeting because I was tired.

I told my client the traffic had been bad. When my partner came home, 2 his haggard face told me his day hadn't gone any better than mine, so when he asked, "How was your day?" I said, "Oh, fine," knowing that one more straw might break his back. A friend called and wanted to take me to lunch. I said I was busy. Four lies in the course of a day, none of which I felt the least bit guilty about.

We lie. We all do. We exaggerate, we minimize, we avoid confrontation, 3 we spare people's feelings, we conveniently forget, we keep secrets, we justify lying to the big-guy institutions. Like most people, I indulge in small falsehoods and still think of myself as an honest person. Sure I lie, but it doesn't hurt anything. Or does it?

4   I once tried going a whole week without telling a lie, and it was paralyzing. I discovered that telling the truth all the time is nearly impossible. It means living with some serious consequences: The bank charges me $60 in overdraft fees, my partner keels over when I tell him about my travails, my client fires me for telling her I didn't feel like being on time, and my friend takes it personally when I say I'm not hungry. There must be some merit to lying.

5   But if I justify lying, what makes me any different from slick politicians or the corporate robbers who raided the S&L industry? Saying it's okay to lie one way and not another is hedging. I cannot seem to escape the voice deep inside me that tells me: When someone lies, someone loses.

6   What far-reaching consequences will I, or others, pay as a result of my lie? Will someone's trust be destroyed? Will someone else pay *my* penance because I ducked out? We must consider the *meaning of our actions*. Deception, lies, capital crimes, and misdemeanors all carry meanings. *Webster's* definition of *lie* is specific:

1: a false statement or action especially made with the intent to deceive;
2: anything that gives or is meant to give a false impression.

7   A definition like this implies that there are many, many ways to tell a lie. Here are just a few.

The White Lie

A man who won't lie to a woman has very little consideration for her feelings.

—*Bergen Evans*

8   The white lie assumes that the truth will cause more damage than a simple, harmless untruth. Telling a friend he looks great when he looks like hell can be based on a decision that the friend needs a compliment more than a frank opinion. But, in effect, it is the liar deciding what is best for the lied to. Ultimately, it is a vote of no confidence. It is an act of subtle arrogance for anyone to decide what is best for someone else.

9   Yet not all circumstances are quite so cut-and-dried. Take, for instance, the sergeant in Vietnam who knew one of his men was killed in action but listed him as missing so that the man's family would receive indefinite compensation instead of the lump-sum pittance the military gives widows and children. His intent was honorable. Yet for twenty years this family kept their hopes alive, unable to move on to a new life.

Facades

> Et tu, Brute?
>
> *—Caesar**

We all put up facades to one degree or another. When I put on a suit to go 10 to see a client, I feel as though I am putting on another face, obeying the expectation that serious businesspeople wear suits rather than sweatpants. But I'm a writer. Normally, I get up, get the kid off to school, and sit at my computer in my pajamas until four in the afternoon. When I answer the phone, the caller thinks I'm wearing a suit (though the UPS man knows better).

But facades can be destructive because they are used to seduce others 11 into an illusion. For instance, I recently realized that a former friend was a liar. He presented himself with all the right looks and the right words and offered lots of new consciousness theories, fabulous books to read, and fascinating insights. Then I did some business with him, and the time came for him to pay me. He turned out to be all talk and no walk. I heard a plethora of reasonable excuses, including in-depth descriptions of the big break around the corner. In six months of work, I saw less than a hundred bucks. When I confronted him, he raised both eyebrows and tried to convince me that I'd heard him wrong, that he'd made no commitment to me. A simple investigation into his past revealed a crowded graveyard of disenchanted former friends.

Ignoring the Plain Facts

> Well, you must understand that Father Porter is only human. . . .
>
> *—A Massachusetts priest*

In the '60s, the Catholic Church in Massachusetts began hearing complaints 12 that Father James Porter was sexually molesting children. Rather than relieving him of his duties, the ecclesiastical authorities simply moved him from one parish to another between 1960 and 1967, actually providing him with a fresh supply of unsuspecting families and innocent children to abuse. After treatment in 1967 for pedophilia, he went back to work, this time in Minnesota. The new diocese was aware of Father Porter's obsession with children, but they needed priests and recklessly believed treatment had cured him. More children were abused until he was relieved of his duties a year later. By his own admission, Porter may have abused as many as a hundred children.

---

* EDS. NOTE—"And you, Brutus?" (Latin). In Shakespeare's play *Julius Caesar*, Caesar asks this question when he sees Brutus, whom he has believed to be his friend, among the conspirators who are stabbing him.

13   Ignoring the facts may not in and of itself be a form of lying, but consider the context of this situation. If a lie is *a false action done with the intent to deceive*, then the Catholic Church's conscious covering for Porter created irreparable consequences. The church became a co-perpetrator with Porter.

Deflecting

> When you have no basis for an argument, abuse the plaintiff.
>
> —*Cicero*

14   I've discovered that I can keep anyone from seeing the true me by being selectively blatant. I set a precedent of being up-front about intimate issues, but I never bring up the things I truly want to hide; I just let people assume I'm revealing everything. It's an effective way of hiding.

15   Any good liar knows that the way to perpetuate an untruth is to deflect attention from it. When Clarence Thomas exploded with accusations that the Senate hearings were a "high-tech lynching," he simply switched the focus from a highly charged subject to a radioactive subject. Rather than defending himself, he took the offensive and accused the country of racism. It was a brilliant maneuver. Racism is now politically incorrect in official circles—unlike sexual harassment, which still rewards those who can get away with it.

16   Some of the most skillful deflectors are passive-aggressive people who when accused of inappropriate behavior, refuse to respond to the accusations. This you-don't-exist stance infuriates the accuser, who, understandably, screams something obscene out of frustration. The trap is sprung and the act of deflection successful, because now the passive-aggressive person can indignantly say, "Who can talk to someone as unreasonable as you?" The real issue is forgotten and the sins of the original victim become the focus. Feeling guilty of name-calling, the victim is fully tamed and crawls into a hole, ashamed. I have watched this fighting technique work thousands of times in disputes between men and women, and what I've learned is that the real culprit is not necessarily the one who swears the loudest.

Omission

> The cruelest lies are often told in silence.
>
> —*R. L. Stevenson*

17   Omission involves telling most of the truth minus one or two key facts whose absence changes the story completely. You break a pair of glasses that are guaranteed under normal use and get a new pair, without mentioning that the first pair broke during a rowdy game of basketball. Who hasn't tried

something like that? But what about omission of information that could make a difference in how a person lives his or her life?

For instance, one day I found out that rabbinical legends tell of another [18] woman in the Garden of Eden before Eve. I was stunned. The omission of the Sumerian goddess Lilith from Genesis—as well as her demonization by ancient misogynists as an embodiment of female evil—felt like spiritual robbery. I felt like I'd just found out my mother was really my step-mother. To take seriously the tradition that Adam was created out of the same mud as his equal counterpart, Lilith, redefines all of Judeo-Christian history.

Some renegade Catholic feminists introduced me to a view of Lilith that [19] had been suppressed during the many centuries when this strong goddess was seen only as a spirit of evil. Lilith was a proud goddess who defied Adam's need to control her, attempted negotiations, and when this failed, said adios and left the Garden of Eden.

This omission of Lilith from the Bible was a patriarchal strategy to keep [20] women weak. Omitting the strong-woman archetype of Lilith from Western religions and starting the story with Eve the Rib has helped keep Christian and Jewish women believing they were the lesser sex for thousands of years.

Stereotypes and Clichés

> Where opinion does not exist, the status quo becomes stereotyped and all originality is discouraged.
>
> —*Bertrand Russell*

Stereotype and cliché serve a purpose as a form of shorthand. Our need for [21] vast amounts of information in nanoseconds has made the stereotype vital to modern communication. Unfortunately, it often shuts down original thinking, giving those hungry for the truth a candy bar of misinformation instead of a balanced meal. The stereotype explains a situation with just enough truth to seem unquestionable.

All the "isms"—racism, sexism, ageism, et al.—are founded on and fu- [22] eled by the stereotype and the cliché, which are lies of exaggeration, omission, and ignorance. They are always dangerous. They take a single tree and make it a landscape. They destroy curiosity. They close minds and separate people. The single mother on welfare is assumed to be cheating. Any black male could tell you how much of his identity is obliterated daily by stereotypes. Fat people, ugly people, beautiful people, old people, large-breasted women, short men, the mentally ill, and the homeless all could tell you how much more they are like us than we want to think. I once admitted to a group of people that I had a mouth like a truck driver. Much to my surprise, a man stood up and said, "I'm a truck driver, and I never cuss." Needless to say, I was humbled.

Groupthink

> Who is more foolish, the child afraid of the dark, or the man afraid of the light?
>
> —*Maurice Freehill*

23 Irving Janis, in *Victims of Group Think*, defines this sort of lie as a psychological phenomenon within decision-making groups in which loyalty to the group has become more important than any other value, with the result that dissent and the appraisal of alternatives are suppressed. If you've ever worked on a committee or in a corporation, you've encountered groupthink. It requires a combination of other forms of lying—ignoring facts, selective memory, omission, and denial, to name a few.

24   The textbook example of groupthink came on December 7, 1941. From as early as the fall of 1941, the warnings came in, one after another, that Japan was preparing for a massive military operation. The Navy command in Hawaii assumed Pearl Harbor was invulnerable—the Japanese weren't stupid enough to attack the United States' most important base. On the other hand, racist stereotypes said the Japanese weren't smart enough to invent a torpedo effective in less than 60 feet of water (the fleet was docked in 30 feet); after all, U.S. technology hadn't been able to do it.

25   On Friday, December 5, normal weekend leave was granted to all the commanders at Pearl Harbor, even though the Japanese consulate in Hawaii was busy burning papers. Within the tight, good-ole-boy cohesiveness of the U.S. command in Hawaii, the myth of invulnerability stayed well entrenched. No one in the group considered the alternatives. The rest is history.

Out-and-Out Lies

> The only form of lying that is beyond reproach is lying for its own sake.
>
> —*Oscar Wilde*

26 Of all the ways to lie, I like this one the best, probably because I get tired of trying to figure out the real meanings behind things. At least I can trust the bald-faced lie. I once asked my five-year-old nephew, "Who broke the fence?" (I had seen him do it.) He answered, "The murderers." Who could argue?

27   At least when this sort of lie is told it can be easily confronted. As the person who is lied to, I know where I stand. The bald-faced lie doesn't toy with my perceptions—it argues with them. It doesn't try to refashion

reality, it tries to refute it. *Read my lips.* . . . No sleight of hand. No guessing. If this were the only form of lying, there would be no such thing as floating anxiety or the adult-children of alcoholics movement.

Dismissal

> Pay no attention to that man behind the curtain! I am the Great Oz!
> —*The Wizard of Oz*

Dismissal is perhaps the slipperiest of all lies. Dismissing feelings, percep- 28 tions, or even the raw facts of a situation ranks as a kind of lie that can do as much damage to a person as any other kind of lie.

The roots of many mental disorders can be traced back to the dismissal 29 of reality. Imagine that a person is told from the time she is a tot that her perceptions are inaccurate. *"Mommy, I'm scared."* "No, you're not, darling." *"I don't like that man next door, he makes me feel icky."* "Johnny, that's a terrible thing to say, of course you like him. You go over there right now and be nice to him."

I've often mused over the idea that madness is actually a sane reaction 30 to an insane world. Psychologist R. D. Laing supports this hypothesis in *Sanity, Madness & the Family*, an account of his investigations into families of schizophrenics. The common thread that ran through all of the families he studied was a deliberate, staunch dismissal of the patient's perceptions from a very early age. Each of the patients started out with an accurate grasp of reality, which, through meticulous and methodical dismissal, was demolished until the only reality the patient could trust was catatonia.

Dismissal runs the gamut. Mild dismissal can be quite handy for forgiv- 31 ing the foibles of others in our day-to-day lives. Toddlers who have just learned to manipulate their parents' attention sometimes are dismissed out of necessity. Absolute attention from the parents would require so much energy that no one would get to eat dinner. But we must be careful and attentive about how far we take our "necessary" dismissals. Dismissal is a dangerous tool, because it's nothing less than a lie.

Delusion

> We lie loudest when we lie to ourselves.
> —*Eric Hoffer*

I could write the book on this one. Delusion, a cousin of dismissal, is the ten- 32 dency to see excuses as facts. It's a powerful lying tool because it filters out information that contradicts what we want to believe. Alcoholics who believe that the problems in their lives are legitimate reasons for drinking rather than results of the drinking offer the classic example of deluded thinking. Delusion uses the mind's ability to see things in myriad ways to support what it wants to be the truth.

33   But delusion is also a survival mechanism we all use. If we were to fully contemplate the consequences of our stockpiles of nuclear weapons or global warming, we could hardly function on a day-to-day level. We don't want to incorporate that much reality into our lives because to do so would be paralyzing.

34   Delusion acts as an adhesive to keep the status quo intact. It shamelessly employs dismissal, omission, and amnesia, among other sorts of lies. Its most cunning defense is that it cannot see itself.

> The liar's punishment . . . is that he cannot believe anyone else.
> —*George Bernard Shaw*

35 These are only a few of the ways we lie. Or are lied to. As I said earlier it's not easy to entirely eliminate lies from our lives. No matter how pious we may try to be, we will still embellish, hedge, and omit to lubricate the daily machinery of living. But there is a world of difference between telling functional lies and living a lie. Martin Buber* once said, "The lie is the spirit committing treason against itself." Our acceptance of lies becomes a cultural cancer that eventually shrouds and reorders reality until moral garbage becomes as invisible to us as water is to a fish.

36   How much do we tolerate before we become sick and tired of being sick and tired? When will we stand up and declare our *right* to trust? When do we stop accepting that the real truth is in the fine print? Whose lips do we read this year when we vote for president? When will we stop being so reticent about making judgments? When do we stop turning over our personal power and responsibility to liars?

37   Maybe if I don't tell the bank the check's in the mail I'll be less tolerant of the lies told me every day. A country song I once heard said it all for me: "You've got to stand for something or you'll fall for anything."

Understanding Context

1. Why do people lie?
2. Does Ericsson see a difference in the severity of lies? Are some lies more harmful than others?

---

* EDS. NOTE—Austrian-born Judaic philosopher (1878–1965).

3. Can people cause unintended harm even when believe they are lying for a valid reason? Consider Ericsson's example of the army sergeant who listed a dead man as missing in action so his family could receive continued benefits.
4. How do people lie by omission?
5. *Critical thinking:* Ericsson includes "group think" and "stereotypes" in her list of lies. Are these really "lies" or merely mistakes in judgment? If people wrongly believe something to be true is that the same thing as consciously stating something they know is untrue?

Evaluating Strategy

1. How important are the labels Ericsson gives each type of lie?
2. How does Ericsson use examples to illustrate each lie?
3. Ericsson includes brief quotations for each example. Are these effective? Do they add authority to her argument?
4. Ericsson uses both historical and hypothetical examples. Are they both effective? Can historical examples appear biased? Are hypothetical examples weak because they are imaginary?
5. Ericsson uses first-person examples of her own lying. What does this admission suggest? What effect does it have on readers?

Appreciating Language

1. What does the style and level of diction suggest about Ericsson's intended audience?
2. *Critical thinking:* Consider the language used to describe lying. What do such terms as *misspoke, fibbed, misstated, gave the wrong impression,* and *white lie* suggest? How do connotations shape our view of lying?

Writing Suggestions

1. Write an essay that provides your personal classification of lies, ranking them from the most to least harmful. Provide examples of each type.
2. Describe a situation in which someone you know told a lie. Did one deception lead to another? Did the lie cause harm he or she never anticipated?
3. *Collaborative writing:* Discuss Ericsson's essay with a group of students and record their responses to this question: If they observed a coworker stealing from their employer, would they say nothing, talk to the employee, or tell a

supervisor? If asked by a superior whether they had seen anyone take anything, would they inform on their colleague or lie? Would their decision be influenced by the value of the theft? Record your group's statements and develop a classification or division essay detailing their responses.

e-reading

Infotrac College Edition
www.infotrac-college.com

ETHICS

Our cheating is the logical conclusion of individualism run amok. When we cheat, we act as if we were alone in the universe, as if the rules that oblige everyone else to play fair did not apply to us. When we cheat, we behave as if we were free to ignore the covenants that tether us to the rest of humanity.

Patrick McCormick

Couple at the Mouth of Truth, Rome   Bettmann/Corbis

In 2005 the White House announced it was requiring staff members to attend ethics classes. The controversy over the leaking of a CIA agent's identity and accusations that the administration misled the public about Iraq's weapons of mass destruction weakened the president's standing in the polls. A decade earlier President Clinton was impeached, charged with perjury and obstruction of justice. He admitted to making misleading statements about a sexual relationship and was suspended from practicing law for five years. Clinton's ambassador to Switzerland, Larry Lawrence, had to be disinterred from the Arlington National Cemetery when records revealed he had lied about being a decorated veteran.

Controversies and charges of ethical misconduct also occur in professional sports, churches, academics, and journalism.

Major league baseball players have been accused of using steroids to enhance their performance. Their denials or explanations about unknowingly taking banned substances disillusion fans and sportswriters.

In 1998 Stephen Glass, a writer for the *New Republic*, admitted that he falsified many of his stories, inventing quotations, people, and events. In 2003 Jayson Blair and several senior editors resigned from the *New York Times* after it was discovered that Blair had fictionalized news reports.

While selling their own holdings in the company, Enron executives urged employees to retain their shares, reassuring them that the firm, then nearing collapse, was fiscally sound. Martha Stewart and other prominent businesspeople were accused or convicted of insider trading or lying to investigators.

Surveys revealed wide-scale cheating and plagiarism in high schools and colleges. Schools themselves were charged with distorting data and misrepresenting test scores to claim higher standards than they could actually document and to secure government funding.

The Internet and the growing blogosphere have created new ethical challenges, allowing individuals to both spread suppressed truths and invented falsehoods.

Before reading these articles, consider these questions:

Do you think people are less honest today than in the past?

Do you believe that high profile scandals give the public a distorted view of the amount of corruption in society?

Have you witnessed ethical violations among your peers at work or school?

Do you consider omitting a truth the same as telling a lie? If someone fails to admit to a sexual partner that he or she is HIV positive or does not tell an employer about a past fraud conviction, is that the same as lying?

Is presenting facts taken out of context to persuade others the same as lying? If a criminal's guilt is clearly proven by DNA evidence, fingerprints, and videotape and his or her attorney appears on television arguing that "no eyewitness links my client to the crime," is that lawyer lying? Why or why not? Can a true statement become a lie if its purpose is to mislead?

E-Readings Online

Search for each article by author or title after entering InfoTrac College Edition through your 1Pass account login.

Stephen Goode. *A Historian Who Lies About His Own Past.*
Goode examines the life of a Pulitzer Prize–winning professor who falsely claimed to have served in Vietnam and to have been a civil rights activist and asks "do his lies as a man cast doubt on his veracity as a historian?"

Jet. *Are Lies More Believable Than the Truth?*
A noted psychologist states that "individuals construct reality in their own mind. If you believe something is true, it becomes true regardless of what the facts are."

Peter H. Schuck. *Free to Lie.*
A Yale Law School professor argues, "In a liberal democracy like ours, law must pursue the truth vigorously but not single-mindedly. Errors—and even some lying—are part of the price we pay for our freedom."

Reilly Dowd. *The Great Pretender: How a Writer Fooled His Readers.*
At twenty-five, Stephen Glass was a promising young journalist at the *New Republic* until he was exposed for making up quotations, people, and covering events that never happened.

Jean-Paul Louisot. *The Implications of "Could I?"*
"Ethics in action," Louisot argues, "is by nature proactive and in constant evolution. It is the debate between the possible and the desirable. In any given situation, the decision maker must ask 'should I?' rather than 'could I?'"

Jeffrey Kluger. *Pumping Up Your Past.*
Background checks of 2.6 million job applicants revealed that 44 percent of résumés contained false statements.

Paul Johnson. *Lies, Damned Lies, Government Statements and What You Read in the Papers.*
"Truth-telling inspires trust," Johnson argues, but when government "feels it cannot trust the public to behave if told the truth, it lies."

Lisa Snell. *How Schools Cheat.*
To comply with the No Child Left Behind Act, public schools must supply data to evaluate their accountability, but in many cases administrators supply false and misleading information to meet the requirements.

Nahal Toosi. *Internet Gives Rise to Bold New Era in College-Student Cheating.*
A survey of 2,100 students from 21 colleges found that 75 percent had cheated the previous year. In another survey, 41 percent admitted to plagiarizing Internet sources.

Patrick McCormick. *Cheaters Never Win: Cheating Has Taken Hold of Our Culture, and We're All the Worse for It.*
"Our cheating," McCormick states, "does more than rob and abuse others, it dissolves the glue that holds communities together, making us enemies and strangers."

Critical Reading and Thinking

1. According to these authors, what motivates people to lie?
2. Do these authors see situations in which deception and lying are justified?
3. Are lies about personal behavior and achievements viewed as being less serious than lies that cause harm to others?
4. What do various authors view as the value of telling the truth?
5. According to these authors, what can guide people to avoid deception?

Writing Suggestions

1. Write an essay about a deception or lie that affected you or someone you know. Did a friend's lie hurt your feelings? Did an employer's lie mislead or cheat employees or customers?
2. *Collaborative writing:* Working with a group of students, conduct a poll, asking them or a larger group of students to rate a list of falsehoods on a scale from highly unacceptable to highly acceptable. Sample falsehoods could include:
   - a husband's lying to his wife about a past affair
   - parents' omitting to tell a child he or she is adopted

- the government's withholding reports of a possible terrorist threat to prevent panic
- a drug company's faking results to get government approval
- a homosexual's lying about being gay to his elderly grandparents
- the government's deciding not to release results from a study that reveals shortcomings and overspending in a federal program
- a job applicant with two years' experience claiming to have five years' experience
- a police officer's posing as a child in an online chat room to identify sexual predators
- a woman's concealing having an abortion from her parents
- a principal's inflating test scores to obtain grant money to assist disadvantaged students
- a doctor's exaggerating chances of a full recovery to a depressed patient considering suicide

3. *Other modes*
   - Write a *cause-and-effect* essay that explores reasons why people lie or that describes the effects that being lied to has on people.
   - Develop a *persuasive* essay that proposes a standard for ethical behavior.
   - Write a *definition* of a "white lie."
   - Write a *process* essay that directs people how they should respond when when they are lied to.

Research Paper

You can develop a research paper about ethics by conducting further research to explore a range of issues:

- How did falsehood play a role in a recent political scandal?
- Are lie detectors reliable? Should their results be admissible in court?
- How does deception affect marital or parent-child relationships?
- What ethical standards do defense attorneys follow when their clients insist on presenting false testimony in court?
- How can schools and colleges prevent and detect cheating?
- How has the Internet been used to both reveal truth and spread falsehood?
- What are some of the ethical issues, challenges, or standards in the career or profession you intend to enter?

For Further Reading

To locate additional sources on ethics, enter these search terms as InfoTrac subjects:

Ethics
Subdivisions: analysis
criticism and interpretation
laws, regulations and rules
management
political aspects
psychological aspects
research
standards

Truthfulness and Falsehood
Subdivisions: analysis
evaluation
personal narratives
political aspects
psychological aspects

Additional Sources

Using a search engine such as Yahoo!, Google, or Alta Vista, enter one or more of the following terms to locate additional sources:

ethics	scandals	lying
cheating	plagiarism	falsehoods
deception	insider trading	steroids in sports
the Big Lie	white lies	perjury

See Evaluating Internet Source Checklist on page 752. See Chapter 30 for using and documenting sources.

MARTIN LUTHER KING JR.

Martin Luther King Jr. (1929–1968) was a leading figure in the civil rights movement in the 1950s and 1960s. A noted minister, King blended his deeply felt religious values and his sense of social justice. He created the Southern Christian Leadership Conference, organized many demonstrations, and lobbied for voting rights. In 1964 he received the Nobel Peace Prize. He was assassinated in 1968.

Ways of Meeting Oppression

In this section from his 1958 book Stride Toward Freedom, *King classifies three ways that oppressed people have responded to their condition. King uses classification as a method to make a persuasive argument urging readers to accept his recommended choice of action.*

1   Oppressed people deal with their oppression in three characteristic ways. One way is acquiescence: The oppressed resign themselves to their doom. They tacitly adjust themselves to oppression, and thereby become conditioned to it. In every movement toward freedom some of the oppressed prefer to remain oppressed. Almost 2,800 years ago Moses set out to lead the children of Israel from the slavery of Egypt to the freedom of the promised land. He soon discovered that slaves do not always welcome their deliverers. They become accustomed to being slaves. They would rather bear those ills they have, as Shakespeare pointed out, than flee to others that they know not of. They prefer the "fleshpots of Egypt" to the ordeals of emancipation.

2   There is such a thing as the freedom of exhaustion. Some people are so worn down by the yoke of oppression that they give up. A few years ago in the slum areas of Atlanta, a Negro guitarist used to sing almost daily: "Been down so long that down don't bother me." This is the type of negative freedom and resignation that often engulfs the life of the oppressed.

3   But this is not the way out. To accept passively an unjust system is to cooperate with that system; thereby the oppressed become as evil as the oppressor. Noncooperation with evil is as much a moral obligation as is cooperation with good. The oppressed must never allow the conscience of the oppressor to slumber. Religion reminds every man that he is his brother's keeper. To accept injustice or segregation passively is to say to the oppressor

that his actions are morally right. It is a way of allowing his conscience to fall asleep. At this moment the oppressed fails to be his brother's keeper. So acquiescence—while often the easier way—is not the moral way. It is the way of the coward. The Negro cannot win the respect of his oppressor by acquiescing; he merely increases the oppressor's arrogance and contempt. Acquiescence is interpreted as proof of the Negro's inferiority. The Negro cannot win the respect of the white people of the South or the peoples of the world if he is willing to sell the future of his children for his personal and immediate comfort and safety.

A second way that oppressed people sometimes deal with oppression is 4 to resort to physical violence and corroding hatred. Violence often brings about momentary results. Nations have frequently won their independence in battle. But in spite of temporary victories, violence never brings permanent peace. It solves no social problem; it merely creates new and more complicated ones.

Violence as a way of achieving racial injustice is both impractical and im- 5 moral. It is impractical because it is a descending spiral ending in destruction for all. The old law of an eye for an eye leaves everybody blind. It is immoral because it seeks to humiliate the opponent rather than win his understanding; it seeks to annihilate rather than to convert. Violence is immoral because it thrives on hatred rather than love. It destroys community and makes brotherhood impossible. It leaves society in monologue rather than dialogue. Violence ends by defeating itself. It creates bitterness in the survivors and brutality in the destroyers. A voice echoes through time saying to every potential Peter, "Put up your sword."* History is cluttered with the wreckage of nations that failed to follow this command.

If the American Negro and other victims of oppression succumb to the 6 temptation of using violence in the struggle for freedom, future generations will be the recipients of a desolate night of bitterness, and our chief legacy to them will be an endless reign of meaningless chaos. Violence is not the way.

The third way open to oppressed people in their quest for freedom is 7 the way of nonviolent resistance. Like the synthesis in Hegelian philosophy, the principle of nonviolent resistance seeks to reconcile the truths of two opposites—the acquiescence and violence—while avoiding the extremes and immoralities of both. The nonviolent resister agrees with the person who acquiesces that one should not be physically aggressive toward his

---

* The apostle Peter had drawn his sword to defend Christ from arrest. The voice was Christ's, who surrendered himself for trial and crucifixion (John 18: 11).

opponent; but he balances the equation by agreeing with the person of violence that evil must be resisted. He avoids the nonresistance of the former and the violent resistance of the latter. With nonviolent resistance, no individual or group need submit to any wrong, nor need anyone resort to violence in order to right a wrong.

8   It seems to me that this is the method that must guide the actions of the Negro in the present crisis in race relations. Through nonviolent resistance the Negro will be able to rise to the noble height of opposing the unjust system while loving the perpetrators of the system. The Negro must work passionately and unrelentingly for full stature as a citizen, but he must not use inferior methods to gain it. He must never come to terms with falsehood, malice, hate, or destruction.

9   Nonviolent resistance makes it possible for the Negro to remain in the South and struggle for his rights. The Negro's problem will not be solved by running away. He cannot listen to the glib suggestion of those who would urge him to migrate en masse to other sections of the country. By grasping his great opportunity in the South he can make a lasting contribution to the moral strength of the nation and set a sublime example of courage for generations yet unborn.

10   By nonviolent resistance, the Negro can also enlist all men of good will in his struggle for equality. The problem is not a purely racial one, with Negroes set against whites. In the end, it is not a struggle between people at all, but a tension between justice and injustice. Nonviolent resistance is not aimed against oppressors but against oppression. Under its banner consciences, not racial groups, are enlisted.

Understanding Context

1. Briefly describe the three ways people respond to oppression, according to King. Do you know of other ways? Do some people respond to oppression by blaming each other?
2. Humility is a Christian value. How does King, a minister, argue that humble acceptance of injustice is immoral?
3. King admits that nations have achieved freedom through violence, but why does he reject violence for African Americans?

Evaluating Strategy

1. Why does King use classification to suggest a solution instead of writing a simple persuasive argument?

2. What transitional statements does King use to direct his readers?

3. How does King use religious values to advance his argument?

Appreciating Language

1. How does King define the difference between "acquiescence" and "non-violent resistance"?

2. What do King's use of biblical analogies and reference to Hegelian philosophy reveal about his intended audience?

Writing Suggestions

1. Use this essay as a model to write your own classification paper persuading people to accept one method over others to respond to a common problem—the end of a relationship, the loss of a loved one, being victimized, or discovering a partner's infidelity. Discuss why other responses are less desirable than the one you recommend.

2. *Collaborative writing:* Discuss King's classifications with a group of students. How many people suffering oppression in the world today appear to be following the "third way"? Have a member take notes; then work together to draft a short paper dividing or classifying, if possible, your group's observations.

BLACK'S LAW DICTIONARY

Black's Law Dictionary is a standard reference used by attorneys, paralegals, administrators, and law enforcement personnel. Like any dictionary, it serves to define terms.

Homicide

In reading this entry, pay attention to the special use of language. Note how the legal definition of homicide differs from the common assumption that homicide is synonymous with murder.

1 **Homicide.** The killing of one human being by the act, procurement, or omission of another. A person is guilty of criminal homicide if he purposely, knowingly, recklessly or negligently causes the death of another human being. Criminal homicide is murder, manslaughter or negligent homicide. Model Penal Code, §210.1; 18 U.S.C.A. §1111 et seq. *See* Manslaughter; Murder.

2 Homicide is not necessarily a crime. It is a necessary ingredient of the crimes of murder and manslaughter, but there are other cases in which homicide may be committed without criminal intent and without criminal consequences, as, where it is done in the lawful execution of a judicial sentence, in self-defense, or as the only possible means of arresting an escaping felon. The term "homicide" is neutral; while it describes the act, it pronounces no judgment on its moral or legal quality. People v. Mahon, 77 Ill.App.3d 413, 395 N.E.2d 950, 958. *See Excusable homicide; Justifiable homicide, below.*

Classification

3 Homicide is ordinarily classified as "justifiable," "excusable," and "felonious." For the definitions of these terms, and of some other compound terms, see *below.*

4 *Culpable homicide.* Described as a crime varying from the very lowest culpability, up to the very verge of murder.

5 *Excusable homicide.* The killing of a human being, either by misadventure or in self-defense. Such homicide consists of a perpetrator's acting in

a manner which the law does not prohibit, such as self-defense or accidental homicide. Law v. State, 21 Md.App. 13, 318 A.2d 859, 869. The name itself imports some fault, error, or omission, so trivial, however, that the law excuses it from guilt of felony, though in strictness it judges it deserving of some little degree of punishment. It is of two sorts,—either *per infortunium*, by misadventure, or *se defendendo*, upon a sudden affray. Homicide *per infortunium* is where a man, doing a lawful act, without any intention of hurt, unfortunately kills another; but, if death ensues from any unlawful act, the offense is manslaughter, and not misadventure. Homicide *se defendendo* is where a man kills another upon a sudden affray, merely in his own defense, or in defense of his wife, child, parent, or servant, and not from any vindictive feeling. *See* Self-defense; also *Justifiable homicide, below.*

Felonious homicide. The wrongful killing of a human being, of any age or either sex, without justification or excuse in law; of which offense there are two degrees, manslaughter and murder. 6

Homicide by misadventure. The accidental killing of another, where the slayer is doing a lawful act, unaccompanied by any criminally careless or reckless conduct. The same as "homicide *per infortunium*." *See* Manslaughter. 7

Homicide by necessity. A species of justifiable homicide, because it arises from some unavoidable necessity, without any will, intention, or desire, and without any inadvertence or negligence in the party killing, and therefore without any shadow of blame. *See* Self-defense. 8

Homicide per infortunium. Homicide by misfortune, or accidental homicide; as where a man doing a lawful act without any intention of hurt, accidentally kills another; a species of excusable homicide. *See* Negligent homicide. 9

Homicide se defendendo. Homicide in self-defense; the killing of a person in selfdefense upon a sudden affray, where the slayer had no other possible (or, at least, probable) means of escaping from his assailant. A species of excusable homicide. *See* Self-defense. 10

Justifiable homicide. Such as is committed intentionally, but without any evil design, and under such circumstances of necessity or duty as render the act proper, and relieve the party from any shadow of blame; as where a sheriff lawfully executes a sentence of death upon a malefactor, or 11 where the killing takes place in the endeavor to prevent the commission of felony which could not be otherwise avoided, or, as a matter of right, such as self-defense or other causes provided for by statute. *See* Self-defense; also *Excusable homicide, above.*

12 *Negligent homicide.* Criminal homicide constitutes negligent homicide when it is committed negligently. Model Penal Code, §210.4. *See* Negligent homicide; also *Vehicular homicide, below.*

13 *Reckless homicide.* See that title.

14 *Vehicular homicide.* The killing of a human being by the operation of an automobile, airplane, motorboat or other motor vehicle in a manner which creates an unreasonable risk of injury to the person or property of another and which constitutes a material deviation from the standard of care which a reasonable person would observe under the same circumstances.

Understanding Context

1. Does it surprise you to learn that homicide may not be a crime? What does this teach you about the differences between common and specialized uses of words?
2. What does the law regard as the most serious, most criminal forms of homicide?
3. *Critical thinking:* What values seem to play a role in determining what is excusable and what is criminal homicide?

Evaluating Strategy

1. How well organized is this entry? Is it easy to follow?
2. How important are the examples used to support the definitions?

Appreciating Language

1. What do the tone, style, and word choice reveal about the intended audience?
2. How might you reword this passage for a general audience?

Writing Suggestions

1. Select one of the types of homicide and illustrate it with a hypothetical narrative. Make sure your example follows the definition.
2. *Collaborative writing:* Working with a group of students, rework this passage, restating it in plain English for a creative writing class interested in writing detective stories.

1. Describe your immediate reaction to this photograph. How does the image of Jesse Owens, an African American, contrast with that of a German athlete giving a Nazi salute?

2. *Visual analysis:* Refer to Chapter 13, which discusses perception. Given the symbolism of this photograph, would you assume that Owens and the German athlete were hostile toward one another? (In fact, Carl Ludwig Long, despite objections by the Nazis, befriended Owens during the Games.)

Japanese, American, and German athletes, 1936 Berlin Olympics © AP

3. What is the historic significance of this event? In a few years Japan and Germany, nations that claimed racial superiority, would be at war with the United States, here represented by an African American. Does this photograph represent the triumph of democracy?

4. The Olympic Games, in theory, are supposed to represent universal brotherhood, demonstrating the ability of athletes from around the world to compete fairly and in peace. Can the games escape politics? Consider the black athletes protesting in 1968 and the terrorist attacks at the Munich Olympics four years later. In 1980 the United States boycotted the Moscow games to protest the Soviet invasion of Afghanistan. Four years later, the Soviets responded by refusing to participate in the Los Angeles Olympics. Are international events like the Olympics bound to be used for political purposes?

5. What role have African American athletes played in the long struggle for civil rights? Why have sports been a field where minorities could triumph?

6. *Critical thinking:* What does this photograph show about the divisions in the world? In 1936 Fascist Italy, Nazi Germany, and Imperial Japan formed a bloc against the Western democracies. Following the end of the Second World War, a Cold War pitted the West against the Soviet bloc. With the fall of Communism, a conflict has emerged between the West and the Muslim world. Does it seem natural or understandable that the world tends to be divided into opposing forces? Why or why not?

7. *Collaborative writing:* Work with a group of students to draft a short essay to accompany this photograph for a high school history book. How would you explain this event to young people today?

8. *Other modes*

   ■ *Compare* how the Olympics have changed since 1936. How have television, commercial endorsements, and judging scandals altered perceptions of the Games? Do they retain any of the idealism that launched the modern Olympics in 1896?

   ■ Write a short *narrative* about an athletic event you participated in or attended, focusing on the behavior of the winning team, the highest scoring players. Did their triumph seem to be a personal one or did they represent something larger—a school, a city, a nation?

   ■ Use this photograph as an *example* to discuss racial conflict. Although the Japanese and Germans were of different races, they allied themselves in World War II, sharing a belief in their racial superiority over others. Have differing racial or ethnic groups in our country overcome their differences by sharing racist attitudes about African Americans or other groups?

Division and Classification Checklist

Before submitting your paper, review these points:

✔ Have you clearly defined your goal—to write a division or classification paper?

✔ Do you make meaningful divisions or classifications? Does your paper oversimplify a complex subject?

✔ Are your categories clearly defined?

✔ Do you avoid overlapping categories?

✔ Do you use parallel patterns to develop categories and items?

✔ In classification, do you use a single standard of evaluation?

✔ Do all the parts of your subject clearly fit into a single category? Are there any items left over?

Companion Website

See **http://www.thomsonedu.com/english/sundance** for additional information on division and classification.

25

CAUSE AND EFFECT
DETERMINING REASONS AND MEASURING RESULTS

WHAT IS CAUSE AND EFFECT?

What led to the stock market crash of 1929? What motivated terrorists to attack the World Trade Center? What caused the Soviet Union to collapse? How did Microsoft dominate the software market? Did the antipoverty programs of the 1960s work? How will budget cuts affect education? Would a handgun ban lower street crime? What effect will a recent Supreme Court ruling have on women's rights? What causes addiction? Would legalizing drugs reduce crime or create more problems? What caused you to choose this college? How did being fired, having an accident, or breaking up with someone affect you? The answers to all these questions call for the use of *cause and effect*, writing that seeks to determine reasons why something occurred or measure and predict results.

Historians devote much of their work to analyzing the causes of events. Did Lenin cause the Russian Revolution or did the revolution create Lenin? Why did Hitler rise to power? How did the Vietnam War affect American military planning during the Gulf War? What led to the women's movement of the 1970s? Historians also consider the ramifications of current events and speculate about the future. Will another oil crisis occur? What role will China play in the twenty-first century? Will a global economy diminish national sovereignty? How will the growing number of Hispanics influence presidential primaries?

Nearly all professions and disciplines engage in cause-and-effect reasoning. Marketers try to determine why a product succeeded or failed. Engineers work to discover why a test motor exploded. Medical researchers seek to discover what causes normal cells to become cancerous and examine the results of experimental treatments. City planners predict the effect a major earthquake would have on emergency services. Social workers study the results of welfare reform. Educators consider if curriculum changes will cause students to achieve higher SAT scores. Crash investigators examine the wreckage of an airliner to diagnose the cause of an accident.

Many of the papers you will be assigned in college and much of the writing you will do in your careers will be developed using cause and effect. Identifying the reasons that something occurred can be formidable. Determining future outcomes, no matter how much evidence you may have to work with, can remain largely guesswork. Critical thinking skills are essential to successfully produce cause-and-effect writing.

 To read more about cause and effect, along with interactive examples and opportunities to work with interactive texts, click on "The Rhetorical Patterns of Inquiry" from the main menu of *Comp21*.

Determining Causes

During the 1920s physicians and surgeons noticed that many of their lung cancer patients were heavy smokers. An observable association was discovered, but no clear proof of a cause-and-effect relationship. Not all lung cancer patients smoked, and millions of smokers were free of the disease. Though many scientists were concerned, they had no clear evidence that tobacco caused cancer. In fact, for the next twenty years cigarette advertisements featured endorsements by doctors who claimed the calming effect of nicotine reduced stress and prevented stomach ulcers. It was not until 1964 that researchers had assembled enough data to convince the surgeon general of the United States that smoking caused cancer, leading him to proclaim cigarettes a health hazard.

In some instances causes can be established through investigation and research. Doctors can diagnose an infection as the cause of a fever. Accountants can study financial records to discover why a company lost money. But many controversial issues remain subject to debate. For decades social commentators have cited violence on television as a cause of juvenile crime. Noting that children witness thousands of killings on television, they have argued that young people have become desensitized to violence and suffering. William F. Buckley, however, questions whether television violence is a cause of criminal behavior:

> We do not in fact know whether this is so. As has been pointed out by critics of television critics, the same stuff we see here on TV is seen in Great Britain and Japan, yet we have more than three times as much crime as Great Britain, and

nine times as much as Japan: So why didn't all that violence corrupt the Brits and the Japanese?

WRITING ACTIVITY

Select one of the following topics and develop ideas using a variety of prewriting strategies.

1. The reasons you or your parents selected this college or university
2. Causes of domestic violence, poverty, racism, or other social problem
3. Reasons why many Americans do not vote
4. The major causes of conflict between parents and children
5. Why a team won or lost a recent game
6. The reason you hold a certain belief about abortion, capital punishment, or any other highly debated issue
7. Why teenagers start smoking
8. Reasons explaining a current fad, fashion trend, popularity of a television show, or a celebrity's success
9. Why people gamble
10. The reason for America's high homicide rate

Measuring and Predicting Effects

Writers use cause and effect to measure and predict effects. By gathering evidence, evaluating data, and considering alternative interpretations, experts attempt to determine the effect of a new drug, a change in social policy, or technological innovation. John Brooks, for instance, studied the effects of the telephone:

> What has the telephone done to us, or for us, in the hundred years of its existence? A few effects suggest themselves at once. It has saved lives by getting rapid word of illness, injury, or famine from remote places. By joining with the elevator to make possible the multistory residence or office building, it has made possible—for better or worse—the modern city.

As with determining causes, measuring effects can be challenging. How can a company measure the effects of an advertising campaign? If sales increase, can this be attributed to the new commercials, a competitor's price increase, or a drop in interest rates?

Predicting future outcomes can be challenging because evidence can be difficult to collect or may be subject to various interpretations. In addition, numerous unforeseen factors can take place to alter expected events. A school board that decides to close schools because of a declining birthrate may fail to account for an influx of immigrants or the closure of private schools that would place more students into the public system. In 1936 the *Literary Digest* predicted that Alf Landon would defeat Franklin Roosevelt in his bid for a second term as president. The editors based their assertion on a detailed telephone survey. By randomly selecting names from phone books and asking people whom they planned to vote for, the surveyors assumed they would obtain an accurate prediction. Their responses from men and women, government employees and business executives, Italians and Jews, farmers and autoworkers, young and old strongly indicated a preference for Landon. But their research failed to accurately assess the results of the upcoming election because the survey method did not measure a significant population. In 1936 many Americans could not afford telephones, and these economically deprived voters tended to favor Roosevelt.

WRITING ACTIVITY

Select one of the following topics and develop ideas using a variety of prewriting strategies.

1. The effect of cable television on popular culture

2. The result of a recent policy change at your college or job

3. Effects you have experienced from exercising or changing your diet

4. The ways a Supreme Court ruling changed law, society, people's attitudes

5. The long-term effects of a past scandal, confrontation, strike, or demonstration in your community

6. The effects losing a job can have on a person's self-worth

7. Side effects you or someone else experienced from medication

8. How an affair affects a marriage or long-term relationship

9. The impact of graffiti on a neighborhood

10. The effects of television advertising on children

STRATEGIES for Writing Cause and Effect

Critical Thinking and Prewriting

1. **Review critical thinking.** Before beginning to write, review Strategies for Increasing Critical Thinking (page 49) and Common Errors in Critical Thinking (pages 50–56).
   - Read about deduction and induction (see pages 638–640).
   - Appreciate the importance of close observation and objective evaluation.
   - Remind yourself to distinguish between fact and opinion in developing topics.
   - Avoid jumping to conclusions, making sweeping generalizations, and mistaking time relationships for cause and effect.

2. **Develop potential topics using the following devices.**

   List events, situations, actions, and decisions; then explore their causes.

   Examples:

Homelessness	Causes:
Illiteracy	Causes:
Changing your major	Causes:
Addiction	Causes:
Suicide bombers	Causes:
Teen obesity	Causes:
Your decision to quit a job	Causes:

   List events, situations, actions, and decisions; then explore their effects.

   Examples:

Recent changes in financial aid policy	Effects:
Rising or decreasing crime rate	Effects:
Your parents' divorce	Effects:
Being downsized	Effects:
A speech by a president or mayor	Effects:
Antismoking, antidrug campaign	Effects:
Moving into your own apartment	Effects:

3. **Determine the goal of your paper—to establish causes, measure results, or predict future outcomes.**

4. **Select topics suitable to your purpose.** Consider the scope of the assignment and the amount of time you can devote to research and writing.
   - Writing about the causes or effects of social, political, environmental, and technological issues may require extensive research. Without factual

evidence, your paper can simply become a list of unsupported assumptions and generalizations.

- Consider writing cause-and-effect papers based on personal experience and observation.
- Keep the length of your paper and the due date in mind as you develop your topic.

5. **Talk with your instructor about possible topics.** Make sure the subjects you are considering meet the instructor's expectations.
6. **List as many causes or effects as you can.**
   - Use prewriting techniques—clustering or freewriting—to develop a list of causes or effects.
   - Do not edit this list; jot down ideas that may seem irrelevant. Because your topic may change, don't discard ideas that might stimulate further thought.
7. **Search for supporting material.** Conduct a computer search using key words in your topic to discover additional insights and supporting material for your paper.
   - Evaluate sources carefully. Look for signs of bias, unproven assumptions, or mistakes in logic.
8. **Determine whether visuals can enhance your paper.** Photographs, charts, and graphs can illustrate or document causes and effects.

Planning

1. **Write a clear thesis statement listing the main causes or effects at the top of the page to guide planning.**
2. **Qualify your approach.** It can be difficult to discuss all the causes or effects of a complex subject. Limit your discussion, stating in the introduction how you intend to establish causes or measure results.
   - If you are writing about a controversial or complex issue, it may be helpful to admit that other interpretations exist and justify your thesis.
3. **Evaluate your reader's needs.** What evidence does your reader require to accept your conclusions? Are government statistics more impressive than expert testimony? Does any background information have to be presented? Are there misconceptions that must be addressed or terms needing definition?
4. **Offer logical, acceptable evidence.** Present support from reliable sources your readers will respect. Use brief narratives and examples to dramatize data.
5. **Revise your list of causes and effects.**
   - Delete minor, repetitive, or marginal ideas.

- Highlight those points needing further development—use prewriting techniques to explore these issues further.
  - Examine each item on your list. Can some be separated into two causes or three separate effects? Can closely related points be combined?
6. **Write a new list, ranking points by order of importance.** Examine the number of points you have developed in light of the scope of the document. Would it be better to discuss one or two causes in depth or provide a list of eight reasons with only light support and explanation?
7. **Organize causes and effects by order of importance, moving from most to least or least to most significant.** You can either open or close your paper with the most important ideas, but avoid placing significant points in the middle of the document where the reader's attention is weakest.

Writing the First Draft

1. **Keep your goal or thesis in mind as you write.** Writing cause-and-effect papers can raise numerous issues, and it is easy to write off topic, to explore interesting but unrelated ideas.
   - Focus on the top two or three points you want to emphasize.
2. **Keep the scope of the paper in mind as you write and consider limiting the topic if the draft becomes too lengthy.** If your 500-word essay begins to expand so that it would require 2,000 or 3,000 words to fully discuss each item on your list, consider focusing on the principal causes or effects.
   - You do not have to discuss all the causes of crime or every effect of bilingual education. You may list a series of causes or effects in your introduction and then focus on the one or two items you think are most important.
3. **Qualify remarks, noting possible exceptions or alternative interpretations.** Avoid making absolute statements that can be easily refuted by readers recognizing a single exception.
4. **Use other modes to organize your discussion of cause and effects.** You can use comparison to discuss alternative interpretations, classification to present a spectrum of causes or effects, and example to illustrate ideas.
5. **Use transitional statements and paragraph breaks to signal shifts between separate causes or effects.**
6. **Make notes as you write.** As you write, new ideas may occur to you, ideas you thought significant may become harder to explain than you thought, or minor points can expand in importance. Note changes in your chain of thought to signal further revisions, taking care to mark these notes clearly so that you'll remember to come back to them. The order of your paragraphs may change because new ideas take priority.

Revising

1. **Review the entire essay.**
   - Does your paper meet the needs of the writing assignment?
   - Did your topic prove suitable for the scope of the assignment?

2. **Examine your thesis and list of causes or effects.**
   - Is the thesis clearly stated? Can it be further refined?
   - Have you supplied enough supporting evidence?

3. **Review your discussion of causes and effects.**
   - Does your paper devote too much space to minor points? Do more causes and effects need to be presented?
   - Does your paper offer only a superficial list of ideas? Should you narrow the thesis and discuss fewer causes or effects in greater detail?

4. **Examine your critical thinking.**
   - Review your use of induction and deduction. Do you jump to conclusions or ignore alternative interpretations? Do you base your reasoning on untested assumptions?
   - Have you avoided making errors in logic (see pages 50–56)?

5. **Review your introduction and conclusion.**
   - Does the first paragraph clearly announce your purpose, limit the topic, and qualify your approach?
   - Does the conclusion end the paper on a strong point by emphasizing the significance of your causes and effects?

6. **Review the use of visual aids.**
   - Are they appropriate for this paper?
   - Do they accurately and effectively illustrate or document the causes or effects you discuss?

7. **Use peer review to identify areas needing improvement.**

Editing and Proofreading

1. **Read your paper aloud.**
   - Are ideas stated in concrete language readers can understand?
   - Do some terms require further clarification or definition?
   - Do the tone and style of your words reflect your purpose?

2. **Review the structure of your paper.**
   - Are transitions clear? Could changes in paragraphing or revised transitional statements make the essay easier to follow?

3. **Use peer editing to locate errors you may have missed.**

STUDENT PAPER

Why Do They Hate Us?

In the months following 9/11 many shocked Americans wondered why people hated the United States. The horror of watching planes flying into buildings was matched by the disbelief and anger many felt watching people in the Middle East dancing in the streets, honking car horns, and passing out candy to children like it was a holiday. Polls taken in the Middle East revealed that vast numbers of Arabs and Muslims approved of Osama bin Laden whose image appeared on posters and T-shirts.

© Reuters/Corbis

As President Bush prepared for war in Iraq, many people in Europe began to criticize the United States. The anti-American feeling in countries like Britain, France, and Germany troubled many Americans.

Why do they all seem to hate us? Scholars, reporters, and diplomats have given us a lot of reasons. They suggest that anti-Americanism is caused by jealousy, resentment over the way American culture is eroding traditional cultures, America's support for Israel, and the exploitation of workers and resources.

But none of these reasons is new. America

has been making movies that offend foreign tastes for eighty years. The United States has supported Israel since 1948. The main cause for rising anti-Americanism, I think, is the end of the Cold War. For almost fifty years the world was controlled by two superpowers—the US and the USSR. This conflict made America look less threatening and violent in contrast to a Communist dictatorship that killed and jailed millions.

People in West Germany may have grumbled about being under America's shadow, but they only had to look over the Berlin Wall to realize it was a lot better than being in East Germany under Communist rule. There was no comparison between living in South and North Korea, either. The Arabs may have resented America's support for Israel, but they knew the United States believed in freedom of religion. The Soviets were atheists and denounced all religion. The spread of American influence may have weakened Islamic values, but the growth of Soviet-sponsored Communist movements in Pakistan, Iran, and Egypt threatened to abolish Islam.

The Cold War made America look like the lesser of two evils. We were the good cop in the good cop–bad cop scenario. People resented American influence, but they had reasons to fear the Communists.

Now that the Cold War is over, the world has one superpower. We no longer look like the good cop or the lesser evil. To many people in other countries the United States is a global bully, an economic giant, and a cultural titan—all of which make other nations feel intimidated and second-rate. And no people like feeling second-rate.

Questions for Review and Revision

1. How effective is the introduction?
2. Why does the student dismiss many of the causes given for anti-Americanism suggested by others?
3. Does the student focus on causes or effects?
4. What does the student mean by "the good cop-bad cop scenario"?
5. How did the end of the Cold War create problems for the United States?

6. How does the student organize the essay? What role do paragraph breaks play?
7. What effect does the photograph the student uses have?
8. Can you think of additional examples that could illustrate or support the student's thesis?
9. Read the paper aloud. Could revisions or reorganization clarify the writer's purpose?

Writing Suggestions

1. Using this student's essay as a model, write a cause-and-effect paper detailing results of an environmental, technological, or social change. How has the Internet changed communication or the news media?
2. *Collaborative writing:* Working with a group of students, discuss the causes or effects of an American policy that you think will cause greater or lesser animosity toward the United States.

SUGGESTED TOPICS FOR WRITING CAUSE AND EFFECT
General Assignments

Write a cause-and-effect paper on any of the following topics. Your paper can focus on determining causes, measuring effects, or explaining both causes and effects. Cause-and-effect papers often require research to present evidence. It is possible to use cause and effect in less formal papers, in which you offer personal experience and observations as support. Review Critical Thinking Strategies (page 591–594).

Write a paper explaining the causes of the following topics:

- Teenage pregnancy
- Domestic violence
- Your choice of major or career goal
- A recent campus or local scandal, incident, or controversy

- The success or failure of a local business, organization, or event
- The victory or defeat of a political candidate
- Your decision to take a course of action—to quit smoking, to begin exercising, to join or leave an organization, to pursue a job, to end a relationship
- Apathy toward the poor
- Current attitudes about an ethnic, political, religious, or social group
- Divorce

Write a paper measuring the effects of the following topics:

- The Internet
- Immigration
- Harsher drunk-driving laws
- Cell phones
- Welfare reform
- Living in a dorm
- Airport security
- A recent policy change at the federal, state, local, or college level
- Single-parent families
- Terrorism

To create your own interactive writing project, use the textual, visual, and video libraries on *Comp21*. For the main menu, choose "Build Your Own Occasion for Writing."

Writing in Context

1. Analyze in a short essay a recent event on your campus, in your community, or at your place of work. Examine what caused this event to take place. If several causes exist, you may use division to explain them or classification to rank them from the most to least important.
2. Write a letter to the editor of the college newspaper predicting the effects of a current policy change, incident, or trend in student behavior.
3. Imagine a job application asks you to write a 250-word essay presenting your reasons for choosing your career. Write a one-page essay that lists your most important reasons. As you write, consider how an employer would evaluate your response.

STRATEGIES | for Reading Cause and Effect

As you read the cause-and-effect entries in this chapter, keep the following questions in mind.

Context

1. What is the writer's purpose—to establish causes, measure results, or predict outcomes? Does the writer use cause and effect to simply report a change or to support a persuasive argument?
2. Subject the essay to critical reading. Does the writer avoid logical fallacies (see Chapter 4)? Are causes and effects clearly linked—or can they simply be time relationships or the results of coincidence?
3. Does the writer qualify his or her conclusions? Does he or she acknowledge alternative interpretations?

Strategy

1. Where does the author place the thesis—at the outset or after presenting evidence? Could it be located elsewhere in the essay?
2. What evidence does the author present—personal observations, statistics, scientific studies, the testimony of experts? Is the evidence sufficient? Is it fairly and accurately presented?
3. How does the author organize the essay? Could the entry be easier to follow if causes or effects were presented in numbered lists?
4. Does the writer practice critical thinking? Does the writer mistake symptoms for causes, assume past trends will continue, or rest conclusions on unproven assumptions?
5. What other modes does the writer use—narration, comparison, definition?

Language

1. Does the author's choice of words indicate bias?
2. What role does diction and connotation play in stating causes and results?
3. What do the tone and style suggest about the writer's intended audience? Are technical terms defined?

JOHN BROOKS

John Brooks (1920–1993) published his first novel, **The Big Wheel,** in 1949. His second novel, **The Man Who Broke Things,** appeared in 1958. Brooks's nonfiction book about corporations in the 1980s, **The Takeover Game,** became a best-seller. Brooks, who served as a trustee of the New York Public Library for fifteen years, contributed articles to the **New Yorker** for four decades.

The Effects of the Telephone

In this brief essay, Brooks outlines how the telephone has shaped human lives and perceptions. Before reading this article, consider what your life would be like without a telephone. How much do you depend on the phone?

opening question
obvious effect

1   What has the telephone done to us, or for us, in the hundred years of its existence? A few effects suggest themselves at once. It has saved lives by getting rapid word of illness, injury, or famine from remote places. By joining with the elevator to make possible the multistory residence or office building, it has made possible—for better or worse—the modern city. By bringing about a quantum leap in the speed and ease with which information moves from place to place, it has greatly accelerated the rate of scientific and technological change and growth in industry. Beyond doubt it has crippled if not killed the ancient art of letter writing. It has made living alone possible for persons with normal social impulses; by so doing, it has played a role in one of the greatest social changes of this century, the breakup of the

possible effects

multigenerational household. It has made the waging of war chillingly more efficient than formerly. Perhaps (though not probably) it has prevented wars that might have arisen out of international misunderstanding caused by written communication. Or perhaps—again not probably—by magnifying and extending irrational personal conflicts based on voice contact, it has caused wars. Certainly it has extended the scope of human conflicts, since it impartially disseminates the useful knowledge of scientists and the babble of bores, the affection of the affectionate and the malice of the malicious.

2   But the question remains unanswered. The obvious effects just cited seem inadequate, mechanistic; they only scratch the surface. Perhaps the crucial effects are evanescent and unmeasurable. Use of the telephone

600

involves personal risk because it involves exposure; for some, to be "hung up on" is among the worst of fears; others dream of a ringing telephone and wake up with a pounding heart. The telephone's actual ring—more, perhaps, than any other sound in our daily lives—evokes hope, relief, fear, anxiety, joy, according to our expectations. The telephone is our nerve-end to society.

psychological effects

In some ways it is in itself a thing of paradox. In one sense a metaphor 3 for the times it helped create, in another sense the telephone is their polar opposite. It is small and gentle—relying on low voltages and miniature parts—in times of hugeness and violence. It is basically simple in times of complexity. It is so nearly human, re-creating voices so faithfully that friends or lovers need not identify themselves by name even when talking across oceans, that to ask its effects on human life may seem hardly more fruitful than to ask the effect of the hand or the foot. The Canadian philosopher Marshall McLuhan—one of the few who have addressed themselves to these questions—was perhaps not far from the mark when he spoke of the telephone as creating "a kind of extra-sensory perception."

paradoxical effects

closing quotation

Understanding Context

1. What does Brooks see as the principal effects of the telephone? Has it had any negative consequences?
2. Why does he see the telephone as "a thing of paradox"?
3. *Critical thinking:* What lessons about the telephone can be applied to cyberspace? Does the Internet connect people in more ways than the typical one-on-one connection of a telephone conversation?

Evaluating Strategy

1. Most people have grown up with telephones. Many carry cell phones in pockets and purses. How does Brooks prompt readers to question something they take for granted? Could you imagine writing a similar essay about cars, ballpoint pens, or supermarkets?
2. *Critical thinking:* Brooks states that the telephone and elevator made the high-rise and the modern city possible. Does this suggest that it can be difficult to isolate a single cause? Do technological and social changes intertwine and interact to create unintended results?

Appreciating Language

1. Brooks states that the telephone is "nearly human." How does he personalize the telephone, linking it to human emotions?
2. Brooks avoids technical language in his essay. Would the introduction of scientific terminology weaken his essay?
3. Consider Brooks's observation that the "telephone is our nerve-end to society." Does the telephone link you to others, to the world? When you need to reach someone, do you instinctively think of calling instead of writing or visiting them?

Writing Suggestions

1. Using Brooks's article as a model, write your own essay explaining the effects of another common invention—newspapers, television commercials, mail-order catalogs, shopping malls, or calculators.
2. *Collaborative writing:* Work with a group of students to discuss the effects of computers on children and society. Develop a list of positive and negative effects and write a brief essay comparing the benefits and dangers.

Norman Cousins (1915–1990) was born in Union City, New Jersey, and became a writer and editor who addressed a range of social and political issues. He edited the *Saturday Review* magazine for decades. After overcoming a life-threatening illness, he became a noted advocate of positive thinking. His books include *Anatomy of an Illness* (1979), *The Healing Heart* (1983), and *Head First: The Biology of Hope* (1989).

Who Killed Benny Paret?

In this 1962 article Cousins examines what caused the death of a prize-fighter during a televised boxing match.

Sometime about 1935 or 1936 I had an interview with Mike Jacobs, the prize-fight promoter. I was a fledgling reporter at that time; my beat was education but during the vacation season I found myself on varied assignments, all the way from ship news to sports reporting. In this way I found myself sitting opposite the most powerful figure in the boxing world.

There was nothing spectacular in Mr. Jacobs' manner or appearance; but when he spoke about prize fights, he was no longer a bland little man but a colossus who sounded the way Napoleon must have sounded when he reviewed a battle. You knew you were listening to Number One. His saying something made it true.

We discussed what to him was the only important element in successful promoting—how to please the crowd. So far as he was concerned, there was no mystery to it. You put killers in the ring and the people filled your arena. You hire boxing artists—men who are adroit at feinting, parrying, weaving, jabbing, and dancing, but who don't pack dynamite in their fists—and you wind up counting your empty seats. So you searched for the killers and sluggers and maulers—fellows who could hit with the force of a baseball bat.

I asked Mr. Jacobs if he was speaking literally when he said people came out to see the killer.

"They don't come out to see a tea party," he said evenly. "They come out to see the knockout. They come out to see a man hurt. If they think anything else, they're kidding themselves."

6   Recently, a young man by the name of Benny Paret was killed in the ring. The killing was seen by millions; it was on television. In the twelfth round, he was hit hard in the head several times, went down, was counted out, and never came out of the coma.

7   The Paret fight produced a flurry of investigations. Governor Rockefeller was shocked by what happened and appointed a committee to assess the responsibility. The New York State Boxing Commission decided to find out what was wrong. The District Attorney's office expressed its concern. One question that was solemnly studied in all three probes concerned the action of the referee. Did he act in time to stop the fight? Another question had to do with the role of the examining doctors who certified the physical fitness of the fighters before the bout. Still another question involved Mr. Paret's manager; did he rush his boy into the fight without adequate time to recuperate from the previous one?

8   In short, the investigators looked into every possible cause except the real one. Benny Paret was killed because the human fist delivers enough impact, when directed against the head, to produce a massive hemorrhage in the brain. The human brain is the most delicate and complex mechanism in all creation. It has a lacework of millions of highly fragile nerve connections. Nature attempts to protect this exquisitely intricate machinery by encasing it in a hard shell. Fortunately, the shell is thick enough to withstand a great deal of pounding. Nature, however, can protect a man against everything except man himself. Not every blow to the head will kill a man—but there is always the risk of concussion and damage to the brain. A prize fighter may be able to survive even repeated brain concussions and go on fighting, but the damage to his brain may be permanent.

9   In any event, it is futile to investigate the referee's role and seek to determine whether he should have intervened to stop the fight earlier. That is not where the primary responsibility lies. The primary responsibility lies with the people who pay to see a man hurt. The referee who stops a fight too soon from the crowd's viewpoint can expect to be booed. The crowd wants the knockout; it wants to see a man stretched out on the canvas. This is the supreme moment in boxing. It is nonsense to talk about prize fighting as a test of boxing skills. No crowd was ever brought to its feet screaming and cheering at the sight of two men beautifully dodging and weaving out of each other's jabs. The time the crowd comes alive is when a man is hit hard over the heart or the head, when his mouthpiece flies out, when the blood squirts out of his nose or eyes, when he wobbles under the attack and his pursuer continues to smash at him with pole-axe impact.

10   Don't blame it on the referee. Don't even blame it on the fight managers. Put the blame where it belongs—on the prevailing mores that regard

prize fighting as a perfectly proper enterprise and vehicle of entertainment. No one doubts that many people enjoy prize fighting and will miss it if it should be thrown out. And that is precisely the point.

Understanding Context

1. What is Cousin's thesis?
2. What did the famous boxing promoter tell Cousins about boxing fans?
3. What damage does a blow to the head inflict on boxers?
4. Who does Cousins ultimately hold responsible for the boxer's death?
5. *Critical thinking:* Can the public also be blamed for pornography, illegal drugs, and gun violence? Why or why not?

Evaluating Strategy

1. Before discussing Benny Paret's death, Cousins tells readers what a famous boxing promoter told him as young reporter? Is this an effective opening?
2. Cousins points out that crowds boo referees who stop fights. How does this support his thesis?
3. Cousins presents and dismisses several causes before he states the real cause. Is this an effective device? Why or why not?

Appreciating Language

1. What words does Cousins use to describe the human brain? How do they work to support his point that boxing is inherently dangerous?
2. What words does Cousins use in paragraph 3 to compare boxing artists with fighters who are "killers and sluggers and maulers"?

Writing Suggestions

1. Write a similar essay that identifies what you think is the "real cause" for a problem, such as binge drinking, terrorism, gangs, domestic violence, or the popularity of a controversial celebrity.
2. *Collaborative writing:* Work with other students to develop an essay that addresses the responsibility fans have at sporting events or concerts. Who is responsible for rowdy behavior, drug use, and violence in stadiums and clubs?

JOHN TAYLOR GATTO

John Taylor Gatto taught in New York City public schools for twenty-five years and was named the city's Teacher of the Year three times. He has published several books about public education, including *Dumbing Us Down, The Exhausted School,* and *The Empty Child.* Since leaving teaching, Gatto has become a public speaker, addressing audiences at the White House and NASA's Goddard Space Flight Center.

Why Schools Don't Educate

In this section from a speech Gatto presented after receiving an award, he outlines the effects schools and television have had on children. As you read his list, consider if there could be other causes for the symptoms he observes.

1 Two institutions at present control our children's lives—television and schooling, in that order. Both of these reduce the real world of wisdom, fortitude, temperance, and justice to a never-ending, nonstop abstraction. In centuries past, the time of a child and adolescent would be occupied in real work, real charity, real adventures, and the real search for mentors who might teach what one really wanted to learn. A great deal of time was spent in community pursuits, practicing affection, meeting and studying every level of the community, learning how to make a home, and dozens of other tasks necessary to becoming a whole man or woman.

2 But here is the calculus of time the children I teach must deal with:

3 Out of the 168 hours in each week, my children must sleep fifty-six. That leaves them 112 hours a week out of which to fashion a self.

4 My children watch fifty-five hours of television a week, according to recent reports. That leaves them fifty-seven hours a week in which to grow up.

5 My children attend school thirty hours a week; use about eight hours getting ready, going, and coming home; and spend an average of seven hours a week in homework—a total of forty-five hours. During that time they are under constant surveillance, have no private time or private space, and are disciplined if they try to assert individuality in the use of time or space. That leaves twelve hours a week out of which to create a unique consciousness. Of course my kids eat, too, and that takes some time—not much, because we've lost the tradition of family dining. If we allot three hours a week to

evening meals we arrive at a net amount of private time for each child of nine hours.

It's not enough. It's not enough, is it? The richer the kid, of course, the 6 less television he watches, but the rich kid's time is just as narrowly proscribed by a broader catalogue of commercial entertainments and his inevitable assignment to a series of private lessons in areas seldom of his choice.

And these things are, oddly enough, just a more cosmetic way to create 7 dependent human beings, unable to fill their own hours, unable to initiate lines of meaning to give substance and pleasure to their existence. It's a national disease, this dependency and aimlessness, and I think schooling and television and lessons—the entire Chatauqua idea—have a lot to do with it.

Think of the things that are killing us as a nation: drugs, brainless competi- 8 tion, recreational sex, the pornography of violence, gambling, alcohol, and the worst pornography of all—lives devoted to buying things—accumulation as a philosophy. All are addictions of dependent personalities and that is what our brand of schooling must inevitably produce.

I want to tell you what the effect is on children of taking all their time— 9 time they need to grow up—and forcing them to spend it on abstractions. No reform that doesn't attack these specific pathologies will be anything more than a facade.

1. The children I teach are indifferent to the adult world. This defies 10 the experience of thousands of years. A close study of what big people were up to was always the most exciting occupation of youth, but nobody wants to grow up these days, and who can blame them. Toys are us.

2. The children I teach have almost no curiosity, and what little they 11 do have is transitory; they cannot concentrate for very long, even on things they choose to do. Can you see a connection between the bells ringing again and again to change classes, and this phenomenon of evanescent attention?

3. The children I teach have a poor sense of the future, of how tomor- 12 row is inextricably linked to today. They live in a continuous present; the exact moment they are in is the boundary of their consciousness.

4. The children I teach are ahistorical; they have no sense of how the 13 past has predestined their own present, limiting their choices, shaping their values and lives.

5. The children I teach are cruel to each other; they lack compassion for 14 misfortune, they laugh at weakness, they have contempt for people whose need for help shows too plainly.

15   6.   The children I teach are uneasy with intimacy or candor. They cannot deal with genuine intimacy because of a lifelong habit of preserving a secret self inside an outer personality made up of artificial bits and pieces, of behavior borrowed from television or acquired to manipulate teachers. Because they are not who they represent themselves to be, the disguise wears thin in the presence of intimacy, so intimate relationships have to be avoided.

16   7.   The children I teach are materialistic, following the lead of schoolteachers who materialistically "grade" everything—and television mentors who offer everything in the world for sale.

17   8.   The children I teach are dependent, passive, and timid in the presence of new challenges. This timidity is frequently masked by surface bravado or by anger or aggressiveness, but underneath is a vacuum without fortitude.

18   I could name a few other conditions that school reform will have to tackle if our national decline is to be arrested, but by now you will have grasped my thesis, whether you agree with it or not. Either schools, television, or both have caused these pathologies. It's a simple matter of arithmetic. Between schooling and television, all the time children have is eaten up. That's what has destroyed the American family; it no longer is a factor in the education of its own children.

Understanding Context

1. How, in Gatto's opinion, are education and television linked in children's lives?
2. How has television affected children's views of the world and their attitudes toward others?
3. Gatto states that schoolchildren are "cruel" and "passive." Can one be both cruel and passive?
4. *Critical thinking:* Gatto states that "children live in a continuous present" without a sense of past and future. Is this a natural attribute of childhood or something induced by television? Doesn't television at least portray popular history?

Evaluating Strategy

1. How effective are Gatto's use of numbered steps?
2. All of Gatto's eight points open with the statement, "The children I teach . . ." Does this repetition become redundant or build emphasis?

3. What risk does a writer run in criticizing children? How might parents respond?

Appreciating Language

1. Gatto uses the word *ahistorical*. How would you define this word?
2. Gatto calls "being devoted to buying things" the "worst pornography of all." Is *pornography* an effective word choice?

Writing Suggestions

1. Write your own essay detailing the effects television has had on your generation or children you observe. Do your observations parallel those of Gatto?
2. *Collaborative writing:* Discuss Gatto's article with a group of students. Record their observations on school reform. Select the major ideas and use them to draft a letter to a local school board suggesting ways of improving education.

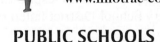

InfoTrac College Edition

www.infotrac-college.com

PUBLIC SCHOOLS

> If an unfriendly foreign power had attempted to impose on America the mediocre educational performance that exists today, we might well have viewed it as an act of war. . . . We have, in effect, been committing an act of unthinking, unilateral educational disarmament.
>
> *A Nation at Risk*

In 1983 the Reagan administration released *A Nation at Risk*, a study that charged, "Our society and its educational institutions seem to have lost sight of the basic purposes of schooling, and of the high expectations and disciplined effort needed to attain them." The report claimed that a "rising tide of mediocrity" in public schools threatened America's position in a world of "determined, well-educated, and strongly motivated competitors."

A Nation at Risk has fueled two decades of debate about education. Jonathan Kozol, author of *Savage Inequalities*, argues that urban schools

© Royalty-Free/Corbis

fail because of unfair distribution of resources. While suburban districts allocate up to $15,000 a year on each student, urban schools provide less than $8,000. Critics of public schools argue that funding alone does not explain poor performance. Blake Hurst, a former school district president, notes that although Missouri spent nearly two billion dollars to reduce class sizes and build new schools in Kansas City, there was little change in test scores. At one point the state devoted 44 percent of its education budget to 9 percent of the student population. Despite this infusion of added resources, the Kansas City School District failed to improve and lost its accreditation in 2000.

Teachers are at the center of the education debate. Damon Moore, a public school teacher, states that legislators, administrators, and parents cannot improve education. "Reform's last chance," he argues, "rests in the hearts and minds of those who are fighting the battle up front—in the classroom." Others claim that teachers and teachers unions are responsible for failing schools. "Some teachers," Sheila Cherry states, "would sacrifice students' futures to save their jobs." Such critics as Lisa Snell charge that teachers and schools disguise their failures by labeling children learning disabled. Special education classes, originally designed to serve the mentally retarded, now teach 12 percent of all students, 90 percent of whom have been diagnosed with learning disabilities.

Frustrated by bureaucracy, lowered standards, and unsafe schools, educators have called for a range of alternatives to traditional public schools. Charter schools, special schools set up independently within a public school system, now serve half a million students. They promised to be more rigorous and accountable, but *American School and University* found that "like traditional public schools, charter schools run the gamut from inspiring successes to disappointing failures." Some cities have experimented with choice or voucher systems, which provide low-income families with vouchers that can be applied to public or private schools. Like charter schools, choice schools have produced mixed results. A growing number of parents now educate their children at home, arguing that Internet resources, educational videos, and museum trips can provide a richer and more challenging educational experience than overcrowded public schools plagued with shortages and violence.

Although advocating different strategies to improve schools, educators and education critics still see America as a nation at risk.

Before reading these entries, consider these questions:

> Do Americans value education? Do you know parents who never attend a parent-teacher conference or PTA meeting but never miss their children's football or soccer games?
>
> How should schools be funded? Is it fair that suburban schools receive more funds than urban schools? Should school funding be based on something other than property taxes?
>
> Do teachers have enough or too much influence?
>
> Do standardized tests improve education? Tests, proponents assert, identify a school's strengths and weaknesses. Critics argue tests are unfair and lead schools to simply suspend marginal students so they won't be tested and lower the school average.

E-Readings Online

Search for each article by author or title after entering InfoTrac College Edition through your 1Pass account login.

Gregory Shafer. *What's Literacy Got To Do With It?*
In practice, the schools designed to assist the poor "actually constitute the engine that stultifies change and hinders revolt."

Mike Kennedy. *Charter Schools: Threat or Boon to Public Schools?*
Charter schools, which now enroll 575,000 students, "run the gamut from inspiring successes to disappointing failures."

Jonathan Kozol. *Malign Neglect.*
A specialist in basic education uses statistics to demonstrate dramatic funding disparities between urban and suburban schools.

Blake Hurst. *End of an Illusion.*

A former school district president concludes from a study of the Kansas City School District that more money is not the answer to ailing schools.

Gregory Kent. *Celebrating Mediocrity? How Schools Shortchange Gifted Students.*

In attempting to provide all children with equal educational opportunities, public schools fail to help gifted students reach their full potential.

Lisa Snell. *Special Education Confidential: How Schools Use the "Learning Disability" Label to Cover Up Their Failures.*

Two million students would not have been labeled learning disabled "if the public schools they attended had provided proper, rigorous, and early reading instruction."

Joe Klein. *How the Teachers Killed the Dream.*

A journalist explains how a multimillionaire in Michigan tried to endow several charter schools in Detroit—and how the teachers stopped him.

Jodie Morse. *Learning While Black.*

A staff writer for *Time* magazine points to evidence that black students are more likely to be disciplined than white students for the same behavior.

Damon Moore. *Hold Us to Higher Standards.*

A middle-school teacher and activist agrees with the proposition that teachers should be held to the highest professional standards but argues they should also have a greater role in determining educational policies.

Critical Reading and Thinking

1. What do these authors see as the major problems in our schools?
2. Do these authors believe that the solution to failing schools is providing more money or creating new systems?
3. What role do teachers play in school reform? Should they have more or less influence in educational policies?
4. How can schools be held more accountable? Do standardized tests work?
5. How effective are educational alternatives, such as charter and choice schools?

Writing Suggestions

1. Write an essay evaluating your own high school experience. Did you attend a public, private, or charter school? Do you feel your school adequately prepared you to enter college or obtain a job? What would have made your high school better?

2. *Collaborative writing:* Work with a group of other students and discuss the causes for the poor performance of many of the nation's schools. Why do so many students drop out? Why are so many high school graduates unprepared for college? Why do American students score lower on standardized tests than students from many Third World countries? List the major causes. Your group may use division to organize them in categories or classification to rank them by importance.
3. *Other modes*
   - Write a *description* essay about your best learning experience.
   - Develop a *comparison* essay contrasting two schools or two teachers.
   - Create a *definition* of an ideal school or teacher.
   - Write a *process* essay giving parents suggestions how they make sure their children get a good education.

Research Paper

You can develop a research paper about public schools by conducting further research to explore a range of issues:

- How effective has the No Child Left Behind initiative been in reforming education?
- Have schools made effective use of new technology?
- What role have teachers unions played in recent educational debates?
- What role have special interest groups had in shaping educational policy?
- What are the current problems, concerns, or controversies in your local schools?

For Further Reading

To locate additional sources on public schools, enter these search terms as InfoTrac subjects:

Public Schools
Subdivisions: analysis
evaluation
finance
forecasts and trends
management
political aspects
public opinion

Education
Subdivisions: beliefs, opinions and attitudes
comparative analysis
evaluation
government finance
parent participation
personal narratives
research
surveys

Charter Schools
Subdivisions: analysis
finance
standards

School, Choice of
Subdivisions: analysis
personal narratives
research

Home Schooling
Subdivisions: analysis
personal narratives
social aspects

Additional Sources

Using a search engine, such as Yahoo!, Google, or Alta Vista, enter one or more of the following terms to locate additional sources:

public schools	teachers unions	school choice
charter schools	school standards	No Child Left Behind
home schooling	PTA	public school funding
dropout rates	standardized testing	SAT scores

See Evaluating Internet Source Checklist on page 752. See Chapter 30 for using and documenting sources.

Brent Staples (1951–) was born in Chester, Pennsylvania, and graduated from Widener University in 1973. He received a doctorate in psychology from the University of Chicago in 1982. After writing for several Chicago publications, he joined the **New York Times** in 1985 and became a member of its editorial board in 1990. He has also contributed articles to **Ms.** and **Harper's.** In 1994 he published a memoir, **Parallel Time: Growing Up in Black and White,** recalling a childhood of violence and poverty.

Black Men and Public Space

In this Harper's *article Staples recounts the effects he has had on white pedestrians. As a black male, he realized he had the power to cause fellow citizens to alter their behavior by simply walking in their direction.*

My first victim was a woman—white, well-dressed, probably in her early 1 twenties. I came upon her late one evening on a deserted street in Hyde Park, a relatively affluent neighborhood in an otherwise mean, impoverished section of Chicago. As I swung onto the avenue behind her, there seemed to be a discreet, uninflammatory distance between us. Not so. She cast back a worried glance. To her, the youngish black man—a broad 6 feet 2 inches with a beard and billowing hair, both hands shoved into the pockets of a bulky military jacket—seemed menacingly close. After a few more quick glimpses, she picked up her pace and was soon running in earnest. Within seconds she disappeared into a cross street.

That was more than a decade ago. I was 22 years old, a graduate student 2 newly arrived at the University of Chicago. It was in the echo of that terrified woman's footfalls that I first began to know the unwieldy inheritance I'd come into—the ability to alter public space in ugly ways. It was clear that she thought herself the quarry of a mugger, a rapist, or worse. Suffering a bout of insomnia, however, I was stalking sleep, not defenseless wayfarers. As a softy who is scarcely able to take a knife to a raw chicken—let alone hold one to a person's throat—I was surprised, embarrassed, and dismayed all at once. Her flight made me feel like an accomplice in tyranny. It also made it clear that I was indistinguishable from the muggers who occasionally seeped into the area from the surrounding ghetto. That first encounter, and those that followed, signified that a vast, unnerving gulf lay between nighttime pedestrians—particularly women—and me. And I soon gathered that being perceived as dangerous is a hazard in itself. I only needed to turn a corner into a dicey situation, or crowd some frightened, armed person in a foyer somewhere, or make an errant move after being pulled over by a policeman. Where fear and weapons meet—and they often do in urban America—there is always the possibility of death.

3   In that first year, my first away from my hometown, I was to become thoroughly familiar with the language of fear. At dark, shadowy intersections, I could cross in front of a car stopped at a traffic light and elicit the *thunk, thunk, thunk, thunk* of the driver—black, white, male, or female—hammering down the door locks. On less traveled streets after dark, I grew accustomed to but never comfortable with people crossing to the other side of the street rather than pass me. Then there were the standard unpleasantries with policemen, doormen, bouncers, cabdrivers, and others whose business it is to screen out troublesome individuals *before* there is any nastiness.

4   I moved to New York nearly two years ago and I have remained an avid night walker. In central Manhattan, the near-constant crowd cover minimizes tense one-on-one street encounters. Elsewhere—in SoHo, for example, where sidewalks are narrow and tightly spaced buildings shut out the sky—things can get very taut indeed.

5   After dark, on the warrenlike streets of Brooklyn where I live, I often see women who fear the worst from me. They seem to have set their faces on neutral, and with their purse straps strung across their chests bandolierstyle, they forge ahead as though bracing themselves against being tackled. I understand, of course, that the danger they perceive is not a hallucination. Women are particularly vulnerable to street violence, and young black males are drastically overrepresented among the perpetrators of that violence. Yet these truths are no solace against the kind of alienation that comes of being ever the suspect, a fearsome entity with whom pedestrians avoid making eye contact.

6   It is not altogether clear to me how I reached the ripe old age of 22 without being conscious of the lethality nighttime pedestrians attributed to me. Perhaps it was because in Chester, Pennsylvania, the small, angry industrial town where I came of age in the 1960s, I was scarcely noticeable against a backdrop of gang warfare, street knifings, and murders. I grew up one of the good boys, had perhaps a half-dozen fistfights. In retrospect, my shyness of combat has clear sources.

7   As a boy, I saw countless tough guys locked away; I have since buried several, too. They were babies, really—a teenage cousin, a brother of 22, a

childhood friend in his mid-twenties—all gone down in episodes of bravado played out in the streets. I came to doubt the virtues of intimidation early on. I chose, perhaps unconsciously, to remain a shadow—timid, but a survivor.

The fearsomeness mistakenly attributed to me in public places often 8 has a perilous flavor. The most frightening of these confusions occurred in the late 1970s and early 1980s, when I worked as a journalist in Chicago. One day, rushing into the office of a magazine I was writing for with a dead-line story in hand, I was mistaken for a burglar. The office manager called security and, with an ad hoc posse, pursued me through the labyrinthine halls, nearly to my editor's door. I had no way of proving who I was. I could only move briskly toward the company of someone who knew me.

Another time I was on assignment for a local paper and killing time be- 9 fore an interview. I entered a jewelry store on the city's affluent Near North Side. The proprietor excused herself and returned with an enormous red Doberman pinscher straining at the end of a leash. She stood, the dog extended toward me, silent to my questions, her eyes bulging nearly out of her head. I took a cursory look around, nodded, and bade her good night.

Relatively speaking, however, I never fared as badly as another black 10 male journalist. He went to nearby Waukegan, Illinois, a couple of summers ago to work on a story about a murderer who was born there. Mistaking the reporter for the killer, police officers hauled him from his car at gunpoint and but for his press credentials would probably have tried to book him. Such episodes are not uncommon. Black men trade tales like this all the time.

Over the years, I learned to smother the rage I felt at so often being taken 11 for a criminal. Not to do so would surely have led to madness. I now take pre-cautions to make myself less threatening. I move about with care, particularly late in the evening. I give a wide berth to nervous people on subway plat-forms during the wee hours, particularly when I have exchanged business clothes for jeans. If I happen to be entering a building behind some people who appear skittish, I may walk by, letting them clear the lobby before I re-turn, so as not to seem to be following them. I have been calm and extremely congenial on those rare occasions when I've been pulled over by the police.

And on late-evening constitutionals I employ what has proved to be an 12 excellent tension-reducing measure: I whistle melodies from Beethoven and Vivaldi and the more popular classical composers. Even steely New Yorkers hunching toward nighttime destinations seem to relax, and occa-sionally they even join in the tune. Virtually everybody seems to sense that a mugger wouldn't be warbling bright, sunny selections from Vivaldi's *Four Seasons*. It is my equivalent of the cowbell that hikers wear when they know they are in bear country.

Understanding Context

1. What is Staples's thesis? What is Staples saying about race, class, crime, prejudice, and fear in our society?
2. What attitudes does the writer have to the way women respond to him? What causes their reactions?
3. Staples reports that both black and white drivers lock their doors when they encounter him. What is he saying about racial perceptions and fear?
4. How do you interpret the conclusion? Why would people be reassured by a black man whistling classical music? What does this say about prejudice, stereotyping, and class? What else would make a black man less threatening—singing spirituals, carrying the *Wall Street Journal*, walking a poodle? Why?

Evaluating Strategy

1. What is the impact of the first sentence?
2. Staples shifts the chronology several times. How does he prevent readers from being confused? How important are transitional statements and paragraph breaks?
3. *Other modes:* How does Staples use narration, comparison, and example in developing his essay?

Appreciating Language

1. Staples avoids using such words as *racist*, *prejudice*, and *stereotypes* in his essay. Do words like these tend to be inflammatory and politically charged? Would it detract from his message?
2. What do the tone and style of the essay suggest about the response Staples hoped to achieve from his readers?

Writing Suggestions

1. Write an essay narrating your own experiences in public space. You can explore how you cause others to react to your presence or how location affects your behavior. What happens when you cross the campus late at night, drive alone, or enter a high-crime neighborhood?

2. *Collaborative writing:* Discuss this essay with a group of students. Consider if a white man in shabby clothing or a black man in a business suit would provoke the same or different responses in white pedestrians. Is class or race the defining factor in provoking fear? Develop an outline for a sociological experiment measuring people's reactions to a variety of test figures engaged in the same actions. Write a process paper explaining how the experiment might be set up and the results evaluated.

WILLIAM F. BUCKLEY JR.

William F. Buckley Jr. (1925–) was born in New York and graduated from Yale. Shortly after graduation he published **God and
Man at Yale,** a book that outlined his political and religious values.
He has published over twenty books, including spy novels and
books about sailing. He founded and edited the **National Review,**
a conservative political magazine. Buckley is probably best
known as host of **Firing Line,** a weekly television debate program
that has been broadcast for over thirty years.

Don't Blame Violence on the Tube

In this TV Guide *article Buckley asserts that television violence does not cause
crime and violent behavior. As you read the article, notice where Buckley uses comparison, example, and argument to develop his thesis.*

1 There's something about violence that—abstractly—appeals. Children
reflect this most directly. Children don't lie: They haven't reached the age
of guile, so when they gravitate to toy guns and gory comics, and movies
with arrows through chests, and boiling oil and exploding turrets, the eyes
marvel with fascination, and the nickels pour out for more. One needs to
reflect on the phenomenon, and apply it not to children, but to their parents.

2 The chestnut about how if you kill one person you're a murderer, if you
kill a million you are a great general, applies, if indirectly, to the uproar about
TV. What hurts is the *particularization* of violence. When what you see on
the screen is machine guns or artillery blazing forth and dozens, even hundreds, of people—Indians, or Nazis, or Japanese—dropping in their tracks,
that's stuff you look at without ever disturbing the rhythm of your hand passing from the popcorn to your mouth. It's when the screen focuses on an individual that one's emotional attention is arrested.

3 And then it's what happens to the victim that makes the difference. If
he is merely going to be shot, that doesn't, in most cases, bother people or
even grip their imagination. Especially if he is the fifth or 15th person shot
in that television hour. It is when the act of violence causes the viewer to fas-
ten his attention not so much on the capacity of so many people to kill, but
on the capacity of some people to engage in individuated cruelty—that's

when you feel the impulse to close your eyes, and when the memory is haunting. These are distinctions Attorney General Reno didn't make when she yakked about how the TV world has to clean up its act, or she will report it to Congress.

Consider the elementary distinction: We are viewing *Roots*, the story of 4 slavery in the United States. A mean white master sets out to punish the unruly or insolent or courageous slave, and somebody steps up with a big long whip. The first stroke brings out an instant diagonal welt on the slave's back and as you see it, you hear his grunt of pain. What then does the camera do?

What it ought to do is what it generally does—turn to look in on the faces 5 of the bystanders; or of the slavemaster's wife, mistress, children; whatever. And what you hear is the repeated slash of the whip and the yelps of pain.

That is violence going on, no question about it, but it is a violence that 6 at least has the grace to blush. It is the lady's fan lifted up to conceal the view of the bull's horn that has got the matador in the groin and is tossing him skyward, the shuttered eyes of the man viewing the same scene. It is what distinguishes the sadist from the viewer who wants realism and excitement and drama but doesn't want that element of violence that indulges instincts it is the purpose of civilization to quieten.

The 6-year-old who takes pleasure in seeing his brother disciplined will, 7 if all goes well with his moral development, want to avoid seeing any such scene by the time he is 16. What he has learned in the interval is that pain is something we seek to avoid. Pain—violence—is what is done by people who aren't socialized, and are insensible to the pain of others. When pain is unavoidable, the doctors are there with narcotics. When it is unnecessary— as with the crime that surrounds us—it is nevertheless the stuff of real life, and we learn about real life primarily, these days, from television.

The statistic is that by the time the average child finishes elementary 8 school, he will have seen some 8,000 people "killed" on TV. And the fuss seems to be about the impact that viewing has on the young American growing up. It is tempting to postulate a correlation: (1) We live in a society in which crime is rampant and generally increasing. And (2) we live in a society in which crime-on-TV is increasing. There are, granted, little oscillations in both generalities: Crime has slightly decreased this year, in several categories. And violence is less frequent on network television, but it is nevertheless all over the place, on TV as in city streets. (3) Therefore: Television is responsible for the proliferation of crime.

We do not in fact know whether this is so. As has been pointed out by 9 critics of television critics, the same stuff we see here on TV is seen in Great Britain and Japan, yet we have more than three times as much crime as

Great Britain, and nine times as much as Japan: So why didn't all that violence corrupt the Brits and the Japanese?

10   It isn't easy to answer that objection, not if your design is like that of Sen. Hollings of South Carolina. He seems to want to hold television responsible for national violence. And of course it springs quickly to mind that if a politician denounces somebody or something for the crime wave, people will get the impression that he is *doing something* about crime, which is generally not the case. It can't be established that crime on the screen has zero connection with crime on the street. No one can tell us how much crime we would have in America, or in England or Japan, if there were *no* crime on television. Perhaps less. Certainly a little less, because we know that specific acts of violence depicted on television have been imitated.

11   We can't know what it is in the nature of some individuals that causes them to take insane risks. We can't know why early in December a jilted ensign shot his girlfriend and one of his Annapolis classmates and then himself, instead of behaving like however many other jilted ensigns who *don't* slaughter the girl who draws away from them. And we cannot establish that he was attracted to violence because of all the killings he saw on television. The Hutus and Tutsis twice in 30 years have killed each other in tribal warfare on a scale that dwarfs American murder (23,750 per year) into insignificance. During most of that time there was no television in Burundi.

12   Our problem is this insensibility to others' feelings, to their rights, to their person. The Christian religion, like most others, teaches us that it is sinful to cause pain, except as civil punishment. We develop in such a way as to cultivate this moral sense that tells us violence is wrong. And if our education succeeds, we feel a progressive distaste for any lascivious treatment of pain. If that moral development isn't cultivated, we are callous. To the extent that we are that, we indulge ourselves in gross forms of realism, and involve ourselves in bloody spectacles that seemed routine to the Romans, who enjoyed witnessing the torture of Christians by lions. It wasn't television that moved the crowds to shout out their joy at seeing men and women torn limb from limb, or that caused Elizabethan society to devise excruciating ways in which to end the lives of heretics. These were the fruit of different, and undeveloped, moral perspectives.

13   *Roots*, I have heard it said, caused many Americans to realize just what it was that Americans were capable of doing to other human beings during the days of slavery. I don't doubt that the horror we feel for the Holocaust is significantly the responsibility of such scenes as Herman Wouk gave us in the miniseries based on his great *Winds of War* novels. The thing to keep your eyes on, surely, is just that one detail: the barring of the entirely redundant detail. *GoodFellas* told us a story of life in the Mafia. It is as violent

as violence gets. But there was a single scene in it that startled the viewer. Or put it this way: One hopes not to encounter anyone who saw it and *wasn't* startled when one of the protagonists opened the trunk of the car where the wounded antagonist lay and plunged a kitchen knife borrowed from his mother into his whimpering prisoner. The viewer saw it—almost all. There was no closeup of the blade entering the stomach and chest—that much was left to the imagination. And such are the critical distinctions in a society that affirms some threshold in matters of taste.

That taste can never be generated by acts of Congress or claps of thun- 14 der issuing from the Attorney General. We suffer from many ailments in America, and a whole lot can be said about the insufficiencies of TV, but not that it is responsible for original sin, whose harvest in every human being varies from season to season, leaving us only to know that here and there, there will always be sin. Don't blame it on the tube. Television violence can do as much to enhance our inclination to oppose violence as to reinforce any inclination to engage in it.

Understanding Context

1. Why does Buckley refute the commonly held belief that television violence leads viewers, especially young viewers, to imitate what they see on the screen?
2. What does Buckley mean by the "*particularization* of violence"?
3. What, in Buckley's opinion, is the real cause for crime and violence?
4. Does Buckley assert that television violence can have positive effects? Can violence teach as well as excite?

Evaluating Strategy

1. How does Buckley support his thesis? What evidence does he present?
2. How does Buckley refute the argument that viewing violent acts leads children to become violent?
3. *Other modes:* How does Buckley use example, comparison, and argument to develop his essay?

Appreciating Language

1. Consider the audience and format of *TV Guide*. Is this article suited for that magazine, its readers, its style? Are there any words or references that seem out of place?

2. Buckley, a highly refined stylist, uses slang words such as *stuff* and *Brits*, in this article. Do these words make his article seem superficial, or do they make the article more readable to a wide audience?

Writing Suggestions

1. Write an essay about how television shaped your world in childhood. What impressions did television give you about the Wild West, New York City, money, marriage, or doctors? Select a single subject and provide examples of how your views were influenced by depictions you saw on television.
2. *Collaborative writing:* Discuss Buckley's article with a group of students. Determine how many agree or disagree with his thesis. Record comments by the group; then write a brief letter to *TV Guide* supporting or criticizing Buckley's view. If students disagree, divide into two groups and write opposing letters.

THOMAS JEFFERSON ET AL.

During the hot summer of 1776, the Second Continental Congress met in Philadelphia. Following a call for a resolution of independence from Great Britain, John Adams, Thomas Jefferson, Benjamin Franklin, Robert Livingston, and Roger Sherman were charged with drafting a declaration. Jefferson wrote the original draft, which was revised by Adams and Franklin before being presented to the entire Congress. After further changes, the Declaration of Independence was adopted and signed.

The Declaration of Independence

The Declaration of Independence presents a theory of government greatly influenced by the concept of natural rights espoused by Locke and Rousseau and then provides evidence that the British have failed to respect these rights. Notice that most of the declaration is a list of causes for the colonies to seek independence.

In Congress, July 4, 1776. The unanimous Declaration of the thirteen united States 1 *of America,*

When in the Course of human events, it becomes necessary for one 2 people to dissolve the political bands which have connected them with another, and to assume among the powers of the earth, the separate and equal station to which the Laws of Nature and of Nature's God entitle them, a decent respect to the opinions of mankind requires that they should declare the causes which impel them to the separation.

We hold these truths to be self-evident, that all men are created equal, 3 that they are endowed by their Creator with certain unalienable Rights, that among these are Life, Liberty and the pursuit of Happiness.

That to secure these rights, Governments are instituted among Men, 4 deriving their just powers from the consent of the governed,

That whenever any Form of Government becomes destructive of these 5 ends, it is the Right of the People to alter or to abolish it, and to institute new Government, laying its foundation on such principles and organizing its powers in such form, as to them shall seem most likely to effect their Safety and Happiness. Prudence, indeed, will dictate that Governments long established should not be changed for light and transient causes; and accordingly all experience hath shown, that mankind are more disposed to suffer, while evils are sufferable, than to right themselves by abolishing the forms to which they are accustomed. But when a long train of abuses and usurpations, pursuing invariably the same Object evinces a design to reduce them under absolute Despotism, it is their right, it is their duty, to throw off such Government, and to provide new Guards for their future security.

6   Such has been the patient sufferance of these Colonies; and such is now the necessity which constrains them to alter their former Systems of Government. The history of the present King of Great Britain is a history of repeated injuries and usurpations, all having in direct object the establishment of an absolute Tyranny over these States. To prove this, let Facts be submitted to a candid world.

7   He has refused his Assent to Laws, the most wholesome and necessary for the public good.

8   He has forbidden his Governors to pass Laws of immediate and pressing importance, unless suspended in their operation till his Assent should be obtained; and when so suspended, he has utterly neglected to attend to them.

9   He has refused to pass other Laws for the accommodation of large districts of people, unless those people would relinquish the right of Representation in the Legislature, a right inestimable to them and formidable to tyrants only.

10   He has called together legislative bodies at places unusual, uncomfortable, and distant from the depository of their public Records, for the sole purpose of fatiguing them into compliance with his measures.

11   He has dissolved Representative Houses repeatedly, for opposing with manly firmness his invasions on the rights of the people.

12   He has refused for a long time, after such dissolutions, to cause others to be elected; whereby the Legislative powers, incapable of Annihilation, have returned to the People at large for their exercise; the State remaining in the mean time exposed to all the dangers of invasion from without, and convulsions within.

13   He has endeavoured to prevent the population of these States; for that purpose obstructing the Laws for Naturalization of Foreigners; refusing to pass others to encourage their migrations hither, and raising the conditions of new Appropriations of Lands.

14   He has obstructed the Administration of Justice, by refusing his Assent to Laws for establishing Judiciary powers.

15   He has made Judges dependent on his Will alone, for the tenure of their offices, and the amount and payment of their salaries.

16   He has erected a multitude of New Offices, and sent hither swarms of Officers to harrass our people, and eat out their substance.

He has kept among us in times of peace, Standing Armies without the 17
Consent of our legislatures.

He has affected to render the Military independent of and superior to 18
the Civil power.

He has combined with others to subject us to a jurisdiction foreign to 19
our constitution, and unacknowledged by our laws; giving his Assent to their
Acts of pretended Legislation:

For quartering large bodies of armed troops among us: 20

For protecting them, by a mock Trial, from punishment for any Murders 21
which they should commit on the Inhabitants of these States:

For cutting off our Trade with all parts of the world: 22

For imposing Taxes on us without our Consent: 23

For depriving us in many cases, of the benefits of Trial by Jury: 24

For transporting us beyond Seas to be tried for pretended offences: 25

For abolishing the free System of English Laws in a neighbouring Prov- 26
ince, establishing therein an Arbitrary government, and enlarging its Boundaries so as to render it at once an example and fit instrument for introducing
the same absolute rule in these Colonies:

For taking away our Charters, abolishing our most valuable Laws, and al- 27
tering fundamentally the Forms of our Governments:

For suspending our own Legislatures, and declaring themselves in- 28
vested with power to legislate for us in all cases whatsoever.

He has abdicated Government here, by declaring us out of his Protec- 29
tion and waging War against us.

He has plundered our seas, ravaged our Coasts, burnt our towns, and de- 30
stroyed the lives of our people.

He is at this time transporting large Armies of foreign Mercenaries to 31
compleat the works of death, desolation and tyranny, already begun with circumstances of Cruelty & perfidy scarcely paralleled in the most barbarous
ages, and totally unworthy the Head of a civilized nation.

He has constrained our fellow Citizens taken Captive on high Seas to 32
bear Arms against their Country, to become the executioners of their friends
and Brethren, or to fall themselves by their Hands.

He has excited domestic insurrections amongst us, and has endeav- 33
oured to bring on the inhabitants of our frontiers, the merciless Indian Savages, whose known rule of warfare, is an undistinguished destruction of all
ages, sexes and conditions.

In every stage of these Oppressions We have Petitioned for Redress in 34
the most humble terms: Our repeated Petitions have been answered only by
repeated injury. A Prince, whose character is thus marked by every act
which may define a Tyrant, is unfit to be the ruler of a free people.

35   Nor have We been wanting in attentions to our British brethren. We have warned them from time to time of attempts by their legislature to extend an unwarrantable jurisdiction over us. We have reminded them of the circumstances of our emigration and settlement here. We have appealed to their native justice and magnanimity, and we have conjured them by the ties of our common kindred to disavow these usurpations, which, would inevitably interrupt our connections and correspondence. They too have been deaf to the voice of justice and consanguinity. We must, therefore, acquiesce in the necessity, which denounces our Separation, and hold them, as we hold the rest of mankind, Enemies in War, in Peace Friends.

36   We, therefore, the Representatives of the united States of America, in General Congress, Assembled, appealing to the Supreme Judge of the world for the rectitude of our intentions, do, in the Name, and by Authority of the good People of these Colonies, solemnly publish and declare, That these United Colonies are, and of Right ought to be, Free and Independent States; that they are Absolved from all Allegiance to the British Crown, and that all political connection between them and the State of Great Britain, is and ought to be totally dissolved; and that as Free and Independent States, they have full Power to levy War, conclude Peace, contract Alliances, establish Commerce, and to do all other Acts and Things which Independent States may of right do.

37   And for the support of this Declaration, with a firm reliance on the protection of divine Providence, we mutually pledge to each other our Lives, our Fortunes and our sacred Honor.

Understanding Context

1. What were the principal causes for the Congress to declare independence?
2. Why do Jefferson and the other authors argue that these grievances cannot be resolved in any other fashion?
3. *Critical thinking:* When was the last time you read the Declaration of Independence? Do some items strike you as relevant to current conditions? Should Americans be more familiar with a document that helped create their country and establish its values?

Evaluating Strategy

1. How does the Declaration of Independence use induction and deduction?
2. How much of the document is devoted to listing causes? Is enough evidence presented to provide support for the decision to sever ties with Britain?

Appreciating Language

1. How does this document refer to the king?
2. This document was drafted in 1776. How has the language changed in 200 years?

Writing Suggestions

1. The Declaration of Independence states that the "pursuit of Happiness" is an unalienable right. Write an essay discussing the effects this pursuit of happiness has had on generations of Americans. How has the guarantee for the search for happiness shaped American culture and society?
2. *Collaborative writing:* Discuss the Declaration of Independence with a group of students. Does the current government reflect Jefferson's ideals? Work together and record your observations. What has been the long-term impact of Jefferson's document?

Responding to IMAGES

Patient in mental asylum, Turin, Italy

© Magnum

1. *Visual analysis:* What is your immediate reaction to this image? Does the man's pose suggest humor, wit, defiance, or desperation? How does the caption influence your response?
2. What does this photograph represent to you in terms of mental illness? Do most people understand how disabling mental disease can be for both patients and their loved ones?
3. Would you consider using this photograph in a fund-raising brochure for a mental health campaign? Why or why not?
4. Write a fictional narrative to accompany this photograph. Write the patient's diary entry, a consoling letter by a friend, a doctor's patient history.

5. *Collaborative writing:* Discuss this photograph with a group of students and measure reactions. Do any of them know someone who has suffered from a severe mental illness? Work together to write a brief statement about how the public should be educated about mental illness. Do people consider mental disorders true disabilities?

6. *Other modes*
   - Develop a *comparison* essay contrasting the way people view physical and mental illnesses. Do people suffering from a mental disorder receive less support, sympathy, and acceptance than those with physical handicaps? Why or why not?
   - Create a *definition* paper that establishes the severity of mental illness required for a patient to receive disability payments.

Cause-and-Effect Checklist

Before submitting your paper, review these points:

✔ Is your thesis clearly stated?

✔ Are causes clearly stated, logically organized, and supported by details?

✔ Are conflicting interpretations disproven or acknowledged?

✔ Are effects supported by observation and evidence? Do you avoid sweeping generalizations and unsupported conclusions?

✔ Do you anticipate future changes that might alter predictions?

✔ Do you avoid making errors in critical thinking, especially hasty generalization and confusing a time relationship for cause and effect?

✔ Have you tested your ideas through peer review?

Companion Website

See **http://www.thomsonedu.com/english/sundance** for additional information on writing cause and effect.

ARGUMENT AND PERSUASION
INFLUENCING READERS

26

WHAT IS ARGUMENT AND PERSUASION?

We are bombarded by argument and persuasion every day. Newspaper editorials encourage us to change our opinions about capital punishment or immigration. Sales brochures convince us to invest in stocks or purchase life insurance. Fund-raising letters ask us to contribute to medical research or an alumni fund. Billboards, e-mails, magazine ads, and television commercials urge us to buy computers, automobiles, perfumes, and soft drinks. Political candidates solicit our votes. Public service announcements warn us against the dangers of cigarette smoking and drunk driving.

As a student you have to develop persuasive arguments in essays and research papers to demonstrate your skills and knowledge. After graduation you will need a persuasive résumé and cover letter to enter the job market. In your career you will have to impress clients, motivate employees, justify decisions, defend actions, and propose new ideas with well-stated arguments and persuasive appeals.

Arguments are assertions designed to convince readers to accept an idea, adopt a solution, or change their opinions. Writers use reason and facts to support their arguments, often disproving or disputing conflicting theories or alternative proposals in the process. Attorneys prepare written arguments stating why a client has a valid claim or deserves a new trial. Scientists present the results of experiments to argue for new medical treatments or to disprove current assumptions. Economists assemble data to support arguments to raise or lower interest rates.

 To read more about argument and persuasion, along with interactive examples and opportunities to work with interactive texts, click on "The Rhetorical Patterns of Inquiry" from the main menu of *Comp21*.

Persuasive Appeals

In ancient times Aristotle and other philosophers established three classic persuasive appeals to convince people to accept ideas or take action: *logos*, *pathos*, and *ethos*. Today these appeals appear in television commercials, political campaign speeches, business proposals, and ordinary e-mail. Because each appeal has advantages and disadvantages, writers often use more than one.

Logos

Logos (Logic) supports a point of view or proposed action with critical thinking (see chapter 4), reasoned arguments, and evidence:

> *Test results*—Findings established by experiments or research
> *Statistics*—Data represented as numbers and percentages
> *Documents*—Materials such as diaries, letters, reports, photographs, and videos generated by participants or witnesses of specific events or situations
> *Expert testimony*—Opinions by respected authorities
> *Eyewitness testimony*—Statements by those who observed or experienced an event or situation
> *Interpretation*—Critical reading and analysis of accepted laws, principles, contracts, and other documents, such as the Constitution
> *Examples*—Specific instances, events, or cases
> *Hypothetical examples*—Fictional examples used to illustrate ideas
> *Surveys*—Polls of public opinion or interviews with sample audiences

Logic is widely used in academic, business, and government writing. Attorneys use expert testimony, forensic evidence, and interpretations of legal principles to persuade judges and juries. Environmentalists will cite scientific data to argue that a certain pesticide is harmful to wildlife and should be banned. You probably used logic in preparing high school research papers.

Advantages   Logical appeals provide evidence needed for major decisions, especially group decisions. In addition, the facts used to support an argument can be verified by readers.

Disadvantages   Logic can demand a high degree of reader attention and specialized knowledge. Readers may not be motivated to study statistics or follow a complex train of thought.

Pathos

Pathos (**Emotion**) uses images, sensations, or shock techniques to lead people to react in a desired manner. Emotional appeals call on people's deeply felt needs and desires:

Creativity—The desire for recognition and self-expression

Achievement—The desire to attain money, fame, or professional accomplishments

Independence—The drive to be unique, to stand out, to be an individual

Conformity—The need to be part of a group, to have friends, to be one of the "in" group

Endurance—The desire to be recognized for bearing burdens others have avoided or could not bear, feeling successful by simply surviving

Fear—The need to resist, avoid, or defeat threats to self, family, or the community, to fight crime, cancer, or terrorism

Popularity—The desire to be accepted, respected, admired by friends, coworkers, or the opposite sex

Emotional appeals are widely used in public relations, marketing, advertising, and political campaigns. Sex appeal is used to sell products ranging from cars to shampoo. Images of starving children will provoke pity and empathy, encouraging people to donate money or lobby politicians for government action. Fear of crime, terrorism, disease, or job loss can be used to motivate audiences to vote for a candidate or support a change in policy.

Advantages Emotional appeals produce immediate, often powerful, responses.

Disadvantages Emotional appeals tend to be short-lived, can easily backfire, and provide limited factual support for readers to share with others.

Ethos

Ethos (**Ethics**) uses shared values to influence readers. Appeals based on ethics may call upon reasoning but do not rest wholly on the logical analysis of evidence. Like emotional appeals, those based on ethics reflect deeply held convictions rather than personal motivations:

Religion—The desire to follow the rules and behavior espoused by one's faith—to be a good Jew, Christian, or Muslim

Patriotism—The drive to place one's country above personal needs, to sacrifice for community ("Ask not what your country can do for you, ask what you can do for your country.")

Standards—The desire to be a good citizen, a good lawyer, or a good parent, to express the higher ideals of a community, profession, or social role

Humanitarianism—A secular appeal to help others, save the environment, protect the weak, or be "a citizen of the world"

Ethical appeals form the basis of many sermons, editorials, and political speeches that emphasize shared values and beliefs.

Advantages   Ethical appeals call upon people's core values and can be powerful motivators.

Disadvantages   Ethical appeals work only on audiences with common moral philosophies. A Muslim cleric's appeal, for example, may have little influence on Roman Catholics. A pacifist may ignore or oppose an appeal to nationalism and militarism.

Blending Appeals

To create effective persuasive messages, writers frequently blend factual details with emotionally charged human interest stories. A fund-raising letter for a children's shelter might use the emotional story of a single child to arouse sympathy, provide facts and statistics to demonstrate the severity of the problem, then conclude with an ethical appeal for financial support:

Make a Difference

Pathos
emotional
example
demonstrating
a problem

Thirteen-year-old Sandy Lopez will not have to sleep in a doorway tonight. Abandoned by abusive parents, she spent six weeks living in subway stations and alleys before she came to Safe Haven. Today she has a warm bed, clean clothes, and regular meals. She is back in school, making friends, and studying music.

Logos
factual support
presenting a
solution

Since 1986 Safe Haven has helped thousands of homeless children find shelter, counseling, and support. Eighty percent of our clients complete high school and almost a third graduate from college.

But Safe Haven has only 90 beds and every day has to turn away dozens of the 2,000 homeless children who live in the streets, where they often succumb to drugs, prostitution, and alcohol abuse. To meet the growing need, Safe Haven needs your help to build a new dorm, hire more counselors, and expand its job training center.

Ethos
ethical call
to action

Living in one of the richest cities in the world, can we ignore the children who sleep in our streets? Make a difference. Contribute to Safe Haven today.

WRITING ACTIVITY

Select one or more of the following writing situations and give examples of the best appeal or appeals. Note advantages and disadvantages of each appeal.

1. A fund-raising brochure for a day care center to be distributed in churches

2. An announcement encouraging students to avoid binge drinking

3. A congressional candidate's letter to voters advocating privatizing Social Security

4. A school board's letter urging parents to attend parent-teacher meetings

5. The text of a public service announcement reminding people to vote

6. A minister's appeal to his or her congregation to donate money to victims of a natural disaster

7. A scientist's statement to Congress urging further funds for genetic research

8. A homeowner's appeal to an alderman for street repairs in his or her neighborhood

9. An automobile manufacturer's letter to car owners explaining the need for a recall to repair an engine defect

10. An environmental group's letter requesting that the city cease using lawn chemicals in public parks

UNDERSTANDING LOGIC

Of the three persuasive appeals, logic is the probably the most important one you will use in college and professional writing. You can take entire courses devoted to logic, reasoning, statistics, and probability. But even a brief overview of logic can sharpen your critical thinking and writing skills.

Two of the basic terms in logic—*deduction* and *induction*—are commonly misunderstood and are worth reviewing in some detail. Many of the problems we encounter as students, consumers, employees, family members, and citizens involve deductive and inductive thinking. Whether you are constructing an argument using deduction or induction, it is important to avoid the *logical fallacies*—errors in critical thinking (see pages 50–56).

Deduction

Deduction is a logical argument stated in a formula or syllogism. A major premise presents a statement of what is true or assumed to be true. Then a minor premise—a sample case or specific example—is measured against it. A conclusion is then drawn from the comparison. Many textbooks offer this age-old illustration:

MAJOR PREMISE: All cows are mammals.
MINOR PREMISE: Bessie is a cow.
CONCLUSION: *Bessie is a mammal.*

Unfortunately, this standard example fails to show how often we use this form of logic. Deduction is basic in solving algebra problems: if $x = 10$ and $a = 5$, we know that x is greater than a. You confront deduction every time you enter a convenience store and see a sign reading "You must be 21 to buy beer." In checking a young person's ID, the sales clerk practices an exercise in simple deduction:

MAJOR PREMISE: Customers must be 21 to buy beer.
MINOR PREMISE: Sharon Smith is 19.
CONCLUSION: *Sharon Smith cannot buy beer.*

Warranties, contracts, lease agreements, wills, and insurance policies are all examples of major premises. Union grievances, for instance, are deductive arguments. An employee complaining that he or she was unfairly fired has to prove that the company violated the contract's termination policy. The Supreme Court devotes all its time to hearing test cases, determining if they are constitutional or not. The justices test each questionable law or lower court decision against their major premise, the U.S. Constitution. Does a handgun ban infringe on the right of citizens to bear arms? Does a city's plan to provide public transportation to parochial school students violate the separation of church and state? Does a campus hate-speech code conflict with the constitutional protection of free speech?

If the major premise in deductive reasoning is incorrect or vaguely worded, problems can emerge. Many lawsuits concern disputed interpretations of a major premise. Apartment leases, for example, usually include bans against making "excess noise," but what actually constitutes "excess noise"? Do the standards differ between an apartment building housing the elderly or one filled with college students? Can you argue against eviction if the police were never called and no neighbor filed a complaint? Is the landlord the sole judge of a tenant's behavior? If landlords and tenants have different interpretations of the terms of a lease, conflicts can occur.

By developing an understanding of deduction, you can prevent potential disputes in business and personal relationships by clearly defining the major premise and making sure all parties accept a common definition. For example, before signing a contract or making a verbal agreement with an employer or contractor, review it carefully. Any clause two parties accept will become a major premise.

Questions

1. Can you think of instances where you have encountered problems in deduction? Have you had disputes based on conflicting interpretations of a lease, warranty, tax regulation, or school policy?
2. Do you see any potential problems with the following rules or major premises? Could different interpretations create confusion or conflicts?
   - Disadvantaged students have priority for on-campus jobs.
   - Students must have completed a substantial amount of work to be eligible for a course extension.
   - Family members of employees can receive a 20 percent discount.

Induction

Unlike deduction, induction does not begin with a premise or assertion of what is true. Instead, an inductive argument starts with evidence, bits of information. From these specifics, a conclusion is drawn. Induction can be illustrated by a simple diagram:

XXX   XXX   XX   X

    XXX   XXX   XXX

XXX   XX   X   XX

    XXX   XXX XXX   X

—————————*inductive leap*—————

CONCLUSION

These X's could represent satellite photographs, blood tests, interviews with rock stars, sales of used cars, snowmobile accidents in Wisconsin, or responses to a questionnaire. From a study of this data, a conclusion is drawn that identifies a cause or observes a general trend.

Physicians use induction to make a diagnosis. Based on observations, test results, and the patient's history, they establish the reason for a medical complaint. Detectives investigating a crime scene collect evidence that is examined to identify suspects. Pollsters conduct voter surveys to determine the likely outcome of an election. Stockbrokers review a company's current sales, debts, market share, and competition to advise potential investors. In all these cases, professionals assemble data, analyze it, and then make an "inductive leap" to draw a conclusion. No one can be 100 percent sure that he or she has properly assembled and interpreted the information; there is always a degree of doubt.

A criminal trial best illustrates the inductive process. In a murder case, the prosecutor presents evidence of the defendant's guilt—eyewitness testimony, fingerprints, expert witnesses, and so forth—and tells the jury that all the evidence adds up to a clear guilty verdict. The defense attorney may introduce contradictory evidence or question the interpretation of the prosecution's evidence to argue that there is not enough proof to conclude that the defendant is guilty. Lawyers don't use the term *inductive leap*—but the legal concept of *reasonable doubt* is very close.

We use inductive logic in making decisions. In choosing a new apartment, we weigh a number of factors—rent, location, appearance, appliances, and the like—then make a decision based on our observations. To determine if a used car is worth $5,000, we take a test drive, check the tires for wear, determine the mileage, ask the previous owner about problems, and check the car's blue book value. From this information we conclude whether the car merits its price.

As with deduction, problems occur with inductive logic. Evidence may be overlooked or misinterpreted. Textbooks frequently refer to the famous *Literary Digest* telephone survey that confidently predicted that Alf Landon would defeat Franklin Roosevelt in his bid for a second term in 1936. Although the results were carefully analyzed, the measuring device was flawed because during the Depression many people could not afford telephones. Any poll that did not include poor voters would fail to provide an accurate survey of public opinion. By questioning only those people listed in telephone directories, the researchers made a fundamental error that generated accurate but misleading information.

Questions

1. How often have you used induction in solving problems or making decisions? What problems have you encountered?
2. Have you observed the use of inductive reasoning during televised trials? How effective have cross-examinations been in raising reasonable doubt?
3. Do your textbooks in other courses offer methods of collecting and evaluating evidence? Do separate disciplines place different values on types of evidence?

PERSUASION AND AUDIENCE

Whenever you write, you should consider your audience—the people who will read your papers, e-mails, reports, and letters. A narrative or description will only be effective if readers understand the definitions, examples, and details you present to support your thesis. In writing persuasion, however, you have to consider your readers more carefully. Unlike a narrative or a description, an argument seeks not to simply tell a story or share information but influence people to change their minds or take action. Readers of persuasive writing are more likely to be critical, even hostile to your viewpoints. To win support, you may have to refute alternative arguments, dismiss competing interpretations of evidence, or admit the value of opposing ideas. The psychologist Carl R. Rogers studied problems in communications and emphasized the importance of building trust by addressing audience concerns and objections. *Rogerian* arguments work to build consensus by showing respect to people holding opposing viewpoints.

Appealing to Hostile Readers

Perhaps the most challenging problem writers face is attempting to persuade a hostile audience—readers you know or expect will have negative attitudes about you, the organization you represent, or the ideas you advocate. Although no technique will magically convert opponents into supporters, you can overcome a measure of hostility and influence those who may be undecided with a few strategies:

1. **Openly admit differences.** Instead of attempting to pretend that no conflict exists, frankly state that your view may differ from that of your readers. This honest admission can achieve a measure of objectivity and respect.
2. **Responsibly summarize opposing viewpoints.** By fairly restating your opponents' views, you are more likely to lead readers to agree with you and demonstrate impartiality.
3. **Avoid making judgmental statements.** Don't label people with differing views with hostile or negative language. Use neutral terms to make distinctions. If you call your views "right" and your readers' "wrong," you will have difficulty getting people to accept your thesis because in the process they will have to accept your insults as valid. Demeaning language will only alienate your audience.
4. **Stress shared values, experiences, and problems.** Build bridges with your readers by emphasizing past cooperation and common concerns.

5. **Ask readers to maintain an open mind.** Don't demand or expect to convert readers, but keep in mind that almost everyone will agree to try to be open-minded and receptive to new ideas.

6. **Overcome negative stereotypes.** Play the devil's advocate to determine what negative stereotypes your readers might have about you, the organization you represent, or your thesis. Include examples, references, evidence, and stories in your paper to counter these negative impressions.

WRITING ACTIVITY

Select one of the following writing contexts and list some strategies to overcome hostile reactions. What facts, narratives, appeals, or approaches would help advance the writer's thesis? What issues does the writer have to address? How can he or she counter objections? What information would the writer have to include?

1. An African American writing a letter to the editor of a conservative business magazine arguing for stronger affirmative action policies

2. A feminist writing an article about sexual harassment directed to business owners and managers

3. A real estate developer writing to a community group opposing the building of a new shopping mall in their neighborhood

4. A student group writing to alumni to suggest that funds being raised for a new athletic facility be spent on computer labs

5. A district attorney explaining to a crime victim why his or her attacker has been allowed to plead to a lesser charge and receive probation rather than a prison sentence

6. A defense attorney drafting opening remarks to a jury in a highly publicized child abuse case

7. A tenant writing to a landlord urging him or her to add security features, such as deadbolts, to apartments

8. A college administrator developing an open letter to students defending a campus organization's decision to invite a controversial public speaker

9. A person acquitted but believed by many to be guilty of a violent sexual offense addressing a school board about why he or she should keep a teaching position

10. A director of the Food and Drug Administration explaining to AIDS patients why a new drug requires further testing before being approved for human use, even for the terminally ill

STRATEGIES | for Writing Argument and Persuasion

Critical Thinking and Prewriting

1. **List as many topics, problems, issues, controversies, debates, and decisions you can think of.** Brainstorm, freewrite briefly, and list questions to isolate promising topics.

2. **Review the scope of the assignment.** Effective argument-and-persuasion papers require substantial evidence and reasoning.
   - Such topics as capital punishment, gun control, abortion, and sexual harassment are difficult to address in a short paper unless you take a unique approach or develop a new angle. Avoid writing papers that simply repeat commonly stated positions.
   - Review your list and discard topics that require extensive research or are simply too complex be fully addressed given the limits of your paper.

3. **Determine the goal of your essay—to persuade readers to accept your opinion or to motivate readers to take action or alter behavior.** Unlike a description or narrative, an argumentative paper has a specific goal.
   - Define the effect you want your paper to have on readers. Do you want them to entertain a new idea, change their minds, or direct them to take action?

4. **Consider your audience.** To craft an effective argument, it is important to consider your audience.
   - Define your readers and their perceptual world. List the past experiences, social roles, values, norms, attitudes, and reference groups that may influence their thinking.
   - Consider their immediate attitude toward your topic. Are your readers likely to be open-minded and neutral or bring strongly held opinions to the issue?
   - List questions and concerns your readers may have.
   - List appeals readers will relate to and respond to.

5. **Develop a thesis statement and a list of principal appeals with your readers in mind.**
6. **List evidence needed to support your thesis.** Conduct a computer search using keywords to locate current sources about your topic.
   - Evaluate sources carefully for accuracy and bias.

Planning

1. **Review critical thinking.** Before writing a plan, review Strategies for Increasing Critical Thinking (page 49) and Common Errors in Critical Thinking (pages 50–56).
2. **Write your thesis statement at the top of the page to guide planning.** Qualify your thesis, avoiding generalizations, absolute statements, and unsupported assumptions.
3. **Develop an introduction that arouses attention, establishes your approach, and uses persuasive appeals to create a favorable relationship with readers.**
   - You may wish to open your essay with a question, a narrative, a quote, or a statistic that illustrates or dramatizes the issue.
   - Consider carefully whether you wish to announce your thesis immediately or present supporting details or answer potential objections before presenting an opinion that may alienate readers.
4. **Do not mistake propaganda for persuasion.** Do not assume that hurling accusations, using inflated statistics, employing shock tactics, or demonizing your opponents will make your argument successful. People resent manipulation, and potential supporters may be alienated by overstated arguments and appeals they find objectionable or false.
5. **Organize ideas in order of importance.** Place the most convincing appeal or argument at the beginning or end of your paper, where reader attention is strongest.
6. **Consider using visuals.** Photographs, charts, and diagrams can add effective support to a persuasive message—provided they are carefully selected and properly presented.
   - Select images that suit the appeals you are using. The image of a starving child may offer moving support for a fund raising poster using emotional appeal but would be inappropriate in an academic paper. Charts, diagrams, and graphs can help readers appreciate data in a business report but add little to an essay based on ethical appeals.
   - Avoid using images that may alienate readers. (See Strategies for Using Visuals on page 211).

7. **Conclude the paper with a thought-provoking impression or a clear call to action.** End the paper with a final fact, example, or quotation that will influence readers to consider your thesis, perhaps even read more to fully understand your point of view. If your goal is to direct people to alter their behavior, present explicit instructions so that motivated readers can take immediate action.

Writing the First Draft

1. **Keep your thesis and audience in mind as you write.** Effective persuasive arguments are directed to a specific audience. As you write, concentrate on your readers.
   - Select appeals, ideas, and facts your readers will understand and respond to. You may come up with ideas or references that may be convincing to you but will be lost on your readers. Work with their frame of reference.
2. **Qualify remarks, noting possible alternative views.** Avoid making absolute statements that can be easily refuted by citing a single exception.
3. **Recognize the strength and weakness of each appeal.** Balance emotional appeals with facts. Dramatize statistics with human interest. Tailor ethical appeals to your readers' perceptual world.
4. **Present factual detail in ways readers can understand.** To present facts, use methods such as example, analogy, and narrative to illustrate and dramatize facts.
5. **Use transitional phrases and paragraph breaks to signal shifts between main points of your argument.**
6. **Keep the scope of the assignment in mind as you write, and consider limiting the topic if the draft becomes too lengthy.** If your draft begins to expand so that it will require ten pages rather than the thousand words you intended to fully address the topic, limit the scope of your paper.
   - Revise your thesis, narrowing your argument.
   - Tighten your introduction, mentioning ideas and then selecting one or two principal points for the focus of your paper.
7. **Anticipate reader objections as you write.** Play the devil's advocate as you write. Consider how you can overcome or counter readers' negative assumptions about your thesis.

Revising

1. **Review the needs of the writing assignment; then examine your entire essay.**
   - On first reading, does your essay meet the needs of the assignment?
   - Is the topic suitable?

- Is the thesis clearly stated?
- If you are motivating readers to take action, are they given a clearly defined course of action?

2. **Examine your use of appeals.**
   - Are logical appeals clear, accurate, and suitable to your task?
   - Do you present clear, convincing evidence your readers will accept?
   - Do emotional appeals avoid bias or propaganda that may offend or backfire?
   - Are ethical appeals suited to your audience? Do your readers share the values you call upon?

3. **Review critical thinking.** Do you avoid Common Errors in Critical Thinking (see pages 50–56)?

4. **Examine the placement of your thesis.** Should the thesis be placed at the opening or end of the essay? Would it be more effective to present background information, address reader objections, and clear up misconceptions before announcing your point of view?

5. **Review your introduction and conclusion.**
   - Does the first paragraph clearly announce your purpose, limit the topic, and qualify your approach? Does it grab attention and prepare readers to accept your message?
   - Does the conclusion urge readers to consider your thesis or direct them to take action?

6. **Examine the paper's structure.**
   - Are there clear transitions between main points?
   - Could paragraph breaks be altered to demonstrate shifts and emphasize ideas?

7. **Review your use of visuals.** Do they support your message? Are they appropriate, effective, and clearly presented?

8. **Use peer review to identify areas needing improvement.**

Editing and Proofreading

1. **Read your paper aloud.**
   - Are ideas stated in concrete language readers can understand?
   - Do any words have connotations unsuited to your purpose or audience?
   - Do the tone and style suit your topic, audience, and message?

2. **Use peer editing to locate errors you may have missed.**

STUDENT PAPER

This paper was written in response to the following assignment:

Write a 500- to 750-word persuasive essay about a current social or political issue. Avoid writing about such subjects as abortion or capital punishment unless you can provide a new or unique angle. Document use of any outside sources.

Why a Black Student Union?

Before any controversial issue can be discussed, there is usually a certain amount of misinformation to deal with. This is clearly the case with the Black Student Union. Many students have voiced concern and written letters to the editor since the college paper revealed that $540,000 was being allocated to the Union (Kane 1). The article stated that $52,000 was going to salaries, making the Black Student Union the only student organization with a paid staff.

First of all, the bulk of the money allocated to the Union is dedicated to renovating the building, which is university property. Constructed in 1962, the building has not had major repairs since 1974. Roof leaks, first reported to the administration three years ago have led to substantial and costly damage. In addition, it is the only building that was not retrofitted with new heating and air conditioning systems in 1996 (*CSU* 22). Also, the building still does not comply with the Americans with Disabilities Act. Wheelchair ramps must be installed by court order (*CSU* 23).

Second, no one at the Union receives a salary for student activities. Five graduate students are paid to tutor remedial classes. Given the lack of space in the cramped Academic Support Center, use of the Black Student Union makes sense and creates more openings in the Center. Many non-black students attend classes and remedial seminars at the Union. Less than half the graduates of the internet course last semester were African-American (Kane 2).

But there are other objections to the Union. Why should blacks have their own facility? Many on campus see the presence of a black student union as a kind of self-imposed apartheid. The Union has also been criticized for being the center of racially hostile militancy.

The Black Student Union hardly threatens to impose a new kind of segregation. We live in integrated dorms, attend integrated classes, participate in integrated sports, and serve on mostly white and Asian academic committees. The few hours a week a student might spend at the BSU hardly threatens racial isolation—any more than the women's center risks ending co-education or the Newman Center pits Catholics against Protestants. From my own observations, I see little evidence of the radical and extremist politics union opponents mention. The most popular event the Black Student Union holds is Career Week when black students line up to meet representatives from AT&T, IBM, Bank One, and 3M. Most students are concerned about academic performance and career options rather than radical politics. True, the Union has sponsored some controversial speakers, but so has the university itself. Much of the "extremist literature" cited in a campus editorial is not distributed by the union. The union receives a lot of free literature in the mail, which has been traditionally displayed in the lobby. When it was brought to the attention of the board that some of the pamphlets were anti-Semitic, members took quick steps to screen incoming publications and discard "hate literature."

The real purpose of the Union is to assist African-Americans to succeed on campus. Comprising less than 5% of the student body, blacks easily feel alienated, particularly those who graduated from predominately black high schools. According to Dean Smith, "Since only one of eight black males entering a university will graduate, it is imperative that we seek remedies to support their academic achievement and professional advancement" (12). Many black students have difficulty forming friendships and joining organizations. Often there were only a handful of college-bound students in their schools. To survive, they had to isolate themselves, studying alone to avoid associating with peers resentful of their dedication to academics. Outcasts in high school, these students find college bewildering. They are not accustomed to participating in class or working in groups. They often discover that they are woefully unprepared for college. Coming from schools with 50–75% dropout rates, many suffered from "social promotion." They discover that their A's and B's are only equal to C's and D's in better suburban schools. The Black Student Union offers African-American students a place to relax, interact with older students, and work to make the university a more hospitable place to minorities.

Given the history of discrimination and disadvantage faced by African- Americans, the Union can be a positive asset. Is it a crutch, an undeserved luxury? No one can deny that black students feel handicapped on campus. No one complains about the cost of wheelchair ramps and elevators which benefit a handful of physically disabled students. Why should we ignore the crippling legacy of racism?

Sources

CSU Facilities Report: 1999 Sacramento: State University Budget Office, 1999.
Kane, Kelly. "BSU Funding Furor." *Campus Times* May 24, 1999, 1–2.
Smith, Dean. *Black Males in Crisis.* New York: Random House, 1998.

Questions for Review and Revision

1. What is the student's thesis?
2. What negative assumptions does the student seek to address? How does he counter them?
3. What audience does the writer appear to address? What appeals does the student use?
4. How much of the paper is driven by responding to opponents' criticisms? Is this an effective device?
5. How effective is the conclusion? Does comparing disabled students to African Americans make a valid point? Would you suggest an alternative ending?
6. Read the paper aloud. Are there passages that should be deleted or expanded? Do the tone and style suit the writer's purpose?

Writing Suggestions

1. Using this paper as a model, write a similar essay taking a position on a current campus controversy. Assume you are addressing a hostile audience. Address their objections without criticizing or demeaning those who disagree with your thesis.
2. *Collaborative writing:* Discuss this paper with a group of students. Have a member record comments by the group. Work to write a short statement approving or disapproving of the concept of establishing separate student unions. If members disagree, consider writing pro and conversions.

SUGGESTED TOPICS FOR WRITING ARGUMENT AND PERSUASION

General Assignments

Write a persuasive argument to a general audience on one of the following topics. You may use one or more appeals. You can frame your paper in the form of an essay, letter, flyer, advertisement, or other document.

- Community and police relations
- The drinking age
- The way colleges prepare or fail to prepare graduates for the job market
- Censorship of the Internet

- Affirmative action
- Minimum wage
- Welfare programs
- Medical malpractice
- Family values
- The insanity defense

Select one of the following issues and craft a persuasive essay targeted to one of the audiences listed.

Issues	Audiences
Medicare reform	Suburban residents
Distribution of condoms in public schools	Minority police officers
	Senior citizens
Gun control	Public health workers
Recycling	Retired school teachers
Legalization of marijuana for medical purposes	Small business owners
	Inner city teenagers
Prayer in public schools	Young parents
Bilingual education	
Internet consumer fraud	

To create your own interactive writing project, use the textual, visual, and video libraries on *Comp21*. From the main menu, choose "Build Your Own Occasion for Writing."

Writing in Context

1. Imagine you have become close to a highly respected member of your community. This person is well regarded by your family and may have a key role in your future. He or she invites you to join an organization that actively supports a view on abortion that is opposite to yours. Write a letter persuading this person to understand your reasons for declining the offer. State your disagreement in neutral terms without creating animosity or angering someone you wish to remain on friendly terms with.
2. Write a letter to the editor of the campus newspaper about a problem or situation you have observed but no one seems willing to address. Urge the college community to take notice and possibly take action.

STRATEGIES | for Reading Argument and Persuasion

As you read the argument and persuasion entries in this chapter, keep these questions in mind.

Context

1. What is the author's thesis? What does he or she want readers to accept? Is the writer persuading readers to accept an opinion or motivate them to take action?
2. How credible is the thesis? Does it make sense? Are alternative views discussed?
3. How does the author characterize those who advocate differing views?
4. Does the writer appear to have an unfair bias?

Strategy

1. Which appeals does the writer use? Does he or she blend logic and emotion, evidence with ethics?
2. Do the appeals seem effective, given the intended audience?
3. Where does the author place the thesis?
4. Are emotional appeals suitable or do they reflect bias?
5. Are errors in critical thinking avoided?
6. Does the reader appear to anticipate a sympathetic, neutral, or hostile audience?

Language

1. What role does connotation play in shaping arguments using logical, emotional, or ethical appeals?
2. What does the author's choice of words reveal about the intended audience?
3. Does word choice indicate bias?

ANNA QUINDLEN

Anna Quindlen (1952–) graduated from Barnard College in 1974 and began working as a reporter in New York. After writing articles for the *New York Post,* she took over the "About New York" column for the *New York Times.* In 1986 she started her own column, "Life in the Thirties." Her collected articles were published in *Living Out Loud* in 1988. She has written numerous op-ed pieces for the *Times* on social and political issues and in 1992 received the Pulitzer Prize. The following year she published another collection of essays, *Thinking Out Loud: On the Personal, the Political, the Public, and the Private.* Quindlen has also written three novels, *Object Lessons, One True Thing,* and *Black and Blue.*

Uncle Sam and Aunt Samantha: It's Simple Fairness: Women as Well as Men Should Be Required to Register for the Draft

Although women now serve in many combat roles in the military, unlike males, they are not required to register for the draft on their eighteenth birthday. As you read this article, consider if registering for the draft should be an obligation shared by both sexes. Does exempting women from the draft give them a separate, less significant status, even in peacetime?

opening fact about women in military

1 One out of every five new recruits in the United States military is female. The Marines gave the Combat Action Ribbon for service in the Persian Gulf to 23 women. Two female soldiers were killed in the bombing of the USS Cole.

2 The Selective Service registers for the draft all male citizens between the ages of 18 and 25.

current policy question

3 What's wrong with this picture?

4 As Americans read and realize that the lives of most women in this country are as different from those of Afghan women as a Cunard cruise is from maximum-security lockdown, there has nonetheless been little attention paid to one persistent gender inequity in U.S. public policy. An astonishing anachronism, really: while women are represented today in virtually all

comment on current policy

fields, including the armed forces, only men are required to register for the military draft that would be used in the event of a national-security crisis.

Since the nation is as close to such a crisis as it has been in more than 60 years, it's a good moment to consider how the draft wound up in this particular time warp. It's not the time warp of the Taliban, certainly, stuck in the worst part of the 13th century, forbidding women to attend school or hold jobs or even reveal their arms, forcing them into sex and marriage. Our own time warp is several decades old. The last time the draft was considered seriously was 20 years ago, when registration with the Selective Service was restored by Jimmy Carter after the Soviet invasion of, yep, Afghanistan. The president, as well as the Army chief of staff, asked at the time for the registration of women as well as men.

Amid a welter of arguments—women interfere with esprit de corps, women don't have the physical strength, women prisoners could be sexually assaulted, women soldiers would distract male soldiers from their mission— Congress shot down the notion of gender-blind registration. So did the Supreme Court, ruling that since women were forbidden to serve in combat positions and the purpose of the draft was to create a combat-ready force, it made sense not to register them.

But that was then, and this is now. Women have indeed served in combat positions, in the Balkans and the Middle East. More than 40,000 managed to serve in the Persian Gulf without destroying unit cohesion or failing because of upper-body strength. Some are even now taking out targets in Afghanistan from fighter jets, and apparently without any male soldier's falling prey to some predicted excess of chivalry or lust.

women in combat

Talk about cognitive dissonance. All these military personnel, male and female alike, have come of age at a time when a significant level of parity was taken for granted. Yet they are supposed to accept that only males will be required to defend their country in a time of national emergency. This is insulting to men. And it is insulting to women. Caroline Forell, an expert on women's legal rights and a professor at the University of Oregon School of testimony Law, puts it bluntly: "Failing to require this of women makes us lesser citizens."

argument to requiring women to register

testimony

Neither the left nor the right has been particularly inclined to consider this issue judiciously. Many feminists came from the antiwar movement and have let their distaste for the military in general and the draft in particular mute their response. In 1980 NOW released a resolution that buried support for the registration of women beneath opposition to the draft, despite the fact that the draft had been redesigned to eliminate the vexing inequities of Vietnam, when the sons of the working class served and the sons of the Ivy League did not. Conservatives, meanwhile, used an equal-opportunity draft

reasons why issue not discussed

as the linchpin of opposition to the Equal Rights Amendment, along with the terrifying specter of unisex bathrooms. (I have seen the urinal, and it is benign.) The legislative director of the right-wing group Concerned Women for America once defended the existing regulations by saying that most women "don't want to be included in the draft." All those young men who went to Canada during Vietnam and those who today register with fear and trembling in the face of the Trade Center devastation might be amazed to discover that lack of desire is an affirmative defense.

10   Parents face a series of unique new challenges in this more egalitarian world, not the least of which would be sending a daughter off to war. But parents all over this country are doing that right now, with daughters who enlisted; some have even expressed surprise that young women, in this day and age, are not required to register alongside their brothers and friends. While all involved in this debate over the years have invoked the assumed opposition of the people, even 10 years ago more than half of all Americans polled believed women should be made eligible for the draft. Besides, this is not about comfort but about fairness. My son has to register with the Selective Service this year, and if his sister does not when she turns 18, it makes a mockery not only of the standards of this household but of the standards of this nation.

11   It is possible in Afghanistan for women to be treated like little more than fecund pack animals precisely because gender fear and ignorance and hatred have been codified and permitted to hold sway. In this country, largely because of the concerted efforts of those allied with the women's movement over a century of struggle, much of that bigotry has been beaten back, even buried. Yet in improbable places the creaky old ways surface, the ways suggesting that we women were made of finer stuff. The finer stuff was usually porcelain, decorative and on the shelf, suitable for meals and show. Happily, the finer stuff has been transmuted into the right stuff. But with rights come responsibilities, as teachers like to tell their students. This is a responsibility that should fall equally upon all, male and female alike. If the empirical evidence is considered rationally, if the decision is divested of outmoded stereotypes, that's the only possible conclusion to be reached.

[margin annotations:]
counters opposing views
challenge
personal examples
comparison
final argument

Understanding Context

1. Why does Quindlen believe that women should be required to register with the Selective Service?
2. Why, in Quindlen's view, have feminists failed to focus on this example of gender inequality?

3. Does exempting women from the draft, in Quindlen's reasoning, result from a traditional belief that women are delicate and require special protections?
4. Should military service be a social responsibility shared by all citizens?
5. Quindlen points out that one of five recruits is female. How does this support her argument for requiring both women and men to register?
6. *Critical thinking:* Would drafting women in time of war make sense for a reason other than equality? Now that many women are entering fields critical to the military such as health care, computers, aviation, and other occupations, would it not double the pool of talent the country needs to wage war in a high-tech world?

Evaluating Strategy

1. Quindlen mentions her own children. Does the fact that she is willing to have her own daughter register support her argument?
2. How effective is the list of opening facts? Do these statistics anticipate reader objections that women should not have to register for the draft?
3. *Blending the modes:* Where does Quindlen use *narration, comparison,* and *cause and effect* to build her argument?

Appreciating Language

1. Look up the word "anachronism." Is this an effective word for Quindlen to use to characterize the "men only" requirement?
2. Quindlen is writing about a serious issue but includes statements like "What's wrong with this picture?" and "yep." Do these informal expressions weaken her argument in your view? Why or why not?

Writing Suggestions

1. Write an editorial for your campus newspaper clearly stating your views on whether women should be required to register for the draft.
2. Quindlen writes specifically about registering for the Selective Service. Many nations have a national service program that requires young people to devote a year or two to military or social service. Do you think every citizen should serve the country in some capacity, be that defending the nation or teaching disadvantaged children how to read? Write a persuasive essay arguing for or against a national service plan.

ARMANDO RENDÓN

Armando Rendón (1939–) was raised in San Antonio, Texas. He is currently vice president of ATM Systems, a Chicago-based counseling firm. He has published articles in the *Washington Post* and *Civil Rights Digest.* Rendón also wrote a film script, *El Chicano.* In 1971 he published *Chicano Manifesto,* which outlined his views of the place of Mexicans in American society.

Kiss of Death

In this passage from Chicano Manifesto, *Rendón uses a personal narrative to argue the importance of Hispanic resistance to assimilation into mainstream American society. Hispanics, he argues, should maintain their language and heritage to avoid being "sucked into the vacuum of the dominant society."*

1 I nearly fell victim to the Anglo. My childhood was spent in the West Side barrio of San Antonio. I lived in my grandmother's house on Ruiz Street just below Zarzamora Creek. I did well in the elementary grades and learned English quickly.

2 Spanish was off-limits in school anyway, and teachers and relatives taught me early that my mother tongue would be of no help in making good grades and becoming a success. Yet Spanish was the language I used in playing and arguing with friends. Spanish was the language I spoke with my *abuelita,* my dear grandmother, as I ate *atole* on those cold mornings when I used to wake at dawn to her clattering dishes in the tiny kitchen; or when I would cringe in mock horror at old folk tales she would tell me late at night.

3 But the lesson took effect anyway. When, at the age of ten, I went with my mother to California, to the San Francisco Bay Area where she found work during the war years, I had my first real opportunity to strip myself completely of my heritage. In California the schools I attended were all Anglo except for this little mexicanito. At least, I never knew anyone who admitted he was Mexican and I certainly never thought to ask. When my name was accented incorrectly, Réndon instead of Rendón, that was all right; finally I must have gotten tired of correcting people or just didn't bother.

4 I remember a summertime visit home a few years after living on the West Coast. At an evening gathering of almost the whole family—uncles, aunts, nephews, nieces, my *abuelita*—we sat outdoors through the dusk until the dark had fully settled. Then the lights were turned on; someone

brought out a Mexican card game, the *Lotería El Diablito*, similar to bingo. But instead of rows of numbers on a pasteboard, there were figures of persons, animals, and objects on cards corresponding to figures set in rows on a pasteboard. We used frijoles (pinto beans) to mark each figure on our card as the leader went through the deck one by one. The word for tree was called *Arbol!* It completed a row; I had won. Then to check my card I had to name each figure again. When I said the word for tree, it didn't come at all as I wanted it to; AR-BOWL with the accent on the last syllable and sounding like an Anglo tourist. There was some all-around kidding of me and good-natured laughter over the incident, and it passed.

But if I had not been speaking much Spanish up until then, I spoke even 5 less afterward. Even when my mother, who speaks both Spanish and English fluently, spoke to me in Spanish, I would respond in English. By the time I graduated from high school and prepared to enter college, the break was nearly complete. Seldom during college did I admit to being a Mexican-American. Only when Latin American students pressed me about my surname did I admit my Spanish descent, or when it proved an asset in meeting coeds from Latin American countries.

My ancestry had become a shadow, fainter and fainter about me. I felt 6 no particular allegiance to it, drew no inspiration from it, and elected generally to let it fade away. I clicked with the Anglo mind-set in college, mastered it, you might say. I even became editor of the campus biweekly newspaper as a junior, and editor of the literary magazine as a senior—not bad, now that I look back, for a tortillas-and-beans Chicano upbringing to beat the Anglo at his own game.

The point of my "success," of course, was that I had been assimilated; 7 I had bought the white man's world. After getting my diploma I was set to launch out into a career in newspaper reporting and writing. There was no thought in my mind of serving my people, telling their story, or making anything right for anybody but myself. Instead I had dreams of Pulitzer Prizes, syndicated columns, foreign correspondent assignments, front-page stories—that was for me. Then something happened.

A Catholic weekly newspaper in Sacramento offered me a position as a 8 reporter and feature writer. I had a job on a Bay Area daily as a copyboy at the time, with the opportunity to become a reporter. But I'd just been married, and there were a number of other reasons to consider: there'd be a variety of assignments, Sacramento was the state capital, it was a good town in which to raise a family, and the other job lacked promise for upward mobility. I decided to take the offer.

My wife and I moved to Sacramento in the fall of 1961, and in a few 9 weeks the radicalization of this Chicano began. It wasn't a book I read or a great leader awakening me, for we had no Chávezes or Tijerinas or

Gonzálezes at the time; and it was no revelation from above. It was my own people who rescued me. There is a large Chicano population in Sacramento, today one of the most activist in northern California, but at the time factionalized and still dependent on the social and church organizations for identity. But together we found each other.

10   My job soon brought me into contact with many Chicanos as well as with the recently immigrated Mexicans, located in the barrios that Sacramento had allocated to the "Mexicans." I found my people striving to survive in an alien environment among foreign people. One of the stories I covered concerned a phenomenon called Cursillos de Cristiandad (Little Courses in Christianity), intense, three-day group-sensitivity sessions whose chief objective is the re-Christianization of Catholics. To cover the story properly I talked my editor into letting me take a Cursillo.

11   Not only was much revealed to me about the phony gilt lining of religion which I had grown up believing was the Church, but there was an added and highly significant side effect—cultural shock! I rediscovered my own people, or perhaps they redeemed me. Within the social dimension of the Cursillo, for the first time in many years I became reimmersed in a tough, *macho ambiente* (an entirely Mexican male environment). Only Spanish was spoken. The effect was shattering. It was as if my tongue, after being struck dumb as a child, had been loosened.

12   Because we were located in cramped quarters, with limited facilities, and the cooks, lecturers, priests, and participants were men only, the old sense of *machismo* and *camarada* was revived and given new perspective. I was cast in a spiritual setting which was a perfect background for reviving my Chicano soul. Reborn but imperfectly, I still had a lot to learn about my self and my people. But my understanding deepened and renewed itself as the years went by. I visited bracero camps with teams of Chicanos; some times with priests taking the sacraments; sometimes only Chicanos, offering advice or assistance with badly needed food and clothing, distributed through a bingo-game technique; and on occasion, music for group singing provided by a phonograph or a guitar. Then there were barrio organization work; migrant worker programs; a rural self-help community development project; and confrontation with antipoverty agencies, with the churches, with government officials, and with cautious Chicanos, too.

13   In a little San Francisco magazine called *Way*, I wrote in a March 1966 article discussing "The Other Mexican-American":

The Mexican-American must answer at the same time: Who am I? and Who are we? This is to pose then, not merely a dilemma of self-identity; but of self-in-group-identity. . . . Perhaps the answer to developing a total Mexican-

American concept must be left in the hands of the artist, the painter, the writer, and the poet, who can abstract the essence of what it is to be Mexican in America. . . . When that understanding comes . . . the Mexican-American will not only have acculturized himself, but he will have acculturized America to him.

If anyone knew what he was talking about when he spoke of the 14 dilemma of who he was and where he belonged, it was this Chicano. I very nearly dropped out, as so many other Mexican-Americans have, under the dragging pressure to be someone else, what most of society wants you to be before it hands out its chrome-plated trophies.

And that mystique—I didn't quite have it at the time, or the right word 15 for it. But no one did until just the last few years when so many of us stopped trying to be someone else and decided that what we want to be and to be called is Chicano.

I owe my life to my Chicano people. They rescued me from the Anglo 16 kiss of death, the monolingual, monocultural, and colorless Gringo society. I no longer face a dilemma of identity or direction. That identity and direction have been charted for me by the Chicano—but to think I came that close to being sucked into the vacuum of the dominant society.

Understanding Context

1. What kind of childhood did Rendón have?
2. What represented his early success? What does Rendón mean by the statement, "I had bought the white man's world"? What were his goals?
3. What is the "Anglo kiss of death"?
4. *Critical thinking:* Rendón describes the Gringo society as "monolingual, monocultural, and colorless." Does he overlook the diversity of Irish, Jewish, Italian, French, Greek, and Russian cultures that make up mainstream America?

Evaluating Strategy

1. What tone does the first sentence create? What effect does the word *victim* have?
2. Rendón includes a quote from one of his own articles. Is this an effective device or would it be better to restate these ideas within "Kiss of Death"?
3. *Other modes:* How does Rendón use narration, description, and comparison in developing his essay?

Appreciating Language

1. What does the term *kiss of death* mean to you? Do you associate it with the Bible or movie images of the Mafia?
2. Rendón uses several Spanish words without providing definitions in English. What does this suggest about his idea of America becoming "acculturized" to the Mexican American?
3. What does Rendón mean by "cautious Chicanos"?

Writing Suggestions

1. Write your own version of a "kiss of death" you avoided in your own life. Perhaps you nearly lost yourself or compromised your future by taking a job, entering a relationship, or moving to a location that was initially appealing but would have had negative consequences. Emphasize how this experience could have altered your identity.
2. *Collaborative writing:* Discuss Rendón's essay with a group of students, asking each one to briefly respond to the concept of an "Anglo kiss of death." Does joining mainstream middle-class America require people to shed or deny their ethnic identity? Record the ideas of the group and collaborate on a response, agreeing or disagreeing with Rendón. If members of the group disagree, consider writing alternative responses.

Barbara Ehrenreich (1941–) was born in Butte, Montana, and attended Reed College in Oregon, where she received a bachelor's degree in chemical physics. In 1968 she completed a doctorate in cell biology at Rockefeller University in New York. While in graduate school, she became active in political and social issues, such as education, low income housing, and the war in Vietnam. She has published numerous articles in *Time, Ms., Mother Jones, New Republic,* and the *Nation.*

Cultural Baggage

Unlike Armando Rendón, who embraces his ethnic heritage, Barbara Ehrenreich refuses to accept an ethnic identity, calling herself one of "the race of 'none.'"

An acquaintance was telling me about the joys of rediscovering her ethnic 1 and religious heritage. "I know exactly what my ancestors were doing 2,000 years ago," she said, eyes gleaming with enthusiasm, "and *I can do the same things now.*" Then she leaned forward and inquired politely, "And what is your ethnic background, if I may ask?"

"None," I said, that being the first word in line to get out of my mouth. 2 Well, not "none," I backtracked. Scottish, English, Irish—that was something, I supposed. Too much Irish to qualify as a WASP; too much of the hated English to warrant a "Kiss Me, I'm Irish" button; plus there are a number of dead ends in the family tree due to adoptions, missing records, failing memories and the like. I was blushing by this time. Did "none" mean I was rejecting my heritage out of Anglo-Celtic self-hate? Or was I revealing a hidden ethnic chauvinism in which the Britannically derived serve as a kind of neutral standard compared with the ethnic "others"?

Throughout the 60's and 70's, I watched one group after another— 3 African-Americans, Latinos, Native Americans—stand up and proudly reclaim their roots while I just sank back ever deeper into my seat. All this excitement over ethnicity stemmed, I uneasily sensed, from a past in which *their* ancestors had been trampled upon by *my* ancestors, or at least by people who looked very much like them. In addition, it had begun to seem almost un-American not to have some sort of hyphen at hand, linking one to more venerable times and locales.

4   But the truth is, I was raised with none. We'd eaten ethnic foods in my childhood home, but these were all borrowed, like the pasties, or Cornish meat pies, my father had picked up from his fellow miners in Butte, Mont. If my mother had one rule, it was militant ecumenism in all matters of food and experience. "Try new things," she would say, meaning anything from sweetbreads to clams, with an emphasis on the "new."

5   As a child, I briefly nourished a craving for tradition and roots. I immersed myself in the works of Sir Walter Scott. I pretended to believe that the bagpipe was a musical instrument. I was fascinated to learn from a grandmother that we were descended from certain Highland clans and longed for a pleated skirt in one of their distinctive tartans.

6   But in "Ivanhoe," it was the dark-eyed "Jewess" Rebecca I identified with, not the flaxen-haired bimbo Rowena. As for clans: Why not call them "tribes," those bands of half-clad peasants and warriors whose idea of cuisine was stuffed sheep gut washed down with whisky? And then there was the sting of Disraeli's remark—which I came across in my early teens—to the effect that his ancestors had been leading orderly, literate lives when my ancestors were still rampaging through the Highlands daubing themselves with blue paint.

7   Motherhood put the screws on me, ethnicitywise. I had hoped that by marrying a man of Eastern European-Jewish ancestry I would acquire for my descendants the ethnic genes that my own forebears so sadly lacked. At one point, I even subjected the children to a seder of my own design, including a little talk about the flight from Egypt and its relevance to modern social issues. But the kids insisted on buttering their matzohs and snickering through my talk. "Give me a break, Mom," the older one said. "You don't even believe in God."

8   After the tiny pagans had been put to bed, I sat down to brood over Elijah's wine. What had I been thinking? The kids knew that their Jewish grandparents were secular folks who didn't hold seders themselves. And if ethnicity eluded me, how could I expect it to take root in my children, who are not only Scottish-English-Irish, but Hungarian-Polish-Russian to boot?

9   But, then, on the fumes of Manischewitz, a great insight took form in my mind. It was true, as the kids said, that I didn't "believe in God." But this could be taken as something very different from an accusation—a reminder of a genuine heritage. My parents had not believed in God either, nor had my grandparents or any other progenitors going back to the great-great level. They had become disillusioned with Christianity generations ago—just as, on the in-law side, my children's other ancestors had shaken their Orthodox Judaism. This insight did not exactly furnish me with an "identity," but it was at least something to work with: we are the kind of

people, I realized— whatever our distant ancestors' religions—who do *not* believe, who do not carry on traditions, who do not do things just because someone has done them before.

The epiphany went on: I recalled that my mother never introduced a 10 procedure for cooking or cleaning by telling me, "Grandma did it this way." What did Grandma know, living in the days before vacuum cleaners and disposable toilet mops! In my parents' general view, new things were better than old, and the very fact that some ritual had been performed in the past was a good reason for abandoning it now. Because what was the past, as our forebears knew it? Nothing but poverty, superstition and grief. "Think for yourself," Dad used to say. "Always ask why."

In fact, this may have been the ideal cultural heritage for my particular 11 ethnic strain—bounced as it was from the Highlands of Scotland across the sea, out to the Rockies, down into the mines and finally spewed out into high-tech, suburban America. What better philosophy, for a race of migrants, than "Think for yourself"? What better maxim, for a people whose whole world was rudely inverted every 30 years or so, than "Try new things"?

The more tradition-minded, the newly enthusiastic celebrants of Purim 12 and Kwanzaa and Solstice, may see little point to survival if the survivors carry no cultural freight—religion, for example, or ethnic tradition. To which I would say that skepticism, curiosity and wide-eyed ecumenical tolerance are also worthy elements of the human tradition and are at least as old as such notions as "Serbian" or "Croatian," "Scottish" or "Jewish." I make no claims for my personal line of progenitors except that they remained loyal to the values that may have induced all of our ancestors, long, long ago, to climb down from the trees and make their way into the open plains.

A few weeks ago, I cleared my throat and asked the children, now mostly 13 grown and fearsomely smart, whether they felt any stirrings of ethnic or religious identity, etc., which might have been, ahem, insufficiently nourished at home. "None," they said, adding firmly, "and the world would be a better place if nobody else did, either." My chest swelled with pride, as would my mother's, to know that the race of "none" marches on.

Understanding Context

1. Why does Ehrenreich have difficulty defining her heritage?
2. Does Ehrenreich see something negative in embracing one's ethnic roots?
3. *Critical thinking:* Armando Rendón (page 656) suggests that he avoided the "vacuum of the dominant society" that would have erased his identity. Does Ehrenreich suggest that embracing "nothingness" is liberating, freeing

one from cultural mind-sets, Old World limitations, bias, and inhibiting traditions?

Evaluating Strategy

1. What is Ehrenreich's thesis? How would you restate it in your own words?
2. How effective is the opening narrative?
3. *Other modes:* Where does Ehrenreich use comparison and narration to develop her essay?

Appreciating Language

1. What do the tone and style about this essay suggest about the intended audience?
2. What words does Ehrenreich use to describe those who embrace their cultural heritage?

Writing Suggestions

1. Write an essay explaining your attitude about your own ethnic identity. Persuade readers to accept your view of identity. Do you embrace a culture or celebrate being "none"?
2. *Collaborative writing:* Discuss Ehrenreich's essay with a group of students. Do they share her views on race and identity or do they see it as a form of denial? Does the "race of none" risk masking racial injustice and oppression? Record members' comments and work to create a response. If members have differing opinions, draft opposing essays.

ALAN M. DERSHOWITZ

Alan M. Dershowitz (1938–) was born in Brooklyn and graduated from Yale Law School in 1962. He was a law clerk for Supreme Court Justice Arthur Goldberg and joined the faculty of Harvard Law School in 1964. As a defense attorney, he has participated in many high-profile cases, representing Claus von Bulow, Mike Tyson, and O. J. Simpson. His recent books include *Chutzpah, Contrary to Popular Opinion, The Abuse Excuse, Reasonable Doubts,* and *Why Terrorism Works.*

The "Abuse Excuse" Is Detrimental to the Justice System

In this essay Alan M. Dershowitz argues that attorneys and defendants who use abuse as an excuse for violent acts damage the justice system by endorsing vigilante behavior.

The "abuse excuse"—the legal tactic by which criminal defendants claim a 1 history of abuse as an excuse for violent retaliation—is quickly becoming a license to kill and maim. More and more defense lawyers are employing this tactic and more and more jurors are buying it. It is a dangerous trend, with serious and widespread implications for the safety and liberty of every American.

Among the recent excuses that have been accepted by at least some 2 jurors have been "battered woman syndrome," "abused child syndrome," "rape trauma syndrome," and "urban survival syndrome." This has encouraged lawyers to try other abuse excuses, such as "black rage." For example, the defense lawyer for Colin Ferguson—the black man convicted in March 1995 of killing white commuters on the Long Island Railroad on December 7, 1993—has acknowledged that his black rage variation on the insanity defense "is similar to the utilization of the battered woman's syndrome, the post-traumatic stress syndrome and the child abuse syndrome in other cases to negate criminal accountability."

The Danger of Vigilantism

On the surface, the abuse excuse affects only the few handfuls of defen- 3 dants who raise it, and those who are most immediately impacted by an acquittal or reduced charge. But at a deeper level, the abuse excuse is a symptom of a general abdication of responsibility by individuals, families, groups, and even nations. Its widespread acceptance is dangerous to the very tenets of democracy, which presuppose personal accountability for choices and actions. It also endangers our collective safety by legitimating a sense of vigilantism that reflects our frustration over the apparent inability of law enforcement to reduce the rampant violence that engulfs us.

4   At a time of ever-hardening attitudes toward crime and punishment, it may seem anomalous that so many jurors—indeed, so many Americans—appear to be sympathetic to the abuse excuse. But it is not anomalous at all, since the abuse excuse is a modern-day form of vigilantism—a recognition that since official law enforcement does not seem able to prevent or punish abuse, the victim should be entitled to take the law into his or her own hands.

5   In philosophical terms, the claim is that society has broken its "social contract" with the abused victim by not according him or her adequate protection. Because it has broken that social contract, the victim has been returned to a "state of nature" in which "might makes right" and the victim is entitled to invoke the law of the jungle—"kill or be killed." Indeed, these very terms were used in a 1994 Texas case in which one black youth [Daimion Osby] killed two other blacks in a dangerous urban neighborhood. The result was a hung jury.

6   But vigilantism—whether it takes the old-fashioned form of the lynch mob or the new-fashioned form of the abuse victim's killing her sleeping husband—threatens the very fabric of our democracy and sows the seeds of anarchy and autocracy. The abuse excuse is dangerous, therefore, both in its narrow manifestation as a legal defense and in its broader manifestation as an abrogation of societal responsibility.

Affirmative Action in the Justice System

7   The other characteristic shared by these defenses is that they are often "politically correct," thus reflecting current trends toward employing different criteria of culpability when judging disadvantaged groups. In effect, these abuse-excuse defenses, by emphasizing historical discrimination suffered by particular groups, seek to introduce some degree of affirmative action into our criminal-justice system.

8   These abuse-excuse defenses are the daily fare of the proliferating menu of TV and radio talk shows. It is virtually impossible to flip the TV channels during the daytime hours without seeing a bevy of sobbing women and men justifying their failed lives by reference to some past abuse, real or

imagined. Personal responsibility does not sell soap as well as sob stories. Jurors who watch this stuff begin to believe it, despite its status as junk science. The very fact that Sally Jessy Raphael and Montel Williams repeat it as if it were gospel tends to legitimate it in the minds of some jurors. They are thus receptive to it in the courtroom, especially when the defendant is portrayed as sympathetic, and his dead victim is unsympathetic. William Kunstler is quick to point to public-opinion polls that show that "two-thirds of blacks and almost half the whites surveyed recognize the validity of our [black rage] theory of Mr. Ferguson's defense."

Most Victims Do Not Commit Violence

But neither public-opinion polls nor TV talk shows establish the empirical 9 or normative validity of such abuse-excuse defenses. The basic fallacy underlying each of them is that the vast majority of people who have experienced abuses—whether it be sexual, racial, or anything else—do not commit violent crimes. Thus the abuse excuse neither explains nor justifies the violence. A history of abuse is not a psychological or a legal license to kill. It may, in some instances, be relevant at sentencing, but certainly not always.

Lest it be thought that the abuse excuse is credited only by radical de- 10 fense lawyers, lay jurors, and talk-show-watching stay-at-homes, a quotation from the attorney general of the United States illustrates how pervasive this sort of thinking is becoming. In April 1993, Janet Reno was quoted as commenting on urban riots as follows: "An angry young man who lashes out in violence because he never had a childhood might do the right thing," and when the "right thing" is in contradiction with the law, "you try to get the law changed." I wonder if the angry young man's innocent victim agrees that the violence directed against his shop was the "right thing" and that the law protecting his property should be "changed."

The worst consequence of these abuse excuses is that they stigmatize 11 all abuse victims with the violence of the very few who have used their victimization as a justification to kill or maim. The vast majority of abuse victims are neither prone to violence nor to making excuses.

Understanding Context

1. How does Dershowitz define "the abuse excuse"?
2. Does Dershowitz believe that victims do not have the right to retaliate?
3. Do those who use abuse as an excuse for their violent behavior demean the majority of victims who do not seek revenge?

4. *Critical thinking:* Does the "abuse excuse" extend throughout society? Do employees, students, and parents give excuses rather than take responsibility for their actions? Have we become a nation of victims?

Evaluating Strategy

1. What examples does Dershowitz use as illustrations of the abuse excuse?
2. Dershowitz places his thesis at the opening of the essay. Is this effective? Can you think of situations in which it would be better to place the thesis at the conclusion?

Appreciating Language

1. Dershowitz is an attorney. How many legal terms does he use in the essay? What does this reveal about his intended audience?
2. Consider the term *abuse excuse.* Does this glib phrase risk trivializing a serious problem?

Writing Suggestions

1. Write an essay expressing your own view of the abuse excuse. Do people seem to dodge or deny responsibility for their actions by making excuses? Has almost any criminal or uncivil behavior been excused as the result of some mental or emotional disorder or an abusive past?
2. *Collaborative writing:* Discuss this essay with a group of students. Have a member record group comments. Write an essay expressing your group's view of Dershowitz's essay. If the members disagree, consider writing pro and con statements.

Leslie Abramson (1944 –) was born in New York, attended Queens College, and graduated from the UCLA Law School. She worked as a public defender for seven years before entering private practice in Los Angeles. Abramson achieved national attention defending Erik Menendez, who was accused of conspiring with his brother to murder their wealthy parents. Twice named Trial Lawyer of the Year by the Los Angeles Criminal Courts Bar Association, she is a frequent commentator on *Court TV*. In 1997 she published *The Defense Is Ready: Life in the Trenches of Criminal Law,* which recounts her experiences as a defense attorney.

The Abuse Defense Balances the Justice System

In this article, Abramson argues that victims are fully justified to use past abuse as a factor in their defense when charged with a crime of retaliation. As you read her essay, consider how Alan M. Dershowitz would regard her position.

I never learned about "male justice" in school. 1

During my education in the New York City public schools, the City 2 University of New York and the University of California, Los Angeles, School of Law, I was taught the noble fictions of our justice system. I was told that American justice is equal for all. I was instructed that the accused always is presumed innocent until proven guilty, and that the prosecution bears the burden of proving that guilt beyond a reasonable doubt.

By the end of my first year of practice I also had learned that much of 3 what I'd been taught was naive. Most important, I discovered that the racism and sexism deforming so many of our institutions also infect the courts, producing a double standard of justice.

Much has been written about racism's insidious role in our criminal jus- 4 tice system. But the recent cases of O.J. Simpson [acquitted of murder in October 1995], Lyle and Erik Menendez [charged with murdering their parents, their trial resulted in hung juries in January1994], and Lorena Bobbitt [acquitted of maiming her husband in January 1994] have opened a public debate on how gender bias influences the way we perceive crime, criminal responsibility and justice.

Justice for "Wronged" Men and Abused Women

5   "Texas justice" was what we criminal lawyers used to call cases in which a man was acquitted after killing his wife and her lover *in flagrante delicto*. It mattered not if the victims were unarmed or asleep when the "wronged" man blew them away in his fit of jealous rage. No one went to the talk shows to decry the "heat of passion" defense employed by men expressing their possessory rights over the women of their choice—including the right to kill. Of course, no such right to kill was expressly provided in the written law, but the unwritten law—what might be called the male bill of rights—was implicitly understood by sympathetic male jurors.

6   The law of macho, of course, does not extend to women and children who kill. They rarely kill, but when they do, they don't do it out of wounded pride or from affronts to their sexuality or in the anger of the rejected. The forces that drive them to act are fear and terror, the motivations of the weak, the oppressed, the tortured and the broken. And they are scorned and ridiculed and hated for it.

7   We guiltily admire the successful barroom brawler, the fastest gun, the aggressive forechecker, the crushing lineman. The law of self-defense as currently codified in most states recognizes this, and is a male version of survival—two physical and emotional equals duking it out or facing off *High Noon* style, pistols at the ready. Burning beds, parents united in abuse in their family den—these are not the images our male legislators had in mind when the criminal codes were written.

8   We've learned a lot since then about the psychology of abusive relationships, about the cruelty, oppression and inescapability of child abuse and molestation, about the terror that marks virtually every moment for the victims of chronic domestic violence. Despite this knowledge, the media, the self-anointed pundits and the self-promoting denizens of the law schools' ivory towers sanctimoniously declare their outrage when an abused person recounts a life of torment to explain why he or she succumbed at last to terror and struck out at the abuser. These critics label such explanations the "abuse excuse." They lament our loss of "personal responsibility."

9   This male model of justice pervades the public consciousness and explains why many people say they would sympathize with O.J. Simpson even if they believe he killed Nicole Brown Simpson and Ronald Goldman. It wouldn't matter, they say, even if they believed that these killings followed years in which this strong, physically fit professional athlete beat and

emotionally abused his five-foot-eight 125-pound wife. O.J. Simpson may indeed be innocent, as he is now legally presumed to be. What makes much of his support in the community troubling, however, is that it derives not from this presumption, but from the undercurrent of entitlement that the killing of an ex-wife engenders.

A Case of Psychological Abuse

The best and worst example of this double standard was graphically dis- 10 played to me in a case I handled a decade ago. My client, then a woman of fifty, had been raped on her way home from work years before and trauma-tized by the experience. Twenty years later she married a widower with a four-year-old daughter—and a shadowy past. Only after marrying this wealthy, domineering man did my client discover that he had produced his widowerhood by shooting his unarmed first wife to death as she spoke to a friend on the telephone while his infant daughter slept in the next room. He was convicted of manslaughter, served less than two years in prison and re-gained custody of the little girl upon his release.

During the course of their ten-year marriage the husband's highest form 11 of amusement was to play the role of my client's former rapist by sneaking up on her from behind and grabbing her. He was the textbook battering hus-band, jealous, possessive, controlling his wife's every movement and human contact, belittling, explosively angry, sexually demanding. Finally, after a period of especially frequent outbursts, he threatened to do to my client what he had done to his first wife. She shot him, once, in the head while he was sleeping. She ran screaming down the hallway, called the police, con-fessed her crime. At her first trial she was convicted of second-degree mur-der and sentenced to five years to life in state prison. Her conviction was re-versed on appeal due to prosecutorial and judicial misconduct.

That's when I entered the case. In her second trial, we presented evi- 12 dence of the extreme psychological impairment this woman suffered. The jury hung; subsequently, she pleaded guilty to manslaughter and the judge granted her probation. At the sentencing hearing, the male deputy D.A. took my client's hand and said: "I want to apologize to you for that first con-viction. You are not a murderer. I just didn't understand."

Score one for equal justice. 13

Understanding Context

1. What is Abramson's thesis? How would you restate it in your own words?
2. What does Abramson mean by "male justice"?

3. Why does Abramson believe that the justice system is unbalanced, favoring men over women? Does the justice system give men special entitlements?

4. *Critical thinking:* Does Abramson see any risk of an "abuse excuse" encouraging vigilante justice? How should society deal with those who act violently in response to abuse?

Evaluating Strategy

1. Abramson includes personal experiences in her essay. Does this give her writing greater credibility? Does firsthand experience provide powerful support?

2. What appeals does Abramson use to support her thesis?

3. Abramson provides several examples to support her thesis. Do you find them effective?

Appreciating Language

1. Abramson uses the term *abuse defense* rather than *abuse excuse.* Consider the connotations these words have. How does Abramson use language to justify use of the abuse defense?

2. *Critical thinking:* How does word choice and connotation affect the way people view criminal cases? When does a "defendant" become an "accused killer" and how do those accused of crimes use the word *victim* to defend their actions?

Writing Suggestions

1. Write an essay stating your opinion on the use of the abuse defense. Support your thesis with examples of situations in which people's past abuse should be considered a justifiable defense for violent behavior.

2. *Collaborative writing:* Discuss a recent criminal case in which the abuse excuse was used as a defense with a group of students. Have a member record comments. Write an essay advocating your group's opinion. If members have differing views, consider drafting pro and con versions.

e-reading

InfoTrac College Edition
www.infotrac-college.com

© Royalty-Free/Corbis

THE CRIMINAL JUSTICE SYSTEM

What Winston Churchill once said about democracy can probably also be said about the adversary system of criminal justice: It may well be the worst system of justice, "except [for] all the other [systems] that have been tried from time to time."

Alan M. Dershowitz

The system is seriously flawed. It disproportionately affects the poor and the African-American community. It makes too many mistakes. Too many prisoners are unjustly placed on death row because of poor representation at trial. Too many others spend irretrievable chunks of their lives behind bars because of false identifications or shoddy police work or inadequate legal representation.

National Catholic Reporter

During the last decade violent crime has steadily dropped, particularly in major cities. Safer streets have, in part, help revitalize urban America, which has experienced a rapid growth in upscale housing and commercial redevelopment. At the same time, the nation's prison population has risen dramatically. Over six million citizens — one in every 32 Americans — are in jail, on probation or parole, or in prison. While many Americans cite falling crime statistics as signs of progress, others, like Paul Butler, a former prosecutor, examine the social cost on those communities in which one in three males are under the supervision of the criminal justice system and more young men are in prison than in college:

> These costs are both social and economic, and they include the large percentage of black children who live in female-headed, single-parent households; a perceived dearth of men "eligible" for marriage; the lack of male role models for black children, especially boys; the absence of wealth in the black community; and the large unemployment rate among black men.

Elizabeth Palmberg argues that the war on drugs has increased racial disparities in the criminal justice system, so that "four out of five state drug prisoners are African American or Latino, although these groups comprise only 22 percent of drug users. . . . and these disparities permeate every level of the criminal justice system, from policing to parole."

Popular television programs have highlighted the use of DNA to identify the guilty and exonerate the innocent. By proving the innocence of convicts, DNA has demonstrated the unreliability of other forms of evidence such as eyewitness testimony. But even when DNA evidence conclusively proves that someone has been wrongly convicted, it does not always lead to immediate release. Bob Herbert noted in *The New York Times* that "once an innocent person is trapped in the system, it's extremely difficult to get him — or her — extricated." Complicating the use of DNA evidence is the fact that many of the current experts who testify in court have as little as two weeks training.

The introduction of cameras in courtrooms in the 1990s allowed Americans who had only seen fictionalized courtroom dramas to witness real trials. Anna Quindlen argues that cameras should be allowed in courtrooms to let people see how the legal process "takes this messy stew of evidence and egos and transmutes it finally through order, instruction and deliberation into a system that gets it right a good bit of the time." In contrast, Jack Litman, a defense attorney, believes that cameras can intimidate witnesses and harm victims because "there is an enormous difference between . . . testifying before 12 people and 12 million people."

Before reading these articles, consider these questions:

> Do you think the criminal justice system is basically fair to victims, witnesses, and defendants?

Do you think trials should be televised? Have you ever watched Court TV or other televised trials? What did you learn by watching actual courtroom proceedings? How do they differ from courtroom dramas?

Do you think juries should ever refuse to convict someone they know is guilty? In rare cases juries have acquitted people they knew were guilty because they believed the law was unjust or that the defendant was unfairly charged. Can you think of any situations in which you would vote to acquit someone you knew was guilty?

Do celebrity and high-profile trials give the public a distorted view of the criminal justice system?

Have you ever served on a jury or appeared in court? How did your experiences shape your view of the criminal justice system?

E-Readings Online

Search for each article by author or title after entering InfoTrac College Edition through your 1Pass account login.

Anna Quindlen. *Lights, Camera, Justice for All.*
Because the point of public trials was to let people in, Quindlen argues "in the 21st century, letting the people in means letting the cameras in."

Felicity Barringer. *Lawyers Are Divided on Cameras in the Courtroom.*
Jack Litman, a defense attorney, questions the impact televised trials can have on witnesses and victims.

Leonard Post. *Citing Low Pay, Lawyers Refuse Indigent Cases.*
Because of low pay, many lawyers refuse to represent poor defendants, denying them adequate counsel and leading judges to dismiss charges against criminals when lawyers cannot be found to defend them.

Elizabeth Palmberg. *Seeing Green: Why the Penal System Isn't Colorblind.*
The war on drugs has increased racial disparities in the justice system so that black teenagers convicted of drug crimes are 48 times more likely to be sent to prison than white teenagers.

Martin L. Haines. *Psst, Jurors: You Have the Power to Nullify.*
Even when presented with conclusive evidence of a defendant's guilt, juries can refuse to convict because "once a jury acquits, its verdict cannot be appealed, its deliberations are private and cannot be investigated, and no juror may be arrested for voting to acquit."

Paul Butler. *Black Jurors: Right to Acquit?*
A former federal prosecutor believes "that for pragmatic and political reasons, the black community is better off when some non-violent law-breakers remain in the community rather than go to prison" and that black jurors have a "moral responsibility" to "emancipate some guilty black outlaws."

National Catholic Reporter. *Flawed Prison System Hurts Us All.*
Noting that over six million Americans are currently in jail, on parole, or probation, the *National Catholic Reporter* argues that "we can't keep locking people away and trying to forget they exist. Humans, even those who have broken the law, deserve better, and even tough sentences eventually end."

Bob Herbert. *Trapped in the System.*
Despite conclusive DNA evidence that he did not commit the crime, Ryan Matthews remains on death row because "freeing someone who has been wrongfully convicted is a torturously slow and difficult process, with no guarantee at any time that it will end positively."

Adam Liptak. *You Think DNA Evidence Is Foolproof? Try Again.*
DNA evidence has proven the unreliability of other forms of evidence, but it cannot create a "foolproof" system of justice because DNA tests are conducted by fallible technicians and presented in court by poorly trained "experts."

Thomas N. Faust. *Shift the Responsibility of Untreated Mental Illness Out of the Criminal Justice System.*
Noting that 16 percent of inmates are severely mentally ill, the executive director of the National Sheriffs' Association, argues that prisons "have started to become psychiatric hospitals."

Critical Reading and Thinking

1. What do the various authors see as strengths and weaknesses in the criminal justice system?
2. How has DNA evidence changed perceptions of the fairness of the criminal justice system?
3. What do some authors view as causes for racial disparities in the justice system?
4. What are the benefits and risks of televising trials?
5. Why do few Americans appear to be concerned about the large numbers of people in prison? Do people feel safer? Do they see

imprisoning large numbers of mostly young and poor males as an acceptable tradeoff for lowered crime rates?

Writing Suggestions

1. Write an essay about one aspect of the criminal justice system that you have observed. Have you ever been a victim of crime, appeared in court, or served on a jury? Describe your most surprising finding or observation. Was the system better or worse than you expected?

2. *Collaborative writing:* Working with other students, develop an essay outlining what your group believes would be the best ways to improve the criminal justice system to make sure victims are fairly treated and defendants adequately represented.

3. *Other modes*
   - Write a *comparison* paper that contrasts the ways that different people view the police, courts, or prison system.
   - Use a single trial, crime, defendant, or victim as an *example* of a problem in the criminal justice system.
   - Write an essay that explores the *causes* or *effects* of racial disparities in sentencing offenders.
   - Develop a *division* paper that discusses three or four of the most pressing challenges to the criminal justice system.
   - Write a *classification* essay that outlines the most to least effective ways of dealing with people who break the law.

Research Paper

You can develop a research paper about the criminal justice system by conducting further research to explore a range of issues:
- Why has crime dropped?
- Why has the prison population expanded?
- What flaws in the justice system have been revealed by the use of DNA evidence? Has it, for example, led more people to oppose capital punishment?
- What representation do poor defendants receive in your area? Are state or local public defenders adequately funded and supported? Do the poor get fair trials?
- Examine media coverage of a sensational criminal trial. Are the stories balanced? Do you detect bias for or against the defendant, witnesses, the attorneys, or the victim?

For Further Reading

To locate additional sources on the criminal justice system, enter these search terms as InfoTrac subjects:

Criminal Justice, Administration of
Subdivisions: beliefs, opinions and attitudes
                       comparative analysis
                       economic aspects
                       evaluation
                       forecasts and trends
                       moral and ethical aspects
                       political aspects
                       public opinion

DNA Testing
Subdivisions: analysis
                       cases
                       laws, regulations and rules
                       methods
                       usage

Prisons
Subdivisions   analysis
                       demographic aspects
                       history
                       personal narratives
                       psychological aspects
                       social aspects

Additional Sources

Using a search engine, such as Yahoo!, Google, or Alta Vista, enter one or more of the following terms to locate additional sources:

DNA testing	prisons	insanity defense
public defenders	televised trials	criminal justice system
capital punishment	parole	community service
Innocence Project	juvenile justice	mandatory sentencing

See Evaluating Internet Sources Checklist on page 752. See Chapter 30 for using and documenting sources.

MANNING MARABLE

Manning Marable is the founding director of the Institute for Research in African American Studies at Columbia University. He attended Earlham and received his doctorate from the University of Maryland in 1976. His books include *Black Liberation in Conservative America, Speaking Truth to Power: Essays on Race, Radicalism and Resistance, The Crisis of Color and Democracy,* and *What Black America Thinks: Race, Ideology, and Political Power.*

An Idea Whose Time Has Come: Whites Have a Moral Obligation to Recognize Slavery's Legacy

In recent years people have sought compensation for past injustices. Congress awarded $20,000 to each Japanese American interned during World War II. Korean women forced into sexual slavery during the war have sought restitution from the Japanese government. Germany has paid billions of dollars to survivors of the Holocaust. Many writers, including Manning Marable, believe that African Americans should be compensated for centuries of slavery and discrimination.

In 1854 my great-grandfather, Morris Marable, was sold on an auction block 1 in Georgia for $500. For his white slave master, the sale was just "business as usual." But to Morris Marable and his heirs, slavery was a crime against our humanity. This pattern of human-rights violations against enslaved African Americans continued under Jim Crow segregation for nearly another century.

The fundamental problem of American democracy in the 21st century 2 is the problem of "structural racism": the deep patterns of socioeconomic inequality and accumulated disadvantage that are coded by race, and constantly justified in public discourse by both racist stereotypes and white indifference. Do Americans have the capacity and vision to dismantle these structural barriers that deny democratic rights and opportunities to millions of their fellow citizens?

This country has previously witnessed two great struggles to achieve a 3 truly multicultural democracy.

4   The First Reconstruction (1865–1877) ended slavery and briefly gave black men voting rights, but gave no meaningful compensation for two centuries of unpaid labor. The promise of "40 acres and a mule" was for most blacks a dream deferred.

5   The Second Reconstruction (1954–1968), or the modern civil-rights movement, outlawed legal segregation in public accommodations and gave blacks voting rights. But these successes paradoxically obscure the tremendous human costs of historically accumulated disadvantage that remain central to black Americans' lives.

6   The disproportionate wealth that most whites enjoy today was first constructed from centuries of unpaid black labor. Many white institutions, including Ivy League universities, insurance companies and banks, profited from slavery. This pattern of white privilege and black inequality continues today.

7   Demanding reparations is not just about compensation for slavery and segregation. It is, more important, an educational campaign to highlight the contemporary reality of "racial deficits" of all kinds, the unequal conditions that impact blacks regardless of class. Structural racism's barriers include "equity inequity," the absence of black capital formation that is a direct consequence of America's history. One third of all black households actually have negative net wealth. In 1998 the typical black family's net wealth was $16,400, less than one fifth that of white families. Black families are denied home loans at twice the rate of whites.

8   Blacks remain the last hired and first fired during recessions. During the 1990–91 recession, African Americans suffered disproportionately. At Coca-Cola, 42 percent of employees who lost their jobs were black. At Sears, 54 percent were black. Blacks have significantly shorter life expectancies, in part due to racism in the health establishment. Blacks are statistically less likely than whites to be referred for kidney transplants or early-stage cancer surgery.

9   In criminal justice, African Americans constitute only one seventh of all drug users. Yet we account for 35 percent of all drug arrests, 55 percent of drug convictions and 75 percent of prison admissions for drug offenses.

10   White Americans today aren't guilty of carrying out slavery and segregation. But whites have a moral and political responsibility to acknowledge the continuing burden of history's structural racism.

11   A reparations trust fund could be established, with the goal of closing the socioeconomic gaps between blacks and whites. Funds would be targeted specifically toward poor, disadvantaged communities with the greatest need, not to individuals. Let's eliminate the racial unfairness in capital

markets that perpetuates black poverty. A national commitment to expand black homeownership, full employment and quality health care would benefit all Americans, regardless of race.

Reparations could begin America's Third Reconstruction, the final 12 chapter in the 400-year struggle to abolish slavery and its destructive consequences. As Malcolm X said in 1961, hundreds of years of racism and labor exploitation are "worth more than a cup of coffee at a white cafe. We are here to collect back wages."

Understanding Context

1. What is Marable's thesis? Restate it in your own words.
2. Marable states that white wealth was "first constructed from centuries of unpaid black labor." How does one explain the wealth obtained by Carnegie, Ford, Edison, and Rockefeller—people who started with modest means? Did they indirectly benefit from the legacy of slavery?
3. Marable does not suggest paying funds to individuals. Would such funds make reparations more effective in resolving racial discrimination? Why or why not?
4. According to Marable, what is the moral obligation of whites?
5. Hasn't America already devoted billions to achieving Marable's goal of "closing the socioeconomic gaps between whites and blacks"? Although the term "reparation" was not used, didn't affirmative action seek to undo the legacy of slavery and discrimination?
6. *Critical thinking:* Marable discusses this issue in terms of white and black. As America becomes more diverse, will this argument resonate with the growing number of Asians and Hispanics? Do the millions of Americans whose ancestors immigrated after slavery ended have a sense of moral responsibility for the past wrongs committed against African Americans?

Evaluating Strategy

1. Marable opens his essay with a personal narrative. Does this effectively dramatize a historical issue?
2. What facts does Marable include to demonstrate the lasting effects of slavery?
3. How effective is the Malcolm X quotation that ends the essay? Does it leave you with a lasting impression? Why or why not?

Appreciating Language

1. How does Marable define the term "structural racism"?
2. What does the term "reparations" mean? How does it frame the debate about African Americans and poverty?

Writing Suggestions

1. After reading Shelby Steele's article (page 683), consider your own views on reparations for slavery and write a persuasive letter to the editor arguing for or against reparations.
2. *Collaborative writing:* Working with a group of students, consider this aspect of reparations—who should pay? Should West African tribes who sold other Africans into slavery be held liable? Should the British government bear some measure of responsibility since most of the slaves were imported during the colonial era? Because the government did not own slaves, can Congress appropriate money or should only those families or institutions that owned slaves have to pay?

Shelby Steele is a research fellow at the Hoover Institution who specializes in race relations. He received a degree in political science from Coe College and a doctorate in English from Southern Illinois University. His 1990 book *The Content of Our Character: A New Vision of Race in America* received the National Book Critic's Circle Award. His most recent book is *A Dream Deferred: The Second Betrayal of Black Freedom in America.* He has published articles in the *Wall Street Journal* and the *New York Times.* Steele has appeared on numerous television programs, including *Sixty Minutes* and *Nightline.*

A Childish Illusion: Reparations Enshrine Victimhood, Dishonoring Our Ancestors

Shelby Steele opposes the payment of reparations for slavery, arguing that it reflects what he calls a "crippling sense of entitlement." The problem, he asserts, is not white responsibility but black responsibility.

My father was born in the last year of the 19th century. His father was very 1 likely born into slavery, though there are no official records to confirm this. Still, from family accounts, I can plausibly argue that my grandfather was born a slave.

When I tell people this, I worry that I may seem conceited, like some- 2 one claiming a connection to royalty. The extreme experience of slavery— its commitment to broken-willed servitude—was so intense a crucible that it must have taken a kind of genius to survive it. In the jaws of slavery and segregation, blacks created a life-sustaining form of worship, rituals for every human initiation from childbirth to death, a rich folk mythology, a world-famous written literature, a complete cuisine, a truth-telling comic sensibility and, of course, some of the most glorious music the world has ever known.

Like the scion of an aristocratic family, I mention my grandfather to 3 stand a little in the light of the black American genius. So my first objection to reparation for slavery is that it feels like selling our birthright for a pot of porridge. There is a profound esteem that comes to us from having overcome four centuries of oppression.

4   This esteem is an irreplaceable resource. In Richard Wright's *Black Boy,* a black elevator operator makes pocket money by letting white men kick him in the behind for a quarter. Maybe reparations are not quite this degrading, but when you trade on the past victimization of your own people, you trade honor for dollars. And this trading is only uglier when you are a mere descendent of those who suffered but nevertheless prevailed.

5   I believe the greatest problem black America has had over the past 30 years has been precisely a faith in reparational uplift—the idea that all the injustice we endured would somehow translate into the means of uplift. We fought for welfare programs that only subsidized human inertia, for cultural approaches to education that stagnated skill development in our young and for affirmative-action programs that removed the incentive to excellence in our best and brightest.

6   Today 70 percent of all black children are born out of wedlock. Sixty-eight percent of all violent crime is committed by blacks, most often against other blacks. Sixty percent of black fourth graders cannot read at grade level. And so on. When you fight for reparational uplift, you have to fit yourself into a victim-focused, protest identity that is at once angry and needy. You have to locate real transformative power in white society, and then manipulate white guilt by seducing it with neediness and threatening it with anger. And you must nurture in yourself, and pass on to your own children, a sense of aggrieved entitlement that sees black success as an impossibility without the intervention of white compassion.

7   The above statistics come far more from this crippling sense of entitlement than from racism. And now the demand for reparations is yet another demand for white responsibility when today's problem is a failure of black responsibility.

8   When you don't know how to go forward, you find an excuse to go backward. You tell yourself that if you can just get a little justice for past suffering, you will feel better about the challenges you face. So you make justice a condition of your going forward. But of course, there is no justice for past suffering, and to believe there is only guarantees more suffering.

9   The worst enemy black America faces today is not white racism but white guilt. This is what encourages us to invent new pleas rather than busy ourselves with the hard work of development. So willing are whites to treat us with deference that they are a hard mark to pass up. The entire civil rights establishment strategizes to keep us the wards of white guilt. If these groups had to rely on black money rather than white corporate funding, they would all go under tomorrow.

10   An honest black leadership would portray our victimization as only a condition we faced, and nurture a black identity around the ingenuity by

which we overcame it. It would see reparations as a childish illusion of perfect justice. I can't be repaid for my grandfather. The point is that I owe him a great effort.

Understanding Context

1. Why does Steele, who is probably a descendent of a slave, object to reparations?
2. How does Steele look back on slavery? What legacies does he see?
3. Marable (page 679) argues that whites need to recognize past injustices. Steele believes the real problem is white guilt, not white racism. Do both writers sense that white attitudes ultimately shape the destiny of African Americans?
4. According to Steele, what are the greatest problems African Americans face?
5. *Critical thinking:* Steele notes that he can't be repaid for his grandfather. Reparations for victims of the Holocaust, for example, are limited to survivors, not their offspring. Is it fair for descendants to be compensated if the generation of victims died without redress? Should Native American tribes be compensated for lands lost in the nineteenth century?

Evaluating Strategy

1. Like Marable (page 679), Steele opens his essay with a narrative about an ancestor who was a slave. How effective is this device? Is it necessary to establish his authority to speak on a controversial issue such as slavery?
2. What statistics does Steele present? How important are they in supporting his thesis?
3. How does Steele attempt to shift the focus away from reparations to African American responsibility?

Appreciating Language

1. Steele uses the term "entitlement." What does the word mean? Why, in his view, is it "crippling"?
2. *Critical thinking:* Steele uses the term "victimhood." In recent years words and phrases such as "victimization," "victimhood," and "blaming the victim" have become popular. What is a "victim"? Do people use the designation of "victim" to justify actions or demand compensation?

Writing Suggestions

1. Write a persuasive paper outlining how public schools should address the legacy of slavery. How should textbooks present the issue? Can it be taught without bias? What, if anything, do all Americans need to know about slavery?

2. *Collaborative writing:* Working with a group of students, discuss the arguments of Marable and Steele. Imagine that your group wants to poll students in your school to determine their attitudes about slavery reparations. Write a process paper detailing how you would conduct a poll. How would you word questions to avoid bias? What background information would you present before asking students to give their opinions? What would be the most effective way of conducting a poll to make sure that it accurately reflected campus attitudes?

AMERICA'S SECOND HARVEST

America's Second Harvest is a nonprofit organization dedicated to "create a hunger-free America." It distributes food, increases public awareness, and advocates policies to benefit the hungry. Each year America's Second Harvest provides two billion pounds of food and supports 50,000 local charitable agencies that operate shelters, food pantries, after-school programs, and soup kitchens.

Childhood Hunger in the United States

The web page on page 688 is part of a group presenting facts about hunger in various American communities. Note that unlike many appeals to help people needing relief, this web page relies on logical rather than emotional appeals.

America's Second Harvest – Childhood Hunger In the United States

http://www.secondharvest.org/learn_about_hunger/child_hunger_facts.html

Google

THE LARGEST MOST COMPREHENSIVE STUDY
EVER CONDUCTED ON DOMESTIC HUNGER

DONATE ■ ADVOCATE ■
Email signup   GO

America's
Second Harvest
The Nation's
Food Bank Network
Ending Hunger.

We are

Search the site   GO

Home | About Us | Who We Help | How We Work | How to Help | Who Helps Us | Learn About Hunger | News Room | Get Help

LEARN ABOUT HUNGER

Learn About Hunger

Child Hunger Facts ■

Hunger in the Suburbs

Rural Hunger

Senior Hunger

Working Poor

Katrina & Rita Aftermath

Hunger in America 2006

Hunger Study 2001...

Hunger Study 2001 Fact Sheet

Issue Briefs

Related Links

CHILDHOOD HUNGER IN THE UNITED STATES ■

🖨 Print
✉ Email

The problem of childhood hunger is not simply a moral issue. Scientific evidence suggests that hungry children are less likely to become productive citizens.

A child who is unequipped to learn because of hunger and poverty is more likely to be poor as an adult. As such, the existence of childhood hunger in the United States threatens future American prosperity.

Current Statistics

• 13 million, or approximately 17.8% of children in the U.S. live in poverty. The rate of poverty for children under 18 remains higher than those aged 18– to– 64 and for those aged 65 and over [i].

• In 2004 over 13.8 million, or 19.0%, of American children resided in food insecure households, meaning they were hungry or at risk of hunger. Over a half–million children lived in food insecure households with hunger [ii].

• According to USDA estimates, 7.0 million or 17.6% of households with children under age 18 were food insecure in 2004 [iii].

• Research indicates that even mild undernutrition experienced by young children during critical periods of growth may lead to reductions in physical growth and affect brain development [iv].

• In fiscal year 2004, the Food Stamp Program served approximately 5.5 million households with children each month, representing more than half of all participating households [v].

• During the 2004 fiscal year, 16.9 million low–income children received free or reduced–price meals through the National School Lunch Program. Unfortunately, just under two million of these same income–eligible children participated in the Summer Food Service Program that same year [vi].

[i] DeNavas-Walt, Carmn, B.D. Proctor, C.H. Lee. U.S. Census Bureau,. Income, Poverty, and Health Insurance Coverage in the United States: 2004 (P60-229), August 2005.

[ii] Nord, Mark, M. Andrews, S. Carlson. United States Department of Agriculture, Household Food Security in the United States, 2004 (ERR-11), October 2005.

[iii] Nord, Mark, M. Andrews, S. Carlson. United States Department of Agriculture, Household Food Security in the United States, 2004 (ERR-11), October 2005.

[iv] The Links Between Nutrition and Cognitive Development of Children, 1998, Tufts University School of Nutrition Science and Policy.

[v] Poikolainen, Anni. United States Department of Agriculture/Office of Analysis, Nutrition and Evaluation. Characteristics of Food Stamp Households: Fiscal Year 2004, September 2005.

[vi] United States Department of Agriculture Food and Nutrition Service.

Understanding Context

1. What does America's Second Harvest want people to know about childhood hunger?
2. How can malnutrition affect a child's future?
3. What facts does the website present?

Evaluating Strategy

1. How does Second Harvest persuade readers to appreciate that childhood hunger "is not simply a moral issue?"
2. What appeals are used in this website?
3. What evidence is presented as support?
4. *Critical thinking:* This web page includes documentation, citing the U.S. Department of Agriculture and U.S. Census Bureau as sources for it statistics. Is this important? Does it add credibility to the message? Do most websites provide documentation for the evidence they present? Does the use of government statistics make a website appear more credible and the organization more reliable?

Appreciating Language

1. This web page avoids emotional language, such as "crisis" or "desperate need." What does this suggest about the intended audience? Would including emotional language make the web page more effective or detract from its credibility?
2. How is the term "food insecure" defined?

Writing Suggestions

1. Create a similar web page that educates the public of another social problem by presenting factual details.
2. *Collaborative writing:* Working with a group of students, create a fund-raising ad or e-mail that uses emotional appeals to raise funds to fight child hunger. Your group may search Internet stock photo sites for appropriate photographs to accompany your text. Make sure your ad not only dramatizes the problem but demonstrates how readers' contributions can make a difference.

Responding to IMAGES

World Trade Center, September 11, 2001   © AFP/Corbis

1. What is your first reaction to this now famous image? Can you remember how you felt on September 11, 2001? Write a brief autobiographical narrative about the events of that day.
2. How do you think history will recall this event? Will it become as important as Pearl Harbor, an event that transforms American values, attitudes, and its position in the world? Or will the World Trade Center attack be remembered only as a tragedy like the sinking of the *Titanic* or the crash of the *Hindenburg*?
3. What does this image reveal about the power of global media? Would a terrorist attack or atrocity in a remote region that claimed thousands of lives but produced few pictures receive less attention? Why or why not? Does the unequal distribution of cameras and computers affect people's lives in the information age almost as much as the unequal distribution of food and fuel?

4. Does this photograph serve as an international Rorschach test of people's attitudes about terrorism, American influence in the world, politics, or religion? How might people around the world respond differently to this image?

5. *Critical thinking:* How would you define "terrorism" or "terrorists"? When do "resistance" or guerrilla fighters become terrorists? If an armed group of dissidents attacked military and economic targets, such as barracks, bridges, or uniformed personnel, would they be defined as "terrorists" in your view? Write a clear definition of "terrorists" and provide examples to illustrate your thesis.

6. *Visual analysis:* Airline commercials have frequently shown jets flying across city skylines or over famous landmarks. How does the image alter our perceptions? Do buildings and landmarks now appear vulnerable? Do airliners now seem threatening?

7. *Collaborative writing:* Discuss this image with a group of students and craft a short essay explaining how September 11, 2001, should be remembered. Should newspapers, television networks, magazines, and public schools treat September 11 as a special day in the future? If so, how should the events be depicted—as a tragedy or an act of war? If members of your groups have differing opinions, write a comparison or division essay.

8. *Other modes*
   - What are the *causes* of suicidal terrorism? Write an essay that details, in your view, the forces that lead people to believe that attacking civilians is a justifiable means to achieve their goals.
   - Write an essay that details the *effects* of terrorism on the public. Can terrorist attacks make any government appear weak and helpless?
   - Write a *division* paper that outlines the different methods of responding to terrorism. Provide examples of technological, military, diplomatic, and other responses.

Argument and Persuasion Checklist

Before submitting your paper, review these points:

✔ Is your message clearly defined?

✔ Does your paper meet readers' needs? Do you provide the support they need to accept your thesis?

✔ Do you support your views with adequate evidence?

✔ Do you anticipate reader objections and alternative points of view?

✔ Do you balance the strengths and weaknesses of logical, ethical, and emotional appeals?

✔ Do you avoid overstated, sentimental, or propagandist appeals?

✔ Do you avoid preaching to the converted? Will only those who already agree with you accept your arguments?

✔ Do you make it easy for undecided readers to accept your position without feeling manipulated or patronized?

✔ Have you tested your argument with peer review?

Companion Website

See **http://www.thomsonedu.com/english/sundance** for additional information about argument and persuasion.

Part Four

Writing In College

THE ESSAY EXAMINATION

27

> Vigorous writing is concise.
> —William Strunk Jr.

WHAT ARE ESSAY EXAMS?

Throughout your college career you will most likely face essay examinations. They can be frustrating, especially if you realize afterward how easily you could have improved your grade by studying lecture notes instead of your textbook or by reading the questions more carefully. Writing papers out of class allows you to select a topic, conduct research, write numerous drafts, and edit. But essay exams force you to truncate the writing process to meet a deadline. Learning to write essay exams can teach you to work under pressure in your profession, when you may have to provide immediate answers to questions or draft statements to manage a crisis with little time for reflection.

Few people feel confident about writing under pressure, but there are strategies that can improve your performance.

The Purpose of Essay Examinations

Instructors use objective tests consisting of multiple choice and true-or-false questions to measure your ability to recall factual information. Essay questions allow instructors to accomplish additional goals:

- measure your understanding of facts by asking you to restate information in your own words
- evaluate your ability to assimilate and analyze material
- analyze your critical thinking skills in diagnosing problems, proposing solutions, comparing situations, outlining causes, and predicting outcomes
- judge your ability to discriminate or classify ideas by isolating essential information from incidental details
- determine your ability to apply knowledge to test cases or hypothetical situations

In asking essay questions, instructors seek more than a simple recital of memorized facts. The literature student who provides an accurate definition of *dramatic irony* in his or her own words better demonstrates an understanding of the concept than one who simply remembers enough from the textbook to recognize a familiar statement appearing on a multiple choice test.

STRATEGIES | for Studying for Essay Examinations

1. **Determine the scope of the examination.** You don't want to spend hours studying only to discover that you have been reviewing the wrong chapters. Many instructors are reluctant to answer the direct question, What's on the test? But most will respond favorably to two critical questions that you should ask: What does the examination cover? What is the best way to prepare? Asking these questions can help you target your studying and avoid reviewing the wrong material.

2. **Begin studying at once. Don't attempt to cram the night before.** Two hours of studying spread over a week will give you more opportunity to learn and recall information than attempting to absorb the same amount of information in four hours of last-minute cramming.
   - If you delay studying until the night before the examination, you run the risk that an unexpected problem will disrupt your plans and leave you unprepared.
   - Studying in advance gives you the opportunity to ask questions before the examination. If you discover that your instructor defines a term differently than the textbook, for example, you can ask which one he or she thinks is accurate.

3. **Talk to other students about the upcoming examination.** Discuss possible topics, methods of studying, and lecture notes. When you talk to classmates, you may realize that you have forgotten or misunderstood information or failed to recall an instructor's recommendation.

4. **Consider the nature of the discipline.** The kind of response that instructors consider acceptable is greatly determined by the discipline. In the humanities, students may be free to advance highly personal interpretations of a work of art or historical event. Creative essays, provided they are well supported, are highly valued. However, in such fields as law, psychology, sociology, and nursing, students are expected to only advance ideas that follow specific standards and practices and that can be scientifically proven. Individual interpretations and subjective opinions reflect poorly on a student preparing for a field grounded in strict adherence to facts and objectivity.

5. **Review your syllabus, notes, textbooks, and handouts.** Highlight important passages for easy review just before the exam. Note significant facts, statistics, and quotations that may serve as support for your responses.

   - Take notes as you study. Essay exams require that you state ideas in your own words, not simply identify what you have read. If definitions are important, close your book and write a brief version of your own and then compare it to the text. Writing about the material is the best way to prepare for an essay test.

   - If you are taking an open book examination, highlight passages and use labeled bookmarks so you can quickly locate information while writing. Familiarize yourself with the book's index.

6. **Recall the types of questions your instructor has asked in class.** The kinds of questions asked to prompt class discussion may provide a clue about the way the instructor may word questions on essay examinations.

   - Does your instructor focus on comparing issues, analyzing problems, debating alternative interpretations or theories?

   - Does he or she concentrate on presenting in-depth analysis of narrow topics or providing a sweeping, inclusive overview of the subject?

7. **Think in terms of the modes.** Most essay questions ask students to *define* elements, *compare* related topics, *explain* a process, or detail *causes* or *effects*.

   - In reviewing your notes and textbook, consider what major items require definition, which subjects are often compared, what ideas are presented as causes or effects.

8. **Prewrite possible responses.** Select the key issues or topics you expect to appear on the examination and freewrite, cluster, or brainstorm possible essays. List possible thesis statements.

   ■ Remember that an essay test requires that you express what you know in writing. Fifteen minutes of prewriting can help you assimilate information, identify facts, generate ideas, and reveal knowledge that you may have overlooked more quickly than hours of reading and memorizing. *Prepare yourself to write.*

9. **Get as much rest as possible the night before.** Late-night cramming may help you identify facts and figures that appear on multiple choice tests, but essay questions demand thinking. If you are not rested, you may find yourself unable to quickly analyze issues, generate ideas, make connections, and present your thoughts in an organized fashion.

STRATEGIES for Writing the Essay Examination

Writing under pressure can frustrate even the most prepared student. If you tend to become rattled or nervous, you may wish to take a walk between classes, call a friend, eat a high-energy snack, or listen to your favorite song just before the test to put you in a positive frame of mind.

1. **Come to the examination prepared to write.** Bring two pens, paper, and, unless prohibited, a dictionary and handbook.

2. **Read the entire exam.** Go over *all* the questions carefully before starting to write. Determine how much each question is worth. Some instructors will indicate the point value of each question.

3. **Budget your time.** Determine how much time you should devote to each question. Give yourself enough time for planning and editing each question.

4. **Answer the easiest questions first while thinking about the more difficult ones.** The easiest questions will take less time to answer and may stimulate ideas that will help you confront more challenging questions.

5. **Read each question twice.** Students often miss points by failing to fully read the question. They respond to a word or phrase out of context and begin writing an energetic essay that does not address the question.

6. **Study the verbs or command words that direct your response.** Most essay questions contain clues to the kind of response the instructor expects:

Question	Desired Response
List reasons for the rise of labor unions in the 1930s.	A series of reasons rather than an in-depth analysis of a single factor
Distinguish the differences between ancient Athens and Sparta.	A comparison/contrast, highlighting differences
What led to the collapse of the Soviet Union?	A cause-and-effect essay, perhaps related in a narrative or organized by division or classification
Describe three common forms of depression.	Three short definitions or descriptions organized by division
Discuss the effects of global warming on the environment.	An essay consisting of cause and effect, process, description, or division

7. **Study questions that require more than a single response.** Some essay questions contain more than one command and require a two- or three-part response:

Question	Desired Response
Provide a definition of chemical dependency and explain why treatment remains problematic.	1. Define term. 2. List causes for problems in treatment.
Select three key economic proposals made by the president in the State of the Union address and predict how they will affect both the trade deficit and unemployment.	1. Describe or define three points. 2. Discuss each point listing effects on trade deficit and unemployment.

8. **Provide a clear thesis statement.** Your response should do more than simply list or discuss ideas. A strong thesis statement will give your response direction and can help organize ideas. This is very important if instructors present you with general questions or topics.

Question:

How has the concept of separation of church and state affected American society?

Possible Thesis Statements:

The separation of church and state has allowed American public schools to accommodate students from diverse religious backgrounds with little of the conflict found in other countries.

Unlike state-supported religious institutions in other nations, American churches are independent and able to take active roles in criticizing government policies regarding discrimination, capital punishment, American foreign policy, and abortion.

9. **Explain or justify your response to broad questions.** Sometimes instructors ask sweeping questions that cannot be fully addressed with a brief response:

    What caused the American Civil War?

    If you respond with a detailed explanation of slavery, an instructor may assume you believe it to be the sole cause of the war. If you present a list of a dozen reasons, however, an instructor may feel that your response is superficial and lacks substance. You can achieve a higher grade if you justify your response:

    There were numerous political, social, economic, philosophical, and moral causes of the Civil War. But clearly the most significant and enduring cause for the conflict was the problem of slavery. . . .

    Although most Americans cite slavery as the main reason for the Civil War, it is difficult to isolate a single factor as a cause for the conflict. To understand why the states went to war, one must appreciate the full range of social, economic, commercial, foreign policy, and moral disputes that separated North and South. . . .

10. **Keep an eye on the clock.** Pace yourself. Don't "overdo" a response simply because you are knowledgeable about the topic. Provide enough information to address the question, and then move on.

11. **Keep writing.** If you become blocked or stalled on a question and can't think, move on to other questions or review what you have answered. Often rereading the response to one question will spark ideas that aid in another.

12. **Provide space for revisions.** Write on every other line of the page or leave wide margins. You will not have time to write a full second draft, but you can make neat corrections and slip in ideas if you give yourself space for changes and additions.

SAMPLE QUESTIONS AND ESSAYS

Read these questions and then examine the responses. How effectively do these students address the questions? Even if you are unsure of the content, you can still evaluate the essay for clarity, organization, and development.

From an economics midterm:

> During the prosperity caused by government spending during World War II both workers and business leaders feared a Depression would follow the end of hostilities. Many envisioned millions of jobless veterans camped in abandoned defense plants. Why were these predictions wrong? What led to the economic expansion after 1945?

It was understandable that many Americans, most of whom had a living memory of the Depression of the 1930s, would fear the end of wartime spending would lead to massive unemployment and poverty. But these dire predictions failed to consider the political, social, and economic forces that would change the American economy for the rest of the twentieth century.

> *Introduction*

The doomsayers overlooked two powerful economic forces that would propel post-war prosperity: pent up consumer demand and personal savings.

> *Thesis*

During the Second World War nearly every industry focused on military production. Civilian automobile production ceased in 1942. At war's end most Americans were driving cars that were three to six years old. The manufacture of other goods such as washing machines, dishwashers, refrigerators, and radios was curtailed. Clothing, shoes, and tires were rationed. The infant television industry was stalled by the war. At war's end the civilian population and returning veterans needed and wanted to replace worn-out goods. The plants that produced military supplies were rapidly put to use to manufacture a range of consumer products in high demand.

> *Evidence*

This pent-up demand was coupled with tremendous buying power. With rationed goods, the war workers, many of whom earned substantial overtime pay, had little outlet for spending. Personal savings exploded during the war. Highly publicized bond drives encouraged people to purchase billions of dollars of government bonds to support the war effort. In addition, millions of veterans returned from combat zones where there was no place to spend the money they earned. Many soldiers had saved six months' to a year's salary.

> *Evidence*

The demand for new goods and services and the ability to pay for them fueled a booming post war consumer economy.

> *Evidence*

Other factors such as the GI Bill helped finance new homes and businesses. The fact many veterans chose to attend college after the war limited the number of men and women seeking jobs immediately after the war. The Marshall Plan, implemented shortly after the war, created a strong overseas demand for American machinery, vehicles, and other goods.

Questions for Review

1. How effective is the thesis? Should it be placed elsewhere in the essay?
2. Is the thesis clearly supported? Are the details convincing?
3. How effective is the conclusion?

From a psychology final exam:

Distinguish between schizophrenia and multiple personality disorder.

The common confusion of these two psychological disorders stems in part from the name "schizophrenia" which literally means "split mind." Many people assume this "split" refers to a Dr. Jekyll and Mr. Hyde duality, a splitting of an individual into two distinct personalities.

But the "split" schizophrenia refers to is a patient's split or disassociation of reality. The schizophrenic can suffer from a number of symptoms affecting their thoughts, emotional reactions, motions, and relationships. Often schizophrenics display inappropriate reactions—failing to appear moved at a funeral while later becoming tearfully agitated over losing a bus transfer. In broiling summer they may bundle themselves in coats and blankets, claiming to be cold. They may suffer hallucinations, frequently reporting they hear their thoughts spoken out loud or a voice commanding them to do certain things. Schizophrenics may also be paranoid, claiming that the FBI or Martians are controlling their thoughts, spying on them, or attempting to kill them.

Schizophrenia is a common mental illness, affecting 1–2 percent of the population. Research has proven a strong link to genetics, since it does run in families. Scientists have identified chemical imbalances in the brains of schizophrenics. Psychologists also believe that social and family factors influence the development of the disease.

Multiple personality disorder has been far less documented since it is believed to be rarer than schizophrenia and harder to diagnose. The 1950s movie "The Three Faces of Eve" was based on an actual case of a woman with three distinct personalities. Psychiatrists of the era believed that overwhelming emotional stress or trauma caused people to develop multiple personalities as a defense mechanism. Frequently, one personality will dominate or protect another. Patients often have both male and female personalities. Under hypnosis, patients will alter their behavior, body language, and speech as each personality emerges. In recent years multiple personality disorder has been used as a defense in several high profile murder cases. Because the condition is rare and research is difficult, the condition is hard to diagnose and study.

The main thing is to realize that schizophrenics do not have more than one personality but are split from reality. Drugs are now available to reduce hallucinations in schizophrenics, but treatments for multiple personality disorder are experimental at best.

Questions for Review

1. How effectively does this essay address the question?
2. What is the thesis? Is it clearly stated?
3. Does the student support the thesis with sufficient detail?
4. Does the student adequately address both disorders?
5. Do you sense the student ran out of time?
6. Consult a psychology text or encyclopedia and then evaluate this essay. How accurately does the student define the two disorders? What grade would you give this response?

WRITING ACTIVITY

1. Review essay exams you have taken in the past. How could you have improved your responses? Read the question and write a fresh response within the time limits of the original test.

2. Select one of the following questions and write for fifteen minutes, drawing on your personal experience, reading, and past courses.

> What, in your opinion, is the principal cause for poverty in America?
> How has immigration shaped American society?
> What effects has the Internet had on education?
> Contrast the messages of Malcolm X and Martin Luther King Jr. What lasting impact have they had on race relations?
> Identify the key abilities needed for someone to succeed in your future profession.

Examine your completed response.
- Is the thesis clearly stated?
- Is the thesis supported by detail?
- Is the response logically organized?
- Are there irrelevant ideas that should be deleted?
- How effective is the conclusion?

How could you improve your ability to write under pressure?

3. Select a textbook chapter you have recently studied and use one of the questions at the end to prompt a fifteen-minute response. If your book does not offer questions, summarize one or more of the chapter's key points in a short essay without looking at the book.

- Were you able to develop a thesis and support it with detail?
- What problems did you encounter in writing?
- How could you improve your studying?

For Further Reading

Burns, Richard. *Pass Exams and Write Top Essays.*
Galica, Gregory. *The Blue Book: A Student's Guide to Essay Exams.*
Lesyk, Susan Burgess. *The Blue Book: Achieving Success on Essay Exams.*

E-Sources

Common Words Used in Essay Questions
http://gwired.gwu.edu/counsel/asc/index.gw/Site_ID/46/Page_ID/14566/
The Essay Exam
http://www.studygs.net/tsttak4.htm
Essay Exams
http://www.unc.edu/depts/wcweb/handouts/essay-exams.html

Companion Website

See http://www.thomsonedu.com/english/sundance for further information on writing essay examinations.

28

WRITING ABOUT LITERATURE

> We need two powers in literature, a power to create and a power to understand.
> —Northrop Frye

WHAT IS LITERATURE?

Literature consists of works of imagination. Poems, short stories, novels, and plays present writers' visions of the world. Chaucer's poetry, Shakespeare's *King Lear*, Alice Walker's *The Color Purple*, Frost's "Stopping by Woods on a Snowy Evening," and Lorraine Hansberry's *Raisin in the Sun* are all examples of literature.

Writing about literature can be challenging, especially if you are accustomed to reading only for pleasure or information. Literature courses require you to understand not only what happens in a work but also how it is stated.

Writers who study literature, like writers in any discipline, use technical terms to discuss their subject. In order to write about a work of literature, it is helpful to understand definitions of key words and concepts.

Major Literary Terms

Characters

characters Individuals appearing in a story, novel, poem, or play.

protagonist The main figure, often called the hero—Hamlet, Huckleberry Finn, Hedda Gabler.

antagonist   A person or force working against the protagonist. This could be a villain or a hostile environment or element like the sea or a blizzard.

stock characters   People representing recurring types—the hard-boiled detective, the innocent child, the vengeful spouse, young lovers.

foils   Minor characters who serve to define the qualities of another figure by contrast. The idealism of a young attorney can be demonstrated to readers by surrounding him or her with cynical or uncaring coworkers.

flat characters   Minor characters who are two-dimensional. Unlike the major figures, they are only superficially developed.

Plot

plot   The events that occur in the work. In an adventure or detective novel, the plot dominates the work and is often more important than the characters. In other works, the events are less important than the protagonist's thoughts or feelings. *Julius Caesar* has a strong plot marked by conspiracy, assassination, civil war, and suicides. In contrast, Beckett's *Waiting for Godot* has no discernible plot but a series of interchanges between two characters.

conflict   The struggle or tension that is a key element of the plot. The conflict can be between individuals, an individual and society or nature, or between contrasting forces within a character. Hemingway's *The Old Man and the Sea* pits a character against nature. In Kafka's *The Trial*, the protagonist battles mysterious forces he cannot understand. Charles Jackson's *The Lost Weekend* depicts the internal conflicts faced by an alcoholic.

climax   An event signaling a turning point in the plot, usually when the conflict reaches its greatest intensity. This may be followed by an **anti-climax,** a less dramatic event that occurs after the climax, often providing a final resolution of the conflict.

setting   The time and place of the work—nineteenth-century Paris, Kansas in the Depression, or present-day New York. In some instances setting is simply a backdrop to events that could occur anywhere. In some works, the setting is essential to the characters and action. In *All Quiet on the Western Front* the First World War engulfs all its characters and shapes the plot. In contrast, the setting of *Who's Afraid of Virginia Woolf?* is relatively incidental to the conflict between spouses.

Theme

genre   A form or type. In literature, genres include poetry, the short story, the novel, the play.

theme   The major issue, problem, or controlling idea. *Invisible Man* concerns racism. *Of Mice and Men* reveals the cruelty and insensitivity often shown to the weak and vulnerable. The author's treatment of theme may include political commentary or a call for social reform.

tone   The author's attitude toward events, characters, or plot. The tone of a play, story, or poem can be somber, humorous, sarcastic, or sympathetic. An alcoholic character, for instance, could be portrayed with empathy or held up to ridicule.

tragedy   A work of literature in which the protagonist moves from a position of power and respect within a society downward to destruction, usually marked by exile, death, or suicide. In literature tragedy involves choice, not random disaster. A character killed in an airplane crash is not considered "tragic." Macbeth, however, makes a decision to kill the king and sets into motion the forces that ultimately destroy him. Traditionally, the tragic hero is a nobleman or person of high standing. *Death of a Salesman* poses the question, can an unsuccessful man, a little man like Willy Loman, be considered tragic? In classic Greek tragedy the heroes often suffer from hubris, or pride, which leads them to assume that they can break laws and control events. Often, as in *Oedipus*, the hero learns too late that no mortal can control destiny.

comedy   A work of literature in which the characters, often a pair of young lovers, overcome obstacles to form a new society, often culminating in a wedding, festivity, or new understanding. Comedies, although they usually have "happy" endings, may not be filled with jokes. Chekhov, for instance, labeled *The Cherry Orchard* and *The Seagull* comedies, even though one play involved a family's being dispossessed and the other involved suicide.

Point of View

point of view   The perspective from which the story is told.

first-person narrator   A narrator who experienced or witnessed the events in the story. The narrator may be the protagonist or a bystander. *Huckleberry Finn* is narrated by the hero. In contrast, events in *The Great Gatsby* are told not by the hero, Jay Gatsby, but by his neighbor, Nick Carroway.

unreliable narrator   A narrator who may have biases or misunderstandings that distort the way readers perceive events. Huckleberry Finn, for example, is unsophisticated and superstitious, and thus often draws erroneous conclusions about what he observes.

third-person narrator   In third person, the narrator may be **omniscient** or all-knowing, entering the minds of several characters, or may have limited knowledge of characters and events. Often the third-person narrator may show the inner thoughts and feelings of major characters and only report the actions and dialogue of minor figures.

Technique

exposition   Supplies readers with background information about setting, characters' past lives, or events that occurred before the plot begins. Exposition is challenging to develop in drama because details have to be communicated to the audience through dialogue.

foreshadowing   Clues or hints of action to follow. Shirley Jackson's "The Lottery," which culminates in a woman being stoned to death, opens with a brief description of small boys piling up stones.

flashback   A scene in a novel, play, story, or poem that returns to earlier events to suggest a character's memory, provide a historical perspective, or clarify the present.

allusion   A casual reference to a famous literary or historical event or figure. Biblical allusions might include a character receiving "thirty pieces of silver" to betray a friend or "parting the Red Sea" to overcome an overwhelming obstacle.

irony   The contrast between anticipated and actual elements. **Verbal irony** consists of remarks in which the spoken words differ from their intended meaning, often for comic or sarcastic effect. An undercover officer arresting a drug dealer might state ironically, "This is your lucky day." In **dramatic irony** there is a discrepancy between what a character believes to be true and what the author or audience knows. In *A Doll's House* Helmer tells his wife that most criminals have mothers who lie, unaware that his wife has been living an elaborate falsehood.

image   A person, object, scene, or situation that creates a strong impression, usually one that relies on the senses. Edgar Allan Poe used images of skulls, bones, tombs, blood, darkness, and death to create sensations of horror and fear.

symbol   A person, object, scene, or situation that represents something else: an idea, quality, or concept. A lion might symbolize courage. A cross represents Christ. Symbols may be obvious or complex. In *Death of a Salesman* Biff Loman steals a fountain pen and a suit, symbols of success in the business world that has eluded him. For many readers the whale in *Moby-Dick* symbolizes nature; for others it represents a destructive obsession.

simile   A comparison of two unlike things using the words *like* or *as*:

> The unpaid bills hit him *like*   The coffee was *as* cold as ice.
>   a tidal wave.

metaphor   A direct comparison of two unlike things made without using *like* or *as*:

> He was hit by a tidal wave of   We drank ice-cold coffee.
>   unpaid bills.

stanza   A unit of poetry named for the number of lines it contains:

> couplet: two lines   sestet: six lines
> triplet: three lines   septet: seven lines
> quatrain: four lines   octave: eight lines
> quintet: five lines

epiphany   A sudden realization or burst of insight by an author or character.

STRATEGIES | for Reading Literature

1. **Survey the work and read available biographical or introductory material.** Many college anthologies include headnotes similar to those in the reader portion of this book. Examine the biography carefully and review any questions that might appear after the text. Consult an encyclopedia or scan the Internet for biographical information about the author or background material about time and setting.
2. **Read the work once to get a first impression.** Allow yourself to read for pleasure. Enjoy the poem or story, noting passages you find interesting, difficult, powerful, or confusing.
3. **Review the overall work and ask questions.**
4. **Examine details in context.** Avoid allowing personal or contemporary attitudes to color your perceptions of the work or the author's intention. Statements by a nineteenth-century writer may strike you as being racist or sexist. Poetry by someone of another culture may puzzle or offend you. Don't allow isolated statements to distort your impression of the entire work.

5. **Identify possible topics for discussion or writing.** Highlight significant passages for easy reference.

6. **Note aspects of the work you find puzzling or confusing.** Sometimes an author will present an image or make a historical reference you do not understand. Characters may use regional or slang expressions you are unfamiliar with. Look up confusing words in a dictionary. Discuss the work with other students. They may know the meaning of a word or the significance of a reference or detail. Another reader may have an alternative interpretation that sharpens your analysis of the work.

Questions for Literary Analysis

✔ What significance, if any, does the title have? What does it suggest?

✔ What is the time and setting of the story? Is it significant or only incidental?

✔ Who are the principal characters? Are any of them archetypes? Do they remind you of characters in other works? What motivates their actions and influences their thoughts?

✔ How would you characterize the protagonist? Does he or she have internal or external conflicts? Does the protagonist appear to represent a group of people, a cause, or a set of values? What motivates the protagonist?

✔ How is the plot developed? What is the central conflict? Does the author use devices such as foreshadowing?

✔ Does the writer use imagery and symbols? What are they? What impact do they have?

✔ Who is the narrator? Is the story related in the first or third person? Does the narrator have limited or full knowledge of events and characters? If told in the first person, is the narrator the protagonist, a minor character, or simply a witness or recorder?

✔ What seems to be the author's message? Does he or she appear to have a clearly stated opinion about events and characters? Is the author making a social or political statement?

✔ What are the significant themes in the work? If you had to write an essay about it, would you focus on a character, a pattern of imagery, the use of language, or the author's message?

✔ What lasting impression does the work create? What strikes you as being the most significant element of the work—a scene, a symbol, a character, the conflict, the author's message?

STRATEGIES for Writing about Literature

Students often make the mistake of beginning to write about something they have read without giving themselves time to think and analyze the work. If you finish reading "The Pit and the Pendulum" and start writing, you are likely to want to recapture what you have just experienced and produce little more than a plot summary. But retelling each twist of Poe's tale adds little to anyone's knowledge or appreciation of the story.

1. **Avoid summarizing the work.** Although most writers analyzing a story, play, or poem will refer to the text, they do more than restate the plot.
   ■ Assume that everyone you are writing to has already read the work. Your job, then, is not to retell the story but to reveal something that other readers may have missed.
2. **Narrow the scope of your response by answering questions.** If you focus on answering specific questions about a character, the author's use of symbols, or the point of view, you can prevent yourself from merely writing a summary.
3. **Prewrite to explore the topic and develop a thesis.** Use brainstorming, clustering, or freewriting to investigate your topic. As you sketch out ideas, you may have to narrow or expand your approach.
4. **Develop a working thesis.** Your thesis should express a clear opinion about the meaning, structure, or style of the work:
   In *Death of a Salesman* Miller uses Uncle Charlie's relationship with his successful son Bernard to emphasize Willy Loman's failure as a father.
   The Great Gatsby presents a world in which marriage, the stock market, and even the World Series are corrupted by selfish greed.
   Ralph Ellison's "Battle Royal" highlights the bankruptcy of Booker T. Washington's "separate but equal" approach to race relations.

5. **Support your thesis with evidence from the text.** Works of literature are subject to a variety of interpretations—but they should not be viewed as abstract sculptures that can mean anything you want. Your opinions must be based on evidence presented in the story or poem. If you assert that a character is mentally ill, you must cite passages where the individual's speech, actions, or thoughts exhibit symptoms of a psychological disorder.

6. **Avoid extensive direct quotes.** Because your readers have read the work, there is no reason to repeat large sections of the text.
   - Use quotations when the author's image or a character's statement is so impressive that a paraphrase would weaken its impact.
   - Refer to passages or statements rather than quote them. Assuming your reader is familiar with the work, you can provide reminders rather than reproduce text.
   - Abbreviate longer quotations by selecting key words or phrases: Montresor leads Fortunato underground to the catacombs of "piled skeletons," guiding him through "low arches" where the narrow chambers are "lined with human remains."

7. **Quote poetry accurately.** Unless a poem is very long, you can present the full text within your paper or a section in a block quotation. When you quote a few lines within a paragraph, use slash marks to indicate original line breaks:
   > Eliot's Prufrock muses at one point, "I should have been a pair of ragged claws / Scuttling across the floors of silent seas."

8. **Write in the present tense.** Although most works are stated in the past tense, writers usually describe an author's views and a character's action in the present tense:
   > Shakespeare *presents* his audience with a dramatic dilemma. How *does* an indecisive character like Hamlet *avenge* his father's death? Hamlet *muses* and *ponders* long before taking action to confront the king.

9. **Identify the most effective mode for you to use to organize your supporting details.** You can structure your analysis by comparing two characters or events, defining a problem the protagonist faces, or discussing the causes or effects of a character's actions.

10. **After writing a first draft, review the work and then examine your thesis and support.**
    - Does your paper have a clear focus? Should the topic be narrowed? A literary paper does not have to address every aspect of a play or story. An in-depth examination of a minor character has more value than a superficial accounting of the plot, characters, setting, and theme.

- Does your paper have a clear thesis?
- Do you support the thesis with sufficient evidence from the text?
- Is the support clearly organized? Would another mode be a better method of structuring the essay?

WRITING ABOUT FICTION

Read the following story; then review the questions on page 716. Though short and starkly told, with little reference to time and setting, "The Bread" presents a strong plot marked by both a climax and anticlimax.

Wolfgang Borchert (1921–1947) was born in Hamburg, Germany, and worked as an actor and bookseller. During the Second World War he served in the German army in Russia and was wounded. An anti-Nazi, he was twice imprisoned for expressing defeatist views. He captured the despair and deprivation of the war in poems and short stories. Borchert died of a fever contracted during the war the day after the premiere of his play *Outside the Door*.

The Bread

Borchert wrote this story when food was strictly rationed, forcing many families to survive on a few slices of bread a day.

1 Suddenly she woke up. It was half past two. She considered why she had woken up. Oh yes! In the kitchen someone had knocked against a chair. She listened to the kitchen. It was quiet. It was too quiet and as she moved her hand across the bed beside her, she found it empty. That was what had made it so particularly quiet: she missed his breathing. She got up and groped her way through the dark flat to the kitchen. In the kitchen they met. The time was half past two. She saw something white standing on the kitchen cupboard. She put the light on. They stood facing one another in their night-shirts. At night. At half past two. In the kitchen.

2 On the kitchen table lay the bread-plate. She saw that he had cut himself some bread. The knife was still lying beside the plate. And on the cloth there were bread-crumbs. When they went to bed at night, she always made the table-cloth clean. Every night. But now there were crumbs on the cloth. And the knife was lying there. She felt how the cold of the tiles crept slowly up her. And she looked away from the plate.

3 "I thought there was something here," he said and looked round the kitchen.

4 "I heard something, too," she answered and thought that at night, in his night-shirt, he really looked quite old. As old as he was. Sixty-three. During the day he sometimes looked younger. She looks quite old, he thought, in her night-dress she really looks pretty old. But perhaps it's because of her hair. With women at night it's always because of their hair. All at once it makes them so old.

"You should have put on your shoes. Barefoot like that on the cold tiles! 5 You'll catch cold."

She didn't look at him, because she couldn't bear him to lie. To lie when 6 they had been married thirty-nine years.

"I thought there was something here," he said once more and again 7 looked so senselessly from one corner to the other, "I heard something in here. So I thought there'd be something here."

"I heard something, too. But it must have been nothing." She took the 8 plate off the table and flicked the crumbs from the table-cloth.

"No, it must have been nothing," he echoed uncertainly. 9

She came to his help: "Come on. It must have been outside. Come to 10 bed. You'll catch cold. On the cold tiles."

He looked at the window. "Yes, it'll have been outside. I thought it was 11 in here."

She raised her hand to the switch. I must now put the light out, or I shall 12 have to look at the plate, she thought. I dare not look at the plate. "Come on," she said and put out the light, "it must have been outside. The gutter always bangs against the wall when there's a wind. I'm sure it was the gutter. It always rattles when there's a wind."

They both groped their way along the dark corridor to the bedroom. 13 Their naked feet slapped on the floor.

"It is windy," he said, "it's been windy all night." 14

As they lay in bed, she said: "Yes it's been windy all night. It must have 15 been the gutter."

"Yes. I thought it was in the kitchen. It must have been the gutter." He 16 said it as though he were already half asleep. But she noticed how false his voice sounded when he lied.

"It's cold," she said and yawned softly, "I'll creep under the covers. 17 Good night."

"Night," he replied and added: "Yes, it really is pretty cold." 18

Then it was quiet. Many minutes later she heard him softly and cau- 19 tiously chewing. She breathed deeply and evenly so that he should not notice that she was still awake. But his chewing was so regular that it slowly sent her to sleep.

When he came home the next evening, she put four slices of bread in 20 front of him. At other times he had only been able to eat three.

"You can safely eat four," she said and moved away from the lamp. "I 21 can't digest this bread properly. Just you eat another one. I don't digest it very well."

She saw how he bent deep over the plate. He didn't look up. At that mo- 22 ment she was sorry for him.

23   "You can't eat only two slices," he said to his plate.

24   "Yes, I can. I don't digest this bread properly in the evening. Just eat. Eat it."

25   Only a while later did she sit down at the table under the lamp.

Questions for Analysis

1. Consider the title. How would your reading of the story differ if Borchert had titled it "The Betrayal" or "The Sacrifice"?
2. The author presents no details about time and location. Would they be helpful? Does the author seem to assume his readers understand the significance of a few slices of bread?
3. What characterizes the conflict between the husband and wife?
4. Review the dialogue between the two characters in the kitchen. Why doesn't the wife confront her husband? Why does she go along with his obvious lie?
5. How do you interpret the wife's final gesture?
6. Which event would you label the climax? Which scene represents an anticlimax?
7. What point of view does the author use in telling the story?

STUDENT ESSAY

Denial

At first reading Wolfgang Borchert's story about an old couple and a few slices of bread seems trivial, especially when cast against the mass murder and suffering of the Second World War. But by focusing on this small incident, Borchert is able to create a tightly focused drama that explores the toll hunger and deprivation can take on a person's character, morality, and self respect.

More pointedly, Borchert's story is a study in denial, demonstrating the defense mechanisms people employ to protect themselves from something too painful to acknowledge.

"The Bread" presents a classic case of what current psychologists call "enabling." Awakened by a noise, a woman enters the kitchen and discovers clear evidence that her husband has cut a slice of bread, stealing food from her. Her husband, whom she knows is lying, offers a childishly clumsy explanation, claiming to be investigating a noise in the dark.

Instead of confronting her husband, the wife changes the subject, abruptly scolding him for not wearing shoes. When her husband haltingly explains that he heard a noise, she quickly agrees, enabling his deception. To leave the scene of the crime—the kitchen with its signs of his betrayal—she urges him to come to bed. Even when she hears him chewing the stolen bread, she remains silent.

In helping him lie, in going along and playing dumb, the wife is masking her pain and anger. It is a form of denial, a way of wishing this theft not to be true. This behavior is common in spouses who discover their partners are unfaithful or parents who encounter a child's drug abuse. The wife certainly must feel betrayed on many levels.

First, her husband was stealing food from her. Suffering severe hunger, he evidently did not ask for more bread or even discuss it with her. Instead, he stole. Second, when caught, he did not admit his guilt but lied. She must feel anger at this betrayal and perhaps disgust at his weakness, his inability control his hunger and his failure to muster the courage to tell the truth and apologize.

The wife's final gesture is a wordless confrontation, letting her husband know that she is aware of his theft. Guilt-stricken, her husband cannot look her in the eye and asserts that she needs to eat more than two slices. The wife lies, claiming to have digestion problems. Her inability to sit at the table, however, reveals the extent of her anger. After decades of life together, the couple can only communicate with shared acts of deception.

Borchert's point is that hunger will drive one to steal from a loved one, to break the trust and love that held a couple together for almost forty years.

Questions for Review and Writing

1. What is the student's thesis? Is it clearly stated?
2. Does the student provide enough support from the story?
3. The student introduces a psychological term. Is it suited to this essay? Should it be better explained?
4. Do any passages need expansion? Are there needless details that should be deleted?
5. How would you improve this commentary? Do you have an alternative interpretation of the woman's final gesture?

WRITING ABOUT POETRY

Poetry is a literary form many students find challenging to analyze. You can compare poems to paintings. Unlike the sweep of fiction, which offers a movielike flow of events, a poem usually captures a scene, a moment, or a mood, like a painting or still photograph. Some poems are narratives and can be analyzed almost like a short story. Other poems, much like impressionist or abstract paintings, offer images and statements that resist literal interpretations.

STRATEGIES for Writing about Poetry

1. **Read the poem aloud.** Poems rely on subtle relationships between words and meanings. You may find it easier to understand the patterns and language devices the poet uses by hearing the way the poem sounds. Read difficult lines several times, emphasizing different words.
2. **Use peer review.** Ask other students or friends about their understanding or interpretation of a poem, line, or image.
3. **Prewrite by writing a prose summary if possible.** Put the meaning or basic action of the poem in your own words. This may help you identify the literal meaning of the poem as well as topics for writing.
4. **Review the rhyme, meter, and form of the poem.** Notice how the cadence of words affects the poem's meaning.
5. **Look up key words in a dictionary.** Words may have subtle meanings or associations you may be unfamiliar with. Because poems are brief, almost every word is significant.

Richard Cory

Whenever Richard Cory went down town,   1
We people on the pavement looked at him:
He was a gentleman from sole to crown,
Clean favored, and imperially slim.

And he was always quietly arrayed,   2
And he was always human when he talked;
But still he fluttered pulses when he said,
"Good-morning," and he glittered when he walked.

And he was rich—yes, richer than a king—   3
And admirably schooled in every grace:
In fine, we thought that he was everything
To make us wish that we were in his place.

So on we worked, and waited for the light,   4
And went without the meat, and cursed the bread;
And Richard Cory, one calm summer night,
Went home and put a bullet through his head.

Questions for Analysis

1. What kind of person is Richard Cory? What attitude does the narrator
   have toward him?
2. The narrator refers to himself or herself as representing the "people on
   the pavement." What kind of people would they be?
3. What does this poem say about wealth and envy?
4. What impact does the final line have? What does it leave unanswered or
   unexplained?

STUDENT PAPER

One Calm Summer Night: Contrast and Irony in Robinson's "Richard Cory"

"Richard Cory" endures as one of the most memorable and widely anthologized American poems, largely because of its surprise ending. The "lesson" of the poem—that you can't judge a book by its cover—is quite simple but so powerfully stated that it makes a profound impression on most readers. Robinson uses contrast and irony in both content and form to maximize the impact of the unexpected and unexplained suicide of his admired protagonist.

First, there is the ironic contrast of Richard Cory's wealth and his eventual suicide. The title character is handsome, slim, wealthy, elegant, yet "always human." The poem, told from the standpoint of the "people on the pavement," celebrates Richard Cory as someone who embodies everything people admire. Cory, though wealthy and aristocratic, appears modest and graceful. Although poor, the townspeople do not resent Cory's wealth. Like a celebrity, Cory has the power to flutter their pulses by simply acknowledging their presence when he passes them on the street. Working, waiting for the light, living without meat, these common people continue with their pedestrian lives while on a calm summer night the admired Cory shoots himself. Seeing his wealth and grace only from a distance, Cory's poor admirers had no knowledge of his inner life, no hint of the turmoil or depression that led him to commit suicide.

Second, the impact of the poem is heightened by the contrast between syntax and subject matter. In telling the story of a suicide, Robinson writes in the unadorned language of a children's poem. The lines read easily in the simple hum drum pattern and flow of a Mother Goose rhyme. The sing-song effect of the poem makes the violent ending unexpected. In addition, the tone and mood of the poem is largely positive and cheerful. The royal connotations of words describing Cory—"king," "imperially," and "crown"—all contrast with the despair and desperation associated with suicide. All these elements work to create a stunning and memorable ending, making both townspeople and readers perplexed by the mystery of Cory's suicide.

Questions for Review and Writing

1. What is the student's thesis?
2. Does the student provide enough detail from the poem to support the thesis?
3. How do you interpret the poem's meaning?
4. Robinson entitled the poem with the protagonist's name. Would a more descriptive title give the end away and weaken the impact of the last line?
5. The reasons for Cory's suicide are never explained. What is Robinson's point?
6. How would you improve or expand this student's analysis?

WRITING EXERCISE

Read the following poem, and then write a short analysis of its meaning, structure, or imagery.

My Life Had Stood—A Loaded Gun—

My Life had stood—a Loaded Gun—
In Corners—till a Day
The Owner passed—identified—
And carried Me away—

And now We roam in Sovereign Woods—
and now We hunt the Doe—
And every time I speak for Him—
The Mountains straight reply—

And do I smile, such cordial light
Upon the Valley glow—
It is as a Vesuvian face
Had let its pleasure through—

And when at Night—Our good Day done—
I guard my Master's Head—
'Tis better than the Eider-Duck's
Deep Pillow—to have shared—

To foe of His—I'm deadly foe—
None stir the second time—
On whom I lay a Yellow Eye—
Or an emphatic Thumb—

Though I than He—may longer live
He longer must—than I—
For I have but the power to kill,
Without—the power to die—
                                        —*Emily Dickinson*

WRITING ABOUT DRAMA

Although most plays relate a narrative with a strong emphasis on plot and character development, they differ from stories and novels because the events must be presented through dialogue. If you are unaccustomed to reading plays, you can easily become lost in the interplay between characters.

STRATEGIES | for Writing about Drama

1. **Study the set and character descriptions.** Read and review the opening descriptions of each character so you can easily identify each one.
2. **Review the playwright's biography, other works, or information about the time and place.** If you know something about the writer's concerns or the setting of the play, you may be able to more easily identify key themes or appreciate subtle details.
3. **Visualize the set and actors.** Plays are meant to be seen, not read. Study the set descriptions and imagine what the stage would look like. Is this a living room, warehouse, nightclub, or battlefield? Would it be darkly or brilliantly lit? Does the background suggest a conflict with or between the characters? After reading descriptions of the characters, imagine the actor or actress who might play the part. If you can imagine faces instead of names, you can more easily follow the plot and understand the interplay between characters.

4. **Read important lines aloud.** Hearing the words of a protagonist's final speech can bring the text to life and help you appreciate the impact it would have on a live audience.
5. **Study the structure of the play.** Plays are usually divided into acts and scenes, many of which end with an important turn of events, revelation, or conflict. Focus on the way each act ends.

WRITING EXERCISE

Read this scene from Clifford Odets's 1935 play *Paradise Lost* and write a short analysis of one of the following: the conflict between characters, the exposition of the plot, the struggle between the two partners, or the author's implied message.

Background: *Paradise Lost* follows the decline of a middle-class family. The protagonist, Leo Gordon, is a small manufacturer who has mortgaged his house to keep his struggling business afloat. A deeply moral man, he has increased wages for his impoverished workers, unaware that his partner of twenty years has been embezzling funds. In this scene, his partner, Sam Katz, has brought home a professional arsonist, hoping to convince Gordon to set fire to their business to collect the insurance money. The arsonist, Mr. May, speaks with a slight Swedish accent and is described as a neatly dressed man carrying an umbrella and briefcase.

Sam: I brought May on a little business.
May: There you got it in a nutshell, Mr. Gordon. Assimilated: business!
Leo: What kind of business?
May: (May *has the quality of apricot cordial*): Well, there is a historical perspective in these things. Delicate!
Leo: What?
Sam: Delicate!
May: For these last three years I handled upward of fifty-three cases. Some of them will pay as triflin' a fee as two hundred dollars. These are cheap jobs—adulterated, what we call. (*Hastily adds*): But don't misunderstand, no prices now. The recommendation is purely suggestive, what we call. (*Leans back with satisfaction. Sam waits with bated breath. Leo does not understand a word of the speech.*)

Leo: (*finally*): I see, but what is your business?

May: (*leaning forward*): You don't ever know who's listening, do you?

Leo: Listening to what?

May: Mr. Gordon. Tell the truth—you're a puzzled gent.

Leo: If you don't mind my saying . . .

May: Business with us is what we call purely a state of mind. You take the average small manufacturer. He pays his bills on the first of the month. Right? (*Answers himself.*) Right! (*Again lowers voice.*) Suppose when the first comes, he can't pay. What then?

Leo: (*after waiting for the answer*): Yes . . . ?

May: Won't it make a state of mind?

Leo: Without doubt.

May: "Without doubt!" The manufacturer will not sleep! Won't eat! Irritation in the business and at home. The wife who is often a thing of beauty, he hits her! In this condition the respected citizen makes a werry foolish mistake. Some charlatan will sell him headache pills.

Sam: (*in an outburst*): But a smart man—!

May: (*chiding* Sam *gently before continuing to* Leo): Mr. Katz! . . . But the man of sensitivity, does he leave unturned the rare gold and silver of experience? Does he? No! Six feet away stands the safe. A certain drawer within those swinging doors. Therein he finds what we call "insurance policy." Protection against theft . . . against fire, Mr. Gordon . . . (*Leans back again.*)

Leo: Fire . . . ?

May: Purely suggestive . . . (*Waits for* Leo, *who first looks to* Sam, *and then begins to scrape crumbs with his fingers.*) Yes, you guessed it: Should the respected citizen take aspirins? (Leo *continues to shovel nutshells together. The two watch him closely. Finally* Leo *says*):

Leo: Your profession is making fires?

May: Incorrect! No! (*Suddenly throws orange from table to* Leo.) See how quick you catched it? Not a thought in your head and you catched it! Fires happen like that.

Leo: In the last three years you made fifty fires—*happen*?

May: Fifty-three.

Leo: Human life is not important?

May: (*with flashing pride*): Nobody was burned—*ever*! (Leo *slowly replaces the orange.*) Don't be afraid, Mr. Gordon. In every case—

Leo: (*quietly, trembling*): Please leave my house.

Sam: Don't be in such a hurry, Leo.

May: Everything has a first time, my friend. The respected citizen . . .

Leo: Please leave!

May: Don't take umbrage, my friend. Tomorrow's another day. Here's my card—Edgar F. May. (*Places card on table.*) Purely suggestive . . .

Leo: (*shouting*): Get out of here!!

Sam: Don't insult humanity with your ignorance!!

May: No, he's right. It's his prerogative in his own house. (*Puts his glasses in their case now.*)

Sam: (*bitterly*): Any day now he won't have a house!

May: (*at the door*): Remember . . . May—between April and June— May. Good night . . .

Literary Paper Checklist

Before submitting a literary paper, review these points:

✔ Have you selected a work that is appropriate for the assignment?

✔ Does your paper *analyze* or only *summarize* a literary work?

✔ Does your paper focus on a specific element of the work, such as the imagery, structure, character development, or plot—or does it attempt to explain everything the writer presents?

✔ Is the thesis clearly stated and supported by details taken from the text?

✔ Do you avoid reading passages out of context?

For Further Reading

Barnet, Sylvan. *A Short Guide to Writing about Literature.*

Callaghan, Patsy, and Ann Dobyns. *Literary Conversation: Thinking, Talking, and Writing about Literature.*

Frye, Northrop. *The Educated Imagination.*

Griffith, Kelley. *Writing Essays about Literature: A Guide and Style Sheet.*

Kurata, Marilyn Jane. *Models and Methods for Writing about Literature.*

McMahan, Elizabeth, Robert Funk, and Susan Day. *The Elements of Writing about Literature and Film.*

Meyer, Michael. *Thinking and Writing about Literature.*

Proffitt, Edward. *Reading and Writing about Literature: Fiction, Poetry, Drama, and the Essay.*
Roberts, Edgar. *Writing Essays about Literature: A Guide and Style Sheet.*

E-Sources

Writing about Literature
> **http://owl.english.purdue.edu/handouts/general/gl_lit.html**

Literature
> **http://www.unc.edu/depts/wcweb/handouts/literature.html**

Poetry Explications
> **http://www.unc.edu/depts/wcweb/handouts/poetry-explication.html**

Drama
> **http://www.unc.edu/depts/wcweb/handouts/drama.html**

 ## Companion Website

See **http://www.thomsonedu.com/english/sundance** for additional information about writing about literature.

The Research Paper

29

CONDUCTING RESEARCH

> The research paper is, in the fullest sense, a discovery and an education that leads you beyond texts, beyond a library, and encourages you to investigate on your own.
>
> —Audrey J. Roth

WHAT IS RESEARCH?

The words *research paper* on a syllabus can instill anxiety and dread. Perhaps you found writing term papers in high school a frustrating and time-consuming chore. Even if you received good grades in the past, you may feel wholly unprepared for the level of work expected in college. For most students research papers imply endless hours spent locating sources, photocopying articles, downloading databases, taking notes, selecting facts, organizing quotations, writing, and rewriting—all while trying to remember when to use endnotes.

Your ability to write effective research papers will greatly determine your success in college. In some courses the research project accounts for more than half the final grade. Instructors assign research papers because, unlike objective tests, they measure your ability to solve problems, apply knowledge, gather evidence, and interpret data.

Learning how to write a good research paper will not only improve your academic performance but sharpen the critical thinking skills needed in most careers. Although few people write traditional research papers once they leave college, almost every professional uses the same methods to produce annual reports, market studies, product evaluations, proposals, and letters. Executives, administrators, attorneys, entrepreneurs, and scientists must base their decisions and recommendations on information. The ability to locate accurate sources, evaluate evidence, and interpret findings is essential for success in any field.

Common Misconceptions

Before undertaking a research paper, it is important to understand what a research paper is *not*. Many students work very hard collecting material and writing pages of text only to receive low grades because the paper they produce fails to meet the instructor's requirements. Even students who do well on research papers often make the project more burdensome and time-consuming than necessary.

A research paper is not a summary of everything you can find about your topic.   The goal in writing a research paper is not to present a collection of facts and quotations "about" a topic but to state a clear thesis supported by evidence. Although it is important to survey information, using twenty sources instead of ten will not necessarily improve the quality of your paper. The goal of a research paper is to present carefully selected evidence that supports your thesis.

A research paper does not simply repeat what others have written.   A research paper is more than a string of related quotations and summaries. Research writers not only collect evidence but also evaluate and interpret it. The focus of a research paper is your thesis and commentary—not pages of text you have cut and pasted from the Internet.

A research paper does not merely support a preconceived point of view. Honest research begins with a topic or question. You should only reach a conclusion and develop a thesis after carefully examining the evidence. Taking the ideas of others out of context to support your position on abortion or the death penalty is not research.

A research paper does not include the ideas of others without documentation.   Including the ideas and words of others in your text without attribution is plagiarism. Whenever you add facts, quotations, and summaries of outside sources, you must identify them (see Chapter 30).

CONDUCTING RESEARCH: AN OVERVIEW

Writing a research paper can be made less intimidating and less arduous if you break the process into key steps:

- Understand the scope of the assignment.
- Select an appropriate topic.

- Conduct preliminary research.
- Limit the topic and develop a working thesis.
- Create a timeline.
- Collect and evaluate relevant evidence.

Understand the Scope of the Assignment

Even when instructors allow students to select topics themselves, most still provide directions or guidelines that outline the scope of the assignment. Students may be required to use a certain number of sources, present evidence in a specific manner, or address a particular issue:

> Write an eight- to ten-page research paper using APA documentation that compares past and present treatments of a common psychological disorder. Your sources must include at least two professional interviews.

> Analyze a critical theme, character, or technique used by the author of one of the works we have studied in this class. Do not summarize the work or repeat what you may have presented in your oral report. Your paper should be six to eight pages long, include a minimum of three electronic sources, and documented in MLA style.

> Select a noted trial, Supreme Court decision, or scandal and examine its lasting impact on the law, American institutions, or perceptions of justice. Your paper should be ten pages long and documented in APA style.

- **It is important to fully understand all the requirements of an assignment and refer to them throughout the process.** Perhaps the most common mistake students make is failing to address the needs of the assignment. Once you begin looking up sources and examining data, you can be easily led astray and write a paper that is interesting but fails to meet the instructor's requirements. The psychology student writing about schizophrenia may be impressed by some recent medical articles and write a thorough research paper outlining genetic factors. Although it may be well written and properly documented, if it fails to draw a comparison between past and present treatments and does not include interviews, the paper may be wholly unacceptable.
- **Ask your instructor for clarification of any points you find confusing.** If your instructor does not supply handouts, take careful notes to record specific requirements and directions. If your instructor does not assign topics, you may wish to ask for suggestions. Ask your instructor which topics to avoid.
- **Make copies of any instructor handouts or notes and keep them next to your computer or in your backpack or briefcase for quick reference.**

Refer to these guidelines when visiting the library or searching the Internet. Make sure your research remains focused on sources that address the needs of the assignment.

Select an Appropriate Topic

The first step in writing a research paper is selecting a topic or topics. Until you begin collecting evidence, you may not be sure if the subjects you start with are workable. Often, subjects that you might find interesting at first become unmanageable because sources are lacking or too numerous to handle.

STRATEGIES | for Selecting a Topic

1. **Select a topic that matches the assignment.** If your instructor requires you to include personal interviews, you may find it difficult to locate people who can provide insights on highly specialized issues. You may find local mental health professionals or volunteers who can tell you about depression, addiction, or mental illness among the homeless. But it may be difficult to locate anyone with knowledge of multiple-personality disorder.
2. **Select a topic that interests you.** If you don't really care about your subject, you may find it difficult to sustain a long research effort. If you choose a topic that you have little knowledge about, you will have to conduct extensive background research. Brainstorm to discover whether your existing knowledge and experiences apply to the assignment. Discuss possible topics with your instructor or friends and ask for suggestions.
3. **Consider your long-term goals.** Writing a research paper offers an opportunity to explore issues and subjects related to personal and career goals. Many doctoral dissertations and business proposals began as research projects. In addition to fulfilling a course requirement, your research may help shape your career goals or locate information that you can use in your job or business. Just make sure that your personal interests do not conflict with the goals of the assignment —refer to the instructor's guidelines to keep your project on track.
4. **Select a topic that is flexible.** Until you begin researching, you cannot tell how much information is readily available. Think of your topic as an accordion, something that may have to be compressed or expanded.

5. **Be willing to alter or reject topics.** Your first topic is only a starting point. If you find it difficult to work with, drop it and select another. Do not feel obligated to stick with something unless required by your instructor. Use such prewriting techniques as clustering, brainstorming, and asking questions to develop new approaches to your topic.

6. **Select more than one topic to start.** At this point no decision is final. Until you begin investigating ideas, you may not know whether a topic will be suitable. If you are unsure which topic to pursue, sketch out two or three for preliminary research.

Topics to Avoid

Difficulties commonly arise from the following kinds of topics, which are often best avoided altogether.

- **Topics that rely on a single source.** Research papers coordinate information from several sources. If you select an event covered in one news story or a process explained by a single set of instructions, you will not be able to achieve a major goal of a research paper. Check with your instructor if you are interested in a topic with only a single source.

- **Highly controversial topics—unless you can develop a new approach.** It is unlikely you can write anything about capital punishment or abortion that has not already been stated—unless you look at the issue from a unique perspective. You might research murder rates, comparing states with or without the death penalty, or examine Islamic views on abortion. Controversial subjects may be difficult to research because many of the sources are biased. Discuss your topic with your instructor and ask for recommended approaches or alternative subjects.

- **New topics.** Issues raised by events that have just happened may be difficult to research because little has been published except news reports and fragmentary comments. A quick Internet search might locate the amount of reliable material currently available.

- **Topics lacking credible sources.** Conducting research about UFOs, psychic phenomena, and alternative medicine can be difficult because sources may be anecdotal and unscientific. Avoid "conspiracy"-related issues. By their nature, these topics resist objective investigation. A reference librarian can suggest sources or a new topic.

- **Popular topics.** Like writing about a controversial topic, it may be difficult to find something new to say about an issue many students have written

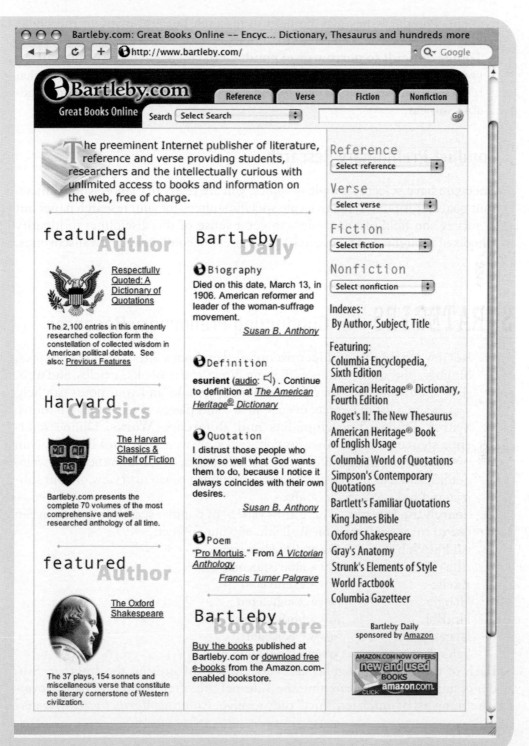

about. Popular issues may be hard to research because many of the books may already be checked out of the library.

■ **Topics difficult to narrow or expand.** Until you begin discovering sources, you will not know how complex your task will be. If you select a topic that resists alterations, you may be forced to reject it in favor of a more manageable subject.

Conduct Preliminary Research

Once you have selected a topic or topics, you are ready to explore your subject. Your goal at this point is not to locate specific sources for your research paper but to survey the field of knowledge, to get a sense of the discipline, to identify schools of thought, and to research trends, areas of conflict, and new discoveries.

STRATEGIES | for Conducting Preliminary Research

1. **Review textbooks and lecture notes.** Textbooks often include endnotes, bibliographies, and footnotes that can direct you to books, articles, and websites about specific issues. In addition, textbooks and your notes can help you create a list of people, events, ideas, and places to use as search terms.

2. **Search Online Encyclopedias and Reference Works.** Online reference sources, such as Answers.com (www.answers.com) and Bartleby.com (www.Bartleby.com), offer online dictionaries, cross-referenced encyclopedias, and lists of websites that can provide a broad overview of your subject and links to specific sources.

3. **Search the Internet.** There are a variety of popular search engines you can use to survey information available on your subject:

AllTheWeb	www.alltheweb.com
AltaVista	www.altavista.com
Excite	www.excite.com
Google	www.google.com
HotBot	www.hotbot.com
Lycos	www.lycos.com
Yahoo!	www.yahoo.com

   Each of these search engines accesses millions of sites on the Internet. Students unfamiliar with searching the Internet are often frustrated by the overwhelming list of unrelated "hits" they receive. Entering *Martin Luther King* may generate a list of thousands of websites about Billy *Martin, Martin Luther,* and *King* George III.

Search engines provide tools to narrow your search. To use these tools efficiently, keep the following suggestions in mind:

- Check the spelling of search terms, especially names.
- Make search terms as specific as possible.
- Put quotation marks around search words or phrases. Entering "Leopold and Loeb" will locate only documents containing this phrase, eliminating documents about King Leopold or Loeb Realty. See page 738 for a sample Internet search using "Leopold and Loeb".
- Use Boolean Search Operators AND, OR, NOT.
  Entering *Orwell* AND *Nature* locates sites containing both terms.
  Entering *Orwell* NOT *Nature* excludes sites containing the second term.
  Entering *Orwell* OR *Nature* locates sites containing either term.
- Check to be sure information is up-to-date by entering **javascript:alert (document.lastModified)** in the Internet Explorer Box from the page you want to check. A dialog box will pop up that indicates the date and time of the latest update for that page.
- Take advantage of subject directories, offered by many search engines, such as Yahoo! and AltaVista. Surveying the subject categories related to your preliminary topic may help you search more efficiently.

4. **Review specialized encyclopedias, dictionaries, and directories.** A general encyclopedia, such as the *Encyclopedia Britannica* can offer only brief commentaries on subjects and will not include minor people, events, or subjects. The reference room of your library is likely to have specialized encyclopedias that may offer substantial entries:

Art
Encyclopedia of World Art
The Oxford Companion to Art

Biography
Who's Who in the World
Contemporary Authors

Business/Economics
Dictionary of Banking and Finance
Encyclopedia of Economics

Education
Encyclopedia of Education
The International Encyclopedia of Education

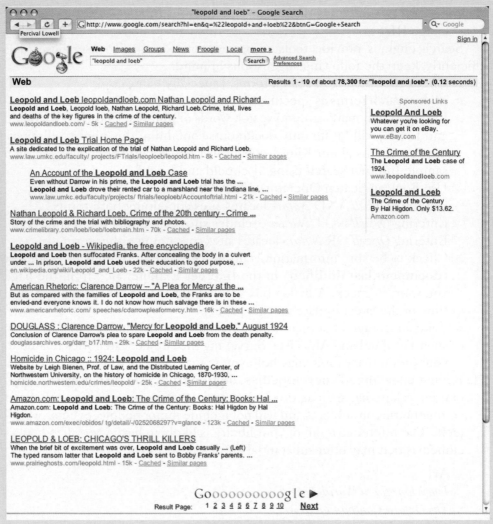

Google search using "Leopold and Loeb".

© 2006 Google

Engineering
The Engineering Index
Information Sources in Engineering

History
Dictionary of American History
Dictionary of Historical Terms
An Encyclopedia of World History

Sample website from "Leopold and Loeb" search.   © 2006 Scott A. Newman

Literature/Film
Cassell's Encyclopedia of World Literature
The Oxford Companion to American Literature

Music
Dictionary of Musical Technology
The New Oxford History of Music

Philosophy
The Concise Encyclopedia of Western Philosophy and Philosophers
Encyclopedia of Philosophy

Political Science
The Blackwell Encyclopedia of Political Thought
Encyclopedia of American Political History

Psychology
Dictionary of Psychology
Encyclopedia of Human Behavior

Religion
The New Catholic Encyclopedia
The Encyclopedia of American Religions

Science/Technology
Dictionary of Mathematics
Encyclopedia of Medical History

Social Sciences
Dictionary of Anthropology
Encyclopedia of Crime and Justice

5. **Review indexes, databases, and abstracts.** Available in print, online, or on CD-ROM, these are valuable tools in conducting research. Databases list articles. Many provide abstracts that briefly summarize articles, usually in a single paragraph. Still other databases are especially useful because they include the entire article in addition to abstracts. If the complete text is available, you may download and save the file for later reading and note taking. Skimming abstracts allows you to quickly review a dozen articles in the time it would take to locate a magazine and find a single article. Abstracts not only list the source of the full article but also indicate its length and special features, such as photographs or tables. Such sources as *Chemical Abstracts*, *Psychological Abstracts*, and *Criminal Justice Abstracts* provide summaries in specific disciplines.

Sample Abstract from *Expanded Academic Index*

Database: Expanded Academic Index

Subject: aids (disease) in motion pictures

Title   TV Movies of the first decade of AIDS (American Values and Images)

Magazine   Journal of Popular Film and Television, Spring 1993 v 21 n 1 p19 (8) (indicates this is an eight-page article)

Authors   Author: Frank Pilipp and Charles Shull

Summary   Abstract: The decade of 1983–1993 has produced several full-length feature films which respond to the AIDS epidemic. Three of them, 'As Is,' 'Andre's Mother,' and 'An Early Frost' undoubtedly portray the virus as non-partisan when it comes to gender, color, or sexual orientation, although they fail to destroy the image of AIDS as being a purely homosexual disease. The disease instead is viewed as punishment inflicted on the main characters and their families for their violation of middle-class norms and values.

Listings for
related
articles

Subjects: Gays—portrayals, depictions,etc.

Motion pictures—criticism, interpretation, etc.

AIDS (disease) in motion pictures—criticism, interpretation, etc.

Features: illustration; photograph

AN: 14558418

Some common online indexes and databases include:

ABC Political Science
ABI/Inform
Academic Search
Art Index
Associations Unlimited
Biography & Genealogy Master Index
Business Abstracts
Business Newsbank
CARL UnCover
Contemporary Authors
Dissertation Abstracts
Education Index
ERIC
General Science Index
Historical Abstracts
Humanities Index
Masterplots
Medline
MLA Bibliography
National Criminal Justice Reference Service
Newspaper Abstracts
Psychological Literature
Reader's Guide Abstracts
Sociological Abstracts
Women's Resources International

e-research activity

Exploring Preliminary Research Online

Explore the sources available online or at your library.

1. Search answers.com (http://www.answers.com) for articles on the following topics. Scroll through the entire article to locate cross references and links.

Chicago	Leopold and Loeb	plagiarism
George Orwell	General Motors	global warming

2. Search the Internet for websites on the same topics using one or more of the following search engines:

www.google.com	www.altavista.com	www.yahoo.com
www.hotbot.com	www.excite.com	www.alltheweb.com

   Follow the search engine's directions to focus your search and reduce the number of unrelated sites.

3. Examine the list of online databases available in your library.

4. Search a business database for a company you have worked for or done business with (such as Taco Bell, Coca-Cola, Home Depot, Bath and Body, or Proctor and Gamble).

5. Use Medline to generate a list of articles about a medical problem you or a family member has experienced (for example, carpal tunnel syndrome, diabetes, or arthritis).

6. Use a general database, such as Reader's Guide, InfoTrac, or Infoseek, to obtain a list of recent articles on one or more of the following topics:

caffeine	federal witness protection program
Alzheimer's disease	high-definition television
Denzel Washington	Hubble Space Telescope

7. Using one of the articles you identified in Research Activity 1, save the file to a disk and then print a hard copy of the first page of the text.

8. Send the file you created in Research Activity 2 as an e-mail attachment to your own e-mail address for later retrieval. This method might be necessary if you locate an article on a database but have no way to save the file.

A Note on Conducting Preliminary Research

Remember, your goal at this point is to simply survey the field, to get an overall feel for your subject. Don't get bogged down with details or allow yourself to become overwhelmed by the complexity or number of sources.

- Determine whether there is sufficient material on your subject to work with.
- Look for ways to limit your topic.
- Identify patterns in the data—conflicting points of view, clusters of related articles, key figures or authors, current theories, or research trends.
- Allow sources to direct you to new topics or new approaches to your subject.

Continually refer to your instructor's guidelines to keep your search on track.

Limit the Topic and Develop a Working Thesis

After surveying the field of knowledge, consider whether your topic is worth pursuing. If you cannot find enough material or if the sources are too diverse or scattered, you may wish to consider a new subject. In most instances, the preliminary material you have located may help you further limit your topic.

Orwell's *Nineteen Eighty-Four*
Loss of Freedom Predicted by Orwell in *Nineteen Eighty-Four*
Role of Technology in Orwell's *Nineteen Eighty-Four*
Orwell and the Loss of Nature in *Nineteen Eighty-Four*

Famous Trials
Role of Media in High Profile Trials
Leopold and Loeb Case
Role of the Press in the Leopold and Loeb Case

Asking questions can help target your paper and prevent you from simply summarizing the work or the ideas of others:

What effect does the loss of nature have on humanity in *Nineteen Eighty-Four*?

Did media coverage affect the outcome of the Leopold and Loeb case?

At this point you may be able to develop a working thesis, a starting point for your research paper. Although it may be general and subject to change, the working thesis moves beyond a narrowed topic or question to make a tentative statement:

Orwell considered contact with nature essential to individual liberty.

Excessive media coverage influenced the outcome of the Leopold and Loeb case.

A working thesis is a tentative statement subject to change. A working thesis is a tool to guide your research; keep an open mind and be willing to alter your opinion.

Create a Timeline

When you write an essay examination, it is important to keep your eye on the clock to avoid running out of time and leaving critical questions unanswered. Similarly, when you begin a long research project, it is important to carefully budget your time and resources. In developing a long paper, make sure you devote enough time for each stage in the writing process. Don't spend six weeks gathering materials and try to write, revise, edit, and proofread a ten-page paper over a weekend.

- **Note the due date and work backward to create a schedule that allows sufficient time for each stage in the writing process.**

May 10	Paper due
May 5	Target date for completion
May 1	Final draft prepared for final editing and proofreading
April 25	Second draft completed
April 15	First draft completed for revision and rewriting
April 10	Final outline completed, final thesis
April 5	Research completed and sources selected
March 15	Topic narrowed, working thesis, and research initiated
March 10	Topic selected and preliminary research started
March 5	Research project assigned

- **Chart your progress on a calendar to keep on track.**
- **Establish cutoff dates for major stages in the process.** If you cannot find enough material by a fixed date, talk with your instructor and consider changing topics. If you find too much material, narrow your topic.
- **Don't allow the research stage to expand past a specific date.** Keep the scope of the assignment and the length of the paper in mind to guide the quantity of material you collect. The advent of the photocopier and the Internet have made it too easy to copy and print more articles than you may need.

Collect and Evaluate Relevant Evidence

The type of evidence you will need to support your thesis will depend on the discipline, the topic, and the scope of the assignment. There are two kinds of sources: primary and secondary. Primary sources are original documents and observations and include works of art, such as novels, poems, and plays; historical documents; letters; diaries; autobiographies; speeches; interviews; raw data, such as polls or observations of experiments; eyewitness testimony; and photographs of events. Secondary sources are interpretations of primary sources and include literary criticism, commentaries, biographies, analytical studies, reviews, and editorials. You may use only primary or secondary sources or a combination. A literary paper might focus on a novel (primary source) and include biographical material about the author and critical interpretations (secondary sources). An economics paper on a recent market trend may examine stock market statistics (primary sources) and comments by experts (secondary sources).

How to Locate Library Sources

Large university libraries may have their collections separated by discipline or department. Look for maps or guides to locate materials. Though the books may be arranged on different floors or even in different buildings on your campus, all libraries will use either the Library of Congress or Dewey Decimal system. Libraries organize books, magazines, videos, and other sources by *call numbers*. Call numbers are standard. *The Grapes of Wrath*, for example, will have the same Library of Congress call number in the Boston College Library as it does at the University of New Mexico.

Library of Congress System

A	General Works
B	Philosophy/Religion
C	History/Auxiliary Sciences
D	History/Topography (except America)
E–F	America
G	Geography
H	Social Sciences (Psychology, Sociology, etc.)
J	Political Science
K	Law
L	Education
M	Music
N	Fine Arts
P	Language and Literature
Q	Science
R	Medicine
S	Agriculture
T	Technology
U	Military Science

| V | Naval Science |
| Z | Bibliography and Library Science |

Dewey Decimal System

000–099	General Works
100–199	Philosophy and Psychology
200–299	Religion
300–399	Social Science
400–499	Language
500–599	Pure Science
600–699	Technology/Applied Sciences
700–799	The Arts
800–899	Literature
900–999	History

Computerized Catalogs

Online catalogs list a library's holdings of books, magazines, videos, and other sources. The exact instructions for searching a catalog will vary slightly. Most systems provide onscreen directions to locate specific works by subject, author, or title.

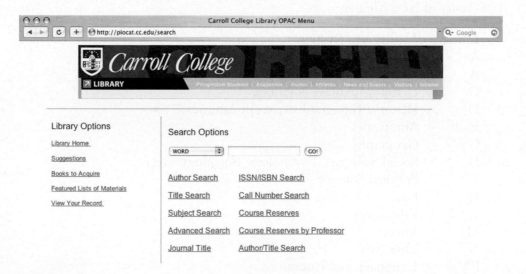

If you do not have a particular source in mind, you can enter a subject or topic:

Leopold and Loeb

LIST OF ITEMS   12 ITEMS MATCH YOUR SEARCH

	-AUTHOR-	TITLE	
ITEM			
1	Bellak, Leopold, 1916-	The schizophrenic syndrome, Leo	1967
2	Busch, Francis X	Prisoners at the bar: an accou	1952
3		Compulsion [videorecording]	1995
4	Darrow, Clarence, 1857-	Clarence Darrow pleas in defen	1926
5	Darrow, Clarence, 1857-	The plea of Clarence Darrow in	1924
6	DeFord, Miriam Allen 18	Murderers sane and mad	1965
7	Geis, Gilbert	Crimes of the century: from Leo	1998
8	Higdon, Hal	The crime of the century	1975
9	Levin, Meyer, 1905-	Compulsion--New York, Simon	1956
10	Loeb, Leo, 1869-	The venom of Heloderma	1913
11	McKernan, Maureen	The amazing crime and trial	1924
12	Vaughn, Betty Ann Erick	The forensic speaking in the	1948

By highlighting or entering the number of the source, you can access specific information about it:

AUTHOR	Higdon, Hal.
TITLE	The crime of the century : the Leopold and Loeb case / by Hal Higdon.
	New York : Putnam, [c1975]
LOCATION	College Library Main Book Collection 3rd Floor West, Room 3191
CALL NO.	HV6245 H46
STATUS	Not checked out
DESCRIPTION	380 p., [8] leaves of plates: ill; 24 cm.

NOTES   Includes index. Bibliography: p. 368

ISBN: 0399114912
OCLC NUMBER: 01801383

Once you have located the call number for a source, you can search for it in the library. Large university libraries may have collections divided by discipline or department. Look for maps or guides to locate where materials are located.

■ When you locate the book, look at the books next to it. Libraries organize books by subject, so you may find other useful titles on the same shelf.

Computerized catalogs are often linked to other libraries so you can search for sources located at other campuses or in local public libraries. They also list databases of abstracts and articles. Ask a librarian if you can access the library's databases from a remote site (for example, at home, in your dorm room, or from a laptop with Internet connection).

■ If this option is available, you may need a current user name and password to gain access.

Locating Periodicals

Libraries refer to magazines and journals as *periodicals* or *serials*. You can locate a magazine or a newspaper in the catalog or *serials holding list*. But this will simply explain where *Newsweek* or the *New York Times* is located in the building, in bound volumes, microfilm, or online. To find which articles and issues to search for, you have to consult specific databases (see pages 740–741). Databases list articles under key words. The *MLA Bibliography*, for instance, lists articles about literature and authors:

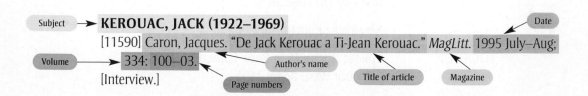

KEROUAC, JACK (1922–1969)
[11590] Caron, Jacques. "De Jack Kerouac a Ti-Jean Kerouac." *MagLitt.* 1995 July–Aug;
334: 100–03.
[Interview.]

Subject · Date · Volume · Author's name · Title of article · Magazine · Page numbers

Fiction
[11590] Oates, Joyce Carol; Dauzat, Pierre-Emmanuel, translator. "Au bout de la route."
MagLitt. 1995 July–Aug; 334: 96–99.

Letters

[11591] "Letters from Jack Kerouac to Ed White, 1947–68." *MissR.* 1994; 17(3): 107–60 [Includes letters (1947–1968) to White, Ed.]

Prose/Some of the Dharma

[11592] Sampas, John, foreword; Stanford, David, ed. and introd. *Some of the Dharma.* New York, NY: Viking; 1997. 420pp. ISBN 0-670-84877-8 [And poetry.Edition.]

Other Secondary Sources

In addition to books and periodicals, secondary sources include government documents, statistics, microfilms, audio and video recordings, photographs, and film. Your library may have special collections of artifacts not included in most databases. Depending on your topic, you may be able to obtain valuable information from corporations, organizations, federal agencies, state and local governments, or historical and professional societies.

SELECTING AND EVALUATING SOURCES

Database and Internet searches may provide you with hundreds, even thousands, of sources. Before you begin printing or photocopying, consider the type and number of sources needed. Without planning a list, you may waste a great deal of time collecting sources that may be interesting but unsuited to your paper.

STRATEGIES | for Selecting and Evaluating Sources

1. **List the types of sources needed to support your working thesis.** Review the assignment, instructor's directions, your preliminary research, and your working thesis to develop a list of needed sources:

   Working Thesis:

   Orwell considered contact with nature essential to individual liberty.

   Sources needed:

   Orwell's attitudes toward nature
   Orwell's view of technology
   Biographical commentary on Orwell's views
   Letters, essays, journals showing Orwell's views of nature and human liberty

Working Thesis:

Excessive media coverage influenced the outcome of the Leopold and Loeb case.

Sources needed:

Background/summary of Leopold & Loeb case
Biographical information of principal figures in Leopold and Loeb case
Description of press in Chicago in 1920s
Actual 1924 newspaper accounts
Assessment of effects of press on judge's decision

For a ten-page paper, you may need only one or two biographical sources—not five or six. Make sure you select enough sources for each item on your list.

2. **Collect a variety of evidence.** If you are writing a paper about the homeless, you may wish to balance personal accounts with statistics and expert opinions. A paper about *Native Son* might benefit from sources from black history or accounts of contemporary race relations in addition to critical studies of the book and biographies of Richard Wright.

3. **Avoid collecting needless or repetitive data.** The Internet has made it possible to access thousands of documents. Although it is important to grasp the sweep and range of material about your subject, avoid printing more items than you need for your paper.

   ▪ Select the most useful sources, briefly noting similar articles for confirmation.

   ▪ Refer to the assignment and your working thesis to keep your research focused.

   ▪ Skim books and long documents by examining tables of contents and indexes to measure their usefulness before checking them out.

4. **Select reliable sources.** Recognized publishers, magazines, and established databases such as MLA, West Law, and Psychological Abstracts are edited by professionals who follow established standards. Articles appearing in *The New England Journal of Medicine*, *The Harvard Law Review*, or *Nursing* have been reviewed by physicians, attorneys, and nurses. Small press publications and individual websites, however, may produce material based solely on rumor, anecdotal observation, and facts taken out of context. Do not assume that all the books in the library or sites found on the Internet are of equal value.

   ▪ Books can be evaluated by checking reviews, many of which are available online. You can also examine the author's use of sources. Does the book include a bibliography? Does the author provide endnotes and support his or her conclusions with facts, quotations, or statistics? Is the author's biography available in *Who's Who* or other databases? Does the author seem biased?

- You can get a sense of the quality of a magazine by reviewing other issues and examining the editorial staff. Determine the audience for the magazine. Publications designed for general readers, such as *Reader's Digest* or *People,* are less rigorous about checking specific facts than professional journals in law or medicine.

- Verify information you may find on the web by seeking confirming articles on established databases. Examine the server or producer of the website. Is it a professional organization, university, or government agency? Or is it a small, amateur, or personal site? Does the information seem biased or objective?

5. **Verify controversial conclusions.** A book or website might offer a striking piece of evidence or make a dramatic conclusion. Before using this material, consider the source. Was the book published by a recognized publisher? Did the article come from a biased publication? Did you find this website using an established database, such as InfoTrac or Medline, or by searching the web with a general search engine, such as Yahoo! or AltaVista?

- Review other books, articles, or material presented by this source.

- Read a periodical's editorial page for signs of obvious bias. Even the tone of a publication's advertising can indicate whether the source is biased or objective.

- Select keywords from the material and search established databases for confirmation.

- Ask a reference librarian or your instructor to assist you in evaluating sources.

6. **Distinguish between fact and opinion.** In evaluating sources it is important to separate factual data from interpretation and analysis. The author of a book, magazine article, or website might accurately report a change in oil prices but present a highly personal and subjective interpretation or prediction.

7. **Examine sources for lapses in critical thinking.** Remember that all the books, articles, and studies you discover were created by human beings who, despite their degrees or expertise, may be biased or mistaken.

- Do not assume that everything you read is accurate or true.

- Facts may be misrepresented, conclusions misguided, and alternative interpretations ignored. Review Strategies for Increasing Critical Thinking on page 49.

Evaluating Internet Sources Checklist

As you search for sources online, determine their value and reliability:

✔ **Source:** What is the domain name of the source? The URL—the site's Internet address—can help you evaluate an online source.

Domain	Source
.com	company or for profit organization
.edu	college or university
.gov	federal government
.mil	military
.net	Internet provider or individual
.ny.us	New York state government
.org	nonprofit organization or individual

Does a reputable organization sponsor the site? Is this organization likely to be impartial in its examination of the information? Does the organization benefit from persuading you to accept its position? Do you detect inflammatory language that reveals bias or prejudice?

✔ **Authorship:** Does the site mention the author or webmaster? This information is often noted at the bottom of the site's home page, but does not always appear on Internal pages. Does the author or webmaster include an e-mail address? An e-mail to the author or webmaster can yield valuable insights.

✔ **Credibility:** If you are able to identify the site's author, can you also determine whether he or she has significant knowledge about the topic? Does the site present objective information or express personal? Does the author include his or her résumé?

- To check if the author has also published books, check your library's online catalog or Amazon.com (www.amazon.com), which lists books and often includes reader reviews.

- Place the author's full name in quotation marks and use it as a search term using a search engine like Yahoo!, Google, or Alta Vista to locate biographical information.

✔ **Purpose:** Can you determine the site's intended purposes? Is the site designed to present all available evidence? Does it seem to take a side? Is the site intended to inform readers or to sell a product or service?

✔ **Audience:** Does the site expect its reader to have an opinion before visiting the site? Does the site encourage its reader to form an opinion based solely on the information presented? Or does the site invite further investigation by providing links to related sites?

✔ **Language:** Is the information presented in a manner that allows virtually any reader to understand it? Is specialized terminology included? Does its presence have a negative effect on the presentation on the general reader's comprehension?

✔ **Presentation:** Has the site been planned and designed well? Is it easy to navigate? Are the links active, current, and relevant? Does the text reflect that careful planning has been devoted to it, including thorough proofreading? Don't allow impressive graphics, sound, and video to substitute for accuracy in the information.

✔ **Timeliness:** Many sites are not dated, making it difficult to determine the currency of the information. If dates do not appear, test links to see if they are still active. Place key terms and phrases in quotations and use them as search terms using search engines, such as Yahoo!, Google, or Alta Vista, to locate determine dates and perhaps locate more recent sources.

✔ **Critical Thinking:** Do you detect errors in critical thinking, such as hasty generalizations, dependence on anecdotal evidence, faulty comparisons, false authorities, or attacking personalities? See pages 50–56.

STRATEGIES for Overcoming Problems with Research

Students frequently encounter common problems in conducting library research.

1. **There are no sources on the topic.** If your library and Internet search fails to yield sufficient results, review the subject and search words you are using.

- Check the spelling of your keywords.
- Check a thesaurus for synonyms.
- Review the Library of Congress Subject Headings for alternative search terms.
- Review textbooks, encyclopedias, and other reference sources for search terms.
- Ask a reference librarian or your instructor for suggestions.

2. **There are sources about the subject but none are related to the specific topic or working thesis.** If you are analyzing the role of the mother in *Death of a Salesman*, you may find numerous articles on the play or Willy Loman but nothing on his wife. You do not have to find articles that exactly match your topic or thesis. Because one of the goals of a research paper is originality, your thesis may address unexplored territory. You can still use related or background sources. Biographies of Arthur Miller might yield insights into the attitudes represented by Linda Loman. Critical commentaries may provide views about the Loman family that relate to Linda's role in the play.

   - Pointing out the lack of sources can be crucial in demonstrating the value of your paper and the uniqueness of your approach.

3. **Sources present conflicting findings or opinions.** Experts often disagree. Biographers and historians evaluate people and events differently. Scientists dispute theories and present different interpretations of data. Economists argue whether tax cuts would increase or decrease the national debt.

   - As a student you are not expected to resolve conflicts among experts, but you should report what you find.
   - On the basis of your evaluation of the evidence, you may side with one group or alter your thesis to conclude that at present it is impossible to make a definitive statement.

4. **There are several books and articles, but they present the same information or refer to a common original source.** If you discover that the five books you have selected about teenage suicide or a person's life present virtually the same material, select the most representative, relevant, or best-written book.

   - Although you may select only a single source, it is important to comment on the consistency of expert opinion.

5. **The only available sources are fragmentary, biased, outdated, inaccurate, or unprofessional.** In some instances the only available sources will lack substance or quality. A controversial historical incident may have

produced a rash of inflammatory editorials, biased newspaper accounts, or subjective memoirs by adversaries.

- Ask your instructor whether you should consider changing your topic.
- Consult a reference librarian for alternative sources.
- As a researcher you are not responsible for the lack of evidence or the quality of sources you can locate—but you should comment on the limited value of existing evidence.

TAKING NOTES

Traditional textbooks suggest students record notes on index cards. Placing single facts or quotations on separate cards makes it easy to shuffle and reorder them after developing an outline. Today most students photocopy or print pages and highlight selected passages. Others will scan text directly onto a computer disk. Yet another option is to download and save full-text articles from databases. Useful passages can be highlighted in bold or other colors for later incorporation into a research paper.

Whatever method you use to record information from outside sources, it is essential to accomplish three tasks:

1. **Accurately record information you will need to cite the source.**
   Books: author's full name, full title (including any subtitle), publisher, place of publication, and year.
   - If a publisher lists several cities, choose the first location listed.
   - Note editions, translators, editors, or forewords.
   Articles: author's full name, full title (including any subtitle), full title of the magazine or newspaper, edition, volume, pages, and date.
   - If you photocopy pages from a book or magazine, write the information directly on the copies for future reference.
   Motion pictures: title, director, studio, city, year of release.
   Videotape: title, director, production company, city, date of production or original broadcast.
   Electronic sources: author's (or editor's) full name, title of website or document, sponsoring organization, date you accessed the source, the full Internet address or URL—http://www.cnn.com/2005/US/12/01/new.orleans .open.ap/index.html, not simply www.cnn.com.
   - Make sure that website addresses appear on the printed version. If they do not, record the information.

2. **Double-check your notes for accuracy.** If you take notes rather than photocopy a source, make sure that you have properly copied facts, numbers,
and names. Understand the difference between quoting and paraphrasing
sources:

Original text:

> When Robert Moses began building playgrounds in New York City, there
> were 119. When he stopped, there were 777. Under his direction, an army of
> men that at times during the Depression included 84,000 laborers reshaped
> every park in the city and then filled the parks with zoos and skating rinks,
> boathouses and tennis houses, bridle paths and golf courses, 288 tennis courts
> and 673 baseball diamonds.
>
> The Power Broker *by Robert A. Caro*

Student notecard, full direct quotation:

Robert A. Caro, <u>The Power Broker</u>. New York: Vintage, 1975.

"When Robert Moses began building playgrounds in New York City, there were
119. When he stopped, there were 777. Under his direction, an army of men
that at times during the Depression included 84,000 laborers reshaped every
park in the city and then filled the parks with zoos and skating rinks, boat-
houses and tennis houses, bridle paths and golf courses, 288 tennis courts and
673 baseball diamonds." Pg. 7

Student notecard, partial direct quotation using ellipsis (. . .) to show omitted text:

Robert A. Caro, <u>The Power Broker</u>. New York: Vintage, 1975.

"When Robert Moses began building playgrounds in New York City, there were
119. When he stopped, there were 777. Under his direction, an army of
men . . . reshaped every park in the city. . . ." Pg. 7

- In deleting details, make sure that your notes accurately reflect the
  meaning of the original text. Do not take quotations out of context
  that alter the author's point of view.

Student notecard, paraphrase, putting text into your own words:

Robert A. Caro, <u>The Power Broker</u>. New York: Vintage, 1975.

Robert Moses increased the number of New York City playgrounds from 119 to 777. During the Depression as many as 80,000 workers restored every city park, embellishing them with zoos, playgrounds, and hundreds of tennis courts and baseball diamonds. Pg. 7

Even though the student is not copying Robert Caro word for word, he or she will have to cite Caro in the research paper to acknowledge the source of the statistics.

3. **Label research materials.**
   - Make sure that you print or photocopy all the material needed. To save paper, some library printers do not automatically print the last page of an article. Make sure your copies are complete.
   - Clip or staple articles to prevent pages from becoming mixed up.
   - Label, number, or letter your sources for easy reference. You may find it useful to write notecards for some or all of your sources so that they can be easily arranged on your desk.
4. **Organize database files.**
   - For files you've downloaded from databases, consolidate them and make a back-up disk.
   - As a quick and easy reference, consolidate abstracts of the articles to form a single file that provides an overview of the items that you've identified as potentially useful.

PRIMARY RESEARCH

Conducting Interviews

Interviews allow you to collect information from professionals, eyewitnesses, and others with direct experience about your topic. Interviews, however, can be challenging to conduct and analyze.

1. **Determine whether interviews will provide useful information.** Not all subjects are conducive to interviews. You may be unable to identify a local expert on your topic. Print and electronic sources may be more useful.

- Many print articles serve as interviews because they are written by experts and eyewitnesses. In addition, in writing an article a person has the opportunity to check facts, verify recollections, and evaluate responses more carefully than in an interview.

2. **Locate backup sources if possible.** Because interviews can be difficult to arrange and subjects may have to cancel a meeting at the last moment, avoid basing your whole paper on interviews.
   - Search for print or electronic sources that can provide information needed to support your working thesis.

3. **Identify possible subjects.** You may ask your instructor or network with local organizations, corporations, and government agencies to locate people who may be willing to provide interviews.
   - Because scheduling meetings may be difficult, locate several prospects.

4. **Determine the information or insights you wish to obtain from an interview.** There is no reason to use an interview to gather background information that you can easily obtain from other sources. Conducting an interview gives you an opportunity to ask questions, to interact with a source, to ask an expert or witness to comment on other sources, or to help you locate resources you may have overlooked.

5. **Schedule interviews in advance.** Because it may be difficult to find a time and place to meet people and last-minute changes can occur, schedule interviews well in advance. If you can, offer the subject additional dates and times in case the first appointment you arrange must be postponed.

6. **Provide subjects with questions in advance.** Reporters and television interviewers usually prefer not to give people questions in advance because they seek spontaneous reactions. As a researcher, however, you are seeking information. Giving subjects a few days or a week to consider the topic of your interview may help them focus their thoughts or locate information.

7. **Ask specific questions.** An interview is not a conversation or an endless monologue. You should ask specific questions to produce comments that you can use in your paper:

   > As a director of a program for the homeless, could you say how many of the homeless suffer from mental illness?

   > What is the biggest obstacle preventing the homeless from gaining independence?

8. **Ask consistent questions.** If you are interviewing more than one subject, don't ask one person, "How many of the homeless are mentally ill?" and then ask another, "How many of the homeless are schizophrenic?" If you use conflicting terms, you will not be able to compare results.

9. **Do not tape-record the interview without permission.** For professional or legal reasons, many subjects will not allow you to tape an interview. Ask in advance whether they will permit recording.

10. **Ask how the subject wishes to be credited.** An attorney working for the U.S. Department of Labor may not wish to be viewed as speaking for the federal government. A physician may prefer not to have his or her hospital mentioned in your paper.

11. **Review the interview material with your subject to ensure accuracy.** Make sure you have accurately recorded names, facts, and statistics. Take careful notes during the interview and verify that you have accurately represented the subject's thoughts.

12. **Use the interview to verify print evidence or seek new sources.** If you have the opportunity to interview a practicing psychiatrist, you can ask him or her whether he or she is familiar with a book you have read or a new study found on the Internet. You might also ask the physician for suggested readings or other interview subjects.
    - Although you do not want a single source to heavily influence how you shape your final paper, you may wish to ask an expert to review your sources and thesis.

13. **Recognize the limits of interviews.** Interviews can be compelling because they bring you face to face with your topic. But remember, an interview presents a single person's experiences or point of view. The observations of one person may be highly individualistic and not representative of others. His or her views should be given no more weight than a book or article.

Conducting Surveys

Surveys can be used to gather specific information about a particular population or to measure that population's knowledge, beliefs, or attitudes about a particular person, issue, or problem. A sociology student researching the homeless could, for example, survey the residents of a local shelter to determine their level of education. A business student studying consumer attitudes toward Internet shopping might distribute a questionnaire to new car buyers, asking if they would consider buying a car from an online dealer.

Like interviews, surveys can be time-consuming and very challenging.

1. **Measure your ability to conduct a survey.** Surveys require time and effort to conduct as well as collect and analyze their results.
   - Will you have enough time to conduct a survey?
   - Will conducting a survey detract from your ability to search for library and online sources?

■ Will the survey reveal valuable information? Is it necessary?

■ Ask your instructor for guidance.

2. **Develop backup sources.** Determine if you can support your working thesis with other forms of evidence in case you have to terminate the survey.

■ Much of the data available in the library or online consists of surveys.

3. **Determine clearly what you are seeking to measure.** A survey should have a clear goal—for example, to assess the education level of the residents of a homeless shelter or measure the attitudes of car buyers toward online car dealers.

4. **Craft the measuring instrument carefully.** Whether surveys are conducted online, on paper, over the phone, or in personal interviews, they must use a standard instrument. Your results will only be valid if all the subjects respond to the same questions.

■ Questions or categories should be as specific as possible. If you simply ask residents of a homeless shelter if they completed high school, negative responses will include people who left school in sixth grade and those only a few credits short of a high school diploma. It would be more effective to ask respondents to record the last year of school completed or check off a box referring to a specific level of education. Asking car buyers, "Would you consider buying a car from an online dealer?" will only produce simplistic responses. More detailed questions would more adequately reflect consumer attitudes:

1. Would you consider buying a car from an online dealer?

____ Definitely ____ Possibly ____ Probably not ____ Definitely not

2. If you answered "Probably not" or "Definitely not," check the reasons for this response. Check all items that apply:

_____ Fear of revealing personal or financial information online

_____ Reluctance to deal with new or unknown businesses

_____ Loyalty to local car dealers

_____ Desire to develop personal relationship with sales staff

_____ Concern for service and warranty repair

_____ Unfamiliarity with Internet

■ Review your instrument carefully for unconscious bias. Examine your use of diction; avoid words with unintended subjective connotations.

- Do not ask "loaded questions" that prompt a desired response, such as "Should we stop wasting money on welfare?" or "Do you support the mayor's urban renewal program that will destroy the city's low income housing?"
- Use peer review to test your instrument for lapses in critical thinking, missing questions, or misleading statements.

5. **Clearly identify your subjects.** Surveys will be useful only if the population being evaluated is clearly defined. Who will you consider homeless—long-term residents of a shelter, or those seeking refuge for a single night? How will you determine who is a "car buyer"?

6. **Determine how to conduct the survey.** You can conduct a series of personal interviews, distribute questionnaires in person or by mail or e-mail, or contact subjects by telephone.
    - If you talk with people directly or by phone, make sure you ask the same questions in the same order. Use a standard form to record responses.
    - Distribute questionnaires in person, if possible, to standardize the time and manner respondents answer.
    - Realize that in many instances only 5 percent of people will respond to a survey. Be prepared to mail or e-mail hundreds of questionnaires to develop a useful number of responses.

7. **Develop a workable method of collecting and interpreting responses.** A sheaf of handwritten responses will be difficult and time consuming to read and interpret. Consider using forms that can be visually or electronically scanned. Many computer programs will collect, organize, and record responses to each question or survey item.

8. **Document your research methods.** Surveys have value only if you carefully record how you selected subjects, the rationale used to construct the measuring instrument, and the number of responses collected.

9. **Maintain a timeline.** Keep an eye on the calendar. You must allow sufficient time not only to conduct surveys, but to analyze results and edit and present your findings. Don't devote too much time to a single step in the process.

10. **Review Common Errors in Critical Thinking (pages 50–56) to test your methods of research and analysis.**

LOCATING AND EVALUATING VISUALS

In some assignments graphs, charts, tables, and photographs are essential sources that should be included in your paper. In other instances, you may develop your own graphics to highlight data or include your own photographs. In other courses, assignments focus primarily on text and visuals can be of limited value.

STRATEGIES | for Locating and Evaluating Visuals

1. **Determine the importance of visuals.** If visuals provide essential information, scan, download, or photocopy tables, photographs, graphs, and charts you find in print or online documents for future use.
   - Make sure you note the source of the visual.

   If visuals will only dramatize a point in your text or supply added interest to your paper, scan, download, and photocopy visuals as you come across documents but do not devote time to locating additional visuals at this point.
   - Do not spend time looking for visuals that is better spent locating text sources.

2. **Search online library galleries, educational websites, and stock photo services for images.** Libraries, educational websites, and stock photo services offer millions of commercial, historical, and news photographs, illustrations, and graphics:

   New York Public Library Digital Gallery
   > http://digitalgallery.nypl.org/nypldigital/index.cfm

   Libraryspot.com
   > http://libraryspot.com/images.htm

   Visual Resources: Photos and Clip Art
   > http://www.eduscapes.com/tap/topic20.htm

   - Study the site's search engines to narrow your search. Most sites list links and allow you to search for images in specific categories, such as historical, commercial, art, news, people, or graphics.

3. **Before selecting visuals, examine them for relevance, distortion, or bias.**
   - See Strategies for Analyzing Visual Images (pages 186–187)
   - See Strategies for Analyzing Graphics (page 192)

4. **If you take your own photographs, document the subject, location, and date for each image.**

RESEARCH ACTIVITY

1. **Use library or online sources to answer the following questions:**
   a. Where is the headquarters for B. F. Goodrich?
   b. When and where was Jack Nicholson born?

   c. Who is the current mayor of San Diego?
   d. When did Ford produce the Edsel?
   e. Who developed methadone?

2. **Create a list of sources for one of the following topics:**
   a. The construction of the Lincoln Tunnel
   b. The role of the green monkey in AIDS
   c. The 1919 World Series scandal
   d. Protecting elephant herds from ivory poachers
   e. Reviews of a current Broadway play or new motion picture

3. **Review selections in the reader section of this book to develop topics and identify sources.**
   a. Use databases or the Internet to search for information about an author.
   b. Use one of the questions following an article to develop a topic.
   c. Examine an article you have read for keywords to guide a database or online search.

Research Checklist

As you conduct your research, consider these questions:

✔ Do you fully understand the needs of the assignment? Do you know what your instructor expects in terms of topic, content, sources, and documentation?

✔ Have you narrowed your topic sufficiently to target a search for sources?

✔ Has your preliminary research given you a global view of the field? Can you detect trends or patterns in the research, prevailing theories, or conflicts?

✔ Have you developed a flexible working thesis to guide your research?

✔ Have you explored database and online sources as well as books and articles?

✔ Are you keeping the final paper in mind as you conduct research? If you sense your paper expanding beyond its target length, narrow your topic.

✔ Does the material you select accurately and fairly represent the wider spectrum of research material, or are you taking material out of context to support a preconceived thesis?

✔ Are you recording the data needed to document your sources in the final paper?

If you have difficulties locating material, ask your instructor or reference librarian for assistance.

For Further Reading

Badke, William. *The Survivor's Guide to Library Research.*
Berdie, Douglas R., et al. *Questionnaires: Design and Use.*
Converse, Jean M. *Survey Questions: Handcrafting the Standardized Questionnaire.*
Dillman, Don A. *Mail and Telephone Surveys: The Total Design Method.*
Harmon, Charles. *Using the Internet, Online Services, and CD-ROMs for Writing Research and Term Papers.*
Harnack, Andrew, and Eugene Kleppinger. *Online! A Reference Guide to Using Internet Resources.*
Roth, Audrey J. *The Research Paper: Process, Form, and Content.*
Rubin, Herbert J., and Irene S. Rubin. *Qualitative Interviewing: The Art of Hearing Data.*
Shepherd, Robert D. *Writing Research Papers: Your Complete Guide to the Process of Writing a Research Paper, from Finding a Topic to Preparing the Final Draft.*
Woodward, Jeannette A. *Writing Research Papers: Investigating Resources in Cyberspace.*

E-Sources

The Library of Congress
http://www.loc.gov
Reference Desk
http://www.ashland.edu/library/internet/refres.html
A Student's Guide to Research with the WWW
http://www.slu.edu/departments/english/research/
Critically Analyzing Information Sources
http://www.library.cornell.edu/olinuris/ref/research/skill26.htm

Companion Website

See **http://www.thomsonedu.com/english/sundance** for additional information on conducting research.

WRITING THE RESEARCH PAPER

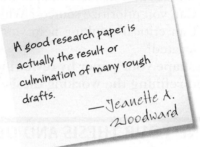

A good research paper is actually the result or culmination of many rough drafts.

—Jeanette A. Woodward

WHAT IS A RESEARCH PAPER?

The research paper is the standard method of demonstrating your skills in most college courses. Collecting data, assembling quotations, finding evidence, and developing a thesis are essential to laying the groundwork for your paper. But before you plunge into working with sources and making citations, it is important to take three preliminary steps:

1. **Review the needs of the assignment.** If you have not examined the instructor's requirements recently, refresh your memory. Study any handouts or notes you may have made.
    - Do you fully understand what is expected in terms of topic, content, sources, and format? If you are unsure, talk with your instructor.
    - Do your working thesis, sources, and notes fit the scope of the assignment? Should some sources be discarded? Should other avenues of research be pursued?
2. **Take a global look at your sources and notes.** Review the full scope of what your research has revealed. Consider the whole body of evidence you have discovered, including those items you examined but did not select.
    - What have you learned about the subject? Have you uncovered information that leads you to further narrow your topic or refine the thesis?

- Do sources contradict or disprove your assumptions? Should you re-think your point of view?
- What do the sources reveal about the state of knowledge about your topic? Is there consensus or conflict? Are there patterns in the evidence?
- How reliable are the sources? Are they based on a careful reading of the subject, thorough research, and controlled experiments, or are they biased and/or do they rely on anecdotal data?
- Are there sources that can be grouped together, such as articles by experts who share the same opinion or similar statistics? Can some sources be considered duplicates?
- Can you prioritize sources? Which are the most important?
- Can critical thinking help you analyze the value of what you have located?

3. **Reshape your paper by reviewing your topic, examining the evidence, and refining the working thesis.**

REFINE YOUR THESIS AND DEVELOP AN OUTLINE

After examining your sources, refine the thesis. If you have limited the original topic, you may need to develop a thesis that addresses the new focus of your paper. In writing shorter papers, you may have needed only a brief plan or list of ideas to guide the first draft. But in writing a research paper, it is useful to develop a full outline to organize your ideas and sources.

Working Thesis

Orwell considered contact with nature essential to individual liberty.

Revised Thesis

Winston Smith's humanity and individual autonomy are stunted not only by the brutality of Oceania and the ever-present Thought Police, but by his lack of contact with nature.

Working Outline

A working outline is a rough guide to direct your first draft. Because it is not likely to be read by anyone other than yourself, it does not have to follow any particular format. Use it as a blueprint to organize your main points and sources. (See pages 791–792 for a sample formal outline.)

    I   INTRO—Conventional readings of <u>1984</u>
       A   Simes quote
       B   Wolzheck quote

      C   Janeson quote

      D   Goodman quote

II   Transition/Thesis—Important Role of Nature Overlooked

III Unnatural/Artificial Life in Oceania
      A   "Golden Country Dream" quote (<u>1984</u> pg. 29)
      B   Smith and Julia in nature
      C   Nature and sexual passion—(<u>1984</u> quote pg. 105)

IV Nature as Orwell's Moral Gold Standard
      A   Sandison quote
      B   Letter to Henry Miller quote (<u>Collected Essays</u> 4:80)

V   Orwell's Lack of Faith in Technology
      A   Electricity quote (<u>Road</u> pg. 84)
      B   Bugs quote (<u>Road</u> pg. 71)

VI Orwell's Doubts about Progress
      A   Pleasure Spots quote (<u>Collected Essays</u> 4:80)
      B   Radio quote (<u>Collected Essays</u> 4:80)

V   Conclusion
      A   Sandison quote (pg. 10)
      B   Final Point—<u>1984</u> relevant for 21st century

Along with an outline, develop a timeline to chart your progress. Make sure you budget enough time for each stage of the writing process, including revising and editing.

STRATEGIES | for Developing an Outline

1. **Write a clear thesis statement.** The thesis is the mission statement of your paper. It should provide a clear focus for the paper and direct your first draft.
   - Use the thesis statement as a guide for selecting outside sources.
2. **Write an outline in light of your thesis and the needs of the assignment.** Make sure that your outline addresses the goals of the paper and the instructor's requirements.
3. **Don't expect that your sources will neatly fall into place like pieces of a puzzle.** In many instances, the evidence you find may be fragmentary and lead in different directions. Outline your ideas and observations, weaving into the text those sources that confirm your point of view.

4. **Use sources to support your views; don't simply summarize them.** An outline forms a skeleton or framework for the first draft. Indicate where you will place source material such as quotations, facts, or statistics.

   - Do not feel obligated to include all the sources you have located.

5. **In writing an outline, leave ample space for alterations.**

6. **Label your sources for easy reference.** You may wish to develop a short-hand reference for each source, labeling sources A, B, C or giving them descriptive names to guide your outline.

7. **Separate longer sources for use in multiple places.** If you have located a long quotation, do not feel obligated to place it in a single block of text. Instead, you may select two or three sections and distribute them throughout the paper.

   - In separating longer passages, make sure you do not distort the source's meaning by taking ideas out of context.

8. **Design an introduction that announces the topic, sets up the thesis, and prepares readers for the direction of the paper.** Because research papers can be long and complex, it is important to give readers a road map, an explanation of what will follow.

   - An introduction can present the thesis, provide a rationale for the methods of research, or comment on the nature of sources. Your introduction might explain that you will compare two writers, use public opinion polls to track attitudes on race, or limit the discussion of Nixon's presidency to his domestic policies.

   - Introductions can be used to address research problems, commenting on the lack of reliable data or conflicting opinions. Introductions can also include a justification of your approach that anticipates reader objections.

   - As in writing any paper, you will probably come up with new ideas while writing the draft. After revising the body, you may wish to rewrite the opening and closing.

9. **Organize the body by using the modes of organization.** Clear structure plays an important role in making your paper readable and convincing. Without a clear pattern of organization, your paper may become a confusing list of quotations and statistics.

   - Use modes, such as *comparison* and *division*, to organize evidence.

   - Use transitional statements and paragraph breaks to signal changes in direction.

10. **Craft a conclusion that ends the paper on a strong point rather than a simple summary of points.** Although it may be useful to review critical points at the end of a long paper, the conclusion should leave the reader with a memorable fact, quotation, or restatement of the thesis.

WRITING THE RESEARCH PAPER

Your goal in writing the first draft, as in any paper, is to get your ideas on paper. Using outside sources, however, complicates the writing process. Students often make common errors in approaching the evidence they have collected.

STRATEGIES | for Using Sources

1. **Avoid simply reporting on what you found.** The quotations, facts, and statistics you have selected should support your point of view. Avoid what some writers call the "string of pearls" effect of simply patching together outside sources with little original commentary or analysis:

   When it first opened on Broadway, *Death of a Salesman* had a great impact on audiences (Stein, 19). According to Sally Lyman, "The play captured the hidden anxiety coursing through postwar America" (17). Another critic, Timothy Baldwin, stated, "This play made the audience face its greatest fear—growing old" (98). Fred Carlson said that he walked out of the theater shaken and deeply moved (23).

   - Although outside sources may be interesting and worth quoting or paraphrasing, your ideas, interpretations, and arguments should form the basis of the paper.

2. **Explain any lack of sources.** If you select a new, unknown, or uncommon subject, there may be few sources directly supporting your thesis. Although readers might be impressed by your argument, they may question why you have not supported your ideas with evidence. An instructor may question if you thoroughly researched your topic. Commenting on the lack of sources can both demonstrate the uniqueness of your approach and justify the lack of outside sources:

   Critics of *Death of a Salesman* have concentrated on the male characters, examining Willy Loman's dreams, his relationship to Biff, his sons' conflicts. Of 125 articles published in the last four years about this play, none focus on the essential role of Linda Loman, who serves as the axis for the male conflicts in the play.

3. **Summarize conflicting opinions.** One of the responsibilities of a researcher is to fairly represent the available body of evidence. If respected authorities disagree, you should explain the nature of the controversy:

> Scientists debate whether this disorder is hereditary. Yale researchers Brown and Smith cite the British twin study as evidence of a genetic link (35–41). However, both the American Medical Association and the National Institutes of Health insist the small numbers of subjects in the twin study do not provide sufficient evidence to support any conclusions (Kendrick 19–24).

4. **Indicate whether sources represent widely held views.** Often you will find that sources present similar views or interpretations. If you find four or five sources that present the same information, you may wish to select the source that is the most thorough, most recent, or best written. You can emphasize the significance of this source by mentioning that its ideas are shared by others:

> Nearly all experts on teenage suicide support Jane Diaz's observation that low self esteem, stress, and substance abuse are the principal contributing factors to the current rise in adolescent suicide (Smith 28; Johnson 10–15; King 89–92).

5. **Comment on the quality as well as quantity of your sources.** Not all sources have equivalent value. Sources may be inaccurate, biased, or based on limited evidence. If you conduct research on controversial issues or events, you may find little reliable material. If you are unable to determine which source is closest to the truth or which study is accurate, inform your readers of the dilemma you face:

> Although the 1908 railroad strike received national attention, few major newspapers offered more than superficial reports. Sensational accounts of lynching, rape, and murder appeared in New York and Chicago tabloids. The radical *Torch of Labor* blamed the deaths of two strikers on a plot engineered by Wall Street bankers. The conservative *Daily World* insisted union organizers were bent on overthrowing the government. Most sources, however, do agree that Red Williams played a critical role in organizing a labor protest that ultimately weakened the emerging Transport Workers Union.

GUIDELINES FOR USING DIRECT QUOTATIONS

Direct quotations give power and authority to your research paper by introducing the words of others just as they were written or stated. But to be effective, direct quotations have to carefully chosen, accurately presented, and skillfully woven into the text of your paper.

1. **Limit use of direct quotations.** Avoid reproducing long blocks of text, unless direct evidence is essential for accuracy or emphasis. In many instances, you can summarize and paraphrase information.
   - Use direct quotations when they are brief, memorable, and so well stated that that a paraphrase would reduce their impact. Avoid using direct quotations when you can accurately restate the information in a documented paraphrase.
   - **Remember, the focus of a research paper is your ideas, observations, and conclusions, not a collection of direct quotations.**
2. **Link direct quotations into your commentary.** Avoid isolating quotations:

Faulty:

Television advertising exploded in the Fifties. "Advertising agencies increased spending on television commercials from $10 million in 1948 to $2 billion in 1952" (Smith 16). These revenues financed the rapid development of a new industry.

Revised:

Television advertising exploded in the Fifties. According to Kai Smith, "Advertising agencies increased spending on television commercials from $10 million in 1948 to $2 billion in 1952" (16). These revenues financed the rapid development of a new industry.

Or

Television advertising exploded in the Fifties, with advertising agencies increasing spending "from $10 million in 1948 to $2 billion in 1952" (Smith 16). These revenues financed the rapid development of a new industry.

3. **Introduce block quotes with a complete sentence followed by colon:**

The Quiz Show Scandal of the 1950s shook public confidence in the new medium. The idea that the highly popular shows were rigged to ensure ratings infuriated and disillusioned the public:

> NBC received thousands of letters and telephone calls from irate viewers who felt cheated. Although the public readily accepted that Westerns and soap operas were fictional, they believed that the teachers and housewives who appeared on shows like "Twenty-One" were "real people" like themselves. Having followed their favorite contestants week after week, loyal viewers strongly identified with people they considered genuine. Learning that all the furrowed brows and lip biting were choreographed, they felt duped. (Brown 23)

4. **Provide background information to establish the value of direct quotations.** Bibliographical entries at the end of your paper may explain a source but do not help readers understand its significance:

Faulty:

President Roosevelt showed signs of declining health as early as 1942. Sheridan noted, "His hands trembled when writing, he complained of headaches, and he often seemed unable to follow the flow of conversation around him" (34–35).

Revised:

President Roosevelt showed signs of declining health as early as 1942. George Sheridan, a young naval aide who briefed the White House during the Battle of Midway, was shocked by the President's condition. Sheridan noted, "His hands trembled when writing, he complained of headaches, and he often seemed unable to follow the flow of conversation around him" (34–35).

5. **Indicate quotations within quotations.** Although most writers try to avoid using direct quotations that appear in another source, sometimes it cannot be avoided. You can easily indicate a quote within a quote with (qtd. in).

Original Source:

From Sandra Bert's *The Plague* (page 23)

The medical community of San Francisco was overwhelmed by the sudden increase in AIDS cases in the early 1980s. Tim Watson, a resident at the time, said, "It was like being hit by a tidal wave. We went home every night absolutely stunned by the influx of dying young men."

Research Paper quoting Tim Watson:

Within a few years the number of AIDS cases, especially in the Bay Area, exploded. Physicians were shocked by the rising numbers of patients with untreatable infections. "It was like being hit by a tidal wave," Watson remembered (qtd. Bert, 23).

6. **Accurately delete unneeded material from quotations.** You can abbreviate long quotations, deleting irrelevant or unimportant details by using ellipsis points (. . .). Three evenly spaced periods indicate words have been deleted from a direct quotation.

Original:

> The governor vetoed the education bill, which had been backed by a coalition of taxpayers and unions, because it cut aid to inner city schools.
> *—James Kirkland*

Shortened quotation using ellipsis points:

Kirkland reported that "the governor vetoed the education bill . . . because it cut aid to inner city schools."

- ■ Use a period and three ellipsis points (four dots. . . .) to indicate deletion of one or more full sentences.
- ■ Avoid making deletions that distort the original meaning. Do not eliminate qualifying statements.

Original:

> Given the gang wars, the failure of treatment programs, the rising number of addicts, I regretfully think we should legalize drugs until we can find better solutions to the problem.
> *—Mayor Wells*

Improper use of ellipsis points:

At a recent press conference, Mayor Wells stated, "I . . . think we should legalize drugs. . ."

7. **Use brackets to insert words or indicate alterations.** In some instances, you may have to insert a word to prevent confusion or a grammatical error.

Original:

> George Roosevelt [no relation to the President] left the Democratic Party in 1935, troubled by the deepening Depression. Roosevelt considered the New Deal a total failure.
> *—Nancy Stewart*

Brackets enclose inserted word to prevent confusion:

As the Depression deepened, many deserted the Democratic Party, seeking more radical solutions to the worsening economy. According to Stewart, "[George] Roosevelt considered the New Deal a total failure."

Original:

Poe, Whitman, and Ginsburg are among some of America's greatest poets.
—*John Demmer*

Brackets enclose altered verb:

Demmer states that "Poe . . . [is] among some of America's greatest poets."

STRATEGIES | for Citing Sources

Many students find citing sources one of the challenging aspects of writing a research paper. Mastering the details of accounting for each source can be frustrating. It is important to understand that documenting where you obtained information for your paper serves three key purposes:

1. **Citations prevent allegations of plagiarism.** Plagiarism occurs when you present the facts, words, or ideas of someone else as your own. Students often find it difficult to believe that copying something out of *The World Book* for a term paper can be considered a crime, but plagiarism has serious consequences. In many colleges students who submit a plagiarized paper will automatically fail the course. In some schools, students will be expelled. Outside of academics, plagiarism (often called "copyright infringement") has ruined the careers of politicians, artists, and executives. Prominent columnists and reporters have been fired from newspapers and magazines for using the ideas of others without acknowledging their original source. Hollywood studios have been sued by artists who claim ideas from their rejected screenplays were used in other films.
   - Accurate documentation protects you from plagiarism by clearly labeling borrowed ideas.
2. **Citations support your thesis.** Attorneys arguing a case before a judge or jury present labeled exhibits to prove their theory of a case. As a researcher, you support your thesis by introducing expert testimony, facts, case histories, and eyewitness accounts. Like an attorney, you have to clearly identify the source for evidence for it to be credible. A paper about crime that draws

upon statistics from the FBI and studies from the Justice Department will be more credible than one relying only on personal websites, blogs, and opinions.

■ The more controversial your thesis, the more readers will demand supporting evidence.

3. **Citations refer readers to other sources.** Citations not only illustrate which ideas originated with the writer and which were drawn from other sources, but they also alert readers where they can find more information. Through your citations, readers may learn of a biography or a website offering additional evidence.

Exceptions to Citing Sources

You do not need to use citations for every fact, quotation, or idea you present in your paper:

1. **Common expressions or famous quotations.** Famous sayings by such people as Shakespeare, Jesus, or Benjamin Franklin (for example, "To err is human" or "I am the resurrection") do not have to be cited, even when presented as direct quotations. If you are unsure, ask your instructor.

2. **Facts considered in the "realm of common knowledge."** You do not have to provide a citation if you referred to a source to check a fact that is readily available in numerous sources. You do not have to cite *The Encyclopedia Britannica* if you used it to find out where Arthur Miller was born or when North Dakota became a state. No one will accuse you of stealing facts that are commonly known and not subject to change or interpretation.

In almost every other instance, however, you have to acknowledge the use of outside material:

1. **Direct quotations.** Whenever you quote a source word for word, you must place it in quotation marks and cite its source.

2. **Indirect quotations or paraphrases.** Even if you do not copy a source but state the author's ideas in your own words, you must cite the source. Changing a few words or condensing a page of text into a few sentences does not alter the fact that you are using someone else's ideas.

3. **Specific facts, statistics, and numbers.** Data will be credible and acceptable only if you present the source. If you state, "Last year 54,450 drunk drivers were arrested in California," readers will naturally wonder where

you obtained that number. Statistics make credible evidence only if readers trust their source.

4. **Graphs, charts, and other visual aids.** Indicate the source of any graphic you reproduce.
   - You must also cite the source for information you use to create a visual display.

STRATEGIES | for Revising and Editing Research Papers

1. **Review the assignment, thesis, and working outline.**
2. **Examine your draft for use of sources.**
   - Does the draft fulfill the needs of the assignment?
   - Does the text support the thesis?
   - Is the thesis properly placed? Should it appear in the opening or the conclusion?
   - Are enough sources presented?
   - Is there any evidence that should be included or deleted?
   - Do you provide enough original commentary, or is your paper merely a collection of facts and quotations?
3. **Read the draft aloud.**
   - Does the paper have an even style and tone? Are there awkward transitions between sources and your commentary?
4. **Revise the introduction and conclusion.**
5. **Edit for mechanical and spelling errors. Make sure your paper follows the appropriate style for documenting sources (see pages 777–789 and 797–809 for guidelines).**

DOCUMENTATION STYLES

Writers document their use of outside sources with one of several methods. The MLA and APA formats are commonly used in the humanities and social sciences. Both methods provide guidelines for placing parenthetical notes after quoting or paraphrasing outside sources and listing them at the end of the paper. Many textbooks suggest recording each source on a note card so they can be easily shuffled and placed in alphabetical order. If you are writing on a computer, you may find it easier to scroll down and enter each source as you refer to it.

THE MLA STYLE

The MLA style, created by the Modern Language Association, is used in language and literature courses. Parenthetical notes listing the author or title and page numbers are inserted after quotations and paraphrases. At the end of the paper all the sources are alphabetized on a "Works Cited" page. For full details about using the MLA style, consult Joseph Gibaldi's *MLA Style Manual and Guide to Scholarly Publishing,* second edition; *MLA Handbook for Writers of Research Papers,* sixth edition; or the MLA website http://www.mla.org/publications/style/style_faq7.

STRATEGIES | for Writing Parenthetical Notes

Parenthetical notes usually include an author's last name and a page number. If no author is listed, titles—sometimes abbreviated—are used. To keep the notes as brief as possible, the MLA format does not precede page numbers with *p., pp.,* or commas. The parenthetical note is considered part of the sentence and comes before the final mark of punctuation. Notes should be placed as close to the source as possible without interrupting the flow of the text.

1. **Parenthetical notes include author and page number.** A direct quotation from Ralph Ellison's novel *Invisible Man* is indicated with a parenthetical note placed after it:

   The novel's unnamed character calls himself invisible because society does not recognize him as a human being. He defends his retreat from society, realizing that many would view his decision as a sign of irresponsibility. "Responsibility," he argues, "rests on recognition, and recognition is a form of agreement" (Ellison 14).

2. **Parenthetical notes include only page numbers if the author is clearly identified in the text:**

   Sheila Smitherin praised Ellison's novel, stating that modern black literature "was born on the pages of *Invisible Man*" (32).

3. **If two or more sources are cited within a sentence, notes are inserted after the material that is quoted or paraphrased:**

   Smith stated that the novel "exposed the deep-rooted racism society was unwilling to confront" (34), leading one columnist to argue that the book should be taught in every high school (Wilson 12–13).

4. **Long quotations are indented ten spaces without quotation marks:**

   The Group Theater revolutionized American drama. According to Frank Kozol, the members tried to create something then unseen on the New York stage:

   > Clurman and his followers wanted to develop a new kind of theater. They not only wanted to produce new, socially relevant plays, but create a new relationship between playwright and cast. It would be a collective effort. Designed to be a theater without stars, actors lived together and shared living expenses. They were infused with the revolutionary spirit of the times. The Group Theater soon launched the career of Clifford Odets, whose plays were among the most poignant depictions of life during the Great Depression. (Taylor 34–35)

   Notice that the parenthetical note appears outside the final punctuation of the last sentence.

STRATEGIES | for Writing a Works Cited Page

List all sources you have cited on a separate sheet at the end of your paper, titled "Works Cited." If you include works you have read for background but have not actually cited, title the page "Works Consulted."

NOTE: MLA style underlines titles of books and periodicals rather than placing them in italics (Time magazine not *Time* magazine) and places carets around website URLS (<www.cnn.com>).

■ Arrange the list of works alphabetically by the author's last name or first significant word of the title if no author is listed:

Jones, Wilson. Chicago Today. New York: Putnam, 2002.

"A New Look for Toronto." Toronto Magazine Fall 2003: 21.

- For sources with more than one author, alphabetize by the first author's last name:

Zinter, Mary, and Jan Ames. <u>First Aid</u>. New York: Dial, 2002.

- Begin each citation even with the left margin, and indent subsequent lines five spaces. Double-space the entire page. Do not separate entries with additional spaces:

Abrams, Jane. "Rebuilding America's Cities." <u>Plain Dealer</u> [Cleveland] 21 Jan.

2002: 12.

Brown, Gerald. <u>The Death of the Central City: The Malling of America</u>. New York:

Macmillan, 2003.

- If more than one source is used for an author, alphabetize the works but list the author's last name only once, substituting three hyphens for the name in subsequent citations:

Keller, Joseph. <u>Assessing Blame</u>. New York: Columbia UP, 2003.

---. <u>Quality Control</u>. New York: Miller, 2000.

GUIDELINES FOR LISTING SOURCES IN WORKS CITED AND PARENTHETICAL NOTES

Books

1. Write the author's last name, first name, then any initial. Copy the name as written on the title page. "C. W. Brown" would appear as:

Brown, C. W.

Omit any degrees or titles such as Ph.D. or Dr.

2. State the full title of the book. Place a colon between the main heading and any subtitle. Underline all the words and punctuation in the title, except for the final period.

Brown, C. W. <u>Sharks and Lambs: Wall Street in the Nineties</u>.

3. Record the city of publication, publisher, and date of publication. If the book lists several cities, use only the first. If the city is outside the United States,

add an abbreviation for the country. If an American city may be unfamiliar, you can include an abbreviation for the state. Record the main words of the publisher, deleting words like "publishing" or "press" (Monroe for Monroe Publishing Company). Use the initials "UP" for "University Press." End the citation with the last year of publication.

Works Cited entry:

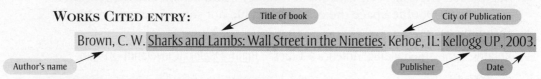

Brown, C. W. Sharks and Lambs: Wall Street in the Nineties. Kehoe, IL: Kellogg UP, 2003.

Book with Two or Three Authors

Works Cited entry:

Smith, David, John Adams, and Chris Cook. Writing On-line. New York: Macmillan, 2000.

Parenthetical note:

(Smith, Adams, and Cook 23–24)

Books with Four or More Authors

Works Cited entry:

Chavez, Nancy, et al. Mexico Today. New York: Putnam, 2003.

Parenthetical note:

(Chavez et al. 87)

Book with Corporate Author

Works Cited entry:

National Broadcasting Company. Programming Standards. New York: National Broadcasting Company, 2002.

Parenthetical note:

(National Broadcasting Company 112)

To avoid a cumbersome parenthetical note, you can mention the author or title in the text:

According to the National Broadcasting Company's Programming Standards, "No single executive should be able to cancel a program" (214).

Book with Unnamed Authors

WORKS CITED ENTRY:

New Yale Atlas. New York: Random House, 2003.

PARENTHETICAL NOTE:

(New Yale 106)

Book with Multiple Volumes

WORKS CITED ENTRY:

Eisenhower, Dwight. Presidential Correspondence. Vol. 2. New York: Dutton, 1960.
6 vols.

PARENTHETICAL NOTE:

(Eisenhower 77)

If you cite more than one volume in your paper, indicate the number:

(Eisenhower 2: 77)

Book in Second or Later Edition

WORKS CITED ENTRY:

Franklin, Marcia. Modern France. 3rd ed. Philadelphia: Comstock, 1987.

PARENTHETICAL NOTE:

(Franklin 12)

Work in an Anthology

WORKS CITED ENTRY:

Ford, John M. "Preflash." The Year's Best Fantasy. Ed. Ellen Datlow and Terri Windling.
New York: St. Martin's, 1989. 65–82.

PARENTHETICAL NOTE:

(Ford 65–66)

Note: If you include more than one work from the same anthology, list the anthology in the Works Cited section separately under the editors' names and list individual entries in a shortened form:

Ford, John M. "Preflash." Datlow and Windling 265–82.

Book in Translation

WORKS CITED ENTRY:

Verne, Jules. <u>Twenty Thousand Leagues Under the Sea</u>. Trans. Michel Michot. Boston: Pitman, 1992.

PARENTHETICAL NOTE:

(Verne 65)

Book with Editor or Editors

WORKS CITED ENTRY:

Benson, Nancy, ed. <u>Ten Great American Plays</u>. New York: Columbia UP, 2002.

PARENTHETICAL NOTE:

(Benson 23)

The preceding parenthetical note would be used to cite Benson's comments.

Book with Author and Editor

WORKS CITED ENTRY:

Gissing, George. <u>Workers in the Dawn</u>. Ed. Jason Day. London: Oxford UP, 1982.

PARENTHETICAL NOTE:

(Gissing 78)

Book in a Series

WORKS CITED ENTRY:

Swessel, Karyn, ed. <u>Northern Ireland Today</u>. Modern Europe Ser. 3. New York: Wilson, 2003.

PARENTHETICAL NOTE:

(Swessel 34)

Republished Book

WORKS CITED ENTRY:

Smith, Jane. <u>The Jersey Devil</u>. 1922. New York: Warner, 2002.

PARENTHETICAL NOTE:

(Smith 23–25)

Periodicals

Newspaper Article

WORKS CITED ENTRY:

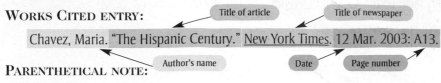

Chavez, Maria. "The Hispanic Century." New York Times. 12 Mar. 2003: A13.

PARENTHETICAL NOTE:

(Chavez)

Note: If an article has only one page, page numbers are not included in parenthetical notes.

Magazine Article

WORKS CITED ENTRY:

Janssen, Mary. "Iran Today." Time 25 Mar. 2003: 34+.

Note: If an article appears on nonconsecutive pages, list the first page followed by a "+" sign.

PARENTHETICAL NOTE:

(Janssen 38)

Scholarly Article

WORKS CITED ENTRY:

Grant, Edward. "The Hollywood Ten: Fighting the Blacklist." California Film Quarterly 92.2 (2002): 14–32.

PARENTHETICAL NOTE:

(Grant 21–23)

Newspaper or Magazine Article with Unnamed Author

WORKS CITED ENTRY:

"The Legacy of the Gulf War." American History 12 Mar. 2003: 23– 41.

PARENTHETICAL NOTE:

("Legacy" 25)

Letter to the Editor

WORKS CITED ENTRY:

Roper, Jack. Letter. <u>Chicago Defender</u> 12 Jan. 2002, sec. B: 12.

PARENTHETICAL NOTE:

(Roper)

Other Print Sources

Encyclopedia Article with Author

WORKS CITED ENTRY:

Author's name → Keller, Christopher. "Lisbon." <u>World Book Encyclopedia</u>. 2003. ← Date

Entry

Title of encyclopedia

Note: Provide edition number if given.

PARENTHETICAL NOTE:

(Keller)

Note: Page numbers are not used with works in which articles are arranged alphabetically.

Encyclopedia Article with Unnamed Author

WORKS CITED ENTRY:

"Lisbon." <u>Columbia Illustrated Encyclopedia</u>. 2002.

PARENTHETICAL NOTE:

("Lisbon")

Pamphlet with Author

WORKS CITED ENTRY:

Tindall, Gordon, ed. <u>Guide to New York Churches</u>. New York: Chamber of Commerce, 1998.

PARENTHETICAL NOTE:

(Tindall 76–78)

Pamphlet with Unnamed Author

WORKS CITED ENTRY:

<u>Guide to New York Museums</u>. New York: Columbia University, 2003.

PARENTHETICAL NOTE:

(<u>Guide</u> 176–82)

The Bible

WORKS CITED ENTRY:

<u>Holy Bible</u>. New International Version. Grand Rapids, MI: Zondervan, 1988.

Note: Titles of sacred texts are not underlined, unless they are specific editions.

PARENTHETICAL NOTE:

(Mark 2 :4–9)

Nonprint Sources

Motion Picture

WORKS CITED ENTRY:

<u>Casino</u>. Dir. Martin Scorsese. Universal, 1995.

Note: You may wish to include names of performers, directors, or screenwriters if they are of special interest to readers. These names should be inserted between the title and the distributor.

Television Program

WORKS CITED ENTRY:

"The Long Goodbye." <u>Law and Order</u>. Dir. Jane Hong. Writ. Peter Wren. Perf. Rita
Colletti, Diane Nezgod, and Vicki Shimi. NBC. WTMJ, Milwaukee. 12 May 2005.

Videotape

WORKS CITED ENTRY:

<u>Colonial Williamsburg</u>. Compiled by Janet Freud. American Home Video, 1996.

Live Performance of a Play

WORKS CITED ENTRY:

> <u>All My Sons</u>. By Arthur Miller. Dir. Anita Dayin. Lyric Theater, New York. 10 May 2006.

Speech

WORKS CITED ENTRY:

> Goode, Wilmont. "America in the Next Century." Chicago Press Club. 12 Oct. 2003.

Personal or Telephone Interview

WORKS CITED ENTRY:

> Weston, Thomas. Personal interview. 21 May 2006.

In the preceding citation, you would substitute "Telephone" for "Personal" if the interview was conducted by telephone.

Parenthetical Notes for Nonprint Sources

Because nonprint sources do not have page numbers and often have long titles, parenthetical notes can be cumbersome. Most writers avoid inserting citations by mentioning the source within the text:

> Multiple personality disorder was featured in a recent episode of <u>Law and Order</u>.

> In <u>Gone With the Wind</u> special effects were used to re-create the burning of Atlanta.

> Interviewed in the fall of 2003, Laura Dornan suggested that many critics failed to see the feminist theme in her play.

Electronic Sources

Web Pages

Web pages vary greatly. In general, include the name of the person or organization that created the site, author (if listed), the title (if there is not a title, you can use a description, such as the one used in the next entry), the date of creation or most recent update, the date of access, and the URL. For a website with a particularly long URL, you may specify the URL of the site's search page, if available, or the sequence of links that took you to the page you cite. See the entry for Joe Rosenthal on p. 789.

WORKS CITED ENTRY:

> Chicago Irish Center. Home page. 5 Apr. 2003. 10 May 2006 <http://www.chi.irish
> .cent.org>.

Electronic Journal Article

WORKS CITED ENTRY:

> Smith, Perry. "Truman Capote and Kansas." Phoenix 2.7 (2003). 15 Mar. 2006 <http://
> www.englishlit.com/hts/phoenix/index>.

Online Newspaper Article

WORKS CITED ENTRY:

> "Long Day's Journey into Night Production Disappointing." New York Times on the Web
> 17 Mar. 2003. 22 Apr. 2005 <http://www.nytimes.com/aponline/a/ap-play.html>.

Reference Database

WORKS CITED ENTRY:

> The Emerald Project: Irish Literature from 1500–2000. 2000 Boston University. 21 Oct.
> 2005 <http://www/bostonuniv/emerald/>.

Electronic Texts

Many books are available online. Because they lack page numbers, mention the title within the text to avoid long parenthetical notes.

WORKS CITED ENTRY:

> Gissing, George. Demos. London, 1892. The Online Books Page. Ed. Charles Al-
> darondo. Jan. 2002. Project Gutenberg Literary Archive Foundation. 5 Mar. 2006
> <http://www.gutenberg.org/dirs/etext03/demos10.txt>

CD-ROM

WORKS CITED ENTRY:

> "Understanding Macbeth." Master Dramas. CD-ROM. New York: Educational Media,
> 2002.

E-mail

WORKS CITED ENTRY:

> Ballard, Morton D. "Rental Cars." E-mail to Germaine Reinhardt. 21 May 2005.

Discussion Group Posting

WORKS CITED ENTRY:

> Humphrey, Doug. "US Radar Coverage." Online posting. 1 Nov. 2005. Coldwarcomms.
> 15 Mar. 2006 <http://groups.yahoo.com/group/coldwarcomms/message/9306>.

Synchronous Communication

To cite a posting from forums such as MOO, MUD, or IRC, include names of speakers, a description of the event, the date, the name of the forum, date of access, and telnet address:

WORKS CITED ENTRY:

> Gladkin, Dorcas. Melville discussion of "Biblical Symbolism in Moby Dick." 19 Oct. 2004.
> MediaMOO. 1 Nov. 2005 <telnet://www.litcafe/homepages/smith/melville.html>.

Linked Sources

MLA does not provide a method of citing hypertext links, but the following format allows readers to follow your search:

WORKS CITED ENTRY:

> Laskowski, Edward. "BMI: Is It Accurate for Weightlifters?" Nov. 15, 2005. Mayo Foundation for Medical Education and Research. 14 Dec. 2005 <http://www.mayoclinic.com>. Path: Ask a Specialist; Fitness.

Visuals

Table, Graph, Chart, or Map

WORKS CITED ENTRY:

> Carlino's Sales. Table. "From Hoboken to Hollywood." The New Yorker 25 May 2006: 21.

PARENTHETICAL NOTES:
Visuals are numbered and captioned:

George Carlino was one of many writers in the Nineties who abandoned writing
highly acclaimed but little read novels to writing lucrative screenplays (see Table 1).

Year	Novel	Publisher's Advance	Movie Rights
1992	*Jersey Angel*	$10,000	$25,000
1995	*Bronxman*	$15,000	$100,000
1997	*Talk Radio*	$18,000	$750,000
1999	screenplay for *Walker's Point*		$1.2 million

Table 1. <u>Carlino's Sales</u>. "From Hoboken to Hollywood." <u>The New Yorker</u>
   25 May 2006: 21.

Advertisement

General Motors. Advertisement. <u>Time</u> 15 Dec. 2005: 12.

Photograph

Include the photographer or original source, title or description, and year, and information about the book, newspaper, or online source of the image. Avoid long
parenthetical notes by referring to the image within the text and its number:

The most famous photograph of World War II was Joe Rosenthal's shot of the flag
raising on Iwo Jima (see Figure 10).

WORKS CITED

Joe Rosenthal. <u>Marines Raising American Flag on Iwo Jima</u>. 1945. Corbis. 12 Feb.
   2006. <http://pro.corbis.com/>.

SAMPLE RESEARCH PAPER USING MLA STYLE

(with Cover Page and Formal Outline)

No page
number

Title
centered
one third
down from
top of page

The Role of Nature in

Orwell's <u>Nineteen Eighty-Four</u>

Writer's
name

by

Maria Perez

Course
Professor's
name,
date

English 102

Professor Brandeis

10 May 2006

Note: If your instructor does not request a separate cover page, the first page of your paper should include the title and your name:

Perez 1

Maria Perez

English 102

Professor Brandeis

10 May 2006

The Role of Nature in

Orwell's <u>Nineteen Eighty-Four</u>

Outline

Thesis statement: Winston Smith's humanity and individual autonomy are stunted not only by the brutality of Oceania and the ever-present Thought Police, but by his lack of contact with nature.

I.   Most commentators view Orwell's last novel as a grim account of perverted Socialism and the abuse of technology.

II. Most readers have overlooked the role of nature in <u>Nineteen Eighty-Four</u>. Winston Smith's lack of contact with nature robs him of his humanity.

III. Smith rebels against both the dictatorship of Big Brother and the artificiality of his environment.

   A. Smith lives in a London of shabby houses and soulless concrete towers.

   B. Food and fiber in Oceania are artificial and dehumanizing.

IV. Smith escapes this world only in dreams of a pasture he calls "The Golden Country."

   A. The dream provides a background for a sexual encounter.

   B. Winston Smith experiences a similar landscape in reality when he travels into the country with Julia.

      1. Nature provides Smith and Julia with inspiration and comfort.

      2. Smith and Julia can only enjoy sex in a natural setting, away from society.

V.   Smith realizes the Party controls its citizens by separating them from reality.

VI. Nature was Orwell's "moral gold standard."

   A. Orwell did not share the Left's faith in scientific progress.

   B. Orwell sensed that even benign uses of technology designed to make life more comfortable had sinister implications.

      1. Artificial environments eliminated contact with nature.

2.   Controlled environments allowed for manipulation and dead-
     ened thought.

VII.   Orwell viewed contact with nature as essential for society to be just, hu-
       mane, and decent. <u>Nineteen Eighty-Four</u> remains relevant in the twenty-
       first century of cyberspace and "virtual" realities.

Last name, page number

The Role of Nature in
Orwell's <u>Nineteen Eighty-Four</u>

Title (1″ from top of page)

Introduction

Review of critical views using selected direct quotations

Most commentators view Orwell's last novel as a grim account of perverted
Socialism, a vision of a society dominated by Big Brother, a god-like Stalin figure.
"Orwell was looking backward, not forward," David Simes argues, "seeing the future as a Nazi state with nuclear weapons." Nancy Wolzheck offers the view that
"Orwell saw the centralization of power as the enemy of human individuality and
liberty" (192). "The principal theme of <u>Nineteen Eighty-Four</u>," Edward Janeson
writes, "is the corruption of political power" (181). Wilson Goodman asserts, "Orwell's novel reveals the horror of totalitarianism coupled with inhuman uses of
technology" (18–19).

Transition

Comment on the lack of critical sources on this theme

Thesis

But most readers have overlooked a central element in <u>Nineteen Eighty-Four</u>,
the role of nature. Winston Smith's humanity and individual autonomy are stunted
not only by the brutality of Oceania and the ever-present Thought Police, but by
his lack of contact with nature.

Summary of novel focusing on student's thesis

Orwell's protagonist Winston Smith rebels not only against the brutal dictatorship of Big Brother but the artificiality of the world created by the Party. Smith
lives in a London of shabby nineteenth-century houses and soulless concrete towers. He moves through a realm of artificial structures and windowless cubicles
devoid of nature. Food and fiber in Oceania bear little resemblance to natural

Perez 2

products; they are manufactured from synthetics. Smith survives on a diet of processed foods and imitation coffee. He only has a childhood memory of lemons, a fruit he has not seen in thirty years. Omnipresent telescreens simultaneously bombard him with propaganda and record his every move. In this artificial world, Smith's natural instincts for comfort, companionship, and freedom are demeaned and criminalized. Sex, the most natural instinct in humans, has been oppressed and sullied so that Smith's only contacts with women since his divorce have been with prostitutes.

In <u>Nineteen Eighty</u>-Four, Smith escapes this grim world only in his sleep, when he dreams of what he calls the "Golden Country":

> It was an old, rabbit-bitten pasture, with a foot track wandering across it and a mole-hole here and there. In the ragged hedge on the opposite side of the field the boughs of the elm trees were swaying very faintly in the breeze, their leaves just stirring in the dense masses like women's hair. (29)

Block quotation

This conventional bit of countryside becomes the setting for eroticism. A dream girl runs toward Smith, tossing aside her clothes in disdainful gestures "belonging to the ancient time" (29).

Smith encounters this dream landscape when he and Julia slip from London to escape the ever-present telescreens that track their every movement and prevent them from consummating their illegal relationship. Meeting in the country, they enter a rabbit-bitten pasture with leaves like "women's hair." Like the girl in the dream, Julia sheds her Junior Anti-Sex League sash in defiance. Smith and Julia can only enjoy sexual intimacy apart from civilization, in the wild where their passion is not blunted by social restraint. This freedom is difficult to maintain in the city, forcing them to hole up like criminals in a dingy room to escape detection.

Nature provides Smith and Julia with inspiration and comfort, vitalizing their sexual instincts. Nature allows them to feel that their biological urges are wholesome and fundamental, elements linking them to the apolitical world of flowers and birds. Smith wants to feel not "merely the love of one person" but "the animal instinct, the simple undifferentiated desire" which will "tear the Party to pieces" (105). Nature gives Smith the spirit to rebel, to energize elements of humanity the Party seeks to eradicate, sully, and trivialize.

Smith realizes that his alienation, his sense of superfluousness is caused not only by political oppression but by his separation from nature. The Party achieves its power not only through surveillance, censorship, and torture, but by distorting natural law. During Smith's interrogation, O'Brien insists that " 'the stars are bits of fire a few kilometers away. We could reach them if we wanted to. Or we could blot them out' " (219). By altering people's concept of nature, the Party assumes all power. Separated from reality, the citizen of Oceania is enveloped in the artificial, managed world of the state, with no independence.

Nature, according to Alan Sandison, was Orwell's "moral gold standard" (10). Nature was an essential part of Orwell's judgment. Writing to Henry Miller, whose books he admired, Orwell chided Miller for wandering off "into a kind of reverie where the laws of ordinary reality were slipped just a little but not too much" (Collected Essays 4:80). Orwell added, ". . . I have a sort of belly-to-earth attitude and always feel uneasy when I get away from the ordinary world where grass is green, stones hard etc." (4:80).

Orwell saw the loss of nature as the inevitable result of mechanical progress. Technology was the major tenet of the ideologies of Orwell's pre-environmentalist era. Mussolini drained the Pontine marshes; Hitler constructed the autobahn; Stalin erected huge hydroelectric dams. Orwell, unlike most Socialists of his generation, did not share the Left's faith in scientific progress. He even doubted the role of electricity, the pet project of Lenin and Stalin, in making the world better. He viewed electricity as a "queer spectacle . . . showering miracles upon people with empty bellies. . . . Twenty million people are underfed but literally everyone in England has access to a radio" (Orwell Road 84).

Marginal notes:

Selected use of direct quotations

Direct quotation of dialogue

Ellipsis indicating deleted words

Ellipsis used to delete unnecessary details

Perez 4

In <u>The Road to Wigan Pier</u>, Orwell decried the slums he saw in Depression-era Britain. He was also distressed by the fact that the poor were deloused before being allowed to move into new low-income housing. "Bugs are bad," he noted, "but a state of affairs in which men will allow themselves to be dipped like sheep is worse" (71).

Orwell found something insidious and dangerous even in the most benign uses of technology. Writing in 1946, he criticized the proposed development of postwar "pleasure spots" in the same way he denounced the "hygiene" in public housing. The planned resorts he read about in "slick magazines" would be comprised of artificial lagoons, heated swimming pools, sunlamps, and glass-covered tennis courts. Examining the characteristics of such artificial playlands, Orwell saw many of the same elements he would later depict in harsher terms in <u>Nineteen Eighty-Four</u>:

1. One is never alone.
2. One never does anything for oneself.
3. One is never within sight of wild vegetation or natural objects of any kind.
4. Light and temperature are always artificially regulated.
5. One is never out of the sound of music. (<u>Collected Essays</u> 4:80)

Orwell found the music to be particularly disturbing and the most important standard ingredient of the modern artificial environment:

Its function is to prevent thought and conversation, and to shut out any natural sound, such as the song of birds or the whistling of the wind, that might otherwise intrude. The radio is already consciously used for this purpose by innumerable people. In very many English homes the radio is literally never turned off, though it is manipulated from time to time so as to make sure that only light music will come out of it. I know people who will keep the radio playing all through a meal and at the same time continue talking just loudly

Block quotation

Block quotation with ellipsis

enough for the voices and the music to cancel each other out. . . . The music prevents the conversation from becoming serious. . . while the chatter of voices stops one from listening attentively to the music and thus prevents the onset of that dreadful thing, thought. (Collected Essays 4:80)

Orwell drew on his observations of the radio in middle class English homes to envision the telescreens of Oceania.

Nineteen Eighty-Four exaggerated trends Orwell saw taking place around him. The danger to humanity was not only totalitarian governments but science and technology. The growing artificiality of life, whether inspired by tasteless commercialism or state planning, threatens human individuality and ability to make rational judgments about the world. In a natural environment all men and women are equal in their response to the world. In the artificial universe created by technology the individual can only respond to an environment created by other humans, a world designed to curtail thought, deceive, and control.

Orwell saw nature as an essential ingredient in any society that wishes to be just, humane, and decent. "Man only stays human," Orwell argued, "by preserving large patches of simplicity in his life" (Collected Essays 4:80). Modern inventions, though they make life easier and more comfortable under the best circumstances, can have severe consequences on the individual and "weaken his consciousness, dull his curiosity, and, in general, drive him nearer to the animals" (Collected Essays 4:81). As Alan Sandison notes in The Last Man in Europe, "the greatest moral danger Orwell can envision for a man is that he should be denied contact with the ordinary world where grass is green, stones hard" (10).

Nineteen Eighty-Four then remains a relevant novel. Orwell's vision of a Stalinist nightmare state may no longer seem compelling, but his observations about the growing artificiality of life and the need for humans to maintain contact with nature are perhaps more pertinent in the twenty-first century world of cyberspace and "virtual" realities.

Conclusion

Perez 6

Works Cited

Goodman, Wilson. <u>Orwell's Dark Vision</u>. New York: Columbia UP, 1992.

Janeson, Edward. "Power and Politics in Nineteen Eighty-Four." <u>Modern Fiction
Studies</u>. May 1999: 179–90.

Orwell, George. <u>The Collected Essays, Journalism and Letters of George Orwell</u>. Ed.
Sonia Orwell and Ian Angus. Vol. 4. New York: Harcourt, 1968. 4 vols.

---. <u>Nineteen Eighty-Four</u>. 1949. New York: New American Library, 1961.

---. <u>The Road to Wigan Pier</u>. New York: Berkley, 1967.

Sandison, Alan. <u>The Last Man in Europe</u>. London: Macmillan, 1974.

Simes, David. "Understanding Orwell's Vision." 22 Jul. 2003. Modern British
Literature Series. 12 April 2006. <http://www.modbritlit.com/orwell-simes/
index.html>

Wolzheck, Nancy. "Orwell Under Fire." <u>Time and Tide</u>. 10 May 2001. 25. Apr. 2006.
<http://www.timeandtide.com>.

Heading centered

First line flush with left margin, then indented

APA STYLE

Most courses in the social sciences, including anthropology, education, political
science, psychology, and sociology, follow the rules for documentation created
by the American Psychological Association. For full details, consult the American Psychological Association's *Publication Manual of the American Psychological
Association*, fifth edition.

STRATEGIES | for Writing Parenthetical Notes

In APA documentation parenthetical notes are placed after material requiring
documentation, and all sources are recorded in a References list at the end of
the paper.

- **Parenthetical notes include author, year of publication, and, for direct
  quotes, page numbers.** Most sources are identified by the author's name

and the year of publication. Page numbers are usually omitted from paraphrases but are always included in direct quotations. The information may be placed in a single note or distributed throughout the text:

Smith (2003) suggested that multiple personality disorder was more common than previously reported.

It has been suggested that multiple personality disorder is more common than previously believed (Smith, 2003).

Based on recent studies, Smith (2003) asserts that "multiple personality disorder is more common than previously reported" (p. 321).

■ **Multiple parenthetical notes indicate more than one source.** If two or more sources are cited within a sentence, notes are inserted after the material quoted or paraphrased:

Johnson (2002) stated that the study "revealed that Chicago schools were adequately staffed" (p. 43), leading Renfro (2003) to reject the teachers' union proposal.

■ **For the first text reference, list up to five authors' names:**

Johnson, Hyman, Torque, and Kaiser (2003) observed that computers enhance student performance.

Note: With multiple authors in a parenthetical cite, use an ampersand (&):

(Johnson, Hyman, Torque, & Kaiser, 2003)

■ **For the first reference of a citation with six or more authors, list the first author's name and "et al." (and others):**

Johnson et al. (2003) examined computer education in Chicago, New York, El Paso, and Philadelphia.

- **List corporate and group authors in full initially; then abbreviate:**

Computers are valuable in teaching higher mathematics (Modern Education Council [MEC], 2002). Textbook publishers now include online support for individual tutoring (MEC, 2002).

- **Assign letters (a, b, c) to indicate use of more than one work by an author with same year of publication:**

Kozik studied students in Chicago bilingual classes (2002a) and later reviewed the performance of an English immersion program in San Diego (2002b).

- **Alphabetize multiple sources and separate with a semicolon:**

Several reports suggest that noise pollution can directly contribute to hypertension (Jones, 1997; Smith, 2002).

- **Websites can be mentioned within the text:**

Chinese educators have attempted to expand Internet access for university students, particularly in the fields of engineering and medicine. Their efforts can be documented by examining Peking University's World Wide Web site at http://www.upkng.eng.edu.

STRATEGIES | for Writing a References Page

List all the sources you have cited on a separate sheet at the end of your paper titled "References" (center the word References and do not italicize it or place it in quotation marks). If you include works you have read for background but not actually cited, title the page "Bibliography."

- **Arrange the list of works alphabetically by authors' or editors' last names, followed by initials. If no authors are listed, alphabetize by the first significant word of the title:**

Jones, W. (2002). *Chicago today.* New York: Putnam.

A new look for Toronto. (2003, Fall). *Toronto Magazine,* 21.

▪ **For sources with more than one author, alphabetize by the first author's last name and list subsequent authors by last names and initials:**

Zinter, M., & Ames, J. (2002). *First aid.* New York: Dial.

▪ **Begin each citation even with the left margin, then indent subsequent lines five spaces. Double-space the entire page. Do not separate entries with additional spaces:**

Abrams, J. (2002, January 21). Rebuilding America's cities. *Cleveland Plain Dealer,* pp. 1, 7, 8.

Brown, G. (2003). *The death of the central city: The malling of America.* New York: Macmillan.

▪ **If more than one source from a given author is used, list the works in chronological order and repeat the author's name:**

Brown, G. (2000). *Hope for renewal.* New York: Putnam.

Brown, G. (2003). *The death of the central city: The malling of America.* New York: Macmillan.

GUIDELINES FOR LISTING SOURCES IN REFERENCES AND PARENTHETICAL NOTES

Books

▪ Write the author's last name, first and subsequent initials:

Brown, C. W.

▪ Place the year of publication in parentheses, followed by a period and one space.

▪ Italicize the full title of the book. Place a colon between the main heading and any subtitle. Capitalize only the first word in the title and any subtitle and any proper nouns or adjectives within the title:

Brown, C. W. (2003). *Sharks and lambs: Wall Street in the nineties.*

■ Record the city of publication and publisher.

> Brown, C. W. (2003). *Sharks and lambs: Wall Street in the nineties.* New York: Kellogg Press.

Note: Do not shorten or abbreviate words like "University" or "Press."

PARENTHETICAL NOTES:

> Brown (2003) stated . . .
>
> (Brown, 2003)
>
> (Brown, 2003, pp. 23–25)

Book with Two or Three Authors

REFERENCES ENTRY:

> Smith, D., Johnson, A., & Cook, F. D. (1989). *Writing for television.* New York: Macmillan.

PARENTHETICAL NOTES:
First note:

> Smith, Johnson, and Cook (1989) stated . . .

Subsequent notes:

> Smith et al. (1989) revealed . . .

First note:

> (Smith, Johnson, & Cook, 1989)

Subsequent notes:

> (Smith et al., 1989)

Book with Corporate Author

REFERENCES ENTRY:

> National Broadcasting Company. (2002). *Programming standards.* New York: National Broadcasting Company.

Parenthetical notes:

According to the National Broadcasting Company's *Programming Standards* (2002), "No single executive should be able to cancel a program" (p. 214).

(National Broadcasting Company [NBC], 2002, p. 214)

Book with Unnamed Author

References entry:

New Yale atlas. (2003). New York: Random House.

Parenthetical notes:

According to the *New Yale atlas* (2003) . . . (p. 106).

(*New Yale atlas,* 2003, p. 106)

Book with Multiple Volumes

References entry:

Eisenhower, D. (1960). *Presidential correspondence.* (Vol. 2). New York: Dutton Books.

Parenthetical notes:

Eisenhower (1960) predicted . . . (p. 77).

(Eisenhower, 1960, p. 77)

Book in Second or Later Edition

References entry:

Franklin, M. (1987). *Modern France* (3rd ed.). Philadelphia: Comstock Press.

Parenthetical notes:

Franklin (1987) stated . . . (p. 12).

(Franklin, 1987, p. 12)

Book in Translation

References entry:

Verne, J. (1992). *Twenty thousand leagues under the sea* (M. Michot, Trans.). Boston: Pitman Press.

Parenthetical notes:

Verne (1992) . . . (p. 65)

(Verne, 1992, p. 65)

Book with Editor or Editors

REFERENCES ENTRY:

Benson, N. (Ed.). (2002). *The absent parent.* New York: Columbia House.

PARENTHETICAL NOTES:

According to Benson (2002) . . . (p. 212).

(Benson, 2002, p. 212)

Book with Author and Editor

REFERENCES ENTRY:

Gissing, G. (1982). *Workers in the dawn* (J. Day, Ed.). London: Oxford University Press.

PARENTHETICAL NOTE:

(Gissing, 1982, p. 78)

Republished Book

REFERENCES ENTRY:

Smith, J. (2002). *The Jersey devil.* New York: Warner Books. (Original work published 1922)

PARENTHETICAL NOTES:

Smith (2002) observes . . . (pp.12–13).

(Smith, 2002, pp. 12–13)

Periodicals

Newspaper Article

REFERENCES ENTRY:

Chavez, M. (2002, August 15). The Hispanic century. *New York Times,* pp. 2A, 8–9A.

Note: List all page numbers, separated by commas.

PARENTHETICAL NOTES:

Chavez (2002) states . . . (p. 8A)

(Chavez, 2002, p. 8A)

Magazine Article

REFERENCES ENTRY:

Janssen, M. (1997, January/February). Iran today. *Foreign Affairs, 64,* 78–88.

PARENTHETICAL NOTES:

Janssen (1997) notes . . . (pp. 80–82)

(Janssen, 1997, pp. 80–82)

Scholarly Article

REFERENCES ENTRY:

Grant, E. (2002). The Hollywood ten: Fighting the blacklist. *California Film Quarterly, 92,* 112–25.

PARENTHETICAL NOTES:

Grant (2002) observes . . . (pp. 121–23).

(Grant, 2002, pp. 121–23)

Newspaper or Magazine Article with Unnamed Author

REFERENCES ENTRY:

The legacy of the Gulf War. (2000, October). *American History, 48,* 23–41.

PARENTHETICAL NOTES:

In "The Legacy of the Gulf War" (2000) . . . ("Legacy," 2000, pp. 22–24)

Note: For parenthetical notes, use shortened titles in quotation marks.

Letter to the Editor

REFERENCES ENTRY:

Roper, J. (1997, June 12). [Letter to the editor]. *Chicago Defender,* p. B12.

PARENTHETICAL NOTES:

According to Roper (1997) . . . (p. B12).

(Roper, 1997, p. B12)

Other Print Sources

Encyclopedia Article

REFERENCES ENTRY:

Keller, C. (2003). Lisbon. In *Encyclopedia of Europe.* New York: Wiley.

PARENTHETICAL NOTES:

Keller (2003) reports . . . (p. 232).

(Keller, 2003, p. 232)

Encyclopedia Article with Unnamed Author

REFERENCES ENTRY:

Lisbon. (2002). In *Columbia illustrated encyclopedia.* New York: Columbia.

PARENTHETICAL NOTES:

In "Lisbon" (2002) . . . (p. 156).

("Lisbon," 2002, p. 156)

Pamphlet

REFERENCES ENTRY:

Tindall, G. (Ed.). (2002). *Guide to New York churches.* New York: New York Chamber of
     Commerce.

PARENTHETICAL NOTES:

Tindall (2002) noted . . . (pp. 34–36).

(Tindall, 2002, pp. 34–36)

Nonprint Sources

Motion Picture

REFERENCES ENTRY:

Scorsese, M. (Director). (1995). *Casino* [Motion picture]. United States: Universal.

PARENTHETICAL NOTES:

Scorsese (1995) depicts . . .

(Scorsese, 1995)

Television Program

REFERENCES ENTRY:

Hong, J. (Producer). (1997, May 12). *Women at work.* [Television broadcast]. New York: Public Broadcasting System.

PARENTHETICAL NOTES:

According to Hong (1997) . . .

(Hong, 1997)

Videotape

REFERENCES ENTRY:

Freud, J. (Producer), & Johnson, K. (Director). (1996). [Video]. *Colonial Williamsburg.* New York: American Home Video.

PARENTHETICAL NOTES:

Freud and Johnson (1996) . . .

(Freud & Johnson, 1996)

Speech

REFERENCES ENTRY:

Goode, W. (2003, October 12). *America in the next century.* Address before the Chicago Press Club, Chicago, IL.

PARENTHETICAL NOTES:

According to Goode (2003) . . .

(Goode, 2003)

Electronic Sources

Web Pages

REFERENCES ENTRY:

Regis, T. (2003, January 5). Developing distance learning. [Electronic version]. *Regis.* Retrieved October 27, 2005, from http://regis.devel/home/distlearng/toc.html.

PARENTHETICAL NOTES:

> Regis (2003) suggests . . .
>
> (Regis, 2003)

Electronic Journal Article

REFERENCES ENTRY:

> Smith, P. (2002, March 2). Help for homeless promised. *Psychology Journal* [Online serial]. Retrieved January 25, 2006, from http://www .psychojourn./hts/index.

Note: Because the content of websites can change, it is important to list the date you retrieved the information.

PARENTHETICAL NOTES:

> According to Smith (2002) . . .
>
> (Smith, 2002)

Online Newspaper Article

REFERENCES ENTRY:

> Gulf war syndrome: Diagnostic survey reveals dangerous trend. (2003, March 11). *New York Times*. Retrieved December 15, 2005, from http://www.nytimes.com/aponline/ap-gulf.html.

PARENTHETICAL NOTES:

> In "Gulf War" (2003) . . .
>
> ("Gulf War," 2003)

Database

REFERENCES ENTRY:

> Criminal Justice Network. (2002). *Capital cases and defense funding*. Retrieved June 23, 2005, from freenet.crimjus.ca. login as guest, go index (2005, June 23).

PARENTHETICAL NOTES:

> According to *Capital Cases* (2002) . . .
>
> ("Capital Cases," 2002)

Electronic Texts

REFERENCES ENTRY:

Weston, T. (1989). *The electronic teacher.* The Education Server at Columbia University. Retrieved May 25, 2005, from http://www.edserv.edu/index.html.

PARENTHETICAL NOTES:

Weston (1989) points out . . .

(Weston, 1989)

CD-ROM

REFERENCES ENTRY:

MedNet, Inc. (2002). *Directory of mental disorders* [CD-ROM]. New York: MedNet.

PARENTHETICAL NOTES:

MedNet (2002) states . . .

(MedNet, 2002)

E-mail

Because e-mail is not recorded in archives and not available to other researchers, it is mentioned in the text but often not included in the list of references. It can be listed if the contents are of scholarly interest:

REFERENCES ENTRY:

Medhin, L. <lmedhin@tat.interport.net>. (2006, March 1).

Budget request [Office e-mail]. (2006, April 2).

PARENTHETICAL NOTES:

Medhin (2006) suggests . . .

(Medhin, 2006)

If you do not list an e-mail source in the References, treat it as a personal communication—mentioned in the text only, as follows.

PARENTHETICAL NOTE:

Medhin (personal communication, March 1, 2006) suggested . . .

Medhin (personal communication, March 1, 2006).

Synchronous Communication

To cite a posting from forums such as MOO, MUD, or IRC, include names of speakers, a description of the event, the date, the name of the forum, date of retrieval and telnet address:

REFERENCES ENTRY:

Goring, D. (2003, May 12). Seminar discussion on alcoholism. Retrieved June 5, 2005, from Telnet://www.drugabuse.parc. edu:8888.

PARENTHETICAL NOTES:

Goring (2003) indicates . . .

(Goring, 2003)

Linked Sources

REFERENCES ENTRY:

Trainer, L. The education of women. Lkd. *Education Today,* at Columbia Network. Retrieved May 10, 2005, from http://www.colwork.net/.

PARENTHETICAL NOTES:

Trainer (2002) . . .

(Trainer, 2002)

Visuals

Table, Map, or Chart

REFERENCES ENTRY:

New Jersey [Map]. (2006) Trenton, NJ: Garden State Tourism.

Photograph

REFERENCES ENTRY:

Jane Mathers. *Fire Sweeps Downtown.* [Photograph]. Retrieved March 21, 2006, from http://www.suntimes.com/images/fire/Mar06/index/html

Number visuals and add caption crediting the original author or source and copyright holder:

Figure 1. Fire Sweeps Downtown.

Note: Retrieved from http://www.suntimes.com/images/fire/Mar06/index/html

SAMPLE RESEARCH PAPER USING APA STYLE

(with Abstract)

Feeding Frenzy 1

Title

Feeding Frenzy:
Journalism and Justice in
the Leopold and Loeb Case

Byline

Sean O'Connell
Brooklyn College

Instructor's
name
Date

Dr. Abazz
May 10, 2006

Abstract single
spaced in single
paragraph block

Abstract

Current popular opinion suggests that recent high profile legal proceedings have been adversely affected by excessive and sensational media coverage. These cases, many argue, have set dangerous precedents which will cause lasting harm to American justice. The 1924 trial of Leopold and Loeb indicates that this is not a new concern. A careful analysis of the role of journalism in what was called "the crime of the century" reveals the media may have undue influence in individual cases but have little lasting influence on the criminal justice system.

Feeding Frenzy 2

Feeding Frenzy:

Journalism and Justice in

the Leopold and Loeb Case

The twentieth century ended with a flurry of highly publicized crimes and trials—the Menendez case, the O. J. Simpson trial, the Jon Benet Ramsey investigation, and the impeachment of President Clinton. In each instance, the media made instant celebrities of suspects and witnesses. Driven by fame or money, even minor figures became household names, publishing books and appearing on talk shows. Commentators continually lamented that justice was being perverted by media attention, that televised trials were turning lawyers into actors and trials into theater. Justice, many argued, was being irrevocably damaged.

An earlier case, however, reveals that this phenomenon is not new. In the spring of 1924 two young men committed a crime that made them nationally known celebrities and sparked a firestorm of media attention, which many at the time insisted "damaged justice forever" (Harrison, 1924, p. 8).

The "Crime of the Century"

On May 21, 1924, Jacob Franks, a wealthy Chicago businessman, received news that his fourteen-year-old son Bobby had been kidnapped. A letter signed George Johnson demanded ten thousand dollars and gave Franks detailed instructions on how to deliver the ransom. Desperate to save his son, Franks complied with the kidnapper's request, but before he could deliver the money, he learned his son had been found dead. Less than twelve hours after the abduction, a worker discovered the naked body in a ditch on the outskirts of the city (Arkan, 1997).

The killing of Bobby Franks created a national sensation. Rumors circulated that the kidnapper had been a jealous teacher or a disgruntled employee or customer of one of Jacob Franks' enterprises. Because the body had been stripped, many speculated the killer was a sexual pervert (Higdon, 1974).

Margin annotations:

page header every page

Full title

Introduction

Direct quotation with author, year, page number

Paraphrase with author and year

Feeding Frenzy 3

The press seized upon the story, printing numerous accounts of the police investigation. One newspaper offered readers a cash prize for submitting the best theory of the case and was swamped with thousands of letters (Higdon, 1974). Figures 1 and 2 illustrate typical headlines that appeared after the discovery of Frank's body.

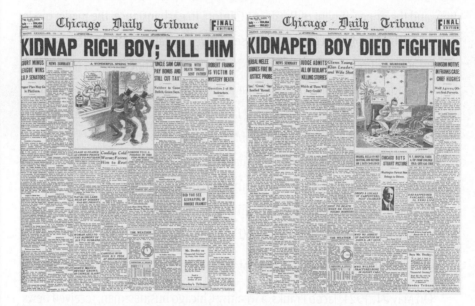

Caption for photograph

Figures 1 & 2. Chicago Daily Tribune *headlines, May 1924*
Note: Retrieved April 7, 2006, from http://homicide.northwestern.edu/documents/5866/19240523trib01.jpg; http://homicide.northwestern.edu/documents/5866/19240523trib03.jpg

The police soon had a strong lead. A pair of eyeglasses had been discovered near the body. Though common in appearance, the glasses, shown in Figure 3, had a newly patented hinge in the frame. Only three pairs had been sold in the Chicago area. The eyeglasses were quickly traced to a neighbor, nineteen-year-old Nathan Leopold ("Born Killers," 1998).

Video listed by title and year

Nathan Leopold explained he had probably dropped the glasses while leading a birding class a few days earlier. At the time of the crime, he claimed to have

Feeding Frenzy 4

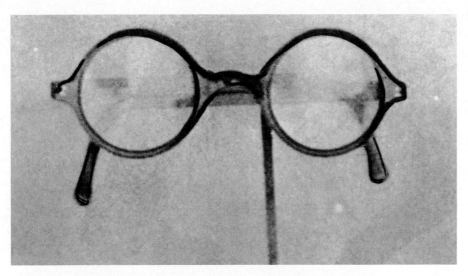

Figure 3. *The key piece of evidence, Nathan Leopold's glasses*　© Bettmann/CORBIS
Note: Retrieved April 10, 2006, from http://pro.corbis.com/search/search.aspx?&i51208223655

been driving with a friend named Richard Loeb and two girls they had picked up in Jackson Park. At first, investigators found Leopold's story believable (Leopold, 1958). Leopold and Loeb seemed unlikely criminals. Like Bobby Franks, they were sons of millionaires; Richard Loeb's father was vice-chairman of Sears & Roebuck. They were gifted students, both having completed college at eighteen. Leopold spoke numerous languages and had become a nationally recognized ornithologist ("Born Killers," 1998). Brought in for questioning, Richard Loeb initially corroborated Leopold's alibi, claiming they spent May 21st with girls they picked up in Jackson Park (Higdon, 1974).

State's Attorney Robert E. Crowe remained unconvinced and continued his investigation. On May 31st, after a long interrogation, Richard Loeb gave a detailed confession, admitting that he and Nathan Leopold were solely responsible for the murder of Bobby Franks. There was no doubt about their guilt. They led police to where they had disposed of the victim's clothing and the lagoon where they had dumped the typewriter used to write the ransom letter (Arkan, 1997). Satisfied he had an airtight case, Richard E. Crowe announced to the press, "'I have a hanging case'" ("Born Killers," 1998). The stunned Loeb family asked the most famous lawyer of the era, Clarence Darrow, to save their son's life (Leopold, 1958).

    The arrest of two wealthy young men, rumors of homosexuality, and the appearance of Clarence Darrow in the case created a media firestorm. Accustomed to reading stories of hardened gangsters, the public was fascinated by the pair of debonair young men who showed no remorse as they chatted with reporters or posed for photographers (see Figure 4).

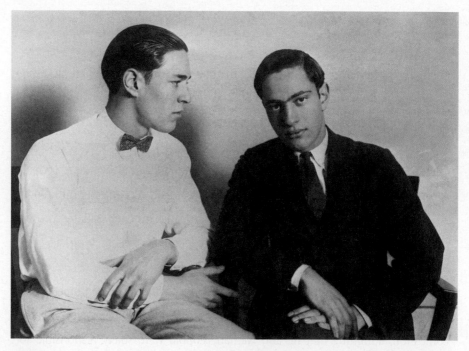

Figure 4.   *Under arrest, Richard Loeb and Nathan Leopold pose for photographers, 1924.* © Bettmann/CORBIS

Note: Retrieved April 10, 2006, from http://cache.corbis.com/CorbisImage/170/12/22/32/12223236/U251458INP.jpg

Feeding Frenzy 6

The Chicago Press of the 1920s

At the time of the Franks kidnapping, Chicago had six daily newspapers, including two Hearst publications known for sensational headlines (Higdon, 1974). Newspapers of the era were highly competitive. In a personal interview, attorney and journalism professor David Evans (2000) noted, "Newspapers in those years were eager to capitalize on crime, sex, and violence to boost sales and increase their advertising rates based on circulation."

Competition led journalists and newspapers to engage in illegal practices. Reporters, whose salaries and bonuses were tied to sales, impersonated police officers to obtain leads, stole documents, and bribed officials for information (Evans, 2000). Major Chicago dailies engaged in brutal circulation wars, hiring gangsters to terrorize news dealers and newsboys from rival papers. The commuter who stopped at a newstand to purchase a *Herald Examiner* might be beaten by a thug working for *The Chicago Tribune* (Higdon, 1974; Evans, 2000).

Feeding Frenzy

The Leopold and Loeb case presented the Chicago press with an unparalleled opportunity for sensationalism. For many, the case represented the moral degeneration of American youth. The 1920s was an era of youthful rebellion, marked by flappers, speakeasies, and open discussions of sex. Prohibition was widely violated, leading millions of Americans to associate with bootleggers and fuel the growing criminal empires of gangsters like Al Capone (Bergreen, 1994).

The Chicago papers had given great press coverage to the gangland killings of the era. But unlike the crude turf battles of the "beer wars," the Leopold and Loeb case gave reporters new avenues to exploit. They quickly dubbed the case a "Thrill Killing," a crime motivated by something darker and more sinister than simple greed (Evans, 2000). After Leopold and Loeb were arrested, Chicago papers

personal interview cited fully in text but not included on References page

reported extensively on their privileged status and their total lack of remorse. *The Chicago Daily News* referred to the defendants as "jealous actors" who "taunted" each other as reporters watched ("Leopold and Loeb," 1924, p. 4). Stories commented on the stylish dress and demeanor of the two young men, who smoked cigarettes and gave impromptu press conferences. Stating the crime had been an experiment, Nathan Leopold told *The Chicago Daily News,* "... it is as easy to justify such a death as it is to justify an entomologist impaling a beetle on a pin" ("Leopold and Loeb," 1924, p. 4).

These comments and images such as the press photograph shown in Figure 5 inflamed the public. Crowds demanded the young men be hanged. Commentators across the country saw the pair as symbols of a corrupt generation without moral consciousness.

Figure 5. Leopold and Loeb laughing during their murder trial. © Bettmann/CORBIS
Note: Retrieved April 10, 2006, from http://cache.corbis.com/ CorbisImage/170/12/51/35/12513500/U252138INP.jpg

Feeding Frenzy 8

The "Trial of the Century"

Despite their confessions, Leopold and Loeb pleaded not guilty. Their attorney, Clarence Darrow, an outspoken opponent of the death penalty, took the case to put capital punishment on trial. Sensing the hostile mood of the jury and cognizant of the crowds milling outside the courthouse demanding the killers be put to death, Darrow changed the plea to guilty (Higdon, 1974).

Darrow's Strategy

Convinced that a jury would not only convict his clients but demand the death penalty, Darrow wanted to avoid a trial. By entering a plea of guilty, Darrow would be able to address the judge directly. He believed he would have a better chance to convince a single individual to spare his clients' lives. A jury, Darrow knew, would make a collective decision. A judge, however, would bear individual responsibility for sending two teenagers to the gallows ("Born Killers," 1998).

Darrow did not consider pleading Leopold and Loeb not guilty by reason of insanity, because this would have required a jury trial. He did, however, argue to Judge Caverly that mental illness should be considered a mitigating factor. He argued that Leopold and Loeb should be imprisoned for life rather than executed (Higdon, 1974).

Press Coverage

The hearing before Judge Caverly became a media circus. Each day thousands of people mobbed the courthouse, hoping to obtain a seat in the courtroom. Admiring women sent flowers to Leopold and Loeb. A despondent man offered to be hanged in their place. A young woman offered to perjure herself, claiming to be one of the girls Leopold and Loeb had picked up in Jackson Park. *The Chicago Tribune,* which owned a radio station, briefly urged readers to demand that the hearing be broadcast over the new medium. Reporters stole a medical report from Darrow's office and printed intimate details about the defendants' sex lives (Higdon, 1974).

When Darrow called psychiatrists to testify on behalf of his clients, William Randolph Hearst offered Sigmund Freud an undisclosed sum to travel to Chicago to comment on the defendants' mental state. Freud declined, but less reputable "experts," including phrenologists, offered opinions to the press. Diagrams of Leopold and Loeb's heads appeared in tabloids with arrows pointing to facial features revealing propensities for falsehood and unnatural sexual appetites (Evans, 2000).

Angered by the crime, the public was outraged by the idea that the killers would be let off because they had unhappy childhoods. Widely viewed as spoiled rich kids, Leopold and Loeb received little sympathy in the press. Hundreds of ministers wrote Judge Caverly insisting they should be put to death. Arguing before the judge, State's Attorney Crowe echoed sentiments expressed in dozens of editorials (Evans, 2000). Having called over a hundred witnesses, Crowe felt confident he had made a compelling case for the death penalty.

Darrow's Use of the Press

Sensing that Judge Caverly would be influenced by community opinion, Darrow sought to defuse some of the negative publicity. Numerous reporters had claimed that Darrow was being paid a million dollars, inflaming public resentment against the affluence of his clients ("Born Killers," 1998; Evans, 2000). Darrow encouraged the fathers of Leopold and Loeb to release a statement to the press asserting that his fee would be determined by the Illinois Bar Association and that their goal was only to secure life imprisonment for their sons. Darrow employed primitive sampling techniques to measure the public mood. He directed pollsters to ask randomly selected men in the Loop if they believed Leopold and Loeb should be executed. Before release of the statement, sixty percent favored the death penalty.

Parenthetical note including two sources

Feeding Frenzy 10

After release of the statement, sixty percent agreed that life imprisonment would be a suitable punishment (Higdon, 1974).

According to Evans (2000), the most significant element of Darrow's strategy was an eloquent twelve-hour closing argument against the death penalty. Quoting the Bible, legal scholars, and great works of literature, he delivered a compelling oration. He stressed the youth of the defendants, arguing that in any other case few would see a life sentence for an eighteen-year-old as lenient. After three weeks of deliberating the case, Judge Caverly shocked the press by sentencing Nathan Leopold and Richard Loeb to life plus ninety-nine years. Despite the severity of the sentence, editorials across the country considered the decision a gross injustice. Edna Harrison (1924) wrote a stinging denouncement of Judge Caverly:

> Nowhere has justice been more blinded than in this city. It is an outrage that perversion, kidnapping, and murder have been rewarded. The science of psychology reduced crime to an ailment and killers to patients. This case has damaged justice forever. (p. 8)

Indented block quotation

The Lasting Influence

The fact that the "outrage" occurred in 1924 illustrates the high profile case made no lasting impact on routine criminal investigations and legal proceedings. David Evans (2000) has argued that the case of Leopold and Loeb, like the sensational trials of the 1990s, had no lasting effect on justice:

> Thousands of trials, both fair and unfair, followed the Leopold and Loeb case. In most instances media attention has had little impact on judges and juries. The insanity plea is rarely used and rarely successful. Psychiatric arguments about diminished capacity have become routine but have not significantly altered the rate of convictions or the severity of sentences, which have steadily become longer.

Feeding Frenzy 11

The case of Leopold and Loeb indicates clearly that excessive media coverage may alter the outcome of a particular sensational trial but has no significant influence on the criminal justice system.

Heading centered

Entries begin flush with left margin

References

Arkan, J. (1997). *Leopold and Loeb*. Retrieved April 10, 2006, from chicago.crime .com/library/article/trials/c15.html.

Bergreen, L. (1994). *Capone: The man and the era.* New York: Touchstone.

Harrison, E. (1924) *The case of Leopold and Loeb.* Chicago: Dearborn.

Higdon, H. (1974). *The crime of the century.* New York: Putnam.

Leopold, N. (1958). *Life plus 99 years.* Garden City: Doubleday.

Leopold and Loeb. (1924, June 2). *The Chicago Daily News,* pp. 1–4.

Meindel, C. (Producer). Born Killers. (1998). <u>In search of history</u>. New York: The History Channel.

WRITING ACTIVITY

1. Using APA style, develop a References page for five of the following sources. Invent needed details such as dates, page numbers, and Internet addresses.
   - one of your textbooks
   - an encyclopedia article
   - a *60 Minutes* episode called "Cyber Crime"
   - a *New York Times* editorial
   - your college's home page
   - a scholarly article from an online journal
   - a corporate Web page
   - the remarks made yesterday by the president on C-SPAN

   Develop a parenthetical note for each of the sources you create.

2. Using MLA style, develop a Works Cited page for five of the following sources. Invent needed details such as dates, page numbers, and Internet addresses.

- a poem by Robert Frost from a book called *100 Poems*
- *Hamlet*
- the Bible
- an interview with John Updike published in this month's *New Yorker*
- a translation of Albert Camus's *The Stranger*
- an essay from the reader portion of this book
- a motion picture
- an online novel

Develop a parenthetical note for each of the sources you create.

Research Paper Checklist

Before submitting your research paper, review these questions:

✔ Does your research paper have a clearly stated thesis?

✔ Do you provide sufficient evidence to support your thesis?

✔ Does the paper focus on your ideas and commentary or does it only summarize other sources?

✔ Do you comment on the quantity and quality of the evidence you have found?

✔ Does the opening introduce the subject, present the thesis, or explain your research method?

✔ Does the conclusion end the paper on a strong point?

✔ Does the paper follow the appropriate style for citing sources?

✔ Questions for your instructor:

- Is my topic acceptable?

- How many sources do I need?

- Does my paper need an outline?

- Which documentation style is required?

For Further Reading

American Chemical Society. *The ACS Style Guide: A Manual for Authors and Editors.*
American Institute of Physics. *AIP Manual of Style.*
American Medical Association. *American Medical Association Manual of Style.*
American Psychological Association. *Publication Manual of the American Psychological Association.*
University of Chicago Press. *The Chicago Manual of Style.*
Council of Science Editors. *Scientific Style and Format: The CBE Manual for Authors, Editors, and Publishers* (note: A 7th edition will be published soon).
Gibaldi, Joseph. *MLA Style Manual.*
Hacker, Diana. *Research and Documentation in the Electronic Age.*
Harvard Law Review. *The Bluebook: A Uniform System of Citation.*
Lester, James D. *Writing Research Papers: A Complete Guide.*
Meyer, Michael. *The Little, Brown Guide to Writing Research Papers.*
Turabian, Kate. *A Manual for Writers of Term Papers, Theses, and Dissertations.*
Veit, Richard. *Research: The Student's Guide to Writing Research Papers.*
Walker, Melissa. *Writing Research Papers: A Norton Guide.*

E-Sources

MLA Style Frequently Asked Questions
   http://www.mla.org/style_faq
Using Modern Language Association (MLA) Format
   http://owl.enlgish.purdue.edu/handouts/research/r_mla.html
APA Style Frequently Asked Questions
   http://www.apastyle.org/faqs.html
Using American Psychological Association (APA) Format
   http://owl.english.purdue.edu/handouts/research/r_apa.html

Companion Website

See **http://www.thomsonedu.com/english/sundance** for additional information on writing research papers.

Grammar and Handbook

GRAMMAR

Grammar is not a set of rules arbitrarily imposed upon writers by dictionary makers, schoolteachers, or anyone else.

— H. J. Tichy

WHAT IS GRAMMAR?

For many students *grammar* means complicated rules, obscure terms such as "nonrestrictive elements," and memories of high school drills about capitals and commas. But grammar is more than rules and regulations. Grammar consists of patterns that organize words into sentences to express ideas. Some people consider grammar to be a set of arbitrary conventions, a form of etiquette. But grammar affects how readers interpret your writing. The following sentences are grammatically correct, but each creates a different impression of the same incident:

> Dr. Green, along with angry patients, protested the closing of the clinic.
> *(Emphasizes the role of Dr. Green in the protest)*

> Dr. Green and angry patients protested the closing of the clinic.
> *(Indicates that the doctor and patients were equally significant)*

> Angry patients, along with Dr. Green, protested the closing of the clinic.
> *(Dramatizes the action of the patients and places the doctor in the background)*

Grammar does have rules and definitions. Although it is not necessary to memorize each detail of this chapter, reviewing and understanding the basic building blocks of grammar will help you not only avoid errors but also improve your ability to write effective sentences.

PARTS OF SPEECH

English consists of nine parts of speech or types of words: nouns, pronouns, adjectives, verbs, adverbs, prepositions, conjunctions, articles, and interjections.

Nouns

Nouns are names of people, places, concepts, and things:

child	*dog*	*automobile*	*computer*
religion	*month*	*ship*	*college*

Proper Nouns   Names of specific people or specially designated places and objects are capitalized:

Nancy	*Bichon*	*Buick*	*Apple*
Islam	*April*	*Titanic*	*Carroll College*

(See pages 888–890 for guidelines on capitalization.)

Gerunds   Gerunds are nouns formed from verbals, usually ending in-*ing:*

Swimming is   He gave up *running.*   She finds *singing* relaxing.
   good exercise.

Pronouns

Pronouns take the place of nouns. They form a kind of shorthand so that Michelle can be referred to as *she*, and the Treaty of Versailles can be called *it*. The noun that the pronoun represents is called the "antecedent."

Personal Pronouns   Personal pronouns refer to specific people, places, or things:

Singular:
I, you, he, she, it   me, you, him, her   mine, yours, his, hers, its

Plural:
we, you, they   us, you, them   ours, yours, theirs

(Antecedents and pronouns must match in number. See pages 854–856 for guidelines on pronoun agreement.)

Indefinite Pronouns   Indefinite pronouns refer to general or nonspecific people, places, or things. Because they don't refer to specific nouns, they do not require an antecedent:

"Can *anyone* help?"

all	any	anybody	anyone	anything
everybody	everyone	everything	few	many
one	something	somebody	someone	some

Demonstrative Pronouns   Demonstrative pronouns point to *antecedents:*

This is my book.   *That* is her car.   *These* are our cards.   *Those* are the boys.

Interrogative Pronouns   Interrogative pronouns introduce questions:

Whose is that?   *Which* is yours?   *What* are you talking about?

Reflexive Pronouns and Intensive Pronouns   Reflexive pronouns add *self* or *selves* to a pronoun to indicate that the subject is also the object:

"He implicated *himself* by lying."

Intensive pronouns add *self* or *selves* for emphasis:

"She baked it *herself.*"

Adjectives

Adjectives modify or describe nouns and pronouns. Adjectives may precede or follow the word they modify:

red car	*old* house	*expensive* tastes	*white* cloth
he was *tired*	she is *young*	they are *angry*	it was *broken*

Verbs

Verbs express action or link ideas.

Action Verbs   Action verbs express both visible action such as running and invisible action such as listening or contemplating:

run	*sing*	*think*	*purchase*
create	*destroy*	*argue*	*support*

Action verbs are *transitive* or *intransitive*. Transitive verbs express action directed toward nouns or pronouns called "direct objects":

> She *purchased* mutual funds.
> <small>Transitive verb   Direct object</small>

Intransitive verbs express action that is not directed to nouns or pronouns:

> She *purchased* recklessly.
> <small>Intransitive verb Adverb</small>

Linking Verbs   Linking verbs express a state of being or relationship. You can think of linking verbs as an equal sign (=), connecting ideas:

> Tom *is* seventeen.   Tom = seventeen.
> They *are* lost.   They = lost.
> Ann *seems* tired.   Ann = tired.

Auxiliary and Modal Verbs   Auxiliary verbs, often called "helping verbs," accompany verbs:

> *had* worked   *has* helped   *is* walking

Modal verbs also accompany verbs to add meaning and indicate tense or time:

> *should* work   *might* help   *will* walk

Time and Number   Verbs are important words in any sentence because they not only express action or a connection but also provide information about the time of the action and whether the subject is singular or plural.

> Tom *works* at Starbucks.   (singular present tense)
> Tom and Nancy *work* at Starbucks.   (plural present tense)
> Tom and Nancy *will get married* in June.   (future tense)
> Tom and Nancy *worked* last semester.   (past tense)

Using singular or plural verbs can help shape meaning:

> A desk and chair *is* on sale.   (indicates the desk and chair are one unit)
> A desk and chair *are* on sale.   (indicates the items are sold separately)

(Subjects and verbs must agree in number. See pages 850–853 for guidelines on subject-verb agreement.)

Adverbs

Adverbs modify verbs, adverbs, adjectives, and entire sentences. They often but not always end in *-ly*.

He ran *quickly*.	(*Quickly* modifies the verb *ran*.)
She sang *very* well.	(*Very* modifies the adverb *well*.)
He bought the *freshly* waxed car.	(*Freshly* modifies the adjective *waxed*.)
Evidently, they refused the offer.	(*Evidently* modifies the whole sentence.)

(See pages 869–870 for guidelines on using adverbs properly.)

Articles

Articles are a form of adjective that limits nouns.
The is a definite article, indicating a specific noun:

We took *the* train to *the* city.

A and *an* are indefinite articles, indicating a general or nonspecific noun.

■ *A* generally precedes nouns beginning with consonants:

She ate *a* banana.　　He read *a* book.　　They bought *a* tent.

■ *An* generally precedes nouns beginning with vowels:

She ate *an* apple.　　He read *an* article.　　They bought *an* awning.

Prepositions

Prepositions express relationships in space and time:

about	*beneath*	*into*	*outside*	*under*
above	*between*	*like*	*over*	*until*
among	*down*	*of*	*past*	*up*
below	*during*	*outside*	*to*	*with*

Prepositions and their objects form prepositional phrases:

above the city	*into the night*	*during the game*
near the car	*to the school*	*until next week*

It is important to recognize prepositional phrases because the subject of a sentence will not be part of a prepositional phrase:

The *cost* of books *is* rising.

(The subject is *cost*, not *books*, so the verb is singular.)

Conjunctions

Conjunctions are connectors.

Coordinating Conjunctions   Coordinating conjunctions—*and, or, yet, but, so, nor, for*—join equivalent words, phrases, and clauses:

Tom *or* Kevin	(*or* connects two nouns)
take the bus *or* walk home	(*or* connects two phrases)
I live in New York, *and* she lives in Miami.	(*and* joins two clauses)

Subordinating Conjunctions   Subordinating conjunctions—*after, although, because, since, though, when, where*—connect main clauses with subordinate clauses:

She failed *because* she did not study.
After the game, we went home.
Though he spoke no French, he moved to Paris.
We moved to Topeka, *where* we opened a cafe.

(Note that when the subordinating clause introduces the sentence, it is set off by a comma.)

Interjections

Interjections are words or phrases that express strong or sudden emotions:

Wow! That's expensive.
Oh! I had no idea.
The paramedics, *alas,* arrived too late.

UNDERSTANDING PARTS OF SPEECH

Words are not automatically nouns or verbs. Parts of speech are determined by the word's role in the sentence. The word *paint,* for example, can be a noun, verb, or adjective:

I bought red *paint*.   (noun)
I will *paint* the bedroom yellow.   (verb)
The brushes are stored in the *paint* room.   (adjective)

A verbal phrase, for instance, can serve as a noun and subject:

Walking along the beach under a full moon is romantic.

Understanding a word's role in the sentence can help you focus on main ideas, avoid common grammar errors, and write more effective sentences.

STRATEGIES | for Determining Parts of Speech

1. Read the sentence out loud.
2. Locate the verb, which either expresses action or links ideas.
3. Determine the subject (noun) that performs the action or is linked to other ideas.
4. Adjectives modify nouns—subjects, direct objects, or indirect objects.
5. Adverbs modify verbs, adverbs, and adjectives.
6. Conjunctions link words, phrases, and clauses—*and, or, yet, but, so, nor, for*.
7. Prepositions express relationships in time and space and often form phrases—*in the mood, around the corner, during the night*.

WRITING ACTIVITY

Identify the parts of speech for each of the italicized words:

The *village* _____ of Holcomb stands *on* _____ the *high* _____ wheat plains of *western* _____ Kansas, a *lonesome* _____ area that other *Kansans* _____ *call* _____ "out there." Some seventy miles east of the Colorado border, *the* _____ countryside, *with* _____ its hard *blue* _____ skies and desert-clear air, has an atmosphere that *is* _____ rather more Far Western than Middle West. The local *accent* _____ is barbed with a *prairie* _____ twang, a ranch-hand nasalness, and the men, many of them, *wear* _____ narrow *frontier* _____ trousers, Stetsons, and *high-heeled* _____ boots with pointed toes. The land is *flat* _____, and views are *awesomely* _____ *extensive* _____; horses, herds of cattle, a white cluster of grain elevators *rising* _____ as gracefully as Greek temples are *visible* _____ long before a traveler reaches them.

—Truman Capote

PHRASES AND CLAUSES

Phrases

Phrases are groups of related words:

Diet and exercise are important.	(noun phrase)
He *sang and danced*.	(verb phrase)
She put the book *on the shelf*.	(prepositional phrase)

Clauses

Clauses are groups of related words that include at least one subject and one verb.

Independent Clauses   Independent clauses can stand alone because they state a complete thought. They are sentences:

We bought a new car.	(subject: *We* verb: *bought*)
She speaks Farsi.	(subject: *She* verb: *speaks*)
Italy produces wine.	(subject: *Italy* verb: *produces*)

Dependent Clauses   Dependent clauses, though they have a subject and verb, do not express a complete thought and cannot stand alone. They are sentence fragments:

after we bought a new car . . .
because she speaks Farsi . . .
since Italy produces wine . . .

You can often detect dependent clauses by reading them aloud. (See pages 841–843 for guidelines on fragments.)

SENTENCES

A sentence contains a subject and verb and expresses a complete thought:

> Mary bought a hat.
> Swimming is good exercise.
> Take cover! (the subject *you* is implied)

Common Sentence Patterns

✔ Subject + Predicate (Verb)
(*Predicates* consist of verbs and related words that express what the subject does.)

> Actors rehearse.

✔ Subject + Predicate (Verb + Complement)
(*Complements* complete the predicate.)

> Actors rehearse daily.

✔ Subject + Predicate (Verb + Direct Object)
(*Direct objects* are nouns or pronouns receiving the verb's action.)

> Actors rehearse dialogue.

✔ Subject + Predicate (Verb + Indirect Object + Direct Object)
(*Indirect objects* are nouns or pronouns that receive the action described by the verb and direct object. They usually precede the direct object.)

> Directors give actors suggestions.

✔ Subject + Predicate (Verb + Direct Object + Complement)

> Directors make actors content.

Types of Sentences

There are four basic types of sentences:

Simple Sentence

A simple sentence consists of a single independent clause:

> George moved to Canada.
> Dublin is the capital of the Republic of Ireland.

Despite years of research and extensive testing, the new computer program, initially promoted as the greatest innovation in decades, has failed to interest experts or consumers.

(Though long, this is a simple sentence consisting of one independent clause.)

Simple sentences can have compound subjects and verbs:

George and Nancy moved to Canada and *opened* a store.
Subject   Subject   Verb   Verb

Compound Sentence

A compound sentence consists of two or more independent clauses. You can think of it as a double or triple sentence. It contains more than one simple sentence:

George moved to Canada, and *Philip returned to Greece.*
Independent clause   Independent clause
Dublin is the capital of the Republic of Ireland; London is the capital of
Independent clause   Independent clause
Great Britain; Belfast is the capital of Northern Ireland.
Independent clause

There are two methods of joining independent clauses to form a compound construction:

■ Link the independent clauses with a comma and a coordinating conjunction—*and, or, yet, but, so, for, nor:*

Independent clause,   *and*   independent clause.
                      or
                      yet
                      but
                      so
                      for
                      nor

■ Link the independent clauses with a semicolon:

Independent clause; independent clause.

Incorrectly punctuated compound sentences can result in run-ons and comma splices. (See pages 843–845 for guidelines on run-ons and comma splices.)

Complex Sentences

Complex sentences consist of one independent clause and one or more dependent clauses:

> *The team won the game* because Chavez made two touchdowns.
> Independent clause   Dependent clause

> After they lost the game, *the team demanded the coach resign.*
> Dependent clause   Independent clause

Note: When dependent clauses begin a complex sentence, they are set off with a comma. (See pages 871–872 for comma rules.)

Compound-Complex Sentences

Compound-complex sentences include two or more independent clauses and at least one dependent clause:

> After she appeared on Broadway, *Fran McCarg opened a jazz club in Kansas*
> Dependent clause   Independent clause
> *City*, but *she never matched her early success.*
>   Independent clause

> *Jack Kerouac wrote* On the Road *based on his American travels; he wrote*
>   Independent clause
> Satori in Paris *after visiting France*, where he sought to learn the origin of his
>   Independent clause   Dependent clause
> family's name.

> *Dean Martin first achieved success as a singer*, but *he became nationally famous*
>   Independent clause   Independent clause
> *when he joined Jerry Lewis*, who did stand-up comedy.
>   Dependent clause

Note: Dependent clauses are set off with commas when they open a sentence.

WRITING ACTIVITY

Label each of the following sentences as simple, compound, complex, or compound-complex.

1. _____ Charles Jackson was born in New Jersey in 1903.

2. _____ He attended Syracuse University but dropped out after his freshman year.

3. _____ While working odd jobs, he developed symptoms of tuberculosis, but he hid his condition from his family.

4. _____ When he was no longer able to conceal his illness, Jackson sought treatment, and he entered a sanitarium in Davos, Switzerland.

5. _____ While he was recovering from tuberculosis, Jackson began drinking to deaden the pain and boredom.

6. _____ Jackson became an alcoholic.

7. _____ Unable to find work during the Depression, he drifted for years, depending on his younger brother for support.

8. _____ In 1936 Jackson entered a hospital; he made a serious effort to stop drinking.

9. _____ Sober, Jackson began writing short stories and radio soap operas.

10. _____ Jackson recorded his experiences in *The Lost Weekend;* the novel became a best-seller, inspiring the Academy Award–winning film starring Ray Milland.

Other Ways of Looking at Sentences

Sentences can also be classified in rhetorical and functional terms.

Rhetorical Forms

Rhetorical sentences can be categorized as *periodic* or *cumulative.*

Periodic sentences end with the main idea, usually stated in an independent clause. Most complex and compound-complex sentences that open with dependent clauses are periodic:

> After he studied for weeks, *George panicked and refused to take the bar exam.*
> Developed by scientists in the 1950s, *the drug,* which many thought had little value for decades, *now is considered a breakthrough in AIDS research.*

Periodic sentences are useful to build tension or highlight a surprise or climactic ending.

Cumulative sentences open with the main idea, usually an independent clause, and add further details in phrases or clauses:

> *Al Capone was tried for income tax evasion* because prosecutors doubted that a Chicago jury would convict him of Prohibition charges.

Cumulative sentences communicate clearly because they state the most important idea first, followed by supporting details. They can be read easily and are less likely to be misinterpreted than periodic sentences.

Alternating between periodic and cumulative sentences can increase the variety in your writing style, reduce repetition, and more clearly emphasize important ideas.

Functional Forms

Functional sentences can be classified as *declarative*, *imperative*, *exclamatory*, and *interrogative*.

Declarative sentences make a statement:

Robert Moses built the Triborough Bridge.
Ottawa is the capital of Canada.
Once banned, absinthe is now legal in some countries.

Imperative sentences give commands:

Bring your books to the exam.
Buy me a ticket to New Orleans.
Don't attempt this at home.

Exclamatory sentences state strong feelings:

That is ridiculous!
He should be fired!
The jury awarded the family $50 million!

Interrogative sentences ask questions:

Can you help?
Where have you been?
Is your home safe?

Grammar Review

Remember these key aspects of grammar to avoid common sentence errors:

✔ Sentences must contain a subject and a verb and must express a complete thought.

✔ Compound sentences join independent clauses either with a comma and *or, and, yet, but, so, for, nor,* or with a semicolon.

✔ When dependent clauses open complex sentences, they are set off with commas.

✔ Personal pronouns—*he, she, they, we, it*—must be clearly linked to nouns (antecedents).

✔ Singular nouns take singular pronouns (*he, hers, it*); plural nouns take plural pronouns (*they, theirs, them*).

✔ Singular subjects have singular verbs; plural subjects have plural verbs.

Companion Website

See **http://www.thomsonedu.com/english/sundance** for additional information about grammar.

THE HANDBOOK

This concise handbook focuses on the most common writing problems you are likely to encounter. Attempting to read and remember all the material in this chapter would be time-consuming and in many cases unnecessary; you probably know more grammar than you realize. Most writers, however, make habitual errors.

STRATEGIES for Using the Handbook

1. Review this chapter to become familiar with its layout.
2. Examine previous assignments to identify mistakes in your writing. Note repeated errors.
3. Highlight sections in the handbook addressing your problem areas. You may wish to jot down page numbers or use Post-its® to tab these pages for quick reference.
4. Review these sections while editing and proofreading papers.
5. Refer to the handbook when instructors return papers with errors in grammar and mechanics.
6. See Companion Website http://www.thomsonedu.com/english/sundance for additional information on mechanics.

CONTENTS

SENTENCE PROBLEMS

There are three common sentence errors:

Fragments	incomplete sentences
Run-ons and comma splices	improperly punctuated compound sentences
Faulty parallelism	words or phrases presented in pairs or lists that do not match in form

You can overcome many errors if you understand basic sentence structure. Review the definitions of *simple* and *compound* sentences on pages 833–834.

Fragments

Fragments are incomplete sentences. They lack a subject, full verb, or fail to state a complete thought. The term *fragment* is misleading because it suggests something short. But even a long group of words can be a fragment:

Sentences:

> Duck! (Note: The subject *you* is implied)
> Ann sings.
> She is seventeen.

Fragments:

> Located by the side of the road just two miles from the main highway.
> (a phrase lacking a subject and verb)

> Worked and toiled for weeks to prepare a new budget before the annual meeting.
> (a verb phrase and complement lacking a subject)

> Kim working until midnight every weekend.
> (incomplete verb. Note: *ing* verbs cannot stand alone.)

> Because Sharon was angered by the voters' lack of support.
> (dependent clause. Note: Although there is both a subject and full verb, the statement does not express a complete thought.)

Writers often intentionally write fragments in fiction and personal essays for special effect:

> He looked out the window. The blizzard had obliterated the farm. There was nothing but snow. *Snow in all directions. Snow on the fields. Snow in the road. Miles of blinding snow. White and unforgiving snow.*

Fragments should be avoided in formal academic, business, and technical writing.

Fragments often occur when you write quickly and either skip a needed word or accidentally break off part of a sentence that cannot stand alone:

> Working at Mister Paul's was frustrating. I had to supervise six employees. *Most of them teenagers.* They had poor work skills and usually arrived late. On the busiest weekend of the year, three waiters failed to show up. *Because they decided to attend a rock concert.*

STRATEGIES | for Detecting and Revising Fragments

1. Read your paper aloud, pausing after each period. Make sure all sentences have a complete subject and verb. Each sentence should express a complete thought. Fragments, especially dependent clauses, sound like introductions to unstated ideas:

   After the game ended.
   Because the examination was canceled.
   Before the Internet was developed.

2. Revise fragments in three ways:
   - Add missing elements

     The house is completely filled with visitors and relatives.
     They are Are unable to locate the source of the pollution.

   - Turn dependent clauses into sentences by deleting subordinating elements (usually the first word or words):

     ~~Because the~~ The president failed to warn Congress.
     ~~Although the~~ The union had won two bitter strikes.

■ Connect fragments to related sentences. Often fragments are just that, pieces of another sentence you have accidentally broken off:

Companies must provide day-care services to recruit employees/~~Who~~ ^{who} have preschool children.

The museum purchased works by some of Europe's greatest painters: *Manet, Monet, Degas, and Chagall.*

Even though he was born in Nigeria, Derrick had little knowledge of African politics.

WRITING ACTIVITY

Locate and revise the ten fragments in the following passage:

The word "Harlem" conjures up a variety of images. To some the neighborhood is one of New York's most distressed slums. While others recall the heyday of the Harlem Renaissance. Cradle of black writers, poets, and jazz musicians. But few realize the unique history of this famous black community. Harlem, ironically, began as an upper-class white residential area. In the late 1800s Harlem was open country. Featuring ponds, woods, and pastures. South of Central Park, Manhattan growing. Additional housing was needed. Because of the new streetcar lines. The land north of Central Park was within easy commuting distance to Manhattan's offices, stores, and businesses. Real estate developers seeing great opportunity. Constructed blocks of expensive townhouses. Unfortunately, speculators overbuilt. Demand had been greatly overestimated. When upper-income white people failed to take interest in the new community. Landlords subdivided the units and rented to blacks. Who traditionally had been forced by discrimination to pay higher rents. Within a decade or so, the planned reserve of white executives became a thriving black community. Its collection of artists, musicians, and intellectuals made it the capital of African American culture. However, as landlords continued to subdivide houses to increase rents. Harlem became overcrowded and began to decay.

Run-on Sentences and Comma Splices

Run-on sentences and *comma splices* are incorrectly punctuated compound sentences. *Compound sentences* (see page 834) consist of two or more independent clauses (simple sentences) joined by a comma and *and, or, yet, but, so, for, nor,* or by a semicolon:

> The teachers edited the magazine, and the students designed the illustrations.
> The runway is closed; it will reopen at noon.

Run-ons occur when two sentences run together without the proper punctuation:

> Administrators are struggling with budget cuts, ^*and*^ they hope private industry will donate computers.
> Patience is important in parenting; children are often defiant.

Comma splices (also called "comma faults") occur when two sentences (independent clauses) are joined with a comma instead of a semicolon. In writing quickly, you may instinctively sense that two complete ideas should be separated but fail to use the proper punctuation:

> The city is responsible for the bridge; the county must repair the onramps.
> Sean Nelson served in the Navy, ^*but*^ he never learned to swim.

STRATEGIES | for Detecting and Revising Run-ons and Comma Splices

- **Read your sentences aloud.** If they contain more than one complete idea or simple sentence, make sure the independent clauses are joined by a comma with *and, or, yet, but, so, nor, for,* or by a semicolon.
- **Revise run-ons and comma splices in four ways:**
  1. **Add missing elements:**

     Celluloid is unstable, ^*and*^ many early films have been lost.

     or

     Celluloid is unstable; many early films have been lost.

  2. **Determine if you have used a comma instead of a semicolon.** In revising sentences, you may wonder if a comma should be semicolon. To determine if you need a semicolon, follow these steps:

a. Read the sentence aloud. Does it sound like more than one complete idea? Are independent clauses properly joined?

b. If a comma seems to join two independent clauses, ask yourself if you can replace the comma with a period and have a complete sentence on the left and on the right. If you can create two simple sentences and a word such as *and, or, yet, but, or, so,* or *nor* is not used, use a semicolon.

3. **Revise the wording of the sentence.** It may be better to stress the relationship between clauses by making one of them dependent:

> *Because* celluloid is unstable, many early films have been lost.

4. **Separate the independent clauses to form two or more simple sentences.** You may have accidentally run sentences together that are not closely related and should be separated. Ideas are given greater emphasis when stated in simple sentences:

Comma splice and run-on:

Creditors were demanding payment,^and^ employees were threatening to strike.^ Franklin Motors declared bankruptcy.

■ **Read your revisions aloud.** Do your new sentences avoid run-ons? Do they effectively express your ideas?

WRITING ACTIVITY

Revise the following comma splices and run-ons. You may add missing elements, separate independent clauses, or reword the sentences for clarity and emphasis.

1. The first computers were large machines they filled entire rooms.

2. They contained thousands of tubes, the tubes blew out constantly.

3. Graduate students ran up and down the computer room they pushed shopping carts filled with replacement tubes.

4. These monstrous computers were marvels they had less power than today's handheld calculators.

5. An early computer expert predicted the United States would need only five computers he could not anticipate the revolution to come.

6. Computers remained mysterious and somewhat sinister machines, most Americans saw them only in science fiction movies.

7. Computers have revolutionized society some experts see problems.

8. The 1960 census was computed on massive reels of tape no modern computer can accommodate them.

9. Only one computer from that era is still operational it is located in a museum.

10. Years of data may be lost future researchers will face a daunting task to retrieve information processed on obsolete equipment.

Faulty Parallelism

When you write about pairs or lists, the words or phrases must match— they have to be all nouns, all adjectives, all adverbs, or all verbs in the same form:

Nancy is *bright, creative*, and *funny*. (adjectives)
Mary writes *clearly, directly*, and *forcefully*. (adverbs)
Reading and *calculating* are critical skills for my students. (gerunds)
She should *lose* weight, *stop* smoking, and *limit* her intake of alcohol.
    (verbs matching with *should*)

Mistakes with parallelism are easy to make. If asked to describe your best friend, you might come up with nouns (*a student*), adjectives (*smart*), or verbs (*sings*). It is often difficult to combine all these ideas into one list and keep them in the same format.

The concert was loud, colorful, and ~~many people~~ well attended.
(the adjective *well attended* matches the adjectives *loud* and *colorful*.)

John failed to take notes, refused to attend class, and ~~his~~ wrote an unreadable final exam ~~is unreadable~~.
(the verb *wrote* matches the verb phrases *failed to take* and *refused to*.)

Quitting smoking and daily ~~exercise~~ exercising are important.
(*exercising* and *quitting* are both gerunds, or *ing* nouns.)

STRATEGIES | for Detecting and Revising Faulty Parallelism

Examine any sentences that include pairs or lists of words or phrases to make sure that they are parallel by applying this simple test:

1. Read the sentence and locate the pair or list.
2. Make sure each item matches the format of the basic sentence by testing each item.

Example:

Students should read directions carefully, write down assignments accurately, and take notes.

> *Students should* read directions
> *Students should* write down assignments accurately
> *Students should* take notes

(Each item matches *Students should . . .*)

This sentence is **parallel.**

Computer experts will have to make more precise predictions in the future to reduce waste, create more accurate budgets, and public support must be maintained.

> *Computer experts will have to* make more precise . . .
> *Computer experts will have to* create more accurate . . .
> *Computer experts will have to* public support must be . . .

(The last item does not link with *will have to*.)

This sentence is **not parallel.**

Review of Faulty Parallelism

Test each of the following to identify unparallel elements:

1. Unemployment can lead to marital problems, alcohol and drug abuse, feelings of depression, and bouts of irrational behavior such as gambling.
2. Maintenance costs are based on labor rates, availability of spare parts, and are subject to inflation.
3. My job entailed word processing, filing, and sales orders had to be verified.

4. An effective resume, a confident interview, and being realistic about hiring salaries will increase your chance of being hired.
5. Born a slave, Booker T. Washington founded a college, led a black businessmen's association, and became the first African American to stay at the White House.

Answers

1. Correct
2. Not parallel: *are based on . . . are subject to inflation* do not match. Substitute *inflation* so the list is composed of all nouns.
3. Not parallel: *My job entailed . . . sales orders had to be verified* do not match. Substitute *verifying sales orders*.
4. Not parallel: *Being realistic* does not match with the nouns *resume* and *interview*. Substitute *a realistic attitude about hiring salaries*.
5. Correct

A Tip on Parallelism

In many cases it is difficult to revise long sentences that are not parallel:

> To build her company, Shireen Naboti is a careful planner, skilled supervisor, recruits talent carefully, monitors quality control, and is a lobbyist for legal reform.

If you have trouble making all the elements match, it may be simpler to break it up into two or even three separate sentences:

> To build her company, Shireen Naboti is a careful planner, skilled supervisor, and lobbyist for legal reform. In addition, she recruits talent carefully and monitors quality control.

The first sentence contains the noun phrases; the second consists of the two verb phrases. Remember, it is often easier to create two short parallel lists than one long one.

WRITING ACTIVITY

Revise the following sentences so that the pairs and lists are parallel. You may break the sentences into two if you are unable to make a single list of items match.

1. The Knights of Labor fought for higher wages, shorter hours, and opposed unsafe conditions.
2. Farmers must anticipate prices, decrease production costs, maintain accurate records, and willing to take risks.
3. The team faces three major problems: the coach's retirement, recurring injuries, and fans unwilling to purchase season tickets.
4. Computers allow entrepreneurs to market products worldwide and competing with major corporations.
5. They saved money to repair the house, purchase a new car, and repayment of debt.
6. Applicants must be intelligent, creative, flexible, and work with little supervision.
7. They decided to drop out of school and seeking adventure in Europe.
8. The employees will be either fined or demotions may be announced.
9. Parents and teachers must agree on the best methods to discipline rude conduct, instruct children with learning disabilities, and determining the role of extracurricular activities.
10. She was spirited, witty, charming, and showed knowledge about the college.

STRATEGIES | for Revising Sentence Problems

1. Read your paper aloud. You can often hear incomplete statements, indicating possible fragments or confusing ideas signaling possible run-ons. Some errors such as comma splices, however, may sound correct because both a comma and a semicolon denote a pause.
2. When you locate sentence errors, do not think of them as a puzzle or math problem you have to solve or "fix." Poorly written sentences may not be easily revised. Reconsider what you were trying to say and express your ideas in a new sentence. Often trying a fresh approach will lead you to not only avoid errors but also create more effective and interesting sentences.
3. Keep track of errors instructors note in your writing and highlight or tab these areas in the handbook for future reference.

Companion Website

See **http://www.thomsonedu.com/english/sundance** for additional information on sentence structure.

AGREEMENT

Subjects and their verbs and nouns and their pronouns must agree or match in number.

Singular subjects have singular verbs; plural subjects have plural verbs:

Singular: The *boy* next door *plays* the piano. (*boy . . . plays*)
Plural: The *girls* across the street *play* the violin. (*girls . . . play*)

Note: An *s* is usually added to indicate plural nouns (cat*s*) and singular verbs (purr*s*).

Singular nouns take singular pronouns; plural nouns take plural pronouns:

Singular: The *boy* next door rides *his* bicycle. (*boy . . . his*)
Plural: The *girls* ride *their* bicycles. (*girls . . . their*)

Maintaining these patterns of agreement emphasizes the relationship between ideas and prevents confusion. Although the concept is basic, agreement problems are very common.

Subject-Verb Agreement

Although matching singulars and plurals appears easy in simple sentences, choosing the right verb can be challenging in longer and more complicated structures. Many words can be singular or plural depending on context. Long noun phrases can easily be misread and assigned the wrong verb form. There are eight common situations that present problems for writers:

1. **Nouns ending in s:** Many words that appear plural because they end with *s* are in fact singular:

   Singular: mathematics   physics   economics

   Words like *statistics* can be singular or plural:

   Singular: *Statistics requires* a keen sense of logic.
   Plural: These *statistics* about homelessness *are* alarming.

2. **Collective or group subjects:** Collective nouns and phrases are singular when they act as a unit:

Singular:
   United Technologies appears to be gaining market share.
   (United Technologies is a single corporation.)

   The *jury deliberates* this weekend.
   (The twelve members act as a unit.)

   Twenty Thousand Leagues Under the Sea is my favorite adventure book.
   (the title of one book)

   The *number* of dropouts *is* less than anticipated.
   (one number or figure)

   Five dollars is not enough for lunch.
   (a single amount of money)

Collective or group nouns are plural when items in the group act separately:

Plural:
   A *number* of parents *were* unable to come.
   (Parents act separately.)

   Five dollars were spread on the table.
   (individual dollar bills)

3. **Subjects joined by *and*:** Subjects linked by *and* are plural if they refer to two separate items:

   My *mother* and *father are* going to Florida.
   (two people)

   His *intelligence* and *hard work are* admirable.
   (two separate qualities)

Subjects linked by *and* are singular if they refer to a single item:

   My *friend and partner is* a skilled designer.
   (a person who is both friend and partner)

   Her *drinking and driving is* very disturbing.
   (a single action)

4. **Subjects joined by *either . . . or*:** The words *either* and *or* indicate that one or the other subject, but not both, is linked to the verb.

If both subjects are singular, the verb is singular:

   My *father* or *mother is* driving us to the airport.
   (Only one parent will drive.)

If both subjects are plural, the verb is plural:

> *Parents* or *teachers supervise* the playground.
> (In both instances, more than one adult watches the playground.)

If one subject is singular and the other is plural, the verb agrees with the subject nearer the verb.

> *Either the letters* or *the package is* insured.
> *Either the package* or *the letters are* insured.

5. **Inverted word order or *There* + verb constructions:** In some sentences the normal word order is inverted so that the verb comes before the subject. In other instances such words as *there, here, when, how, what, which,* and *who* begin constructions that can be singular or plural:

Singular: *There goes* my best friend.
           What is your problem?
           He is a person *who loves* money.
           When is she coming?

Plural: *There go* my best friends.
           What are your problems?
           He is one of those people *who love* money.
           When are they coming?

6. **Indefinite pronouns:** The words *anybody, anyone, someone, each, either,* and *everybody* are singular.

Singular: *Everybody is* encouraged to participate.
           Someone travels downtown every day.

The words *all, any, some, none, most,* and *half* can be singular or plural, depending on the noun preceding the verb:

Singular: *All* of the money *is* missing.
           Some of the snow still *remains* on the field.
           Half of my income *depends* on bonuses.

Plural: *All* of the books *are* missing.
           Some of the children *remain* on the field.
           Half of the stores *close* early on Sunday.

7. **Prepositional phrases:** Prepositional phrases are groups of related words linked to such words as *above, around, over, under, before, after, while,* or

during. The subject of a sentence is not included within a prepositional phrase. The key word or subject usually precedes the prepositional phrase.

Singular: One of *my friends* is absent.
            (The subject is *One*, not *friends*.)

Plural: Children *with a love of poetry* are attracted to these programs.
            (The subject is *Children*, not *a love*.)

8. **Subjects with possessive forms:** Subjects that include a possessive form can be easily misread:

Singular: The parents' main concern *is* school security.
            (*concern* is the subject, not *parents'*.)

            The Europeans' love for American music *is* well known.
            (*love* is the subject, not *Europeans'*)

Plural: Paul's clothes *are* stylish.
            (*clothes* is the subject, not *Paul's*)

            Kim's books *are* overdue.
            (*books* is the subject, not *Kim's*)

STRATEGIES | for Overcoming Problems with Subject-Verb Agreement

1. Recognize sentences that may pose problems—sentences with compound subjects, collective nouns, *either . . . or* constructions, or inverted word order.
2. Read sentences out loud to appreciate their meaning. In a few instances, agreement problems will stand out when spoken.
3. Locate the verb or verbs.
4. Ask who or what is associated with the verb's action or linked to the subject. The answer will be the subject.

In some instances you may have created a long or awkward sentence that should be restated rather than simply repaired. Consider your ideas and express them using different constructions that will avoid agreement errors and state your ideas more clearly.

WRITING ACTIVITY

Circle the correct verb in the following sentences.

1. Children's clothing (is/are) designed for durability, not style.
2. The goal of the parents and teachers (remain/remains) the same.
3. Either the teacher or the substitute (supervises/supervise) the testing center.
4. Neither the lawyers nor the investigators (are/is) confident about solving the case.
5. *Nine Stories* (is/are) on the summer reading list.
6. There (are/is) guests waiting.
7. Either the cities or the federal agency (oversees/oversee) new construction.
8. The teacher's guidelines (provides/provide) strategies for using the library.
9. Fifteen minutes (give/gives) us enough time to evacuate the building.
10. The movies, especially ones filmed before WWII, (was/were) usually in black and white.
11. The lifespan of birds (vary/varies) greatly.
12. Anyone who is interested in helping (is/are) invited.
13. In a small office, located in a battered safe, (lie/lies) secrets of a major conspiracy.
14. The audience, which included teachers and students, (was/were) restless.
15. Half the class (is/are) interested in attending summer school.

Pronoun Agreement

Pronouns must agree or match with their antecedents—the nouns or pronouns they represent:

1. **Pronouns should agree in number and gender with antecedents:**

   Bill took *his* time.   *Nancy* rode *her* bicycle.   The *children* called *their* mother.

2. **Compound nouns require plural pronouns:**

> Both the *students and the teachers* argue that *their* views are not heard.
> *Tom and Nancy* announced that *they* plan to move to Colorado next year.

3. **Collective nouns use singular or plural pronouns:**

Singular: The *cast* played *its* last performance.
      (The cast acts as one unit.)

Plural: The *cast* had trouble remembering *their* lines.
      (Cast members act independently.)

4. **Either . . . or constructions:** The words *either* and *or* indicate that one noun or the other, but not both, is linked to the verb.

If both nouns are singular, the pronoun is singular:

> *Either* the city council *or* the county board will present *its* budget.
> (Only one group will present a budget.)

If both nouns are plural, the pronoun is plural:

> *The board members* or *the city attorneys* will present *their* report.
> (In both instances, several individuals present a report.)

If one noun is singular and the other is plural, the pronoun agrees with the nearer noun:

> *Either the teacher or students* will present *their* findings to the principal.

Note: Place the plural noun last to avoid awkward statements or having to represent both genders with *he and she, his or her,* or *him and her.*

5. **Avoid shifts in person or point of view:** Pronouns should maintain the same person or point of view in a sentence, avoiding awkward shifts:

Awkward shift: To save money, *consumers* should monitor *their* (third person) use of credit cards to avoid getting over *your* (second person) head in debt.

Revised: To save money, *consumers* should monitor *their* use of credit cards to avoid getting over *their* heads in debt.

6. **Indefinite pronouns.** In speaking, most people use the plural pronouns *they, them,* and *their* to easily include both males and females. But in formal

writing, most writers follow the established rule that singular indefinite pronouns agree with singular pronouns:

Singular:

anybody	everybody	nobody	somebody
anyone	everyone	no one	someone
either	neither	each	one

Anybody can bring *his or her* tax return in for review.

Everybody is required to do the test *himself or herself.*

Plural: If *many* are unable to attend the orientation, make sure to call *them.*

Indefinite pronouns like *some* may be singular or plural depending on context:

Singular: *Some* of the ice is losing *its* brilliance.

Plural: *Some* of the children are missing *their* coats.

STRATEGIES | for Avoiding Sexism in Pronoun Use

Singular nouns and many indefinite pronouns refer to individuals who may be male or female. Trying to include both men and women, however, often creates awkward constructions:

If a student has a problem, *he or she* should contact *his or her* adviser.

In editing your writing, try these strategies to eliminate both sexism and awkward pronoun use:

1. **Use plurals:**
   If students have problems, *they* should contact *their* advisers.
2. **Revise the sentence to limit or eliminate the need for pronouns:**
   Students with problems should contact advisers.
   Advisers assist students with problems.

WRITING ACTIVITY

Circle the correct pronoun in the following sentences:

1. The cable television industry or the local stations are responsible for the messages (it/they) convey to children.

2. An attorney should focus on the needs of (his or her/their) clients.

3. The attorney and her advisors claimed (her/their) meeting had to be delayed because (they/it) could not be scheduled before the judge's ruling.

4. A child or (his and her/their) parents may sign the release form.

5. The causes of heart disease demand extensive research because of (its/their) complexity.

6. The jury made (their/its) decision.

7. Neither the United States nor any European country is willing to risk (its/their) prestige.

8. Half the merchandise could not be delivered because of (its/their) cost.

9. Either Mom or Dad can let you into (his or her/their) house.

10. If prices of wheat cannot remain stable (it/they) will drive investors from the market.

Companion Website

See **http://www.thomsonedu.com/english/sundance** for additional information about agreement.

VERBS

Irregular Verbs

Most verbs are *regular: -d or -ed* is added to indicate the past participle.

    pass/passed   walk/walked   create/created   adopt/adopted

Other verbs are *irregular:* other spellings or words indicate the past and the past participle.

    swim/swam/swum   drink/drank/drunk   sing/sang/sung

Common Irregular Verbs

Review this list and highlight any verbs that have given you trouble in the past:

Present Tense	Past Tense	Past Participle (used with helping verb)
arise	arose	arisen (*ex:* have arisen)
be	was/were	been (*ex:* have been)
bear (carry)	bore	borne (*ex:* were borne)
bear (give birth)	bore	borne/born
beat	beat	beaten
become	became	become
begin	began	begun
bend	bent	bent
bet	bet	bet
bite	bit	bitten/bit
blow	blew	blown
break	broke	broken
bring	brought	brought
build	built	built
burst	burst	burst
buy	bought	bought
catch	caught	caught
choose	chose	chosen
come	came	come
do	did	done
draw	drew	drawn
eat	ate	eaten
fall	fell	fallen
find	found	found
fly	flew	flown
forbid	forbade/forbad	forbidden
freeze	froze	frozen
get	got	got/gotten
give	gave	given
go	went	gone
have	had	had
lay (to place)	laid	laid
lie (to recline)	lay	lain
lose	lost	lost
pay	paid	paid

ring	rang	rung
say	said	said
shine	shone/shined	shone/shined
show	showed	shown/showed
sleep	slept	slept
strike	struck	struck
swear	swore	sworn
take	took	taken
tear	tore	torn
tell	told	told
throw	threw	thrown
wear	wore	worn
write	wrote	written

Verb Tense

Verb tense shows the time of an action or event. English verbs have three simple and three perfect tenses or times.

Simple tenses indicate that the action is restricted to one specific time.

Past: I was sick.
           (*suggests the illness was limited to the past*)
Present: I study French.
           (*indicates the speaker is currently studying*)
Future: I will take algebra next semester.
           (*indicates a future action*)

Perfect tenses indicate that the action is not limited to one time period.

Past: I had been traveling for several months before I met my family.
           (*suggests traveling ended before a past date*)
Present: I have been studying French.
           (*indicates recent and current action*)
Future: I will have completed algebra by the time I graduate.
           (*indicates that a future action will be completed by a date further in the future*)

STRATEGIES for Using Verb Tenses

1. **Shift tenses in writing to indicate changes in time:**

   I *was* born in Chicago, but I *live* in New York.

2. **Shift tenses to contrast past with ongoing action or unchanging status:**

   The conference *was* in Trenton, which *is* the capital of New Jersey.

   Note: Stating *was the capital* suggests that the capital has changed.

3. **Add clarifications to prevent confusion:**

   Capone *sold* liquor, which *was then* illegal.

   Note: indicates a subsequent change in the law

4. **Avoid inappropriate shifts in time:**

   Inappropriate: Janet *hosts* lots of dinner parties. They ~~were~~ *are* elegant.

5. **Use either past or present tense to describe actions in a work of art, such as a novel, play, or film.**

   Past
   Hamlet *pondered* his fate. He *was* haunted by the death of his father. Yet he *could* not bring himself to avenge his murder.

   Present
   Hamlet *ponders* his fate. He *is* haunted by the death of his father. Yet he *can*not bring himself to avenge his murder.

WRITING ACTIVITY

Revise the following sentences to avoid incorrect tense or inappropriate shifts in tense.

1. Translators work for years to produce the 1989 edition of *War and Peace*.

2. Students who currently worked full time will be eligible for loans next year.

3. The Holland Tunnel was congested, so we call to postpone our meeting.

4. He wait a full day before calling a doctor, a delay that was almost fatal.

5. The children can't come this weekend because they were sick.

6. Counties in Louisiana were called parishes.

7. Students hated his take-home exams so much they call them "brain-killers."

8. Telephone when you needed a ride.

9. My father was born in Boston, which was a major city on the East Coast.

10. He speaks Greek better than he spoke Turkish.

Companion Website

See **http://www.thomsonedu.com/english/sundance** for additional information on verbs.

PRONOUNS

Pronouns take the place of nouns and other pronouns. Because pronouns can refer to a number of words, they must be used carefully to avoid confusion.

Pronoun Reference

Pronouns should clearly refer to specific antecedents. Avoid unclear references:

> Crime is ruining the community. Cars are stolen. Stores are vandalized. Windows are smashed. *They* just don't care.

Who does *they* refer to? Criminals? Residents? Police? Politicians?

Note: *They* is probably the most often misused pronoun. When editing, make sure that each *they* can be clearly linked to a specific noun or pronoun.

STRATEGIES | for Using Pronouns

1. **Make sure pronouns have clear antecedents.** Avoid constructions in which a pronoun could refer to more than one noun or pronoun, creating alternative possible interpretations.

Unclear: Nancy was with Sharon when *she* got the news.
            (Who received the news—Nancy or Sharon?)

Revised: When Sharon received the news, *she* was with Nancy.

2. **Replace pronouns with nouns for clearer references.**

Unclear: The teachers explained to the students why *they* couldn't attend the ceremony.
            (Who cannot attend the ceremony—teachers or students?)

Revised: The teachers explained to the students why *faculty* couldn't attend the ceremony.
            The teachers explained to the students why *children* couldn't attend the ceremony.

3. **State *either . . . or* constructions carefully.**

Either George or Jim can lend you *their* key.
(George and Jim share one key.)

Either George or Jim can lend you *his* key.
(Both George and Jim have keys.)

Either George or Anna can lend you *a* key.
(avoids need for *his or her*)

4. **Avoid unclear references when using *this, that, it, which,* and *such.***

Unclear: Many people think that diets are the only way to lose weight. *This* is wrong.

Revised: Many people mistakenly think that diets are the only way to lose weight.

Unclear: Sharon used a company car and drove to the airport, *which* was illegal.

Revised: Sharon illegally used a company car to drive to the airport.

5. **Avoid unnecessary pronouns after nouns.**

Thomas Jefferson *he* wrote the Declaration of Independence.

The manual *it* says all emergency calls must be reported.

6. **Avoid awkward use of you.** *You* is acceptable for directly addressing readers. Avoid making awkward shifts in general statements.

Awkward: Freeway congestion can give you stress.

Revised: Freeway congestion can be stressful.

Pronoun Case

Pronouns have different forms—or cases—depending on how they are used in a sentence:

Subjective Case:
I/we   you   he/she/it   they   who/whoever

Subjective pronouns are used as subjects:

I can drive.   *You* look great.   *She* is here.   *They* are moving.
Who is there?

Objective Case:
me/us   you   him/her/it   them   whom/whomever

Objective pronouns are used as direct or indirect objects and objects of verbals or prepositions:

He drove *me.*   Here's to *you!*   Give it to *her.*   Help *them!*
To *whom* it may concern

Possessive Case:
my/ours   your   his/hers/its   their   whose
mine/ours   yours   his/hers/its   theirs

Possessive pronouns indicate ownership:

Take *my* car.   Is that *your* hat?   She likes *her* house.
Their car is stalled.   *Whose* hat?

STRATEGIES | for Using Proper Case

Your use of case is usually automatic. Reading a paper aloud will often help you catch making mistakes between using *he* and *him* or *they* and *them.*

There are a few areas that most writers find confusing:

1. **Using *who/whom:***

   Who and *Whom* are often confused because they are typically used in questions:

   > (Who/Whom) did you call?
   > (Who/Whom) called last night?

   To determine which pronoun to use, answer the question, substituting *they* or *them:*

   > I called *them* (objective case needed)
   > *Whom* did you call?

   > *They* called last night (subjective case needed)
   > *Who* called last night?

   When *they* is appropriate, use *who;* when *them* is appropriate, use *whom.*

2. **Using *whoever/whomever:***

   Whoever and *whomever* often introduce dependent clauses:

   > The director shouted at (whoever/whomever) crossed the stage.
   > The director shouted at (whoever/whomever) she liked.

   To determine which pronoun to use, isolate the dependent clause and substitute *they* or *them:*

   > *they* crossed the stage (subjective)
   > she liked *them* (objective)

   > The director shouted at *whoever* crossed the stage.
   > The director shouted at *whomever* she liked.

   When *they* is appropriate, use *whoever;* when *them* is appropriate, use *whomever.*

3. **Using *we* and *us* before a noun:**

   > (We/us) girls can win this game.
   > They'd better give that trophy to (we/us) winners.

To determine which pronoun to use, delete the noun to see which sounds appropriate:

We can win this game. (subjective)
They'd better give that trophy to *us*. (objective)

We girls can win this game.
They'd better give that trophy to *us* winners.

4. **Using the right pronoun case in compounds:**

Although you may automatically choose the right pronoun in isolation—*I* gave the money to *her*—you may find compounds confusing:

Tim and (I/me) worked with Sandy and (she/her).
We wanted Sharon and (she/her) to attend the seminar.

To determine which pronoun to use, simplify the sentence by isolating each pronoun:

I worked with *her*.
We wanted *her* to attend the seminar.

WRITING ACTIVITY

In the following sentences, apply the strategies to identify sentences with correct use of pronouns and sentences with pronoun problems. In some instances you may correct the problem by simply substituting a word; in others, you may have to rewrite the sentence.

1. Sarah and Nancy spent the day looking for parts for her antique car.

2. The government announced that they should pay their taxes.

3. To prevent workers from being injured by tools, make sure they are examined before each shift.

4. In Martin Luther King's article, he states that people deal with oppression in three ways.

5. Children and parents often feel their feelings are being ignored.

6. The coach rewarded whomever could hit a homerun.

7. I give money to whoever needs it.

8. I hate the way they treat we students.

9. Sharon borrowed my report and made copies for everyone. That was unfair.

10. When Jack and her first opened the store, I was convinced they would be successful.

Companion Website

See **http://www.thomsonedu.com/english/sundance** for additional information on pronoun use.

DANGLING AND MISPLACED MODIFIERS

Modifiers—adjectives, adverbs, prepositions, and verbals—are effective only if they are carefully placed in a sentence:

> She wore a ribbon in her hair, which was *red*.
> (What is *red*, her hair or her ribbon?)
>
> *Drained yesterday*, the guests were disappointed that the pool was empty.
> (Were the guests *drained*?)

Dangling Modifiers

Modifiers that serve as introductions must describe what follows the comma. When they do not, they "dangle," so that what they modify is unclear:

> *Grounded by fog*, airport officials ordered passengers to deplane.
> (Were airport officials *grounded by fog*?)
>
> Revised:
> Grounded by fog, the passengers were ordered by airport officials to deplane.
> Airport officials ordered passengers to deplane the aircraft, which was grounded by fog.

STRATEGIES | to Detect Dangling Modifiers

Sentences with opening modifiers set off by commas fit this pattern:

Modifier, Main Sentence

To make sure the sentence is correct, use the following test:

1. Read the sentence, then turn the modifier into a question, asking who or what in the main sentence is performing the action:

   question, answer

2. What follows the comma forms the answer. If the answer is appropriate, the construction is correct:

   Hastily constructed, the bridge deteriorated in less than a year.

   Question: What was *hastily constructed?*
   Answer: the bridge
   This sentence is **correct.**

   Suspected of insanity, the defense attorney asked that her client be examined by psychiatrists.

   Question: Who was *suspected of insanity?*
   Answer: the defense attorney
   This sentence is **incorrect.**

   Revised: Suspecting her client to be insane, the defense attorney asked that he be examined by psychiatrists.
               The defense attorney asked that the defendant she suspected of insanity be examined by psychiatrists.

Misplaced Modifiers

Place modifying words, phrases, and clauses as near as possible to the words they describe:

   Confusing: Scientists developed new chips for laptop computers *which cost less than fifty cents.*

Do laptop computers cost *less than fifty cents?*

   Revised: Scientists developed laptop computer chips which cost less than fifty cents.

Confusing: Jogging often reduces stress.

Does this mean that frequent jogging reduces stress or that jogging has proven to occasionally reduce stress?

Revised: Frequent jogging reduces stress.
Jogging can reduce stress in some instances.

WRITING ACTIVITY

Revise the following sentences to avoid dangling and misplaced modifiers. In some instances, you can merely move phrases; in others, you may have to rewrite the entire sentence.

1. Spinning out of control, the aeronautical engineer struggled to advise the troubled pilot.
2. She is teaching a course at Cornell on plane geometry.
3. Fearing contamination, all food products were ordered destroyed by inspectors after the flood.
4. Hoping to pass with flying colors, the exam grade stunned Michelle.
5. Shocked by his falling blood pressure, Sam was treated by paramedics.
6. Once regarded with suspicion, marketers see the Internet as a way of increasing sales.
7. No longer endangered, tourists can easily see lions in their natural habitat.
8. Popular with customers, the kitchen staff at the Coffee Trader felt overwhelmed.
9. Chewing often provokes headaches.
10. She designed restorations of old houses that people just loved.
11. The almost developed lots sold for a million dollars.
12. Developed only recently, scientists still doubt the efficacy of the new drug.
13. Demanding a refund, car dealers tried to calm the angry consumers.
14. Understanding these notes completely prepares students for the GED exam.
15. Children only learn what they can experience.

Companion Website

See **http://www.thomsonedu.com/english/sundance** for additional information about dangling and misplaced modifiers.

ADJECTIVES AND ADVERBS

Adjectives modify nouns and pronouns, and can be formed from nouns and verbs:

Nouns: *car* insurance   *field* glasses   *book* report
Verbs: *steamed* rice   *iced* tea   *dyed* shirt

Adverbs modify verbs, adverbs, adjectives, and sentences. Most adverbs are formed by adding *ly* to adjectives:

poor/poorly   angry/angrily   heated/heatedly

STRATEGIES | for Using Adjectives and Adverbs

1. **Understand differences between adjectives and adverbs:**

   She gave us *freshly sliced* peaches.
   (The adverb *freshly* modifies the adjective *sliced*, meaning that the peaches, whatever their freshness, have just been sliced.)

   She gave us *fresh sliced* peaches.
   (The adjectives *fresh* and *sliced* both describe the noun *peaches*, meaning the peaches are both fresh and sliced.)

2. **Review sentences to select the most effective adjectives and adverbs.**
   Adjectives and adverbs add meaning. Avoid vague modifiers:

   Vague: The concert hall was *totally inappropriate* for our group.

   Revised: The concert hall was *too informal* for our group.
              The concert hall was *too large* for our group.

3. **Use adverbs with verbs.**

   Incorrect: Drive *careful*. (adjective)
   Revised: Drive *carefully*.

4. **Avoid unnecessary adjectives and adverbs.**

Unnecessary: We drove down the *old, winding, potholed, dirt* road.
Revised: We drove down the *winding, potholed* road.

5. **Use *good* and *well*; *bad* and *badly* accurately.** *Good* and *bad* are adjectives and modify nouns and pronouns:

The cookies taste *good*. (*good* modifies the noun *cookies*)
The wine is *bad*. (*bad* modifies the noun *wine*)

Well and *badly* are adverbs and modify verbs, adjectives, adverbs:

She sings *well*. (*well* modifies the verb *sings*)
He paid for *badly* needed repairs. (*badly* modifies the adjective *needed*)

WRITING ACTIVITY

Revise adjective and adverb use in the following sentences:

1. I ruined my shoes walking across the fresh tarred parking lot.

2. He played so good last night.

3. That is such a high stressful job.

4. Radical diets are unfortunate popular with teens who feel bad about their appearance.

5. Drive slow because of the ice.

6. He suffered a severely injury in the accident.

7. The soup tasted badly.

8. Without glasses, she sees poor.

9. I was upset at the sloppy decorated banquet hall.

10. That tastes so well.

Companion Website

See **http://www.thomsonedu.com/english/sundance** for additional information on adjectives and adverbs.

PUNCTUATION

Punctuation can seem trivial. But missing or misused punctuation marks, like misspelled words, not only detract from your message and your credibility as a writer but also can alter meaning:

Instructors, say students, complain about the grading policy.

Without commas, faculty members report that students are complaining about the grading policy. With commas, the sentence means the opposite, suggesting that instructors are the ones who are complaining.

, Comma

Commas serve as road signs signaling a change or transition in a sentence. Commas indicate pauses that prevent confusion:

When we reached the theater, patrons were leaving.

Commas are used for ten basic reasons.

1. **Commas come before a coordinating conjunction that joins independent clauses in compound and compound-complex sentences:**

   Independent clause, *and* independent clause
   (simple sentence) *but* (simple sentence)
   or
   nor
   for
   yet
   but

2. **Commas follow introductory words, phrases, and clauses:**

   Angered, the committee read the complaint letters.

   Opened in 1912, the bridge remains the only link to the island.

   Earning ten million dollars in less than a year, she became the highest paid player on the tour.

   To avoid becoming infected, avoid contact with patients.

   Prepared to take decisive action, the firefighters waited for the wind to change.

   Commas follow dependent clauses introducing independent clauses:

   When she graduated from law school, Corinne decided to move to Florida.

Because prices rose faster than investors anticipated, additional stock offerings were postponed.

3. **Commas separate lists of parallel words, phrases, or clauses:**

Words: The gym was *old, dark,* and *musty.*
She *ran, swam,* and *danced.*
Pens, pencils, paper, and *books* were supplied to refugee
children.

Phrases: He *exercises daily, eats lightly,* and *drinks moderately.*
Parents of small children, small business owners, and *real estate
developers* met with the zoning committee.
The changes were *developed too late, explained too poorly,* and
implemented too quickly to solve the problem.

Clauses: In the ideal company *the customers receive respect, the employees are
appreciated,* and *investors are enriched.*
The students were frustrated, the faculty was confused, and *the alumni
were dumbfounded* by the president's speech.
We were convinced that *most of the children were malnourished, the
parents were overworked,* and *the community was nearing collapse.*

4. **Commas come between coordinate adjectives.** Coordinate adjectives
modify the same noun or pronoun and can be joined by a coordinating conjunction. One test is to reverse the order of the adjectives. Another is to
place the word *and* between them. If you can include *and* without changing
the meaning or creating an awkward phrase, insert a comma:

Examples: It was a *hot humid* day. It was a *hot and humid* day. (no change)
add comma
It was a hot, humid day.

I bought a *hot apple* pie. I bought a *hot and apple* pie. (awkward)
no comma
I bought a hot apple pie.

5. **Commas set off nonrestrictive phrases or clauses.** *Nonrestrictive phrases
and clauses* provide nonessential information about a noun or pronoun.
They can be eliminated without changing the meaning of a sentence.
Restrictive phrases or clauses restrict or limit the meaning of nouns or pronouns. They cannot be eliminated without changing the meaning of a
sentence.

Because the terms *nonrestrictive* and *restrictive* are difficult to remember—think of the words *extra* and *ID*. *Nonrestrictive* elements don't *identify* words; they add *extra* or parenthetical information. *Restrictive elements* help *ID*, or *identify*, words:

Nonrestrictive: Tom Green, *who wants to quit smoking,* should consider hypnosis.
          (The proper noun *Tom Green* is clearly identified and the phrase *who wants to quit smoking* merely adds additional or *extra* information. Eliminating the phrase does not alter who should consider hypnosis—Tom Green.)

Restrictive: Anyone *who wants to quit smoking* should consider hypnosis.
          (The pronoun *anyone* is restricted or further *identified* by the phrase *who wants to quit smoking.* Eliminating the phrase alters the meaning, suggesting that everyone should consider hypnosis.)

Nonrestrictive	**Restrictive**
Extra	*ID*
George, *who is my friend,* will help.	Anyone *who is my friend* will help.
Extra	*ID*
Frank's car, *which was repaired last week,* broke down.	The car *that was repaired last week* broke down.
Extra	*ID*
Marquette University, *located in Milwaukee,* will conduct the research.	A university located in Milwaukee will conduct the research.

In some instances the use of commas depends on the writer's meaning:

Teenagers, who like rock music, love this store.
(implies that all teenagers like music and love the store)

Teenagers who like rock music love this store.
(implies that only teenagers who like rock music love the store)

6. **Commas set off appositives, absolutes, and contrasted elements.** *Appositives* provide additional information about a noun or pronoun. Appositives giving nonrestrictive or *extra* details are set off with commas:

George Washington, *the first president,* was born in 1732.

Pennsylvania, *the Keystone state*, has a new lottery.
Morphine, *a highly addictive drug*, is prescribed carefully.

Contrasted elements: Books, *not television*, should inspire our children.

Absolutes: *Designed for speed*, the car was not practical for most drivers.

7. **Commas set off parenthetical expressions, interjections, and direct address.**

Parenthetical expressions:
  The conduct of the judge and, *thus,* the attitude of the jury shocked the defense attorneys.
  Her statement to the press, *no doubt,* alters the whole investigation.

Interjections: *Say,* that is a good idea.
                             She refuses, *I bet,* to share her thoughts.
Direct address: *Mother,* are you coming?
                             I suggest, *Dr. Wilson,* that you talk to the parents.

8. **Commas set off geographical names, items in dates, addresses, and numbers.**

Geographical names: The office in *Baton Rouge, Louisiana,* processes all bills.
                                    He was born in *Ottawa, Canada.*

Items in dates: She retired on *December 15, 2002.*

Addresses: Checks can be sent to *Committee for Refugees, 700 Kings Highway, Haddonfield, NJ 08033.* (Note: No comma between state and ZIP codes.)
                       Drive to Henri Maltrec's warehouse at *3737 North Lakewood, San Diego.*

Numbers: Commas set off units of three numbers: We sold 425,987 cars last year.

Note: Do not insert commas in page numbers, ZIP codes, Social Security numbers, decimals, street addresses, or telephone numbers.

9. **Commas set off quotations:** Winston Churchill said, "Never give in."

10. **Commas are inserted in sentences to prevent confusion.** Writers often add commas simply to prevent readers from being confused.

We assume that by 2005, 500 computers will have to be replaced.

STRATEGIES | for Eliminating Unnecessary Commas

Because commas have so many uses, you may easily place them where they are not needed. Insert commas where needed in the following sentences:

1. **Do not set off prepositional phrases from what they modify:**

   The boy/ *in the last row*/ has a question.

2. **Do not put commas between subjects and verbs unless setting off non-restrictive elements:**

   The mayor/ spoke with the press.
   The mayor, *who denied he was resigning,* spoke with the press.

3. **Do not set off titles in quotation marks with commas:**

   I read/ "The Gold Bug/" last night.

4. **Do not put commas after a series unless it ends a clause needing to be set off from the rest of the sentence:**

   They brought *food, water, and clothing*/ to the church.
   They brought *food, water, and clothing,* and they offered to take the supplies to the flood victims.

5. **Do not separate items in a compound verb unless there are three or more.**

   We *talked*/ and *danced* all night.
   We *talked, danced,* and *played cards* all night.

6. **Do not set off dependent clauses that end a sentence:**

   He sold the house/ *because it was too expensive to maintain.*

WRITING ACTIVITY

Insert commas where needed in the following sentences.

1. Henry Woo who majored in history applied to law school.

2. We can accept cash credit cards and checks for any rentals leases or purchases.

3. She insisted the documents were filed on January 15 2000.

4. In 1989 the company sold 3500 trucks and 32598 cars.

5. J. Edgar Hoover who ran the FBI for almost fifty years used the media to cultivate his image as a tough crime fighter.

6. Warner Oland who played Chinese detective Charlie Chan was Swedish and he translated the works of Strindberg into English.

7. Exercise not diet is the key to losing weight.

8. Las Vegas the fastest growing city in the West may run out of water.

9. San Diego California once known simply as a military town now features an expanding commercial district.

10. They played tennis ran marathons and lifted weights to stay in shape fight boredom and avoid chores.

11. At what point Shelly wondered would her family accept her decision?

12. Taxpayers always eager to complain were surprisingly silent when Fenton New Jersey doubled property taxes.

13. Teenagers including those who show no outward signs often suffer from depression.

14. The small book shop is threatened by Internet booksellers chain bookstores and discount retailers.

15. She was hired because of her willingness to take risks drive to make changes and ability to improvise solutions.

Companion Website

See **http://www.thomsonedu.com/english/sundance** for additional information about commas.

;   Semicolon

Semicolons link related independent clauses and separate items in lists containing internal commas.

1. **Semicolons link related independent clauses. Compound sentences without coordinating conjunctions use semicolons:**

> Lewis drove to El Paso; Frank flew to Chicago.
> He visited France often; however, he never learned French.

2. **Semicolons separate items in a list containing internal commas:**

> The Big Three consisted of Franklin Roosevelt, president of the United States; Josef Stalin, leader of the Soviet Union; and Winston Churchill, prime minister of Great Britain.

The inclusion of semicolons prevents readers from counting an item twice, thinking, for instance, that Roosevelt and the president of the United States were two different people.

■ When you encounter semicolons in a list, all the words and phrases between them are considered one item.

WRITING ACTIVITY

Circle each of the six ingredients of milk chocolate as listed on the wrapper of a Hershey's candy bar:

> MILK CHOCOLATE CONTAINS SUGAR; MILK; COCOA BUTTER; CHOCOLATE; SOYA LECITHIN, AN EMULSIFIER; AND VANILLIN, AN ARTIFICIAL FLAVORING.

WRITING ACTIVITY

Add the missing commas and semicolons in this passage from Bruce Catton's "Grant and Lee." After completing the exercise, check your corrections against the original text on pages 464–468.

> Lee was tidewater Virginia and in his background were family culture and tradition . . . the age of chivalry transplanted to a New World which was making its own legends and its own myths. He embodied a way of life that had come down through the age of knighthood and the English country squire. America was a land that was beginning all over again dedicated to nothing much more complicated than the rather hazy belief that all men had equal rights and should have an equal chance in the world. In such a land Lee stood for the feeling that it was somehow of advantage to human society to have a pronounced inequality in the social structure. There should be a leisure class backed by ownership of land in turn society itself should be keyed to the land as the chief source of wealth and influence. It would bring forth (according to this ideal) a class of men

with a strong sense of obligation to the community men who lived not to gain advantage for themselves but to meet the solemn obligations which had been laid on them by the very fact that they were privileged. From them the country would get its leadership to them it could look for the higher values—of thought of conduct of personal deportment—to give it strength and virtue.

Companion Website

See **http://www.thomsonedu.com/english/sundance** for additional information about semicolons.

: Colon

Colons are used to introduce elements and separate items such as numerals, titles, and time references.

1. **Colons introduce a list, explanation, or an example.** Note that colons are used only after an independent clause.

   We need/computer paper, pens, and pencils.
   We need office supplies: computer paper, pens, and pencils.
   We could resolve all the problems but one: pollution.

2. **Colons introduce long quotations:**

   > Though Harry Truman is highly regarded today, Smith argues that he disappointed many in Washington when he assumed the presidency:

   > Truman lacked the polish and dignity that marked the Roosevelt era. He was a plain-spoken, sometimes earthy Midwesterner who had only a high school education. He struck many as woefully unprepared to conclude a world war and lead the country forward after victory.

3. **Colons are used in common notations:**

Time references:	10:15 a.m.
Ratios:	They chose our product by a 4:1 margin.
Titles and Subtitles:	His book is called *A Nation Apart: The Young in America.*
Bible references:	Ecclesiastes 12:12

" "   **Quotation Marks**

Quotation marks are used for direct quotations, titles of short works, and highlighted words.

1. **Direct quotations.** When you copy word for word what someone has written or said, enclose the statement in quotation marks:

   > Martin Luther King said, "I have a dream."

   Note: The final mark of punctuation proceeds the final quotation mark, unless it does not appear in the original text:

   > Did Martin Luther King say, "I have a dream"?

   Note: The identifying phrase is set off with commas:

   > Maria argued, "We cannot win."
   > "We cannot win," Maria argued.
   > "We cannot win," Maria argued, "unless we practice!"

   Note: Commas do not set off a quotation if the quotation is blended into the sentence:

   > They "do unto others" by volunteering at the clinic.

   Note: Quotations within quotations are indicated by single quotation marks:

   > The president said, "I was only a child when Martin Luther King said, 'I have a dream.'"

   Note: Final commas are placed inside quotation marks:

   > The letter stated, "The college will lower tuition," but few students believed it.

   Colons and semicolons are placed outside quotation marks:

   > The letter stated, "The college will lower tuition"; few students believed it.

   Note: Indirect quotations or paraphrases do not require quotation marks:

   > Martin Luther King stated that he had a vision.

2. **Titles of short works.** Quotation marks are placed around the titles of articles, poems, songs, short stories, essays, individual episodes of television shows, and other larger works. (Titles of longer works such as magazines or books are underlined or placed in italics.)

Did you read "When Are We Going to Mars?" in *Newsweek*?

Note: In titles, capitalize the first and last words, and any middle words that are nouns, pronouns, adjectives, verbs, adverbs, or subordinating conjunctions (such as *if*, *because*, and *that*). Do not capitalize middle words that are prepositions, articles, or coordinating conjunctions (such as *and*, *but*, and *or*). The "to" in infinitives should also not be capitalized in middle words of titles.

3. **Highlighted words.** Quotation marks can be used to focus attention on items, words, or phrases:

I still don't know what "traffic abatement" means.

WRITING ACTIVITY

Insert quotation marks where needed in the following sentences.

1. John F. Kennedy stated, Ask not what your country can do for you, ask what you can do for your country.

2. The film seems to be a modern adaptation of Willa Cather's story Paul's Case.

3. Nancy Lowe argues, The most famous saying of the Depression was Roosevelt's statement We have nothing to fear but fear itself.

4. I can't go, James said, until I register these documents.

5. Advertisements aimed at children should not mention the word sex.

Companion Website

See **http://www.thomsonedu.com/english/sundance** for additional information about quotation marks.

' Apostrophe

Apostrophes indicate possession, missing letters or numbers, and some plurals.

1. **Possessive forms:**
   Add *'s* to show possession for most singular nouns:

   a boy*'s* hat   the book*'s* cover   the dog*'s* collar

   Add *s'* to show possession for plural nouns ending in *s:*

   two boy*s'* hats   the book*s'* covers   the dog*s'* collars

   Add *'s* to show possession for plural nouns that do not end in *s:*

   women*'s* clothing   children*'s* games   men*'s* shoes

   Add apostrophes to the last noun to show joint or mutual possession:

   Smith and Baker*'s* travel agency is providing the tickets.

   Add apostrophes to all nouns to show individual possession:

   The parent*s'* and the teacher*s'* statements were reported by the press.

2. **Missing letters and numbers.** Omitted letters in contractions are indicated by a single apostrophe:

   can't for cannot   *he'll* for he will

   Note: Only one apostrophe is used, even if more than one letter is deleted. The apostrophe is placed over the missing letter or letters, not where words are joined:

   do not = don't   *not*   do'nt

   Deleted numbers are indicated by a single apostrophe:

   He was embued with the Spirit of '76.
   Back in '29, Wall Street collapsed.
   My brother is restoring a '65 Mustang.

   Apostrophes indicate letters dropped to reproduce dialect or slang:

   The London cabby shouted, "'E ain' goin' nowhere!"

3. **Plurals of letters, numbers, or symbols:**

   She got all A's last semester.
   I need a lot of size 7's this week.

Note: Common abbreviations such as UFO and ESP do not require apostrophes:

They claimed he stole two TVs and three VCRs.

Note: Apostrophe use in referring to decades is optional; be consistent:

Incorrect: I grew up in the *1980s* but loved the music of the *1960's.*
Correct: I grew up in the 1980s but loved the music of the 1960s.

Remember: *it's = it is   its = possessive*
                    it's raining   The car will not start because *its* battery died.

WRITING ACTIVITY

Add apostrophes where needed in the following passage.

Charles Lindbergh will always be remembered for 1927s famed flight to Paris. However, his influence on American politics, science, aviation, and medicine cant be underestimated. Fame seemed to follow Lindberghs every move. He pioneered new air routes over some of the worlds most remote areas. Lindberghs marriage to the daughter of Dwight Morrow brought him more fame. The kidnapping of Charles and Annes first son thrust the young couples grief into the headlines. The newspapers lurid coverage and the reporters intrusive behavior soured Lindbergh on America. He moved his family to England in the late 1930s because he felt Britains more genteel society would provide a safe haven. During those years, Lindbergh worked with Dr. Alexis Carrel, a Nobel Prize winning scientist. Lindberghs and Carrels creation of an experimental artificial heart in the 1930s signaled an achievement in medical engineering. Lindberghs visit to Nazi Germany and his opposition to Americas entry into the Second World War led many Americans to question his loyalty. Lindbergh did serve in the South Pacific as an advisor, showing US pilots how to extend their planes range by lowering gas consumption. Though he spent most of his life working with aircraft, Lindbergh opposed the SSTs development in the 1960s because he felt it would damage the earths atmosphere. In his last years, Lindbergh devoted his life to environmental causes, sharing the younger generations concern about pollution.

Companion Website

See **http://www.thomsonedu.com/english/sundance** for additional information about apostrophes.

. . .   Ellipsis

An *ellipsis*, composed of three spaced periods (. . .), indicates that words have been deleted from quoted material:

Original text: The mayor stated, "The city needs a light rail system to overcome freeway congestion and provide efficient transportation between the airport and the convention center."

With ellipsis: The mayor stated, "The city needs a light rail system to . . . provide efficient transportation between the airport and the convention center."

Note: Do not omit words that will alter or distort the meaning of the original text. Delete extra or parenthetical material.

Note: When deleting words at the end of a sentence or an entire sentence, add the final period to the ellipsis, creating four periods:

The mayor stated, "The city needs a light rail system to overcome freeway congestion. . . ." (The quotation marks follow the ellipsis.)

Note: Do not use ellipsis when omitting words from the beginning of a quotation:

The mayor stated the city needs light rail to facilitate "efficient transportation between the airport and the convention center."

Note: If omitting words alters the grammar of a sentence, you may change a verb or pronoun to maintain agreement:

Original: The mayor said, "The convention center and the new hotels are the lifeblood of development."

With ellipsis and alteration in brackets:
The mayor said, "The convention center . . . [is] the lifeblood of downtown development."

( )   Parentheses

Parentheses enclose nonessential but related ideas. Parenthetical information can be located anywhere in a sentence except at the very beginning. It should be placed just after the idea it refers to.

1. **Use parentheses to set off additional or illustrative matter and to enclose abbreviations, explanatory letters, or numerals:**

   Students took the Scholastic Aptitude Test (SAT) last week.

   George Wilson (later joined by Jan Sullivan) argued for a policy change.

   Michael Collins (1890–1922) remains one of Ireland's greatest heroes.

   Primary diagnostic methods (such as blood tests and X-rays) are fully covered by the new insurance policy.

   Because Tom graduates in December (he took a semester off to travel), he won't look for a job until after New Year's.

   Note: When parenthetical comments appear after a word or phrase set off by commas, the commas follow the parentheses:

   Star Trek, which lasted only three seasons (1966–1969), became a TV classic.

2. **Use parentheses to enclose nonessential sentences:**

   College instructors assume students will use computers to conduct research and prepare research papers. (Some professors refuse to accept handwritten documents.) Many colleges guarantee students access to computers.

   Note: The parentheses enclose the entire sentence, including the final mark of punctuation.

[ ]   Brackets

Brackets are used to enclose words inserted into a quotation.

1. **Brackets set off clarifications or explanations:**

   "The main plant [located in Tennessee] will be expanded next year."

   "During the Gulf War, the President kept in touch with Professor Sarah Bush [no relation] at the Middle East Institute."

"The ambassador stated she could not deliver the message until he [Frank Wilson] completed the annual report."

2. **Brackets indicate grammatical alterations or corrections:**

Original: The United States, Canada, and Germany are among the most promising markets.

Quotation with brackets containing alteration:
"The United States . . . [is] among the most promising markets."

Original: After Roosevelt's death, Harry Truman became president.

Quotation with brackets noting error:
After Roosevelt's [*sic*] death, Harry Truman became president. (The Latin term *sic* is used to indicate that an error appears in the original text.)

- Hyphen

A *hyphen* consists of a single short line used to separate or join words and other items.

1. **Use hyphens to break words:**

We attempted to tele-
phone her last night.

2. **Use hyphens to combine words into adjectives:**

Grossman made a last-ditch attempt to save his job.

Do not use a hyphen after an adverb ending in *ly:*

Grossman issued a quickly drafted statement to the press.

3. **Use a hyphen to join words forming numbers:**

The company was forced to pay twenty-two million dollars in back taxes.

4. **Use a hyphen after some prefixes:**

It is dangerous to take these drugs based on a self-diagnosis or the advice of an ex-doctor.

5. **Use a hyphen between a combination of a number and a word:**

He drove a 4.5-ton truck.

— Dash

A *dash* is used to set off words in a sentence. Sometimes a dash appears in print as two hyphens (–) but usually it appears as one continuous line (—) that is about the length of two hyphens. Dashes are dramatic marks of punctuation that emphasize words and phrases:

> The college changed the tuition schedule—driving it to near bankruptcy.
> The college—long pressured by student groups—changed the tuition policy.

Note: Do not place spaces between the dash and the words it connects.

/ Slash

The *slash* is used to separate words when both are applicable and in quotations to signal line breaks in poetry:

> A student should study his/her lessons.
> To test the microphone, she began reciting the simple refrain, "Mary had a little lamb / Its fleece was white as snow / And everywhere that Mary went / The lamb was sure to go."

? Question Mark

Question marks are placed after direct questions and to note questionable items:

> Can anyone truly predict the stock market?
> He read a disturbing article, "What Is to Be Done?"

Note: In the preceding example, the question mark is placed within the quotation marks because it is part of the title.

> Did you read Poe's "The Tell-Tale Heart"?

Note: In the preceding example, the question mark is placed outside the quotation marks because it is not part of the title.

> The children reported they waited two hours (?) for the police to arrive.

Note: To indicate that you doubt the accuracy of a fact, number, or idea, place the question mark in parentheses after the item in question.

! **Exclamation Point**

Exclamation points are placed after emphatic statements:

> I can't go on!
> Get out!

Exclamations, like dashes, should be viewed as special effects that lose impact if overused.

. **Period**

Periods are used after sentences, in abbreviations, and with decimals:

> They moved to Michigan.
> We gave the report to Mrs. Chavez and promised to give an estimate by
>   Jan. 15.
> We promised to pay $134.45 a share.

Note: When a sentence ends with an abbreviation, only one period is used.

Note: Some abbreviations such as CIA, NBA, TWA, and UCLA do not require periods.

WRITING ACTIVITY

Insert punctuation where needed in this passage from Armond Budish's "Fender Benders: Legal Do's and Don'ts." After you finish editing the section, review the original text on pages 507–511.

5. Call the Police
    Its obvious that if its a serious accident in which someone is injured the police should be called immediately. Thats both the law and common sense. But what if the accident seems minor. Say youre stopped another car taps you in the rear. If its absolutely clear to both drivers that there is no damage or injury you each can go your merry way. But thats the exception.
    Normally you should call the police to substantiate what occurred. In most cities police officers will come to the scene even for minor accidents but if they wont you and the other driver should go to the station

of the city where the accident occurred to file a report. Ask to have an officer check out both cars.

If you are not at fault be wary of accepting the other drivers suggestion that you leave the police out of it and arrange a private settlement. When you submit your $500 car repair estimate several weeks later you could discover that the other driver has developed amnesia and denies being anywhere near the accident. If the police werent present on the scene you may not have a legal leg to stand on.

Even if you are at fault its a good idea to involve the police. Why. Because a police officer will note the extent of the other drivers damages in his or her report limiting your liability. Without police presence the other driver can easily inflate the amount of the damages.

MECHANICS

The writing context can dictate or influence the rules of mechanics. Make sure your writing follows the accepted style used in your discipline or profession.

Capitalization

Capital letters signal the beginning of a new sentence and denote proper nouns such as *Alabama*, *Chevrolet*, *Dublin*, *Islam*, and *Dark Ages*. Capitals also help prevent confusion by making distinctions:

> They drove the Dodge to ford the stream.
> We bought china made in Japan.
> The Republican candidate supported democratic principles.

Capitalize proper nouns and their abbreviations and acronyms:

Names of people, specific objects, and trademarks:

Michael Collins	Malcolm X	Coca-Cola	Buick
Xerox	Apollo	Ford Mustang	Apple computer
Titanic	Tommy	Lucky Jim	

Geographical names:

Maple Avenue	Chicago	Lake Michigan	Midwest
Asia	Mars	Mexico	Lee Circle
Grant Park	Moon Beach		

Peoples, nations, and languages:

Asians	Jews	Italian	Chinese
Mexican	Kurds	Germany	Canada
Cheyenne	Iran		

Corporations, organizations, institutions, and government agencies:

FBI	Clark College	NASA	New York
Yankees	IRS	Microsoft	CORE
KLM	NAACP	Campbell Soup	

Historical documents, eras, events, and movements:

Declaration of Independence	the Dark Ages	the Civil War
Existentialism	the Civil Rights Movement	Nazism

Days of the week, months, and special days:

Monday	October	Christmas Eve	Memorial Day

The seasons—winter, spring, summer, fall—are not capitalized.

Religions and their followers, sacred texts, holidays, and names for the
  Supreme Being:

Presbyterian	Islam	Roman Catholic	Hinduism
Muslim	Jews	Buddhists	Mormons
Bible	Talmud	Koran	Book of Mormon
Easter	Christmas	Ramadan	Kwanza
Allah	God	Immanuel	Christ

Special events:

World Series	Super Bowl	Winter Olympics	Founder's Day

Common or generic words when used in titles or part of proper names:

Clark College   Children's Hospital   Chicago Police Department
but "The police took him to a children's hospital after the accident."

Titles of books, films, paintings, and other works of art:

Hamlet   *Starry Night*   *Moon for the Misbegotten*   "Moonlight"

Professional titles preceding a personal name or when used in place of a
  person's name:

"Get Doctor Wilson" but "Get the doctor."

The delegation met with a mayor and Senator James.

The following morning President Wilson met with the premier of France.

Words derived from proper nouns:

Orwellian   Marxism   French

Breeds of animals are not capitalized unless they refer to a geographical region, such as *Irish terrier, French poodle*, and *Labrador*.

WRITING ACTIVITY

Edit this opening passage from Joe Rodriguez's "Mexicans Deserve More Than *La Mordida*" and add capital letters. After completing the exercise, review the original text on pages 381–384.

"i wouldn't give you a dime for mexico!"

my father used to tell us that every time mexico broke his heart. he was *muy indio*, with dark reddish brown skin, huge calloused hands and a handsomely hooked nose. on our occasional trips to tijuana to visit relatives, he'd see indian women begging on the streets, indian kids selling chiclets chewing gum, and white-skinned mexicans owning and running everything.

"not a dime for mexico!"

he was more mexican than i'll ever be, more mexican than any harvard-educated technocrat, any spanish-looking *gachupin*, any middle-class zapatista guerrilla-intellectual, or any bald-headed ex-president crook from mexico city's ritzy polanco district. my father wasn't referring to the nation's people, but to a political and social system that still fosters extreme poverty, discrimination and injustice, and to the privileged and the ruthless who benefit by it.

i should have remembered my dad's dime recently when two mexico city policemen pulled me over for making an illegal left-hand turn at the monument of cuauhtemoc on the famous paseo de la reforma boulevard.

i was driving back into the giant city after three days in the countryside.

i had escaped a traffic accident only minutes earlier. i was hot, tired, grumpy and jumpy. i was driving a rental car. these conditions made me the perfect *pollo* for these two uniformed coyotes.

both cops got out. the older one checked out the rental plates. the younger one wanted to see my driver's license.

"where's your hotel?" he asked.

right over there, i said, the maria cristina hotel on rio lerma street.

Companion Website

See **http://www.thomsonedu.com/english/sundance** for additional information about capitalization.

Underlining and Italics

Traditional typewriters could not change type, so writers used *underlining* to indicate text that would be *italicized* in print. The advent of changeable type and computers have made underlining unnecessary, but MLA still requires its use (see page 778).

Underlining and italics serve to highlight words and phrases for special reasons:

1. **Underlining or italics is used for titles of long works of art.** Books, magazines, newspapers, plays, television programs, and recordings are underlined or italicized:

   We saw <u>Death of a Salesman</u>.   *or*   We saw *Death of a Salesman*.

   Note: Underline the entire title, including spaces between words.

   Note: Religious texts and historical documents are not italicized: The Bible. The Bill of Rights.

2. **Names of ships, trains, aircraft, and space vehicles:**

   My grandmother sailed on the <u>Titanic</u>.

   My father took the *City of New Orleans* to Chicago.

3. **Words being emphasized or highlighted:**

   Patients <u>must</u> sign a release before receiving treatment.

   Your paper is hard to read because the *1*'s and *7*'s look alike.

4. **Uncommon foreign words and phrases:**

   Hitler demanded <u>Lebensraum</u>.

   The hero was undone by his overwhelming *hubris*.

   Note: Once foreign words enter popular English usage, they are no longer underlined or italicized: kindergarten, tortilla, rotisserie, or lasagna. Consult your dictionary if you are unsure.

Abbreviations

Abbreviations are shortened versions of words or phrases:

1. **Names of organizations, names of products, and common phrases:**

   FBI   UPS   GM   NATO   IRA
   USA   VCR   BBC   COD   AFL-CIO

   Note: Capitalize all letters and do not separate them with periods.

   Note: Some writers insert periods between letters or numerals: W.W.II. Consult your handbook or professional style manual. Always be consistent.

2. **Abbreviations of single words:**

   Mon.   Dec.   pg.   fwd.   ms.

   Note: Most abbreviations use lowercase letters except for abbreviations of proper nouns.

3. **Professional titles:**

   Dr. Smith   Ms. Wong   Jim Chavez, M.D.   Nancy Gross, Esq.

   Note: Professional titles preceding names are followed by a period. Professional titles following names are set off with commas.

   Note: Avoid using abbreviations unless associated with a name:

   We saw Dr. Green.
   or
   We saw the doctor.
   not
   We saw the Dr.

   Note: Do not use double titles:

   Dr. Green *or* Sandy Green, M.D.
   not
   Dr. Sandy Green, M.D.

4. **Geographical regions:**
   Do not use periods between letters in state abbreviations used in addresses:

   Haddonfield, NJ   Albany, NY   San Diego, CA

   Note: Use periods in *Washington, D.C.,* and *U.S.* when these are used to modify another word, as in *U.S. regulations.*

5. **Latin expressions:**

    etc.   e.g.   i.e.   vs.   et al.

6. **Certain terms used with dates or numbers:**

80 B.C.	A.D. 95	*or*	80 B.C.E	95 C.E.
35 mph	10 a.m.	*or*	35 MPH	10 AM

Note: Be consistent with alternate forms.

You do not have to identify commonly known abbreviations such as FBI, NYC, or UCLA. When you use an abbreviation your readers may not understand or may misunderstand, define it after its first use:

We reported the incident to the Center for Air Pollution Studies (CAPS). She worked for the CIA (Canadian Insurance Adjusters) for two years.

Numbers

Numbers are either written out (*twenty-two*) or presented as numerals (*22*).

1. **Numbers presented as words.** Write numbers out if they appear infrequently in your writing, can be written in one or two words, or when they begin a sentence:

We drove *forty-two* miles.

Three hundred seventy-five students graduated last week.

Note: Hyphenate numbers between 21 and 99 (except for round numbers such as *forty* and *sixty*).

Note: To avoid long and awkward phrases, avoid opening sentences with large numbers:

Last week 8,998 students graduated from the city's high schools.

2. **Numbers presented as numerals.** Use numerals to represent dates, addresses, large or often repeated numbers, page numbers, most percentages, decimals, and identifications:

She accepted the post on January 25, 2000.

Send the car to the garage at 700 West State Street.

Last year 32,987 complaints were received.

Look on page 23.

Sales rose 34% last year.

The average subject slept less than 7.5 hours a night.

You can find the offices of Channel 36 in Room 300.

3. **Numbers presented in combinations of words and numerals:**

4646 North 47th Street	*or*	2323 Second Avenue
4 PM	*or*	four o'clock in the afternoon
$24,000,000	*or*	24 million dollars

Spelling

Spelling errors, even in the age of computer spell checks, remain one of the most common and most annoying errors that you can make. Poor spelling detracts from the impact and authority of your writing. Readers interpret spelling mistakes as indications of haste, sloppiness, and ignorance.

Understand the Limits of Spell Checking Programs

If you write on a computer, you may be lulled into the belief that you can rely on a spell checking program to locate errors.

1. Spell checkers do not find missing or misused words.
2. Many programs will not detect problems in usage, mistaking *there* for *their* or *conscience* for *conscious*.
3. Spell checkers often flag correctly spelled words, especially proper names. If your spell checker keeps flagging a repeated word, click IGNORE ALL or customize the program by adding the word to its list of correctly spelled words.

STRATEGIES | for Improving Spelling

1. Review the guidelines in the chapter, noting words that you have found confusing.
2. Review the list of commonly confused words on page 898. Underline or highlight pairs that you have found troublesome.
3. Review the list of commonly misspelled words on page 901. Underline or highlight those that you recall misspelling.
4. As you are introduced to new terms in college courses, readings, or your career, make sure to get the correct spelling. If you learn to spell a word correctly as soon as you learn it, you will not have to unlearn or correct a habitual error. Refer to glossaries in your textbooks and specialized dictionaries.
5. Develop a list of words that you commonly misspell.

Spelling Guidelines

1. **Prefixes:** *Prefixes* are added to the beginning of words to form new words. *The spelling of the base word does not change:*

im + moral	=	immoral
re + entry	=	reentry
anti + biotic	=	antibiotic
mayor + elect	=	mayor-elect

   Note: Some combinations use hyphens, especially if the base word is capitalized: *un-American, non-Lutheran, anti-Communism.*

2. **Suffixes:** *Suffixes* are added to the end of words to form new words. If the word ends in a silent *e* and the suffix begins with a vowel, drop the *e:*

continue + ous	=	continuous
pure + ist	=	purist

   If the word ends in a silent *e* and the suffix begins with a consonant, do not drop the *e:*

state + ly	=	stately
state + ment	=	statement

   Note: There are some exceptions to these guidelines:

dye + ing	=	dyeing *not* dying
true + ly	=	truly *not* truely

   If a word ends in *y*, change the *y* to an *i* if preceded by a consonant:

easy + ly	=	easily
play + ful	=	playful

   Note: If the suffix is *-ing*, the *y* is always retained:

cry + ing	=	crying

   Add *-ly* to adjectives to create adverbs. For most words ending in *-ic* add *-ally*. Retain the final *l* in words ending in *l:*

regular + ly	=	regularly
tragic + ally	=	tragically
cool + ly	=	coolly

Double the last consonant if the word ends with a single accented vowel and a single consonant and is joined to a suffix beginning with vowel:

stop + ed   =   stopped
begin + ing   =   beginning

3. *ie* and *ei* words:

When words sound like *ee* as in *see*, write *ie* except after *c:*

belief	field	brief	yield	shield
receive	ceiling	perceive	conceit	

When words sound like *ay* as in *ray*, write *ei:*

weigh   rein   neighbor   eight   vein

Exceptions: ancient, either, foreign, height, science

4. **Plurals:**

Most words in English simply add *s* to create plural forms, but there are a few exceptions:

When words end with a consonant and *y*, add *-ies:*

theory/*theories*   mystery/*mysteries*

When words end in *s*, *sh*, *ch*, *x*, or *z*, add *es:*

bus/*buses*   bush/*bushes*   fox/*foxes*

Many words ending in *f* or *ef* change to *ves:*

leaf/*leaves*   calf/*calves*   self/*selves*

Some words do not have a separate plural form:

deer/*deer*   sheep/*sheep*

Latin and Greek terms ending in *on*, *um*, or *us* change to *a* or *i:*

medium/*media*   alumnus/*alumni*

Add the *s* to the first word in hyphenated words:

mother-in-law/*mothers-in-law*   court-martial/*courts-martial*

5. **British spellings.** If you read material published in the United Kingdom, Canada, or Australia, you may note spelling differences:

American	British
curb	kerb
theater	theatre

color   colour
tire   tyre
labor   labour

Use British spelling only in direct quotes.

WRITING ACTIVITY

Read and correct the spelling errors in this passage from George Orwell's essay "Shooting an Elephant." When you complete the exercise, examine the original text on pages 349–356 to see whether you located all the misspellings and errors in usage.

> In Moulmein, in Lower Berma, I was hated by large numbers of people—the only time in my life that I have been impotant enough for this to hapen to me. I was sub-divisonal police oficer of the town, and in aimless, petty kind of way anti-European feeling was very bitter. No one had the guts to raise a riot, but if a European women went through the bizarres alone somebody would probably spit betel juice over her dress. As a police officer I was an ovious target and was bated whenever it seemed safe to do so. When a nimble Berman tripped me up on the football field and the refere (another Berman) looked the other way, the crowed yelled with hedious laughter. This happen more thcn once. In the end the sneering yellow faces of young men that meet me everywhere, the insults hooted after me when I was at a safe distance, got badly on my nerves. The young Budhist priests were the worst of all. Their ere several thousands of them in the town and none of them seemed to have anything to do but accept stand on street corners and jear at Europeans.

Companion Website

See **http://www.thomsonedu.com/english/sundance** for additional information about spelling.

APPENDIX

Commonly Confused Words

accept	to take	Do you *accept* checks?
except	to exclude	Everyone *except* Joe went home.
adapt	to change	We will *adapt* the army helicopter for civilian use.
adopt	to take possession of	They want to *adopt* a child.
adverse	unfavorable	*Adverse* publicity ruined his reputation.
averse	opposed to	I was *averse* to buying a new car.
advice	a noun	Take my *advice*.
advise	a verb	Let me *advise* you.
affect	to influence	Will this *affect* my grade?
effect	a result	What is the *effect* of the drug?
all ready	prepared	We were *all ready* for the trip.
already	by a certain time	You are *already* approved.
allusion	a reference	She made a biblical *allusion*.
illusion	imaginary vision	The mirage was an optical *illusion*.
all together	unity	The teachers stood *all together*.
altogether	totally	*Altogether*, that will cost $50.
among	relationship of three or more	This outfit is popular *among* college students.
between	relationship of two	This was a dispute *between* Kim and Nancy.
amount	for items that are measured	A small *amount* of oil has leaked.
number	for items that are counted	A large *number* of cars are stalled.
any one	a person, idea, item	*Any one* of the books will do.
anyone	anybody	Can *anyone* help me?
brake	to halt / a stopping	Can you fix the *brakes*?
break	an interruption	Take a coffee *break*.
	to destroy	Don't *break* the window.
capital	money	She needs venture *capital*.
	government center	Trenton is the *capital* of New Jersey.
capitol	legislative building	He toured the U.S. *Capitol*.

cite	to note or refer to	He *cited* several figures in his speech.
site	a location	We inspected the *site* of the crash.
sight	a view, ability to see	The *sight* from the hill was tremendous.
complement	to complete	The jet had a full *complement* of spare parts.
compliment	express praise, a gift	The host paid us a nice *compliment*.
conscience	moral sensibility	He was a prisoner of *conscience*.
conscious	aware of/awake	Is he *conscious* of these debts?
		Is the patient *conscious*?
continual	now and again	We have *continual* financial problems.
continuous	uninterrupted	The brain needs a *continuous* supply of blood.
council	a group	A student *council* will meet Tuesday.
counsel	to advise/advisor	He sought legal *counsel*.
discreet	tactful	He made a *discreet* hint.
discrete	separate/distinct	The war had three *discrete* phases.
elicit	evoke/persuade	His hateful remarks will *elicit* protest.
illicit	illegal	Her use of *illicit* drugs ruined her career.
emigrate	to leave a country	They tried to *emigrate* from Germany.
immigrate	to enter a country	They were allowed to *immigrate* to America.
eminent	famous	She was an *eminent* eye specialist.
imminent	impending	Disaster was *imminent*.
everyday	ordinary	Wear *everyday* clothes to the party.
every day	daily	We exercise *every day*.
farther	distance	How much *farther* is it?
further	in addition	He demanded a *further* investigation.
fewer	for items counted	There are *fewer* security guards this year.
less	for items measured	There is *less* security this year.
good	an adjective	She has *good* eyesight.
well	an adverb	She sees *well*.
hear	to listen	Can you *hear* the music?
here	a place/direction	Put the table *here*.
imply	to suggest	The president *implied* he might raise taxes.
infer	to interpret	The reporters *inferred* from his comments that the president might raise taxes.
its	possessive of *it*	The car won't start because *its* battery is dead.
it's	contraction of *it is*	*It's* snowing.
lay	to put/to place	*Lay* the books on my desk.
lie	to rest	*Lie* down for a nap.
loose	not tight	He has a *loose* belt or *loose* change.
lose	to misplace	Don't *lose* your keys.

moral	dealing with values	She made a *moral* decision to report the crime.
morale	mood	After the loss, the team's *morale* fell.
passed	successfully completed	She *passed* the test.
past	history	That was in my *past*.
personal	private/intimate	She left a *personal* note.
personnel	employees	Send your resume to the *personnel* office.
plain	simple/open space	She wore a *plain* dress.
plane	airplane/geometric form	They took a *plane* to Chicago.
precede	to go before	A film will *precede* the lecture.
proceed	go forward	Let the parade *proceed*.
principal	main/school leader	Oil is the *principal* product of Kuwait.
principle	basic law	I understand the *principle* of law.
raise	to lift	*Raise* the window!
rise	to get up	*Rise* and shine!
right	direction/correct	Turn *right*. That's *right*.
rite	a ritual	She was given last *rites*.
write	to inscribe	They *write* essays every week.
stationary	unmoving	The disabled train remained *stationary*.
stationery	writing paper	The hotel *stationery* was edged in gold.
than	used to compare	I am taller *than* Helen.
then	concerning time	We *then* headed to class.
their	possessive of *they*	*Their* car is stalled.
there	direction/place	Put the chair over *there*.
they're	contraction of *they are*	*They're* coming to dinner.
there're	contraction of *there are*	*There're* are two seats left.
to	preposition/infinitive	I went *to* school *to* study law.
too	in excess/also	It was *too* cold to swim.
two	a number	We bought *two* computers.
wear	clothes/damage	We *wear* our shoes until they *wear* out.
where	a place in question	*Where* is the post office?
weather	climatic conditions	*Weather* forecasts predict rain.
whether	alternatives/no matter what	You must register, *whether* or not you want to audit the class.
who's	contraction of *who is*	*Who's* on first?
whose	possessive of *who*	*Whose* book is that?

Commonly Misspelled Words

absence	career	excellent	immediately	mortgage	psychic
accept	carrying	existence	importance	necessary	psychology
accident	celebrate	experience	incidental	ninety	publicly
accommodate	cemetery	explanation	independence	noticeable	qualify
accumulate	challenge	extremely	influence	obligation	quality
achieve	characteristic	fallacy	intelligence	obvious	quantity
achievement	column	familiar	interest	occasionally	query
acquaint	coming	fantasy	interpret	occupation	quiet
acquire	commitment	fascination	interrupt	occurred	quizzes
across	committee	favorite	involvement	omit	realize
address	competition	February	irrelevant	operate	recede
advertisement	completely	feminine	irresistible	opinion	receive
adolescence	complexion	field	irresponsible	opportunity	reception
a lot	conceive	finally	judgment	oppose	recognition
amateur	consistent	foreign	judicial	optimism	recommend
analysis	continually	forgotten	judicious	ordinarily	refer
analyze	control	forty	knowledge	original	regulation
annual	controversial	fourth	label	paid	relation
anonymous	criticism	frequent	laboratory	pamphlet	religious
apparent	curious	friend	language	parallel	remember
appreciate	dealt	frighten	leisure	particularly	repetition
approach	decision	fulfill	libel	perform	responsible
arctic	definite	fundamental	library	permanent	restaurant
argument	deliberate	further	license	permission	rhythm
article	dependent	generally	lightning	persistent	ridicule
assassination	description	generous	loneliness	persuade	roommate
assistance	difficult	government	luxury	persuasion	sacrifice
athletic	disappear	gradually	lying	philosophy	safety
attention	disappoint	grammar	magazine	physical	scene
attitude	discipline	grateful	maintenance	playwright	schedule
basically	discuss	guarantee	maneuver	politician	seize
basis	dominant	guard	marriage	positive	separate
beautiful	dying	guidance	martial	possession	sergeant
becoming	efficient	happiness	material	possible	severely
beginning	eighth	height	mathematics	precede	significance
belief	eligible	heroes	meant	preference	significant
believe	embarrass	holocaust	mechanical	prejudice	similar
benefit	enough	huge	medieval	presence	simplify
breakfast	environment	humorous	mere	primitive	sincerely
business	equipment	hypocrite	miniature	probably	situation
calendar	essential	identically	mischief	procedure	skillfully
candidate	exaggerate	identify	misspell	prominent	sociology

sophisticated
sophomore
special
specimen
stereotype
straight
strict
studying
success
summary
surprise
synonymous
technique
temperament
tenable
tendency
thorough
thought
throughout
tomorrow
tragedy
tremendous
truly
unfortunate
uniform
unique
until
unusual
useful
using
usually
vacillate
vacillation
vacuum
valuable
various
vengeance
villain
violence
vulnerable
weird
whole
writing
yield

Add other words you often misspell:

Essay Topics

stalking	SAT tests	student unions	ideal job
dieting	privacy laws	day care	women in combat
Internet fraud	lawyers	soap operas	prisons
AIDS	being fired	gay bashing	Iraq war
depression	Social Security	life after death	bilingual education
spring break	fads	funerals	gambling
family values	blind dates	success	pornography
new cars	disabilities	being a victim	malls taxes
exercise	Patriot Act	voting	gangs
gun control	job interviews	hybrid cars	bloggers
racism	oil	wearing fur	minimum wage
immigration	adoption	high school	NFL teams
latest hit movie	drug testing	living wills	camera phones
local singles bars	sex offenders	fast food	the homeless
charity	role models	Wall Street	reality TV
friendship	Hollywood	dreams	car insurance
music videos	Christmas	tobacco	birth control
pensions	summer jobs	terrorism	graffiti
cults	video games	world hunger	stereotypes
drinking age	people you admire	owning a business	sex education
eating disorders	nuclear power	child support	divorce
talk shows	feminism	gay rights	the glass ceiling
morning after pill	car repairs	jealousy	right to die
baseball	affirmative action	worst jobs	interracial dating
single mothers	hate speech	conspiracy theories	labor unions
toxic waste	illegal immigration	politicians	welfare reform
sexual harassment	marriage	drunk driving	plea bargaining
health care	work ethic	professors	military recruiting
digital TV	fatherhood	space exploration	poverty
banks	credit cards	commercials	first apartment
lawsuits	censorship	suicide	addiction
twelve-step programs	ski resorts	local restaurants	chat rooms
sex on the Web	Islam	best teacher	fashion models
child abuse	romance	jogging	celebrities
stadiums	grand juries	crack cocaine	animal rights
churches	the insanity defense	being "in"	cable TV
pets	the Pope	the Holocaust	urban sprawl
suburbs	slavery reparations	busing	legalized prostitution
China	child labor	doctors	school choice
images of women	Congress	Africa	ethnic conflict
steroids	married priests	TV news	e-mail
surveillance cameras	coffee bars	favorite film or book	casinos

school prayer
relationships
alcohol
teen smoking
the Olympics
comedy clubs

foreign aid
mutual funds
bad habits
addiction as disability
art museums
profanity in public

the American Dream
future career
adultery
animal testing
night clubs
children's TV

prayer
alternative fuels
NBA salaries
nostalgia
the president
discrimination

Credits

Abramson, Leslie, "The Abuse Defense Balances the Justice System" from *Newsweek*, July 24, 1994. Copyright © 1994 Newsweek, Inc. All rights reserved. Reprinted by permission.

Adler, Mortimer, "How to Mark a Book" first appeared in *Saturday Review of Literature and Reader's Digest*, August 1940. Article entitled "How to Mark a Book." extracted from Chapter 11 from *How to Read a Book* by Mortimer J. Adler. Copyright © 1940 by Mortimer J. Adler, renewed 1967 by Mortimer J. Adler 1972 by Mortimer J. Adler and Charles van Doren. Reprinted with permission of Simon & Schuster, Inc.

Angelou, Maya, "Champion of the World," copyright © 1969 and renewed 1997 by Maya Angelou, from *I Know Why the Caged Bird Sings*, by Maya Angelou. Used by permission of Random House, Inc.

Baker, Russell, "The Plot Against People" from *The New York Times*, June 18, 1968. Copyright © 1968 by The New York Times. Reprinted by permission.

Borchert, Wolfgang, "The Bread" from *The Man Outside: Play and Stories* by Wolfgang Borchert. Copyright © 1971 by New Directions Publishing Corp. and Marion Boyars Publishers of London.

Brooks, John, "The Effects of the Telephone" from *Telephone: The First Hundred Years*, pp. 8–9. Copyright 1975, 1976 by John Brooks. Reprinted by permission of HarperCollins Publishers, Inc.

Brown, Tony, "Death of a Dream" pp. 266–67, 271–73 from *Black Lies, White Lies* by Tony Brown. Copyright © 1995 by Tony Brown. Reprinted by permission of HarperCollins Publishers, William Morrow.

Buckley, William F., Jr., "Don't Blame Violence on the Tube." from *TV Guide*, March 19, 1994, pp. 38–39. Copyright 1994 by William F. Buckley Jr. Used by permission of the Wallace Literary Agency, Inc.

Budish, Armond, "Fender Benders: Do's and Don't's" as appeared in *Family Circle*, July 19, 1994. Reprinted by permission of the author.

Burciaga, Jose Antonio, "My Ecumenical Father" from *Drink Culture*, by Jose Antonio Burciaga, copyright 1993. Reprinted by permission of Cecilia P. Burciaga.

Capote, Truman, "Out There" from *In Cold Blood* by Truman Capote. Copyright © 1965 by Truman Capote and renewed 1993 by Alan U. Schwartz. Used by permission of Random House, Inc.

Carson, Rachel, "A Fable for Tomorrow" from *Silent Spring* by Rachel Carson. Copyright © 1962 by Rachel L. Carson. Copyright © renewed 1990 by Roger Christie. Reprinted by permission of Houghton Mifflin Company. All rights reserved.

Castro, Janice, Dan Cook, and Cristina Garcia, "Spanglish" from *Time*, July 11, 1988, vol. 132, no. 2, p. 53. Copyright © 1988 Time Inc. Reprinted by permission.

Catton, Bruce, "Grant and Lee" from *The American Story* by Earll Schenk Miers. Reprinted by permission of the U.S. Capital Historical Society

Ciardi, John, "What is Happiness?" Reprinted by permission of John L. Ciardi as Trustee of The Ciardi Family Publishing Trust.

Cousins, Norman, "Who Killed Benny Paret?" from *Present Tense*, p. 452. Reprinted by permission of HarperCollins Publishers, Inc.

Dershowitz, Alan M. "The 'Abuse Excuse' is Detrimental to the Justice System" from *The Abuse Excuse*, pp. 3–6. Copyright © 1994 Alan Dershowitz. Reprinted by permission of Little Brown & Company.

Dickinson, Emily, "My Life Had Stood—A Loaded Gun" from *The Poems of Emily Dickinson*, Thomas H. Johnson, ed., Cambridge, Mass.: The Belknap Press of Harvard University Press. Copyright © 1951, 1955, 1979, 1983 by President and Fellows of Harvard College. Reprinted by permission of the publishers and trustees of Amherst college.

Dillard, James, "A Doctor's Dilemma" from *Newsweek*, June 12, 1995, vol. 125, p. 12. Copyright © 1995 Newsweek, Inc. All rights reserved. Reprinted by permission.

Ehrenreich, Barbara, "Cultural Baggage" originally appeared in the *New York Times Magazine*, "Hers" column, April 5, 1992, vol. 141, pg. 16. Copyright © 1992 by the New York Times.

Index

Bold page numbers indicate material in drawings and photographs.